Buffalo Bill Cody

THE MAN BEHIND THE LEGEND

ROBERT A. CARTER

John Wiley & Sons, Inc.

This book is printed on acid-free paper. ∞

Title page photo: Buffalo Bill and the Wild West show cast, c. 1908. (Buffalo Bill Historical Center, Cody, Wyoming)

Published by John Wiley & Sons, Inc., New York
Published simultaneously in Canada

Library of Congress Cataloging-in-Publication Data

Carter, Robert A.
    Buffalo Bill Cody: the man behind the legend / Robert A. Carter
      p. cm.
    Includes bibliographical references (p. 477) and index.
    ISBN 0-471-31996-1 (cloth : alk. paper)
    ISBN 0-471-07780-1 (paper : alk. paper)
    1. Buffalo Bill, 1846–1917. 2. Pioneers—West (U.S.)—Biography. 3. Entertainers—United States—Biography. 4. Scouts and scouting—West (U.S.)—Biography. 5. West (U.S.)—Biography. 6. Frontier and pioneer life—West (U.S.) 7. Buffalo Bill's Wild West Show—History.   I. Title.

F594.B63   C37   2000
978'.02'092—dc21
[B]   00-020368

Printed in the United States of America

10 9 8 7 6 5 4 3 2 1

For my two beloved sons, Jonathan and Randy—they, too, are westerners

There are many men, but few heroes.

—Herodotus

CONTENTS

PREFACE

Who *was* Buffalo Bill Cody? Most people know, at the very least, that he was a hero of the Old West, like Daniel Boone, Davy Crockett, and Kit Carson—one of those larger-than-life figures from which legends are made. Cody himself provided such a linkage to his heroic predecessors in 1888 when he published a book with biographies of Boone, Crockett, Carson—and one of his own autobiographies: *Story of the Wild West and Campfire Chats, by Buffalo Bill (Hon. W.F. Cody), a Full and Complete History of the Renowned Pioneer Quartette, Boone, Crockett, Carson and Buffalo Bill.* In this context, Cody was often called "the last of the great scouts."

Some are also aware that he was an enormously popular showman, creator and star of Buffalo Bill's Wild West, a spectacular entertainment of the late nineteenth and early twentieth centuries.

It has been estimated that more than a billion words were written by or about William Frederick Cody during his own lifetime, and biographies of him have appeared at irregular intervals ever since. A search of "Buffalo Bill Cody" on amazon.com reveals twenty-seven items. Most of these, however, are children's books, and it is likely that many of them play up the more melodramatic and questionable aspects of his life story; a notable exception is Ingri and Edgar Parin d'Aulaire's *Buffalo Bill*, which is solidly based on fact. Cody has also shown up in movies and television shows, though not in recent years, for whatever else he was, he was never *cool* or cynical. As his latest biographer, I believe his life has a valuable contribution to make in this new millennium—it provides a sense of who we once were and who we might be again. He was a commanding presence in our American history, a man who helped shape the way we look at that history. It was he, in fact, who created the Wild West, in all its adventure, violence, and romance.

Buffalo Bill is important to me as the symbol of the growth of our nation, for his life spanned the settlement of the Great Plains, the Indian

Wars, the Gold Rush, the Pony Express, the building of the transcontinental railroad, and the enduring romance of the American frontier—especially the Great Plains. Consider what he witnessed in his lifetime: the invention of the telephone, the transatlantic cable, the automobile, the airplane, and the introduction of modern warfare, with great armies massed against each other, with tanks, armored cars, flame-throwers, and poison gas—a far cry from the days when Cody and the troopers of the Fifth Cavalry rode hell-for-leather across the prairie in pursuit of hostile Indians. Nor, though it is not usually considered a milestone in American history, should we forget Joseph F. Glidden's 1874 invention of barbed wire, which, more than the rifle or the plow, transformed Buffalo Bill's Great Plains by insuring the survival of thousands of family farms, and making possible the growth of enormous—and enormously profitable—cattle ranches.

In addition, I feel a personal connection.

In April 1855 my great-granduncle Alexander Carter Jr. and his younger brother, Thomas Marion Carter, left their home in Scioto County, Ohio, and headed west. Starting by steamboat, the two brothers floated down the Ohio River until it joined the Mississippi and then traveled upstream to St. Louis. In St. Louis they found little transportation west, so they walked, hitched rides, and rode horseback to reach St. Joseph, Missouri. There they caught a stagecoach to Council Bluffs, Iowa, riding on top of the stage, with seventeen men and women—a three-day ordeal.

On May 14, nineteen days after leaving St. Louis, the brothers crossed the Missouri River and landed on the town site of Omaha, then a community of cotton tents and shanties, where lots were being offered to anyone willing to build on them. They refused this offer and pressed on to their final destination, DeSoto, Washington County, Nebraska Territory, where they found only one completed log house and another under construction. There they homesteaded the town of Blair, Nebraska. For three generations there were Carters in Nebraska, first in Blair and then in Omaha, where I was born.

As a native Nebraskan, I feel a particular affinity for William F. Cody, who lived most of his adult life in Nebraska. My father, George W. Carter, could have seen Buffalo Bill's Wild West when it came to Omaha in August 1908. I wish I had known the old scout personally; I am glad I have come to know him better while writing this book. It is also my fond hope that readers will feel as I do, that Buffalo Bill Cody is well worth knowing.

Writing a biography of someone long dead is always a challenge. You must come to understand the person, the motivations, the key events that altered the course of history. And there are the records, the letters, the reminiscences of contemporaries. In Bill Cody's case the documentation is plentiful but sometimes contradictory. Did Buffalo Bill kill Yellow Hand—the "first scalp for Custer"—for example? There are those who say he did and detractors who say he did not. Who are we to believe? For the most part, if I found two or three accounts that agreed with each other, particularly if there were official government records supporting him, I felt sure I could give the credit to Cody.

Unless some long-lost trove of letters or a forgotten diary turns up, I believe that we probably now know all we are ever likely to know about William F. Cody. What I offer in this book then, based on my reading and research, is what I feel confident is the true story of his life.

In an essay in *American Heritage* magazine for September 1999, John Steele Gordon writes of biography as a genre: "If the subject is a household name, the biographer must separate the facts from the myths that inevitably sprout like mushrooms out of the folk memory of a great individual. Even more important, the biographer must provide both the background—the vast complexity of the civilization in which an individual lived his life—and minibiographies of important people in that life. And this must all be done without wearying the reader or losing the thread of narration."

That has been my goal in this book—to "separate the facts from the myths" and bring back the *real* Buffalo Bill Cody, the man behind the legend—to fascinate and, if I'm especially fortunate, to inspire a new generation of readers.

ACKNOWLEDGMENTS

I have listed in the bibliography the many books that contributed to this volume but would like to single out two for special mention. They are Don Russell's *The Lives and Legends of Buffalo Bill*, which no writer on the Colonel could do without; and Nellie Snyder Yost's *Buffalo Bill: His Family, Friends, Fame, Failures, and Fortunes*, for its mother lode of material about the lives of the Codys in North Platte, Nebraska. Two other volumes have been especially helpful: *Letters from "Buffalo Bill"* by Stella Foote and *The Business of Being Buffalo Bill: Selected Letters of William F. Cody, 1879–1917* by Sarah J. Blackstone.

Prominent among the many people to whom I owe my thanks are Byron Price, director; Paul Fees, curator; Frances Clyner, librarian; and Elizabeth Holmes, associate registrar, all of the Buffalo Bill Historical Center in Cody, Wyoming. Lisa Backman of the Western History Department, Denver Public Library; Jeanie Cook of the Park County Archives, Cody, Wyoming; Graeme Rymer of the Royal Armouries, London; and Tom Morrison, superintendent of Scout's Rest Ranch in North Platte, Nebraska, have been especially helpful in the course of my research, as has Ray Wemmingler, librarian and curator of the Hampden-Booth Library of The Players in New York. The Tuckahoe Branch of the Henrico County Library has been unflagging in supplying me with literature through the Inter-Library Loan Program; thanks also to the Library of Virginia, the Library of Congress, the Smithsonian Institution, and the National Archives. I should also acknowledge the search engine yahoo!; the Internet has made writing a biography much easier.

On a personal note, I should like to thank Stanley R. Moore, Dr. Michael Rostafinski, and John Tebbel for advice and information; my wife and "first reader," Reade Johnson; and my editor at John Wiley, Hana Lane, for support and encouragement.

INTRODUCTION

"WHERE COUNCIL FIRES GLEAMED"

William Frederick Cody, the legendary "Buffalo Bill," died quietly and painlessly at five minutes past noon on January 10, 1917, in the Denver home of his sister May Cody Decker. Cody had four sisters—Julia, Eliza, Laura Ella (known as Helen), and Mary Hannah (May)—and one half sister, Martha. At the time of his death, only Julia and May were still living.

Within minutes the news was telegraphed around the world, having been given "Clear the Line" status by Western Union and the other telegraph companies, a status then reserved only for news of the war raging in Europe.

Joseph Bona of the Olinger Mortuary in Denver was called to the Decker home at 2932 Lafayette Street at about one o'clock. He embalmed the body in the bedroom where it lay. Bona said he found "a man of unusual appearance, tall and straight, with fine, big veins that made the embalming so easy he was finished in about two-and-one-half hours." The young mortician later told how impressed he was by the telegrams and messages streaming in from all over the world: from the king of England, the kaiser of Germany, President Wilson, governors, generals, senators, friends from everywhere.

Indeed, for one day, William Frederick Cody stole center stage from a world war.

The accolades were indeed impressive. Said Lieutenant General Nelson A. Miles: "Colonel Cody was a high-minded gentleman, and a great scout. He performed a great work in the West for the pioneers and for the generations coming after them and his exploits will live forever in history."

1

In the years following, former president Theodore Roosevelt, in accepting an honorary vice-presidency in the Buffalo Bill Memorial Association, called Cody "the most renowned of those men, steel-thewed and iron-nerved, whose daring opened the West to settlement and civilization . . . an American of Americans. . . . He embodied those traits of courage, strength and self-reliant hardihood which are vital to the well-being of the nation."

If Cody's fame and popularity seem strange to us today—he was, after all, celebrated for his prowess in killing, both buffalo and Indians—it is because his virtues were nineteenth-century virtues, and we live in an age of disillusion and cynicism. Cody's death, in a way, along with the First World War, signaled the end of those nineteenth-century values.

COL. CODY'S BODY TO REST ON LOOKOUT'S PEAK ran the headline in the Denver *Post* the next day. FAMOUS SCOUT WILL BE BURIED WHERE COUNCIL FIRES GLEAMED.

"Where the first trembling rays of the morning sun gleam upon the flowers and crags and snow of Mount Lookout's summit," wrote Courtney Ryley Cooper in one of the more florid obituaries occasioned by Cody's death, "there will Pahaska sleep, there will the 'long-haired man' rest, after his long journey of life. Far above the plains, stretching out to the north and east beneath him, far above where the buffalo once thundered in its massive herds, where the echoing whoop of the Cheyenne and the roving Sioux shrilled in its eerie warning, where the prairie schooner once rocked its weary way through the sands and gorges and arroyos, there will Buffalo Bill slumber in eternity, his hands folded, his work done."

Such heated prose might well have been expected from a writer who was once the old showman's press agent.

The announcement of Cody's death spread swiftly with headlines and glowing obituaries from one coast to the other, and across Europe as well.

The New York *Times* editorial writer eulogized—one might say "rhapsodized"—Cody this way: "He delighted millions and became better known than the equator. Will there be anything to equal the Wild West Show, or is it to confess one's self the child of a simpler time to ask? . . . It was a grand show, let the slaves of the movie habit say what they will. . . . We can see him still, a little stiff in the legs latterly, but a gallant figure. . . . He played a good game of poker," the *Times* obituary continued. "He was straight as a trivet. He knew the men and manners of many cities and countries. Emperors, Kings, Princes and Princesses, sculptors, painters, statesman, halfbreeds, papooses, he was at home with all. There was something essentially poetical and artistic about the man. . . . He got a lot out of his long life. Endurance, valor, horsemanship, marksmanship. . . . The symbol of a noble period of American history, a friend of the youth of many of us departs.

"Even as a mother covers her child with her cloth, O Earth, cover thou him!"

It is unclear precisely what William F. Cody's intentions were as to his last resting place. He had planned to travel to his beloved Bighorn country before his final illness and would undoubtedly have chosen to be buried there, on Cedar Mountain above Cody, Wyoming. In the spring of 1902 Cody had written his sister Julia about the Wyoming location: "I have got a mountain picked out big enough for us all to be buried on."

He had expressed the same intention in his will: "It is my wish and I hereby direct that my body shall be buried in some suitable spot of ground on Cedar Mountain. I further direct that there shall be erected over my grave, to mark the spot . . . a monument wrought from native red stone in the form of a mammoth buffalo, and placed in such a position as to be visible from the town. . . . I give to my executors the sum of ten thousand dollars for the cost of the monument and its erection and to carefully keep the ground around it in proper order."

Unfortunately for the Colonel's last wishes, the city of Denver had other plans. As a *Time* magazine staff writer observed on the one-hundredth anniversary of Cody's birth: "Denver's mayor Robert W. Speer was out to claim him. Buffalo Bill, dead and enshrined (on Denver's Lookout Mountain), would obviously be a greater civic asset than Buffalo Bill alive with one foot on the Albany Hotel bar rail."

At first the selection of Cody's burial site was under consideration both by members of his immediate family and by the city of Denver, but the family finally chose to leave the decision entirely up to the city. A committee was appointed to make the selection of the gravesite and to transfer it, when finally agreed upon, to the family. Gene Fowler, a reporter for the Denver *Post* and later a well-known biographer, was put in charge of attendant publicity.

Fowler's opening tribute was a poem, entitled "When the Kids Next Door Called You Buffalo Bill." The first stanza ran like this:

Remember the time when your cheeks were hot
From the Indian raids on the vacant lot?
Remember the rush of the boyhood thrill
When the kids next door called you "Buffalo Bill"?

The poem's last stanza:

And now you've grown to the world of men,
But you long for your boyhood days again.
And today the lips of the scout are still—
For God has taken your Buffalo Bill!

Fowler later described Cody as "indiscreet, prodigal, temperamental as a diva, pompous but naive, vain but generous, bigger than big today, littler than little tomorrow. Cody lived with the world at his feet and died with it on his shoulders."

It was later rumored that Cody did not leave $10,000 in his will but that a payment of $10,000 was made to Cody's widow, Louisa, by Harry Tammen, co-owner of the Denver *Post*, to persuade her to choose Denver rather than Cody, Wyoming, as the Colonel's final home. Louisa had to bear the expenses of his interment; hence it was her privilege to choose the site, although there were actually sufficient funds in Cody's estate to cover the funeral costs. Judge W. I. Walls of Cody, Wyoming, administrator of the estate, announced that after the affairs of the estate were settled, a residue of $65,000 would remain. Walls also divulged that an examination of the Colonel's affairs showed that in the last two years, he had lost between $140,000 and $200,000.

Whether Tammen talked Louisa into letting her husband be buried on Lookout Mountain, or whether the old scout really had changed his mind, we will likely never know. When it comes to Buffalo Bill Cody, it must be noted that anything said about him is possible.

Louisa Cody, in her autobiography *Memories of Buffalo Bill*, written with Courtney Ryley Cooper, asserted that although long ago he had told her that he wanted to be buried on Cedar Mountain, "where the last rays of the sun touched the hills at night," now, on his next to last day on earth, he had changed his mind and wanted to be buried on Lookout Mountain. "It's pretty up there. . . . You can look down into four states," he said.

At any rate, Denver won the old plainsman's remains, and Lookout Mountain in nearby Golden, Colorado, would receive them—but not immediately. The funeral services were scheduled for Sunday, January 14, but the body would be kept in a mortuary vault in Olinger's Funeral Home until Memorial Day, when it would be finally buried on Lookout Mountain.

Cody's funeral, like his life, was carried out on a grand scale. Described as "the most impressive and most largely-attended ever seen in the West," it was a service of such pomp and ceremony as only a head of state would have been granted.

At ten o'clock on the morning of January 14, Cody's body was taken from the Decker home to the state capitol, where it lay in state in the rotunda, beneath the huge dome and its flagpole, on which the Stars and Stripes floated at half mast.

The body was dressed in a frock coat on which were pinned the badges of the Legion of Honor and of the Grand Army of the Republic. The coffin bore the inscription: "Colonel William F. Cody, 'Buffalo Bill.'"

Troopers from Fort Logan formed lines in the rotunda, through which passed the governors of Colorado and Wyoming, delegations from the legislatures from those states, officers of the United States Army, members of the fraternal organizations of which Cody was a member, veterans of the Grand Army of the Republic, thousands of men, women, and children. Among the mourners were a handful of old Indians and former scouts—those who had been performers in Buffalo Bill's Wild West.

The rotunda was open for three hours. During that time, some eighteen thousand people according to the Denver *Post*'s estimates—twenty-five thousand was the New York *Times*'s guess—filed past the casket. At noon the crowd was kept back while the family, including his foster son, Johnny Baker, bade the Colonel farewell. A delegation of Knights Templar from North Platte followed. Next to pass the bier came a large number of old cowboys, greeting the old scout with "Good-bye, old pard," and "Good-bye, Bill." The guard of honor at the casket included members of the Colorado National Guard, the Pioneer Society, the Benevolent and Protective Order of Elks, and Civil War veterans, members of the GAR, the Grand Army of the Republic.

When the doors of the building—kept open half an hour longer than was planned—were finally closed, thousands more still waited outside.

That Sunday was bitterly cold, with a biting wind, but some three thousand people, many of them children, trudged through the snow and ice as the casket, on its horse-drawn caisson, was borne from the capitol to the Elks Home. Among those following in motor cars were the two governors, the lieutenant governor of Nebraska, Elks from Kansas and New Mexico, and Masons from North Platte. Seventy cowboys walked in the procession. Two of them led a riderless horse, with stirrups reversed and the old scout's pistols hanging from the saddlehorn.

Nellie Snyder Yost, one of Cody's most reliable biographers, commented: "Several writers say the horse was McKinley, the Colonel's last mount. . . . Actually, the nameless white horse came from a Denver livery stable, merely window dressing for the funeral of a man who had striven always to keep everything about *his* show strictly *real*."

At the Elks Lodge, the funeral service began at 3 o'clock. In the lodge hall, a quartet sang Cody's favorite song, "Tenting Tonight on the Old Camp Ground." Eulogies were read by John W. Springer, banker, who spoke for the Elks, and Albert U. Mayfield, of the Cowboy Rangers. In his eulogy, Springer waxed grandiloquent; no one connected with Cody's death ever seemed to strike a low key. The banker began by quoting, in full, Arthur Chapman's poem, "Out Where the West Begins": "Out where the skies are a trifle bluer / Out where friendship's a little truer, / That's where the West begins." Springer got the year Cody was born wrong, but even Cody himself, in his first autobiography, put his birth back a year.

The Elks' chaplain, the Reverend Charles H. Marshall, pastor of St. Barnabas Episcopal Church, then read the burial service, after which the coffin was taken to Olinger's mortuary to await its spring burial.

After the services, the many flower offerings sent in Cody's memory were taken to the headquarters of the Denver Flower Girls Association, where they were dismantled, so that each of the several thousand children in the grade schools of Denver could be given a souvenir flower.

Immediately after his death, a bill to erect a monument to Cody was introduced in the state senate. Reported the Denver *Post:* "The bill provided for the erection, by joint subscription of Wyoming, Colorado and Nebraska, of a mausoleum or monument over the place chosen for the last resting place of the scout." The bill called for $25,000 to be contributed by the city, another $25,000 by the state, and $25,000 each from the states of Nebraska and Wyoming.

Even before the funeral services were held, the Denver *Post,* spearheaded by Tammen and his partner Frederick G. Bonfils, started a drive to raise money for a Buffalo Bill memorial, to be built on Lookout Mountain. Before the end of January, a memorial association was permanently organized, with Mayfield of the Cowboy Rangers as president, W. H. Wheadon of the Elks as treasurer, and John C. Shaffer, publisher of the *Rocky Mountain News,* heading the advisory council.

Schoolchildren, too, were urged to contribute their pennies and nickels to the construction of the monument. BUFFALO BILL MEMORIAL TO BE BUILT BY CHILDREN OF U.S. PUBLIC SCHOOLS ran the *Post*'s headline. It was suggested that "no child be permitted to contribute more than 5 cents" to the memorial fund. The first contribution to the fund came the day after the funeral. It included forty buffalo nickels sent by the pupils of the primary and grammar grades of the Maple Grove school in Arapahoe County, "to build a monument to Buffalo Bill."

"Denver has donated a plot for the monument on Lookout Mountain," reported the New York *Times* on February 11, 1917, "and has offered to become custodian of the memorial. The peak chosen for the memorial is to be renamed 'Mount Cody' and on it will be erected a mausoleum, the interior of which will contain the tomb, as well as the trappings, relics, paintings, personal souvenirs, gifts and collections of 'Buffalo Bill.'

"Sculptured groups illustrating episodes in the life of the frontier will flank each corner of the monument. There will also be a heroic equestrian statue of the scout as he looked in youth."

There were actually two plans suggested for the monument. One was a grandiose affair, a domed structure 220 feet high, containing an art museum and a collection of Buffalo Bill's artifacts. The other proposal was a huge bronze sculpture of Colonel Cody as pictured in a painting by Pappacena.

In the end, the $100,000 a suitable monument would cost was never raised, least of all with the pennies of schoolchildren, and neither monument was ever built on Lookout Mountain. Cody's grave bears only a cairn of rough stones and a simple marker with the legend: "In Memoriam. Colonel William Frederick Cody, 'Buffalo Bill.' Noted scout and Indian fighter Born February 26, 1846, Scott County, Iowa. Died January 10, 1917, Denver, Colorado. At rest here by his request." A gift shop, tacky as so many gift shops are, refreshment stands, and a museum containing Cody artifacts called Pahaska Lodge are all that the townspeople of Denver managed to build. For years, Cody's foster son, Johnny Baker, and his wife looked after the souvenirs. Before Baker died in 1931 at the age of sixty-two, his last words to his wife were: "I want you to stay at Pahaska after I'm gone. I want you to keep alive the memory of the Colonel."

The grave was carved from solid granite and lined with cement, with a steel vault, so that the body could not be stolen for Cody, Wyoming, or North Platte, Nebraska, both claiming the Colonel as a native son. He could also have been claimed by Arlington, Virginia, where his military service entitled him to be buried.

The burial itself was another spectacular affair. It was held on June 3, five months after Cody's death. "A day has passed," wrote Gene Fowler rather pompously in the *Post*. "With it we have turned a page that cannot be rewritten. . . . It was the most impressive, the most notable funeral ever witnessed in America. No president could have been more honored by the presence of thousands. To Nature and to God, this afternoon, we Americans of the West surrendered Pahaska to his final slumber. Pahaska, Farewell."

Some twenty-five thousand people toiled up the mountainside to pay their respects. Three thousand automobiles (which included some Sells-Floto circus wagons) also climbed the mountain that day, not without strain, for cars of that time were not the powerful machines we know, and the Lariat Trail they followed, while a splendid achievement for 1913, was daunting. "The roads are excellent in their wealth of view," wrote Fowler. "At first the pitch of the road is gradual. It becomes more abrupt on the ascent. Its trend is ever upward." Mrs. Cody had to stop and rest before reaching the summit.

"It was a remarkable funeral," continued Fowler. "There was a circus atmosphere about the whole thing. A lot of us drank straight rye from bottles while speeches were being made by expert liars. Six of the Colonel's surviving sweethearts—now obese and sagging with memories—sat on camp chairs beside the grave. . . . The glass over the Colonel's amazingly handsome face began to steam on the inside. . . . One of the old Camilles rose from her camp chair. . . . Then, as though she were utterly alone with *her* dead, and while thousands looked on, this grand old lady walked to the casket and held her antique but dainty black parasol over the glass. She stood there throughout the service, a fantastic, superb figure. It was the gesture of a queen."

Fowler's account, while appealingly flamboyant, was disputed by Johnny Baker Jr., the twenty-one-year-old friend of Cody Boal, the Colonel's grandson. "It was hotter than seven hundred dollars that day," said Baker in a newspaper interview years later, "so they put a big umbrella, one of the great big ones like they use at beaches, over the casket to shade it. . . . Some things have been written about six of Buffalo Bill's old girl friends sitting in the front row at the burial, and that one of them stood up and shaded Mr. Cody's face with a little fancy parasol. There were chairs for the family, but I didn't see anyone I thought would have been there because she was an old girl friend of the Colonel's. And there was a big umbrella shading the casket, like I said."

If Johnny Baker Jr. was right, it is possible that Gene Fowler drank more than his share of rye that day, or that his imagination was working overtime. He would later become a chronicler of the Denver *Post*'s publishers Tannen and Bonfils, in his books *Timberline* and *Solo in Tom-Toms*, and of his drinking companion, the great actor John Barrymore, in *Good Night, Sweet Prince*.

Although it had been announced that the coffin would not be opened, it was, at Mrs. Cody's order. For two hours the crowd filed by, two abreast, parents holding their children shoulder high. The ceremonies were in the charge of Golden City Lodge No. 1, Ancient Free and Accepted Masons, acting for the North Platte lodge of which Cody had been a member. The Masonic burial ritual was read, as was an original poem dedicated to the scout by A. F. Beeler. The lambskin Masonic apron was dropped into the grave. Quince Record, chief musician of the Fifth Ohio Infantry in the Spanish-American War, sounded "Taps." The national flag was raised. A salute of eleven guns, that for a brigadier general, was fired by Colorado's Battery B.

"The most notable funeral ever witnessed in America" was over.

In all this hoopla, the citizens of Cody, Wyoming, who had mourned the old scout in their own way, without fanfare, had no part. Still, in one of those ironies of which history is so full, it was the town of Cody that wound up with a museum, the extraordinary Buffalo Bill Historical Center, considered one of the finest collections of western Americana in the country. And it was Cody that also got the monument, a statue of Buffalo Bill on horseback, sculpted by Gertrude Vanderbilt Whitney and set on a rise of ground just outside the center.

In North Platte, Nebraska, the North Side City Park was renamed Cody Park, and the Colonel's beloved Scout's Rest Ranch became a museum and art gallery, and a prime tourist attraction; in 1997, some thirty-five thousand people visited it—an impressive figure, when you consider that North Platte, Nebraska, is not on every traveler's itinerary. Visitors to Scout's Rest, however, will get a poignant and evocative sense of why Buffalo Bill so cherished his Nebraska ranch.

THE CODY
(OR WAS IT COADY?)
FAMILY TREE

If we are to believe Helen Cody Wetmore, one of William Cody's sisters, her family was descended from Spanish and Irish royalty, and were accordingly entitled to a crest. In her book *Buffalo Bill, Last of the Great Scouts: The Life Story of Colonel William F. Cody*, published in 1899, she wrote that her brother was "a lineal descendant of Milesius, king of Spain, that famous monarch whose three sons, Heber, Heremon, and Ir, founded the first dynasty in Ireland about the beginning of the Christian era."

The Cody family, Mrs. Wetmore asserted, came down from the line of Heremon. Their original name was Tireach, which signifies "The Rocks." Murdeach Tireach, one of the first of this line, was crowned king of Ireland in the year 320. Another of the line became king of Connaught in 701, his possessions being located in the present counties of Clare, Galway, and Mayo, whence came the family name, in a contraction of Connaught-Galway to Connelly, Conly, Cory, Coddy, Coidy, and, finally, "Cody."

All this almost makes sense. However, it is only one of the legends Mrs. Wetmore offers up as fact in her book, despite her disclaimer in the preface that "embarrassed with riches of fact, I have had no thought of fiction."

For the truth about William Cody's lineage, we must turn to Don Russell's authoritative biography, *The Lives and Legends of Buffalo Bill*. Russell's research was thorough and exemplary; the notes for his book in the Buffalo Bill Historical Center in Cody, Wyoming, are proof of that.

According to Russell, "Buffalo Bill's most remote definitely known ancestor was one Philip, whose surname appears in various surviving records as Legody, Lagody, McCody, Mocody, Micody . . . as well as Codie, Gody, Coady, and Cody."

Russell traces Philip to Philippe Le Caude of the Isle of Jersey, who married Marthe Le Brocq of Guernsey in the parish of St. Brelades, Isle of Jersey, on September 15, 1692. Although the family names are French, the Channel Islands have been British possessions since the Middle Ages. No Irish or Spanish in sight; just good English stock.

The Cody Family Association's book *The Descendants of Philip and Martha Cody* carries the line down to the present day. Buffalo Bill was sixth in descent from Philip. Philip and Martha purchased a home in Beverly, Massachusetts, in 1698, and occupied it for twenty-five years, farming six acres of adjacent land. In 1720 Philip bought land in Hopkinton, Massachusetts, and he and his family moved there, probably in 1722 or 1723. When he died in 1743, his will was probated under the name of Coady.

The spelling of the family name had stabilized by the time Bill's father, Isaac, the son of Philip and Lydia Martin Cody, was born on September 15, 1811, in Toronto Township, Peel County, Upper Canada. It is Lydia Martin Cody who may have been responsible for the report of an Irish king in the family genealogy; she boasted that her ancestors were of Irish royal birth.

When Isaac Cody was seventeen years old, his family moved to a farm near Cleveland, Ohio, in the vicinity of what is today Eighty-third Street and Euclid Avenue. That move would ultimately embroil William Cody in a lawsuit many years later, one of several suits he was destined to lose.

Six years after arriving in Ohio, Isaac married Martha Miranda O'Connor, who died in 1835, shortly after the birth of a daughter, also named Martha. Isaac married again soon after his first wife's death; his second wife was Rebecca Sumner of Medina County, Ohio. Within a short time Rebecca, too, was dead, leaving no children.

In 1839 Isaac set out for Missouri with his older brother Elijah and Elijah's family, leaving his daughter, Martha, in Cleveland. The travelers went by boat down the Ohio River, stopping along the way in Cincinnati. There Isaac met Mary Ann Bonsell Laycock. The couple quickly became romantically attached to each other, yet Isaac continued his travels nonetheless. However, he did not stay long in Missouri, but returned to Cleveland to pick up his daughter and then headed for Cincinnati, where he and Mary Ann were married in 1840. Unlucky though Isaac had been in his first two marriages, this one proved to be happy and fertile.

Mary Ann was descended from Josiah Bunting, a friend of Willia.
Penn. The Buntings migrated from Derbyshire, England, in 1690 and settled in Derby, Pennsylvania. Mary Ann's mother, Hannah Taylor Laycock, died in 1830; her father, Samuel, a sea captain, remarried and was
lost at sea shortly afterward. When her stepmother remarried, Mary Ann
went to live with her brother William in Cincinnati, and had been there
for three years when she met Isaac Cody. According to Julia Cody Goodman's *Buffalo Bill: King of the Old West*, Mary Ann was a schoolteacher
before her marriage.

Isaac Cody was a good husband and father but afflicted with a bad
case of wanderlust. Like many pioneers, he simply could not remain long
in one place. Shortly after his marriage to Mary Ann, he took his wife
and daughter to Davenport in the Iowa Territory, traveling down the
Ohio and up the Mississippi. There he prospered as an Indian trader, and
inside a year he bought a house in the town of LeClaire. He also filed a
claim on a site two miles west of LeClaire. He used his house as his headquarters for the next fourteen years, and his first son, Samuel, was born
there on February 22, 1841. Meanwhile, Isaac built a four-room log cabin
on his claim, and there his first daughter in his marriage to Mary Ann,
Julia Melvina, was born on March 28, 1843. It is altogether fitting that
William Frederick Cody was born in that same log cabin on February 26,
1846.

In the first of his two autobiographies, *The Life of the Hon. William F.
Cody, Known as Buffalo Bill*, published in 1879 by Frank E. Bliss of Hart-
ford, Connecticut, Cody gives his year of birth as 1845, but the family
Bible and the United States Census of 1850 show it as 1846. The fam-
ily eventually consisted of five daughters and two sons—Martha, Samuel,
Julia, William, Eliza, Helen, and May.

By 1849, when news of the discovery of gold in California reached the
East, Isaac Cody was a solid citizen of his community. In 1847 he contracted with William F. Brackenridge to clear a six-hundred-acre farm on
the Wapsipinicon River. Cody hired twenty-five men to open up the land,
and additional men to cut stone in a quarry on the tract and to build a
house of eight to ten rooms. In this stone house, still standing with additions, Cody lived as farm manager.

The news of the gold strike at Sutter's Mill was quite enough to
inflame Isaac Cody's wanderlust. He resigned as the Brackenridge farm
manager and planned to head to California with two other men, George
Long and Dennis Barnes. However, the trip never took place, either
because Cody became ill, or because Long got cold feet when he heard
reports of Indian attacks. The fate of the Donner Party, snowbound in the
High Sierras and resorting to cannibalism, may also have dampened Long's

he journey. In any event, Cody and Barnes were unable to
themselves, and it was aborted. Isaac Cody then swapped
on for an ambulance—what might be considered an early
version of the station wagon—and contracted to carry the mail and passengers from Davenport to Chicago, making one trip a week. By the year
1852, Isaac had sold both his LeClaire property and his stage business, and
once again hired on with Brackenridge to manage a large farm at Walnut
Grove.

Little Will Cody's Iowa years were filled with the kind of adventures
common to small boys living in the country. He learned to ride at an early
age and owned a dog named Turk. He described himself in his autobiography as something of a scamp, stealing apples and melons from a nearby
orchard, and being "nearly eaten up by a large and savage dog." On
another occasion, he claimed that he went out on the Mississippi River in
a boat with two other boys. They lost their oars, became frightened, and
let out a chorus of piteous yells. A man heard their cries and came to their
rescue, towing them to shore with his canoe.

Helen Cody Wetmore described her brother's dog as "a large and powerful animal of the breed of dogs anciently used in Germany in hunting
the wild boars. . . . His fidelity and almost human intelligence were time
and again the means of saving life and property; ever faithful, loyal, and
ready to lay down his life, if need be, in our service." Curiously, Cody
himself does not mention Turk in his autobiographies.

His early education was haphazard. In 1847 Will's father hired Miss
Helen Goodridge to teach school in a log building with board benches.
She had twelve to fifteen pupils, among them Martha, Samuel, and Julia.
The two-year-old Will went along with his brother and sisters, but his
exposure to book-learning was seemingly imperfect, judging by his spelling
later in life.

Much of his time, however, was not spent in school but in trapping
quails with figure-four traps, which he built himself, and riding horseback.

Helen Cody Wetmore tells a story about her mother that may also belong
more to family legend than to family history. It seems that Mary Ann Laycock and her sister were in a Southern city to which a fortune-teller came.
The two girls visited the seer, who prophesied that Mary Ann "would
meet her future husband on the steamboat by which she expected to
return home; that she would be married to him within a year, and bear
three sons, of whom only the second would live, but that the name of this
son would be known all over the world, and would one day be that of
the President of the United States." Mary Ann Laycock was persuaded by

the fortune-teller that Will Cody would indeed do great things when he grew up.

Either because of this prophecy or because he was so appealing as a child, he was doted on by his older sisters and worshiped by the younger, as well as being much fussed over by his mother.

The first part of the prophecy—if it was actually made—was fulfilled in the fall of 1853 when Samuel Cody, then twelve, died tragically.

One of Samuel's chores was to bring the cows home in the evening from a pasture two or three miles away. To do this, he rode a troublesome mare, Bettie. That day he passed by the schoolhouse just as school was letting out. He probably attempted to show off his horsemanship, and the mare, sensing that her rider had grown careless, reared and toppled over on her back, crushing Sam beneath her. In his 1879 autobiography, Cody wrote that he was riding along with his brother and promptly rode off to inform his father, who took Samuel to the house. A doctor was summoned, who examined the boy and told the family there was nothing he could do. Samuel died the next morning.

Isaac Cody was not long satisfied with the life of a farm manager. Upon learning that the Territory of Kansas was soon to be opened for settlement, he wrote to his brother Elijah, who was then living in Weston, Missouri, across the river from Leavenworth, Kansas, and asked for information. Elijah told him to come and stay with him. Isaac had also been assured by members of Congress, to whom he had written, that the act opening Kansas and Nebraska to settlement would be passed in the winter session. Once again Isaac resigned his job with Brackenridge and prepared to migrate.

On about the first of April in 1854, the Cody family was on the move. They were well equipped for the journey, with a large four-horse wagon, filled mostly with clothing, another wagon filled with goods to trade with the Indians, and a big family carriage, drawn, according to Helen Cody, by "a span of fine horses in silver-mounted harness." Will rode alongside the carriage, acting, as his sister put it, "as an armed escort." He himself described his role as "second in command."

The Codys did not camp out along the way, but went from county seat to county seat, usually staying in makeshift hotels or in private houses. The trip took them a month, for they stopped frequently and once took part in a horse race. In Missouri, young Will had his first encounter with a Negro, a slave who addressed the boy as "Massa."

Elijah Cody's home was in Weston, Platte County, Missouri, at that time a sizable community, where he ran a general store. Elijah welcomed his brother's family and put them up in a house on his farm two miles from town. Elijah suggested that he and his brother and their wives look over the prospects in the Kansas Territory. They took Will along with them.

After crossing the Missouri River by ferry, they stopped at Fort Leavenworth. A regiment of cavalry was there at the time, and young Cody was greatly impressed by a full-dress parade he saw. It is possible that the memory of those dragoons in their brightly colored uniforms came back to Cody when he planned his first Wild West show. At Leavenworth he also saw his first Indians and rode Indian ponies. He described the Indians as "dark-skinned and rather fantastically-dressed people . . . and as I had never before seen a real live Indian, I was much interested in them. I went over and endeavored to talk to them, but our conversation was very limited."

The West that the Codys were seeing for the first time in the 1850s was called "the Great American Desert," and carried that designation on contemporary maps; it was thought to be habitable only by savages and so was at first bypassed for settlement. However, on their way to the Potawatami Indian Reservation, where Elijah Cody had business to negotiate, the Codys crossed over a high hill known as Salt Creek Hill, from which they looked down into what Will Cody considered the most beautiful valley he had ever seen. Isaac and Mary Cody felt the same way; they immediately picked a site in the valley as their future home.

In the Salt Creek Valley, Will was much impressed by the sight of white-covered freight wagons, prairie schooners heading, his father informed him, to Utah and California. Both the Mormon and California emigrants passed through the valley and camped beside its numerous streams. The boy was warned by his father to avoid the Mormons, for a cholera epidemic that had already claimed hundreds of victims was raging in their camp.

On their return to the fort, Isaac Cody met the quartermaster and received permission to graze his horses in the valley. He also was given a contract to provide hay for the army and permission to build a cabin for his family's temporary use. Until the cabin was finished, Isaac and Will camped out in the valley, while Cody's mother and sisters remained in Weston. They traded for Indian ponies, one a gentle mare they named Dolly, the other an unbroken mustang that Will named Prince.

A young man they met shortly after their arrival turned out to be Horace Billings, the son of Isaac Cody's sister Sophia. Billings had left home years earlier and no one knew his whereabouts until he arrived at the Salt Creek Valley. He must have seemed the epitome of the westerner to little Will: Over six feet tall, well built, he wore a beaded buckskin suit and a broad-brimmed hat.

In his years of wandering, Billings had been a circus acrobat, had lived in Hawaii and California, where he worked not as a miner but as a mustanger, breaking horses. He helped Will break Prince and also taught the horse to kneel. He displayed his own skills as a horseman by riding one of the Cody horses bareback and standing up. He did not linger long in the valley, but returned to mustanging. His short stay left a permanent impression on young Cody, who undoubtedly borrowed some of the flamboyance he later displayed from Horace Billings.

On May 30, 1854, President Franklin Pierce signed the act Congress had passed to officially organize the Territory of Kansas. News traveled slowly in those days, and Isaac Cody learned of the Kansas-Nebraska Act only on June 10. He immediately packed up his wife and family and moved them to the cabin he had built in Salt Creek Valley. He could claim to be the first legal settler in Kansas, though there were already squatters in the territory. Isaac dutifully filed his claim at Fort Leavenworth and hired men to build him a seven-room log house.

One common feature of frontier life was the Fourth of July celebration. That first year in Kansas, Isaac Cody organized a patriotic fete, along with a missionary, the Reverend Joel Glover, and M. Pierce Rively, who operated a trading post for the Kickapoo, Delaware, and Cherokee Indians in the region. They decided on a barbecue and picnic and bought the necessary supplies. Except for those Indians, there weren't many neighbors to invite to the celebration. Cody and Rively got two large beeves, one for the whites, who roasted their meat in a pit and served it on a long table constructed of boards and sawhorses, and another for the Indians, who butchered it as they did buffalo and ate it in the same fashion, wasting nothing. The Indians gave war dances, ran horse races, and played games. The whites made patriotic speeches.

Although Isaac Cody may have been the first legal settler in Kansas, squatters from Missouri, most of them slaveholders, had preceded him, setting the stage for a fateful conflict. The Kansas-Nebraska Act of 1854 introduced the doctrine of popular sovereignty, which permitted all U.S. territories to have self-government in all matters, including slavery. It was only a matter of time before a bitter sectional rivalry broke out between free-soil and antislavery factions and the proponents of slavery. The Republican Party was formed by Free-Soilers and was ascendant by 1860.

Between 1854 and 1859, however, the issue figuratively tore Kansas apart and ushered in a period of political chaos and bloodshed. Free-soil forces from the North formed emigrant associations to populate Kansas, while pro-slavery advocates poured over the border from Missouri. Some of them brought bottles of whiskey with them, and when they had drunk the whiskey, they would drive the bottles into the ground to mark their claims. Four logs tied together in a square were called an "improvement" and entered as evidence of legal settlement. The town of Leavenworth consisted of four tents, a steam engine, and a sawmill. It was pro-slavery. Brutal and quarrelsome border men continued to pour into the territory from Missouri, most of them pro-slavery. They held meetings in Rively's trading post, expressing their intention to make Kansas a slave state. Northern abolitionists hurried from Illinois to fight the pro-slavery Missourians with gun and Bowie knife.

"Stake out your claims!" declared a border newspaper. "And woe to the Abolitionist or Mormon who shall intrude upon it!" Every Saturday night, rallies at the local grocery stores stirred the mob spirit around the whiskey barrels whose spigot poured a powerful liquor, said to have the strength of forty jackasses. A southerner waved a hundred-dollar bill, boasting "I just sold a nigger for that and I reckon that's my share for cleaning out them daggone Yankees!"

"If I had my way, I'd hang every damned Abolitionist!" trumpeted an editor named Stringfellow from the Missouri side of the river. "And everyone born north of the Mason-Dixon line is an Abolitionist." At his urging, a mob of horsemen rode into the Salt Creek Valley, where the Codys lived, and declared that slavery was "thereby instituted in the Territory of Kansas."

There was no government to speak of. "Govern Kansas?" said Wilson Shannon, the second territorial governor. "You might as well have attempted to govern hell!" Violence was inevitable. Guerrilla bands were formed by both parties. "Bleeding Kansas" became a reality with the sack of Lawrence, Kansas, in 1856, during which a pro-slavery mob swarmed into town, wrecking and burning the hotel and newspaper office in an effort to wipe out this "hotbed of abolitionism."

Three days later, John Brown led an antislavery band in what was called the Pottawatomi Massacre. Five pro-slavery settlers were dragged from their homes and hacked to death. After this raid, the name of "Old Osawatomie Brown" conjured up a fearful image among pro-slavery apologists. Less than three weeks after the battle, a drama called "Osawatomie Brown" opened on Broadway. Periodic bloodshed along the Kansas-Missouri border followed, as the two factions fought battles, captured towns, and set prisoners free; Brown went on to lead his ill-fated raid on Harpers Ferry in 1859.

Isaac Cody did not consider himself a Free-Soiler, but he was inexorably drawn into the conflict. On the very day he moved his family to Kansas, a group of quarrelsome squatters met in Rively's store to organize for the protection of their rights to illegal claims, a common practice in western settlement. The result was the Salt Creek Valley Resolutions of June 10, 1854. It attracted attention because of two provisions. The first: "That we recognize the institution of slavery as always existing in this Territory and recommend that slaveholders introduce their property as soon as possible." The second provision read: "That we afford protection to no Abolitionists as settlers of Kansas Territory." Rively was clearly a prime mover in these declarations.

Isaac Cody saw no reason to be concerned about the resolutions; he was not, after all, an abolitionist; his main ambition in coming to Kansas was to attain material success, not lead or join a crusade. Moreover, he was no politician. Although his son and daughters later claimed that he had been elected to the Iowa legislature, there is no record of his having ever served there.

Isaac Cody was credited with being a good public speaker, though, and on September 18, 1854, when he was passing Rively's trading post on horseback, he was hailed and asked to address his fellow settlers. He did his best to beg off, but some of the settlers took him to a large drygoods box that served as a platform and demanded a speech. As reported by his son, "as nearly as I can recollect," Isaac Cody explained that he had always voted to make Iowa a *white* state—"that Negroes, whether free or slave, should never be allowed to locate within its limits; and, gentlemen, I say to you now, and I say it boldly, that I propose to exert all my power in making Kansas the same kind of state as Iowa. I believe in letting slavery remain as it now exists, and I shall always oppose its further extension. These are my sentiments, gentlemen, and let me tell you—"

He never finished this sentence, or his speech. He may have intended to mollify the crowd with additional disclaimers, but he was shouted down, and several spectators attempted to drag him from his platform. One hot-headed pro-slavery man named Charles Dunn, an employee of Elijah Cody, stabbed Isaac twice in the chest with a Bowie knife. Dr. Hathaway, a neighbor who also supported the free-soil movement, took Cody into Rively's store and treated his wounds. Mrs. Cody was sent for. When she arrived with a wagon and driver, she took her husband to Elijah Cody's home to recuperate. He stayed there for three weeks. He had been stabbed in the lung.

Isaac Cody eventually recovered and resumed his normal life, but three years later, when he died, the stab wounds were listed as factors contributing to his death.

In his first autobiography, the one published in 1879, Buffalo Bill wrote only that "his father shed the first blood in the cause of freedom in Kansas." Helen Cody Wetmore's account of the episode gave her brother a leading role in the affair. "As father fell," she wrote, "Will sprang to him, and turning to the murderous assailant, cried out in boyhood's fury: 'You have killed my father. When I'm a man, I'll kill you.'" Helen Wetmore added that "supported by Will, father dragged his way homeward, marking his tortured progress with a trail of blood. This path was afterward referred to in the early history of Kansas as 'the Cody Bloody Trail.'"

Cody himself further embroidered the tale in his second autobiography, published after his death, in this fashion: "I saw the gleam of a knife. The next instant, without a groan, father fell forward stabbed in the back. Somehow I got off my pony and ran to his assistance, catching him as he fell. His weight overbore me, but I eased him as he came to the ground."

In this highly unlikely version, Isaac is stabbed in the back, not the chest, and though only eight years old at the time, the future scout is credited with an early act of daring, although his sister Julia later said that Willie was at home at the time of the stabbing.

Some observers took Cody's second account of the stabbing as proof positive that it never took place. The incident was, however, reported in the *Democratic Platform* of Liberty, Missouri, on September 28, 1854, and in a hostile fashion at that:

A Mr. Cody, a noisy abolitionist, living near Salt Creek, in Kansas Territory, was severely stabbed while in a dispute about a claim with a Mr. Dunn, on Monday week last. Cody is severely hurt, but not enough it is feared to cause his death. The settlers on Salt Creek regret that his wound is not more dangerous, and all sustain Mr. Dunn in the course he took. Abolitionists will yet find "Jordan a hard road to travel!"

There was a sequel to the original attack. Isaac Cody's neighbors showed their disapproval of his sentiments by driving off his horses. Then three thousand tons of hay he had put up to fulfill his Fort Leavenworth contract mysteriously burned.

Isaac Cody was not one to be frightened off by threats or violence. He filed his claim in Kickapoo Township, Leavenworth County, in the fall of that year, paying $1.25 an acre for it. He was in Kansas to stay.

Whether the attack on him prompted his future activity or not, in time he did take an active part in the affairs of his adopted state. He was instrumental in founding the new town site of Grasshopper Falls, later Valley Falls. Both a sawmill and a grist mill were built, and Isaac became active in an emigrant society that helped Free-Soilers move to the community to establish their homes. Clearly, Isaac Cody was every bit as memorable a character as his celebrated son.

Once he had finished building his own house in Grasshopper Falls, Isaac Cody established a school in his old log cabin. He hired Miss Jennie Lyons to be the teacher and rounded up a dozen children to attend it, including two Kickapoo Indian boys who became Will's friends. The school didn't last long, however. A group of squatters visited it and told Miss Lyons in no uncertain terms that they weren't going to let a "damned abolitionist" run a school, and that if they came again they would burn the school and everyone in it, since most of them were Cody's brats anyhow. The frightened teacher quit her job, and Will's education was interrupted, not for the last time.

During this period, nine-year-old Will, besides attending school, worked alongside his twelve-year-old sister Julia to plow ten acres and plant corn—perhaps the only time in his life he worked as a farmer.

On May 10, 1855, Charles Whitney, the last of the Cody children, was born. Charlie was always a delicate child and died at the age of nine, on October 10, 1864.

One episode that members of the family agreed took place at about this time concerned a justice of the peace named Sharpe. Apparently Sharpe came to the Cody house one evening and demanded food. He asked Mrs. Cody where "her damned abolitionist husband" was. Mary Cody told him that she thought her husband was in Grasshopper Falls, when actually he was upstairs, lying ill in bed. Sharpe sat in a chair, sharpening a Bowie knife on a whetstone and swearing that he was going to take Isaac Cody's lifeblood when he caught him. Mrs. Cody sent Will and her daughter Julia upstairs, telling the boy to get his gun and Julia to get an ax. They were waiting on the stairs, ready to attack if Sharpe attempted to take their father's life. Mrs. Cody kept on talking to the intruder until finally he left, though not before stealing Isaac Cody's saddlebags or Will's pony Prince, depending on whose version of the story you read.

Meanwhile, the troubles in Bleeding Kansas continued. Pro-slavery vigilantes terrorized the area, lynching and tarring and feathering. An abolitionist lawyer in Leavenworth, now growing rapidly into a city, was seized by a mob, his clothes stripped from him, his head shaved, covered with hot tar, ridden on a rail for more than a mile, and then, the ultimate indignity, sold for a dollar and a half by a Negro auctioneer. Pro-slavery elements endorsed this brutality and described the victim as a "moral perjurer."

On March 30, 1855, an election was held for the state's first legislative body, carried by ballot-box stuffers from Missouri. Free Staters called it "a bogus legislature." Aroused, the various opponents of the pro-slavery forces joined together and held a constitutional convention in Topeka. The so-called Topeka Movement held an election on January 15, 1856, in which Isaac Cody was elected a representative from the Twelfth District.

The pro-slavery men, or Border Ruffians as they were called, made no attempt to vote in this election, but they did commit one of the most atrocious crimes of the border war. At the town of Easton, near Leaven-worth, they threatened to stop the voting. A Free State militia company, led by Reese P. Brown, who was also a candidate for election, was called out to guard the polls. Kickapoo Rangers, the notorious squatters of Cody's hometown, caught Captain Brown unawares and hacked him to death.

Cody was active in the state legislature that year. He was one of the thirty-three members out of sixty who attended the first roll call to estab-lish a quorum. He served on the Ways and Means Committee and the Accounts Committee, and out of fifty roll calls, he was present at all but three.

But the harassment of Isaac Cody by the Kickapoo Rangers had by no means ended. On one occasion, as Will Cody tells it, a hired hand told him that "the pro-slavery men had laid another plan to kill him and were on their way to Grasshopper Falls." According to Helen Cody Wetmore, however, Will was in bed with what was then called "the ague," a malar-ial fever with chills and hot and sweating stages, when he heard about the plot to ambush his father on his return trip from the falls. His mother started him off on Prince, with a warning letter to his father in his sock. Though he was weakened by his illness, and a storm threatened, he set out on his mission. At Stranger Creek, about eight miles out, he saw a camp of armed men. One of them recognized him and cried out: "That's the son of the old abolitionist we're after." Though he was ordered to halt and a pistol shot was fired, young Cody galloped off, pursued by several men. Prince stayed barely a few hundred yards ahead of his pursuers. The storm finally broke; Will lost his hat and began to vomit. Realizing that he could not go much farther, he remembered that friends of his father, a family named Hewlette, had a farm about nine miles from the creek. If he could reach it in time, he would be safe. He arrived at the Hewlette gate just ahead of the Kickapoo Rangers. Although his horse's muzzle was white with foam and Will had puked all over the beast, he insisted on going on to warn his father. Mr. Hewlette told him that Isaac Cody had no intention of returning home before the end of the week, so there was no reason for him to go any farther. Hewlette then put the boy to bed, where he slept soundly and awoke the next morning feeling fine. He then rode on to Grasshopper Falls to join his father, who would remain a hunted man for the rest of his life.

When Isaac Cody and his son returned home several days later, it was felt that Isaac would not be safe in the house, inasmuch as there were watchers visible on a hill not far off. A bed was made up for him in a cornfield. During the day he wore a dress and cape and bonnet, so that he would look like a woman from a distance. Later he walked to Fort Leavenworth, but as he was ill from exposure, it took him three days to walk four miles. Will and Julia accompanied him, carrying food, water, and blankets from one stop to the next.

In early 1857 Isaac journeyed east to recruit settlers for his Grasshopper Falls colony. In Cleveland, he stayed with his brother Joseph. The two brothers went to Chicago to attend a Republican conference, and there Isaac met Abraham Lincoln, who was then still a country lawyer in Springfield but already an influential member of the fledgling political party. Isaac's eastern trip was a success; he brought some sixty families back to Grasshopper Falls with him, inviting them to stay at his house until they were settled. "As a result," wrote Mrs. Wetmore, "our house overflowed, while the land about us was white with tents; but these melted away, as one by one the families selected claims and put up cabins."

Because of the overcrowding, scarlet fever and measles broke out, and four people died; at the time, there was no known treatment for these diseases, no hospital in Grasshopper Falls; loved ones could only attempt, without much success, to alleviate the victims' suffering. While working in the rain in an effort to be helpful, Isaac Cody caught the chill that was to prove fatal. Dr. Hathaway was called but could do nothing; pneumonia had set in. Elijah Cody came from Weston, bringing another doctor with him. Despite all the efforts to save him, Isaac Cody died on March 10, 1857; he was only forty-six. He was buried in Pilot Knob Cemetery, overlooking Leavenworth. At the age of eleven, Will Cody, a handsome youth, conspicuous for his large brown eyes, his fine features, and his mop of blond hair, was a good rider, a crack shot, and the principal breadwinner for a family of six.

"THE YOUNGEST INDIAN SLAYER
ON THE PLAINS"

Frontier life in the nineteenth century did not allow for such indulgences as adolescence; children were considered small adults and expected to do their share of the work at hand. In Will Cody's case, that meant driving the Cody cows home from the meadow and hunting small game to contribute to the family larder—especially important because the Codys suffered from extreme hardship during the winter of 1854–1855. And even before Isaac's death, at the age of ten, the boy went to work to earn money. In his 1879 autobiography, Cody tells of being hired by William H. Russell at a salary of $25 a month. "I worked at this for two months and then came into Leavenworth. . . . Upon my arrival in Leavenworth with the herd of cattle, Mr. Russell instructed his book-keeper, Mr. Byers, to pay me my wages, amounting to fifty dollars. Mr. Byers gave me the sum all in half-dollar pieces. I put the bright silver coins into a sack, which I tied to my mule, and started home, thinking myself a *millionaire*. This money I gave to mother."

There is no verification for this story, though following his father's death, Will went to work for a neighbor, driving an ox team to Leavenworth for fifty cents a day.

The family was badly in need of money. Isaac Cody had died before accumulating the wealth he expected from his sawmill and grist mill in Grasshopper Falls. Also, according to Helen Cody Wetmore, a claim for $1,000, for lumber and supplies, was entered against the estate. Had the claim been allowed, the Codys would have lost their home. Fortunately, it was settled in the late summer. Meanwhile, Mrs. Cody took in boarders.

After his job driving the ox team was finished, Will told his mother that he wanted to work for the freighting company of Majors and Russell. Mrs. Cody took her son along with her to Leavenworth, when she went to shop at the company store. Alexander Majors had known Isaac Cody and was willing to aid his widow and son, but Will was still only a boy. What can a boy of your age do? Majors asked. Will replied that he could ride, shoot, and herd cattle, and that he often ran races in Salt Creek Valley with William H. Russell.

After the two partners discussed the matter, Russell offered young Will a job as an express boy. His duties were to carry messages between the firm and Fort Leavenworth, a distance of three miles. Will was happy to go to work for Majors and Russell. He was given a mule and told to report for work at eight in the morning. Like all the firm's employees, he was also required to sign the following pledge:

> While I am in the employ of A. Majors, I agree not to use profane language, not to get drunk, not to gamble, not to treat animals cruelly, nor to do anything else that is incompatible with the conduct of a gentleman. And I agree, if I violate any of the above conditions, to accept my discharge without any pay for my services.

After this oath was signed, Majors gave each man a Testament. It is unlikely that all of the teamsters, rough men in a rough age, observed all these prohibitions, but at this point in his life it was easy for Cody to cleave to the oath. Even as a grown man he did not use profanity. His favorite expressions were "Thunderation," "By Jiminy," or "You can bet your boots and socks."

Will Cody was at the office right on time and set off for the fort on his mule. He was so quick to get back that Alexander Majors thought he had not left and was about to scold him; instead, Will was complimented on his promptness.

Will kept this job carrying messages between the freighting office and the fort telegrapher for a couple of months, but there was too much sitting around and not enough action for one of his temperament, so he went to work herding oxen for one of the firm's wagon train bosses, John Willis. The oxen grazed about eight miles from the Cody home, so he was able to make frequent visits. His sister Julia recalled that on one visit he came in with a revolver that Willis had given him strapped around his waist, strutting proudly. When this job ended, he went home again.

After Miss Lyons, the schoolteacher, had been frightened off by Border Ruffians, the Codys' community was without a school, until a young man boarding with the Codys while he sought to stake a claim on a piece of land himself told them he had been a teacher in Illinois. That prompted Mrs. Cody to start a school herself. Will and his sister Julia managed to round up eighteen other youngsters, including Will, Eliza, and Helen, who would pay the young teacher two dollars a month each.

Classes opened in midsummer in an empty log cabin on the bank of a creek. Will, in his own words, "made considerable progress in my studies—such as they were—and was getting along well in every other respect, until I became involved in my first love affair."

The object of Will's youthful attentions was a girl named Mary Hyatt, with whom he was "dead in love." His rival for Mary's affection was a boy three years his senior named Stephen Gobel, the bully of the school. The boys in the school all built playhouses for their sweethearts, and Will built one for Mary. Steve Gobel promptly pushed it over. Will fought him and was knocked down. When the teacher learned of the quarrel, he whipped both boys. "This made matters worse than ever," Cody recalled, "as I had received two thrashings to Steve's one." Will built a second playhouse that afternoon, and Steve treated that one in the same fashion. At this point, Will told his rival that "if you ever do that again, I'll hurt you." The next day Will had a third playhouse almost two-thirds constructed when Steve once again pushed it over. The fight that followed found Will once again on his back, pinned down by Steve Gobel. This time he resorted to a small pocket knife he carried and slashed Steve on the thigh. It was not a serious wound by any means, but it did draw blood, as well as Steve's anguished cry that he had been "killed." The other pupils and the teacher came running, and Will decided he'd better make himself scarce. He fled to a wagon train led by John R. Willis, for whom he had herded cattle. When he told Willis what had happened, the wagon master hid the boy in one of his wagons. Soon Steve, his father, an elder brother, and the local constable came to arrest Will Cody. Willis, a Philadelphia lawyer at heart, demanded to see a warrant. When the constable admitted he didn't have one, Willis told him that he thought it was overdoing it to arrest a boy for what was only play. Will was safe—for the moment—but he was afraid to return to school. Willis suggested that young Cody accompany him on the wagon train, which was headed for Fort Kearny, a trip of some forty days, by which time the excitement ought to have cooled down. Will's mother consented to the trip, not without some foreboding; she feared that her son might be attacked by Indians. Cody wrote of this first trip across the plains that "it proved a most enjoyable one for me, although no incidents worthy of note occurred along the way."

John Willis disagreed with Cody about the lack of incidents. Forty years later Buffalo Bill's Wild West played Memphis on October 4, 1897, and Willis, now a judge in Harrisburg, Arkansas, wanted to see it. Unfortunately, he missed the show, but he wrote Cody the following letter: "Dear Old Friend it has been a long time since I have herd from you. . . . I would like very much to shake your hand, Billy, and talk over the old grand hours you rode at my heels on the little gray mule while I was killing Buffalo. oh them were happy days. of course you recollect the time the Buffalo ran through the train and stampeded the teams and you stoped the stampede."

Cody does describe the incident in his second autobiography. The wagon train was strung out over a trail near the Platte River, some two miles away. A large herd of buffalo was grazing between the road and the river. A party of Californians fired several shots, stampeding the herd. "About five hundred of them rushed through the train pell mell," wrote Cody, "frightening both men and oxen. Some of the wagons were turned clear around, and many of the terrified oxen attempted to turn to the hills, with the heavy wagons attached to them. Others turned around so short that they broke the wagons' tongues off. Nearly all the teams got entangled in their gearing, and became wild and unruly, so that the perplexed drivers were unable to manage them. The buffaloes, the cattle, and the drivers were soon running in every direction, and the excitement upset nearly everybody and everything. Many of the cattle broke their yokes and stampeded. One big buffalo bull became entangled in one of the heavy wagon-chains; and it is a fact that in his desperate efforts to free himself, he not only actually snapped the strong chain in two, but broke the ox-yoke to which it was attached, and the last seen of him he was running towards the hills with it hanging from his horns."

Cody wrote that the stampede lasted only a few minutes, but it did so much damage to the train that it took three days to make repairs before the train could move on. Not a word about having stopped the stampede, which would have required an extraordinary and daring feat of horsemanship for a boy of eleven or twelve.

On his return from Fort Kearny, Will was paid the same wages as the rest of the employees, and spent the rest of the summer and fall herding cattle and working for Majors and Russell. He was relieved to learn that his mother had made peace with the Gobel family and that he was no longer threatened with punishment. Moreover, he and Steve Gobel became good friends. "I have since often met Stephen Gobel," Cody wrote, "and we have had many a laugh together over our love affair, and the affray at the school-house." In 1879, the year Cody's first autobiography was written, Mary Hyatt, "the innocent cause of the whole difficulty," was married and living in Chicago.

At the time of Will Cody's plains crossing with John Willis, the firm of Majors and Russell, which later became Russell, Majors and Waddell, was thriving. In 1855 it had obtained a two-year contract from the U.S. Government, giving it a monopoly in carrying supplies to all the army posts west of the Missouri River. The contract was renewed on February 25, 1857, and during April and May their wagons set out loaded with supplies for the forts. Normally they would then have completed their government assignment for the year and turned to private freighting to keep the money coming in. However, in 1857 they were asked to transport three million pounds of additional supplies for the so-called Army of Utah.

At that time, the Mormons were in conflict with the federal government, thanks to the Mormons' determination to establish their own political and social system—and thanks also to the incompetency of federal territorial officials, many of whom had little sympathy for the religion of the Church of Jesus Christ of Latter-day Saints. Conflict was nothing new to the Mormons. Driven out of Missouri and then out of Illinois when their founder, Joseph Smith, was assassinated, they had settled in the Utah desert in the hope of finding peace.

In 1857 President James Buchanan, believing the Mormons to be in a state of open rebellion, ordered some 2,500 soldiers, a sixth of the United States Army, into Utah to replace Brigham Young, who had served as governor during the settlement's early years. This military force consisted of parts of two regiments of infantry, a regiment of dragoons, and a battery of artillery. With this, Buchanan meant to fight the Utah War, also called the Mormon War. The force was under the command of General Albert Sidney Johnston, later to be famous for his service in the Civil War.

Johnston's Army of Utah was organized in July 1857. On July 24 of that year, 2,500 Mormons gathered near Salt Lake City to celebrate the tenth anniversary of their arrival in Utah, which they had named Deseret. There they learned that General Johnston's army was preparing to march. Antagonism toward the Mormons continued unabated despite their exodus West. The reason for the hostility of course was polygamy, against the law then as now, as well as the hostility of the Mormons to the federal government. Polygamy was, in fact, a key issue in the election of 1856. John Fremont, running under the brand-new Republican banner, called for an end to both slavery and polygamy. His opponent, Democrat James Buchanan, concentrated on the inflammatory issue of polygamy.

Brigham Young prepared for what he thought would be an invasion by declaring martial law, mustering his militia, the Nauvoo Legion, and organizing a guerrilla band called the Mormon Raiders. "Woe, woe to those men who [come] here unlawfully to meddle with me and this people," said Young. "I swore in Nauvoo when my enemies were looking me in the face that I would send them to hell . . . if they meddled with me; and I ask no more odds of all hell today." These actions convinced Buchanan that Young was indeed acting like a traitor in open rebellion against his country.

While federal troops slowly moved west, a wagon train of migrants from Arkansas and Missouri entered southern Utah. In the train was a band of horsemen who called themselves the Missouri Wildcats. One Mormon described them this way: "They were the worst set that ever crossed the plains. They swore and boasted openly that they helped shoot the guts out of Joe Smith . . . and that Buchanan's whole army was coming right behind them, and would kill every God Damn Mormon in Utah."

On September 7, 1857, the wagon train reached a grassy area called Mountain Meadows. There are two versions of what happened next. In the first version, which is most probably the true one, two hundred Paiute Indians, thinking mistakenly that the migrants had poisoned their watering holes, attacked the train, were driven off, and then asked their allies the Mormons to join their siege. The Mormons living near Mountain Meadows sent a message to Salt Lake City, asking what they ought to do. Brigham Young sent back a courier with orders to let the migrants go on through Utah. Unfortunately, the courier arrived too late.

Meanwhile, a Missourian who had slipped away from the train to get help was caught and shot dead by the Mormons. Realizing that this death would bring reprisals from the advancing federal army, the Mormons decided to wipe out the entire wagon train to ensure that the story of the Missourian's murder never got out. So they joined the Indians in the attack, claiming later that the Paiute were entirely to blame for what had happened. The migrants were able to hold their own until a Mormon elder, John D. Lee, was ordered by a council of Mormon Elders to lure the emigrants into the open. "The orders were to *decoy* the emigrants from their position," Lee recalled, "and kill all of them that could talk. This order was in writing. . . . I read it and then dropped it on the ground, saying, 'I cannot do this' . . . I then left the Council and went away to myself and bowed myself in prayer before God and asked him to overrule the decision of the Council. . . . If I had then a thousand worlds to command, I would have given them freely to save that company from death."

The Paiute, who were eager to get on with the attack, nicknamed the vacillating Lee "Nah-Ghats"—Cry Baby—but in the end Lee approached the wagon train under a flag of truce and told the emigrants that the Indians had promised not to attack if they would lay down their arms. When they did so, someone gave a signal and the Mormons opened fire on the men, then stepped aside to let the Paiute kill all the women and all the children over the age of five. In under half an hour, 120 people were slaughtered.

"Although covered up at the time and blamed on the Indians," wrote Richard White in his book *It's Your Misfortune and None of My Own: A*

New History of the American West, "the Mountain Meadow Massacre would return to haunt the Mormons later."

It is not clear how much Brigham Young actually knew about the massacre, or when he knew it. Publicly, however, he put the blame for the violence on the Indians. Fearing revenge by the federal troops, he showed no interest in finding out who was responsible for the outrage. "The more you stir a manure pile," he said, "the worse it stinks."

What made the Mountain Meadow Massacre distinctive, other than white men attacking other white men in cold blood, was the rarity of Indian attacks on wagon trains. Despite their frequency in Hollywood movies, Indians rarely attacked the wagons on their way west; they were more inclined to charge the trains tolls or, in some instances, to hang around begging for food. Not all Indians were warriors; nor were all of them proud and independent.

After its late start, Johnston's army was slowed down further by Mormon raids on his supply trains and bad weather. The Mormons also stole army livestock and burned the grass the troops needed to feed their animals. Unable to reach Utah, the army had to halt for the winter at the site of Fort Bridger in Wyoming Territory; the Mormons had already razed that fort as well as Fort Supply.

In the end, the Mormon War was one without any further bloodshed. President Buchanan decided to call the war off, and Brigham Young agreed to step down as governor but remained as president of the Church of Jesus Christ of Latter-day Saints. Although he abandoned his resistance to the presence of federal troops in Utah, he remained in firm control of his church and his people. "The petrified truth is that Utah is an absolute monarchy and Brigham Young is king," wrote Mark Twain.

Twain's report of the massacre in *Roughing It* is the second version. In this version, Mormons dressed themselves as Indians and launched the first attack. When it failed, they withdrew, washed off the warpaint and put on their own clothes, and then thirty of them, heavily armed, approached the wagon train under a white flag. They persuaded the Missourians to lay down their arms and march out of their camp, leaving everything behind. When they were about a mile from the camp, the signal was given and the Mormons opened fire, killing all the men in the first volley.

In the summer of 1857 meanwhile, Majors and Russell had managed to put together the fifty-nine wagons required to transport their supplies. Since the company was short on manpower, they undoubtedly could find use for Will Cody's services. In both his autobiographies, he describes starting for Salt Lake City with a herd of cattle destined as beef for the troops. The wagon train, Cody recalled, was headed by Frank and Bill McCarthy. The McCarthy brothers, in Will's view, were typical westerners: rough but courageous, and with plenty of experience on the frontier.

On this trip, if it actually took place, Will would probably have been a boy "extra," whose job was to ride from one wagon to another, relaying orders. He told of an attack on the wagon train by Indians, near Plum Creek, on the South Platte River, thirty-five miles west of Old Fort Kearny. The teamsters were compelled to take cover in the bed of the Platte River, using the steep banks as breastworks. They decided to make their way on foot to the fort. Clinging to his old Mississippi Yager rifle, a short muzzle-loader that carried a ball and two buckshot, Will soon tired and fell behind the others. "Presently the moon arose, dead ahead," Cody wrote in his second autobiography, "and painted boldly across its face was the black figure of an Indian. He wore the war-bonnet of the Sioux and at his shoulder was a rifle, pointed at someone in the bottom below him. I knew well enough that in another second he would drop one of my friends. So I raised my Yaeger and fired. I saw the figure collapse, and heard it tumbling thirty feet down the bank, landing with a splash in the water."

Thus did Will Cody kill his first Indian—according to Cody. He and his sister Helen both claim that when he got back to Leavenworth, he was interviewed by a reporter for the Leavenworth *Times* and that his adventure was published as a feat of "the youngest Indian slayer on the Plains, making him something of a local hero." Cody identified the reporter as John Hutchinson, who was living in Wichita, Kansas, in 1879 when the first autobiography was published. However, no trace of the story has ever been found in the files of the Leavenworth *Times*, so it was probably one of the adventures that Cody made up, or a story of someone else's encounter, embellished by Cody in the telling. It is equally doubtful that he made that particular trip at all; his accounts of it are confusing. Still, it all makes a good yarn, so good one would wish it to be true.

Don Russell, on the other hand, insists that "Bill's story is not so remarkable as to seem an invention. That the newspaper account of it has not been found proves little, for more frontier newspapers than Indians became casualties in early Kansas. Whether Bill killed an Indian at eleven, or twelve, or thirteen years of age is of scant importance, but [as] he seldom told any tale without some basis of fact, it seems probable that he did."

THE DARK SIDE
OF "MANIFEST DESTINY"

Whether Will Cody shot his first Indian brave at the tender age of eleven or not, it is quite true that the blood in Bleeding Kansas was not shed solely by Border Ruffians or Free-Soilers. The Indians of Kansas were the fierce Cheyenne, Kiowa, and Arapaho, among others, and the warriors of these tribes did not take kindly to the advance of white settlers into their territory.

The history of what became known as the Plains Indian Wars goes back to Major Stephen Harriman Long, who led one of the United States' most important western explorations since the Lewis and Clark expedition. Not only soldiers and adventurers but also men of science accompanied Long's small army, which was ordered to seek sites for military posts that would offset the British strength in the north. Long followed the Platte River across the Nebraska plains in the year 1820 and described the area extending five or six hundred miles east of the Rockies as being "uninhabitable by a people depending on agriculture for their subsistence" and useful to the United States in the future only "as a barrier against too great an expansion of our population westward." It was Long who dubbed this region "the Great American Desert." The mistaken notion that the region was a wasteland kept white settlement to a minimum on the plains west of the Missouri River until the middle of the nineteenth century, when the Indian tribes that had long lived east of the Mississippi were driven west by whites who wanted their rich farmlands for themselves. Since the plains were thought to be a worthless desert by the federal government, why not resettle the unwanted eastern Indians upon these desolate prairies? Tribes from the Alleghenys and the Ohio watershed—the Shawnee, Kickapoo, Delaware, Wyandot, and others—were uprooted and forced to settle in the West. But these plains were not uninhabited, any

32

more than the North American continent was uninhabited when the white man first arrived; and the plains Indians who already populated the region were naturally unhappy at having to share their hunting grounds with tribes they regarded contemptuously as farmers. The situation was bound to erupt in internecine warfare.

At the same time, there was a resurgence of republican imperialism in the mid-1840s. Expansionists argued that extending the nation's boundaries was not only a triumph for liberty but that Canada, Mexico, Cuba, and all the other lands of North America belonged to the United States by right of "manifest destiny."

Manifest destiny in its broadest conception meant that Americans were a chosen people ordained by God to create a model society. It was a nationalist doctrine that asserted a destiny for a united nation. But the country was not united; on the contrary, it was sharply divided into two distinct regions, the North and the South. Manifest destiny also assumed that the continent belonged to the white race no matter who lived on it, yet the West was already occupied and to some extent already developed by non–Anglo-Saxon peoples, both the Indians and the Spanish. Expansionists claimed that expansion would solve both the political problem of slavery and the economic problems that had led to a deep depression. The expansionists did manage to forge a sectional alliance between the slave and the free states to achieve their aims, and Presidents Tyler and Polk were both supporters of expansion during their administrations in the mid-1840s. Although chiefly a tenet of the Democratic Party, individual Whigs and Republicans also supported manifest destiny.

Fearing that warfare among the Indians would threaten the wagon trains moving westward, to what was soon considered the American Eden, the federal government decided that the Indian lands ought to be divided up into tribal "colonies" or "territories" (what later became the reservations). If the Indians were thus sequestered, conventional wisdom had it, they would be safe from whites and could, in the fullness of time, be converted to Christianity and become God-fearing farmers. The Indians were to be wards of the state while they were fashioned into imitation Caucasians.

The first step was to persuade tribes whose entire way of life was built on nomadism and courage in battle to give up both.

The U.S. Indian agent for the Upper Platte and Arkansas Agency was the former mountain man Tom "Broken Hand" Fitzpatrick. He was wise enough in the ways of Indians to know that it would be hopeless to attempt to keep them penned up like domestic animals, that to do so would require a much larger military force than Congress was likely to provide, but he agreed to do the best he could. Accordingly, he summoned the chiefs of the various tribes to meet at Fort Laramie on the North Platte for a conference with the *Wasicus* (whites).

The meeting took place in September of 1851. Some ten thousand Lakota Sioux, Cheyenne, Arapaho, Crow, Gros Ventre, Blackfeet, and a handful of Assiniboin, Mandan, and Hidatsa attended, all decked out in their finest ceremonial costumes, making a dazzling burst of color on the brown, barren prairie. Present to watch over them were 270 nervous soldiers. It was one of the largest gatherings in Indian history, and would have been even larger, had not the Pawnee refused to attend; they were certain the Lakota would kill them all. Similarly, the Kiowa and Comanche stayed away; they had too many horses, one chief said, "to risk among such notorious horse thieves as the Sioux and Crows."

The government heaped the attending Indians with gifts of beads, blankets, and utensils, and promised them $50,000 worth of supplies a year for fifty years, along with the assurance of swift punishment for any whites who invaded their land. "The United States recognized the political right of the Northern Plains tribes to police their own lands," wrote Vine Deloria Jr. in *Custer Died for Your Sins*, "and, until these lands were ceded, they properly belonged to, and were under the control of, these tribes; and intruders took their own risks."

In turn, the Indians were to promise not to harass the white wagon trains and to allow the government to build forts and roads to protect the trains—which they were already doing. The tribes were also to stay within their assigned boundaries and not make war on each other. They were shown a crude map drawn by the mountain man and scout Jim Bridger, showing where their assigned lands would be. These lands were promised to them "as long as grass shall grow and the waters run."

The Lakota wanted no part of this arrangement. They had been used to taking land by conquest, very much like the whites who had driven the eastern Indians across the Mississippi. "You have split my land and I don't like it," said the Lakota chief Black Hawk. "These lands once belonged to the Kiowas and the Crows, but we whipped these nations out of them, and in this we did what the white men do when they want the lands of the Indians." Unable to persuade the Lakota to accept their assigned territory, the Americans backed down and let them remain in their sacred hunting grounds.

When the American delegates sought to get signatures on their treaties with the tribes, they found that no tribe was willing to name a supreme leader; accordingly, the whites appointed chiefs to sign. It is altogether possible that most of the Indians had no idea of what they were signing, and what they were losing—in truth, their birthright.

* * *

Two years later Tom Fitzgerald reported that the constant stream of wagon trains plying the Oregon Trail had caused the tribes to be "in abject want of food half the year. . . . The travel upon the road," the agent wrote, "drives [the buffalo] off. . . . Their women are pinched with want and their children constantly crying with hunger." At the same time, the Indians were falling by the hundreds to cholera and other diseases brought by the white man. Already the Mandan, for one tribe, had been almost exterminated by smallpox. Cholera struck first in 1849 and hung on for nearly a year, killing nearly half the Cheyenne tribe and devastating the Sioux. It was followed by a smallpox epidemic, and measles.

There were no cures for these diseases; they were especially devastating to the Indians because they were unused to them. Moreover, they did not exist among Indians before the whites' arrival in the West.

The Sioux and Cheyenne began to talk of taking vengeance against the whites; they were convinced that the cholera was a wicked magic that had been deliberately introduced among them. It was now only a matter of time before the Indians would actually seek their revenge.

In August of 1854, the Brulé Sioux tribe of the Dakota came to Fort Laramie to collect their supplies. While they were there, a calf wandered off from a Mormon wagon train and was killed by a hungry Dakota. The calf was lame and may have been abandoned, but the owner saw a chance for reimbursement and complained to the fort commandant. Chief Conquering Bear offered more money than the calf was worth and apologized, but the army turned down his offer. A trigger-happy young lieutenant named John L. Grattan, who hoped to win a reputation as an Indian fighter, was sent to arrest the brave who had killed the calf. Grattan marched with thirty men to the Dakota camp. He was resolved "to conquer or die" despite his orders "to avoid unnecessary risks." When the warrior resisted arrest, Grattan, who had two howitzers with him, panicked and opened fire on the Dakota without warning. Conquering Bear was the first to fall. Enraged, the Indians leapt to the attack. Grattan hastily retreated but was soon surrounded, and he and his men were cut down. Only one soldier managed to crawl back to Fort Laramie, where he died.

The Grattan Massacre, to give the incident its unfortunate name (Indian victories in battle were commonly called "massacres," while white victories were always known as "battles"), caused a nationwide furor. Jefferson Davis, the secretary of war, declared the tragedy "the result of a deliberately formed plan" and ordered the army to exact punishment. Troops under General William S. Harney attacked Conquering Bear's people, killing eighty-six and carrying off seventy women and children. Half a century of peace between the Lakota Sioux and the Americans had come to a bloody end; conflict would simmer with small-scale raids and occasional murders on each side. Almost forty years would pass before the Sioux would lay down their weapons for good. Meanwhile, a trip across the plains in a wagon train remained a hazardous enterprise, though more emigrants fell victim to cholera, "milk sickness," or the "puking fever" than to Indian arrows.

Manifest destiny fulfilled its purpose in regard to the Native Americans; between 1852 and 1856 the United States negotiated some fifty-two treaties with tribes of the trans-Mississippi West, that vast area of America that lay west of the Mississippi River. These treaties transferred over 170 million acres of Indian land to the federal government.

In October 1857 Will Cody, determined now to be a plainsman though he was only eleven, again asked Alexander Majors for work. He was assigned to wagon master Lewis Simpson as an "extra hand." Mrs. Cody raised an objection to Simpson, as she had heard that he was "a desperate character, and that on nearly every trip he had made across the plains he had killed someone." Mr. Russell assured her that these stories of Simpson's violent temper were much exaggerated and that Simpson was in fact one of the most reliable wagon masters on the plains. Mrs. Cody also disliked the idea of her young son being away from home for a full year. Will was so determined, however, that he threatened to run away if she would not agree to let him go. After talking with Simpson herself, she finally gave her consent. On this trip, Cody rode his own mule and had the chance to be a relief driver, or bull-whacker, on the wagons.

In his first autobiography Cody gave a description of the wagon train: "The wagons used in those days . . . were known as the 'J. Murphy wagons,' made in St. Louis especially for the plains business. They were very large and were strongly built, being capable of carrying seven thousand pounds of freight each. The wagon boxes were very commodious—being as large as the rooms of an ordinary house—and were covered with two heavy canvas sheets to protect the merchandise from the rain. These wagons were generally sent out from Leavenworth each loaded with six thousand pounds of freight, and each drawn by several yokes of oxen in charge of one driver. A train consisted of twenty-five wagons, all in charge of one man, who was known as the wagon-master. The second man in command was the assistant wagon-master; then came the 'extra hand,' next the night herder, and lastly, the cavallard driver, whose duty it was to drive the lame and loose cattle. There were thirty-one men all told in a train. The men did their own cooking, being divided into messes of seven. One man cooked, another brought wood and water, another stood guard, and so on, each having some duty to perform while getting meals. All were heavily armed with Colt's pistols and Mississippi yagers." The Mississippi yager rifle was a single-shot weapon carrying a conical or Minié ball, and made famous by the Mississippi volunteer regiment commanded by Colonel Jefferson Davis in the Mexican War of 1846–1847.

"The wagon-master," Cody continued, "was called the 'bull-wagon boss,' the teamsters were known as 'bull-whackers,' and the whole train was denominated a 'bull-outfit.'"

It was on the trip with Simpson, Cody recalled, that he first met James Butler "Wild Bill" Hickok. "He was a plainsman in every sense of the word," wrote Cody. "In person he was about six feet and one inch in height, straight as the straightest of the warriors whose implacable foe he was. He had broad shoulders, well-formed chest and limbs, and a face strikingly handsome. . . . His hair and complexion were those of the perfect blonde. The former was worn in uncut ringlets, falling carelessly over his powerfully formed shoulders. Add to this figure a costume blending the immaculate neatness of the dandy with the extravagant taste and style of the frontiersman, and you have Wild Bill. Whether on foot or horseback, he was one of the most perfect types of physical manhood I ever saw."

Cody described an incident involving Hickok in which Will was the victim of one of the teamsters, a notorious bully who slapped him in the face and knocked him off an ox yoke on which he was sitting. Will retaliated by picking up a pot of boiling coffee and tossing the scalding liquid into the teamster's face. The teamster leapt on the boy and "would undoubtedly have torn me to pieces," except that Wild Bill Hickok knocked the man down. When the teamster protested, Hickok declared that he would protect the boy from being kicked or cuffed, and "if you ever again lay a hand on that boy—little Billy there—I'll give you such a pounding you won't get over it for a month of Sundays."

This, said Cody, cemented a friendship that lasted until Hickok's death.

Did this actually happen? Again, one would like to think so. However, Joseph G. Rosa, Hickok's most trusted biographer, writes in *Buffalo Bill and His Wild West: A Pictorial History*: "In fact, neither Cody nor Hickok was with Simpson's train on that occasion. Billy was at home in Leavenworth, while Hickok was at Monticello in Johnson County."

The Codys apparently met Hickok when he lived near Leavenworth for several months in 1856. In 1859 he became a regular visitor to the Cody home. It is a fact that Cody and Hickok were close friends.

Rosa's denial that Cody was a member of the Simpson wagon train is disputed both by Don Russell and, of course, by Cody himself, who described the trip in both his autobiographies. What is unclear is precisely where in his personal history this trip fits. Did it precede the trip with the McCarthy brothers, as Don Russell wrote, or follow it, as Cody himself claimed? Cody describes three trips across the plains, but their chronology is so confusing it's practically impossible to straighten them out.

In his second autobiography, Cody wrote of an incident in which Simpson's wagon train was captured by the Danites, the Mormon militia, in the course of the Mormons' attacks on Albert Sidney Johnston's supply trains. On October 5, 1857, Major Lot Smith's Mormon party captured Lewis Simpson's Train 26. Simpson succeeded in talking Smith out of one wagon, oxen to pull it, provisions, clothing, and even their arms. The Danites then proceeded to set the rest of the wagon train aflame. Lot Smith left his own account of the capture, in which he said, "Captain Simpson was the bravest man I met during the campaign."

In Cody's version of this incident, the teamsters were left without a single weapon and were forced to walk the thousand miles home to Leavenworth. "The wagon was loaded to full capacity," he wrote. "There was nothing to do but walk. I was not yet twelve years old, but I had to walk with the rest the full thousand miles, and we made thirty miles a day."

Cody wrote that he wore out three pairs of moccasins on that journey and learned then that "the thicker are the soles of your shoes, the easier are your feet on a long walk over rough territory."

On the face of it, the story of the thousand-mile walk home seems quite improbable. In fact, Cody's first autobiography contradicts it, claiming that after their wagon train was burned, the wagons, which were loaded with bacon, lard, hardtack, and other provisions, "made a very hot, fierce fire and the smoke to roll up in dense clouds. Some of the wagons were loaded with ammunition, and it was not long before loud explosions followed in rapid succession."

Simpson's party made its way to Fort Bridger and spent the winter there with troops of the Army of Utah and remnants of wagon train personnel who had been attacked by the Danites. Two other trains had been captured and burned in the same fashion as Simpson's. Seventy-five wagon loads, or 450,000 pounds of supplies, never reached General Johnston's command.

Will Cody's presence at Fort Bridger was verified by Trooper Robert Morris Peck of the First U.S. Cavalry, who wrote his reminiscences for the *National Tribune* in 1901. Peck says that Cody "was then a boy of 11 or 12 years old, employed by Lou [sic] Simpson, a bull-train wagon boss, as an extra hand, or 'cavvyard' driver or something of the kind.

"He gave no visible signs then of future fame, and only impressed me as a rather fresh, 'smart-ellick' sort of kid. The bullwhackers had made quite a pet of him and one of them informed me that Billy was already developing wonderful skill at riding wild horses or mules, shooting and throwing a rope, etc. I had almost forgotten that I had ever seen the little dirty-faced bull-whacker when, just after the war, I heard the name of 'Buffalo Bill' mentioned frequently in connection with frontier affairs. I thought at first it was another nick-name that had been conferred on 'Wild Bill,' whom I had known on the plains by several sobriquets, as 'Injun Bill' and 'Buckskin Bill,' but on asking an old comrade who had been with me in Utah, 'Who is this Buffalo Bill I hear so much about?' he answered 'Why don't you remember Bill Cody, that smart little fellow that was with Lou Simpson's bull-train as an extra hand?' my recollection of him was revived."

In the West of that period, apparently men were often called "Bill" whether their first names were William or not, as was the case with Hickok.

In his first autobiography, Cody describes conditions at Fort Bridger during that severe winter. There were about four hundred teamsters there, and they were divided into militia companies, with the wagon bosses as captains. Because they expected to run short of food, they were immediately put on three-quarter rations, then half rations, and finally one-quarter rations. They killed many of the cattle, some of them so emaciated and weak that they had to be stood up to be shot. The mules were the next to be sacrificed for food.

Will returned to Fort Leavenworth in July of 1857. He went back to school intermittently during the winter of 1857–1858, at his mother's insistence. She was determined that her son would have some kind of education. "The master of the school wore out several armfuls of hazel switches," wrote Cody, "in a vain attempt to interest me in the 'three Rs.'"

In the spring, young Will was eager to be on the move again. Simpson gave him a job as a general utility man. In that capacity, he rode horseback and also got a chance to be a relief driver, or bull-whacker, on the wagons.

Simpson believed that oxen were faster than mules, so to entertain his crew he arranged for a race between his wagon train drawn by oxen and one drawn by mules. The winner would be the first train to reach Fort Laramie. Although most bulls couldn't do much better than fifteen miles a day with heavily loaded wagons, Simpson's selected animals, according to Cody, could do twenty-five.

The mule train lost the race at the Platte, when it became mired in the river's soft, muddy banks, while the bulls plunged in through the mud and swam or wallowed their way across on their bellies, using their legs as paddles, with the Conestoga wagons floating behind them.

On this trip, Cody got his first look at Fort Laramie. This splendid bastion of the Old West had been established by a fur-trading company in 1834 and was bought by the government in 1849 and used as a military post. The fort stood eighty air miles to the northeast of the present city of Laramie, Wyoming. Before Cody saw it, thousands of emigrants had already passed through, stopping to rest, to buy supplies, or to wait for others in their party to show up. Forty-niners, the flood of hopeful gold-seekers that poured into California in 1849, had passed through Fort Laramie, as had army detachments and missionaries; both Brigham Young's Mormons and the members of General John C. Fremont's expedition had spent time there.

"Surrounding the adobe walls," wrote Henry Sell and Victor Weybright in *Buffalo Bill and the Wild West*, "was a peaceful settlement of several thousand Indians, Sioux, Arapaho, Cheyennes—many of them sleeping in the sun while their naked children ran up and down the hillside. Blockhouses stood at each corner and there was a fortified tower over the main gate. Inside the walls there was a self-sufficient village, complete with stores, houses, a blacksmith shop, the whole fortress built to resist a siege."

"Laramie had become the most famous meeting-place of the plains," wrote Cody in his second autobiography. "Here the greatest Indian councils were held, and here also came the most celebrated of the Indian fighters, men whose names had long been known to me, but whom I never dared hope to meet. . . . It was here that I had abundant time and opportunity to study the West at first hand."

The famous scouts Kit Carson and Jim Bridger were there during the summer of 1858, and Cody had the chance to meet both of his heroes. Kit Carson was then fifty years old, and his great days as a scout—guiding John C. Fremont and General Phil Kearny—were past. He lived now in Taos, New Mexico, and visited Laramie regularly. He was a small, quiet, dapper man who fascinated young Will. "I used to sit for hours and watch him and the others talk to Indians in the sign language," wrote Cody. "Without a sound they would carry on long and interesting conversations, tell stories, inquire about game and trails, and discuss pretty much everything that men find worth discussing."

While at Laramie, Cody was able to learn "this mysterious medium of speech" and also to pick up a working knowledge of the Sioux language—an acquisition that would stand him in good stead later on. He played with Indian boys and learned something of their ways.

From Jim Bridger, who was the epitome of the mountain man, one who needed no maps, Cody learned that "you could love a mountain as intimately and passionately as a man could love a woman." It was through meeting these two famous men that Cody decided to become a scout.

In January of 1859, Simpson, now a brigade train master, was ordered to return with three trains to Leavenworth, the trains each traveling a day apart. Will Cody decided to return home with Simpson.

Instead of following the trail down the South Platte, Simpson picked a new route along the North Platte. There was no road, but the grass was still long and they needed forage for the cattle.

One morning Simpson took George Wood, his assistant wagon master, and Will to ride with him from the rear train to the one ahead. They had gone about seven miles on their mules and were on a large plateau in back of Cedar Bluffs when a party of Sioux bore down on them. "There was little time to act," wrote Cody in his *Life Story*. "No cover of any kind. For us three, even with our rifles, to have stood up against the Sioux in the open would have been suicide. . . . I thought that our end had come this time sure. Simpson, however, took in the situation in a moment, and knowing that it would be impossible for us to escape by running our played-out mules, he jumped from his own mule and told us to dismount also. He then shot the three animals, and as they fell to the ground he cut their throats to stop their kicking. He then jerked them into the shape of a triangle and ordered us inside the barricade." The Indians, forty altogether, charged. Simpson, Wood, and Cody first fired their Mississippi yager rifles, and then their Colt revolvers. The Indians checked their charge, as they usually did when they met resistance, and began circling the barricade, responding with a shower of arrows and a couple of bullets. Only a few of them had firearms. One of the arrows struck Wood in the shoulder, but the wound was not serious enough to put him out of action. Simpson examined the arrow and decided that it had not been poisoned.

After all the shooting, three Indians and a horse lay dead—not an especially spectacular fight. The Sioux tried to burn their quarry out, but the late-winter buffalo grass was too short to be effective. At dawn the Indians attacked again, but again they retreated when they discovered that the trio were not out of ammunition. "But we were still heavily outnumbered," wrote Cody. "They knew it and we knew it. Unless help came it was only a question of time till it was all over."

At ten o'clock in the morning, the loud crack of a bullwhip was heard, and the lead wagon of the train appeared. The Indians mounted their horses, made a halfhearted charge, fired a last volley of arrows, and rode off.

Cody later reported that Wood's wound had become inflamed and painful. He was put in one of the wagons, while Will and Simpson obtained remounts to replace their dead mules. After securing the orna-ments "and other plunder" from the dead Indians, "we left their bodies and bones to bleach on the prairie."

Will had at least one more adventure before this trip was over. After some buffalo hunting along the Platte near Plum Creek, Simpson sent him with two other men, Charley and Scott, ahead of the wagon trains with the train-book record, so that the teamsters' wages would be ready when they reached Leavenworth. They were pursued by Indians for two hours but succeeded in finding shelter in a deep ravine. Will found a hole in the ravine's bank into which they crawled, but when Charley struck a match to light his pipe, they saw to their horror that the cave was full of skeletons. "Skulls were grinning at us from every corner of the darkness," wrote Cody. They had obviously stumbled into an Indian burying ground, and left as soon as they could.

Back in Leavenworth, Will collected his pay, which was nearly $1,000—a great deal of money in those days.

Thirty years later, on Cody Day at the 1898 Trans-Mississippi Exposi-tion at Omaha, he recalled the pride he had felt at that time. "Ain't it splendid, Mother, that I can get all this money for you and my sisters," he remembered saying as he spread the silver coins on the table. Then, car-ried away by the memory of that moment, he added: "And I've been spreading it ever since!"

Alexander Majors told the same audience at the Omaha Exposition how young Cody practiced his writing skills all along the route of the wagon train, for Majors had found "Will Cody," "Little Billy," "Billy the boy messenger," and "William Frederick Cody" written with the burned end of a stick on tents and wagon covers—and carved on wagon bodies, or wherever Will could find a wooden surface to use his penknife.

In all these adventures, we must realize that Cody was only thirteen years old, a time when other boys of his age were in school. And school is where he went after he got back home and delivered his wages to his mother. Mr. Valentin Divinny was the teacher, Cody said, "and my mother wished me to attend it, and I did for two months and a half—the longest period of schooling that I ever received at any one time of my life." This was the fifth school he is credited with attending.

An amateurish attempt to join the gold rush followed shortly after this period of schooling. Will, dreaming of riches, joined a party headed for Auraria, the future Denver. "We pushed on to the gold streams in the mountains, passing through Golden Gate," said Cody, "and over Guy Hill and thence on to Black Hawk. We prospected for two months, but as none of us knew anything about mining we met with very poor success, and we finally concluded that prospecting for gold was not our forte."

Will and his companions built a raft, hoping to navigate it down the Platte, but the raft sank at Julesburg, with all their baggage and provisions. Fortunately, Will came upon a bull train and, since he knew the wagon master, was able to hire on and return to Leavenworth.

"That fall the Cody family moved into what they called the Big House," wrote Don Russell, "which they planned to run as a hotel." Billy contributed by inviting some of his friends to board there during the winter. Julia names them as James B. Hickok (not yet Wild Bill), Lew Simpson, John Willis, and George Ross.

Cody then decided to try his luck as a fur trapper and trader. He and his partner Dave Harrington, a friend his own age, bought a wagon, a yoke of oxen, provisions, and traps and poison for the wolves, and set out for the Republican River. At the mouth of Prairie Dog Creek, one of the oxen slipped on the ice, dislocating its hip, and had to be shot. The two boys decided to trap beaver. They built a dugout in the hillside, roofing it with brush, long grass, and dirt. A rude earthen fireplace served for cooking and heating. They succeeded in trapping both beaver and otter. Then, the misadventures began to mount. First an unusually savage bear attacked their camp. Harrington shot the bear but only wounded it, and it charged. With a lucky shot, Will killed the bear. A few days later Will slipped on the ice and dislodged a large stone, which broke his leg. Harrington went off to get help, 125 miles away, leaving Will with wood and provisions enough to last twenty days, which they estimated was what the trip would take. Harrington rigged a can on a stick, so that Will could get water from the snow. While he waited for rescue, Will had little to do but lie still. He read through the Bible and a few other books—one of the rare times he mentions ever reading—and cut notches in a stick to keep track of time.

"On the twelfth day after Harrington left me," he wrote in his 1879 autobiography, "I was awakened from a sound sleep by some one touching me upon the shoulder. I looked up and was astonished to see an Indian warrior standing by my side. His face was hideously daubed with paint, which told me more forcibly than words could have done that he was on the warpath. . . . I began to think that my time had come, as the saying is, when into the cabin stepped an elderly Indian, whom I readily recognized as old Rain-in-the-Face, a Sioux chief from the vicinity of Fort Laramie." Rain-in-the-Face recognized Will and persuaded his men to spare the boy, though they took his rifle and pistol, cooking utensils, sugar, coffee, and matches. They cooked some of his provisions; "however, they were polite enough to give me some of the food after they had cooked it."

Two days after the Indians departed it began to snow. The snowfall continued until the entrance was blocked, and the dugout itself was covered with three feet of snow. Snowed in, surrounded by howling wolves, Will waited not twenty but twenty-nine days before Harrington returned with a team of oxen to rescue him.

After using twenty-five of their three hundred beaver skins to pay for another wagon, they went on to Junction City, where they sold the remaining furs and their wagon and joined a government mule train, arriving home in March 1860.

Harrington stayed with the Codys that spring at Will's invitation, and planned to stay on even longer and farm the land, but in the latter part of April he caught a severe cold and was taken seriously ill with lung fever. Despite Mrs. Cody's nursing and the attentions of a local doctor, Harrington died, leaving Will feeling lonely, for he had lost his best friend, the companion who had saved his life.

"THE SWIFT PHANTOM
OF THE DESERT"

Of all the many chapters in the history of the Old West, few hold the romantic afterglow of the Pony Express. Books have been written about it; movies have been made about it; it was immortalized by artists of the period, most notably Frederic Remington in his *Changing Horses*.

William F. Cody was a part of the short, brilliant life of the Pony Express—shorter than one might think. Although its memory has remained fresh for nearly 140 years, the Pony Express itself only lasted for a matter of 19 months, 2 weeks, and 3 days.

This is how Mark Twain, who rode a stagecoach to California in 1860, described a Pony Express rider in his book *Roughing It*:

> In a little while all interest was taken up in stretching our necks and watching for the "pony rider"—the fleet messenger who sped across the continent from St. Joe to Sacramento, carrying letters nineteen hundred miles in eight days! Think of that for perishable horse and human flesh and blood to do! The pony rider was usually a little bit of a man, brimful of spirit and endurance. No matter what time of the day or night his watch came on, and no matter whether it was winter or summer, raining, snowing, hailing, or sleeting, or whether his "beat" was a level straight road or a crazy trail over mountain crags or precipices, or whether it led through peaceful regions or regions that swarmed with hostile Indians he must be always ready to leap into the saddle and be off like the wind!
>
> We had a consuming desire, from the beginning, to see a pony rider, but somehow or other all that passed us and all that met us managed to streak by us in the night, and so we heard only the whiz and a hail, and the swift phantom of the desert was gone before we could get our heads out of the windows. . . .

At last a Pony Express rider appears:

Every neck is stretched further, and every eye strained wider. Away across the endless dead level of the prairie a black speck appears against the sky, and it is plain that it moves. . . . In a second or two it becomes a horse and rider, rising nearer—growing more and more defined— nearer and nearer, and the flutter of the hoofs comes faintly to the ear— another instant, a whoop and hurrah from our deck, a wave of the rider's hand, but no reply, and man and horse burst past our excited faces. . . .

Although Mark Twain had been known to "stretch a thing or two," he was not far off the mark in this anecdote of the incident in which he and the fellow passengers on a stagecoach heading west saw a Pony Express rider "go winging away like a belated fragment of a storm."

The creation of the Pony Express, like so many events in American history, was an irresistible confluence of desire and necessity. It began with the discovery of gold at Sutter's Mill in California on the morning of January 24, 1848. By that year, the United States had claimed virtually all of the West. The Louisiana Purchase, the annexation of Texas and Oregon, the war with Mexico in 1846–1847 had stretched the country's boundaries all the way to the Pacific Ocean. But the West was American in name only. Few people east of the Mississippi were willing to venture into a region that seemed too forbidding—distant and dangerous. The discovery of gold at a bend of the South Fork of California's American River changed all that.

By 1849 some twenty-five thousand avid prospectors were on their way to California by ship—eighteen thousand nautical miles, from the East Coast all the way around South America. Another thirty thousand Americans headed for the goldfields by land—from New York, Pennsylvania, Ohio, and the southern states. Those who set out for the California goldfields had a phrase for what they were about to experience; they called it "seeing the elephant."

Necessity demanded that there be a Way West, that mail somehow be carried east from California and west across the Mississippi to California, where the population had exploded. By 1860 half a million people lived in the regions west of the Rocky Mountains. At that time St. Joseph, Missouri, was the westernmost point that the railroad and telegraph had reached. Beyond St. Joseph lay a vast wilderness inhabited primarily by Indians. How was the mail to be delivered? Mail normally took a month by boat. The first efforts were by mule—fifty-three days from Sacramento to Salt Lake City. Then came the stagecoaches. When carried by overland stagecoaches, mail between St. Louis and San Francisco took twenty-four days.

Necessity again played a deciding role when the Civil War broke out. It was imperative that California, with its goldmines, be kept in the Union.

There were two possible routes to California. One, called the Oxbow Route, went south from St. Louis, Missouri, to El Paso, Texas, almost touched the Mexican border at Fort Fillmore, then went by way of Fort Yuma, Arizona, to San Diego and north up California's interior valley to San Francisco. This route was favored by southerners. The other route ran along what was known as the Egan-Simpson Central Trail, named after Major Howard Egan, a Mormon pioneer and great western explorer, and Captain James Simpson, who followed Egan's Trail to the Ruby Mountains, where he explored a shorter and more direct trail that went almost due west. This route was favored by the North.

In 1858 Postmaster General Aaron V. Brown, a southerner from Tennessee, awarded the first overland mail contract to John Butterfield for a southern route. Butterfield's firm, the Overland Mail Company, was formed by the country's four leading express companies—Adams, American, National, and Wells Fargo. The combined firms had hopes of breaking the grip of the steamship companies on the bulk of passenger and mail traffic to the Pacific Coast.

The Overland Mail Company was a considerable enterprise for the time: eight hundred employees, one hundred Concord coaches, a thousand horses and mules, and many stations. The trip on the Oxbow, 2,800 miles in length, took twenty-one to twenty-three days. Said one traveler: It was "as close to hell as he ever wanted to be." Apache, Comanche, and Kiowa were a constant menace.

Enter the firm of Russell, Majors and Waddell—or rather, enter William H. Russell.

In 1837 William Russell, a Missourian, helped organize the Lexington First Addition Company; another stockholder was William Bradford Waddell. By his middle thirties, Russell was a prosperous landholder. His first venture in shipping came in 1847 with a wagon train of merchant's goods from Westport, Kansas, to Santa Fe. A radical pro-slavery adherent, he wanted Kansas to be a slave state. In 1851 he became a member of the firm of Morehead, Waddell & Company. When Morehead retired the following year, the firm became Waddell & Russell, and in 1855 it became a new copartnership variously known as Majors and Russell and Russell, Majors and Waddell.

Alexander Majors, Cody's mentor, was a Kentuckian who spent his boyhood and young manhood in Missouri, then the newest frontier of the day. According to Mary Lund Settle and Raymond W. Settle in their book *Saddles and Spurs: The Pony Express Saga,* "He [Majors] became intimately acquainted with back-breaking toil in the clearing of land, splitting of rails, erecting log cabins and wrestling with the soil to produce a crop. Unlike Russell he was a typical frontiersman and remained such to the end of his days."

William Bradford Waddell was also a midwesterner. He made his way by steamboat down the Ohio River to Lexington, Missouri, in 1835, drawn by stories of wealth and by his own wanderlust. In 1849 he financed a party to go to the goldfields of California. With Russell he organized the Lexington Marine Fire & Marine Insurance Company.

The partnership of Russell, Majors and Waddell, founded on January 1, 1855, provided "that the firm should engage in the business of selling goods, ware, and merchandise, general trading in stock, wagons, teams and other items used in outfitting persons for crossing the plains, and in freighting for the U.S. government or anyone else."

The partners complemented each other neatly. Russell was the promoter who went East to lobby in Washington and to represent the firm in New York and Philadelphia. Majors was concerned with the wagon trains on the road and was home only when they were not running. Waddell was the business head, in charge of local financial affairs and keeping the books. Majors and Waddell were instinctively conservative; Russell was a polar opposite, daring to the point of recklessness, ever seeking the main chance.

It was Alexander Majors and William Russell who had given young Will Cody his first paying job after his father's death in 1857.

In the early summer of 1859, with John S. Jones as a partner, Russell organized the Leavenworth and Pikes Peak Express Company. He neglected to consult Majors or Waddell about this venture, though they would inevitably become involved with the fortunes of the new company. In order to get a mail contract, Russell bought J. M. Hockaday and Company, which had a government mail contract between the Missouri River and Denver. The overextended new company was bankrupt by October 28, 1859, half a million dollars in debt, and Majors and Waddell unwillingly took it over to save their partner from financial ruin, despite their already straitened circumstances because of losses suffered during the Mormon War. The Leavenworth and Pikes Peak Express Company was then reorganized as the Central Overland California & Pikes Peak Express Company. Since the name was a mouthful, it was quickly abbreviated as COC&PP. New stock was sold, and Russell was named president.

The principal asset of Russell's company was his $130,000 mail contract. The more lucrative $600,000 mail contract had been awarded by the Post Office to Butterfield's Overland Mail Company. Russell set about lobbying in Washington to win a new contract for his firm. He found a willing ally in California Senator William Gwin, then chairman of the Senate Post Office and Post Roads Committee.

To win a mail contract, using the Central Route to California, Russell needed an experiment to prove it could be done—something so dramatic that it would command nationwide attention. That experiment—the primary arrow in Russell's bow, his big idea and the main chance—was the Pony Express.

Who thought of the idea first? Was it William H. Russell? Senator Gwin? Because there have been so many claims and counterclaims in the past 140 years, it is unclear whose brainchild it was. It could even be credited to Ghengis Khan, conqueror of Tartary and China. Marco Polo in his thirteenth-century account of his travels in China, *Il Millione*, wrote that Khan had established stations at twenty-five-mile intervals and that a single horseman would carry messages as far as three hundred miles a day.

A prime American candidate was George Wilkins Kendall, pioneer war correspondent, who established a pony express to send his Mexican War dispatches to the New Orleans *Picayune*.

There was also the intrepid frontier trader Francois Xavier Aubry. "On the night of September 17, 1848," reported Frederic D. Schwartz in *American Heritage* magazine, " . . . Aubry rode his staggering horse through a driving rain into Independence, Missouri. The disheveled rider stopped outside a tavern and, being too stiff to dismount, was lifted from his blood-caked saddle. In his bag was a copy of the Santa Fe *Republican*. Its date was September 12. Incredible as it seemed, Aubry had ridden from Santa Fe to Independence, a journey of 780 miles that normally took a month, in five days and eighteen hours."

Aubry already had a reputation as a fast man in the saddle. The previous winter he rode the same route in fourteen days, breaking the previous record by ten days. In May he had made the same journey in less than nine days. Aubry's rides required almost superhuman endurance; he rode day and night, strapping himself to the saddle in case he nodded off, eating while in motion. On his record-breaking trip, he broke down six horses, slept only three hours the entire time, and walked twenty miles when one of his horses fell dead beneath him.

Whoever had conceived the idea of the Pony Express first, it was William Russell who would get the credit and who would risk everything, including the loss of his liberty, to keep his beloved venture afloat.

In the fall of 1859 Russell sent the following telegram to his son John W., in Leavenworth:

HAVE DETERMINED TO ESTABLISH A PONY EXPRESS TO
SACRAMENTO, CALIFORNIA. TIME TEN DAYS.

As we have seen, Russell's partners Majors and Waddell not only felt no enthusiasm for the project; they doubted it could succeed. They predicted that unless Russell could win a substantial government subsidy, his Pony Express would prove a financial burden and could not possibly turn a profit. There were not only the start-up costs to be considered but monthly expenses of $30,000.

Russell, Majors and Waddell did have an advantage in their race to establish a record time in mail delivery; they had stage stations set up all the way to Salt Lake City, but they were too far apart to serve as Pony Express stations; the distance between them would need to be cut in half. Moreover, they would still need to set up stations between Salt Lake City and California. Altogether there would be 190 stations, 500 horses, between 50 and 80 riders—the total number remains a mystery, because no accurate records were kept, and the Civil War dominated the newspapers at the time, leaving little coverage for the Pony Express. The total cost of the venture was approximately $100,000.

WANTED—young, skinny, wiry fellows, not over 18.
Must be expert riders, willing to risk death daily.
Orphans preferred. Wages $25 a week.

This was the advertisement that appeared in a San Francisco paper early in 1860.

The typical Pony Express rider was slightly built, wiry, and about eighteen to twenty years of age. He was, of course, an accomplished horseman, a requirement quite easy to come by in the West of 1860, where boys virtually grew up in the saddle. That the riders were brave, even fearless, hardly needs to be said, for they had to ride headlong over mountainous terrain, at times through blinding rain or snow, threatened by tornadoes, lightning, floods, rattlesnakes, bears, mountain lions, murdering outlaws, and menaced always by marauding Indians. In winter, they faced snowstorms and hailstones the size of golf balls; in summer there was not only the blistering sun but the danger of a horse stepping into a prairie dog hole and tumbling down, perhaps collapsing on top of the rider.

The route led west out of St. Joseph, Missouri, and along the Oregon Trail from Kansas through what is now Nebraska and Wyoming. Proceeding up the Little Blue River to Fort Kearny, the riders continued up the Platte River, passing Courthouse Rock, Chimney Rock, and Scotts Bluff to Fort Laramie; then along the Sweetwater River past Independence Rock, Devil's Gate, and Split Rock, to Fort Caspar, through South Pass to Fort Bridger and Salt Lake City. The route then crossed the Great Basin and the Utah-Nevada desert, skirting Lake Tahoe, then over the Sierra Nevadas into California. A rugged trail indeed!

Weight was of prime importance in equipping the riders. The ten-day trip from St. Joseph to Sacramento covered a distance of 1,966 miles, and the load had to be light. The ordinary western saddle was considered too heavy, so a modified vaquero model was used. (The *vaquero* is a Mexican cowboy.) Over the seat was placed the expressman's mail bag, his *mochila* (Spanish for purse). Made of a tough, well-tanned hide about an eighth of an inch thick, there were four stiff leather *cantinas*—boxes—sewn to it, to carry the mail, two on each side. Openings in the center of the *mochila* let it fit tightly over the saddle, with only the rider's body weight to fasten it down beneath his seat. The *cantinas* were secured with brass locks. Way stations had access to one of them in which a waybill was placed for recording times of arrival and departure along the route. Riders carried an average of about sixty pieces of mail on lightweight paper, including telegrams, each trip. The cost of sending a letter by Pony Express was $5.00 an ounce. A rider galloping into a station had only to free his *mochila*, throw it over an already saddled fresh horse, and he was on his way.

The riders were to be outfitted with two revolvers, a Bowie knife, and a rifle—but this was far too much artillery for someone traveling light, so in the end they carried only a Colt five-shot revolver with a .31-caliber ball. A rider usually rode fifty to a hundred miles along the trail and changed horses every twelve to fifteen. He prided himself on the speed at which he could drop from one horse and leap atop the next.

The Pony Express was officially under way at 5:15 P.M. on April 3, 1860. The night before the first ride, the young Pony Express riders stayed in the Pattee House, St. Joseph's most luxurious hotel, now a museum recording the exploits of the Pony Express and of the James brothers, Jesse and Frank. St. Joseph also has a statue commemorating the Pony Express.

It is uncertain who the first rider out of St. Joe was, since no one thought to record the man's name, or where in the city he started from—but we do know it was not Will Cody. It was probably either Johnnie Frye—the popular choice in St. Joseph, where a painting of him hangs on the wall of the Johnnie Frye Bar and Grill—or Johnson Richardson, but at least five other riders were named as the possible inaugural rider that April day. The ride should have been under way hours earlier, but it had to await mail from the East. It finally arrived aboard a special locomotive—the *Missouri*—and one car. The train roared out of Hannibal and set a speed record that lasted for fifty years. As the assembled crowd in St. Joseph watched, a cannon boomed, a brass band played, and the mail was stowed in the *cantinas*. There were forty-nine letters, five telegrams, and some special-edition newspapers, written or printed on tissue paper and wrapped in oilskin. As the first rider was about to set off down the cobblestone street, bystanders plucked hair from the horse's mane and tail to make rings and necklaces. The rider then boarded a ferry to take him across the Missouri River.

One apocryphal story has it that some of the women in St. Joe liked to give Johnnie Frye the cookies they had made, but he rode so fast through town that it was difficult for him to take them. One woman is said to have invented the doughnut so Johnnie could pick it up as he rode by, his finger through the hole.

We do know who the first rider was to arrive in Sacramento. It was William Hamilton, making the first, record-breaking delivery of transcontinental mail, only eleven days out of St. Joseph. When Hamilton arrived, the citizens of Sacramento were ecstatic, and the waiting crowd broke into a frenzy of cheering, waving handkerchiefs. Cannon boomed and boys representing the Young America Volunteers of the local fire department struck an anvil with sledgehammers. Hamilton trotted up to the telegraph office. From the eighty letters in his *mochila*, the telegraph agent removed those addressed to Sacramento and entered the time and date on the waybill: 5:30 P.M. April 14, 1860. Mail intended for the residents of San Francisco was placed on a steamer destined for that city.

When the Pony Express got under way, Will Cody was only fourteen; he was sixteen when it ended. Some skeptics contend that he never rode the Pony Express at all, because he was too young. However, most of the riders were young; the average age of the forty riders whose history is known was under nineteen. However, Cody was tall for his age, strong, and already an experienced plainsman and horseman.

In his first autobiography, Cody tells of arriving at the Julesburg ranch in Colorado when "the great pony express . . . was at that time just being started." He writes that the owner of the ranch, George Chrisman, who was also the station agent, was reluctant to hire him as an express rider "as I was so young he thought I would not be able to stand the fierce riding which was required of the messengers . . . he gave me a short route of forty-five miles, with the stations fifteen miles apart, and three changes of horses. . . . I wrote to my mother and told her how well I liked the exciting life of a pony express rider. She replied, and begged of me to give it up, as it would surely kill me. She was right about this, as fifteen miles an hour on horseback would, in a short time, shake any man 'all to pieces';

and there were but few, if any, riders who could stand it for any great length of time."

Nevertheless, Cody stuck with it for two months, until he received a letter informing him that his mother was quite ill. He then gave the job up and went back to the Cody home in Salt Creek Valley.

Cody's autobiographical account of this experience places it *before* his trapping expedition with Dave Harrington, which would make it the summer of 1859—yet we know that the Pony Express did not get under way until the spring of 1860, so Cody was clearly incorrect in his memoir. However, he was correct in naming George Chrisman as the Julesburg agent; Chrisman had bought the Julesburg ranch from the Frenchman Rene Jules, or Jules Reni, for whom the station was named.

In his memoir, Alexander Majors wrote: "Among the most noted and daring riders of the Pony Express was Hon. William F. Cody, better known as Buffalo Bill." Majors also wrote this, in his rather labored and hifalutin style: "The Pony Express was but the forerunner of a more important and greater enterprise, which must soon reach its culmination, viz the construction of a road upon which a tireless iron horse will start his long overland journey, opening up as he goes, the rich meadows of nature, the fertile valleys, and crowning the eminences of the rocky range with evidences of civilization and man's irresistible mania for progression."

In the summer of 1860 Lew Simpson, the master of the wagon train Will had traveled with two years earlier, asked him to join another trip from Atchison to Fort Laramie and points farther west. In Atchison Cody met with William Russell, who offered to hire him for the Pony Express. He was assigned to Joseph Slade's division in Horseshoe Station, Wyoming.

Joseph Alfred "Alf" Slade was a notorious character who attracted the attention of Mark Twain, among other travelers in the Old West. In *Roughing It*, Twain devotes an entire chapter to Slade, who had the reputation of being at once "the most bloody, the most dangerous, and the most valuable citizen that inhabited the savage fastnesses of the mountains."

Slade was born in Illinois in 1824, of good parentage, Twain tells us. He served in the Fifth Illinois Volunteers in the Mexican War. At twenty-six, he killed a man in a quarrel and fled west, where he was hired as a wagon master in St. Joseph. One day on the plains he got into an argument with another driver. Both drew their pistols, but the other driver cocked his weapon first. Slade suggested they both put down their pistols and settle the matter with their fists. The other driver put down his revolver, at which point Slade shot him dead. He was said to have killed twenty-six men. In a vigilante history of the time, it was reported that "stories of Slade's hanging men, and of innumerable assaults, shootings, stabbings, and beatings, in which he was the principal actor, form part of the legends of the stage line."

Sober, Slade could be charming. Mark Twain found him "so friendly and so gentle spoken that I warmed to him in spite of his awful history." Cody too thought well of him. "Slade, though rough at times and always a dangerous character—having killed many a man—was always kind to me. During the two years I worked for him as pony-express rider and stage-driver, he never spoke an angry word to me."

Slade's worst behavior came when he was drunk. On March 10, 1864, after shooting up the town of Virginia City, Montana, while drunk, he was hanged by vigilantes for defying the miner's court.

While working for Slade, Cody made his most celebrated ride— between Red Buttes and Three Crossings in Utah, considered the most dangerous stretch on the whole route. Once at Three Crossings, he found that his relief rider had been killed the night before in a drunken brawl. He changed horses and rode on to Rocky Ridge, seventy-six miles farther, then turned back with the eastbound *mochila*. He reached Red Buttes safely, having covered 322 miles, the third longest Pony Express ride on record. Cody made the ride in twenty-one hours and forty minutes, using twenty-one horses. In his book, Alexander Majors claims that Cody rode a total of 384 miles, making it the longest ride ever recorded on the Pony Express—an attempt, perhaps, to inflate Buffalo Bill's legend. However, the record, 380 miles, belongs to Robert "Pony Bob" Haslam. Haslam, who was one of the first Pony Express riders, was later associated with Buffalo Bill's Wild West. Haslam worked his last years in the Congress Hotel in Chicago, where he passed out cards with drawings of him at the age of twenty. The second longest ride was made by William R. Egan, a run of 330 miles. Most of the Pony Express riders didn't last long; the life was too grueling.

A complete roster of riders of the Pony Express and a reconstruction of their full story cannot be made, since no authentic list dating back to the days when it was in operation has ever been found. Written accounts of the period are also few and far between. The only newspapers of any significance at that time along the Pony Express route were the *Weekly West* and *Missouri Free Democrat* of St. Joseph; the *Free Press* of Elwood, Kansas; the Salt Lake City *Deseret News*; the Sacramento *Union*; and the San Francisco *Alta California*. However, a roster of the Pony Express riders was compiled in the first decade of the twentieth century by individuals in various parts of the country, especially in the West, who investigated the story and wrote down the names of as many riders as they could identify. They did their best against heavy odds, with splendid results.

There are 120 names on the list, including Wm. F. Cody, who was cited five times in the six lists compiled. Only 26 riders were cited all six times.

A witness to Cody's Pony Express riding was Edward E. Ayer, a wealthy contractor who founded the Indian collection in Chicago's Newberry Library. Ayer wrote in his journal: "About six or seven years ago I attended a reception and dinner given by all the diplomats of Paris for Buffalo Bill. I said it wasn't necessary to introduce me to Bill Cody; that I had crossed the plains in 1860, and that he was riding by our train about a month, and would give us the news in a loud voice as he rode by, so that we all became much attached to him. At the reception Bill wouldn't let me get out of his sight, and insisted that I should sit by his side, thereby disarranging the seating plan at the banquet."

This report would seem to buttress Cody's claim to have been a Pony Express rider; one historian, William E. Connelley, secretary of the Kansas Historical Society, denied Cody's claims. And yet there is something odd about Ayer's account. "Riding by our train about a month?" Is it a wagon train that Ayer is referring to? Does that mean he rode by the train frequently? And how often was Ayer on the train? As for giving the news in a loud voice as he rode by, surely the speed of the horse, coupled with the speed and noise of the wagons, would make it impossible for anyone on the train to hear what was said, even if it was shouted in a loud voice. In any event, the Pony Express riders were not necessarily aware of the news; the newspapers were sealed in their *mochilas*.

Young Will had several other adventures during his Pony Express days. As he was leaving Horse Creek, Wyoming Territory, one morning, he was ambushed in a sand ravine by a band of fifteen Indians. They fired repeatedly at him but missed. Cody was mounted on a roan California horse—"the swiftest steed I ever had." He put his spurs and whip to the animal and, instead of turning back to Horse Creek, headed for Sweetwater, eleven miles distant. "The Indians came on, but my horse soon got away from them, and ran into the station two miles ahead of them. The stock-tender had been killed there that morning, and all the stock had been driven off by the Indians."

Unable to obtain a fresh mount, Cody kept riding another twelve miles to Plant's Station, making this a ride of twenty-four miles on the same roan.

Indian raids became quite troublesome around mid-September. Between Split Rock and Three Crossings they robbed a stage, killed the driver and two passengers, and severely wounded the assistant division agent, Lem Flowers. Indians also drove off the horses from different stations and lay continually in wait for stagecoaches and express riders, who had to run a gauntlet to achieve their missions. The Indian tribes involved in these depredations were Gosh Ute, Paiute, and Shoshone.

As a consequence of the Indian raids, the Pony Express ceased to operate for six weeks, while the stations were restocked with horses, and the stages ran only infrequently. It was decided to organize a party of forty well-armed and well-mounted men—stage drivers, express riders, and ranchers—to attack an Indian village and recover as many horses as they could. James Butler "Wild Bill" Hickok, who had been first a stage driver and, being too heavy to be a rider, was now a stock tender, was elected captain of the party.

"Twenty miles out from Sweetwater Bridge, at the head of Horse Creek," wrote Cody, "we found an Indian trail running north towards Powder River, and we could see by the tracks that most of the horses had been recently shod and were undoubtedly our stage stock."

Following the trail, the pursuers soon found themselves in the heart of hostile territory, and moved with extreme caution. Finally, the trail took them to Powder River, Crazy Woman's Fork, and Clear Creek, where they found a large Indian village. Realizing that they were badly outnumbered, the men dared not risk a daylight charge into the village. Instead, Hickok suggested that they wait until it was almost dark, then dash into the Indian camp, opening fire and stampeding the horses.

The plan worked. The Indians were caught completely by surprise, and the raiders succeeded in retaking all their own horses and a hundred Indian horses as well. Later, in Sweetwater Bridge, the victorious stockmen and ranchers began to celebrate: drinking, carousing, fighting. Alf Slade, hearing about the "orgie," as Cody described it, came to join in the fun. He got into an argument with a stage driver and shot the man, "killing him almost instantly."

Will was asked by Slade to become "a sort of supernumerary rider" at Horseshoe Creek, where he occasionally rode with the mail, and where he had time to go hunting as well. On one hunt for bear, he rode through rough country and saw no bear, only bear tracks in the snow. Finally tiring, he shot two sage hens and decided to camp out for the night and resume his bear hunt in the morning. After tying his horse to a tree, he prepared to make camp when he heard a horse whinnying nearby. Not expecting to find any white men in the area, he followed the horse's whinny to a dugout, which he expected belonged to trappers. Instead, it was occupied by eight men, two of whom he recognized as having worked on Lew Simpson's wagon train; they had been discharged and were suspected of having murdered and robbed a rancher.

Though the men hadn't recognized him, Will knew he had to escape or he would probably be killed. He suggested that he leave his rifle with them and go to fetch his horse; instead, two of the men accompanied him and told him to leave his rifle, since he would have no need of it. Cody was still carrying his brace of sage hens and he still wore his pistols. On the path, he dropped one of the hens and asked one of the outlaws to pick it up. When the man bent over, Will struck him on the head with a revolver and shot the second man. Retrieving his horse, he rode down the creek as fast as possible. He was pursued, of course, and knowing that the outlaws would probably catch up with him, he dismounted and sent his horse on without him. As he had hoped, his pursuers followed his horse, while he escaped on foot.

It was twenty-five miles to Horseshoe Station, difficult walking all the way, and when Will arrived he was weary and footsore. Nevertheless, when he told Slade what had happened, the station master insisted they form a party and return to the thieves' dugout. The posse consisted of twenty men; Slade insisted that Will also come along. When they reached the dugout, they found it empty. The outlaws had fled, leaving a newly dug grave where they had undoubtedly buried the man Cody shot.

"The significant part of this story," wrote Don Russell, "is that it is the only one, of anything signed by Cody, in which he tells of killing a white man." Unlike his friend Hickok, Cody, while a marksman, was never a gunfighter.

In the closing days of the Pony Express, Hickok had his encounter with "the McCanles gang," in which he earned his nickname "Wild Bill." The so-called McCanles Massacre was written up in *Harper's Magazine* in 1867 by Colonel George Ward Nichols. According to Nichols, Hickok had slain ten men with his pistol, a rifle, and his knife. A court record shows that on July 12, 1861, David C. McCanles, his nephew James Woods, and James Gordon, a rancher, were killed at Rock Creek Station. Arrested were Hickok, Horace Wellman, station agent, and J. W. Brink, known as "Doc." Hickok had shot all three, killing McCanles and wounding the others, who were then killed by Wellman and Brink. The defendants pleaded self-defense and were acquitted.

What happened was that McCanles had sold his Rock Creek property to Russell, Majors and Waddell to be used as a Pony Express Station. When McCanles wasn't paid, he quite naturally demanded his property back. Wellman, the station agent, attempted to get the money from his employers, but the firm was virtually bankrupt. Wellman then told McCanles he couldn't have his property back, and McCanles threatened to take it by force; when he entered the Rock Creek station to carry out his threat, McCanles was shot by Hickok. When Woods and Gordon, hearing the shots, ran up, they were shot and wounded by Hickok. Describing the incident later, Hickok said that at the time of the shootings, he had "got ugly" and "was wild." McCanles is said to have bullied Hickok, which, as it turned out, was a bad mistake.

By that time, the end of the Pony Express was in sight. As a logistic triumph, it was regarded as a success. Only one *mochila* was lost in the entire nineteen-month run. The ten-day delivery time of the Pony Express was a revolutionary development then, bringing political and social news to an avid readership. President Buchanan's last message to Congress was delivered in eight days from St. Joseph to Sacramento. When Abraham Lincoln was elected president of the United States, California knew about it eight days after the news had reached St. Joseph's telegraph terminal. Details of Lincoln's Inaugural Address covered the 1,966 miles separating the two cities in seven days seventeen hours. In eight days fourteen hours out of St. Joseph, the unionists and separatists in California knew that Fort Sumter had been bombarded in the first shots of the Civil War. The Pony Express could be credited with keeping California in the Union during the dark days when there was a real threat that California would side with the Confederacy. All through the spring and summer of 1861, the Far West followed the news of the ebb and flow of battle, calls for volunteers, the Battle of Bull Run, and the rosters of dead, wounded, and missing. Because of the rapid delivery of news of early Union victories, California and its gold stayed in the Union.

In later years, a Pony Express ride was always a popular highlight of Cody's Wild West. It had all the excitement of a horse race as well as the romance of western history. In fact, much of the glamour adhering to the Pony Express came from Cody's association with it.

Russell, Majors and Waddell went into bankruptcy in January 1861. Only the Central Overland California & Pikes Peak Express Company, the Pony Express, was left. A success as a precious information link between the coasts, yes, but a failure as a moneymaker. One estimate is that the Pony Express lost around $200,000. The financial problems of the COC&PP led Bill Trotter, a driver with a sense of humor, to interpret the company's initials as meaning "Clean out of cash and poor pay." Another wrote this threatening verse:

> On or about the first of May,
> The boys would like to have their pay.
> If not paid by that day,
> The stock along the road may stray.

Riders grumbled that they had been without pay for several months. Russell continued to hope that his partnership would once again haul the lion's share of military supplies; that Congress would grant their claim of $494,000 in losses suffered in 1857 on the way to Fort Bridger, when attacking Mormons destroyed several trains; and, finally, that Congress would quit its interminable bickering and authorize a triweekly service over the Central Route, thus saving the Pony Express. None of these expectations materialized.

In the end, desperation led William Russell to traffic in stolen government bonds, money belonging to the Indian Trust Fund of the Interior Department, where they were held for the benefit of various Indian tribes. Russell "borrowed" the bonds to cover the company's losses. When he learned what had happened, President Lincoln himself insisted on an investigation. Russell was arrested in his New York office and jailed. Called before a congressional committee, he testified freely and frankly, at the suggestion of his lawyer, who knew that by a congressional act of 1857, witnesses who testified before Congress could not be indicted for the matters on which they testified. Although he was saved by a legal technicality from trial and imprisonment, Russell did not escape censure. In a letter to the attorney general a week after his inauguration, Lincoln referred to the matter of the stolen bonds as "the Russell fraud." Though spared the worst punishment, Russell was nevertheless disgraced, and returned to Missouri, where he died broke on September 10, 1872. He was sixty years old. The Pony Express had been Russell's great gamble, the critical turn of the cards, and it had failed.

"That the business men and citizens of Lexington believed in Russell and highly respected him is quite obvious," wrote the authors of *Saddles and Spurs*. "His record for more than two decades was without spot or blemish. During that time he was regarded as one of the town's most progressive citizens. Then, in the year 1860, in the far away city of Washington he, by one act, stained that shining record. Anyone who studies his remarkable life, including this incident, turns from it all with a feeling of intense sadness that a brilliant career such as his should close under a shadow."

William Waddell returned to Lexington and died there on April 1, 1862, at the age of sixty-five.

As for Alexander Majors, he moved to Salt Lake City, where he tried freighting, then prospecting. After 1879, he lived in Kansas City and Denver. Buffalo Bill Cody, then at the height of his fame as a showman, found him in Denver living in a little shack, engaged in writing the story of his life. Cody hired Prentiss Ingraham, the dime novelist, to edit and personally paid for having it printed under the title *Seventy Years on the Frontier*. Cody also supported Majors for the rest of his life. Majors died in Chicago on January 14, 1900, at the age of eighty-six; he was buried in Kansas City, Missouri.

An interesting sidelight of the Pony Express saga was revealed by recent research indicating that Cody's mother was in litigation with William Russell at this time. Mary Cody alleged that Russell and others (among them former U.S. Marshal Elias S. Dennis) had maltreated animals and removed stock and property from her ranch after her husband's death. In court on April 7, 1860, the defendants were acquitted. This was only four days after the start of the Pony Express. Could Russell have held a grudge against Cody? Perhaps, but it seems unlikely; their relationship extended back to 1857.

The final question: Was William F. Cody a Pony Express rider? Though there are historians who doubt his claim, there is enough evidence of his having ridden the route through the records in which his name appears and the recollections of contemporaries such as H. W. Ayer and Alexander Majors.

In 1861 the firm of Russell, Majors and Waddell was bankrupt; however, the story of the Pony Express was not quite finished. It was the telegraph, "the lightning wires," that spelled the end for the daring pony riders. Only a few weeks after the Pony Express had thrilled the nation with its speed, Congress passed a bill offering a subsidy of $40,000 a year for ten years to the company that would connect East and West by "talking wires." Bids to build the telegraph line were submitted to the secretary of the treasury, and in the spring of 1861 construction crews began to work on the telegraph lines. Twenty-five poles for each mile covered were necessary. Contests were held to determine the team of workers that had covered the most ground in a month's time. As in the building of the transcontinental railroads not long after the Civil War, rival gangs from the two coasts—one, the Overland Telegraph Company, from the West; the other, the Pacific Telegraph Company, from the East—vied with each other to be the first to join a telegraph line from coast to coast. As the poles went up, relentlessly, mile by mile, the Pony Express riders continued to carry the news, even, ironically, news of the progress of the telegraph line.

On October 28, 1861, the last Pony Express Rider dismounted from his horse and delivered the mail in Sacramento. An epochal western adventure had ended.

Even before the end came, Will Cody quit the Pony Express. "After a year's absence from home, I began to long to see my mother and sisters again," he wrote in his second autobiography. "In June, 1861 I got a pass over the stage-line and returned to Leavenworth. The first rumblings of the great struggle that was soon to be known as the Civil War were already reverberating throughout the North; Sumter had been fired upon in April of that year. Kansas, as every schoolboy knows, was previously the bloody scene of some of the earliest conflicts."

Soon many thousands of young men—among them Will Cody—would be swept up and plunged into the bloodiest conflict in the annals of American warfare.

FROM HORSE THIEF
TO CAVALRY SCOUT

The Civil War was fought on many fronts and by ragtag bands of guerrillas as well as by disciplined troops. It was as a guerrilla, more specifically a "jay-hawker," that Will Cody first served his country. At least, that's what he thought he was doing at the time.

In the spring of 1861, when Cody arrived back in Leavenworth after his Pony Express riding days had ended, he found his mother gravely ill; she would not survive the war. "A strong Union woman," according to Cody's own account, "she had such great confidence in the government that she thought the war would not last over six months." She asked her son not to join the army, and he respected her wishes. One of Cody's most appealing characteristics was certainly his devotion to his family. As long as she was alive, he was his mother's chief source of support; he felt the same responsibility toward his sisters. In 1862, however, Will Cody had no trade or occupation, only a sketchy education, and few prospects. His lack of education was not unusual at the time; Mark Twain's education, for example, ended at the age of twelve, and as late as 1890 the average American did not go beyond the fifth grade. In any event, it is virtually inarguable that the only education that matters in the long run is self-education.

Had his family still lived in Ohio, Will Cody might have worked in a livery stable or driven a grocer's wagon. As it was, living on the frontier, he was exposed to the life of a teamster and was a wage-earner at an age when other boys were still in school, farming, or serving apprenticeships as printers, perhaps, as Mark Twain had done.

At the time of the Civil War, teenagers were welcome in the ranks of both armies; drummers and fifers could be as young as sixteen and still enlist. Cody was now fifteen, and wanted to serve somehow.

Buffalo Bill as a private in the Seventh Kansas Cavalry, c. 1864 or 1865. (Buffalo Bill Historical Center, Cody, Wyoming)

The State of Kansas in 1861 had twelve official regiments, ten quasi-regimental organizations, but in fact only 1,600 soldiers on active duty. There were home guards for defense against guerrillas, such as those led by Colonel William C. Quantrill, whose men were successors to the Border Ruffians of Bleeding Kansas. Independent companies were raised locally. It was one of those private armies that Will Cody joined.

"A man by the name of Chandler," he wrote, "proposed that we organize an independent company for the purpose of invading Missouri and making war on its people on our own responsibility. He at once went about it in a very quiet way, and succeeded in inducing twenty-five men to join him in the hazardous enterprise. Having a longing and revengeful desire to retaliate upon the Missourians for the brutal manner in which they had treated and robbed my family, I became a member of Chandler's company."

Chandler's plan was that his men should leave their homes in parties of not more than two or three together and meet at a certain point near Westport, Missouri, on a fixed day. "His instructions were carried out to the letter," said Cody, "and we met at the rendezvous at the appointed time. Chandler had been there some days before us, and, thoroughly disguised, had been looking about the country for the whereabouts of all the best horses. He directed us to secretly visit certain farms and collect all the horses possible, and bring them together the next night. This we did, and upon reassembling it was found that nearly every man had two horses."

At once the raiders struck out for the Kansas line, which they crossed at an Indian ferry on the Kansas River, above Wyandotte. As soon as they had set foot upon Kansas soil, they separated with the understanding that they were to meet again one week from that day at Leavenworth.

"Some of the parties boldly took their confiscated horses into Leavenworth," Cody recalled, "while others rode them to their homes. This action may look to the reader like horse-stealing, and some people might not hesitate to call it by that name; but Chandler plausibly maintained that we were only getting our own back, or the equivalent, from the Missourians, and as the government was waging war against the South, it was perfectly square and honest, and we had a good right to do it. So we didn't let our consciences trouble us very much."

Chandler's men continued to make similar raids on the Missourians off and on during the summer, and occasionally had running fights with them; none of the skirmishes, however, amounted to much. Government officials, hearing of their operations, put detectives on their track, and several of the party were arrested. "My mother," said Cody, "upon learning that I was engaged in this business, told me it was neither honorable nor right, and she would not for a moment countenance any such proceedings. Consequently I abandoned the jay-hawking enterprise, for such it really was."

While at Leavenworth, marking time, Will ran into Wild Bill, who had been put in charge of some ox trains bought by the government from Jones and Cartwright—the same John S. Jones who had formed a partnership earlier with William Russell—carrying supplies to the federal post at Rolla, Missouri. Hickok asked Cody to come along, "as a sort of assistant to him," and Will gladly accepted. From Rolla, they took a freight shipment to Springfield, Missouri, after which they returned to Rolla.

"On our return to Rolla," Cody wrote, "we heard a great deal of talk about the approaching fall races at St. Louis, and Wild Bill having brought a fast running horse from the mountains, determined to take him to that city and match him against some of the high-flyers there; and down to St. Louis we went with this running horse, placing our hopes very high on him."

They bet all the money they had on the horse and bet the horse as well against $250.

"I rode the horse myself," said Cody, "but nevertheless, our sure thing, like many another sure thing, proved a total failure, and we came out of that race minus the horse and every dollar we had in the world. . . . We were 'busted' in the largest city we had ever been in, and it is no exaggeration to say that we felt mighty blue."

The next morning, Wild Bill went to army headquarters in St. Louis and landed a job as scout, and Will records, "I being so young failed in obtaining similar employment." Hickok borrowed money from a friend and bought a steamboat ticket to send Will back to Leavenworth, while he went to Springfield, headquarters on his scouting trips.

In the fall of 1861, Will made a trip to Fort Larned, carrying military dispatches, and in the winter he accompanied George Long to buy horses for the government. He was still without any firm goal or sense of purpose, merely drifting. He took a series of temporary jobs, carrying dispatches once more on the wagon trains and working as a teamster.

The following spring, 1862, an expedition against the Indians was organized, consisting of a volunteer regiment, the Ninth Kansas, under Colonel Clark. "This expedition," wrote Cody, "which I had joined in the capacity of guide and scout, proceeded to the Kiowa and Comanche country, on the Arkansas River, along which stream we scouted all summer, between Fort Lyon and Fort Larned, on the old Santa Fe Trail. We had several engagements with the Indians, but they were of no great importance."

Official records show that Lieutenant Colonel Charles C. Clark, with seven companies of the Ninth Kansas Cavalry, was stationed at Ohio City, Kansas, on May 10, and sometime between then and August 7 marched to Fort Lyon and Fort Larned; Colonel Clark was in command of Fort Larned in November. One engagement is recorded, at Locust Grove, Indian Territory, on July 3, in which one enlisted man of the regiment was killed. Will's sister Julia claims that in Santa Fe Cody again met Kit Carson, then a colonel of the First New Mexico Volunteer Infantry.

In the winter of 1862, Cody joined the Red Legged Scouts, so called, according to Don Russell, because they wore red leggings made from the red sheepskin shoemakers used in those days. This was an informal militia, organized by James H. Lane, a veteran of the Mexican War and a politician who, after Fort Sumter, persuaded President Lincoln to give him a commission as a brigadier general. In Kansas he recruited three regiments. The one Cody joined was led by Dr. Charles R. Jennison, who had been a disciple of John Brown and who was a hater of all things and persons Missourian.

Will served with the Red Legs only when called upon; the rest of that winter he went to school once again. Will's commander in the Red Legs was Captain William S. Tough; Cody spells the name "Tuff"; it was also spelled "Tuft" and "Tufft." Tough lived up to his name. He was born in Savannah, Georgia, and lived for a time in Baltimore before moving to St. Joseph, Missouri. At first he leaned toward the Confederate side, but when a band of bushwhackers, as Missouri irregulars were known, shot him, he raised a company of seventy-five men and, without any authority, led them against the bushwhackers and hanged five of them. From that time on, he was considered a Union supporter.

Cody felt he could join the Red Legs without breaking his promise to his mother, since they were irregulars. One of the bushwhacker leaders was the infamous Will C. Quantrill. Quantrill lived at one point in Kansas, where he taught school under the alias of Charlie Hart. Quantrill, a physically repellent man with a huge nose and a mop of coarse blond hair, was given to sadistic rages. In Missouri he led a marauding band of outlaws who, during the war, killed several thousand men, usually from ambush. Originally from Ohio, he was said to have stolen, cheated, and murdered his way West. Disliked by Kansans, he was run out of the town of Lawrence.

He took his revenge for this slight on August 19, 1863, when he invaded Lawrence with three hundred men and sacked the town, burning homes and stores, killing nearly two hundred citizens within four hours. Hearing that a body of Union troops was headed after him, Quantrill and his men escaped over the border into Missouri.

Cody defended the actions of the Red Legs, who included members of Jennison's Jayhawkers, the Seventh Kansas Volunteer Cavalry, and at times were no less predatory than the bushwhackers. "The Red-Legged Scouts," he wrote, "while they cooperated with the regular army along the borders of Missouri, had for their specific duty the protection of Kansas against raiders like Quantrell [sic], and such bandits as the James Boys, the Younger Brothers, and other desperadoes who conducted a guerrilla warfare against Union settlers." These same Jameses and Youngers were to become celebrated—and reviled—as murderous outlaws after the end of the Civil War.

Among the members of his company were "some of the most noted Kansas Rangers, such as Red Clark, the St. Clair brothers, Jack Harvey, an old pony express-rider named Johnny Fry, and many other well-known frontiersmen." Still, despite Cody's version of this paramilitary activity, one observer defined a Red Leg as "more purely an indiscriminate thief and murderer than a Jayhawker."

Cody did not list Wild Bill Hickok as one of the Red Legs, though he is reported to have been one at an earlier time. Cody described "many a lively skirmish with the Younger Brothers, and when we were not hunting them, we were generally employed in carrying dispatches between Forts Dodge, Gibson, Leavenworth, and other posts."

During the summer of 1863, Cody said that he "engaged to conduct a small train to Denver for some merchants," arriving there in September. In Denver Cody received a letter from his sister Julia, telling him that his mother was not expected to live much longer. He hastened home, to find her dangerously ill with tuberculosis. She died on the twenty-second of November 1863. "Thus passed away a loving and affectionate mother, and a noble, brave, good and loyal woman. That I loved her above all other persons, no one who has read these reminiscences can for a moment doubt."

Helen Cody Wetmore describes the trip with their mother's coffin to Pilot Knob Cemetery, "in a rough lumber wagon . . . a long, cold, hard ride, but we wanted our parents to be united in death as they had been in life, so we buried mother in a grave next to father's."

At last Will Cody was free of his promise to his mother, free to enlist in the Union Army, then engaged in some of the fiercest fighting of the war. He was in no great haste to do so, however.

To begin with, there were his sisters to consider. Before his mother's death, sister Julia had married James Alvin Goodman on December 22, 1862. As it turned out, young Will had been the matchmaker. Julia remarked in the fall of 1862 that since he was not likely to spend much time at home, it didn't seem right for the girls to be living alone without a man to protect them. Will then suggested that Julia get married. However, he objected to every candidate for his sister's hand; the only man he found acceptable was James Goodman, then living in a rented farm across the road from the Codys. The young man did not smoke or drink, and he was honest and hardworking—so the mantle fell on him. The marriage seemed more like a business arrangement than a romance. Julia proposed to him, and since he had limited means, he accepted.

Julia took care of the house. Helen and May, the younger sisters, were unhappy with the clothes they had been given after their mother's death, and they appealed to their brother for help. He answered: "My dear sisters:

I am sorry that I cannot help you and furnish you with such clothes as you wish. At this writing I am so short of funds myself that if an entire Mississippi steamer could be bought for ten cents, I couldn't purchase the smokestack. I will soon draw my pay and I will send it, every cent, to you. So brave it out, girls, a little longer. In the meantime, I will write Al [Goodman, his brother-in-law]. Lovingly, Will."

Cody kept his promise; he sent them the money, something he would do often in later life, when his Wild West show was successful.

His home appeared gloomy to Will, now that his mother was gone. So he went to Leavenworth and, as he put it, "entered upon a dissolute and reckless life—to my shame be it said—and associated with gamblers, drunkards, bad characters generally. I continued my dissipation for two months and was becoming a very 'hard case.'"

On February 4, 1864, Jennison's Jayhawkers returned to Leavenworth to reenlist. Volunteers ordinarily served for three years and were then asked to "re-up." If they did so, they were granted a furlough, so they could go home, parade around in their uniforms, and see if they could persuade any of their friends to join them.

That is what happened to Will Cody. Among the veterans, "I met quite a number of my old comrades and neighbors, who tried to induce me to enlist and go south with them. I had no idea of doing anything of the kind; but one day, after having been under the influence of bad whisky, I awoke to find myself a soldier in the Seventh Kansas. I did not remember how or when I had enlisted, but I saw I was in for it, and that it would not do for me to endeavor to back out." Hardly the kind of statement made by a warrior eager for battle.

Nothing is said in *Buffalo Bill's Life Story*, his second autobiography, about this episode, but it must be true, for it is not the sort of thing anyone would make up; more likely it is something a proud man would wish to keep hidden. At any rate, Will enlisted on February 19, 1864, and was mustered in on February 24. He was assigned to Company H, commanded through most of Cody's tour of duty by Captain Charles L. Wall.

In his enlistment papers, Cody gave his occupation as "teamster." His hair was described as "brown," complexion "fair," height "five feet ten." In later life he always appeared taller, but inasmuch as he was only eighteen at the time, he might still have had some growth ahead of him.

Cody said very little in his autobiographies about his Civil War service. Fortunately, both military records and campaign histories shed some light on it. On March 12 his regiment was ordered by way of St. Louis to Memphis, where it arrived on June 6. It was assigned to escort working parties along the Memphis and Charleston Railroad, to protect the workmen from Confederate raids, but the regiment soon found itself under fire.

The spring and summer of 1864 was a perilous time for the Union. Lincoln was up for reelection, facing the "Boy General" George B. Mc-Clellan, the Democratic Party candidate. If Lincoln could not announce an important victory, it appeared that he would lose the election, and McClellan would drop the demand for unconditional surrender and negotiate a peace treaty with the South.

At the time of Bill Cody's enlistment, Grant was leading the mighty Army of the Potomac against Lee's Confederates in the furious, desperately fought battles of the Wilderness in Virginia, while Sherman was beginning his advance from Chattanooga toward Atlanta. Across the Mississippi to the west lay embattled Missouri and "Bleeding" Kansas.

Missouri was a border state, but one with strong Confederate sympathies, as it was a slave state. Since Isaac Cody and his wife had both been ardent supporters of the Union and, if not abolitionists, certainly opposed to the expansion of slavery into Kansas, young Will undoubtedly held the same convictions. True, his feelings for the embattled Union were of less importance to him, surely, than the lure of the frontier, the daring life of a scout, and the great drama of westward expansion.

If Missouri had gone with the Confederacy, the entire course of the war would have been different. As it was, while Missourians despised the Jayhawkers, and many of them owned slaves, they stayed in the Union. At least a third of the white residents sympathized with the Confederacy, however, and many men from the state joined the Confederate army. Guerrilla warfare as well as pitched battles plagued Missouri throughout the war. "More than any other state," wrote Pulitzer Prize–winning historian James M. McPherson in *The Atlas of the Civil War*, "Missouri suffered from a civil war within the Civil War; its bitter legacy was to persist for generations." That legacy was epitomized by the James and Younger gangs' postwar rampages.

Cody's regiment arrived in Memphis about the time that Confederate cavalry general Nathan Bedford Forrest, who seemed always to "get there fustest with the mostest," was once again displaying his brilliant military genius in persistent attacks against federal installations in Kentucky and Tennessee. Forrest captured Fort Pillow, just northeast of Memphis, on April 12. The fort was defended by a mixed garrison of 580 white Tennesseeans and black soldiers; most of the black troops were killed, and Forrest was accused of slaughtering them after they had surrendered.

After Fort Pillow, Forrest fought and soundly defeated Brigadier General Samuel D. Sturgis, who had been sent to Tennessee by General Sherman, fearing that the Confederates would destroy his vital rail supply lines in the central part of the state.

The Seventh Kansas, Cody's regiment, arrived at Colliersville on the Memphis and Charleston Railroad in June 1864, just in time to reinforce Sturgis's retreating troops. On July 5 General Sherman ordered Major General Andrew J. Smith into Mississippi with 14,000 troops, in an attempt to intercept Forrest and protect Union supply lines. A corps of cavalry was formed, including the Seventh Kansas, which moved from LaGrange, Tennessee, to Ripley, Mississippi. The Seventh was the advance guard and skirmished with an enemy brigade for about an hour.

Smith led his forces on to Tupelo, cutting a swath of destruction in his wake. There, in what is known as the Battle of Tupelo or the Battle of Harrisburg, Smith's forces were attacked by Bedford Forrest on July 14. In a number of disorganized frontal assaults, the Confederates suffered a bloody pounding from the entrenched Federals. However, short of rations and ammunition, Smith was forced to withdraw the next day, pursued by Forrest. In a vigorous rearguard action, Forrest was shot in the foot, which put him out of action. The Battle of Tupelo could not be considered a victory for either side, though Smith did seriously damage the Confederate forces, and he successfully protected Sherman's supply line. "There is no doubt," wrote one of Forrest's biographers, "that it was a defeat for the Confederates which, with more dash and boldness on the part of A.J. Smith might have been turned into a disaster." Perhaps.

From July 15 through July 19, 1864, the Seventh Kansas was frequently embroiled in skirmishes. "On several occasions," reported Colonel Thomas P. Herrick, "my regiment was engaged with the enemy and severely punished him, without corresponding loss to ourselves." The Seventh lost two men killed, two wounded, and six horses shot.

The Battle of Tupelo must be considered the most important campaign of Will Cody's Civil War service, if only because it was one of the few battles in which General Forrest was ever defeated. Yet all he wrote about it is this: "General A.J. Smith re-organized the army to operate against Forrest, and after marching to Tupalo [sic] Mississippi, we had an engagement with him and defeated him. This kind of fighting was all new to me, being entirely different from any in which I had ever before been engaged." We must surmise that what Cody meant by this is that his previous battles had been fought guerrilla style with Indians and that he was unaccustomed to marching lockstep with other soldiers and fighting pitched battles over established fronts.

Years later, in 1911, Buffalo Bill's Wild West played Tupelo, Mississippi, famous today as the birthplace of Elvis Presley, and Cody wrote: "Busy day here. The people found out I had been in the Battle of Tupelo—

And a committee of local citizens took me out to the battlefield to explain to them the positions of both armies as I am the first Northern Soldier to do it who was in the battle."

After the excitement of Tupelo, Cody spoke of "skirmishing around the country with the rest of the army for some little time" and then returning with the regiment to Memphis, where they were kept in readiness for a forced march to Missouri. A Confederate force led by Major General Sterling Price threatened to invade St. Louis; the Seventh Cavalry was sent northward to defend the city. While the Seventh was still on the move, Price crossed the Missouri line on September 19, and on the twenty-seventh, the Confederates were stopped in Pilot Knob, eighty miles from St. Louis.

The Seventh was not in this fight, though Cody writes that "the command of which my regiment was a part hurried to the front to intercept Price, and our first fight with him occurred at Pilot Knob. From that time for nearly six weeks we fought or skirmished every day."

Army records show that the defense of St. Louis consisted of 4,500 infantry under General Smith's command, the Seventh Cavalry, just in from Memphis, part of the Thirteenth Missouri, and recruits for Merrill's Horse—a total of 1,500 cavalry. In these days of completely mechanized warfare, it is difficult to imagine how important mounted soldiers were in battle. Not only did they serve as advance scouts, reporting the location and strength of enemy troops, but they frequently led the attacks, charging forward with sabers drawn.

On October 20 the Seventh Kansas became part of a cavalry division and was assigned to the division's Second Brigade, led by Brigadier General John McNeil. Cody claims to have done some scouting for McNeil at that time.

Price's forces were still intact on October 22, 1864, when General McNeil's brigade crossed the Little Blue River and attacked two brigades of Price's army, driving them back to the edge of Independence, Missouri. Pursuing the Confederates, McNeil's men found themselves facing Price's entire force and fell back from the skirmish line, hoping for reinforcements. During the night, however, Price's army withdrew, ending his threat to St. Louis.

What this account of Cody's war service omits is the nature of the Civil War itself. Men marched or rode from one battlefield to another, often spending days in harsh weather. Many succumbed to disease or fatigue, or deserted before their enlistments were up. Wounded men had to depend on the crude medical equipment of the time for survival; a man hit in the arm or leg by a Minié ball was almost certain to lose the limb, because the balls destroyed the bone. More than half the battlefield casualties died, either instantly or later of their wounds. It was the most devastating war ever fought by Americans on their own soil or abroad; some 600,000 on both sides were casualties.

Army records are necessarily perfunctory and coldly factual. It is unlikely that the trans-Mississippi campaigns got much newspaper coverage; they were small bore, compared to Grant's drive toward Richmond and Sherman's toward Atlanta. It was Sherman's taking of Atlanta, in fact, that gave Lincoln the victory he needed to win reelection in 1864.

The year 1864 was a critical one for the United States on another front: the Great Plains. There violence frequently broke out between the Indians and the settlers. During and after the Civil War it was often said that the restlessness and hostility of the Indians was caused by Confederate agents. As we have seen, however, the Indians had more than enough reasons of their own to strike out at the whites. "As the Indian was pushed west toward the Rockies," wrote Sell and Weybright, "he became less reconciled to the white conquest. He continued to resist the effort to occupy his lands."

Prospectors, hunters, trappers, all were a threat to the Indian way of life. Surveyors arrived, planning railroad tracks through virgin forests. Farmers and ranchers built homes along the trails. As they saw more and more covered wagons rolling west across the Great Plains, the Indians could see themselves trampled by a ceaseless flood of settlers.

By August 1864 Ben Holladay's coaches and freighters had been so frequently and savagely attacked that he was nearly put out of business. Indians destroyed his stations, burned farms, massacred small groups of settlers. At Plum Creek ten people were murdered. For nearly four hundred miles almost every ranch along the stagecoach route had to be abandoned; only strongly defended coaches could get through. From Colorado came demands that something be done to quell these Indian uprisings.

Major Jacob Downing set out from Denver with forty men, in search of the Cheyenne. He found an Indian Village near Cedar Bluffs. "We commenced shooting," he reported. "I ordered the men to commence killing them. They lost twenty-six killed and thirty wounded. I burnt up their lodges and everything I could get hold of. We captured about one hundred head of stock, which was distributed among the boys."

This flagrant piece of lunacy, butchery, and thievery committed by Major Downing's "boys" led, inevitably, to a retaliation by the Indians, who promptly burned, scalped, and mutilated a family of settlers within twenty miles of Denver.

About 100 yards from the ranch they discovered the body of the murdered woman and her two dead children, one of whom was a little girl of four years and the other an infant. The woman had been stabbed in several places and scalped, and the body bore evidence of having been violated. The two children had their throats cut, their heads being nearly severed from their bodies. [The bodies were brought to Denver and] placed in a box, side by side, the two children between their parents, and shown to the people from a shed where the City Hall now stands. Everybody saw them, and anger and revenge mounted all day long as people filed past or remained to talk over Indian outrages and means of protection and reprisal.

This so aroused Governor Evans that he declared that there was no hope for peace on the plains until after "severe chastisement." Outright war was imminent. At this point, Black Kettle, chief of the Cheyenne, came forward. Black Kettle was proud, eloquent, diplomatic, and a mighty warrior. He offered to make peace if all the tribes were included in an amnesty.

Black Kettle wanted peace; he was about to encounter an adversary who wanted nothing less than all-out war against his people. This was Colonel John M. Chivington, a towering, bearlike Methodist parson, the presiding elder of the Rocky Mountain District of his church, who sometimes preached with a revolver resting on the pulpit. Rather than serve the Union in the Civil War as a chaplain, Chivington had demanded a "fighting commission" instead. He and his First Colorado Volunteers, mostly gold miners spoiling for a fight, met Confederate Brigadier General Henry H. Sibley and his army of Texans at Fort Union. They were the only Union forces between Sibley and the Colorado goldfields; it was then "on to San Francisco," as their motto had it.

Despite having marched forty miles a day through ice and snow to get to the field of battle, the Coloradans attacked Sibley's forces and halted the Confederate invasion of the Southwest. Chivington could do no wrong—or so he and everyone else in Colorado thought, including Governor Evans. It was Chivington, in command of the Third Colorado Regiment, who was assigned the task of punishing the Cheyenne.

Chivington was warned by William Bent, an old trader married to a Cheyenne woman and the father of three half-Cheyenne sons, that if the Indians were provoked any further they would unite among themselves—Cheyenne and Kiowa, Arapaho and Lakota—and then nothing could protect the whites from their anger. Chivington dismissed Bent's warning contemptuously.

In September of 1864, Black Kettle and six other Cheyenne chiefs came to Fort Weld, near Denver, wanting to talk peace, and bringing with them four white captives they had ransomed from other bands as evidence of their good faith.

Chivington and Governor Evans did not welcome Black Kettle's peaceful overtures. "What shall I do with the Third Colorado Regiment if I make peace?" Evans asked privately. "They have been raised to kill Indians and they must kill Indians."

When Black Kettle brought his band back to the reservation at Fort Lyon, Major Edward Wynkoop, also eager to avoid battle, offered him protection as well as food and supplies. He was overruled by his superiors, who said that the Indians must be made "to suffer more" before they could have peace. Wynkoop was replaced by Major Scott Anthony, who was working with Evans and Chivington. He told Black Kettle to take his people twenty-five miles away, to Sand Creek. They would be safe there, he said. Meanwhile, Anthony waited for reinforcements from Denver.

They weren't long in coming. Chivington and seven hundred volunteers, including mounted troops and howitzers, arrived at Fort Lyon on November 26, 1864. At daybreak on November 29, they reached the edge of Black Kettle's camp, and Chivington ordered his men to "kill and scalp all, big and little. Nits make lice." Many of his men were drunk from the whiskey they had swallowed to keep them warm during an icy, all-night ride. On the way to Black Kettle's camp, Chivington told his half-breed guide, William Bent's son Robert, who had been commandeered against his will to show the way to the Cheyenne camp: "I haven't had an Indian to eat for a long time. If you fool with me, and don't lead us to that camp, I'll have you for breakfast." Three of Bent's children were in the camp: Charles, Julia, and George. George watched the soldiers come down the creek at a rapid trot. In the camp all was confusion; men, women, and children screaming at the sight of the troops. Black Kettle had a large American flag tied to his lodgepole and was standing in front of his lodge. All this time the Cheyenne chief was calling out to his people not to be frightened, that the camp was under protection, and there was no danger.

About six hundred Indians were in the camp; they gathered around the Stars and Stripes. A white flag was also raised, to no avail. The volunteers started firing into the lodges. The warriors did everything they could to defend their families. "I never saw more bravery displayed by any set of people on the face of the earth than by these Indians," one regular soldier recalled later. "They would charge on the whole company, singly, determined to kill somebody before being killed themselves. . . . We, of course, took no prisoners."

"We killed as many as we could," Chivington reported. "The village was destroyed and burned." Black Kettle was spirited away to safety by his young warriors, against his will; he wanted to die with his people. White

Antelope stood before his tent, wrapped in his blanket, folded his arms, and sang his death song as the soldiers beat him down and shot him.

No one among the Indians was spared. One little girl about six years old came out of a hole with a white flag; she had not proceeded a few steps when she was shot and killed. Chivington's troops chased the fleeing Indians up Sand Creek. One interpreter who witnessed the slaughter wrote, "All manner of depredations were inflicted on their persons; they were scalped, their brains knocked out; the men used knives, ripped open women, clubbed little children, knocked them on the head with their guns, beat their brains out, mutilated their bodies in every sense of the word."

Chivington, this appalling excuse for a man of God and a soldier, returned to Denver with his band in triumph, claiming they had killed five hundred Indians. Their actual victims were ninety-eight women and children and a handful of mostly old men. The *Rocky Mountain News* proclaimed it "a brilliant feat of arms." "All did nobly," Chivington said, and one evening during intermission in the Denver opera house, one hundred scalps were put on display, and the audience gave Chivington's men a standing ovation.

Some people on the frontier said this was the only way to treat the Indians. Old Indian scouts Kit Carson and Jim Bridger were indignant, and warned of swift and terrible retribution. Horrified people in the East could not understand such a massacre; editors in New York denounced it.

Regular army officers, too, were outraged by Sand Creek. General Ulysses S. Grant himself privately declared it nothing more or less than murder. There were separate investigations by Congress and by the U.S. Army. "As to Colonel Chivington," said the official report of the Senate Committee on the Conduct of the War, "your committee can hardly find fitting terms to describe his conduct. Wearing the uniform of the United States, which should be a symbol of justice and humanity . . . he deliberately planned and executed a foul and dastardly massacre which would have disgraced the veriest savage among those who were the victims of his cruelty." By the time the reports were in, Chivington was a civilian again and beyond the reach of military justice. No one was ever punished for the Sand Creek Massacre. Twenty years later Chivington, unrepentant to the last, speaking to a reunion of Pikes Peak pioneers, said: "I stand by Sand Creek."

Word of what had happened spread swiftly, and William Bent's dire predictions proved correct. Cheyenne runners carried the news to all the Lakota, Arapaho, and Cheyenne bands. Soon the entire plains region was embroiled in war. Stagecoaches were burned; telegraph wires were cut down. The Indians raided Julesburg, a fort, and burned it. During the summer a wagon train near Platte Bridge was attacked, a rare occurrence for the Indians in ordinary times. A battle ensued when more Indians and soldiers joined in. Among the Indians was a great warrior named Roman Nose. After an all-day fight he rode alone around the wagons. Everybody in the train was either dead or wounded. He motioned to his Cheyenne braves, who killed all who showed any sign of life.

"Since this . . . horrible murder by Chivington," said Major Wynkoop, "the country presents a scene of desolation; all communication is cut off with the States, except by sending bodies of troops, and already over one hundred whites have fallen as victims to this fearful vengeance of these betrayed Indians. All this country is ruined; there can be no such thing as peace in the future."

Black Kettle, on the other hand, still wanted no part of fighting, only peace. "Although wrongs have been done me," he said, "I live in hopes. I have not got two hearts. . . . I once thought that I was the only man that persevered to be a friend of the white man, but since they have come and cleaned out our lodges, horses, and everything else, it is hard for me to believe white men any more." He took the survivors of Sand Creek south, away from the fighting.

The consequences of the Sand Creek Massacre were many and far-reaching. The Cheyenne sent a war pipe north. The northern Cheyenne smoked it, as did the Sioux, among them Sitting Bull. Thirteen years later he would exact his own revenge at the Little Big Horn. And it was certainly the outbreak of Indian warfare that drew Cody back to scouting after the end of the Civil War.

Nearly fifty years after the war, Cody was visiting Colonel D. B. Dyer, a business partner who lived near Kansas City, when he saw what he recognized as the site of the Battle of the Little Blue. He told the colonel that Price's forces were "right on the edge of this bluff." During the battle Major General John Sappington Marmaduke, commander of Price's cavalry, was captured, after having had two horses shot out from under him. In his second autobiography, Cody tells that he approached the general, whose dash and fighting ability he admired, and asked if there was anything he could do to make him more comfortable. The general told him he was hungry, so Cody shared his lunch with him, and a bottle of whiskey, which he had somehow "liberated" from another soldier's saddlebag. Cody then "was put in charge of General Marmaduke and accompanied him as his custodian to Leavenworth." Marmaduke spent the rest of the war imprisoned at Fort Warren, Massachusetts. After the war, Marmaduke was elected governor of Missouri, and he and Cody became good friends.

Cody spoke of two adventures during his Civil War service. The first occurred when he was acting as a scout—a spy, really—riding well ahead of his command to see if he could pick up any information about Price's movements. He was dressed in Confederate gray, or Missouri jeans, when he rode up to a farmhouse and discovered an old friend in the kitchen, eating bread and milk. It was Wild Bill Hickok, wearing the gray uniform of a Confederate officer. "You little rascal," he claimed Hickok said, "what are you doing in those 'secesh' clothes?" While they were both enjoying their bread and milk, Hickok told his friend that he had been spying on Price and had some papers, which he gave to Will to deliver to General McNeil. This story is surely no more improbable than many similar episodes reported during the Civil War. The bread and milk adds a touch of the bizarre to the whole incident. Bread and milk—Wild Bill and Will Cody?

A second adventure took place a few days after Will's encounter with Hickok. He was again riding ahead of his regiment as a scout when he stopped at a farmhouse for a drink of water. There were three women alone in the house, a mother and her two daughters; all three were frightened by the approach of Federal troops. They feared, quite rightly, that the Yankees would make off with everything in the house of any value. Because they had treated him well and given him food, Cody appointed himself sentinel in front of the house and turned away any possible pillagers until the rear guard of the army had passed. The grateful mistress of the house invited him to dinner. While he was eating, three men burst into the kitchen and pointed shotguns at his head. When they learned how Cody had protected the women, the men—the husband of Cody's hostess and their two sons—lowered their weapons; however, the father advised Will to move on before being cut off by bushwhackers. Although there may be a suspicion of blarney in Cody's report of this episode, it does illustrate his innate sense of chivalry, which endeared him to many, as well as his personal appeal and charm. He was then an extremely good-looking young man: clean-shaven, with a full head of brown hair. What was remarkable about Bill Cody, then and later, was that everyone he met apparently liked him.

Following Price's retreat across the Arkansas, Cody undoubtedly did some more scouting. "From this time on," he wrote, "Wild Bill and myself continued to scout together until Price's army was driven south of the Arkansas River and the pursuit abandoned. We then returned to Springfield, Missouri, for a rest and for supplies, and Wild Bill and myself spent two weeks there in 'having a jolly good time,' as some people would express it." We can only guess at what that "good time" might have been.

Cody is recorded as detached for duty in a hospital at Pilot Knob on January 23, 1865, and was assigned special duty as an orderly at Headquarters, District of St. Louis, on February 19. Except for a furlough to Weston, Missouri, beginning on April 5, he remained on this duty until September 13, when he was ordered to return to his regiment.

Throughout the war, Indian attacks had bedeviled the Union army, and while volunteers were still available, a large army expedition was sent against the Sioux in Powder River country, in the hopes of ending Indian raids. The Seventh Cavalry was not a part of the expedition but replaced other troops who were.

On August 25, 1865, the Seventh was ordered to return to Fort Kearny from Fort Leavenworth, arriving there on September 14, one day after Will rejoined their ranks.

On September 29 Will was mustered out with the rest of his regiment. He had served one year seven months and ten days with the Seventh Kansas. The regiment had seen considerable fighting, and Cody missed no battle, campaign, or skirmish during that time. In the seven months he had been on detached duty, his regiment had been in garrison. Although he said he had been a noncom, he was discharged as a buck private, the same rank he had when he enlisted. It is possible that he received the temporary battlefield rank of sergeant, but there is no record of it. The regimental history says of him: "One of the members of Company H has since become famous—W.F. Cody, 'Buffalo Bill.' He entered as a veteran recruit and was mustered out with the regiment."

Despite the dubious beginnings of his military service and the peculiar circumstances of his enlistment, William Cody had served his country if not with distinction, then with diligence.

The Civil War, however, was to prove fateful for nineteen-year-old Will Cody in yet another way, and his life would not be quite the same again.

CODY TAKES A SHOT
AT DOMESTIC LIFE

hile on duty as a hospital orderly in St. Louis in the winter of 1864–1865, Cody met an attractive young woman named Louisa Frederici. There are several versions of their meeting. In her book *Memories of Buffalo Bill*, Louisa says that the fateful encounter took place on May 1, 1865. According to her story, Will was brought to her home on Chateau Avenue in Old Frenchtown by her cousin William McDonald. Finding her dozing over *The Family Fireside* magazine, the two young men pulled the chair out from under her as a joke. Louisa slapped Cody, under the impression that he was her cousin, the guilty party. Together the three young people concocted a practical joke. She and Will would pretend to be engaged, to discourage an admirer with whom she had a date that night. After this first meeting, Will became a regular visitor; her other admirer dropped out of the picture.

Helen Cody Wetmore tells the most romantic and unlikely story of all. She claims that her brother saw Louisa while out horseback riding, and he was impressed by her graceful bearing on her mount; he always appreciated fine horsemanship. How could he meet her? None of his friends knew her. His lucky break came when "her bridle-rein broke one morning; there was a runaway, a rescue, and then acquaintance was easy."

Another version of the meeting, told by Cody's press agent, Major John M. Burke, has it that some drunken soldiers in the streets of St. Louis were making loud comments about a group of schoolgirls, teasing them and making advances. When Cody saw what was going on, he ordered them to stop. While the men argued with him, all the girls ran away except one—Louisa. Will escorted her home and they promptly fell in love. While the chivalrous action described here is certainly in keeping with what we know of Cody's character and his courage, it is hard to credit it, given the source. It was one of Burke's jobs to build up Cody's heroic qualities for the good of the Wild West show's box office receipts.

Cody himself writes that after his discharge and a brief visit in Leavenworth, he returned to St. Louis, "having made up my mind to capture the heart of Miss Frederici, whom I now adored above any other young lady I had ever seen." He declared his sentiments and received her consent to marry him in the near future, "and when I bade her goodbye, I considered myself one of the happiest of men."

But almost any romance may fade in time, and in 1905, when Cody sued unsuccessfully for divorce, he implied that he had been tricked into marriage. "Boylike," he testified in the trial, "I thought it would be very smart to be engaged. I asked her to marry me, or asked her if she would marry me if I would come back after the war was over. And jokingly she said 'yes.' Shortly after that I was ordered away from St. Louis . . . and I had nearly forgotten all about this little engagement when the war was over and I was discharged from the army. I returned to Leavenworth, Kansas, which she knew was my home, and I received several letters from her, asking me to keep my word and I desiring to keep my word if I had asked her to marry me after the war, I concluded to do it. I went to St. Louis and arrived there, I think, two days before we were married, which ceremony was performed by a justice of the peace at her father's house at about eleven o'clock in the morning." The date was March 6, 1866.

Between the time of his discharge and the wedding, Cody had somehow to earn enough money to consider marriage; that meant going back to Leavenworth and finding work. He says that he drove a string of horses from Leavenworth to Fort Kearny. His friend Bill Trotter, division agent of the Overland Stage Line, hired him in Fort Kearny to drive a stagecoach between the fort and Plum Creek.

One adventure from his stint as a stage driver was recorded in *The Great Salt Lake Trail*, a book cowritten by Cody and Colonel Henry Inman. The story, significantly, is not told in the first person, and Cody never claimed that it had happened.

"While driving stage between Split Rock and Three Crossings, he [Cody] was set upon by a band of several hundred Sioux. Lieutenant Flowers, assistant division agent, sat on the box beside Cody, and there were half a dozen well armed passengers inside. Cody gave the reins to Flowers, applied the whip, and the passengers defended the stage in a running fight. Arrows fell around and struck the stage like hail, wounding the horses and dealing destruction generally, for two of the passengers were killed and Flowers badly wounded. Cody seized the whip from the wounded officer, applied it savagely, shouting defiance, and drove on to Three Crossings, thus saving the stage."

It is at about this same time that Cody claims he did his first scouting, for General William Tecumseh Sherman. Shortly after his postwar appointment as commanding general of the Military Division of the Mississippi, Sherman made a tour of his new command. He left St. Louis toward the end of September—about the time of Cody's discharge from the Seventh Kansas—and traveled from Fort Riley to Fort Kearny. Cody claims that he was hired as a dispatch rider for General Sherman, then on his way to a conference with Indian chiefs at Council Springs. Council Springs was on the Arkansas River, about sixty miles beyond Fort Zarrah, or Zara (no one, including Cody, seems to know how to spell the name of the fort correctly; it is "Zarah"), and three hundred miles southeast of Leavenworth. Dick Curtis, a plainsman especially experienced with Indians and familiar with several Indian languages, was the chief scout. However, Curtis apparently lost his way, and Cody volunteered to guide the expedition, which he did, riding along with the general until they reached the Indian camp, which Cody had seen before. At Council Springs, treaties were negotiated with Kiowa and Comanche. After the council, Cody guided General Sherman to Fort Kearny and Leavenworth.

"At Leavenworth," Cody wrote, "I took leave of one of the noblest and kindest-hearted men I have ever known." It is doubtful that any defeated Confederate soldier would agree with this view; nor, in time, would the Plains Indians, who would soon learn that Sherman's objective in his new post was to crush them completely.

After his work as a stage driver and a scout for Sherman, Cody proceeded to St. Louis to be married. Cody was twenty years old; Louisa, a couple of months short of her twenty-second birthday. However romantically it might have begun, it was not a marriage made in heaven. Of French descent, accustomed to a gracious city life, complete with maids and carriages, Louisa Frederici Cody disliked the West, with its rough accommodations and ever-present dangers. Highly volatile and emotional, she had the vanity of a spoiled daughter. A strikingly beautiful young woman, she expected flattery and constant attention; when things did not go as she wished, she became moody. This side of her personality was hard for Cody to comprehend. From the beginning of the marriage, she spent more time in St. Louis with her relatives than with him. Later in the marriage, she disliked show business as much as Cody loved it. The two spent longer periods of time apart; it is doubtful that Cody was ever at home for more than six consecutive months. Louisa would have done better, perhaps, to marry Louis Reiber, the suitor scared off by their practical joke. Reiber would have given her the house in the Old French section of

St. Louis that would have suited her better than a log house on the plains. It is true that Cody the plainsman cut a handsome figure, but for Louisa the Wild West held no allure whatever—nor was she cut out for the pioneer life.

Not that the marriage must be considered a complete failure, however. The couple had four children, two of whom died young. They always—or almost always—spoke affectionately of each other. He called her "Mama" or "Lulu"; to Louisa he was always "Will." Cody, moreover, was always a kind and loving father to his children.

In Cody's life, Louisa occupied a place quite apart from his ambition and his achievements. As Courtney Ryley Cooper put it after Louisa's death, "The poor old woman hardly knew the parade had gone by—Buffalo Bill's life was largely a haze to her."

At the beginning of their marriage, though, the picture was quite different. They left immediately after the wedding ceremony on their honeymoon, a boat trip up the Missouri to Leavenworth, on the luxury steamer *Morning Star*. According to Will, Louisa's parents accompanied the young couple to the boat and bade them "a fond farewell and a God-speed on our journey."

There was a contingent of Missourians aboard the boat who shunned Cody, regarding him as "a Kansas jay-hawker and one of Jennison's house-burners." Cody had no choice but to admit to one of the Missourians that he was from Kansas and that he had been a soldier and a scout in the Union army.

The second day out from St. Louis, the boat pulled up at a desolate landing to put on wood. A band of horsemen rode up, threatening to shoot "the black abolitionist jay-hawker." Cooper reports that Louisa fainted in Cody's arms. The boat pulled out before the riflemen, who were bushwhackers, could carry out their threat. Fearing that his new wife would think him "a hard customer," Cody telegraphed ahead to Leavenworth when the boat docked in Kansas City, to arrange for a reception, so that his bride would know he was not without friends.

The couple were met at the dock in Leavenworth by Will's sister Eliza and her husband, George Myers. About sixty of Will's friends, including a brass band and officers from Fort Leavenworth, were also waiting at the dock to greet the newlyweds with an old-fashioned charivari. As Cooper put it, "they were waiting, with carriages and flowers and greetings and happiness." Thanks to the "cultured men and cultured women she met at the fort," along with dances and carriage rides, Louisa's first weeks in Kansas were quite pleasant.

Vowing to settle down to a more placid existence, Will rented the big house in the nearby Salt Creek Valley that had belonged to his mother, who had taken in boarders to earn a living. The house was then owned by Dr. J. J. Crook, former surgeon with the Seventh Kansas Regiment. Will decided to turn the house into a hotel, which he called "the Golden Rule House"; he attempted to run the place with Louisa's help. In his case, the Golden Rule meant treating all his friends to the food and drink he was himself enjoying; he had to abandon the hotel business six months later as a losing proposition. As his sister Helen put it, "Will radiated hospitality, and his reputation as a lover of his fellowman got so widely abroad that travelers without money and without price would go miles out of their way to put up at his tavern. Socially he was an irreproachable landlord; financially his shortcomings were deplorable."

Cody himself describes the experience differently. "People generally said I was a good landlord, and knew how to run a hotel—a business qualification which, it is said, is possessed by comparatively few men. But it proved too tame employment for me, and again I sighed for the freedom of the plains."

There is undoubtedly some truth in Cody's claim that he had voluntarily quit the hotel business; he was not a man who could be easily broken to the halter of domesticity, and if he had not headed west for one reason, it would certainly have been for another. The life of a frontiersman was in his blood.

Cody wrote that he "started out alone for Salina, Kansas, then the end of the track of the Kansas Pacific Railway," which was at that time being built across the plains. At Junction City, he met Wild Bill Hickok, who had been hired as a scout at Fort Ellsworth, later called Fort Harker. Cody went to the fort with Wild Bill and was also hired as a scout. "During the winter of 1866–67," he says, "I scouted between Fort Ellsworth and Fort Fletcher." Because of the cold weather, there probably wasn't much scouting to be done, and Cody spent the winter in a dugout in Saline County.

Meanwhile, Lulu stayed in Leavenworth, where their first daughter was born on December 16, 1866. Cody returned home to help name the baby girl Arta and then reported back to Fort Ellsworth.

In the spring of 1867, Brevet Major General George Custer arrived at Fort Fletcher, having been appointed a lieutenant colonel of the new Seventh United States Cavalry. Custer was on his way to join an Indian expedition led by Major General Winfield Scott Hancock. In that year hostile bands of Indians were attacking settlers in Kansas, and Hancock was ordered to find them and to negotiate with the tribes. He led an army of fifteen hundred men. "Hancock's Indian War," as it was called, proved to be a dismal failure. Despite some Delaware Indian scouts and the finest white scouts he could hire (Cody was not one of them), Hancock could find few hostile Indians. "Since starting out with Hancock in March," Stephen Ambrose wrote in *Crazy Horse and Custer,* "Custer had covered nearly one thousand miles. More than 1,400 soldiers had scoured the countryside looking for Indians; the net result of this gigantic effort was two Indians killed, and they had been killed by the Kidder party. Meanwhile the Indians had left two hundred or more dead white scattered across Kansas. Custer had not gotten off to much of a start as an Indian fighter."

Later in the spring, while Cody was still at Fort Fletcher, the Big Creek, on which it was located, overflowed its banks, and the fort had to be abandoned. The garrison was moved to Fort Hays, about a mile south of present Hays City, Kansas. There Cody scouted in the vicinity of the fort.

Scouting, like riding the Pony Express, carried a certain romantic quality, an element of glamour that Cody later popularized. Scouts served as the eyes and ears of army units venturing into unsettled territory—what would eventually be called reconnaissance, when maps were finally available. Most of the early scouts were former fur trappers, who turned to scouting after the decline of the beaver trade. The trappers had learned how to survive in the wilderness and applied their many skills to scouting. They knew the ways of the Indians as well as the country. They were good at hunting game to feed their employers. In order to communicate with the Indians, they had learned sign language. Most important, they could "read signs," deciphering the meaning of bent blades of grass and broken twigs, Indian fashion, searching for hoofprints of ponies and buffalo.

Among the most famous of the early scouts were Jim Bridger and Kit Carson, both of them having begun as trappers in the early 1830s. By all accounts they were two of the most trusted and respected men in the West. Will Cody had met them both at Fort Laramie when he was only twelve.

Bridger, born in 1804, was a walking atlas of the West. In the vast expanse of wilderness from the headwaters of the Missouri to the Rio Grande, along the Colorado River and over the Sierra Nevada to California, his knowledge of the land was encyclopedic. Kit Carson, who was five years younger than Bridger, won fame scouting for John Charles Fremont, the foremost western explorer of the mid-nineteenth century. Carson served with Fremont during the Mexican War and in 1853, at the age of forty-four, was appointed Indian agent for the Ute of New Mexico. No one knew Indians better than Kit Carson, and, when not fighting them, he was sympathetic to their needs. At the outset of the Civil War, he left the agency and signed on with the New Mexico Volunteers as a lieutenant colonel.

Scouts and guides in Cody's time were hired by the Quartermaster Department of the army, usually through a post or regimental quartermaster. Scouts were hired by the month, and had no assurance of continuous employment; their pay ranged from $60 to $150 a month, more if they were called upon for hazardous missions. If a regiment or an expedition employed a number of scouts, as was often the case, the most experienced among them would be named chief of scouts. There were also Indian scouts; the Pawnee were especially prized for their scouting ability but also were asked to fight other Indians.

Although scouts were not hired as Indian fighters per se, they might be called upon to fight, along with the soldiers they guided. Their primary function was to lead the troops from one destination to another, by the most expeditious route, and to locate hostiles. "As a scout, Cody had his share of fighting," writes Don Russell, "but in 1866 and 1867, he was employed for the most part as guide and dispatch bearer."

Scouting in an Indian war was extremely hazardous. Scouts, guides, and couriers risked their lives daily, either carrying messages or guiding troops through hostile country. For the most part, scouts rode horses, though mules were sometimes preferred, because they were able to move more easily over rough terrain. Traveling by night if possible rather than by day, scouts were armed with a carbine and one or two revolvers. Courage alone, however, was seldom enough; determination was required, a knowledge of the country, and also luck to avoid death or capture by Indians.

It was while scouting near Fort Hays that Cody took his first ride with "the dashing and gallant Custer, who had come up to the post with an escort of only ten men. He wanted a guide to pilot him to Fort Larned, a distance of sixty-five miles. . . . I was ordered by the commanding officer to guide General Custer to his desired destination."

In his 1879 autobiography, Cody described his ride with Custer as an amusing episode. Custer had patronized Cody for riding a mule and suggested, in so many words, that he ought to "get a horse." Cody defended his mount, saying, "That mule is a good one." In fact, at the beginning of the ride, Cody's mule lagged behind the horses, but by the time they crossed the Smoky Hill River and struck the sandhills, the mule got a second wind and was soon outpacing Custer, on his fine Thoroughbred mount, as well as the other riders. At the end of the ride, Custer had to admit to Cody that "you have a better vehicle than I thought you had."

"General Custer thanked me for having brought him straight across the country without any trail," Cody writes, "and said that if I were not engaged as post scout at Fort Hays he would like to have me accompany him as one of his scouts during the summer; and he added that whenever I was out of employment, if I would come to him he would find something for me to do. This was the beginning of my acquaintance with General Custer, whom I always admired as a man and as an officer."

Be that as it may, this was the only occasion on which Will Cody ever scouted for Custer, though they were to meet again in several years under quite different circumstances. It is no coincidence that the two men are so often linked in western legend. Both wore their hair long and sported luxurious facial hair; both had been nicknamed "Pahaska," or Long-Hair, by the Indians. Both were flamboyant. Here is how Custer in the Union army was described by his biographer Frederick Whittaker in 1876: "In his new apparel, set off by shoulder-length golden curls, he looked 'as if he had just stepped out of Van Dyke's pictures,' the image of the seventeenth century." Cody, too, knew how to dress the part of the dashing westerner. It is unlikely that either of these two peacocks could have borne the company of the other for very long. When you add Wild Bill Hickok, you have three of a kind, all theatrical.

While Cody claims to have scouted for General Custer in 1867, his name does not appear in any official records until 1868.

Custer arrived at Fort Hays on April 19, 1867, after an Indian chase from Fort Larned, and remained there until the first of June. He was back in July on an unauthorized trip to Fort Harker and then went on to Fort Riley to be with his wife; for this trip he was court-martialed as absent without leave.

Custer was also accused of shooting deserters, a charge he defended on the grounds that he had been ordered in a telegram from General Hancock to "capture or kill the deserters."

An editorial in the New York *Times* on December 7, 1867, commended Custer in these terms: "Gen. CUSTER is, to those who know him intimately, the very *beau ideal* of an American cavalry officer. He is a magnificent rider, fearlessly brave, a capital revolver shot, and without a single objectionable habit. He neither drinks, swears, nor uses tobacco in any form."

It should be added for the record that the one occasion on which Custer drank alcohol, by his own admission in My Life on the Plains, he got violently sick, sick enough apparently to turn him into a teetotaler.

"A few days after my return to Fort Hays," says Cody, "the Indians made a raid on the Kansas Pacific Railroad, killing five or six men, and running off about one hundred horses and mules." He wrote that on the first of

August 1867, he was sent as scout and guide to an expedition led by Brevet Major George Augustus Armes, an appropriately named captain of Company F, Tenth United States Cavalry, with his troop and a mountain howitzer. The Tenth was a new regiment made up largely of veterans of the United States Colored Volunteers and other organizations of Negroes raised during the Civil War.

Continued Cody: "On the second day out we suddenly discovered on the opposite side of the Saline River, about a mile distant, a large body of Indians, who were charging down upon us. Major Armes, placing the cannon on a little knoll, limbered it up and left twenty men to guard it; and then, with the rest of the command, he crossed the river to meet the Indians. Just as he had got the men over the stream, we heard a terrific yelling and shouting in our rear, and looking back to the knoll where the cannon had been stationed, we saw the negroes, who had been left to guard the gun, flying toward us, being pursued by about one hundred Indians; while another large party of the latter were dancing around the captured cannon, as if they had got hold of an elephant and did not know what to do with it. Major Armes turned his command back and drove the Indians from the gun. The troops then dismounted and took position there. Quite a severe fight ensued, lasting about two hours. Five or six of the soldiers, as well as Major Armes, were wounded, and several of the horses were shot. . . .

"Major Armes, who was wounded and lying under the cannon—which, by the way, had become useless—called me up and asked me if there was any show of getting back to the fort. I replied that there was. Orders were given by Major Armes for a retreat, the cannon being left behind. During the movement several of our men were killed, but as night came and dense darkness prevailed, we succeeded in making good headway, and got into Fort Hays just at daylight next morning, in a very played-out condition."

When the Tenth Cavalry arrived at the fort, they found that an epidemic of cholera had broken out, as much to be dreaded in those days as the Indian attacks.

Cody's version of this event corresponds with military records, except for a few details in which he was in error: Only one man, Sergeant William Christy, was killed, not "several men," and Major Armes was the only one wounded, not "five or six." Cody also misspelled Armes's name as "Arms."

During this period, the U.S. Government was active in pursuing peace overtures with the Indians as well as sometimes pursuing the Indians themselves. General Hancock's mission, which included Custer's efforts, was designed to intimidate the Indians with a mighty show of force.

A tribe or two, perhaps, were persuaded to make peace; otherwise the mission was a failure. So were Sherman's efforts in the northern plains.

What must be borne in mind through any account of the Indian Wars is that no one in authority questioned the right of the Indians to the land they had occupied for centuries; lip service at least was paid to their claims of ownership, and the government insisted on treaties before appropriating Indian land; at times the tribes were paid for their land, though never what it was worth. At the same time, no one in or out of authority questioned the right of white settlers to move in and develop the land— remember manifest destiny. There could be no peace as long as whites made treaties with the Indians and promptly broke them. Cody himself stated that if the government had ever kept its promises to the Indians, there would have been no warfare.

One of the great Indian warriors of history was Red Cloud of the Oglala Dakota Sioux tribe, who had a reputation for daring and ferocity. In June of 1866, Sherman called Red Cloud and several other Lakota Sioux leaders to Fort Laramie to discuss a new treaty to permit a new road to be built through Sioux territory. Even before an agreement had been reached, however, a battalion of seven hundred infantrymen under Colonel Henry R. Carrington arrived at the fort, with orders to protect travelers along a road that had not yet been built. It was clear to Red Cloud that the whites intended to use his land whether he agreed or not. The chief, along with Man-Afraid-of-His-Horses, refused to sign the treaty; some Lakota and Cheyenne did, for which they were scorned by Red Cloud.

Red Cloud felt that if the Lakota and Cheyenne joined forces to repel this invasion, together they would be able to drive the soldiers out of their country.

Colonel Carrington was able to construct three forts in the Powder River country: Fort C.F. Smith in Montana and Forts Reno and Phil Kearny in Wyoming. But Lakota and Cheyenne warriors raided the forts again and again, seizing supply wagons, attacking the men when they ventured outside, driving off stock. The occupants of the forts were terrorized.

One officer, thirty-year-old Lieutenant Colonel William J. Fetterman, like Lieutenant John Grattan back in August of 1854, refused to be cowed by the Lakota. "Give me eighty good men," he boasted, "and I can ride through the whole Sioux nation." Four days before Christmas, 1866, a daring young Oglala Sioux named Crazy Horse led an attack on a wagon train carrying firewood to the fort. Fetterman saw his chance and asked to be allowed to go to the train's rescue. His superior officer, Colonel Carrington, agreed to let him go but specifically warned him not to be drawn out of sight of the fort. "Support the wood train," said Carrington. "Relieve it and report to me. Do not engage or pursue Indians at its expense. Under no circumstances pursue over Lodge Trail Ridge."

Not long after Fetterman led his men out of the fort, Crazy Horse and other young braves appeared and began to taunt the soldiers, despite a rain of bullets sent their way. Then the Indians remounted and rode over the ridge. Fetterman galloped after them. On the far side, nearly two thousand warriors were waiting for him—mostly Lakota, but also Cheyenne.

Inside the fort, the sounds of battle were heard in the distance and then, after only half an hour, silence, a silence even more frightening to the huddled women than the sound of gunfire. A search party went over the ridge and found Fetterman and all his command lying dead. Fetterman and his second-in-command had shot each other through the temple at close range in order to avoid falling into Indian hands. All the bodies had been horribly mutilated: stripped naked; skulls crushed by war clubs; ears, noses, and legs cut off; scalps torn away; and bodies pierced with arrows and bullets. Soldiers in the rescue party trod unaware on the victims' entrails in the high grass.

The Fetterman Massacre put an end to the thought of an early peace with the Lakota. The warfare would go on, sporadically at times, but always a threat, and the services of a scout like Cody were constantly in demand. There was still, however, some hope for peace south of the Platte.

The question arises: Who began the terrible practice of mutilating the dead after these battles? It must be said that both the whites and the Indians committed atrocities. The Indians claimed that they merely followed the white men's savagery after the massacre at Sand Creek in 1864. It was also a fact that scalping originated not with the Indians but with the Spanish. It doesn't much matter how it started; there was plenty of savagery to go around. A sign posted in the Mohawk Valley of New York when it was still wilderness read: *Nous sommes tous bêtes*—"We are all beasts."

That winter and spring of 1867, after his visit home, Will Cody wrote long letters to his wife, describing his scouting with Custer and other officers, the savage Indian battles, and other feats of daring. Shortly after the Saline River fight, in August 1867, Cody quit scouting again. This time he was about to take another flyer as an entrepreneur, a role he would play many times in his life.

In the autumn of 1867, while carrying dispatches from Fort Hays to Fort Harker, Cody stopped in Ellsworth. There he met William Rose, who had a grading contract with the Kansas Pacific Railroad near Fort Hays. Rose proposed to Cody that they go into partnership and establish a town on the west bank of Big Creek, about a mile from the fort, where the railroad was scheduled to cross. Rose's idea was that they would lay out and sell building lots to the public and then build a saloon and a store. In the West of that period, that was really all it took to get a town going.

Cody was delighted with Rose's scheme. "Thinking it would be a grand thing to be half-owner of a town, I at once accepted his proposition." The two men hired a railroad engineer to survey the site and stake it off into building lots. They named their new town Rome. Rome, Kansas, was almost, but not quite, built in a day. The two partners had the happy inspiration of donating lots free to anyone who would build on them, reserving the choice lots for themselves, which they planned to sell for $50 each. They bought supplies and opened their store.

"In less than one month," said Cody, "we had two hundred frame and log houses, three or four stores, several saloons, and one good hotel." So far, all had gone according to plan, and both Rose and Cody considered themselves millionaires. So certain was Cody that he had become a rich man that he sent for his wife, Louisa, and their daughter, Arta. After their arrival, the Cody family moved into the back of the store.

A number of colorful yarns have been spun about the town of Rome and Cody's part in its brief history. Louisa Cody, in her book written with Courtney Ryley Cooper, *Memories of Buffalo Bill*, claimed that her husband installed her and Arta in a back room of the saloon, and was then summoned to Fort Hays on official business. While he was gone, a violent fight broke out in the saloon, awakening the baby. Louisa was terrified when the men on the other side of the wall heard the baby's cries and wanted to come in and see it. Too frightened to refuse them, Louisa admitted "ten dirty, unkempt, bearded men," who filed in and stared at the baby in awe, after which the bartender closed down the saloon so that mother and daughter could get some sleep.

We can be quite certain this did not happen. Will tells a quite different story. He records that "one day a fine gentleman calling himself Dr. W.E. Webb appeared in town, and dropping into our store introduced himself in a very pleasant way." This Dr. Webb asked to be taken into the partnership with Cody and Rose; they refused. What they did not know is that William E. Webb was an agent for the Kansas Pacific Railroad. The next day Webb staked out a town one mile east of Rome and called it Hays City. He told the inhabitants of Rome that Hays City was where the railroad would pass and where a roundhouse and machine shop would be located. He also offered to move everyone from Rome to Hays City. "A ruinous stampede from our place was the result," said Will. "People who had built in Rome came to the conclusion that they had built in the wrong place; they began pulling down their buildings and moving them over to Hays City, and in less than three days our once flourishing city had dwindled down to the little store that Rose and I had built."

As a matter of fact, Kansas historians deny this story, claiming that Rome actually lasted a year or two, surviving a cholera epidemic in 1868. When the railroad raised its approaches to Big Creek Bridge, a high embankment blocked Rome's view of the tracks, and the city quietly expired.

However it happened, Rome's rise and fall was the first attempt on Will Cody's part to get rich quick; it would not be the last. He was compelled to send his wife and daughter back to St. Louis. Rose still had a five-mile grading contract with the Shoemaker and Miller Company, and the two men turned their hands to that work, which was at least remunerative. At the time, Cody also hunted buffalo. He had a prized stallion named Brigham, after the Mormon patriarch, which he had bought from a Ute Indian in Utah, "the fleetest steed I ever owned." It was on Brigham that Cody rode out after buffalo; the horse had been trained to chase down the animals so his master could shoot them.

Cody later became good friends with William Webb, "the man who stole Rome"; Webb was kind enough to give Cody and his partner each a lot in Hays City, and Cody revised his opinion of the good doctor, finding him "a perfect gentleman, a whole-souled, genial-hearted fellow whom everybody liked and respected." Cody also went buffalo-hunting with Webb, riding out on the prairie almost every morning. Within a year, according to Cody, "there were but few men on the prairie who could kill more buffaloes on a hunt than he."

On one of their hunts, they spotted a band of Indians not two miles away; the braves were attempting to get between the two men and the town, ten miles distant, cutting them off. Cody was mounted on Brigham and Webb on a fine Thoroughbred; they had no doubt they could outrun any Indian ponies. By running their horses hard, they succeeded in placing themselves between the Indians and the town. There they waved their hats at the Indians and fired some shots at them from a distance. The Indians, thirteen in number, began to get a little too close to them for comfort, so they struck out for Hays City. The Indians fired scattered shots at them and gave chase, but Cody and Webb easily left them behind. Webb then wanted to set off after the Indians, but Cody talked him out of it; he was unwilling to hunt Indians for sport.

In 1872 Webb gave Cody his first book publicity in *Buffalo Land*, his own story of life on the plains. He did not, however, mention the story of the thirteen Indians and their cat-and-mouse game with them.

Cody was still working with Rose on the grading contract. At one point, he made an effort to turn Brigham into a work horse, by hitching him to a grader; the experiment was not a success, but Cody was always ready to take off from work, climb on Brigham, and go buffalo hunting, whenever he had the excuse. On one occasion, hearing that a buffalo herd was close by and aware that the Shoemaker and Miller workmen were short of meat, Bill unhitched Brigham from the grader and, having no saddle with him, mounted the horse bareback. He was armed with what was to become his celebrated buffalo-killer, "Lucretia Borgia," an improved needle gun given him by the government. "Needle gun" was the common name given then to a .50-caliber Springfield rifle that had been converted to breechloading. The gun had a needlelike pin that, when the trigger was pulled, went through the powder to strike a primer on the end of the cartridge. The caliber of the gun made it a deadly weapon, which would save Cody's life more than once as well as account for a good deal of wild game.

On the way to the buffalo, Cody came across five officers from Fort Hays, a captain and four lieutenants, also out for buffalo. They struck up a conversation. Looking at Cody's outfit—work clothes, no saddle on his horse, only a bridle—the captain expressed doubt that Cody would be able to kill a buffalo on "that Gothic steed." The officers then offered to share their kill with him, keeping only the tongues and tenderloins for themselves. Cody, feigning ignorance, agreed to tag along behind them.

"There were eleven buffaloes in the herd and they were not more than a mile from us," he said. "The officers dashed ahead as if they had a sure thing on killing them all before I could come up with them; but I had noticed that the herd was making towards the creek for water, and as I knew buffalo nature, I was perfectly aware that it would be difficult to turn them from their direct course. Thereupon, I started towards the creek to head them off, while the officers came up in the rear and gave chase. The buffaloes came rushing past me not a hundred yards distant, with the officers about three hundred yards in the rear. Now, thought I, it's time to 'get my work in,' as they say. . . . I pulled the blind-bridle from my horse, who knew as well as I did that we were out for buffaloes—as he was a trained hunter.

"The moment the bridle was off, he started at the top of his speed, running in ahead of the officers, and with a few jumps he brought me alongside the rear buffalo. Raising old 'Lucretia Borgia' to my shoulder, I fired, and killed the animal at the first shot. My horse then carried me alongside the next one, not ten feet away, and I dropped him at the next fire. As soon as one buffalo would fall, Brigham would take me so close to the next, that I could almost touch it with my gun. In this manner I killed the eleven buffaloes with twelve shots."

Cody could not resist having fun with the officers; he presented them with all the tongues and tenderloins they wished from the buffalo *he* had slain; they themselves had failed to make a single kill.

This was the first reference Cody made in his early autobiography to hunting buffalo, but it is obvious from his description of the hunt that he was already a skilled and experienced hunter. The method he used—coming on the herd from behind, riding close to the animals, and picking them off one by one from the rear before they could panic and stampede—was clearly a practice he had learned from the Indians. Even riding bareback was doing it Indian-style. Still, all due credit must be given to his horse, Brigham, who, it could be argued, was every bit as buffalo-savvy as its rider.

According to Cody, Captain Graham asked him if he would consider scouting for the Tenth Cavalry, but Will doubted he could get out of his grading contract. The two men would meet again, however. Shortly after his conversation with Graham, a band of Indians raided the grading camp and drove off five or six teams of horses. Will went to the fort and reported the theft. The fort's commandant ordered Captain Graham and Lieutenant Emmick, along with one hundred colored troops, to punish the raiders; Cody went along as a civilian, not an official scout. He and his party found the Indian camp, but before they could attack, which Graham was eager to do, seeking to make his reputation, one of the men fired a rifle prematurely and frightened the Indians off. Captain Graham cursed the soldier who had discharged his weapon and forced him to walk all the way back to the fort.

It was in 1867 that the name "Buffalo Bill" first appeared in print. There is a mention in the Leavenworth *Daily Conservative* of November 26, 1867, of a "Captain Graham . . . Buffalo Bill and other scouts." Cody had named Captain Graham of the Tenth U.S. Cavalry as one of the officers he encountered on the hunt in which he killed the eleven buffalo. However, it would not be until he started killing buffalo professionally for the Kansas Pacific that his nickname was widely circulated.

His career as a buffalo hunter began when his work as a grader ended; the twelve hundred tracklayers of the railroad had reached the heart of buffalo country and needed to be fed. The contract for feeding the work-men was awarded to the Goddard Brothers Company, which hired Cody to provide twelve buffalo a day for the railroad. Cody demanded—and received—a large salary for his work: $500 a month, a substantial sum in those days. He was paid so well because the work was dangerous. He had to travel on his faithful Brigham five or ten miles from the safety of the fort every day, accompanied only by one man in a wagon to bring the meat back. There was always the risk of an Indian attack. The com-pany hiring Cody got a bargain in any case, for the meat ended up costing them about a cent a pound. Only the hump and hindquarters were used; the rest was left on the prairie for scavengers.

"During my engagement as hunter for the company—a period of less than eighteen months," said Cody, "I killed 4,280 buffaloes; and I had many exciting adventures with the Indians, as well as hair-breadth escapes." This figure was repeated in biographies and reference books for years—until Don Russell did the arithmetic. Had Cody killed 12 buffalo a day for eighteen months, the total would have been some 6,480 kills. If he killed only 4,280, he would have shortchanged his employers. The likelihood was, Russell concluded, that Cody had worked for Goddard Brothers for only eight months, not eighteen, which also would have agreed with the dates of his other activities. At eight months, 12 buffalo a day would have amounted to only 2,880, indicating that if Cody's total is correct, he killed *more* than his quota in that time frame. This seems the most likely explanation of the discrepancy. It would also mean that Cody began his contract to hunt for the railroad in October 1867 and, as he later recalled, ended it in May 1868, when the tracklayers reached Sheridan.

Confirmation of his skills came in an article in a contemporary news-paper account. The Leavenworth *Conservative* on January 11, 1868, quoted a report in the Hays City *Advance*: "Bill Cody and 'Brigham' started on a hunt Saturday afternoon, and came in Tuesday. The result was nineteen buffalo. Bill brought in over four thousand pounds of meat, which he sold for seven cents per pound, making about $100 a day for his time out." No mention of the railroad in the account; perhaps Bill was "moonlighting" on this occasion.

While Cody was hunting buffalo for the Kansas Pacific, he said that he always brought the best buffalo heads into camp and turned them over to the company, who found a good use for them. "They had them mounted in the best possible manner, and sent them to all the principal cities and railroad centers in the country, having them placed in prominent posi-tions at the leading hotels, depots, and other public buildings, as a sort of trade-mark, or advertisement, of the Kansas Pacific Railroad."

In his 1879 autobiography, Cody described two adventures with the Indians. One of them was recorded by a newspaper reporter on December 12, 1872, seven years before that autobiography was published, in an account apparently taken down verbatim and published in the Omaha *Herald*. At a banquet in Omaha, Cody said: "That was the time of the railroad construction, and the Indian war was going on. One day I rode twenty-one miles from the line of the road, and was alone. Just as I came out on a little rise of ground I saw a lot of Kiowa Indians. They discovered me at the same time, and eighteen or twenty jumped up to go for me. They were at breakfast and their horses were right by their sides. When they are on the war path they are always armed, so that each only had to put a bit of rope into his horse's mouth and he was ready.

"I saw at a glance what they were doing and I wanted to be home. You may bet I would like to be out of that, and I got out as fast as I could. I looked over my shoulders and saw them just a whooping and howling after me. . . . Once when I came to a little hog wallow on the prairie I turned long enough to fire at the fellow that was ahead and I must have hit him for he stoped [*sic*] but I could never find him afterwards. I had every confidence in my horse and I noticed that the Indians soon began to string out . . . though the Indians had a great advantage because their horses were fresh and mine had gone twenty miles before they saw me. It was a long run and a wild one. They fired several shots but they did not happen to hit me at all. One advantage I had was that they carried long muzzle loading guns and could not load again when they had once fired. I could see how they came on and changed places just as the horses gave out. Mine kept ahead. Finally the guard at the camp saw us. At that time there were only six Indians following me. All the rest had played out. Soldiers came out to meet me and we easily killed those six."

At the time, Cody was riding Brigham, and we must assume that he was carrying Lucretia Borgia. On another occasion, when he was not mounted on Brigham, Cody was accompanied by a butcher named Scotty, in a wagon driven by two mules and loaded with the meat from fifteen buffalo Cody had killed. When they saw about thirty Indians riding out of a ravine, they unhitched the mules "more quickly than that operation had ever been performed before," and tied them and the horse to the wagon. They then piled up buffalo hams to form a barricade, and with the extra revolvers and ammunition they carried, prepared to greet an Indian attack. The Indians charged but were stopped about a hundred yards away by the combined fire of rifles and pistols. According to Cody, the Indians charged back and forth several times but were driven off again; three of them who got within fifty yards were shot down. Meanwhile, as a pre-arranged signal to the cavalry troops stationed along the railroad, Cody had lit a brushfire to the windward side of their wagon. After about an hour, while the Indians continued to fire at them, Cody and Scotty saw cavalry coming toward them at full gallop over the prairie. The Indians saw the troops about the same time, mounted their horses, and rode off. The meat had a few arrows sticking in it but was otherwise all right, and was loaded into the wagon and taken to camp. Five Indian dead were left on the field.

The money Will Cody was earning as a hunter made it possible for him to bring his young family back to Hays City, although it is doubtful he was able to spend much time with them.

About this time, contemporary newspaper stories took notice of Cody. In the Lawrence, Kansas, *Weekly Tribune* on February 14, 1868, he was cited as "Cody, the noted guide and hunter" in a story about a buffalo-hunting party he led. Another item in the Topeka *Leader* of March 28, 1868, reported: "W.F. Cody, government detective, and Wm. Haycock, Deputy U.S. Marshal, brought eleven prisoners and lodged them in our calaboose on Monday last—a band of robbers having their headquarters on the Solomon, charged with stealing government property and desertion." The Wm. Haycock mentioned in the article was, of course, Cody's friend Wild Bill Hickok, whose name was frequently misspelled as Wm. Hitchcock, Wm. Hancock, Wm. Hickok, Wm. Haycock, as well as "Jim Hickock," according to an article by Theodore R. Davis, a correspondent for *Harper's Weekly*.

Some of the publicity for Buffalo Bill's later enterprises claimed that he had hunted for the Union Pacific, linking him to the transcontinental railroad. Actually, the line he worked for was called the Union Pacific, Eastern Division. This caused so much confusion that the name was changed in 1868 to the Kansas Pacific. That line was absorbed into the Union Pacific in 1880, which hardly clarified matters.

In any event, the work he did for the railroad surely helped to spread the name "Buffalo Bill" across Kansas. As he put it in his *Life Story*: "It was not long before I acquired a considerable reputation, and it was at this time that the title 'Buffalo Bill' was conferred upon me by the railroad hands. Of this title, which has stuck to me through life, I have never been ashamed." Actually, in one of the books attributed to Cody, *True Tales of the Plains*, he implied that the nickname was not entirely complimentary. Apparently, the road-workers began to tire of a steady diet of buffalo meat and would say "Here comes this old Bill with more buffalo." At last, said

Cody, "they connected the name buffalo and Bill together, and that is where the foundation to the name 'Buffalo Bill' was laid." At the same time, a jingle appeared and became popular:

> Buffalo Bill, Buffalo Bill,
> Never missed and never will;
> Always aims and shoots to kill
> And the company pays his buffalo bill.

As a matter of fact, there were other Buffalo Bills out West. One, William J. "Buffalo Bill" Wilson, was hanged at Lincoln, New Mexico, on December 10, 1875, for murder. Another was the "Buffalo Bill" reported on March 30, 1876, to have killed, "a few weeks ago," the sheriff of Young County, Texas. There was also a Buffalo Billy Brooks, buffalo hunter and peace officer at Dodge City, Kansas, in the 1870s.

The most determined and vocal candidate for the title was William C. Mathewson, a frontiersman who actually appears to be the "original" Buffalo Bill, and who had a life every bit as adventurous as Cody's. Mathewson was born in Broome County, New York, on January 1, 1830. His boyhood was spent hunting and trapping through the Northeast, venturing as far west as Wisconsin and as far north as Canada. When he was nineteen, he headed west. He was first employed by the Northwestern Fur Company, with headquarters at Fort Benton, Montana. Trapping furs, trading with friendly Indians and fighting hostiles, he spent two years in Montana, the Dakotas, Nebraska, and Wyoming.

After leaving the fur company, he joined Kit Carson's expedition and explored the Rocky Mountain region, crossing into Colorado and back down through the plains. In 1853 he settled in Kansas, on the old Santa Fe Trail, where he opened a trading post on the site of what would become the city of Wichita.

In 1860 and 1861 he saved a good many pioneer families in Kansas from starvation. A drought and a severe winter had ruined their crops. In O. H. Bentley's *History of Wichita, Kansas*, published in 1910, his story is told:

> All from the area were grateful and ever retained memories of the man who saved them from starvation in that terrible winter of 1860 and 1861. Till February, William Mathewson remained on the buffalo range, some days killing and sending eastward as many as eight carcasses of fat cows. Each day brought its quota of gaunt, penniless settlers, and each day, no matter what the weather, Mathewson shouldered his rifle and with a few miles of tramping sent his guests rejoicing homeward with all the choicest buffalo roasts and steaks they could carry.

In 1867 Mathewson saved 155 lives and recaptured 147 wagons of government supplies from a band of hostile Indians. In recognition of the valiant deed, which he achieved by riding through the Indians as they circled the wagon train, Mathewson was presented with a magnificent cased set of etched, inscribed, silver- and gold-plated, ivory-handled Colt model 1861 Navy revolvers.

In 1911 Mathewson wrote Cody the following letter: "You have no right to call yourself 'Buffalo Bill' and you know you haven't. . . . You know I am the original Buffalo Bill and was known by that name ten years before you ever worked for the Kansas Railroad. When I was post trader I was called Buffalo Bill because I killed buffaloes to supply meat for them that didn't have any meat or couldn't get it and I never charged them a cent for it. When you and your show come to Topeka I aim to tell you to your face that you are using a title that doesn't belong to you."

"I was shooting buffalo," Mathewson also declared, "when Cody was shooting jackrabbits." He also claimed that "Cody worked for me when he was a young fellow. I reckon he had begun to read Indian stories and see how much was to be made by that kind of reputation, and he was always fond of talk and show. I was never any hand to wear my hair long and go swaggering around the country blowing about what I had done. Cody knows he has no real right to the name, but if he wants to show off as a dime novel hero, I have no objection."

These reports of Mathewson's claim surfaced in 1894, when Cody was at the height of his fame. When reporters questioned Cody about Mathewson, he replied: "I never laid eyes on him and of course never worked for him. But this is the first intimation that I have ever had that any reputable person other than myself has ever claimed the title of Buffalo Bill. A few years ago there were as many claimants for my name as there were wild yellow flowers that gave their name to the State."

However, Cody was concerned for his reputation and for the protection of his name, which now had considerable capital invested in it. So Cody's press agent for the Wild West, Frank Winch, was sent ahead to Kansas to see if he could straighten things out. Cody didn't want any unfavorable publicity for his show arising from Mathewson's claims. Winch discovered that the old plainsman was having serious financial problems and had pawned a valuable rifle. Winch retrieved the rifle and presented it to "the original Buffalo Bill" with Cody's compliments. When Cody got to Topeka, he met with Mathewson and acknowledged his claim to the title. He installed Mathewson as an honored guest in a box for the opening performance, and later, without letting Mathewson know about it, Winch arranged with a local newspaper to "buy" the plainsman's life story, with money supplied by Cody.

Although Cody went to some lengths to protect his name, which had become virtually a trademark by the 1890s, at one point suing a rival showman who was using the name "Buffalo Bill," his kindness toward Mathewson was clearly more a heartfelt gesture of respect and admiration for the old man than a publicity maneuver. In his lifetime, Cody was accused of many things—braggadocio, lying, self-aggrandizement, and more—but no one ever accused him of being anything less than generous.

What must be realized is that the title "Buffalo Bill" belonged to more than one man; Cody, as Mathewson himself ruefully acknowledged, was the only one to capitalize on it. "Considering that in the 'sixties the plains were black with fifteen million buffalo," wrote Richard J. Walsh and Milton Salsbury in *The Making of Buffalo Bill*, "and that thousands of men were killing them, it was not strange that many a nickname was based on the magic word. There was Buffalo Jones, there was Buffalo Chips, and there were other Buffalo Bills. But Cody seems to have won the title fairly."

In order to clinch the title of Buffalo Bill, Cody had to face and overcome one serious challenge. It came from William Comstock, who was not commonly known as Buffalo Bill but as Billy "Medicine Bill" Comstock. Comstock, a post guide and interpreter at Fort Wallace, was said to have been part Cheyenne. He was a special favorite of George Armstrong Custer, who used him as chief scout in his campaign of 1867.

The buffalo-hunting contest between Cody and Comstock was apparently initiated by the officers of Fort Hays, backing their favorite scout, Cody, and the officers of Fort Wallace, backing Comstock. Some writers doubt the contest ever took place; no one seems to know when, although there is circumstantial evidence of where, it happened. Don Russell places the location about two and one-half miles west of Monument, Kansas; Cody says it was twenty miles east of Sheridan. An advertisement for the event reproduced by Courtney Ryley Cooper in Louisa Cody's book reads: "Grand excursion to Fort Sheridan, Kansas Pacific Railroad. Buffalo shooting match for $500 a side and the championship of the world between Billy Comstock (the famous scout) and W.F. Cody (Buffalo Bill), famous buffalo killer for the Kansas Pacific Railroad."

There is no date given on this poster, which has led at least one historian, John Gray, to conclude that it is an "obvious forgery." Don Russell accepts Cody's account of the episode, and it is included in all the biographies of Buffalo Bill, but the only first-person accounts of the contest appear in Cody's autobiographies and in Louisa Cody's book. No newspaper account of it has ever been found, although surely some paper somewhere would have mentioned it. In addition, while there was a town named Sheridan, there was no *Fort* Sheridan.

The railroad reached Sheridan on May 8, 1868; the match would have had to take place after that date. According to Cody's first autobiography, the excursion party consisted of "about a hundred gentlemen and ladies, and among the number was my wife, with little baby Arta, who had come to remain with me for a while." This was the first occasion on which the Cody family was together since the fall of Rome, Will's Kansas real estate venture. The hunt was to last from eight o'clock in the morning until four in the afternoon. The two hunters were to go after the same herd at the same time, each "making a run," and killing as many buffalo as possible. An official referee, or scorekeeper, was to follow each hunter. Cody rode Brigham, his favorite mount, and carried Lucretia Borgia, and Comstock was armed with a Henry rifle that, while it could fire shots faster than Cody's .50-caliber needle gun, was not as powerful.

"Comstock and I dashed into a herd," said Cody, "followed by the referees. The buffalo separated; Comstock took the left bunch and I the right. My great *forte* in killing buffaloes from horseback was to get them circling by riding my horse at the head of the herd, shooting the leaders, thus crowding their followers to the left, till they would finally circle round and round. On this morning the buffaloes were very accommodating, and I soon had them running in a beautiful circle, when I dropped them thick and fast, until I had killed thirty-eight; which finished my run. Comstock began shooting at the rear of the herd, which he was chasing, and they kept straight on. He succeeded in killing twenty-three, but they were scattered over a distance of three miles, while mine lay close together. I had 'nursed' my buffaloes, as a billiard-player does the balls when he makes a big run."

After the first run was finished, the spectators from St. Louis set up a round of champagne "which proved a good drink on a Kansas prairie," said Cody, "and a buffalo hunter was a good man to get away with it." On the second run Cody killed eighteen, and Comstock, fourteen: the score was Cody fifty-six and Comstock thirty-nine. Then came lunch, and once again the champagne of the excursion party was tapped. After a ride of some three miles, another herd of buffalo was sighted, and the chase was on once more, for the final run. At this point, knowing he was far ahead in the contest, Cody decided to show off for the ladies; he would ride without a saddle or bridle. Cody proceeded to kill thirteen more, "the last one of which I had driven down close to the wagons, where the ladies were. It frightened some of the tender creatures to see the buffalo coming at full speed directly toward them; but when he had got within fifty yards of one of the wagons, I shot him dead in his tracks." The final score was Cody sixty-nine, Comstock forty-six. Comstock and his backers gave up the idea that they could beat Will, "and thereupon the referees declared me the winner of the match, as well as the champion buffalo-hunter of the plains."

Shortly after General "Fighting Phil" Sheridan took over command of the Missouri Department on March 2, 1868, William Comstock was sought out to scout for him. Along with Abner Sharp Grover and Richard Parr, Comstock was enlisted as a mediator under Lieutenant Fred H. Beecher; it was thought that their influence among the Cheyenne might help keep the peace. Beecher sent Comstock and Grover to the Cheyenne village of Chief Turkey Leg, with whom they had long been friendly, but while they were there, a runner came with news that four Indians had been killed and ten wounded in a fight on the Saline. Comstock and Grover were told to leave the camp. When they had gone about two miles, they were joined by seven young Cheyenne whom they thought to be friendly. As they were all riding along together, the Indians suddenly opened fire, killing Comstock instantly and severely wounding Grover. Comstock was scalped and his pearl-handled Colt revolver was taken from him. Grover played dead, hiding in the grass the night of August 16 and all the next day, then dragged himself to the railroad, where he was picked up by a passing train and taken to Fort Wallace.

The problems Sheridan faced were formidable, far greater perhaps than any he confronted during the Civil War. The size of the Indian forces was unknown—what was known was that thousands of nomadic warriors and their families wandered over the trackless plains and hills of Kansas and Nebraska. These Cheyenne, Kiowa, Wichita, Arapaho, and Comanche tribes were self-sustaining; they could live off the land, do as they pleased. They had nothing but contempt for the white man and his laws and way of life. They could live somehow in a largely arid country and protect themselves from sandstorms and blizzards. If necessary, they could live on jackrabbits, terrapins, packrats, and even snakes.

Sheridan's troops were poorly disciplined and badly paid. Sixteen dollars a month didn't go very far on the plains, even if it was only spent on whiskey, which is where most of a soldier's pay went. The troops found Indian fighting, like any other war, a life that alternated between utter boredom and sheer terror. Yet with these motley forces, Sheridan was instructed to keep the ranches from being raided, the settlements safe, and the roads clear so that the transcontinental railroads could be built without harassment.

At a meeting in October 1867 at Medicine Lodge, the Indian chiefs were told that they must become sedentary and conform to the white man's ways of living. A reservation of 3 million acres between the Red

River and the Washita was offered to the Comanche and Kiowa and another 4.3 million acres to the Cheyenne and Arapaho. They were to live on government rations of beef, flour, coffee, and sugar. In time they were to have homes, farms, agricultural tools, and instructors to teach them how to grow crops.

Satanta, the most powerful of the Kiowa chiefs and the most eloquent, rose and said, "The white chief seems not to be able to control his braves. He sometimes gets angry when he sees the wrongs his people commit on the red men, and his voice is as loud as the roaring wind; but like the wind, it soon dies away and leaves the sullen calm of unheeded oppression. The white man grows jealous of his red brother. He once came to trade; he now comes as a soldier. He once put his trust in our friendship . . . but now he covers his face with a cloud of jealousy and anger, and he tells us to be gone as the offended master speaks to his dog.

"You know what is best for us; do what is best. Teach us the road to travel and we shall not depart from it forever. For your sakes the green grass shall not be stained with the blood of whites; your people shall again be our people and peace shall be our mutual heritage."

Five thousand Indians were present at the final ceremonies—the peace commissioners in Prince Albert coats and silk top hats; the Indian chiefs in breechcloths, moccasins and leggings, their necks adorned with wampum, bracelets on their arms and war bonnets on their heads.

Despite the commissioners' promises, this peace was not destined to last long. The Indians had promised to go to their designated reservations but made no move toward them. Because of delays in ratifying the treaty in the Senate, the goods and annuities promised the Indians were not immediately forthcoming. Sheridan did all he could to meet the treaty obligations. "An abundant supply of rations is usually effective to keep matters quiet in such cases," he wrote in his *Memoirs*, "so I fed them pretty freely." The Indians had food in any case, for the buffalo still roamed the plains, despite the herds killed by Cody and other professional hunters. The Indians themselves were responsible for some of the slaughter inflicted on the buffalo. On occasion they would stampede a herd over a cliff, to pile up in heaps of meat.

A German visitor to the plains in 1853, Baron Mollhausen, described the typical Indian buffalo hunt: "The buffalo has many enemies, but the most dangerous is still the Indian who has all manner of wily tricks. Buffalo hunting for the Indian is a necessity; but it is also his favorite pastime. Life holds no higher pleasure than to mount one of the handy, patient little ponies . . . and gallop into a herd dealing death and destruction. Everything which might interfere with the movements of man or horse is flung away. Clothing and saddle are cast aside; all the rider retains is a big leather strap . . . which is fastened around the pony's neck and allowed to trail behind. This trailrope acts as a bridle, and as a life-line too, for recapturing the horse should its rider be dismounted. In his left hand the hunter carries his bow and as many arrows as he can hold; in his right a whip with which he belabors his beast without pity. Indian ponies are trained to gallop close alongside the buffalo, providing an easy shot; the instant the bow twangs the pony instinctively dodges to escape the buffalo's horns, and approaches another victim. Thus the hunt continues until his pony's exhaustion warns the hunter to desist."

Buffalo Bill often followed the Indian's hunting tactics closely, riding in near his target, bareback and with only a bridle to control his mount.

Originally the several species of bison ranged from the Great Slave Lake in Canada to the Chihuahua in Mexico; they were also found in northern Nevada and eastern Oregon. Sometimes in pre-Columbian days they wandered into the grasslands of Kentucky, Tennessee, and even as far east as Ohio. A few may even have migrated as far as the shores of Lake Erie in New York, or even into Pennsylvania.

As settlers invaded their grazing lands, their range shrank. White men did not hunt them much before 1850, and then at first not for sport but to provide meat for the railroad workers. The picture changed drastically in the 1850s. According to David A. Dary in *The Buffalo Book*, "Many sportsmen traveled to Kansas during the 1859's to shoot buffalo. Of all who came west in that decade, perhaps the most famous was Sir St. George Gore of Ireland. Gore outfitted his hunting expedition in St. Louis in the spring of 1854, then headed west. By the time his party returned to St. Louis nearly three years later, Gore had spent more than $500,000 and traveled at least 6,000 miles with forty servants, about fifty hunting dogs, numerous wagons and horses, and a number of companions, including scientists and mountain men." The Gore kill totaled 105 bears, 1,600 elk and deer, and more than 2,000 buffalo.

During the winter of 1855–1856, Gore and his party killed so many buffalo in eastern Montana that the Indians complained to their agent. "The federal government," wrote Dary, "ordered Gore to stop hunting buffalo in that area. This was the first and only time that the U.S. government moved to stop the wholesale slaughter of the buffalo while large numbers of the animals still roamed the plains and prairies. But it appears that the government was more concerned about Gore's safety among the Indians than it was about the killing of so many buffalo. Whether Gore himself shot many buffalo is doubtful. Accounts of his almost unbelievable slaughtering expedition indicate he was a bad shot and had to have help to bring down even one shaggy." At the time, buffalo were customarily called "shaggies."

In due course buffalo hunting became a popular pastime—and almost anyone could shoot one. To raise money for their church, one congregation in Lawrence, Kansas, organized a buffalo excursion: Three hundred people signed up for a two-day trip, blasting away wildly from the windows of their railroad chair cars.

It was not until the 1870s that the wholesale slaughter began, and it was to continue until the bison were almost extinct on this continent. In the early 1870s it was possible to travel through herd after herd and in one day see from half a million to 12 million bison. The Republican River herd in Kansas alone was estimated to contain more than 12 million buffalo. The total Great Plains herd may have contained more than 75 million head. By the end of that decade, however, buffalo were hard to find. What had once been an apparently inexhaustible meat supply, unrivaled by anything else known to man before or since, had vanished—and less than one-thousandth part of their meat was ever used.

The early inhabitants of the plains only had to add the available wild vegetables and fruits to the buffalo meat to have all they needed to support life. The tongue of the buffalo was considered a special delicacy. Moreover, when proper use of the buffalo was made, it provided most of the other necessities of Indian life. The skins provided shelter and clothing; weapons, utensils, and even toys for the children could be fashioned from the bones. The buffalo even provided a supply of fuel for the treeless prairie—dried buffalo droppings, called chips, or *bois de vache,* as General Fremont delicately described them, were burned in campfires.

Extermination of the buffalo meant the certain decline of the Indians. As the railroad reached deeper into buffalo country, hunters reduced the herds, shipping the hides to the East, where they found an eager market, to be made into coats and robes. In this way, the herds would be swiftly decimated, and the Indians would have to go on reservations or starve. When official Washington realized this, the slaughter was bound to continue until the herds were gone. A few people questioned the morality of civilizing the Indians by starving them to death, but their protests were in vain. General Sherman, who served on the Medicine Lodge peace commission, did not want to make peace with the Oglala Sioux and the Cheyenne; he wanted to punish them for humiliating the army. As he told his brother, the commission would have to "concede [to the Indians] a right to hunt buffaloes as long as they last, and this may lead to collisions, but it will not be long before all the buffaloes are extinct. . . . "

The white hunters, killing a thousand and more buffalo a week for each gun they carried, were the Plains Indians' real enemies, not the army. In slightly more than ten years, a continental herd of 50 million buffalo was reduced to a few thousand stragglers. The hunters' only weak point was the railroad line; without the iron horse, the hides could not reach the market. If the Indians had concentrated on disrupting the railroad, they might have stopped the slaughter. As it was, except for one occasion on which the Cheyenne derailed a Union Pacific train, apparently finding the experience a great treat, the Indians left the line largely alone, so the hunters were able to reach the range and then ship their hides east, thereby ensuring the extinction of both buffalo and Indian. Seldom did the slaughtering contain any element of sportsmanship. With the blessing of the government and the army, it became a war against a whole race, a deliberate policy of genocide, mandated by President Ulysses S. Grant and carried out with systematic, cold-blooded determination by Generals Sherman and Sheridan.

In the face of this policy, Will Cody's buffalo count, whether it was 4,280 or only 2,850, is negligible.

Could historians have been wrong all these years about the decline of the buffalo? Was the slaughter by white hunters and sportsmen, encouraged by government officials and army officers, possibly *not* the primary factor in bringing the American bison to near extinction? According to a report in the New York *Times* of November 16, 1999, recent research suggests that even without the white hunters, the buffalo would have become extinct. Among the factors involved in the decline of the species: changes in climate, competition for forage, and cattle-borne disease. "Another major factor," writes the *Times*'s Jim Robbins, "were Indian tribes, empowered by the horse and gun and driven to hunt buffaloes for the profits that came from the hides and meat." Apparently Indians began to hunt buffalo for entrée into the market economy as early as the 1840s.

Several contemporary Western history scholars share this view that even without the white hide hunters, the buffalo probably would have disappeared within thirty years. Nevertheless, this fact does not mean that the hide hunters are "off the hook" regarding culpability in the Indians' problems, according to Dan Flores, professor of western history at the University of Montana.

Vine Deloria Jr. of the University of Colorado and a member of the Standing Rock Sioux finds these new theories "nonsense. The Indians did not make any appreciable dent in buffalo numbers in the Northern Plains. It's anti-Indian stuff."

When the Kansas Pacific Railroad reached Sheridan in May 1868, there was no further need for Cody's services as a buffalo hunter, and he no longer needed his horse Brigham. As an army scout, he would now ride U.S. Government horses and mules. He raffled off the horse by selling chances at $30 each. Ike Bonham of Wyandotte, Kansas, held the lucky number. After Brigham won a long-distance race against five Thorough-bred horses, Bonham sold the animal to Superintendent of Construction Wilcox of the Kansas Pacific. In 1876 Cody met Wilcox in Memphis, Tennessee, and was invited to see Brigham once again. "It seemed as if he almost remembered me," Cody recalled.

In May of 1868 Louisa and Arta returned to Leavenworth, and Cody was hired by the quartermaster at Fort Larned, Kansas, then commanded by Captain Daingerfield Parker of the Third Infantry.

At Fort Larned, Cody served as a guide and courier for Brevet Major General William B. Hazen, superintendent of Indian affairs for the Southern Plains, who was charged with carrying out the provisions of the Medicine Lodge Treaty. "The post at that time," Cody wrote, "was garrisoned by only two companies of infantry and one of cavalry." Each company in the army consisted of a headquarters and two platoons; the platoon usually numbered fifteen men, led by a lieutenant. The garrison at Fort Larned was clearly not a strong force.

Trouble broke out in July of 1868, when Cheyenne robbed the houses of several white settlers near Council Grove. After this raid, the post commander at Fort Larned refused to issue weapons and ammunition to the Kiowa and Comanche, as the treaty had promised them. The Indians scorned the food and other supplies they were offered in place of arms. When Brevet Brigadier General Alfred Sully came from Fort Dodge, Kansas, to investigate, Chief Satanta of the Kiowa, pleading that the Indians needed guns to hunt buffalo, convinced Sully that only a few bad young warriors of the tribe had misbehaved and that the rest were peaceful. Sully then issued the promised arms. On August 10, while the Comanche and Kiowa were still encamped near Fort Larned, two hundred Cheyenne, four Arapaho, and twenty Sioux went on the warpath and committed a series of rapes and murders. Altogether, thirteen men and two women were murdered before troops arrived to rescue the survivors. That same month Billy Comstock was slain by Cheyenne who wanted his pearl-handled revolver.

Although Will Cody may have done little or no scouting between May and August, with the Indian uprisings there was soon to be plenty of work for him.

SCOUTING WITH SHERIDAN

By August both Will Cody and Wild Bill Hickok were employed as scouts, this time for Brevet Major General (regular rank Major) George Armes of the Tenth Cavalry at Fort Hays. Major Armes recorded in his journal for August 21 that his rival, Major M. H. Kidd, had "failed to pay attention to the advice of Wild Bill our scout and guide, in regard to the course we should take when we left camp yesterday, he appearing to know more about the country than those who have lived here for years." Major Kidd found himself ten miles off course with no sign of Indians. Kidd was later relieved of his command and discharged from the army at his own request in 1870.

On August 24 Major Armes wrote in his diary: "We marched out at sunrise, met Lieutenant Colonel Frederick W. Benteen, Seventh Cavalry, en route to [Fort] Harker. He was relieved in the field by Colonel L. H. Carpenter, who marched twenty-five or thirty miles and has discovered quite a number of Indian signs.

"Bill Cody (Buffalo Bill)," Armes continued, "one of our scouts and one of the best shots on the plains, keeps us well supplied with plenty of buffalo and deer. He gets $60 per month and a splendid mule to ride, and is one of the most contented and happy men I ever met."

Eight years later Colonel Benteen became a prominent player in the Battle of the Little Big Horn.

On the day Major Armes recorded his appreciation of Buffalo Bill's prowess as a hunter, General Sheridan augmented his forces by directing his assistant inspector-general, Brevet Colonel George A. Forsyth, to enroll "fifty first-class hardy frontiersmen to be used as scouts against the hostile Indians," with Lieutenant Fred H. Beecher as second-in-command. Within five days this company was organized at Fort Hays and Fort Harker and took the field, scouting across the headwaters of the Solomon River and along Beaver Creek.

Cody, at left, with his favorite buffalo-hunting rifle, Lucretia Borgia, and three unidentified men, c. 1867–1870. (Buffalo Bill Historical Center, Cody, Wyoming)

At Fort Wallace, Colonel Forsyth learned of an attack on a wagon train by a small band of Indians. While following the raiders' trail, Forsyth's company ran into Chief Roman Nose with 970 warriors. A fight ensued at an island on the Arickaree Fork of the Republican River—later named Beecher's Island, after Lieutenant Beecher, who was killed in the fighting. In the battle, mounted Indians charged the small force of soldiers and were driven off by volleys of carbine fire. The Indians rallied and attacked again, and were again driven off; Roman Nose fell in the second charge. The scouts were under siege from September 25 to September 27, when they were rescued by a Tenth Cavalry detachment led by Colonel L. H. Carpenter. Cody never claimed to have been in the Beecher's Island fight, though some books placed him there without any corroborating evidence.

On September 2 Major Armes left Fort Hays on an expedition to Walnut Creek, this time with Wild Bill Hickok as his guide. Army records show that from September 9 to 14, 1868, William F. Cody was hired as a laborer, at a salary of $30 a month, paid by Second Lieutenant L. W. Cooke, acting assistant quartermaster at Fort Larned. The fact that this job lasted only a matter of five days is evidence that he probably was employed in this menial capacity to keep him occupied at the fort until his services as a scout were needed again—as they soon were. The records indicate that on September 15 Lieutenant Cooke discharged W. F. Cody as a laborer sacking forage at $30 a month and put him on the payroll as a scout at a salary of $75 a month—the top pay authorized for a scout at that time.

In his first autobiography, Cody tells of being asked by General Hazen to guide him and a small party from Fort Larned to Fort Zarah. At Zarah, the general decided to proceed on to Fort Harker without an escort and ordered Cody and the infantrymen in the party to return to Larned the next day.

"After the General had gone," wrote Cody, "I went to the sergeant in command of the squad and told him I was going back that very afternoon, instead of waiting till the next morning; and I accordingly saddled up my mule and set out for Fort Larned. I proceeded uninterruptedly until I got halfway between the two posts, when at Pawnee Rock I was suddenly 'jumped' by about forty Indians . . . some of the same Indians who had been hanging around Fort Larned in the morning. I saw that they had on their war-paint, and were evidently now out on the warpath."

Cody was captured by the Indians, who took his weapons and struck him on the head with a tomahawk, stunning him. He was taken before Chief Satanta, who asked him where he had been. Cody, in a sudden inspiration, told the chief that he had been out looking for cattle, or "whoa-haws" as the Indians called them—the cattle promised to the Kiowa. Satanta bought the story and directed Cody to bring the cattle to him. This ruse enabled Will to put the river between him and Indians, and he set out for Larned, riding as fast as his mule would take him. When the Indians realized they had been duped, they took up the chase. About six miles from the fort, Cody met a small party of soldiers led by a scout named Denver Jim. They set a trap for the pursuing Indians, ambushed them, and killed two of the braves. After scalping the Indians and taking their arms and their horses, the men proceeded to the fort.

Shortly after this incident, Cody was ordered to ride from Larned to Fort Hays, a distance of sixty-five miles, to advise General Sheridan that the Kiowa and Comanche were on the warpath. In his memoir, Sheridan wrote: "This intelligence required that certain orders should be carried to Fort Dodge, ninety-five miles south of Hays. This too being a particularly dangerous route—several couriers having been killed on it—it was impossible to get one of the various 'Petes,' 'Jacks,' or 'Jims' hanging around Hays City to take my communication. Cody learning of the straits I was in, manfully came to the rescue, and proposed to make the trip to Dodge, though he had just finished his long and perilous ride from Larned. I gratefully accepted his offer, and after four or five hours' rest, he mounted a fresh horse and hastened on his journey, halting but once to rest on the way, and then only for an hour, the stop being made at Coon Creek, where he got another mount from a troop of cavalry. At Dodge he took six hours' sleep, and then continued on to his own post— Fort Larned—with more despatches. After resting twelve hours at Larned, he was again in the saddle with tidings for me at Fort Hays, General Hazen sending him this time, with word that all the villages had fled to the south of the Arkansas. Thus, in all, Cody rode about 350 miles in less than sixty hours, and such an exhibition of endurance and courage was more than enough to convince me that his services would be extremely valuable in the campaign, so I retained him at Fort Hays till the battalion of the Fifth Cavalry arrived, and then made him chief of scouts for that regiment." It was the beginning of what would be a lifelong friendship, based on the two men's respect for each other's abilities, not their stations in life.

Cody's first memoir gives the distance he rode as 355 miles. In his book, Don Russell calculates the distance Cody actually rode as 290 miles and the elapsed time as fifty-eight hours. Still, an average ride of 116 miles a day is no small achievement, even for an accomplished horseman. It is not surprising that Cody, whose ride of 322 miles in twenty-one hours and forty minutes, using twenty-one horses, was the third longest ride in Pony Express history, was able to achieve this feat. Nor was Sheridan's designation of Cody as chief of scouts for the Fifth Cavalry the only recognition he would receive for his ability as a scout.

In 1868 Major General Philip Henry Sheridan was one of the most admired and respected officers in the American army. The quartermaster turned cavalry officer, Sheridan was the hero of Missionary Ridge in the Civil War's Battle of Chattanooga, and the man who became the scourge of the Shenandoah Valley, as Sherman was of Georgia.

Sheridan, the son of an Irish tenant farmer, was trained at West Point—from which he had been suspended for a year for trying to stab

another cadet with his bayonet. He was considered an unprepossessing little man, five foot five inches tall, with a large, bullet-shaped head and
coarse black hair. Abraham Lincoln described him as "a brown, chunky
little chap, with a long body, short legs, not enough neck to hang him,
and such long arms that if his ankles itch he can scratch them without
stooping." He was often patronized by people who let his physical appearance deceive them as to his courage and competence under fire. Grant,
however, knew differently, saying: "You will find him big enough for the
purpose before we get through with him." His subordinates called him
"Little Phil" affectionately, but not within his hearing. He was hardworking, demanding, profane, patriotic, and brave. He was also hot-tempered
and ruthless. "The proper strategy," he once said, "consists in the first
place in inflicting as telling blows as possible upon the enemy's army, and
then causing the inhabitants so much suffering that they must long for
peace, and force their government to demand it. The people must be left
nothing but their eyes to weep with over the war."

He did not say, as the widely believed version has it, that "the only
good Indian is a dead Indian." What he did say, whether jokingly or in
earnest, was "the only good Indians I saw were dead." It's not quite the
same thing as the accepted citation, though it is slightly alarming in view
of his later conduct toward the Indians. In the first version of the quote,
Sheridan could have meant that only dead Indians were "good"; therefore,
they ought to be killed. In the second version, he meant that only dead
Indians are good, in the sense of "good behavior."

Whatever Sheridan's true feelings were, however, he merely carried
out U.S. policy, as defined by his superior, General in Chief of the Army
William Tecumseh Sherman. Sheridan himself was to achieve that same
post in 1883. By the year that he died, 1888, no Indian tribe dared to
challenge the U.S. Army; the white man's conquest of the West was complete, in large measure because of Sheridan's generalship, especially his
"scorched earth" policy when it came to the slaughter of the buffalo.

Shortly after Cody's long ride for Sheridan, the Fifth Cavalry arrived
at Fort Hays, reinforcing the troops Sheridan already had in place for his
planned winter campaign against the Indians: 2,600 men—the Seventh
and Tenth regiments of cavalry, the Third and Fifth regiments of infantry,
and four companies of the Thirty-eighth regiment of infantry.

The Fifth Cavalry had been organized in 1855 as the Second Cavalry—
before that, mounted regiments in the army were known as dragoons and
mounted riflemen—and served against the Indians in 1860. With the outbreak of the Civil War, the newly christened Fifth lost some of its most
distinguished officers to the Confederacy—among them Robert E. Lee,
Albert Sidney Johnston, and John B. Hood.

When the Fifth, with Cody as their scout, left Fort Hays on October 5, 1868, they were led by Major (Brevet Colonel) William B. Royall. The battalion proceeded along the Kansas Pacific Railway toward Prairie Dog Creek, where signs of an Indian camp had been seen. In Cody's first autobiography, he wrote that Sheridan was anxious to punish the Indians for their attack on General Forsyth's troops at Beecher Island. Cody quickly struck up warm personal relations with several of the officers and scouts of the Fifth. "I was very favorably struck with the appearance of the regiment," he wrote. "It was a beautiful command, and when strung out along the prairie with a train of seventy-five six-mule wagons, ambulances and pack mules, I felt very proud of my position of guide and chief of scouts of such a warlike expedition."

The ambulances Cody mentioned were, on the frontier, light, canvas-topped army wagons for carrying personnel, wounded or healthy, and could have meant almost any government wagon for transporting people. Also called "prairie wagons," they were not primarily considered medical transport, as we know it today. Officers frequently rode in ambulances rather than on horseback.

After they had marched for a couple of days, Major Royall asked Cody to go out and shoot some buffalo to provide food for the command.

"All right, Colonel," Cody said, addressing Royall by his brevet rank, as was considered proper, "send along a wagon or two to bring in the meat."

"I am not in the habit of sending out my wagons until I know there is something to be hauled in; kill your buffalo first and then I'll send out the wagons" was the colonel's reply.

"I said no more," wrote Cody, "but went out on a hunt, and after a short absence returned and asked the Colonel to send his wagons over the hill for the half-dozen buffaloes I had killed."

The next afternoon Royall asked Cody again to go out and get fresh buffalo meat. Cody did not request wagons this time, but rode out some distance, until he came upon a herd. This is how Cody tells the story: "I managed to get seven of them headed for the encampment, and instead of shooting them just then, I ran them at full speed right into the camp, and then killed them all, one after the other, in rapid succession." Royall asked Cody for an explanation.

"I didn't care about asking for any wagons this time, Colonel; so I thought I would make the buffaloes furnish their own transportation" was his reply.

There is no evidence other than Cody's own account for this story, so it may well have been one of his tall tales, but the deed as he described it was not beyond his demonstrated abilities as a hunter, and the bravado implicit in his reply to the colonel is typical Buffalo Bill.

Three days' march brought the Fifth to Beaver Creek, where they made camp. Royall sent two detachments out in search of Indians; they returned without having made contact, to find that the camp had been attacked in their absence by Tall Bull and his band of Cheyenne, who killed one trooper, wounded another, and drove off six horses belonging to Company H.

The expedition Cody was a part of was after the Dog Soldier Indians, a band of Cheyenne and unruly members of other tribes who would not enter into a treaty or keep a treaty if they made one, and who had always refused to live on a reservation. They were strong, warlike, daring, and restless braves, who were determined to hang on to the country in the vicinity of the Republican and Solomon rivers. They were called Dog Soldiers because they were principally Cheyenne, a name that suggests *chien*, the French word for dog.

Not long after the Indian raid on Beaver Creek camp, the command set out in pursuit of the raiders. Two companies, led by Major Brown with three days' rations, set out in advance of the main force. Cody was not with Brown but remained with the command. On the eighteenth day out, and running out of rations, the battalion marched toward the nearest railroad station and camped on the Saline River, three miles from Buffalo Tank.

While the command was waiting for rations, Brevet Major General Eugene A. Carr, senior major of the Fifth Cavalry, who outranked Royall, arrived to take command. Carr was a distinguished officer, of whom it was said that he would rather be colonel of a cavalry regiment than president of the United States. He was well versed in Indian warfare; from the time he graduated from West Point in 1850 until the Civil War, he made almost annual expeditions against the tribes. He was severely wounded in a fight against the Mescalero Apache in Texas; served in 1857 in Kansas during the troubles there; was a captain in the Mormon War of 1858. His Civil War service was outstanding. As a colonel commanding the Third Illinois Volunteer Cavalry, in the Battle of Pea Ridge he was awarded the Medal of Honor for "directing the deployment of his command and holding his ground under brisk fire of shot and shell in which he was several times wounded." Carr was the officer under whom Cody would serve during most of his time with the Fifth Cavalry.

When the regiment was joined by its new commander, it was Buffalo Bill Cody who met Carr at the train station.

Carr recalled:

While I was unloading my horses and baggage, I saw a man in buckskin with a broad hat sitting on a horse on some rising ground not far from the station. Thinks I "There is one of those confounded scouts posing." Some of them mostly fakes are apt to hang around railroad stations & tell big stories to tenderfeet. Pretty soon he rode down to me & said Col. Royall's command was camped on the Saline about 3 miles off, & if I wished he would ride down & tell him and he would send an ambulance for me. I said "you may if you want to."

Carr was soon to correct his first impression of Cody as "one of those confounded scouts." That first meeting led to a long association and another of Cody's lifelong friendships. Carr remembered Cody as "a wonderful shot" who "killed antelope running" and who had "eyes as good as a fine field glass, and was the best white trailer I ever saw. One of his qualities was a trained knowledge of the country . . . and he could pick the best route for a wagon train. He rode down a good many horses; but it paid to furnish them as it saved the rest."

With Carr when he arrived at Buffalo Tank were the celebrated Forsyth's scouts, now commanded by Lieutenant Silas Pepoon of the Tenth Cavalry. The morning after Carr's arrival, the entire command started out toward the Republican River on a hunt for Indians. Carr directed Cody to guide him to Elephant Rock on Beaver Creek. On the second day of the march, the men came upon a large Indian trail, still fresh, and following this trail for eight miles, they saw a large body of Indians on the bluffs ahead of them.

Carr ordered the Forsyth's scouts, under Lieutenant Pepoon, and Company M, led by Lieutenant Jules C. A. Schenofsky, to move forward as advance guard. On October 25 Pepoon and Schenofsky's troops struck a party of Sioux and Cheyenne estimated at four or five hundred. Cody describes Schenofsky as "a Frenchman by birth and a dare-devil by nature, who was anxious to have a hair-lifting match." A running fight ensued, in which the entire command took part, continuing until dark. One cavalryman was wounded and thirty Indians were reported killed in the day's fighting.

That evening Indians fired on the camp, while Cody and three officers were having dinner, and he reports that a bullet struck and broke Lieutenant Alfred B. Bache's plate.

The following morning the pursuit of the Indians was resumed along Prairie Dog Creek, with skirmishes throughout the day. That night, however, the Indians took off, and were rarely seen the following day. By the end of October, only the scattered trails left by migrating villages were in evidence.

One of the command's marches pursuing the Indians was toward the headwaters of the Beaver, and General Carr asked Cody how far it was to the river; Cody told him it was twenty-five miles. After they had gone a considerable distance, Carr rode out and asked Cody how far they were from water. "Seven or eight miles," said Cody. Carr told him that Pepoon's scouts thought he was heading in the wrong direction to find water and that they would find that the Beaver had gone dry. "General, I think the scouts are mistaken," said Cody, "for the Beaver has more water near its head than below; and at the place where we will strike the stream, we will find immense beaver dams." Carr told Cody to proceed but warned him that he did not want "a dry camp."

Cody's reckoning proved correct. He found an ideal campsite along a tributary of the Beaver, with plenty of fresh water and good grass. Learning that the stream had no name, Carr located it on his map and christened it Cody Creek.

The following morning there was a skirmish when the command pulled out to reach the Beaver. "When we were approaching the stream," said Cody, "I rode out ahead of the advance guard, in order to find a crossing. Just as I turned a bend of the creek, 'bang!' went a shot, and down went my horse—myself with him. I disentangled myself, and jumped behind the dead body. Looking in the direction whence the shot had come, I saw two Indians, and at once turned my gun loose on them, but in the excitement of the moment I missed my aim. They fired two or three more shots, and I returned the compliment, wounding one of their horses."

A rare occurrence: It was not often that Cody missed a shot, or admitted that he had.

He saw a few lodges moving away, as mounted warriors kept shooting at him. "I sent a few shots after them to accelerate their speed, and also fired at the one on the other side of the stream." Apparently he did not hit anyone.

"When General Carr came up, he ordered Company I to go in pursuit of the band. I accompanied Lieutenant Brady, who commanded, and we had a running fight with the Indians, lasting several hours. We captured several head of their horses, and most of their lodges." At nightfall, the company returned to the command, which by this time had crossed the creek on a beaver dam.

At the end of October, the command returned to Fort Wallace, Kansas, for three weeks. As usual, Cody hunted buffalo, and on one of these hunts he and a small party "were 'jumped' by about fifty Indians. We had a severe fight of at least an hour, when we succeeded in driving the enemy. They lost four of their warriors. . . . We finished our hunt and went back to the post loaded down with plenty of buffalo meat, and received the compliments of the General for our little fight."

Meanwhile, General Sheridan was so dissatisfied with the performance of the Seventh Cavalry under Major Joel H. Elliott that he petitioned the secretary of war to rescind Custer's suspension from duty; the sentence of his court-martial still had several months to run. Carr's battalion marched to Fort Lyon, Colorado Territory, where it was ordered to prepare for a winter campaign.

When he was sent to the Department of the Missouri by Sherman, Sheridan concluded that the best way to deal with the Cheyenne was to attack them in the winter, when they were most vulnerable. "In taking the offensive," Sheridan advised Sherman, "I have to select that season when I can catch the fiends; and if a village is attacked and women and children killed, the responsibility is not with the soldiers, but with the people whose crimes necessitated the attack." Thus did Sheridan transform victims into aggressors.

Sherman wholeheartedly approved of this approach. "Go ahead in your own way," he told Sheridan, "and I will back you with my whole authority. . . . I will say nothing and do nothing to restrain our troops from doing what they deem proper on the spot, and will allow no mere vague general charges of cruelty and inhumanity to tie their hands, but will use all the powers confided to me to the end that these Indians, the enemies of our race and our civilization, shall not again be able to begin and carry out their barbarous warfare on any kind of pretext they may choose to allege."

Sheridan's strategy in his 1868 winter campaign was to launch a three-pronged attack of converging columns from three principal forts, designed to keep the Indians from breaking out of their normal range. The main column, as Sheridan himself explained it, "was to push down into the western part of the Indian Territory [present-day Oklahoma], having for its initial objective the villages which, at the beginning of hostilities, had fled toward the head-waters of the Red River, and those that had gone to the same remote region after decamping from the neighborhood of Larned at the time General Hazen sent Buffalo Bill to me with the news." This column included the Seventh Cavalry under Custer, who had been reassigned to active duty. Sheridan expected Custer to do the bulk of the fighting. "I rely in everything upon you," Sheridan had told the younger man, "and shall send you on this expedition without giving you any orders, leaving you to act entirely on your own judgment." This main column, which Sheridan accompanied, would set up a base camp at Fort Supply, Indian Territory.

Before the column reached Fort Supply, however, the trail of a returning war party was seen, and Custer was ordered to follow it. The result was the Battle of the Washita, the only substantial fight of the campaign. It was a fight in which both Custer and Major Joel H. Elliott hoped to redeem themselves—Custer from his court-martial and Elliott from Sheridan's distrust of his leadership in an earlier Seventh Cavalry expedition, when the major was faulted for excessive caution.

Custer drove his men relentlessly through the snow. An old Osage scout asked him what he would do if they were to find "more Indians than we can handle."

"All I'm afraid of is that we won't find half enough," Custer replied. "There are not Indians enough in the country to whip the Seventh Cavalry."

Then his scouts reported that they had found a Cheyenne village of some fifty lodges. The village was Black Kettle's, located along the Washita River, well within the Cheyenne reservation. Black Kettle wanted peace, and to protect his people he flew a white flag of truce above his tepee. Custer ordered his men to prepare an attack. At dawn on November 27, 1868, just two days short of the fourth anniversary of the Sand Creek Massacre, Custer's six hundred mounted men charged the village, firing as they went. Shortly before the attack, the morning star emerged from a ground fog, rising with such brilliance that at first the men mistook it for a rocket—though why they thought the Indians might employ rockets is a mystery. The morning star was to figure prominently in the rest of Custer's life. After his furious assault on Black Kettle's village, the Indians called him *Ouchess*, Creeping Panther. Five years later, in Dakota Territory, the Arikara christened him "Son of the Morning Star." This was the name he liked to be called. His men, on the other hand, referred to him as "Hard Ass," "Iron Butt," or "Ringlets."

Custer's report read:

> The Indians left on the ground 103 warriors, including Black Kettle, whose scalp was taken by an Osage guide. 875 horses and mules were captured, 241 saddles . . . 573 buffalo robes, 390 buffalo skins, 160 untanned robes . . . [All] the winter supply of dried buffalo meat, all the meal, flour and other provisions; in fact, all they possessed was captured, as the warriors escaped with little or no clothing. Everything of value [to them] was destroyed.

Cheyenne survivors said that only eleven warriors were killed. The rest of the dead were women, children, and old men.

Sheridan sent the following message to Custer:

The battle of the Washita River is the most complete & successful of all our private battles, and was fought in such unfavorable weather & circumstances as to reflect the highest credit on Yourself & Regt.

There was no irony in this message, although in truth Custer had attacked a village on a reservation flying a white flag and had killed primarily women, children, and old men.

On December 3, when Custer returned to the base camp on the Canadian River to join Sheridan, his band played "Garry Owen," Custer's favorite song. He had arranged the order of march in the most dramatic fashion possible, like a conquering Roman general returning to Rome. He himself was dressed in buckskin and riding a dancing black stallion. His officers and enlisted men were followed by a line of fifty-three captive Indian widows and orphans bundled up in blankets and robes; they thought they were going to be shot.

Major Elliott was not so fortunate as Custer. He charged into a group of Indians saying "here goes for a brevet or a coffin." He was killed—along with nineteen of his men.

"If we can get in one or two more [such] blows," said Sheridan, "there will be no more Indian troubles in my department." The secretary of war, J. M. Schofield, sent a wire to General Sherman: "I congratulate you, Sheridan, and Custer on the splendid success with which your campaign is begun. Ask Sheridan to send forward the names of officers and men deserving of special mention."

Custer's victory was not totally untarnished. He was accused of abandoning Elliott and his men by escaping from Black Kettle's village under cover of darkness while his troops were under attack by Indians who were camped nearby.

The second column of Sheridan's forces in the winter campaign came from Fort Bascom, New Mexico, under the command of Captain A. W. Evans, consisting of six troops of the Third Cavalry and two companies of infantry from New Mexico. The third column departed from Fort Lyon, Colorado, led by General Carr with Cody as chief of scouts. Their mission was to join five troops of cavalry already in the field under Brevet Brigadier General William H. Penrose, captain of the Third Infantry. The combined forces would then move toward the Antelope Hills and the headwaters of the Red River.

Penrose's command consisted of some 250 men and 18 scouts and guides, one of whom was Cody's friend Wild Bill Hickok. Penrose had only a small pack train and was expected to run short of supplies. By December the command had gotten lost and snowed in on Paloduro Creek, on what is now the southeast corner of Texas County, in the Oklahoma Panhandle.

Carr's troops left Fort Lyon three weeks behind Penrose. The Fifth Cavalry usually traveled with a full wagon train, which never seemed to slow its advance down; it made some astonishing marches in pursuit of Indians. According to Cody, there were seventy-five six-mule wagons, in addition to ambulances and pack mules. They followed Penrose's trail for three days, when they were caught in Freeze-out Canyon by a heavy snowstorm and forced to go into camp for a day. The ground was covered with deep snow, making it impossible to follow Penrose's trail any farther. General Carr ordered Cody to take four scouts and push on ahead to see if he could find any sign of Penrose.

After riding twenty-four miles through a snowstorm, Cody found traces of one of Penrose's camps. He rode back alone to inform Carr, who was pleased with the news, because he was concerned for the safety of General Penrose. The next morning the command headed out, through snow so heavy that a way had to be shoveled through snowdrifts for the wagons. Penrose's trail led along the west side of the Cimarron River, but that route appeared too rough for the wagons, so Carr elected to follow along the opposite bank. A day's march brought them to a high tableland in the Raton foothills, overlooking a creek valley. The bluff was not too steep for mounted men to descend, but Carr didn't believe the wagons could make it. Cody assured him that the wagons would be there when he and his men arrived. When the train came up, Cody ordered one of the drivers to "run down, slide down or fall down—any way to get down." The driver feared the wagons would overrun the mules, but Cody, having had long experience with wagons during his work with the drivers of Russell, Majors and Waddell, knew better.

"Telling Wilson, the chief wagon-master, to bring on his mess wagon, which was at the head of the train, I said I would try the experiment at least. Wilson drove the team and wagon to the brink of the hill, and following my directions he brought out some extra chains with which we locked both wheels on each side and then rough-locked them. We then started the wagon down the hill. The wheel-horses—or rather the wheel-mules—were good on the hold-back, and we got along finely until we nearly reached the bottom, when the wagons crowded the mules so hard that they started on a run and galloped down into the valley and to the place where General Carr had located his camp. There was not the slightest accident. Three other wagons followed the same way. In half an hour, every wagon was in camp. It was an exciting sight to see the six-mule teams come almost straight down the mountainside and finally break into a run. At times it seemed certain that the wagon must turn a somersault and land on the mules, but nothing of the kind happened."

The wagon train's daring descent of the hill gained seven days on Penrose, who had been halted by a cliff that even pack mules could not descend. He had been forced to turn back, losing three days each way. Carr's force continued to follow Penrose's trail, which was now well marked. Along San Francisco Creek, Cody ran into two soldiers from the Tenth Cavalry, who greeted their old scout Buffalo Bill. The two deserters reported that Penrose's command was out of rations and nearly starving. Carr ordered Major Brown with two troops of cavalry and fifty pack mules loaded with provisions to push on ahead, with Cody as guide. Three days later Penrose's command was found on Paloduro Creek. Penrose's men had been on one-quarter rations for two weeks, and two hundred horses and mules had died of fatigue and starvation. The rations Major Brown had brought came none too soon.

Because he outranked Penrose, General Carr was now in command of the combined forces. He proceeded to unload his wagons and set up camp on December 30. The wagons were then sent back for more supplies. A force of five hundred of his best men and horses was assembled, including Cody and Wild Bill, to be sent with the pack train on a forty-mile march due south into the Texas Panhandle, toward the Canadian River. They camped at the south fork of the river, where scouts from Evans's column joined them. The scouts told Cody that a bull train well supplied with beer was expected at any time. Cody and Wild Bill decided to hijack the shipment. The Mexicans who had brought the beer from Fort Union were happy to sell it twelve miles short of their final destination.

"It was sold to our boys in pint cups," said Cody, "and as the weather was very cold we warmed the beer by putting the ends of our picket-pins heated red-hot into the cups. The result was one of the biggest beer jollifications I ever had the misfortune to attend." The picket pins Cody mentioned were small iron rods with sharpened points and a ring on top; they were driven into the ground and a horse would be tied to the ring so that it could graze but not run away.

General Carr recorded that "during the winter of 1868, we encountered hardships and exposure in terrific snow storms, sleet, etc., etc. On one occasion that winter, Mr. Cody showed his quality by quietly offering to go with some dispatches to General Sheridan, across a dangerous region, where another principal scout was reluctant to risk himself." According to Cody, the general declined his offer, saying that he wished Cody to remain with the command, as he could not spare him. Wild Bill, a half-breed called Little Geary, and three other scouts carried the dispatches.

After scouting along the Canadian River without sighting hostiles, Carr returned to his supply camp. Meanwhile, Cody and Hickok were set for a spell of riot.

"Among the scouts of Penrose's command," said Cody, "were fifteen Mexicans, and between them and the American scouts there had existed a feud, when General Carr took command of the expedition—uniting it with his own—and I was made chief of all scouts, this feud grew more intense, and the Mexicans often threatened to clean us out; but they postponed the undertaking from time to time, until one day, when we were all at the sutler's store, the long-expected fight took place, and resulted in the Mexicans getting severely beaten.

"General Carr, having heard of the row, sent for Wild Bill and myself, he having concluded, from the various statements which had been made to him, that we were the instigators of the affair. But after listening to what we had to say, he thought that the Mexicans were as much to blame as we were.

"It is not to be denied that Wild Bill and myself had been partaking too freely of 'tanglefoot' that evening; and General Carr said to me: 'Cody, there are plenty of antelopes in the country, and you can do some hunting for the camp while we stay here.'" Although Cody implied that he may have been sent out hunting as a disciplinary measure, in fact, the command badly needed fresh meat. According to Sergeant Luke Cahill, who commanded the hunting party, scurvy had broken out among the men, and many were sick. Twenty wagons with drivers, a wagon master, and twenty infantrymen were assigned to accompany Cody. After a march of four days, a buffalo herd was sighted. Cody stampeded the herd into a deep, snow-filled arroyo, and fifty-five were killed. The next day Cody killed forty-one buffalo, exhausting two horses. The recoil of his Springfield rifle left his shoulder so bruised and sore that he could not put his coat on without help. It took the men two days to collect all the buffalo carcasses, and by that time Cody was ready to take up the hunt again.

The Fifth Cavalry returned to Fort Lyon on February 19, 1869, according to the regimental history, "without having encountered hostile Indians or accomplished any material results, although the companies were conspicuous for their energy, untiring pursuit, and rapid movements. Company L made one march of seventy-five miles in twenty-six hours during a blinding snowstorm." Carr's column, however, did accomplish what Sheridan wanted it to do: It blocked the Indians from drifting westward while the other two columns pursued their missions, Custer at the

Battle of the Washita, and Evans at a village of Nakoni Comanche on the North Fork of Red River, which his men captured on Christmas Day. Custer then moved against the Cheyenne but did not attack because two white women prisoners were in their camp. The women were surrendered and a peace was concluded on March 15, 1869. For the time being, the fighting was over.

Carr's relief of Penrose's command, along with the subsequent campaign in snow, with temperatures twenty-eight to thirty degrees below zero, were no mean feats. Cody's contributions included his guiding, his hunting, and his handling of the wagon train. For these achievements, he received a monetary reward. On February 26 General Carr, by Special Order No. 46, Headquarters, Expedition from Fort Lyon, Colorado Territory, commanded Lieutenant Hayes, quartermaster of the Fifth Cavalry, to employ William Cody as a scout at $125 a month to date from October 5, 1868. Since his salary at that time was only $75 a month, and the order was retroactive, its effect was to give him a $50 a month raise for all his service with the Fifth Cavalry. Then, said Cody, "General Carr, at my request, kindly granted me one month's leave of absence to visit my family in St. Louis."

In her book *Memories*, Cody's wife recalled that she heard her husband's "booming" voice as he burst into her parents' home. "I could only stare at him," she recorded. "Where the close cropped hair had been were long, flowing curls now. A mustache weaved its way outward from his upper lip, while a small goatee showed black and spot-like on his chin."

"What on earth did you grow it for," Louisa recorded having said to her husband.

"Why, I had to," he explained. "It's the fashion out West now. You're not a regular scout unless you've got this sort of rigout."

This was true. It had become a point of honor with all who fought the Indians to let their hair grow long enough to form a respectable scalplock, so that if one should be so unfortunate as to fall in battle, the warrior might not be cheated of his victim's scalp.

Louisa was later to remark that "even with the stories of his prowess on the plains, Buffalo Bill would not have been Buffalo Bill without that long hair, without that mustache and that little goatee—at least, he would not have been the unusual appearing character that he was, nor would he have been as handsome."

In any event, the winter campaign, the long locks, and the facial hair had transformed Will Cody into the dashing figure he was to be for the rest of his life.

THE BATTLE OF
SUMMIT SPRINGS

When Cody left the Fifth Cavalry to travel to St. Louis to see his family, he was allowed to take a horse to ride and a mule to carry his personal belongings. He was told to leave the animals at the quartermaster's corral at Fort Wallace. Instead of following orders, Cody, in typical fashion, decided to leave them with his friend Dave Perry, a hotelkeeper in Sheridan; he then took a train to St. Louis. While Will was gone, a quartermaster's agent at Fort Wallace reported to Brevet Brigadier General Henry C. Bankhead, Captain Fifth Infantry, who commanded the fort, that Cody had sold government property to the hotelkeeper. The animals were seized by the quartermaster, Captain Samuel B. Lauffer, and taken to Fort Wallace.

When Cody returned to Sheridan, Perry told him what had happened. "I immediately went over to the office of the quartermaster's agent," said Will, "and had Perry point him out to me. I at once laid hold of him, and in a short time had treated him to just such a thrashing as his contemptible lie deserved."

Cody then went to the fort and demanded the horse and mule, which were the property of the quartermaster at Fort Lyon, who had let Will take them. Both General Bankhead and Captain Lauffer accused the scout of lying and ordered him off the fort. Will went back to town, found the government clerk again, and gave him a second beating. That night, while sleeping at the Perry House, Cody was awakened by soldiers from the Thirty-eighth Infantry, under Captain Israel Ezekiel, an old friend. The soldiers' guns were pointed at him, and he was told he was under arrest. He protested to Ezekiel that he could have made the arrest without bringing the Negro regiment with him, but Ezekiel, according to Cody, said: "I know that, Bill, but as you've not been in very good humor the last day or two, I didn't know how you would act."

Cody was taken to the guardhouse; however, since Captain George Graham's company was on guard duty, he was not locked in a cell but allowed to sleep in a sergeant's bunk. The next morning Graham told Will that he would intercede for him with General Bankhead. Bankhead refused to see Cody, who then addressed a telegram to General Sheridan, but the telegraph operator took it to the general, who tore it up. Hearing of this, Cody returned to the telegraph office and demanded that his wire be sent. The hapless clerk, knowing that he might be fired if he didn't send the telegram, again went to General Bankhead. Bankhead, who had exceeded his authority by arresting a civilian scout and putting him in the guardhouse, agreed to give Cody his horse and mule back if he would let the quartermaster's agent alone. Will accepted these terms and left for Fort Lyon.

We know that Buffalo Bill was not a gunfighter and seldom resorted to violence; this is one of the few occasions on which he did. His behavior seems excusable, though it is harder to find excuses for his disregard of army regulations. In this respect, he was very much like Custer, who enforced the rules strictly with his subordinates but flouted them himself.

Upon his return to Fort Lyon, Will was commissioned a "United States Detective," a designation that does not have any counterpart in today's army. General Carr wanted Cody to see if he could track down the thieves who had stolen some horses and mules from the post, including a horse belonging to General Carr and a mule belonging to Lieutenant W. C. Forbush. Another scout, Bill Green, had tracked the thieves to the vicinity of Old Fort Lyon, abandoned when the new fort was built. There Green lost the trail in the tall grass. Cody, with Green, Jack Farley, and a man identified only as "Long Doc," was ordered to pursue. Will picked up the trail farther along and followed it to the Arkansas River, which the thieves had crossed at Sand Creek, heading in the direction of Denver. It was there Cody was sure he would find them, at the Saturday horse auction.

Arriving in Denver, Cody and the other scouts stabled their horses at the Elephant Corral and rented a hotel room overlooking the corral. Will took up an observation post in the room and was soon rewarded by seeing Lieutenant Forbush's mule put up at auction. Cody immediately went down and arrested the thief, a man named Williams. "He recognized me and endeavored to escape," said Cody, "but I seized him by the shoulder. He was armed with a pair of pistols, which I took away from him."

Cody, Green, and Jack Farley took Williams out of town and threatened to hang him if he did not tell them the name of his accomplice. Williams was swift to betray his partner, one William "Bill" Bevins, who was hiding out in a house three miles farther down the Platte River. Cody and his companions proceeded to the house, and Bevins was covered with Cody's rifle before he could draw his revolver. The stolen animals were rounded up, and the two prisoners were taken to Denver, where they were jailed overnight. The next day the two prisoners were tied to mules, and the party started for Fort Lyon. The first night out, while Farley was on guard, he was kicked into the fire by Bevins, who jumped over the fire with his shoes in his hand. While Cody knocked Williams out with the butt of his revolver, Bevins managed to escape, dropping one of his shoes as he fled. He was followed for eighteen miles through snow and finally run down on the banks of the Platte. Cody expressed admiration for "the most remarkable feat of the kind ever known either of a white man, or an Indian. A man who could run bare-footed in the snow eighteen miles through a prickly pear patch, was certainly a 'tough one' and that's the kind of person Bill Bevins was." Cody let Bevins use his Bowie knife to cut the thorns out of his foot, and he was allowed to ride Will's horse back to camp, by which time his foot had swollen to an enormous size and was useless, making it impossible for him to escape again. Williams, however, managed to trick Long Doc and got away on a "dark, stormy night."

Bevins was turned over to civil authorities at Boggs's Ranch on Picket Wire Creek. As soon as he recovered the use of his foot, he escaped from a log jail where he was awaiting trial. Later Bevins was notorious for a series of stagecoach holdups in 1876 along the Black Hills Trail, between Cheyenne and Deadwood. He was arrested and sentenced to ten years in prison. Once again he escaped from jail in Laramie and resumed stagecoach robbing but was caught again. In 1879, when Cody wrote his first autobiography, Bevins was confined in the Nebraska state prison, to which he had been transferred from Laramie. Bevins was finally released in 1886 and died shortly afterward.

In May 1869 the Fifth Cavalry under General Carr was ordered to Fort McPherson in Nebraska. Cody recorded that en route to their new post, the Fifth stopped at Fort Wallace for a day to pick up supplies and that he had occasion to pass General Bankhead's headquarters. He claimed that Bankhead sent for him and hoped that the scout had "no hard feelings for him for having you arrested." According to Don Russell, Bankhead was one of those who, in later years, endorsed Cody's Wild West in glowing terms. After leaving Fort Wallace, the command proceeded to Sheridan, where Major Brown and Cody were sent for provisions for the mess. "Unfortunately we were in too jolly a mood to fool away money on 'grub,'" said Cody. When the company cook went to get the provisions out of an ambulance, he found "a five-gallon demijohn of whiskey, a five-gallon demijohn of brandy, and two cases of Old Tom-Cat gin." All was not lost, however, for another mess, well provided with solid food, offered to trade their supplies for the booze. "It is a fact," said Cody, "we got more provisions for our whiskey, than the same money, which we paid for the liquor, would have bought; so after all, it proved a very profitable investment."

As the battalion went into camp on May 13, Cody discovered a large Indian trail. Carr sent Lieutenant Edward W. Ward and twelve troopers with Cody to investigate. Some five miles downstream, Ward and Cody crawled to the top of a high knoll, from which they spotted an Indian village three miles away, with what appeared to be thousands of ponies grazing. Toward the left, they saw a party of Indians bringing in buffalo meat. Ward then wrote a note addressed to General Carr and sent it back to the base camp with one of the troopers. As Ward and his men slowly retreated, they heard shots and saw the messenger galloping back toward them, pursued by Indians. The detachment charged and drove off the Indians; Cody then volunteered to take the dispatch back to Carr himself.

When Cody reached camp, General Carr mounted five companies of troopers, leaving two companies to guard the camp, and moved off toward the Indian village, picking up Ward's detachment on the way. At three o'clock the battalion attacked some five hundred Indians at Elephant Rock. One company, commanded by Lieutenant C. A. Schenofsky, whom Cody described as "rattle-brained and daredevil," was cut off and had to be rescued. Schenofsky's company lost three or four men; three others were wounded. Thirty Indians were killed. After dark the Indians retreated toward the Republican River.

The Indians' trail was followed for three days. At noon on May 16, the advance guard of forty soldiers guided by Cody was surrounded and attacked at Spring Creek by two hundred Indians. The troopers dismounted and formed a circle, holding their mounts while firing and dropping back to the main body of troops, three miles away.

In 1878 General Carr said: "They all, to this day, speak of Cody's coolness and bravery. . . . Reaching the scene we could see the Indians in retreat. A figure with apparently a red cap rose slowly up the hill. For an instant it puzzled us, as it wore the buckskin and had long hair, but on seeing the horse, I recognized it as Cody's 'Powder Face' and saw that it was Buffalo Bill without his broad-brimmed sombrero. On closer inspection I saw his head was swathed in a bloody handkerchief, which served not only as a temporary bandage, but as a chapeau—his hat having been shot off, the bullet plowing his scalp badly for about five inches. It had ridged along the bone and he was bleeding profusely—a very 'close call' but a lucky one."

Cody said nothing of this wound in either autobiography, a striking omission in view of the criticism sometimes leveled against him for vainglory. "I am a modest man," he wrote later, "and I can prove it."

The Cheyenne were fighting to cover the retreat of their women and children, and they abandoned ponies, lodges, and possessions as they fled across the Republican River. Toward evening the troops halted; their horses were giving out and they were out of supplies. Fort Kearny was the nearest depot. General Carr says that "Cody decided it would be best to undertake the job himself—a point characteristic of him as he never shirked duty or faltered in emergencies. . . . Cody made a ride of fifty miles during the night, arriving at Fort Kearny at daylight. He had chased and fought Indians all day, been wounded, and when, through his rare frontier instinct, he reached us he had been almost constantly in the saddle for forty hours."

The troops resumed their march up Spring Creek and across the divide to the Platte River, arriving at Fort McPherson on May 20, 1869.

At the conclusion of this campaign, General Carr filed an official report in which he said: "Our scout William Cody, who has been with the Detachment since last September, displayed great skill in following it [the trail] and also deserves great credit for his fighting in both engagements, his marksmanship being very conspicuous. He deserves honorable mention for this and other services and I hope to be able to retain him as long as I am engaged in this duty."

Carr's official report was accompanied by a separate letter in which he said, "I have the honor respectfully to request that authority be given to pay my scout William Cody, one hundred dollars extra for extraordinarily good services as trailer and fighter in my late pursuit of hostile Indians; see my report of this date, page 6."

This letter went through the usual military channels to the War Department in Washington and resulted in an order signed by E. D. Townsend, the adjutant general of the army, dated June 1 and addressed to Brevet Major General C. C. Augur, commanding the Department of the Platte. It read: "Referring to your endorsement of the 27th ultimo, forwarding copy of Report of Brevet Major General E.A. Carr, Major 5th Cavalry, of his request that authority be given to pay his scout William Cody $100 extra for extraordinarily good services as a trailer and fighter in the pursuit of hostile Indians, I have the honor to inform you the Secretary of War authorized the $100 to be given Mr. Cody."

There are several remarkable features of this episode. One, of course, familiar enough to anyone who has served in the army but perhaps surprising to anyone who has not, is the amount of red tape required to pay Cody his hundred dollars. It is also remarkable in that no other scout was so commended and so rewarded during the Indian Wars. Remarkable finally is that Cody makes no mention of it in his autobiographies, though he could easily have patted himself on the back had he chosen to do so.

When Cody first saw Fort McPherson, he was still only twenty-three years old, and he had already begun to be famous as a scout and a dead shot. All of Cody's biographers agree that at the time he was tall and handsome, but no one seems to know how tall. As measured by a friend, Major M. C. Harrington, in 1888, at his home, Scout's Rest Ranch in North Platte, Nebraska, he was six foot three-quarters inch tall, although others have recorded his height as everything from five foot ten to six foot three. His hair has been described as both black and brown, but was probably dark brown and wavy. He weighed about two hundred pounds, but his carriage was always ramrod-straight. His complexion was often described as exceptionally smooth and fine, and his hands as soft and well shaped, rather surprising in one who spent so much of his life outdoors.

Fort McPherson, on that spring day when Cody first saw it, was still a raw frontier post. It was a bustling, busy place, with thirty-nine buildings, some log, some frame, and extensive horse corrals and stables, spread over a thirty-eight-acre square, or "reservation," as it was called. The parade quadrangle, 844 by 560 feet, was the center of the fort, and above it flew the thirty-seven-star flag of the United States; Nebraska's was the thirty-seventh star.

The only major army post between Fort Kearny in Nebraska and Fort Laramie, Wyoming, Fort McPherson was responsible for patrolling east toward Kearny, west to Julesburg, Colorado, and south to the Republican River, a vast territory. Because of hostile Indians, this sector of the Overland Trail—south of the Platte River and Union Pacific Railroad—was considered the most dangerous between the Missouri River and the Pacific coast; thus the need for more troops, including the Fifth Cavalry.

Fort McPherson was to be Will Cody's station until 1872, and Nebraska was to be his home for most of the next forty-four years. He was to find the fort both busy and exciting in the days ahead. The last spike in the Union Pacific Railroad had been driven at Promontory, Utah, ten days before his arrival on the Platte, but wagon travel was still heavy on the trail during the grass season, and would be for years to come. Troops were continually coming and going. Eastern government officials and military brass, riding the cars to McPherson Station, about four miles north across the river, visited the fort almost daily, some anticipating a bit of hunting, others making tours of inspection or performing other official duties. From reveille and the morning gun salute at daylight until taps sounded at nine in the evening, there was always something doing.

For entertainment there were two company libraries, one for the officers, furnished with 362 volumes, another for the enlisted men, who were presumably not heavy readers, with 26 books; and the post theater. Performances were given at the theater every Saturday night. Both "dramas and comedies were rendered exceedingly well for amateurs," wrote Louis A. Holmes in *Fort McPherson, Nebraska*. Dances, too, were popular at the fort. Neighbors and settlers from outside were invited, as were cowboys from ranches far and wide.

Young Cody fraternized freely with the officers and was on good terms with the other ranks, so he most likely attended all the dances. It is quite probable that he had a good time, for his friends said that there was always something doing where Will Cody was.

"It was a somewhat demoralized army that took the field against the Indians in the spring of 1869," according to Don Russell. "Congress by an act of March 3 cut the army from 54,641 to 37,313, reducing the number of infantry regiments from forty-five to twenty-five, although retaining the five regiments of artillery and ten of cavalry."

At that time, a cavalry regiment would muster between 1,024 and 1,240 men. The enlisted men included a few veterans of the Civil War, many immigrant foreigners who found no other jobs open to them, a few adventurous young men, and some who joined the army to get free transportation to the Far West for various reasons, not all of them praiseworthy. Desertion rates were high, reenlistments, or "re-ups," low, with the result that every summer campaign was manned by a lot of raw recruits.

As for Will Cody, the army retrenchment affected him as well; his pay was cut from $125 a month back to $75.

Cody and the Fifth had little time to get acquainted with their new quarters, for serious trouble broke out on the Republican River the day after they reached Fort McPherson. During the week of May 21 to 28, 1869, Indians killed thirteen whites in raids along that river, and on

May 29 they derailed a Kansas Pacific train and killed most of the crew—one of the few Indian derailments recorded. On the thirtieth of May a band under Tall Bull raided a German settlement on the Solomon River in Kansas, killed several people, and took two white women prisoner, Mrs. Thomas Alderdice and Mrs. G. Weichel, killing the former's baby and the latter's husband. On June 7 Carr and his troops received orders to leave Fort McPherson on June 9 and clear the Republican country of hostile Indians.

In his 1879 autobiography Cody records that General Carr recommended to General Augur, who was in command of the department, that "I be made chief of scouts in the Department of the Platte, and informed me that in this position I would receive higher wages than I had been getting in the Department of the Missouri. This appointment I had not asked for." When the Fifth Cavalry was relieved from the Department of the Missouri, all the scouts were discharged with the exception of Cody. Although he had received a promotion and an extraordinary commendation, his salary remained at $75 a month.

At McPherson, Cody met Major Frank North, who was to become a good friend, a business partner, and, much later, a member of Cody's Wild West. With North were three companies of Pawnee scouts and another company of Pawnee led by Frank's brother Luther. North himself was a veteran of the Civil War; he and his company of Pawnee were mustered out of service in June 1866. An act of Congress of July 28, 1866, authorized the enlistment of Indian scouts "who shall receive the pay and allowances of cavalry soldiers, and be discharged whenever the necessity for their further employment is abated, or at the discretion of the department commander." A battalion of four companies of Pawnee scouts under Major Frank North was raised in the winter of 1866–1867 to guard construction of the Union Pacific Railroad.

Cody thought highly of Major North and the Pawnee scouts in particular. The Pawnee "had made quite a reputation for themselves as they had performed brave and valuable services, in fighting against the Sioux, whose bitter enemies they were; being thoroughly acquainted with the Republican and Beaver country, I was glad they were to be with the expedition." Toward Luther North, Cody's feelings were less warm, and Luther would later show enmity toward Cody while challenging claims to some of Will's exploits.

General Carr also appreciated the Pawnee, though he said that he had "always been opposed to the enlistment of Indians and negroes." Nevertheless, he remained loyal to government policy, realizing that good scouts and trailers were essential and that the very best should be employed regardless of race, for there were "very few Buffalo Bills" to choose from.

On June 8, the day before the expedition was to take the field, the "Dandy Fifth," at Carr's command, put on a full-dress review. Eugene A. Carr, a West Point graduate, class of 1850, a tall, handsome "bearded Cossack," in Don Russell's description, and an experienced Indian fighter, loved such military displays and provided them at the slightest excuse. General Augur was there to review the troops, along with Brevet Brigadier General Thomas Duncan, commandant at the fort and lieutenant colonel of the Fifth. The entire McPherson garrison and their families, as well as all the villagers of Cottonwood Springs, turned out to watch the parade. The day was warm and sunny. Drums rolled, the regimental band struck up a military march, and sabers glittered in salute as the Fifth passed in review. Following the blue and yellow ranks of cavalry came the Pawnee Battalion. Cody himself was undoubtedly mounted on some splendid horse, for he enjoyed pomp every bit as much as Carr. Cody was amused by the odd assortment of uniforms worn by the Pawnee. Some wore only breechclouts; others had donned heavy overcoats; some were minus pantaloons; others wore pantaloons but no shirts and were bareheaded. Under Major North's commands, however, given them in Pawnee, which North spoke fluently, they drilled well and were obviously proud to be soldiers. That evening they gave an exhibition of Pawnee dances, which were much enjoyed by the ladies of the post.

The next day the battalion marched out of McPherson, setting a rapid pace. Marching for three hundred miles under a broiling sun and through heavy sandhills, the eight companies of the command finally came up with their objective, Tall Bull's Dog Cheyenne, "notoriously the worst band of Indians on the plains," according to Holmes in *Fort McPherson, Nebraska*. The Dog Men Society was a warrior group that set itself up as a separate band of outlaws. The main body of the Cheyenne had already made peace with Custer, but Tall Bull had not, and continued to fight and raid. Tall Bull had been joined by a band of Arapaho, traditional allies of the Cheyenne, and a band of Sioux. On May 30, while the Fifth Cavalry was still at Fort McPherson, Tall Bull's renegade band had made the attack on the settlers along the Solomon River, carrying off Mrs. Alderdice and Mrs. Weichel. Carr's mission was to attack Tall Bull and rescue the two women.

The first encounter came at 5:00 P.M. on June 15 when the Indians attempted to stampede the expedition's mules while they were being watered. According to Cody, "One of the herders came dashing into camp with an arrow sticking into him. My horse was close at hand and mounting him bareback, I at once dashed off after the mule herd. . . . I supposed certainly that I would be the first man on the ground. I was mistaken, however, for the Pawnee Indians, unlike regular soldiers, had not waited to receive orders from their officers, but had jumped on their ponies without bridles or saddles, and placing ropes in their mouths, had dashed off in the direction whence the shots had come, and had got there ahead of me."

Colonel Royall, with three companies, took up the pursuit of the Indians, a band of fifty Sioux, until darkness set in. In this first raid two privates were wounded.

On most of his scouting forays, Cody rode a mule; this time he was on horseback, because General Carr had requested two good horses for the guides and scouts, so they would run fewer risks than if they were mounted on mules. During the chase, Cody saw a Pawnee riding a horse that he admired, and he later arranged for a trade. The horse became famous as Buckskin Joe, and Cody continued to ride him until the end of his service in 1872. Buckskin Joe, of course, belonged to the government, not to Cody.

A few days after the mule raid, the Pawnee hunted for buffalo and, by surrounding a small herd, killed thirty-two. Cody then asked Major North to hold back the Pawnee while he saw what "he and Buckskin Joe" could do. Following his usual method of driving the buffalo into a circle and picking them off one by one, he killed thirty-six in a half-mile run. From then on, he said, he was a big chief among the Pawnee.

After two skirmishes with Indians in which Cody took no part, the command set out to follow an Indian trail. It was about this time that it became definitely known to Carr's command that Tall Bull's Cheyenne held Mrs. Alderdice and Mrs. Weichel captive. "Wherever they had encamped we found the print of a woman's shoe," said Cody. Will was sent out ahead of the force with six of the best Pawnee and instructed to keep ten or twelve miles in advance. After they had gone about ten miles, Cody and his Pawnee, sensing they were nearing the Indian encampment, began to move cautiously, looking over the tops of hills before showing themselves. At last they discovered the Indian village, in the sandhills south of the South Platte River at Summit Springs. "Here I left the Pawnee scouts to keep watch," said Cody, "while I went back and informed General Carr that the Indians were in sight."

There are several versions of what happened at what became known as the Battle of Summit Springs, and conflicting stories concerning the death of Tall Bull, the leader of the Dog Cheyenne. What is inarguable is that Summit Springs was a classic Indian fight, the kind immortalized by Hollywood, with hundreds of cavalrymen riding in a charge against an equal number of Indian braves, capped with a large slaughter of Indians and the rescue of a captured white woman. The fight was the last one in that section of the plains, freeing Kansas and some surrounding country of serious Indian troubles. It was unusual in that it involved eight companies of cavalry; most of the 968 actions against Indians recorded between 1865 and 1898 involved only an understrength company or two, and some were fought by even smaller detachments. In all these battles the army suffered only 1,944 casualties.

One version of Summit Springs is Cody's account, told first in his 1879 autobiography and repeated later in slightly different accounts in other books bearing his name though not necessarily written by him. Cody says that he first changed his horse for Buckskin Joe, who was comparatively fresh. He suggested that the general move his troops to the north, which Carr did. Carr later wrote: "Cody's idea was to get around, beyond, and between [the Indians] and the river." "By this maneuver we avoided discovery by the Sioux scouts," said Cody, "and we were confident of giving them a complete surprise." Captain George F. Price of the Fifth credits Cody with the intelligence that was instrumental in the ensuing victory. Wrote Price:

> . . . the arrival of the guide, William F. Cody, who reported large herds of ponies about six miles distant in a southwesterly direction, which was indubitable evidence that Tall Bull and his warriors were encamped and unconscious of approaching peril, as the pickets, who were watching their rear, had made no danger signals. . . . [Cody] guided the Fifth Cavalry to a position whence the regiment was enabled to charge the enemy and win a brilliant victory.

Another endorsement of Cody's contribution to the battle came from Lieutenant Edward M. Hayes, quartermaster, who recalled that Cody had "discovered the village and led the troops to the position they were to occupy in the attack without the knowledge of the Indians. This was considered the greatest of the many achievements of this wonderful scout."

Cody's account then described how the troops halted at the top of a hill overlooking the village. It was about two o'clock in the afternoon. The line moved forward at a slow trot; a heavy gale blowing from the west kept the sound of hoofbeats from arousing the camp. A fifteen-year-old Indian boy who was guarding a herd in the hills beyond the village saw the troops coming and began a wild dash on a white pony to sound the alarm. His shouts could not be heard because of the gale, but if he reached the village first, surprise would be lost. Carr ordered his bugler to sound the charge. Apparently the bugler forgot how to do so, and Quartermaster Hayes—who had obtained permission to attend the expedition—seized the bugle and sounded it himself, "in clear and distinct notes," said Cody.

"As the troops rushed forward, he threw the bugle away, then drawing his pistols, was among the first men that entered the village."

As the Indian herder reached the south side of the ravine in which the village lay, the troops were at the north edge, only fifty yards away. Shouting, the cavalrymen struck. The Cheyenne had no time to seize their weapons or get their horses, and fled panic-stricken in all directions. The young herder who might have warned them was killed fighting in the middle of the village. Major Frank North's Pawnee scouts charged head-long through the village, driving all before them. It was a short, savage fight that completely broke the strength and spirit of the Dog Soldiers.

Carr appointed the officers of the battalion to determine the casualties and account for any captured property. They reported fifty-two Indians killed on the field and seventeen women and children captured. In Carr's forces, one man was slightly scratched by an arrow. Property taken included 85 lodges, 274 horses, and 144 mules—as well as rifles, revolvers, bows and arrows, and powder. Thirteen hundred dollars in cash was found in the village, the plunder taken by Tall Bull's raids on the settlers.

As for the captive women, one, Mrs. Alderdice, was slain by Tall Bull's wife, brained with a tomahawk. Mrs. Weichel, though wounded in an abortive attempt to kill her, survived; Cody says she was rescued by the company ordered to seize the village. She recovered from her injuries at Fort Sedgwick, where she married the hospital steward who took care of her there. Of the money found in the village, $900 was given to her. In Buffalo Bill's Wild West re-creation of this battle in later years, he was portrayed as having taken part in Mrs. Weichel's rescue, though he never personally claimed any credit.

Tall Bull, or Tatonka Haska as he was called, was killed in the fight. There will probably always be some question as to who fired the fatal shot. In the Fifth Cavalry, credit was always given to Buffalo Bill. Only one person present at the battle challenged this assertion: Frank North's brother Luther.

Cody said that while the loot seized in the camp was being burned, some Indians returned, and a fight went on all around the camp. "I was in the skirmish line, and I noticed an Indian, who was riding a large bay horse, and giving orders to his men in his own language—which I could occasionally understand—telling them that they had lost everything, that they were ruined, and he entreated them to follow him, and fight until they died. His horse was an extraordinary one, fleet as the wind, dashing here and there, and I determined to capture him if possible, but I was afraid to fire at the Indian for fear of killing his horse.

"I noticed that the Indian, as he rode around the skirmish line, passed the head of a ravine not far distant, and it occurred to me that if I could dismount and creep into the ravine I could, as he passed there, easily drop him from his saddle without danger of hitting his horse. Accordingly I crept into and secreted myself in the ravine, reaching the place unseen by the Indians, and I waited there until Mr. Chief came riding by.

"When he was not more than thirty yards distant I fired, and the next moment he tumbled from his saddle, and the horse kept on without its rider. Instead of running toward the Indians, however, he ran toward our men, by one of whom he was caught. Lieutenant Mason, who had been very conspicuous in the fight and who had killed two or three Indians himself, single-handed, came galloping up the ravine and jumping from his horse, secured the fancy war bonnet from the head of the dead chief, together with all his other accoutrements. We both then rejoined the soldiers and I at once went in search of the horse; I found him in the possession of Sergeant McGrath, who had caught him. The Sergeant knew that I had been trying to get the animal and having seen me kill his rider, he handed him over to me at once.

"I jumped on his back," Cody continued, "and rode him down to the spot where the prisoners were corralled. One of the squaws among the prisoners suddenly began crying in a pitiful and hysterical manner at the sight of this horse, and upon inquiry I found that she was Tall Bull's wife, the same squaw that had killed one of the white women and wounded the other. She stated that this was her husband's favorite warhorse, and that only a short time ago she had seen Tall Bull riding him. . . . I informed her that henceforth I should call the gallant steed 'Tall Bull' in her husband's honor."

One might wonder what possible consolation the poor bereaved widow could find in this gesture, but it is typically Codyesque that he would at first be more interested in the horse than in the chief and would matter-of-factly report that he killed Tall Bull only in order to obtain the horse. It is unlikely that he even knew at the time that the Indian he had killed was Tall Bull.

Years afterward, whenever Cody was asked how many Indians he had killed in his frontier career, he would never give a direct answer but would only say "I never shot anyone who wasn't shooting at me." That was surely not true in the case of Tall Bull; not only was he no threat to the scout, Cody ambushed him—and all for a horse. It is still true, however, that Tall Bull and his Dog Cheyenne had to be taken out, and Tall Bull would surely have died in any case, whether Cody or someone else killed him; he did not, like Black Kettle, intend to surrender and seek peace with the whites. So his death was necessary, to leave the Dog Soldiers leaderless and demoralized.

As captured Indian property, the horse would now belong to the army, but Cody rode him during his scouting service and the horse "four years afterward, was the fastest runner in the state of Nebraska."

The second version of the Battle of Summit Springs is attributed to Luther North, who was interviewed frequently in later years. Many of these interviews were given after Luther reached the age of eighty-three, some sixty years after the fight, and a number were inconsistent with the others. He told interviewers, most notably Richard Walsh, the coauthor of *The Making of Buffalo Bill*, that Cody and General Carr had both missed the fight altogether and that his brother Frank, not Cody, had killed Tall Bull. By the time of the interviews, Luther had become a minor celebrity as one of the few survivors of the Indian Wars; both Cody and Frank North were long dead. Luther's reminiscences provided material for at least nine printed versions of Summit Springs, though no two of them agreed with each other, and none agreed with official army records of the fight.

Why would Luther North have so distorted the historical record? It can be surmised that he was jealous of Cody's reputation and growing fame as a scout. Jealousy of William F. Cody was common among scouts of the period, because he was shown such favoritism and was so admired by the officers he served with. In Luther's case jealousy seems to have become a positive hatred. We know that Luther was also prejudiced against General Carr. Frank North discharged his brother on August 7, less than a month after the fight, and Luther says that "I had a few words with General Carr and when we got to the fort I resigned and came home." Luther continually disparaged the cavalry and its officers, and claimed that his brother Frank and the Pawnee scouts were primarily responsible for the victory. His partiality for his brother, and his defense of Frank's reputation, must also be taken into account. Don Russell believes that "in a court of law the discrepancies in Luther North's stories would be sufficient to discredit him as a witness. Certainly they show that he was no reliable authority on either the Battle of Summit Springs or the death of Tall Bull."

The third version of Cody's contribution to the battle was recorded by the officers who took part in it. Most of the officers and enlisted men of the Fifth Cavalry who rode with Cody that summer gave him high marks as a scout on the basis of his accomplishment in the campaign and the

Battle of Summit Springs. Brigadier General William P. Hall, who joined the Fifth Cavalry as a second lieutenant, or "shavetail" (the term comes from the custom of shaving the tail of a mule that had not yet been properly trained and was not yet ready for action), immediately after the fight, wrote Cody in 1907: "I recall that you shot Tall Bull, and captured his celebrated gray race horse which you named Tall Bull and with which you captured the stakes in a great many horse races afterward." Brigadier General Charles King, who joined the Fifth Cavalry as a first lieutenant within two years of the fight, wrote in 1929, "Never before this year did I hear of it being doubted or questioned that Cody killed Tall Bull." William H. McDonald of North Platte lived near Fort McPherson as a boy and told Don Russell: "I know it was generally understood at Fort McPherson, where the 5th Cavalry came immediately after the Battle of Summit Springs in July, 1869, that Cody killed Tall Bull."

The killing of Tall Bull has become a part of Buffalo Bill's history and of his legend. However, it was not his supreme achievement at Summit Springs; that was the masterful way in which he found Tall Bull's camp and guided the troops of the Fifth Cavalry in their attack, for which he quite properly received abundant credit. Among the booty Cody received, besides the chief's gallant steed, was "a pony which I called 'Powder Face,' and which afterward became quite celebrated, as he figured prominently in the stories of Ned Buntline."

The victory at Summit Springs was hailed as freeing Kansas, and Nebraska south of the Niobrara River, from the danger of Indian attacks—although Indians continued to steal horses and in turn continued to be pursued by the cavalry. General Carr's expedition, its mission accomplished, marched to Fort Sedgwick, near Julesburg, Colorado, for rest and refitting. "From there," said Cody, "the particulars of our fight . . . were telegraphed to all parts of the country. We remained at this post for two weeks, during which General Augur, of the Department of the Platte, paid us a visit, and highly complimented the command for the gallant service it had performed." Cody added that the command was complimented not only in general orders but also received a vote of thanks from the legislatures of Nebraska and Colorado, for Tall Bull had long been a terror to the border settlements.

On July 10, while Cody and the troops were off on the Summit Springs campaign, Brevet Major General William H. Emory had arrived at Fort McPherson to establish regimental headquarters for the Fifth Cavalry. When the expedition returned, the general assured Cody that his employment as scout would be permanent and that a log house would be built on the post for him and his family. Happy over this good news, he immediately wrote Lulu, telling her to be ready to come west again soon.

While the Summit Springs expedition was still at Fort Sedgwick, General Carr received a telegram that Indians had raided O'Fallon's Station on the Union Pacific Railroad, killing several section men and running off stock. A detachment led by Brevet Major William H. Brown was ordered to pursue the Indians and punish them if possible. Carr instructed Cody to proceed by train to join the expedition as scout.

The expedition was of little consequence, except that it led to another fateful meeting in the life of William F. Cody. Major Brown introduced him to "Colonel" Edward Zane Carroll Judson, the author of blood-and-thunder dime novels under the pseudonym Ned Buntline. (Judson took his pseudonym from the term for one of the ropes attached to the foot of a square sail to haul it up to the yard for furling, chosen surely because of his youthful service as a midshipman in the navy, and the series of sea stories with which he launched his writing career.) Judson was an extraordinary figure, famous in his own right, and certainly one of the most colorful writers who ever put pen to paper. Inspired by James Gordon Bennett, a foreigner and a Catholic, who had built the New York *Herald* from nothing to an income of over $130,000 annually, Ned started his own paper, *Ned Buntline's Own*, which went in and out of bankruptcy during several incarnations.

Judson served as a private in the First New York Rifles for two and a half years during the Civil War, but he fought in no battles. Army records show that on October 24, 1862, he was promoted to the rank of sergeant and that on February 12, 1863, he was reduced to the ranks. He was under arrest from March 22 to April 11. While under arrest, he pleaded his case to the commanding general of the Seventh Corps, asserting that while "on my way voluntarily to return to my regiment, after having overstayed my furlough through unavoidable circumstances (sickness), I have been arrested and held . . . as a deserter." Later he claimed to have been "chief of scouts with the rank of colonel"; there is no basis for the claim. His pseudonym was legitimate, acquired by churning out an enormous amount of cheap fiction and by editing *Ned Buntline's Own* magazine.

As Ned Buntline, Judson was an able and prolific storyteller and boasted that he wrote as many as six novels a week. In his lifetime he reeled off the equivalent of two hundred volumes—more than Dickens and Sir Walter Scott together. He boasted that he once wrote a book of six hundred pages in sixty-two hours, during which time he scarcely ate or slept. His income was reputed to be as high as $20,000 a year, and he supported half a dozen wives, some of them simultaneously. After killing a Nashville man in a duel over the Tennessean's wife, he was hanged, but the rope broke or was cut and he was spared to commit other outrages on his fellow man. One was to instigate what has become known as the Astor Place Riot.

In 1848 the noted British actor William Charles Macready made the last of his three visits to America. During this visit, a "feud" was initiated by the American actor Edwin Forrest, attacking Macready as a foreigner and an aristocrat, making him the scapegoat of the Nativist movement. Edwin Forrest was considered by many Americans to be the ideal Macbeth. New York's Bowery "b'hoys" idolized him and scorned Macready. Yet intelligent Americans preferred Macready to Forrest, who was disliked by his fellow players for his insistence on such things as rehearsals and performing Shakespeare's plays as they had been written. Walt Whitman said of actors of the day, "If they have to enact passion, they do so by all kinds of unnatural and violent jerks, swings, screwing of the nerves of the face, rolling of the eyes, and so on." He might have been describing Edwin Forrest.

The attacks on Macready culminated in a riot outside the Astor Place "opera house" in New York City, where the English actor was playing in *Macbeth*, during which more than twenty people were killed by the militia. The rioters were led by Judson/Buntline. Judson was arrested and spent a year in jail, but when released he was treated as a hero. In St. Louis, Buntline staged another riot, this time as an organizer for the American, or "Know-Nothing," party, stirring up a mob against the Germans in the city. After being indicted by a grand jury, Buntline fled the city.

As a writer, Buntline had a particular technique. In his own words:

> I take a bound book of blank paper, set my title at the head of it, and begin to write about the fictitious character who is to be the hero of it. I push ahead as fast as I can write, never blotting out anything I have once written, and never making a correction or modification. If you will examine the leaves of my manuscript you will see that the pages are clean with no erasures—no interlineations. If a book does not suit me when I have finished it, or at any stage of its progress, I simply throw it in the fire and begin again, without any reference to the discarded text.

It is easy to see from this prescription for what might be called speed writing why Buntline was so prolific. His unusual approach to the writer's craft resulted in some four hundred novels and novelettes, many under such additional pseudonyms as Edward Minturn, Jules Edwards, and Julia Manners. Verse and tracts on political and temperance subjects (he was as strong a champion of temperance as he was of strong drink) were part of his prodigious output.

Buntline's success owed much to the immense popularity of dime novels from 1860 to 1900; during that period they were the favorite reading of Americans both rich and poor. In Ned's youth people spoke of "bits"—as in "two bits"—and "shillings"—as in "shilling shockers." During the Civil War, dime novels "came to the camp in bales like hay," and soldiers read them hour after hour. They were published by a firm known as Beadle and Company. The Beadle brothers, Erastus and Irwin, had achieved success in Buffalo, where they published *The Dime Songbook*. In 1861 they published the first dime novel, entitled *Malaeska, The Indian Wife of the White Hunter*, by a woman named Ann Sophia Winterbotham Stephens. The Beadle Company published the book with a saffron cover ornamented with the picture of a ten-cent piece to prevent sutlers from overcharging soldiers. In 1862 the firm reorganized as Beadle and Adams. The company was not without its competitors, most notably Street & Smith, publishers of the *New York Weekly*, where Buntline's first Buffalo Bill novel appeared.

This colorful if unsavory rogue has been credited in some accounts as having "discovered" Buffalo Bill and having given him his famous name in one of his dime novels. One story, related by the notoriously unreliable Luther North, has it that Buntline ventured west to Fort Sedgwick, Colorado, in search of an authentic frontier hero. Having read the newspaper reports of the Battle of Summit Springs, Buntline sought out the hero of the battle, Major Frank North. North declined the honor and pointed out Cody, who was lying asleep under a wagon, saying "there's your hero." Buntline woke the young scout, according to Luther, and dubbed him "Buffalo Bill."

In truth, as Don Russell points out, Cody was known as Buffalo Bill a full two years before Buntline wrote his novel *Buffalo Bill, the King of Border Men*. On November 26, 1867, the Leavenworth *Daily Conservative* recorded that "Buffalo Bill, with fifteen or twenty citizens volunteered to go out and look for" Judge Corwin, who had strayed from a hunting party of Ohio and eastern Kansas gentlemen who left Fort Hays on November 22. After a long ride, the lost man was found about five miles from the fort, nearly starved and exhausted. The same newspaper on January 11, 1868, mentions "Buffalo Bill and 'Brigham'" hunting buffalo from Fort Hays. There is no room for doubt that Buffalo Bill received his famous handle while hunting buffalo for the railroad contractors, and not from Buntline's novel.

In fact, Ned Buntline was not in search of a hero when he arrived at Fort McPherson; he was returning from a temperance lecture he had given in California and was en route to giving another such lecture in Cotton- wood Springs. When Ned arrived in Fort Sedgwick, Major North had already gone home and Cody was on his way to Nebraska.

This is how Cody described his meeting with Buntline, when Major Brown introduced the two:

"Just then I noticed a gentleman, who was rather stoutly built, and who wore a blue military coat, on the left breast of which were pinned about twenty gold medals and badges of secret societies. He walked a little lame as he approached us . . . 'Colonel Judson, I am glad to meet you,' said I; 'the Major tells me that you are to accompany us on the scout.' 'Yes, my boy, so I am,' said he; 'I was to deliver a temperance lecture to-night; but no lectures for me when there is a prospect for a fight.'"

The command, led by Major Brown with Cody as scout and Buntline as supernumerary riding Cody's horse Powder Face, headed for O'Fallon's Station on July 24, 1869, where Cody succeeded in finding the Indian trail. However, as the Indians had a head start of two days, Major Brown abandoned the pursuit, while Cody went back to Fort Sedgwick, accom- panied by Buntline.

Cody was much impressed by Buntline when Ned, though diffident about his horsemanship, was the first to swim his mount across the South Platte, wide and high because of recent rains. "During this short scout, Buntline had asked me a great many questions," Cody said, but that was apparently the end of the encounter, and Cody was genuinely surprised when Buntline's novel appeared, heralding him as a frontier hero.

Shortly after the aborted expedition with Buntline, Cody discovered that his horse Tall Bull was an extraordinarily swift runner, and he began to race him, first against Lieutenant George F. Mason, who owned a racer. Cody saw at once that Tall Bull would win the race, but kept him in check so that no one would know quite how fast his horse ran, thereby ensuring that he would find other takers. In a short time, he was up $700 in winnings. He then raced Powder Face against one of Luther North's horses. Powder Face proved to be "one of the swiftest ponies I ever saw," and he won his first race so decisively that Cody could get up no more races. "Thus passed the time while we were at Fort Sedgwick," he said.

The July expedition with Buntline was followed by another led by Major Royall on August 2, with seven companies of the Fifth Cavalry, Pawnee scouts, "and the guide, William F. Cody," on a scout toward Frenchman's Fork of the Republican River. Chief Pawnee Killer's band of Sioux was discovered within ten miles of the fort. A running fight followed, and the Sioux were pursued across Frenchman's Fork and northward across the South Platte. The chase continued across the North Platte and eight miles through the sandhills toward the Niobrara, but since the Indians were making much better time than the cavalry, the pursuit was hopeless. Forty-two Indian ponies were found abandoned, but the expedition also had its troubles in the sandhills. "I have lost 17 animals and am leading many barely able to walk," Royall reported. Rations were also exhausted, so on August 11 the pursuit was called off. The troops returned to Fort McPherson, arriving there on August 22.

It is easy to see how frustrating such a campaign must have been for soldiers trained and eager to fight, pursuing an elusive foe who constantly fled, vanishing as swiftly as smoke in a high wind. It was always the Indians who decided when the battle would be joined, if at all—and when they made the decision, they usually won the battle.

When he got back to Fort McPherson, Will Cody found that the house he had been promised was not yet finished, but letters from Louisa informed him that she and their daughter, Arta, were on their way to Nebraska. When they reached the fort a few days later, Will found lodging for them with William Reed at the trading post until the house was ready.

The Codys' two-room cabin and small log barn were located a short distance east of the post reservation, between the last post buildings and the McDonald trading post. Like the officers' houses, the Cody cabin had a rain barrel at one corner to catch runoff water from the roof for laundry purposes; when it did not rain, a big tank wagon manned by enlisted men brought water from the river to fill the barrels. In either case, before it could be used, the water had to be carefully poured off the mud that settled to the bottoms of the barrels.

Mrs. Cody said that the walls of the cabin were lined with condemned tents after the logs had been chinked with mud. Will tried to hang wallpaper he had brought from Cheyenne, but made a mess of it. An old army stove served for cooking and heating.

Louisa Cody and Mrs. Charles McDonald, wife of the trader, became good friends. "Together," Lulu wrote in her memoir, "we would do our sewing or laundry, [for] servants were an unknown quantity at Fort McPherson." As a matter of fact, servants were abundant at the fort, and could be hired for fifty cents to a dollar a week, with room and board thrown in. All the officers' wives had servant girls, many of whom married settlers or enlisted men and stayed to make their homes in the valley.

With lodgings and a salary equal to an officer's, Will Cody could easily afford to hire help for his wife, and undoubtedly did. He was not a man to see his wife bent over a washboard if domestic help was available.

On one occasion, Louisa says she had prepared a special dinner for some friends her husband had invited to their home. Mrs. McDonald helped her prepare the meal, the finest that could be put together on the frontier at that time. The guests, according to Louisa and Courtney Ryley Cooper, were "Lord and Lady Dunraven from England and Lord Finn from Australia." When the guests arrived, the Codys met them at the front door. Lulu soon excused herself to go to the kitchen to serve the dinner, politely declining Lady Dunraven's offer of assistance. When she stepped into the kitchen, she found six Indians finishing off the meal.

Frances Sims Fulton, in her book *To and Through Nebraska*, wrote that in 1883, when she visited Mrs. Cody in North Platte, Mrs. Cody told her that she had prepared a dinner "at great expense for six officers at Fort McPherson," and that while she and her husband were receiving their guests at the front door, six Indians entered by the kitchen door, "sur-rounded the table and without ceremony or carving knife," ate her roasted chickens and other delicacies. Concluded Mrs. Cody, "the dinner was com-pletely spoiled, but while I cried with mortification the officers laughed and enjoyed the joke."

The story, while true, did not involve British royalty. The lords and ladies were provided by Cooper, who probably felt that army officers in the Cody cabin would not be as impressive to readers as aristocracy.

"When the scouting ended in October 1869, Cody found himself stranded at Fort McPherson, with no occupation and no income," accord-ing to Richard Walsh in *The Making of Buffalo Bill*. Walsh added that Cody was reduced to making a living for himself and his family by racing his horse as long as he could find anyone to match a race against him, and that his wife had to take in washing to keep groceries on their table.

Walsh's version of Cody's plight is groundless. Army records show that from the day Cody joined the Fifth Cavalry as scout on October 5, 1868, until he resigned in December 1872, he was never off the govern-ment payroll. To recap his service: During the first part of this period, October 5, 1868, to October 28, 1869, as chief of scouts he took part in seven expeditions against Indians and in nine Indian fights. Few if any men in the regiment he served in saw this much action. He was acclaimed for his able and efficient scouting service by four generals—Carr, Sheridan, Emory, and Augur—and even by order of the secretary of war. Red tape had been stretched to the breaking point to keep Cody on the payroll, in a time when a scout's employment was always casual and by the job.

That he raced his horses there is no doubt, but for sport and not because he was penniless. Fort McPherson had a properly laid-out one-mile racetrack, and the men enjoyed racing whenever their duties permitted.

Cody himself wrote that he "found Fort McPherson to be a lively and pleasant post to be stationed at, especially as there was plenty of game in the vicinity, and within a day's ride there were large herds of deer, antelope and elk."

During the winter of 1869–1870, Cody spent a great deal of time hunting. During the season, the fort played host to two hunting parties of Englishmen; Cody names them as a "Mr. Flynn, and George Boyd Houghton, of London—the noted caricaturist." The visitors were entertained by horseraces, among other things, arranged by Cody. His horses Tall Bull and Powder Face were invariably the winners, and soon he could no longer attract bettors.

Cody, mounted as usual on Tall Bull, did run a rather novel race against a horse from Captain Spaulding's Company of the Second Cavalry. He made a bet that Tall Bull would beat that horse around a one-mile track and, during the time that he was running, he, Cody, would jump on and off the horse eight times. "I rode the horse bareback," he related, "seized his mane with my left hand, rested my right on his withers, and while he was going at full speed, I jumped to the ground, and sprang again upon his back, eight times in succession. Such feats I had seen performed in the circus and I had practiced considerably at it with Tall Bull, so that I was certain of winning the race in the manner agreed upon."

On September 15 another expedition set forth, this time with General Duncan in command. According to the regimental history, it consisted of four companies of the Fifth Cavalry, three companies of the Second Cavalry, Major North's Pawnee Scouts, "the guide, William F. Cody," and another scout, John Y. Nelson, whom Cody called "a good fellow though as a liar he has few equals and no superior." In later years Nelson traveled with Cody's stage show as interpreter and was a fixture with Buffalo Bill's Wild West—a number of photographs taken at the show were of full-bearded John Nelson, his Sioux wife, and their children.

Will Cody was always quite open about his drinking, although none of the officers he served under ever went on record to accuse him of drinking on duty. Off duty it was another matter altogether. On the morning after the first day's march, General Duncan, whom Cody called "a jolly, blustering old fellow," proposed a shooting match. Says Cody, "I can assure the reader that I did not feel like shooting anything except myself, for on the night before I had returned to Fort McPherson and spent several hours in interviewing the sutler's store, in company with Major Brown. I looked around for my gun, and found that I had left it behind. The last I could remember about it was that I had left it at the sutler's store." Cody had to borrow a gun from John Nelson in order to shoot in the match with the general, "which resulted in his favor"—another of the rare occasions in which Will was outshot, perhaps deliberately.

This September expedition was a pursuit of the remnants of the Cheyenne and Sioux led by Chiefs Pawnee Killer, Whistler, and Little Bull. Cody and Major North bagged a good many buffalo, undoubtedly to augment the command's rations. On September 23 North recorded, "Cody and I killed 13 Buffalo our men killed lots." On September 26, at Prairie Dog Creek, which Cody says was not far from the place where he had been laid up with a broken leg while trapping with Dave Harrington, Buffalo Bill and Major North went hunting and killed a few buffalo while looking for a campsite. Frank dismounted to rest, while Will rode back over the next hill to look for the advance guard. As soon as he spotted it, he too dismounted and lay down to rest.

"Suddenly I heard three or four shots," Cody recalled, "and in a few moments Major North came dashing up towards me, pursued by eight or ten Indians. I instantly sprang to my saddle, and fired a few shots at the Indians, who by this time had all come in sight, to the number of fifty. We turned our horses and ran, the bullets flying after us thick and fast— my whip being shot from my hand and daylight being put through the crown of my hat."

In his *1869 Diary of Frank North*, the story is told in much the same way: "Today we marched 24 miles and I and Cody came ahead to the creek and 6 Indians got after us and gave us a lively chase you bet. I got my men out and they killed one Indian and got two ponies a mule and lots of trash."

When the troops came to the rescue, led by Lieutenants Price and Volkmar, the pursuing Indians retreated. North rode his horse in a circle, according to Cody, "a traditional plains signal for 'enemy in sight.'" North's Pawnee scouts "broke ranks pell mell and, with Major North at their head, started for the flying warriors," pursuing them so closely that they completely abandoned their village, which was destroyed next morning. "It was afterwards learned," says Price, "that the band traveled ninety miles without stopping, and thereafter marched as rapidly as possible until they arrived at Standing Rock Agency."

This last engagement marked the end of the campaign. By October 23 there seemed little hope of overtaking this hostile band. Rations were running low and snow impeded movement, so the expedition turned back toward Fort McPherson, where it arrived on October 28 and was disbanded, going into winter quarters. General Sheridan wrote to Sherman in Washington: "I am now able to report that there has been a fulfillment of all the conditions which we had in view when we commenced our winter's campaign last November—namely, punishment was inflicted; property destroyed; the Indians disabused of the idea that winter would bring security; and all the tribes south of the Platte forced on to the reservations."

William F. Cody was discharged as scout on October 31, 1869, but was hired as chief herder the next day, at the same salary. Why the change in job description? Probably because the army had no need of scouts during the winter, and it would have looked peculiar to the powers-that-be if Cody was carried on the rolls as a scout when there was no scouting for him to do. Cody remained on the payroll as chief herder at $75 a month until July 1, 1870, when he again became a scout, this time at a salary of $100 a month.

This last expedition also closed one brief chapter of the conquest of the plains. Indian resistance was not ended, and there would be warfare north of the Platte, and Cody would have a part in it—but he was about to play a completely different role, one for which his entire life had prepared him.

"BUFFALO BILL, THE KING
OF BORDER MEN"

Although Ned Buntline may not have specifically come out west to find a new hero—a successor to Davy Crockett and Kit Carson in the American pantheon, or to James Fenimore Cooper's Natty Bumppo in American literature—he serendipitously found one in William F. Cody. Buntline and Cody might have been meant for each other: both larger than life, both the best of their kind and at the top of their games, both gifted tellers of tall tales.

On December 23, 1869, the first installment of Ned Buntline's serial story *Buffalo Bill, the King of Border Men* appeared in the *New York Weekly*. It was advertised as "the wildest and truest story he ever wrote." At least the first part of that claim had some validity.

This is how Buntline began his "truest story":

Chapter I

An oasis of green wood on Kansas prairie—a bright stream shining like liquid silver in the moonlight—a log house built under the limbs of great trees—within this humble home a happy group. This is my first picture.

A noble-looking, white-haired man sits by a rough table, reading the Bible aloud. On stools by his feet sit two beautiful little girls—his twin daughters—not more than ten years of age, while a noble boy, twelve or thirteen, stands by the back of the chair where sits the handsome, yet matronly-looking mother.

It is the hour for family prayer before retiring for the night, and Mr. Cody, the Christian as well as patriot, always remembers it in the heart of his dear home.

He closes the holy book, and is about to kneel and ask heaven to bless and protect him and his dear ones.

Hark! The sound of horses galloping with made speed toward the house falls upon his ear.

"Is it possible there is another Indian alarm?" he says, inquiringly.

Alas! worse than red savages are riding in hot haste toward the door.

"Hallo—the house!" is shouted loudly, as a large cavalcade of horsemen halt before the door.

"What is wanted, and who are ye?" asked the good man, as he threw wide open the door and stood upon its threshold.

"You are wanted, you black-hearted nigger-worshipper, and I— Colonel M'Kandlas—have come to fetch you! And there's the warrant!"

As the ruffian leader of the band shouted these words, the pistol already in his hands was raised, levelled, fired, and the father, husband and Christian fell dead before his horror-stricken family.

The band is about to ride off, when:

"Stop!"

It was but a single word—spoken, too, by a boy whose blue eyes shone wildly in a face as white as any new-fallen snow, and full as cold— spoken as he stood erect over the body of his dead father, weaponless and alone.

Yet that ruffian—aye, and all of his mad, reckless crew—stopped as if a mighty spell was laid upon them.

"*You*, Jake M'Kandlas, have murdered my father! You base cowards, who saw him do this dark deed, spoke no words to restrain him. I am only little Bill, his son, but as God in heaven hears me now, I will kill every father's son of you before the beard grows on my face!"

Say what you will about Buntline's style, he certainly knew how to hook a reader from the get-go. Nor did he forget his ride with Buffalo Bill mounted on Powder Face:

"One is as good on a scout as twenty" [Buntline's Buffalo Bill is speaking], "especially when he has got such an insect as my Powder Face under him, for that pony can out-smell, out-see and out-hear any livin' thing, be it man, dog, or catamount, that ever yelped. Look at him standing there, one eye open and t'other one shut—but see how his ears pint. He knows I'm talking about him. Come here, Powder Face, and let the folks look at you."

The horse, a rather large-sized pony of full Indian breed, in color a regular light buckskin, with long black mane and tail, walked up to the porch and rested his nose on the shoulder of his young master.

Clean-limbed, deep in the chest, heavy in the arms and quarters, full of muscle, he was a splendid specimen of that breed.

"Isn't he a rare insect? He can run ten hours and never flag, swim any current this side of the big hills, and he knows as much as I do about hide and seek. Powder Face, go bring your saddle and bridle—we're going on a hunt."

History does not tell us how long Ned labored over his first "Buffalo Bill," but it could not have taken him long, for he did not have to waste any time dealing with the facts. As for his readers, the East was just beginning to feel the full thrill of the West. In reaction to the long anxiety and tragic news of the Civil War, people craved fresh sensations daily. The Indian campaigns had been vividly reported in the newspapers. The transcontinental railroads and the telegraph had brought the frontier quite near. America wanted a new hero, and the country responded to what Don Russell called "the alliterative magic of the name Buffalo Bill."

As to his own career, Buntline summed it up in his typically disingenuous way: "I might have paved for myself a far different career in letters but my early lot was cast among rough men on the border; they became my comrades, and when I made my name as a teller of stories about Indians, pirates, and scouts, it seemed too late to begin over again. And besides, I made more money than any Bohemian in New York or Boston."

Cody was flattered and appreciative of Buntline's efforts to spread his fame. When his first and only son was born on November 26, 1870, Will planned to name him Elmo Judson Cody, in honor of Ned Buntline, but this the other scouts and the officers of the fort, especially Major Brown, objected to. Cody wisely gave in and named the boy after Kit Carson.

How well did Buntline's story do? Don Russell believes that it was probably more advertised than sold, for *Buffalo Bill, the King of Border Men* appeared only in a "story paper" and was not published in book form until 1881, under a new title: *Buffalo Bill and His Adventures in the West.* A two-column by eleven inch ad announcing the book appeared in the New York *Times* on November 16, 1869. There was apparently no demand for a sequel, and although Buntline wrote three other Buffalo Bill dime novels, they did not appear until the scout was at the height of his fame.

In the end, Ned Buntline's true contribution to Buffalo Bill's legend would come later, in 1872. Meanwhile, Cody's fame owed even more to General Sheridan than it did to Buntline, for it was Fighting Phil who introduced Will to the movers and shakers of New York society and European royalty. His life would never be the same again.

In 1870 Cody also met "Texas Jack" Omohundro. John Burwell Omohundro, a Virginian only five months younger than Cody, had served in the Confederate army during the war. His war record was distinguished. He served initially with former U.S. Secretary of War (later Major General)

John B. Floyd, C.S.A., as a mounted orderly. In February 1864 the young Omohundro joined Company G, Fifth Virginia Cavalry, which rode under Major General Fitzhugh Lee and Lieutenant General J. E. B. Stuart. In the Shenandoah Valley campaigns, Omohundro was both courier and scout. Afterward he drifted to Florida, taught school there for a while, and moved on to Texas where he did a little Indian fighting before coming up the trail to North Platte with three thousand longhorns in the summer of 1869. This was the first big herd of "commercial" cattle to reach the town. After the cattle were sold, the tall cowboy decided to stay on in North Platte, to tend bar for Lew Baker in one of the many saloons in the three-year-old village. Cody persuaded Texas Jack to quit his bartender's job and become a scout at Fort McPherson, where he was a popular square-dance caller at the post but was best known as a scout, trail agent for the Pawnee, and close friend of Buffalo Bill. Texas Jack was also a pal of Wild Bill Hickok. Two years later the three men would be reunited in a way they could never have foreseen.

Another close friendship that began that same year and was to last through the years was that of Cody and Dr. Frank Powell, also known as "White Beaver," contract surgeon at the post. Powell, a Kentuckian a year younger than Cody, obtained his medical education at the University of Louisville. He was a thirty-second-degree Mason who conferred the various degrees of the lodge on Buffalo Bill; he was also a newspaper reporter who supplied the Omaha papers with accounts of any worthwhile news from McPherson.

The Fifth Cavalry had only one major Indian fight in 1870—but it was one in which Buffalo Bill played an important part. Early on the morning of June 7, a band of rogue Indians raided four ranches near the mouth of Fremont Creek, on the North Platte. After scooping up horses from these ranches, they proceeded to the Fort McPherson herd, which was grazing above the post, and took more horses, including Cody's Powder Face.

"When the alarm was given, 'Boots and Saddles' was sounded," said Cody. "I always kept one of my best horses by me, and was ready for any surprise. The horse that I saddled that day was Buckskin Joe." Cody galloped for the herd, in time to see the Indians disappearing over a range of hills. He hurried back to the camp and told General Emory that he could pick up the trail.

The first troop ready for a pursuit was Company I, led by Second Lieutenant Earl D. Thomas. Thomas had graduated from West Point on September 30, 1869, and thus had missed out on the Fifth Cavalry's campaigns of that year, but he was no raw shavetail. Though inexperienced in

Indian warfare, he had served three years with the Army of the Potomac in the Civil War, rising from private to sergeant-major. Cody described him as "a little red-headed chap." Thomas's instructions from the general were to "follow Cody and be off quick." Emory added that more troops would follow as soon as they were saddled.

Starting at eight o'clock in the morning without rations, Thomas's troop pushed ahead at a gallop wherever possible. By dark they had covered sixty miles, when the lieutenant ordered his men to dismount and had them "stand to horse"—that is, be ready to remount instantly—until daylight. Cody felt confident that the Indians would camp at Red Willow Creek, four miles away. He scouted in that direction and discovered horses feeding along the creek.

"The Indians were encamped on a little knoll," Cody said, "around which was miry ground, making a cavalry charge difficult. The Indians numbered as many as we did. . . . We approached very cautiously till we got within a quarter of a mile of the Indians. Then the charge was sounded."

In a commendatory order written by General Carr, the district commander, it was said that "The whole Command rushed across the stream which owing to the miry swamps on each side was a difficult and hazardous undertaking, worthy of the highest commendation." The Indians fired a few shots and then fled, abandoning everything except the horses they rode. Cody tells of keeping a sharp lookout for Powder Face. Spotting his horse with two Indians riding him, he fired a shot at a range of thirty feet that passed through the backs of both braves. Both were wearing beautiful war bonnets, which Cody took and later presented to the daughters of General Augur. The troops rounded up thirty-three horses and mules, more than had been stolen.

When Cody urged Thomas to have his men saddle up and return to the fort, Thomas suggested instead that they ought to remain where they were, rest up, and wait for reinforcements. Will reminded him that his orders were to "follow Cody." The scout then led the troop back to McPherson by a different trail. "I knew a shorter route," Cody explained, "and besides, I didn't want to meet the support that was coming. I knew the officer in command, and was sure that if he came up he would take all the glory of the capture away from Lieutenant Thomas. Naturally I wanted all the credit for Thomas and myself as we were entitled to."

When the reinforcements arrived, their scout, Texas Jack Omohundro, reported that Cody had taken a different trail to the fort. "The major was hotter than a wounded coyote," said Cody. "He told the general that it was all my fault, and that he did not propose to be treated in any such manner by any scout, even if it were General Sheridan's pet, Buffalo Bill.

He was told by the general that the less he said about the matter the better it would be for him."

Cody could easily be accused of self-aggrandizement for his actions in this case, but he was aware that the senior officer in an episode of this kind would quite naturally take the credit for it, and he may have had some animus against that officer, who was later dismissed from the army. In any case, Cody did not need the glory, having already earned enough of it for two men.

Official reports show that Company I returned to the post on the day of the fight, June 8, arriving at 7:00 P.M. after a march of 120 miles in two days. Said Cody: "This being the first fight Lieutenant Thomas had ever commanded in, he felt highly elated over his success, and hoped that his name would be mentioned in the special orders for gallantry; sure enough when we returned both he, myself, and the whole command received a complimentary mention in a special order." In this order General Carr wrote: "Lieutenant Thomas especially commends scout Cody for the manner in which he followed the trail, particularly at night, during a storm of rain, and for gallant conduct in the fight."

Although this was Cody's only Indian fight of 1870, he was kept busy hunting buffalo and other game to supplement the rations provided by the army's Subsistence Department. Other duties included guiding hunting parties of VIPs who arrived at Fort McPherson and expected to find game, with their guides provided at government expense. It is probable that Cody supplemented his income in this fashion, while also building on his already imposing stature as a hunter and a celebrity in his own right.

As a boy in Leavenworth, Cody had marveled at the company and equipment of Sir St. George Gore, who had slaughtered 2,500 buffalo on one trip, disgusting Jim Bridger and bringing the disapproval of the federal government, who feared he was killing game that properly belonged to the Indian tribes. When the transcontinental railroad was completed in 1869, it stimulated the visits of foreign sportsmen. One hunter, Sir John Watts Garland, established permanent camps in 1869, where he left horses and dogs with caretakers. Thereafter, according to Don Russell, he came from England for hunts at about two-year intervals. He would pay as much as $1,000 for a trained buffalo horse. Cody guided Sir John in the winter of 1870–1871. "Sir John adapted the California saddle and the American frontier habit of drinking a cocktail before breakfast rather than brushing one's teeth," wrote Cody in an article for Cosmopolitan magazine in 1894.

Among the other notable British sportsmen was the Earl of Dunraven, who was Lord Adair when Cody first guided him in 1871. He was the author of several books, including Canadian Nights and Past Times and Pastimes, and was a foreign correspondent for the London Daily Telegraph.

Buffalo Bill with his wife, Louisa, and daughter Arta, 1870. (Buffalo Bill Historical Center, Cody, Wyoming)

It was General Sheridan who arranged Dunraven's first hunting trip. In Sheridan's office, Dunraven saw the head of an elk, or wapiti, which had been given to the general by the officers of Fort McPherson. Dunraven immediately wanted such a prize himself. Sheridan wrote to the fort's commander, in Dunraven's words, "requesting him to give me any assistance in his power, and if possible to let me have the valuable services of Mr. William Cody, otherwise known as Buffalo Bill, the government scout at the fort."

Dunraven was met at the railroad station by Buffalo Bill and Texas Jack Omohundro. "Bill was dressed in a pair of corduroys tucked into high boots," Dunraven wrote, "and a blue flannel shirt. He wore a broad-brimmed felt hat, or sombrero, and had a white handkerchief folded like a little shawl loosely fastened round his neck, to keep off the fierce rays of the afternoon sun. Jack's costume was similar, with the exception that he wore moccasins, and had his lower limbs encased in a pair of comfortably greasy deer-skin trousers, ornamented with a fringe along the seam. Round his waist was a belt supporting a revolver, two butcher knives, and in his hand he carried his trusty rifle, the "Widow."

"Jack, tall and lithe," continued Dunraven, "with light brown close-cropped hair, clear laughing honest blue eyes, and a soft and winning smile, might have sat as a model for a typical modern Anglo-Saxon—if ethnologists will excuse the term. Bill was dark, with quick searching eyes, aquiline nose, and delicately cut features, and he wore his hair falling in long ringlets over his shoulders, in true Western style."

Clearly, the earl was a first-rate reporter, with an excellent memory.

Dunraven accompanied a scouting party along the Platte River to Little Sandy Creek. On the second day he got his first elk, which was cut up for meat with axes. Cody describes an elk hunt this way: "Six or seven of us would start at sunrise on our prairie horses and get as close as possible to the elk, which would be feeding in the open, two or three hundred, perhaps, in a bunch. These long-legged beasts were swifter than the buffalo, and they would let us get within half a mile of them before they would give a mighty snort and dash away after their leader. Then came the test of speed and endurance. They led the horses a wild race, and it put our chargers to their mettle to overtake the game. Right in among them we would spur, and, dropping the reins, use the repeating rifle with both hands. The breech-loading Springfield piece of fifty-calibre, the same as used in the regular army, was our favorite rifle at that time."

In the summer of 1870, the army outfitted and escorted a different kind of hunter, Yale University's Othniel Charles Marsh, first professor of paleontology in the United States. With a party of students, Marsh came to the Great Plains to hunt fossils and old bones. Cody and Major Frank North, along with North's Pawnee, were to be the scouts for this expedition. The previous year the Pawnee had unearthed some immense fossil bones, and Professor Marsh was eager to find the same kind.

The day before Marsh's arrival, Cody had been out hunting on the north side of the North Platte River, near Pawnee Springs, with several companions, when they were suddenly attacked by Indians, who wounded one of their number, John Weister. "We stood the Indians off for a little while," said Cody, "and Weister got even with them by killing one of their party. The Indians, however, outnumbered us, and at last we were forced to make a run for our lives. In this we succeeded, and reached the fort in safety." General Emory wanted to have the Indians pursued and said he could not spare Cody to accompany Professor Marsh. Cody did ride out with Marsh for a few miles on the first day, however, and their conversation on the ride was the beginning of a long friendship. In later years, whenever his Wild West was in New Haven, Cody visited Marsh at Yale.

"He gave me a geological history of the country," Cody wrote of Marsh's visit, "told me in what section fossils were to be found; and otherwise entertained me with several scientific yarns, some of which seemed too complicated and too mysterious to be believed by an ordinary man like myself; but it was all clear to him."

That same summer another hunt was arranged for four special guests: his sisters May and Helen and General Augur's two daughters. Twenty-nine years later, in her book *Last of the Great Scouts*, Helen Cody Wetmore told the story of the hunt. "A gay party it was," she wrote. "For men, there were a number of officers . . . and Dr. Frank Powell . . . for women, the wives of two of the officers, the daughters of General Augur, May, and myself." Buffalo Bill was away from the post at the time and was unaware of the outing that had been planned.

After twenty miles on horseback, the party sighted a herd of buffalo. Dr. Powell proposed that the ladies do the shooting, and a gun was put into May's hands. After being given "explicit directions as to its handling," she fired, wounding the buffalo, which promptly dropped its shaggy head and charged. The officers then fired into "the mountain of flesh," but this only enraged the buffalo more. May was handed another rifle, which she discharged at random.

At this point in her narrative Helen left the hunting party with the vicious buffalo still charging at them and returned to the post, where her brother, Will, had just returned from a scouting trip. When he learned about the family junket, he was furious; the women should never have left the post, for there was always the danger of capture by Indians. He rode off to find the party, just in time to fire at the charging buffalo and bring it down.

In the Omaha papers the next day, an account by Dr. Powell gave the credit for the kill to May Cody. Were it not for the presence of Frank Powell and his newspaper account, it would be hard to believe that this incident took place at all.

In the fall of 1870 Cody was a witness in a court-martial at Fort D.A. Russell, Wyoming. "I woke up one morning," he said, "and found that I was dead broke. . . . to raise necessary funds I sold my race horse Tall Bull to Lieutenant [actually Captain Julius W.] Mason, who had long wanted him." Cody had promised Lulu to buy furniture, but lost the money at roulette. When he reached home, he told his wife that he was dissatisfied with the furniture he had seen in Wyoming and would order it elsewhere; Lulu was mollified.

On November 13, 1870, Cody visited Omaha, Nebraska, and the *Daily Herald* of that city wrote:

> Buffalo Bill is in town. Our readers are no doubt familiar with some of the exploits of this famous scout and guide. One of our reporters interviewed the gentleman yesterday and found him a modest, quiet man. His real name is William Cody. He was born in Davenport, Ia., and is 34. [He was 24.] He has been on the plains 27 years and for the last seven has been an army scout. He is a strongly built man, 6 feet 1 inch, and rather good looking. . . . Although Buffalo Bill is able to "hoe his own row" on the plains, he feels rather strange in a city, and consequently has engaged a guide to "take him around" while he remains in Omaha.

The Fifth Cavalry had only one Indian fight in 1871: on May 24 at Birdwood Creek, Nebraska. Lieutenant Hayes, the Fifth's quartermaster, led thirty men in surprising and capturing six renegade Sioux with sixty horses and mules. Cody was the scout on the foray and was mentioned for "conspicuous and gallant conduct in the fight," though he said nothing of the episode in his writings. He would not take part in another Fifth Cavalry fight until 1876.

Meanwhile, the hunting continued. Among the hunters was a Mr. McCarthy from Syracuse, a relative of General Emory, and two Englishmen. Cody led McCarthy into a fake ambush, concocted by Frank North's Pawnee scouts. McCarthy was so terrified that he dropped his hat and gun and could not be stopped until he had ridden back into camp. Cody's practical jokes sometimes could be quite crude.

The 1871 expedition that most enhanced Buffalo Bill's growing reputation in the East was the one the newspapers called General Sheridan's party of buffalo hunters or, facetiously, "New Yorkers on the Warpath." The party included James Gordon Bennett, editor of the New York *Herald;* Charles L. Wilson, editor of the Chicago *Evening Journal;* and General Henry Eugene Davies, who wrote a pamphlet, *Ten Days on the Plains,* describing the hunt. Among the others rounding out the group were Leonard W. and Lawrence R. Jerome; General Anson Stager of the Western Union Telegraph Company; Colonel M. V. Sheridan, the general's brother; General Charles Fitzhugh; and Colonel Daniel H. Rucker, acting quartermaster general and soon to be Phil Sheridan's father-in-law. Leonard W. Jerome, a financier, later became the grandfather of Winston Churchill when his second daughter, Jenny, married Lord Randolph Churchill.

The party arrived at Fort McPherson on September 22, 1871. The New York *Herald*'s first dispatch reported: "General Sheridan and party arrived at the North Platte River this morning, and were conducted to Fort McPherson by General Emery [*sic*], commanding. General Sheridan reviewed the troops, consisting of four companies of the Fifth Cavalry. The party start[s] across the country tomorrow, guided by the renowned Buffalo Bill and under the escort of Major Brown, Company F, Fifth Cavalry. The party expect[s] to reach Fort Hays in ten days."

After Sheridan's review of the troops, the general introduced Buffalo Bill to the guests and assigned them to their quarters in large, comfortable tents just outside the post, a site christened Camp Rucker. The remainder of the day was spent entertaining the visitors at "dinner and supper parties, and music and dancing; at a late hour they retired to rest in their tents." The officers of the post and their ladies spared no expense in their effort to entertain their guests, to demonstrate, perhaps, that the West was not all that wild. The finest linens, glassware, and china the post afforded were brought out to grace the tables, and the ballroom glittered that night with gold braid, silks, velvets, and jewels.

Buffalo Bill dressed for the hunt as he had never done before. Despite having retired late, "at five o'clock next morning . . . I rose fresh and eager for the trip, and as it was a nobby and high-toned outfit which I was to accompany, I determined to put on a little style myself. So I dressed in a new suit of buckskin, trimmed along the seams with fringes of the same material; and I put on a crimson shirt handsomely ornamented on the bosom, while on my head I wore a broad sombrero. Then mounting a snowy white horse—a gallant stepper, I rode down from the fort to the camp, rifle in hand. I felt first-rate that morning, and looked well."

In all probability, Louisa Cody was responsible for the ornamentation on his shirt, for she was an expert with a needle. General Davies agreed with Will's estimation of his appearance that morning. "The most striking feature of the whole was . . . our friend Buffalo Bill. . . . He realized to perfection the bold hunter and gallant sportsman of the plains."

Here again Cody appeared as the showman emergent. The sombrero, already remarked on by the Earl of Dunraven, was the forerunner of the ten-gallon cowboy hat that Cody is credited with popularizing in his Wild West show days.

In his pamphlet, General Davies also reported: "At the camp we were introduced to the far-famed Buffalo Bill, whose name has lately been used to 'point a moral and adorn a tale' in the New York *Ledger,* and whose life and adventures have furnished the material for the brilliant drama that under his name has drawn crowded and delighted audiences at one of our metropolitan theatres. . . . William Cody, Esquire, which title he holds of right, being in the county in which his home is a justice of the peace, was a mild, agreeable, well-mannered man, quiet and retiring in disposition though well informed and always ready to talk well and earnestly on any subject of interest, the reverse of the person we had expected to meet.

"Tall and somewhat slight in figure," continued Davies, "though possessed of great strength and iron endurance; straight and erect as an arrow, and with strikingly handsome features, he at once attracted to him all with whom he became acquainted and the better knowledge gained of him during the days he spent with our party increased the good impression he made upon his introduction."

The expedition itself was as elaborately turned out as Buffalo Bill. It consisted of a train of sixteen wagons for baggage, supplies, and forage, including one wagon solely for ice; three four-horse ambulances in which members of the party who were weary might rest; and a light wagon drawn by a pair of Indian ponies belonging to quartermaster Lieutenant Hayes, in which General Sheridan occasionally liked to ride. Five greyhounds were brought along to course antelopes and rabbits. Among the supplies were linen, china, and glassware for the multicourse dinners prepared by French chefs and served by waiters in evening dress. It was recorded by Cody that "for years afterward travelers and settlers recognized the sites upon which these camps had been constructed by the quantities of empty bottles which remained behind to mark them."

Hunting in the Gilded Age clearly did not mean that you had to rough it. Sheridan's party brought all their creature comforts along—and left some of them behind to litter the plains.

This imposing cavalcade made seventeen miles the first day and went into camp on Fox Creek, a tributary of the Republican River. General Davies records that "a good deal of time and some trouble were required to pass our teams over to the south of the stream on which our camp for the night was to be established, as a bridge had to be built for the wagons to cross on, and it was necessary to double all the teams to pull up the steep hill that formed the northern bank. At this work our friend Buffalo Bill proved as skillful as he was in killing buffalo, and by his science in bridge building and success as teamster, acquired new titles to our confidence and respect."

The much-publicized hunt lasted ten days, moving on down a ladder of rivers by way of Medicine Creek and the Republican River in Nebraska, across Beaver and Prairie Dog creeks to the Solomon and Saline rivers in Kansas, arriving at Fort Hays on October 2, nearly two hundred miles from its starting point.

Along the way, the party hunted. And hunted. And hunted yet again. General Fitzhugh was awarded a silver drinking set as a trophy for downing the first buffalo. Lawrence Jerome was allowed to ride Cody's favorite buffalo-hunting mount, Buckskin Joe, described by Davies as "a dismal-looking, dun-colored brute . . . but like a singed cat, much better than he looked. He was a wonderful beast for hunting, as his subsequent conduct proved, and on his back Jerome did wonders for one brief day among the buffalo." On the following day, however, Jerome made the mistake of dismounting to make a steady shot with his rifle, and he carelessly let go of the bridle. Buckskin Joe, trained to chase buffalo, promptly took off, stranding Jerome, who had to be given another mount. Joe meanwhile made his own way back to Fort McPherson.

That night, at Camp Cody—named, says General Davies, "after our guide, philosopher, and friend"—Lawrence Jerome was tried by a kangaroo court for "aiding and abetting in the loss of a government horse." In his defense Jerome contended that the horse had lost him. Cody was appointed chief justice and delivered a verdict of "suspended judgment."

During the course of the hunt, the party killed more than six hundred buffalo and two hundred elk, along with unnumbered quantities of rabbit, prairie dog, and wild turkey. The company bagged so much game, in fact, that the Salt Lake *Tribune,* looking ahead to rumors of a much more grandiose hunt soon to take place, commented: "Enough game will be left, we hope, for the Grand Duke Alexis when he takes a scurry over the hunting grounds."

In his first autobiography, Cody quoted liberally from General Davies's pamphlet without using quotation marks, but he never included anything complimentary Davies said about him; again, if he were the braggart some called him, he would surely have done so. He included a menu of one of the party's dinners; the Bill of Fare began with Buffalo Tail Soup, and included Salmi of Prairie Dog, Stewed Rabbit, Fillet of Buffalo aux Champignons, Elk, Antelope Chops, Buffalo-Calf Steaks, Young Wild Turkey, Black-tailed Deer, Teal, and Mallard. The beverages consisted of Champagne Frappe, Champagne au Naturel, Claret, Whiskey, Brandy, and Bass Ale. Delmonico's or Tony Pastor's of New York City could not have provided a more sumptuous repast—a dinner that surely would have delighted a gourmand like Diamond Jim Brady.

With such splendid cooks and plenty of wine, the New Yorkers had a wonderful time on the hunt and marveled at Buffalo Bill's competence and self-assurance. Each day out he somehow led them to game, always bringing them to a pretty, tree-bordered stream at camping time. At Fort Hays, as General Sheridan and his guests prepared to board the train that would take them home, Bennett and his fellow New Yorkers urged Buffalo Bill to come visit them in their stomping grounds at the first opportunity. General Sheridan agreed to give Cody leave, but not until after the visit of Grand Duke Alexis of Russia, for he was appointing Cody as guide for that royal extravaganza, the most famous western buffalo hunt of all time.

With James Gordon Bennett on the hunt, Buffalo Bill was bound to get publicity in the New York *Herald,* and he probably would have received the same attention in Chicago, were it not for the Great Chicago Fire, which broke out only days after the Chicago contingent arrived home. As a consequence, the pages of Charles Wilson's *Evening Journal* were devoted to reports on the devastation caused by the fire, and General Sheridan was faced with the problems of administering a city under martial law.

Still, with the invitation to visit New York in hand and the coveted assignment to guide a royal hunt to come, Cody was riding high—his reputation as a scout and hunter solidly established both on the plains and nationally.

When Cody returned to Fort McPherson, he learned that Mr. Royal Buck's father and his party had been killed on Beaver Creek by Indians led by Pawnee Killer. "Two companies of cavalry were sent," said Cody, "and I accompanied them as a guide." The troops had little success, finding no hostiles, but they did discover "some of the remains, which we buried; but nothing further. It was now getting late in the fall and we accordingly returned to Fort McPherson." The Fifth Cavalry was soon ordered to Arizona. Cody wanted to go with the friends he had made in the preceding three years, and the Fifth Cavalry wanted to retain him, despite his lack of knowledge of the terrain or Apache ways of warfare, but a letter was received from General Sheridan instructing the commanding officer "not to take Cody." Sheridan wanted to ensure the services of the country's most famous hunting guide, Buffalo Bill, for the January hunt of Grand Duke Alexis. "During the next few weeks I had but little to do," Cody recalled.

Grand Duke Alexis, fourth son of Alexander II, the Czar of All the Russias, was a handsome young man of twenty-one, six foot two inches tall, with luxuriant side whiskers and a good command of English. His father decided in 1871 to send him on a goodwill tour, perhaps also to get him away from an inappropriate romantic attachment. Alexis was an avid sportsman, and the U.S. Government wanted to show him every courtesy and consideration. Relations between Russia and the United States were good, especially because five years before Russia had sold Alaska to the United States at a bargain price, a transaction then known as Seward's Folly, after the American secretary of state. Although his homeland, ruled by the Romanoffs, had little in common with democratic America, when Alexis did arrive, the country rolled out the red carpet and showed him the time of his life. In the late nineteenth century, royal visits were rarer than they became after the turn of the century.

A Russian frigate brought Alexis to New York late in November 1871. Within a few days he and his entourage visited Washington, D.C., where President Grant, according to the New York *Times* for November 24, did little more than shake the duke's hand at an afternoon stand-up reception. The chief executive, reportedly irritated by the inept, interfering Russian minister to America, Constantine Catacazy, was not about to extend himself for Muscovite royalty, the acquisition of Alaska notwithstanding. Ulysses S. Grant was a singular exception to Alexis's "red carpet" reception in the United States.

Early in December Alexis began a lengthy stay in Boston, where the hospitality he received was much warmer than in the nation's capital. From Boston he traveled to Montreal, Ottawa, Toronto, and Niagara; then to Buffalo for Christmas. Cleveland and Detroit were next on his schedule. On New Year's Day the royal party was in Chicago, visiting the stockyards and shooting pigeons. The duke's choice of winter as his time to visit the American West seems odd, except that it was probably warmer there than in his homeland.

At this point Sheridan comes into the picture. The following dispatch from Chicago, dated January 4, appeared in the Lincoln (Nebraska) *Daily State Journal*:

> The Grand Duke Alexis returns here [Chicago] from Milwaukee this afternoon and leaves tomorrow for St. Louis. Gen. Sheridan has completed plans for a buffalo hunt. The parties will leave the railroad at Fort McPherson and expect to be on the hunt six or eight days. No servants, carriages, or luxuries will be indulged in, the design being to rough it.

Although roughing it may have been the plan, and despite Commander in Chief Grant's lack of interest in Russians, the affair turned out to be as lavish a one as the military could provide at the time.

Sheridan was aboard the duke's special train when it left St. Louis on January 11, bound for Omaha, where the party was joined by other army brass, including the boy wonder of the Union army, George Armstrong Custer, now thirty-two, with shoulder-length hair and a scraggly mustache. Custer had brought along his best suit of fringed buckskins for the occasion.

Even before the duke's train departed St. Louis, preparations were under way at Fort McPherson. Early in January General George Forsyth and Dr. Morris Asch of Sheridan's staff arrived at the fort. For the camp-grounds, Cody suggested Red Willow Creek, forty miles south of the fort, and guided the two officers, along with Lieutenant Hayes, Fifth Cavalry quartermaster, who had also been retained for the hunt, to the chosen site. There they established Camp Alexis, not far from the present location of Hayes Center.

The staff officers asked Cody to find the Sioux chief Spotted Tail, whose warriors were then at peace with the United States, and persuade him to bring one hundred Indians to a camp nearby for the entertainment of the royal visitor. This was not a simple errand for Cody; there was the possibility that he would run into one of Spotted Tail's militant young braves who would want to kill him for his gun and horse, not to mention his scalp. Cody managed to locate the Indian camp, and said he slipped in covered with a blanket, so he might be taken for a redman rather than a white. In the chief's lodge, he was made welcome by Spotted Tail. Todd Randall, agent and interpreter, explained the request to the chief, who readily agreed to put on a buffalo hunt and a war dance "in ten sleeps . . . for the great chief from across the water."

The duke's special chugged onto a siding at North Platte on the night of January 12. Next morning the eager hunters, including actor Lawrence Barrett, breakfasted in their dining car. The *Daily State Journal* report continues from there, with a dispatch datelined North Platte, January 13:

> Five ambulances and a light wagon for baggage and a carriage for the duke met the party, and they immediately started for camp. The camp consists of two hospital tents, ten wall tents, and "A" tents for the servants and soldiers. Three of the wall tents are floored, and the duke's is carpeted. Box stoves and Sibley stoves are provided for the hospital and wall tents. The hospital tents are used as dining tents. An extensive culinary outfit also is taken along. Ten thousand rations of flour, sugar and coffee and 1,000 pounds of tobacco are being taken along for the Indians. . . . A few days ago 400 Indians were reported at the camp, with their families, and others coming in rapidly.

The ambulances, of course, were for transportation, not medical emergencies, and the Sibley stove mentioned was a popular army tent heating device about the size of a water bucket. "Roughing it," Russian style, was not half bad.

In the welcoming party at the station was a splendid array of brass and gold braid, along with fifteen or twenty extra saddle horses, two companies of cavalry, two of infantry, and the regimental band of the Second Cavalry. Cody conservatively estimated the entire party at five hundred people. Most of North Platte also turned out to see the train come in.

According to an unidentified newspaper dispatch from North Platte, as the royal party left the train General Sheridan singled out the tall figure of Buffalo Bill and presented him to the duke in this manner: "Your highness, this is Mr. Cody, otherwise and universally known as Buffalo Bill. Bill, this is the Grand Duke." "I am glad to know you," said the hero of the plains.

Cody described Alexis as "a large, fine-looking young man," and newspaper reporters present found the prince "a fine democratic fellow" and "a live one," and "a jovial lively body." In his belt the duke carried a Russian hunting knife and a .44-caliber Smith and Wesson revolver, inlaid with gold and pearl with the seals of the United States and Russia engraved on it. The gun was a gift from the manufacturer.

A Cincinnati reporter wrote: "Buffalo Bill is a famous Western scout, employed by Sheridan for Indian service, and one who is efficient and reliable. Bill is about 30 years of age [he was twenty-five], is over six feet in height. . . . Bill was dressed in a buckskin coat, trimmed with fur, and wore a black slouch hat, his long hair hanging in ringlets over his shoulders."

According to the Omaha *Herald* reporter, the party moved immediately to the camp at Red Willow, preceded by the Second Cavalry band, which played "Hail to the Chief." Spotted Tail and 265 lodges, or nearly one thousand of his people, were waiting. That night the Indians put on the war dance Will had arranged, to the admiration of the visitors. Cody says that Alexis paid much attention to a handsome redskin maiden and that Custer carried on a mild flirtation with one of Spotted Tail's daughters.

Buffalo Bill's skills as a raconteur were also noted. A New York *Herald* headline referred to "Buffalo Bill as Guide, Tutor, and Entertaining Agent."

The grand duke questioned Cody closely about buffalo-hunting methods. Was a rifle or a pistol used, and was a trained horse necessary? Cody assured the duke that he would be riding Buckskin Joe, his personal buffalo-hunting mount, and that he could use either weapon.

The first hunt started at nine o'clock in the morning, and the hunters rode seventeen miles before finding any game; then, reported the *Daily State Journal*, "they came upon a fine herd upon a splendid hunting ground." The same reporter mentioned the "fine weather" the group was having. Sheridan's authority apparently extended to the elements, for one week later western Nebraska was hit by a howling blizzard.

Sheridan wasn't feeling well, so Cody, Custer, and the grand duke led the way, through snow that was eighteen inches deep in places. Spotted Tail and eight of his warriors came along. A newspaperman reported that

Custer wore "his well-known frontier buckskin hunting costume, and if, instead of the comical seal-skin hat he wore, he had feathers fastened in his flowing hair, he would have passed at a distance for a great Indian chief."

Every effort was made to ensure that the grand duke would have the first shot. It wasn't easy. He had decided to use his pistol and, according to Cody, "he fired six shots from this weapon at buffaloes only twenty feet away from him, but as he shot wildly, not one of his shots took effect. Riding up to his side and seeing that his weapon was empty, I exchanged pistols with him. He again fired six shots without dropping a buffalo. Seeing that the animals were bound to make their escape without his killing one of them, unless he had a better weapon, I rode up to him, gave him my old reliable 'Lucretia' and told him to urge his horse close to the buffaloes, and I would give him the word when to shoot. At the same time I gave old Buckskin Joe a blow with my whip, and with a few jumps, the horse carried the Grand Duke to within about ten feet of a big buffalo bull.

"'Now is your time.' said I. He fired and down went the buffalo. The Grand Duke stopped his horse, dropped his gun on the ground and commenced waving his hat. Very soon the corks began to fly from the champagne bottles, in honor of the Grand Duke Alexis, who had killed his first buffalo."

Some newspapers reported that Cody actually killed the buffalo for Alexis, "while in some," said Cody, "it was stated that I held the buffalo while His Royal Highness killed it. But the way I have related the affair is the correct version."

"The hunt was continued for some two hours," reported the *Journal*, "and resulted in the killing of between 20 and 30 buffaloes. Generals Custer and Forsyth were both distinguished in the chase. The duke was in splendid spirits and expressed his great delight at the sport."

Sheridan finally called an end to the first day's hunt, and Cody was guiding the company back to their camp when several of them broke off and began riding wildly over the plains in search of buffalo. Alexis bagged his second shaggy when a small herd, startled by the wayward hunters, rode by. The duke raised his pistol and fired; a cow fell. "It was either an extraordinarily good shot or it was a 'scratch,'" says Will, "probably the latter, for it surprised the Grand Duke as well as everybody else." Once again the champagne was brought out, and Cody "was in hopes that he [the duke] would kill five or six more buffaloes before we reached camp, especially if a basket of champagne was to be opened every time he dropped one."

According to Cody, the grand duke killed eight buffalo altogether during the hunt.

On the last day of the hunt, Spotted Tail and his eight Indians were given a chance to show what they could do. They performed magnificently, driving a herd of buffalo into a canyon with high hills on either side, forming a splendid arena. A newspaper reporter described what followed: "Spotted Tail and his chosen Sioux, with a wild whoop, charged into the midst of the fleeing herd, and with unerring aim let fly the feathered arrows from their bows. . . . It was difficult to decide which to admire the more, the skill of the Indian in managing his horse, or the rapidity and accuracy with which he let fly his feathered darts into the side of the doomed buffalo."

Alexis saw Two Lance, celebrated for this exploit, shoot an arrow entirely through a buffalo; the duke later retrieved the arrow as a souvenir. Another Indian, with a lance ten feet long, its steel head a foot long and the shaft possibly three inches in diameter, was seen by Cody "singling out a gigantic bison and thrusting his spearhead, while both raced at full speed, straight into the creature's heart. . . . Considerable skill was necessary to apply the momentum of the horse in just the right way to send the stroke home, it being necessary for the hunter instantly to let go the lance or be pulled from his steed."

On the second day of the hunt, which happened to be the grand duke's twenty-second birthday, Custer and Alexis became close companions. Custer regaled the duke with stories about how it had been in the old days on the plains, before the coming of the railroad. Alexis was disappointed at not seeing any of the enormous herds he had heard so much about. Custer explained that the grand duke got there just in time; in another few years there would be no more buffalo left on the central plains. Hides were being sent east from Fort Riley and other points at the rate of forty thousand per shipment. If the ground had been bare instead of covered with snow, Alexis would have seen for himself—the plains were covered with buffalo bones. Indeed, a minor but flourishing industry was springing up; settlers in need of cash would gather wagonloads of bones and take them to the railroad station, where they were shipped east by the tons to be ground up for fertilizer.

Cody had one more bravura performance in store for the royal party. On the return trip, as Cody told it, the grand duke and Sheridan rode in "a heavy, double-seated open carriage . . . drawn by six cavalry horses which were not much used to the harness. The driver was Bill Reed, an old overland stage driver. . . . The Grand Duke frequently expressed his admiration of the skillful manner in which Reed handled the reins. General Sheridan informed the Duke that I also had been a stage driver in the Rocky Mountains, and thereupon His Royal Highness expressed a desire to see me drive. I was in advance at the time, and

General Sheridan sang out to me, 'Cody, get in here and show the Duke how you can drive.'"

Cody and Reed changed places and "in a few moments I had the reins and we were rattling away over the prairie. When we were approaching Medicine Creek, General Sheridan said, 'Shake 'em up a little Bill, and give us some old-time stage driving.'"

Cody shook 'em up all right, and soon they were flying over the ground. "At last we reached a steep hill, or divide, which led down into the valley of the Medicine. There was no brake on the wagon, and the horses were not much on the hold back. I saw that it would be impossible to stop them. All I could do was to keep them straight in the track and let them go it down the hill, for three miles which . . . I believe was made in about six minutes. Every once in a while the hind wheels would strike a rut and take a bound, and not touch the ground again for fifteen or twenty feet. The General and the Duke were kept rather busy in holding their positions on the seats, and when they saw I was keeping the horses straight in the road, they seemed to enjoy the dash. . . . I was unable to stop the team until they ran into the camp where we were to obtain a fresh relay."

Cody concluded his version of the hunt with this statement: "On arriving at the railroad the Duke invited me into his car, and made me some valuable presents, at the same time giving me a cordial invitation to visit him, if ever I should come to his country. At the same time, General Sheridan took occasion to remind me of [the] invitation to visit New York which I had received . . . in September. . . . Said he, 'You will never have a better opportunity to accept that invitation than now. I have had a talk with General Ord concerning you, and he will give you a leave of absence whenever you are ready to start.'"

Elsewhere Buffalo Bill told how, upon arriving at North Platte, "the Grand Duke invited me into his car, and there, over a few bottles of champagne, we went over all the details of the hunt. . . . As I was leaving the car one of his suite approached me, and, extending a big roll of green-backs, begged me to accept it." Cody refused the money but did accept the magnificent overcoat, made of many fine Russian furs, which the duke had worn on the hunt. Cody's story also had Alexis telegraphing "the most famous of New York jewelers, to order a set of cufflinks and a scarf pin, studded with diamonds and rubies, each piece in the form of a buffalo head as large as a silver half-dollar." In another account, Cody received a purse of gold and a diamond stickpin. The fur coat, cuff links, and studs are the more likely presents, since the family still has the cuff links.

The most important gift to Cody from this hunt was the publicity he received. The account of the first day's hunt in the Kansas City *Times* read:

AT IT

Alexis on the Untamed Bison's

Native Heath

He is introduced to Buffalo Bill And

Follows His Lead

Another said "General Sheridan and 'Buffalo Bill' Lead the Way."

Louisa told Courtney Ryley Cooper that all that winter Will had been growing famous, due to the Buntline tales. "Every week, some new thrilling story, in which Buffalo Bill rescued maidens in distress, killed off Indians by the score and hunted buffalo in his sleep, appeared in the romantic magazines."

After Alexis left North Platte, he went by rail to Denver, accompanied by Generals Sheridan and Custer and other staff members. In Colorado he was met and escorted by the governor and former governor and other territorial officials; on the evening of January 18, 1872, the Pioneer Club of Colorado hosted a grand ball for the distinguished visitor.

The Coloradans had heard of the Nebraska buffalo hunt, and local pride demanded a reprise in their state. At the town of Kit Carson, Colorado, the duke's train pulled to a stop and discharged its passengers for Colorado's version of buffalo hunting. Overly enthusiastic reporters announced that "the exciting hunt on the Nebraska Plains in the early part of the week dwindles into insignificance compared with the chases, uncertainties and final triumphs of this last campaign." Even the buffalo in Colorado were considered better. "Unlike the sluggard animals of the Nebraska Plains, these were disposed to make a desperate effort for escape." Still, the duke only "brought down five buffaloes altogether, and retained the tail of each as trophies of the day's sport."

Even Buffalo Bill, though not present, got into the press coverage. The newspaper reported an exciting confrontation during the Colorado hunt when a buffalo turned upon Alexis and charged with great ferocity. "The Grand Duke and his experienced horse were equal to the emergency," the report concluded, "and although they dodged the infuriated animal every time, the escapes were sufficiently narrow for even a Buffalo Bill to boast of."

At any rate, Alexis had killed eight buffalo in Nebraska and five in Colorado—a respectable tally. And the following day, as the train jogged along . . . "leisurely" across Kansas, he, General Sheridan, General Custer, and other passengers fired, unsportsmanlike, from the car windows at buffalo herds along the track; "the Duke probably brought down no less than half a dozen of the animals."

Custer's wife, Libbie, joined the party at Louisville, Kentucky, where there was a long series of grand balls. Libbie danced with his imperial highness and was the center of attention throughout the night. The duke liked Custer and his wife and invited them to accompany him to New Orleans, by way of Louisville, Kentucky, and Mammoth Cave, which the duke wanted to visit. In her diary, Libbie recorded: "The Admiral [Custer] is all sunshine and sweet simplicity. He strives to interest Alexis in the towns we pass, length of rivers, and the like. But in boat or on the train Alexis is not concerned with the outside, only with the pretty girls, with music—he sings magnificently, and has already learned Lydia Thompson's Music Hall ditty—which he renders 'If efer I cease to lufe . . . '—in his eternal cigarette, and in joking with his suite and with the General [Custer]." In New Orleans, the grand duke honored the couple with a suite adjoining his own. But all too soon, the Russian fleet arrived in Pensacola, Florida, where the duke had traveled from Louisiana, and on February 22, 1872, Alexis was on his way home.

Sheridan was so pleased with Cody's starring role in the royal entertainment that he offered the scout a commission. Louisa, with her strong desire for social status, probably would have wanted him to accept it; however, either mindful of his lack of formal education, or because he was already making about as much as a second lieutenant anyway, Cody declined the offer. "All I looked forward to was the life of the Plains," said Cody. "It was enough for me to be in the saddle, trusting each day to find some new adventure. Army life would mean a great deal of routine, and routine was something I could not endure."

Now he was free to travel east. General Ord gave him a thirty-day leave, to begin whenever he wished. General Stager sent Cody railroad passes—and James Gordon Bennett sent him $500 for expenses. His days as a scout were far from over—but a brilliant new chapter of his life was about to open.

MORE FAME—
AND THE MEDAL OF HONOR

February of 1872 was the perfect time for Buffalo Bill to take advantage of his invitation to visit the East. There were only two companies of cavalry at Fort McPherson, making it unlikely there would be any Indian expeditions until the arrival of the Third Cavalry, which was exchanging posts with the Fifth. Cody was given a month's leave of absence with pay.

His wife, Louisa, being pregnant ("a beautiful little reason why I could not accompany him" is how she expressed it), he would travel alone. Wanting to make sure that he was properly dressed when he mixed in eastern society, Lulu set to work. "We procured some blue cloth at the commissary and, sewing day and night, I made Will his first soldier suit, with a Colonel's gold braid on it, with stripes and cords and all the other gingerbread of an old-fashioned suit of 'blues.'"

Cody's first stop was in Chicago, where he was met at the depot by Colonel M. V. Sheridan, the general's brother, who told him that he would be a guest at their house. "I spent two or three days very pleasantly," he said. General Sheridan provided him with a dress suit at Marshall Fields, and his buffalo-hunting friends took him to a ball in Riverside, a Chicago suburb. "On this occasion I became so embarrassed that it was more difficult for me to face the throng of beautiful ladies than it would have been to confront a hundred hostile Indians. This was my first trip to the East, and I had not yet become accustomed to being stared at." His embarrassment would soon wear off.

On the train to New York he ran into Professor Henry A. Ward of Rochester, whom he had first met while Ward was collecting fossils in Nebraska. Ward showed him Niagara Falls, and he also got his first look at Rochester, which was to be his family's home some years later. In New York Cody was met at the station by J. G. Hecksher and Schuyler Crosy, who took him to the Union Club on fashionable Fifth Avenue at Twentieth Street, where he was greeted by James Gordon Bennett of the *Herald,* Leonard Jerome, and other buffalo-hunters, who gave him a dinner and informal reception. The New Yorkers disapproved of his Chicago wardrobe, insisting he go to Hecksher's New York tailor for a fitting. The plan was for him to make their club his headquarters while he was in New York.

After dinner Cody, with Hecksher as his guide, set off in search of Ned Buntline. They found the dime novelist at the Brevoort Place Hotel, where he was staying with his fourth wife; his third had yet to divorce him. Buntline was pleased to see Cody and insisted that the scout stay at the Brevoort with him; Overton and Blair, the proprietors, offered him a room. Will decided to divide his time among the Union Club, the Brevoort, and Buntline's quarters.

The Union Club crowd did not approve of Buntline or his many marriages, which resulted in a faux pas on Cody's part. James Gordon Bennett gave a dinner party in his honor one night, and, apparently distracted by Buntline, he forgot to attend. Bennett forgave him this oversight, however, and he did manage to attend another dinner given by August Belmont. Bennett also took him to the Liederkranz masked ball, where, dressed in his buckskin suit, he "exhibited some of my backwoods steps, which, although not as graceful as some, were a great deal more emphatic." Cody reported that he also spent some evenings at Niblo's Garden, where *The Black Crook* was playing, and he saw Edwin Booth, the greatest Shakespearian actor of the time, at the Booth Theater in Shakespeare's *Julius Caesar*. The actor Lawrence Barrett, a good friend of General Custer and whom Cody knew from the hunt with Grand Duke Alexis, played Cassius.

The most memorable of his New York experiences was provided by Ned Buntline. Buntline and Fred Maeder had dramatized Buntline's first Buffalo Bill novel and, as *Buffalo Bill, the King of Border Men*, the melodrama was being revived at the Bowery Theater. On opening night, Cody occupied a private box, and saw the actor J. B. Studley as "Buffalo Bill," with Mrs. W. G. Jones as his sister. Studley was a popular and versatile actor whose recent hits had been *A Dream of Destiny, Money and Misery, The Irish Outlaw*, and other melodramas, in which he appeared almost continuously at Niblo's, the Bowery Theater, Hooley's, and the Olympic in Brooklyn.

The drama critic of the New York *Herald* described the drama on its opening night this way: "J.B. Studley played his part to perfection. The laudable desire he exhibits to avenge the murder of his paternal ancestor and the coolness he displays when encompassed by dangers and difficulties is superb . . . the highest pitch of excitement was reached in the third act when Jack McKandless, a noted border ruffian, meets Buffalo Bill and a terrific hand-to-hand conflict with Bowie knives three feet long ensues. The audience were spellbound, breathless, during this fierce encounter; but when it was brought to a conclusion by the death of the villain and the victory of Buffalo Bill, the burst of enthusiasm that followed would have rivaled the roar of Niagara."

When the audience learned that the celebrated scout was among them, a cheer went up, and Cody was asked by Freleigh, the theater manager, to stand on the stage and say a few words. "I finally consented," he said, "and the next moment I found myself standing behind the footlights and in front of an audience for the first time in my life. . . . I confess that I felt very much embarrassed—never more so in my life—and I knew not what to say. I made a desperate effort, and a few words escaped me, but what they were I could not for the life of me tell, nor could anyone else in the house. My utterances were inaudible even to the leader of the orchestra, Mr. Dean, who was sitting only a few feet in front of me. Bowing to the audience, I beat a hasty retreat. . . . That evening Mr. Freleigh offered to give me five hundred dollars a week to play the part of Buffalo Bill myself. . . . I told him it would be useless for me to attempt anything of that kind, for I never could talk to a crowd of people like that, even if it was to save my neck, and that he might as well try to make an actor out of a government mule." Ned Buntline's powers of persuasion—and money—were enough to make Cody change his mind several months later.

When Cody had been in New York for several weeks, General Sheridan arrived, and Cody told him "I had struck the best camp I had ever seen" and asked for a ten-day extension of his leave. Sheridan obliged but insisted that Cody then hurry back to Fort McPherson, as the Third Cavalry would have need of his services. Cody took advantage of the extra ten days to visit relatives in West Chester, Pennsylvania, with Ned Buntline in tow. An interview with Cody appeared in the *Philadelphia Public Record* on February 26, which happened to be his twenty-sixth birthday. The interview was probably arranged by Buntline.

Cody was described as "a young man who has obtained considerable celebrity as a daring hunter and an Indian fighter on the plains." The story continued: "From the wild cognomen, 'Buffalo Bill,' it has been the impression of many persons that he was a sort of semi-barbarian, or a regular border ruffian. On the contrary Mr. Cody is a fine specimen of a well-bred, bright-minded western pioneer. In fine, one of a class of men to whom the country owes much in its occidental developments. . . . [He is] rather slim and wiry, and over six feet high. He wears a mustache and goatee, and allows the hair of his head to hang in ringlets over his shoulders."

All the publicity given to Cody because of Grand Duke Alexis's hunt and his trip east inspired Ned Buntline to write a second Buffalo Bill novel. *Buffalo Bill's Best Shot; or, The Heart of Spotted Tail* started serially in Street & Smith's *New York Weekly* on March 25, 1872. This work was followed swiftly by *Buffalo Bill's Last Victory; or, Dove Eye, the Lodge Queen,* which ran from July 8 to October 14.

In that same year W. E. Webb's *Buffalo Land* was published, the first time Cody's name appeared in a hardbound book as distinguished from the dime novel. Webb is generous in his tribute to Buffalo Bill. "Cody," he wrote, "is spare and wiry in figure, admirably versed in plain lore, and altogether the best guide I ever saw. The mysterious plain is a book that he knows by heart. He crossed it twice as a teamster, while a mere boy, and has spent the greater part of his life on it since. He led us over its surface on starless nights, when the shadow of the blackness above hid our horses and the earth, and though many a time with no trail to follow and on the very mid-ocean of the expanse, he never made a failure." Webb added that "Cody had all the frontiersman's fondness for practical jokes."

Meanwhile, even as Ned Buntline was hatching a scheme that would put Cody even more deeply in the spotlight, the scout was on his way west to join an Indian expedition, though not without both adventures and misadventures along the way.

Cody received a telegram from Sheridan ordering him to proceed immediately to Fort McPherson while he was being entertained at one of Bennett's dinners, but he put off his departure for twenty-four hours because his West Chester relatives had arranged a fox hunt for him, their opportunity to see the great hunter on horseback. Cody was ill at ease. "I was familiar neither with the horse, the saddle, the hounds, nor foxhunting, and was extremely nervous," he wrote in his *Life Story.* Instead of joining the master of the hunt and other riders as they galloped off in search of the fox, vaulting over stone fences, Cody trotted along sedately with his elderly relatives. "Shortly we came to a tavern," he said, "and I went in and nerved myself with a stiff drink, also I had a bottle filled with liquid courage, which I took along with me. Just by way of making another fiasco impossible I took three more drinks while I was in the bar, then I galloped away and soon overtook the hunters. . . . I was in at the death and was given the honor of keeping the brush."

There followed what is most likely one of Cody's tall tales. Frank Thompson of the Pennsylvania Railroad lent Cody a private car to speed him to Chicago. On arriving there, he found orders waiting from Sheridan; he was to proceed immediately to Fort McPherson, as an expedition was waiting for him. True to form, Bill engaged in one more lark. At Omaha he was entertained by friends who insisted on seeing Buffalo Bill in a dress suit. He was still wearing it when they put him aboard the train, filling his compartment with champagne, but forgetting his trunk, left behind at the Hotel Paxton. Cody arrived at Fort McPherson dressed not for an Indian fight but for a ball, stovepipe hat and all. So attired, his hair tucked up under his top hat, he reported in the field to his new commanding officer, Brevet Major General J. J. Reynolds, colonel of the Third Cavalry, who didn't recognize him until he had let his hair down.

This was the kind of story that almost had to be true because it put Cody in such a ridiculous light. Army records suggest there was no expedition waiting for him, but soon after his arrival he did indeed see action.

"Shortly after my return," said Cody, "a small party of Indians made a raid on McPherson Station, about five miles from the fort, killing two or three men and running off quite a large number of horses." Company B of the Third Cavalry, with Captain Charles Meinhold commanding, was sent in pursuit of the marauders. Cody and Texas Jack Omohundro were the scouts on the expedition.

On April 26, after two days on the trail, Company B reached the South Fork of the Loup River, Nebraska. The troop encamped while Cody, with a detachment of six men led by Sergeant Foley, scouted the area. Cody discovered an Indian camp and horses grazing scarcely a mile away. Captain Meinhold's report read: "Mr. Cody had guided Sergeant Foley's party with such skill that he approached the Indian camp within fifty yards before he was noticed. The Indians fired immediately upon Mr. Cody and Sergeant Foley. Mr. Cody killed one Indian; two others ran toward the main command and were killed."

Cody said that the Indians headed for their horses across a creek and that he, riding Buckskin Joe, followed, but that the cavalry horses refused to jump. The troopers dismounted and came to Cody's aid. Two mounted warriors fired at him. He returned the fire and saw one Indian tumble from his horse. Cody pursued the other, rode alongside, and shot him through the head. When the rest of the troop arrived, the Indians, who had fresh horses, fled. In the course of this skirmish, Cody says that he received a slight scalp wound and that Buckskin Joe was also shot in the breast. Don Russell thinks that he may have confused this fight with the one in 1869 in which General Carr vividly remembers Will's scalp wound.

"While this was going on," ran the official report, "Mr. Cody discovered a party of six mounted Indians and two led horses running at full speed at a distance of about two miles down the river. I at once sent Lieutenant Lawson with Mr. Cody and fifteen men in pursuit. He, at the beginning of the chase, gained a little upon them, so that they were compelled to abandon the two led horses, which were captured, but after running more than twelve miles at full speed, our jaded horses gave out and the Indians made good their escape."

Captain Meinhold's report concludes: "Mr. William Cody's reputation for bravery and skill as a guide is so well established that I need not say anything else but that he acted in his usual manner." On the basis of this report, Cody was awarded the Medal of Honor on May 22, 1872. Because he had served as a civilian and not a soldier, however, his name was stricken from the rolls under an act of Congress of June 16, 1916, "on the ground that at the time of the act of gallantry he was neither an officer nor an enlisted man, being at that time a civilian."

It is also true that at the time Cody received his Medal of Honor, the award had been shamefully abused; it was being given out almost indiscriminately, on the recommendation of officers of low rank. After having been revoked, Cody's Medal of Honor was again reinstated, but it is doubtful he even knew of the act of Congress that revoked it, while its subsequent reinstatement followed his death.

Said Cody: "I made several other scouts during the summer with different officers of the Third Cavalry, one being with Major Alick Moore, a good officer, with whom I was out for thirty days. Another long one was with Major Curtis, with whom I followed some Indians from the South Platte river to Fort Randall on the Missouri river in Dakota, on which trip the command ran out of rations and for fifteen days subsisted entirely on the game we killed."

On August 15, 1872, the post surgeon at Fort McPherson noted: "3 p.m. Mrs. Cody, wife of Mr. William Cody, Post guide and interpreter, delivered of a daughter." This was Orra Maude, the Cody's third child and second daughter.

That fall the Earl of Dunraven returned for a hunting trip with three friends, with Cody as their guide. This is how the earl describes his arrival at North Platte:

> At one of those lonely little stations I was deposited [from the train] one fine evening in the early fall just before sundown. For a few moments only the place was all alive with bustle and confusion. The train represented everything that was civilised, all the luxuries that could be carried in a train were to be found on board of it, the people were all clothed in fashionable dresses, it was like a slice cut out of one of the Eastern cities

set down bodily in the midst of a perfect wilderness. In a few seconds it was gone, civilisation vanished with it, the station relapsed into its normal condition of desolation, and I found myself almost alone in the heart of the desert.

Before their hunt was over, a party of General Sheridan's Chicago friends arrived, and, of course, they had to have Buffalo Bill as their guide. Cody turned over his duties as the earl's guide to Texas Jack. "The Earl seemed somewhat offended at this, and I don't think he has ever forgiven me for 'going back on him.'" Texas Jack proved a worthy substitute, however, and was hired by the earl again in 1874.

Cody returned to Sheridan's Chicago party, which included a man named Milligan, of the firm of Heath and Milligan. Milligan is described by Cody as "a regular velocipede, so to speak, and was here, there and everywhere," the life of the party. Milligan was eager for an Indian fight until Cody spotted a band of thirty mounted Indians. "Milligan, here's what you've been wanting for some time." Milligan decided that it wasn't one of his fighting days and that he had urgent business back in camp.

On another hunt, Cody says, "I lariated, or roped, a big buffalo bull and tied him to a tree—a feat which I had often performed, and which the gentlemen requested me to do on this occasion for their benefit."

In the fall of that same year, some of Cody's friends at a convention in Grand Island secured his nomination as Democratic candidate to represent the Twenty-Sixth District in the Nebraska legislature. As the district was predominately Republican, and Cody had always been a Democrat, he had no hope of being elected and did not campaign. However, the returns showed that Buffalo Bill had won by forty-four votes. "That is the way in which I acquired my title of Honorable," he wrote in his final autobiography. He used that title until he was given the honorary rank of colonel in the Nebraska militia.

Cody's only previous political experience had been as a justice of the peace at Cottonwood Springs in 1871. Since the army had little jurisdiction beyond the limits of its own military grounds, outlaws and sharpers of various descriptions hung about the fringes of the reservation, preying on soldiers, settlers, and travelers. Crooked gambling and the theft of government property had become so rife that General Emory decided something had to be done. He recommended the appointment of W. F. Cody to the office, figuring that someone also sympathetic to the army's problems would be most helpful, although Cody insisted that "he didn't know any more about law than a mule knows of singing." Louisa put it differently, saying that Cody accepted the appointment "with glee," assuring her that "I know as much law as I need to know around here."

In one unverified episode, Cody was required to deal with the matter of a stolen horse. He was told he needed a writ of replevin to recover the animal. Since he didn't know what the writ was, he decided that his faithful Lucretia Borgia would make an acceptable substitute. He found the thief, recovered the horse, and fined the offender $20—which he pocketed. On another occasion, it was said that he performed a marriage ceremony. Unable to locate the words of the ceremony, he recited what he could remember, ending up with "whomsoever God and Buffalo Bill have joined together, let no man put asunder."

Although pleased that he had been elected to the legislature, Cody did not bother to show up at the capitol to claim his seat, and the following year a recount showed that the votes from an unorganized territory had been improperly counted and that Cody had actually lost the election by forty-two votes. Although he was served written notice of this outcome, he did not comment on it. His election, however, provided him with an honorific; henceforth, he could call himself "the Honorable" W. F. Cody.

In any case, he had more pressing business to attend to than Nebraska politics. Ned Buntline, ever resourceful, was about to surface with another tempting scheme.

During the summer and fall of 1872, Cody received a number of letters from Buntline urging him to go on the stage and play himself. "There's money in it," wrote Ned, "and you will prove a big card, as your character is a novelty on the stage." If Cody hesitated, it was because he remembered his stage fright at the Bowery Theater in New York. Still, "there's money in it," Buntline had said, and that thought was tempting. Like his father before him, Cody was always attracted by glittering financial prospects.

The officers at Fort McPherson, including General Reynolds, advised him to stay where he was. Buntline kept up his overtures, assuring Cody that he would get over his stage fright in good time. He asked Cody to join him in Chicago, where he would organize a theatrical company—and if the venture failed, the scout could always return to the army. There were other considerations swaying his decision. Texas Jack, who was eager to go on the stage, "whether the audience said he could act or not," did his best to persuade his friend. His wife wished to return to St. Louis to spend time with her family. Louisa's reaction to Buntline's offer was favorable. In her memoirs, she quotes Cody as saying "I don't know just how bad I'd be at actin'. I guess maybe I'd better find out." So, on November 30,

Cody resigned his post, and on December 12, he and Texas Jack arrived in Chicago.

An advertisement in that day's Chicago *Journal* announced the appearance at Nixon's Amphitheatre on Monday, December 18, of "The real Buffalo Bill, Texas Jack and Ten Sioux and Pawnee chiefs in Ned Buntline's great drama *Buffalo Bill*." Buntline was disappointed when his stars arrived without any Indians in tow—bringing them would have been impractical and prohibitively expensive—but he cheered up when he realized that Buffalo Bill was his real attraction.

Jim Nixon's "Amphitheatre" was one of the side-boarded, canvas-topped affairs that had been put up after the great Chicago fire had destroyed all the old theaters. It soon became apparent, when Buntline and his two stars arrived there, that Buntline didn't have a play, and the theater manager canceled his contract. According to Cody, Buntline offered to rent the Amphitheatre for $600 for one week. He then proceeded to his hotel room, where he hired several clerks as copyists and wrote his melodrama—in four hours. Its title was *The Scouts of the Prairie*, but its source was Buntline's own serial *Buffalo Bill's Last Victory; or Dove Eye, the Lodge Queen*, then running in installments in the *New York Weekly*.

On December 17 the Chicago *Evening Journal* heralded "The real heroes of the Plains, Buffalo Bill and Texas Jack in a great sensation drama entitled *The Scouts of the Prairie*, written expressly for them by Ned Buntline. Morlacchi as Dove Eye. Matinees Wednesday and Saturday—Every lady visiting the matinees will be presented with portraits of the boys."

Cody and Texas Jack were now committed to learning their lines by the following morning, when they would have the first rehearsal. Both were convinced they would never be able to learn a line of the play. When Buntline cautioned them not to read the cues, Cody retorted: "Cues be d——d, I never heard of anything but a billiard cue."

The press had fun with the so-called Sioux and Pawnee chiefs, said to be fresh from the plains, greased, painted, and dangling fresh scalps from their belts. What the audience saw on stage, however, was "a selection of talented supers in tan-colored frocks and cambric pantalettes." The real Indians were "off on a horse-stealing expedition."

It was not so much opening night for *The Scouts of the Prairie* as amateur night. Cody described it this way:

> Buntline, who was taking the part of "Cale Durg" appeared, and gave me my "cue" to speak "my little piece," but for the life of me I could not remember a single word. Buntline saw I was "stuck," and a happy thought occurred to him. He said—as if it were in the play:

"Where have you been, Bill? What took you so long?"

Just then my eye happened to fall on Mr. Milligan, who was sur-rounded by his friends, the newspaper reporters, and several military offi-cers, all of whom had heard of his hunt and "Indian fight"—he being a very popular man, and widely known in Chicago. So I said:

"I have been out on a hunt with Milligan."

This proved to be a big hit. The audience cheered and applauded; which gave me greater confidence in my ability to get through the per-formance all right. Buntline, who is a very versatile man, saw that it would be a good plan to follow this up, and he said:

"Well, Bill, tell us about the hunt."

I thereupon proceeded to relate in detail the particulars of the affair. I succeeded in making it rather funny, and I was frequently interrupted with sounds of applause. Whenever I began to "weaken," Buntline would give me a fresh start by asking some questions. In this way I took up fif-teen minutes, without once speaking a word of my part; nor did I speak a word of it during the whole evening. The prompter, who was standing between the wings, attempted to prompt me, but it did no good; for while I was on the stage, I "chipped in" anything I could think of.

So much for the dialogue; what about the action of the play? Cody describes Jack and himself "blazing away" at the ersatz Indians with blank cartridges, and "when the scene ended in a hand-to-hand encounter—a general knock-down and drag-out—the way Jack and I killed Indians was a 'caution.' We would kill them all off in one act, but they would come up again ready for action in the next. Finally the curtain dropped; the play was ended, and I congratulated Jack and myself on having made such a successful *debut*. There was no backing out after that."

Although Cody's version of his debut typically pokes fun at himself, it does not conceal the kind of innate genius he possessed that was to make him a superstar: By obscuring the fine line between make-believe and reality, between his and Jack's actual experiences on the frontier and the derring-do they improvised on the stage, he was unknowingly creating the myth of the Wild West, the archetype of the Western, a genre that persists to this day. The play in itself was an absurdity, not really worth mounting without its stars, and certainly not worth reviving.

Cody would have scoffed at a formulation like this. Archetype? Genre? Nonsense! He was only doing his best to make money by cashing in on his fame. Still, it is characteristic of an innovator, a pioneer, that he does not always know what he has done. According to Sell and Wey-bright, "Imitators were soon presenting melodramas of the West manufac-tured according to his formula, which also found increasing popularity in the dime novels of the 1870s. Buffalo Bill had shown them the way, with his *Scouts of the Prairie*. The show was copied by enterprising producers in the stock companies of all the large cities. All these shows involved Indians, cowboys, scouts, frontiersmen, a lost maiden to be rescued, and some kind of comic relief. The more violent and absurd, the more shooting, the more coincidences and predicaments, the better the audiences liked them. The pattern of latter-day western movies was emerging. But Buffalo Bill's show was the most conspicuous and successful, for no one could compete with Buffalo Bill in person. Overnight heroes usually enjoy a short reign, but Buffalo Bill was winning a lasting audience. He was the original; his imitators were stereotypes."

In addition, Cody's monologues in the play, prompted by Ned Buntline, and the stories Texas Jack and Buffalo Bill told around their fake campfire, actually created a new entertainment formula that years later reached its peak in the cowboy monologues of Will Rogers in the Ziegfeld Follies.

What actually took place on stage is subject to conjecture, but a synopsis appearing in a New York program later in the season outlines what was *supposed* to happen:

> Act I. On the Plains—Trapper and the Scouts. The Renegade's Camp—Peril of Hazel Eye. Ned Buntline's Temperance Lecture. Cale Durg at the Torture Post. The Indian Dance—The Rescue.
>
> Act II. Texas Jack and his Lasso. The Loves of Buffalo Bill. The Death of Cale Durg. The Trapper's last Shot.
>
> Act III. The Scout's Oath of Vengeance. The Scalp Dance—The Knife Fight. The Triumph of the Scouts. The Prairie on Fire.

Certainly there was no shortage of action or special effects.

As for Chicago's reactions to what must have been an astonishing spectacle, "the papers gave us a better send-off than I expected," said Cody, "for they did not criticize us as actors." The *Evening Journal*, whose editor Charles Wilson had been on Sheridan's hunt and was favorably disposed toward Cody, treated the play generously, with a review that took into consideration the amateur status of nearly all of the leading players:

> Nixon's Amphitheatre was last night the scene of a most extraordinary character and one in which the audience bore quite as prominent a feature as did the occupants of the stage. The occasion was the first appearance of Ned Buntline's play with the blood-curdling and hair-raising title of *The Scouts of the Prairie; or, Red Deviltry As It Is*, being a descriptive affair of life on the plains and in the mountains of the West, and in which the noted characters "Buffalo Bill" and "Texas Jack" in their own original selves were presented, as well as "Ned Buntline," the author of the play. Last night not less than 2,500 boys and young men crowded the

amphitheatre to catch a glimpse of their heroes. Mlle. Morlacchi, the Italian danseuse, essayed the part of the Indian maiden Dove Eye with great success . . . largely sustained the dramatic interest from first to last and was an interesting connecting link in the chain of events.

Guiseppina Morlacchi, born in Milan in 1846, studied dance at La Scala and made her debut at the Carlo Felice Theatre in Genoa in 1856. She appeared in Naples, Florence, Turin, London, and Lisbon before coming to America in 1867. In Boston that year, she introduced the cancan to America. Her part in Buntline's play was summed up by the Chicago *Tribune* as that "of a beautiful Indian maiden with an Italian accent and a weakness for scouts." That last line was right on the mark, for within a few months she married Texas Jack.

Cale Durg, the part Buntline played, was an alias he had invented earlier for a recital at Stamford, New York, his sometime home. His contribution was summed up by the *Tribune:* "Buntline delivered some opinions on the use of liquor which he said was injurious and had done a great deal of harm." According to Cody, the newspaper *Inter-Ocean* said that it was regrettable that Cale Durg had not been killed in the first act—before the temperance speech—instead of in the second—and the *Times* opined that if Ned Buntline actually spent four hours in writing that play, it was difficult to see what he had been doing all that time. The *Times* also said: "On the whole it is not probable that Chicago will ever look upon the like again. Such a combination of incongruous drama, execrable acting, renowned performers, mixed audience, intolerable stench, scalping, blood and thunder, is not likely to be vouchsafed to a city for a second time— even Chicago."

Buntline had promised money to Cody, and the first night's box office was $2,800. If this particular critic had a crystal ball, he would have known that Chicago was going to see a lot of this particular combination again, from Buffalo Bill for the next decade and from his successors from that time to this. The Western had been born, and there would be no turning back—"no backing out," as Cody put it. "Buffalo Bill won no laurels as an actor," wrote Don Russell, "but from the first night he proved his showmanship."

Cody's recollections of that first night also included a mixture of powder smoke (when dispatching all the extras dressed as Indians), rough-and-tumble fights, and tall tales around a fake campfire.

Part of the play's success could be attributed to the curiosity in the East about the western way of life, involving as it did Indians, buffalo, cowboys, and scouts of the plains. But it was Cody himself who was most responsible for the show's popularity. Cody's genuine exploits on the frontier

Richmond Theatre.

FOUR NIGHTS ONLY!

THIS EVENING,

JENNY LIND ᴬᵀ LAST!

JENNY LEATHERLUNGS	BESSIE SUDLOW
GRANBY GAG	G. C. DAVENPORT
Mr. Leatherlungs	G. C. Beach
Baron Swigitoffbeery	W. Fletcher
Herr Scheroot	J. Johnson
Herr Kanaster	J. Jefferson
Herr Spittoon	W. Cunningham
Herr Meershaum	J. Smith

To conclude with Ned Buntline's Great Realistic Drama of THE

Scouts of the Prairie!

BUFFALO BILL, by the Original Hero,	Hon. W. F. CODY
TEXAS JACK, by the Original Hero,	J. B. OMOHUNDRO
CALE DURG	NED BUNTLINE
Mormon Ben	Harry Wentworth
Phelim O'Laugherty	Geo. C. Davenport
Carl Pretzel	Walter Fletcher
Hazel Eye	Senorita Eloe Carfano

INDIANS.

Wolf Slayer	W. J. Fleming
Big Eagle	Jos. P. Winter
Little Bear	Mr. Harper
Ar-fiar-Ka	Grassy Chief
As-ge-tes	Prairie Dog
As-sin-an-wa	Water Chief
Te-co-tic-pown	Big Elk
Kit-kot-tons	Great River
Ko-ku-su	Swamp Fox
Dove Eye	BESSIE SUDLOW

MATINEE THURSDAY 2 O'C.

Thursday Evening,

FAREWELL PERFORMANCE OF THE SCOUTS,

As they play in Norfolk on Friday and Saturday
Nights.

WHIG JOB PRESS.

*Jeff & Booth witnessed the above plays &
were well pleased — May 1873 —*

Broadside for a performance of *The Scouts of the Prairie* in
Richmond, Virginia, May 1873. (Library of Virginia
Collection, Richmond, Virginia)

181

combined with the bogus feats in Ned Buntline's dime novels about him, along with his friendships with generals and millionaires, made him a natural box office draw. It was, after all, also an era when schmaltz was king and melodrama ruled the stage. *The Scouts of the Prairie* was hardly worse than any number of "ten-twenty-thirts" as they were called, plays designed to please the crowds that packed the cheap seats.

After a performance was played for the benefit of Buffalo Bill and Texas Jack on Friday night, and one on Saturday night for Ned Buntline, the show took to the road, heading for St. Louis. Buntline's benefit marked the first appearance of Senorita Eloe Carfano as "Hazel Eye," not to be confused with "Dove Eye," played by Morlacchi. In St. Louis, the show opened at DeBar's Opera House on December 23. The night was bitterly cold and snowy, but Buntline's show drew the biggest theater crowd in town. In all probability Lulu was in the audience. Although Will does not mention her, she says she was there:

> With Arta on my lap, I sat in the audience, watching the performance, and waiting for Will to appear. At last, three or four Indians pranced across the stage, turned, waved their tomahawks, yelled something and then fell dead, accompanied by the rattle-te-bang of a six-shooter. Out rushed Will, assured himself that all three of the Indians were thoroughly dead, turned just in time to kill a couple more who had roamed on to the stage by accident, and then faced the audience.
>
> I was sitting in about the third row, and Will saw me. He came forward, leaned over the gas footlights and waved his arms.
>
> "Oh Mamma," he shouted, "I'm a *bad* actor!"
>
> The house roared. Will threw me a kiss and then leaned forward again, while the house stilled.
>
> "Honest, Mamma," he shouted, "does this look as awful out there as it feels up here?"
>
> And again the house chuckled and applauded. Some one called out the fact that I was Mrs. Buffalo Bill.

When the crowd began to urge her to get on the stage, her husband joined in with "Come on up . . . you can't be any worse scared than I am." Someone placed a chair in the orchestra pit, hands reached to help, and she was boosted onto the stage, and Arta after her. Her stage fright plainly showed, and Will boomed, "Now you can understand how hard your poor old husband has to work to make a living!" And again the audience applauded. After that, Louisa says, whenever she went to see her husband's show, she chose a seat in the farthest and darkest part of the house.

But it did little good. For invariably Will would seek her out and call, "Hello, Mamma. Oh, but I'm a bad actor."

A writer on the *Missouri Democrat*, which had deplored the Buntline riot twenty years earlier, wrote: "Buffalo Bill is a beautiful blonde, and wears the Alexis diamond on a shirt, whose fastenings are in the rear."

On December 27, 1872, the Chicago *Evening Journal* reported: "Ned Buntline of the Buffalo Bill troupe was arrested at St. Louis yesterday for having participated in a riot there twenty years ago." Buntline had jumped bail after organizing the anti-German riot for the Know-Nothing party. Circuit Court Judge Primm told Buntline that he was still liable for trial on the rioting indictments in spite of the passage of twenty years. A thousand dollars would be required in bail to release him from custody. Ned did not have the money, but a friend, Captain George D. Martin, hurried away to raise it, and before the evening performance, Ned's bail had been posted. Ned jumped bail again, of course, and his bondsman had to pay a forfeit.

The Scouts of the Prairie traveled on to Cincinnati, where it opened at Pike's Opera House on December 30. The *Daily Gazette* critic caught the essence of the show this way: "The play is beyond all precedent in the annals of stage lore. . . . It has in it all the thrilling romance, treachery, love, revenge, and hate of a dozen of the richest dime novels ever written. . . . The play bids fair to have a most wonderful run, for its novelty is so striking, and its subject is such a popular one with many readers of thrilling border tales, that the temptation to see the real actors in those tragedies can not be resisted." Hundreds had to be turned away from the overflowing theater every night.

In the New York *Herald*, people who had been following the progress of *The Scouts of the Prairie* read this notice:

CINCINNATI. W.J. Halpin, actor, died at noon today from the effects of injuries received last Thursday night when playing his part as Big Wolf with Ned Buntline's company.

Neither Cody nor Buntline ever offered any explanation of this actor's death, but the troupe went into seclusion for a month, then traveled to Cincinnati in February.

The troupe then moved east, through Rochester and Buffalo. A week in Boston, where the play opened on March 3, 1873, grossed $16,200. Said the Boston *Traveler*: "The Indian mode of warfare, their hideous dances, the method they adopt to 'raise the hair' of their antagonists, following the trail, etc., or in the way their enemies deal with them, manner of throwing the lasso, etc., are forcibly exhibited, and this portion of the entertainment alone is worth the price of admission." The Boston *Transcript* chimed in with "Those who delight in sensations of the most exciting order will not fail to see the distinguished visitors from the western plains before they leave"; and, said the Boston *Journal*: "The play of itself is an extraordinary production with more wild Indians, scalping knives and gun powder to the square inch than any drama ever before heard of."

Somewhere along the line, the Chicago South Side Indians had been replaced by twenty-one (the playbill lists twenty-five) presumably real Indians, played by Pawnee chiefs.

It was on to New York, then, as now, the theatrical capital of America. There too, the competition for audiences was keener. When *The Scouts of the Prairie* arrived in town to open at Niblo's Garden, Edwin Booth was playing in *Julius Caesar* and Joseph Jefferson in *Rip Van Winkle*. Bennett's *Herald* could have been expected to look favorably on Cody, but Bennett had a long-standing feud with Ned Buntline, whose part was described by the *Herald*'s critic as being represented "as badly as is possible for any human being to represent it. . . . Ned Buntline is simply maundering imbecility. Ludicrous beyond the power of description is Ned Buntline's temperance address in the forest." As for Buffalo Bill, "he is a good-looking fellow, tall and straight as an arrow, but ridiculous as an actor. Texas Jack is not quite so good-looking, not so tall, not so straight, and not so ridiculous." The *Herald* critic summed up the evening this way: "Everything is so wonderfully bad it is almost good." Once again, nothing succeeded like excess.

Said the critic on the *World*: "As an exhibition of three remarkable men it is not without interest. The Hon. W.F. Cody enters into the spectacle with a curious grace and a certain characteristic charm that pleases the beholders. He is a remarkably handsome fellow on the stage, and the lithe, springy step, the round uncultured voice, and the utter absence of anything like stage art, won for him the good-will of an audience which was disposed to laugh at all that was intended to be pathetic and serious." The *Times* credited Buffalo Bill's success with the way he exhibited "a surprising degree of aplomb, notable ease of gestures and delivery, and vocal power quite sufficient readily to fill a large theatre. . . . His use of the revolver and rifle indicated extensive practice, and were vastly relished by the audience. . . . It is only just to say that the representation was attended by torrents of what seemed thoroughly spontaneous applause; and that whatever faults close criticism may detect, there is a certain flavor of realism and of nationality about the play well calculated to gratify a general audience." In using the word "nationality" the *Times* critic sounded a note that would also describe Cody's Wild West show: It was in the American grain. As for the realism, Cody would also learn from his stage experience that audiences were hungry for something that either was or seemed authentic.

The play remained in New York for two weeks, March 31 to April 13, and then moved on to the Arch Street Theatre in Philadelphia. On April 21 the critic of *The Age* remarked that "Buffalo Bill looks able and willing to do many of the deeds in earnest which are represented on the stage." Not surprising, since he'd already done a number of them "in earnest." On May 12 the Richmond, Virginia, *Whig* published a rave review. "The best thing in the sensational way that has ever visited us. . . . all who miss seeing and hearing this company will have to regret having missed one of the most striking and stirring dramas of the age, performed by men who have gone though in stern reality what they simulate on the stage." The Richmond *Enquirer* was not quite as enthusiastic. "Were it not . . . that they represent in a measure real scenes of which they have been the actual heroes, the performance would be tame and unprofitable indeed."

"We closed our tour on the 16th of June, 1873, at Port Jervis, New York," said Cody, "and when I counted up my share of the profits I found that I was only about $6,000 ahead. I was somewhat disappointed, for, judging from our large business, I certainly had expected a greater sum. . . . There was not a single city where we did not have crowded houses."

Louisa suggests why Will's share of the season's take was so slim. Although the money flowed in,

> Unheard extravagances became ours. And Will, dear, generous soul that he was, believed that an inexhaustible supply of wealth had become his forever. One night . . . we entered a hotel, only to find that the rooms we occupied were on a noisy side of the house. Will complained. The manager bowed suavely [and explained]: "The only way you could have absolute peace would be to rent the whole floor and, of course, you don't want to do that—"
>
> "Don't I? . . . How much is it?"
>
> The manager figured. Then he smiled.
>
> "Two hundred dollars would be a pretty stiff price to pay for peace and quiet."
>
> "Paid! . . . Now, let's see how quick you can make things comfortable for us. I've got a wife and babies and we're all tired."

This pattern, periods of affluence followed by reckless extravagance, was one Cody would follow for the rest of his life.

Cody does not mention that his family traveled with him, but it would appear from Louisa's *Memories* that they did, at least part of the time, for she says she often took little Kit to watch his father on stage. At the end of the season, since their home at Fort McPherson had been sold, it is likely that Louisa and the children moved to the new home Will had purchased in Rochester after the first tour. He was already looking forward to a return to the stage. Meanwhile, according to Cody, "Texas Jack and myself longed for a hunt on the Western prairies once more; and on meeting in New York a party of gentlemen who were desirous of going with us, we all started westward, and after a pleasant trip arrived at Fort McPherson."

Before he arrived at Fort McPherson, Cody was interviewed by the local press. Cody allowed, surely with tongue in cheek, that

> We have played New York until we forced Edwin Booth to go West. He said it would not do for him to try to buck against us, and he was right. I propose to [be] . . . playing Shakespeare right through, from beginning to end, with Ned Buntline and Texas Jack to support me. I shall do Hamlet in a buckskin suit and when my father's ghost appears "doomed for a certain time," &c., I shall say to Jack, "Rope the cuss in, Jack!!" and unless the lasso breaks, the ghost will have to come. As Richard the Third I shall fight with pistols and hunting knives. In "Romeo and Juliet" I will put a half-breed squaw on the balcony, and make various interpretations of Shakespeare's words to suit myself.

Shakespeare has had to endure many indignities over the years: bowdlerizations, bizarre directorial concepts, and costume choices of all kinds, but theatergoers, fortunately, were spared Hamlet in buckskin or the balcony scene in a Western saloon. On the other hand, it is possible that Cody, with his genius for showmanship, might have won over a whole new audience to the plays.

During the run of *The Scouts of the Prairie*, Cody had not only overcome his initial stage fright but had developed enough self-confidence to feel comfortable onstage. Moreover, he knew that audiences responded favorably to him. Although he still did not consider himself an actor, he had begun to wear the more becoming mantle of "showman."

Ned Buntline had all kinds of plans for his show. He spoke of playing it on horseback under a tent, of taking it to London. Texas Jack and Buffalo Bill had other ideas, however. They would return to the stage, but without Ned. The author had fulfilled his role in Cody's career, by launching the scout in show business; now, in June 1873, it was time for Ned to recede into the wings.

Ned Buntline's contribution to the legend of Buffalo Bill has often been exaggerated; it must be said that he exploited Cody more than Cody exploited him. Still, his dime novels all added to Cody's celebrity—and he did succeed in getting Buffalo Bill on a stage, though he probably never realized how big a star he had.

Ned wrote a new play based on another dime novel, *Dashing Charlie, the Texas Whirlwind*, and produced it with Dashing Charlie in person, backed up by Arizona Frank, another real-life hero. Without Buffalo Bill, though, the formula failed to work. In 1885 Buntline wrote the fourth and last of his Buffalo Bill dime novels, *Buffalo Bill's First Trail, or, Will Cody, the Pony Express Rider*. Ned also wrote two novels based on the career of Texas Jack: *Texas Jack, the White King of the Pawnees*, and *Texas Jack's Chums, or, The Whirlwind of the West*. He was not, however, one of the most prolific writers of the dime novel western—that achievement belonged to Colonel Prentiss Ingraham, who is credited with 211 of the 557 original dime novels, though we can only be certain of 121 of these—and Don Russell, who has made an exhaustive study of the Buffalo Bill dime thrillers, questions more than half of this number.

Cody and Texas Jack did not remain out west hunting for long; by August they were back in Rochester, to begin preparations for the next theatrical season. Texas Jack had another reason to return. He had fallen in love with Signorina Morlacchi, and they were now engaged.

Omohundro and Morlacchi were married in St. Mary's Roman Catholic Church in Rochester on the last day of August 1873. Immediately following the wedding, preparations for the next play went into high gear. Now that Ned Buntline was out of the picture, they needed another factotum, a dogsbody. That indispensable jack-of-all-trades turned out to be Major John M. Burke, who was Morlacchi's manager. Although his name was to be associated with Buffalo Bill's until his death, Burke would never have signed on with Cody had it not been for Morlacchi. Some histories of the Wild West considered him Buffalo Bill's press agent (the term did not exist at the time); actually, he served a number of useful functions: advance man, advertising representative, company manager. However, his primary role at the beginning was to shepherd Signorina Morlacchi's career. In fact, when Texas Jack and Cody finally went their separate ways, Burke cast his lot with Jack and Giuseppina. In time, he would return to assume the same role for Buffalo Bill, whom he worshiped all his life. As Arizona John, Burke also acted at times, growing his hair long and adopting the mannerisms of a scout, although he had never been west of the Missouri River before signing on with Cody. Burke would, in time, be even more important than Ned Buntline in shaping Buffalo Bill's legend—for better or for worse.

* * *

For the next ten years, Cody would divide his life and his work neatly in two. From fall through spring he mounted a play, or what was called a "combination," touring the cities of the North and Southeast. Combinations were not repertory companies, but groups of actors organized to put on only one drama, with a second one possibly kept in reserve in case it was needed. During these months Cody lived a trouper's life. The man who had sat in the saddle from fort to fort now sprawled on the dusty seats of railway cars that bore him from one city to another. He who had slept in tents and dugouts and caves and rolled up in a blanket on the open prairie now learned the stuffiness and untidiness of hotel bedrooms, decrepit theaters, and tiny dressing rooms without running water or electricity. All these conditions required that he adopt new habits, find new pastimes, turn himself into a businessman who must watch his expenses and count his box office receipts. The old manners of chuck wagon and saloon gave way to the new manners of ballroom and gilded barroom.

Then every summer, after the season ended, Cody returned to the plains, either to guide hunting parties or to serve as an army scout. As a scout, he would be able to take part in adventures that could provide material for his plays and also reinforce the publicity he received as an actor, reenacting his own valorous deeds on the frontier. His audiences always took him for "the real thing," and so he was.

The first of the "Buffalo Bill combinations" was *The Scouts of the Plains*, hardly to be distinguished from *The Scouts of the Prairie*, with one notable exception. Cody invited his old friend Wild Bill Hickok to join the company. Hickok's fame equaled and at times perhaps surpassed Cody's in those early years.

Since *Harper's* magazine had thrilled its readers with Hickok's adventures back in 1867, he had added considerably to his reputation. He and Buffalo Bill had met again during General Sheridan's 1868–1869 winter campaign against the Indians; they were both members of the Carr-Penrose commands. In 1869, while carrying dispatches alone, Hickok was jumped by Indians at Sand Creek, Colorado Territory, and was severely wounded by a lance before he escaped. He was released as a scout at Fort Wallace and returned to his home in Troy Grove, Illinois, to recuperate. Wild Bill was in Hays City, Kansas, shortly after Sheriff Thomas Ganlon was killed; Hickok was persuaded to become acting sheriff of Ellis County on August 23, 1869, and was also named city marshal. He served until January 3, 1870. There, and in Abilene, Kansas, where he was city marshal from April 15 to December 13, 1871, he made his reputation as a frontier peace officer.

Western and eastern newspapers alike had avidly followed Wild Bill's career, and there is no doubt he was a drawing card for *The Scouts of the*

Wild Bill Hickok. (Western History Collection, University of Oklahoma Library)

Plains. In fact, Ned Buntline had included a character named "Wild Bill Hickok" in the first season's run of *The Scouts of the Prairie*; the character was played by a professional actor. And of course Wild Bill had figured in Buntline's dime novel *Buffalo Bill, the King of Border Men*, as Cody's best friend. Hickok accused Buntline of using most of his adventures in that book as well as killing him off. "Ned Buntline has been trying to murder me with his pen for years," Hickok recalled in a newspaper interview in 1873, "having failed, is now, so I am told, trying to have it done by some Texans, but he has signally failed so far."

Cody's combination was not Hickok's first experience with show business. After he left Hays City in 1870, he went north along the Republican River to Beaver Creek, where he captured six buffalo. He then hired a number of Comanche Indians and took them and the buffalo to Niagara Falls, where he advertised a buffalo chase on July 20. He attracted a crowd estimated at five thousand, but he had neglected to build a fence around his show and was forced to pass the hat. He did not collect enough to pay his expenses. Moreover, one spectator turned loose a trained bear belonging to one of the Comanche, which promptly took off after a vendor of baked sausages, ancestors of the hot dog. The bear disposed of the sausages, and Hickok was forced to make good their cost. That was the end of his show, which, in its way, was a forerunner of Buffalo Bill's Wild West before Cody ever thought of the idea.

In *The Scouts of the Plains* Cody and Texas Jack again played themselves; Mlle. Morlacchi was Pale Dove this time instead of Dove Eye. The play was written by Fred G. Maeder, author also of the play version of *Buffalo Bill, the King of Border Men*, which became the alternate offering during the 1873–1874 season. Maeder was a member of a well-known theatrical family of the time.

According to Cody, Wild Bill "told us from the start that we could never make an actor out of him. Although he had a fine stage appearance and was a handsome fellow, and possessed a good strong voice, yet when he went upon the stage before an audience, it was almost impossible for him to utter a word. He insisted that we were making fools of ourselves, and that we were the laughing-stock of the people. I replied that I did not care for that, as long as they came and bought tickets to see us."

The play opened in Williamsport, Pennsylvania, on September 8. In Titusville, Pennsylvania, on November 6, the hotel owner asked them to stay out of the billiard room, where a crowd of drunks had threatened to clean out the Buffalo Bill Combination. Cody as usual wanted to avoid trouble, but Wild Bill couldn't resist the temptation. He slipped into the billiard room, laid out four or five of the drunks with a chair, and drove the rest from the hotel.

Hiram Robbins, who managed the combination, says that Hickok was given a secondary part because "he had a voice like a girl." At Philadelphia a calcium limelight was used, and Hickok was much impressed by its effects on Buffalo Bill and Texas Jack. He demanded that it be thrown on him as well, threatening to shoot the lighting man if it was not. When it was turned on him full center, Wild Bill, "with his weak eyes blinded by the intense light," shouted "Turn the blamed thing off" and spoiled the scene.

From the beginning of the run, Hickok delighted in playing tricks on the other actors, and he especially enjoyed tormenting the "supers," who played the Indians. He liked to shoot blank cartridges close to their legs, causing powder burns that interfered with their death throes on stage. Cody remonstrated with his friend, but Wild Bill continued the practice until March 10, in Rochester, where Hickok again powder-burned a super. Cody told him he must stop it or leave the troupe, which Hickok promptly did. He turned up in the audience, watching the show. Cody and Omohundro were sorry to see him go, but they had little choice. Texas Jack and Buffalo Bill each gave Hickok $500 and a pair of .44 Smith and Wesson revolvers to take with him out West.

Many years later Mr. D. J. Antonides, a North Platte hardware merchant, reminisced:

> In New York, where I was raised, I saw Texas Jack and Buffalo Bill and Wild Bill. There had been several shows put on with real (professional) actors (playing the parts of Buffalo Bill, et al.) so nobody would believe these were the *real* scouts, but thought they were just more actors. But I saw them. The way it happened, our show was out before theirs was. We had gone to one on a neighboring street and we walked down that way. They had come out and were standing under a lamp post for advertising. They were dressed in regular citizen's dress and they were handsome. Texas Jack was a very handsome blonde fellow and Wild Bill was of a different build but good looking, and Buffalo Bill was always tops for looks. But we couldn't believe they were the real scouts. The funny thing about it was that, unlike the real actors, none of the scouts could memorize a thing. They had their parts written out for them, and the different things they could do, but it was no good. So they just "put on" about the things they did when they were scouting.

A reporter for the Rochester *Democrat and Chronicle* spotted Wild Bill on the street after the combination had left town and stopped him for an interview. Hickok implied that General Sheridan had recalled him for service as a scout. "He will first proceed to New York where he has some business to transact," the interviewer reported, "remain there a few days and then go direct to the frontier. He had nothing but kind words to speak of the boys, as he familiarly termed the other scouts." His business in New York turned out to be signing up with another theatrical troupe, the Stevens Daniel Boone Company, and when it turned out that he didn't make enough money, Hickok quit. The theater manager, who had invested good money in posters advertising Wild Bill, hired an actor to play the part. Hickok demanded that the impersonation of him be stopped. When his demand was ignored, he went up on the stage in Binghampton and threw the bogus Wild Bill through a set of scenery and then, for good measure, tossed the manager over the footlights. He was arrested but was fined only three dollars and costs.

Although Wild Bill never again appeared onstage, he did have one last fling with show business. He traveled to Cheyenne, where he spent most of his time gambling until he met a widow, Mrs. Agnes Thatcher Lake, whom he had befriended when her circus played Abilene. They were married on March 5, 1876, in Cheyenne, and Hickok toured with the circus as far as Cincinnati. A gold strike drew him next to Deadwood, Dakota Territory.

Deadwood was the raw, roaring capital of the Black Hills mining camps. Founded in April 1876, it had a population of ten thousand in two months. It became the wildest, most lawless mining camp in history. Gamblers, gunmen, and outlaws flocked there, along with the prospectors and traders. Doc Pierce, the busy undertaker, said, "Deadwood was then hog-wild; duels and gunfights in the streets, and one often had to duck or fall flat on the ground to escape a shower of lead."

When Wild Bill reached the top of the divide and looked down on the raw mining town, he turned to his friend Colorado Charlie and said, "I have a hunch that I am in my last camp and will never leave this gulch alive."

Sans Hickok, Cody's show continued its run, playing in Lockport, Buffalo, and Erie, until May 13, 1874, when the show closed in Boston. After the end of the run, Texas Jack went to New England to spend the summer with his new wife; in August he returned west to guide the Earl of Dunraven on another hunt. Cody returned west even earlier to guide a hunt. He was engaged in New York by "an English gentleman, Thomas P. Medley of London. . . . He was a very wealthy man . . . a relative of Mr. Lord of the firm of Lord & Taylor, of New York. . . . He offered to pay the liberal salary of one thousand dollars a month while I was with him. . . . of course I accepted." Dr. W. F. Carver, "who then resided at North Platte, and who has recently acquired considerable notoriety as a rifle-shot, hunted with us for a few days," said Cody. Cody and Carver would meet again.

Once out in Nebraska, Medley informed Buffalo Bill that he did not wish to hunt in the manner of Grand Duke Alexis, with carriages, servants, and other lavish equipment, but that he wished to rough it, in the open air, and do his share of the work. Cody found him "a very agreeable gentleman and an excellent hunter."

The Medley hunt ended, it was now time for Cody to go back to his first love, scouting.

TRIUMPH—AND TRAGEDY

In July 1874, after his show closed in Boston, Cody went back to Fort McPherson, where he was hired as a guide at $150 a month for the Big Horn Expedition commanded by Brevet Lieutenant Colonel Anson Mills. Will's tour of duty with Mills lasted from August 7 to October 2. The expedition did not result in any Indian fights and thus received little attention. The command consisted of five companies of cavalry, two companies of infantry, four Pawnee scouts, and "citizens: Two guides (Mr. Cody or 'Buffalo Bill' and Tom Sun), six scouts, twenty packers, and thirty teamsters; one ambulance, 28 wagons, and 70 pack mules"—a substantial force.

A man named White was mentioned by Colonel Mills as one of the scouts; his grave marker reads "Jonathan White." White had come to Fort McPherson for medical treatment of an injured leg but was refused admission to the post hospital until Cody intervened and offered to pay the bill. White, who had served the Confederacy under J. E. B. Stuart, was a fine rifle shot and an excellent horseman. After his recovery, he attached himself to Cody.

Said Captain King in *Campaigning with Crook*: "For years he had been Cody's faithful follower—half servant, half 'pardner.' He was Bill's 'Fidus Achates'; Bill was his adoration. . . . He copied Bill's dress, his gait, his carriage, his speech—everything he could copy; he let his long yellow hair fall low upon his shoulders in wistful imitation of Bill's glossy brown curls. He took more care of Bill's guns and horses than he did of his own and so, when he finally claimed, one night at Laramie, the right to be known by some other title than simple Jim White—something descriptive, as it were, of his attachment for Cody and life-long devotion to his idol 'Buffalo Bill,' a grim quartermaster dubbed him 'Buffalo Chips,' and the name was a fixture." Buffalo chips, or *bois de vache*, were the dried dung that was used for fuel on the plains, so the nickname may have been less uncomplimentary than it sounds today. White was killed by Indians at Slim Buttes in 1876, an Indian fight that Cody missed.

One day while the troops were resting on a prairie near the head of the Powder River, Cody tells of seeing a solitary horseman approaching them in the distance. At first the rider was thought to be an Indian, but it turned out to be California Joe Milner, armed with a heavy old Sharps rifle, a revolver, and a knife. Cody introduced California Joe to the officers and then asked the old plainsman where he was going. Although he actually had been out prospecting, Joe preferred to say that he was "out for a morning ride." Joe accompanied the expedition for several days, at which point Colonel Mills suggested to Cody that he hire Joe as a scout, so that he might earn some money. Cody put him on the payroll at a salary of five dollars a day. Said Cody: "It was worth the money to have him along for company's sake, for he was a droll character in his way, and afforded us considerable amusement." California Joe had scouted for George Armstrong Custer, who seems to have regarded Joe as a drunken buffoon, although useful. Asleep or awake he wore a huge sombrero and carried a long breech-loading Springfield musket, and as Custer wrote in *My Life on the Plains*, he always rode a mule "in whose speed and endurance he had every confidence." On October 29, 1876, Joe was shot in the back at Fort Robinson by a man with whom he had quarreled.

The Big Horn Expedition scouted the Powder River, Crazy Woman's Fork, and Clear Fork, and then pushed westward through the mountains to the Wind River. On the first day of September a severe snowstorm hit the command. It lasted for thirty-six hours and brought snow two feet deep. One horse died where it stood that night, and Colonel Mills attributed the loss of twenty-three horses to this one storm. In the end, the expedition found that the Indians they were searching for had abandoned their villages. Thereupon General E. O. C. Ord, the department commander, ordered the expedition dissolved, its object having been accomplished—to be certain that the Indians had left the area.

An encounter with a hostile bear accounted for the expedition's only casualty. On September 28 Colonel Mills recorded: "Marched at 10 a.m. and camped at 3 p.m. on Little Creek, distance 12 miles. During the day's march the men of Major Moore's company encountered a bear on the muddy Creek, wounded and chased him into a clump of Willows on the creek when Private Miller dismounted and entered the willows against the remonstrance of California Joe, when he was seized by the bear and horribly mangled and would have been killed had not some of the men rode in and dispatched the bear, firing three shots at him, while the bear and Miller were on the ground struggling together. Miller died of these wounds soon after reaching his post—Fort McPherson, Nebraska. One man riding too close had several pounds torn from his horse by a stroke of the bear's paw." In concluding his report, Colonel Mills mentioned only three of his civilian employees: "Mr. Cody (Buffalo Bill) sustained his old reputation as an excellent and invaluable guide, Mr. Sun also is a good guide, and I will recommend him for future employment should occasion require it. Mr. Parker acquitted himself well with the pack train."

After his discharge as guide on October 2, Cody headed east to organize his next combination. Since Texas Jack was still hunting with the Earl of Dunraven, Bill had to find an actor to play Texas Jack in *The Scouts of the Plains*. The new scout was billed as "Kit Carson, Jr.," though no member of the great scout's family was ever in show business. As soon as he had completed an abbreviated tour, Buffalo Bill spent the summer of 1875 in his new home in Rochester, a rare occurrence in his peripatetic lifestyle, according to Don Russell. However, the *Nebraskian* of July 23 states that he was to start for the Black Hills in a few days with ten men for a six-week buffalo hunt. Accompanying him were the New Yorkers J. F. Hecksher and Robert Adams of Beadle and Adams, the dime novel publishers, and several men and women of the Buffalo Bill Combination. Texas Jack was to go along. Nothing more is reported of this hunt, so more than likely it did not take place.

During the next theatrical season, the fall of 1875, Texas Jack was back, along with Mlle. Morlacchi, for what turned out to be the last tour of the old combination. Morlacchi again played Pale Dove, and Major Burke was back as manager. As *The Scouts of the Plains* opened a two-day engagement at Springfield, Massachusetts, on April 20, 1876, Cody was handed a telegram from Colonel G. W. Torrence of Rochester, informing him of the serious illness of the Codys' only son, five-year-old Kit Carson, or "Kitty," with scarlet fever. Cody played the first act, after which Major Burke substituted, so that Will could take a nine o'clock train. According to his sister Helen, on the journey, despite his fear and anxiety, he recalled those times when Kit attended one of his father's performances. The boy knew how important, from the management's point of view, a large audience was. He would watch while the house filled up and then, once his father appeared onstage, call out, "Good house, Papa!" Audiences apparently learned to expect and enjoy this bit of byplay between father and son.

"At ten o'clock the next morning I arrived in Rochester," said Cody, "and was met at the depot by my intimate friend Moses Kerngood who at once drove me to my home. I found my little boy unable to speak but he seemed to recognize me and putting his little arms around my neck he tried to kiss me. We did everything in our power to save him, but it was of no avail. The Lord claimed his own, and that evening at six o'clock my beloved little Kit died in my arms. We laid him away to rest in the beautiful cemetery of Mount Hope amid sorrow and tears."

In a letter to his sister Julia, written at three o'clock in the morning a few hours after his son's death, his sentiments are simple and tender as he struggled to understand why the gay little Kit had been taken, telling her that the boy "was too good for this world. We loved him to[o] dearly he could not stay." He attempted to picture the boy in a bright and better world, "where he will wait for us." Cody wrote that he reached home a few hours before Kit died, and Lulu, worn out from her long vigil with three sick children, was sleeping, while he watched at the bedside of his little girls.

Cody's grief at the death of his only son is easy to understand; perhaps no tragedy is more devastating to a parent than the death of a young child. When Will returned to the cast of *The Scouts of the Plains* in Rochester, it was to honor the show business tradition that the show must go on, though it is sometimes hard for the audience to understand *why* it must go on. Still, his heart was not in it. He began receiving requests from Colonel Anson Mills to join General Crook's command as a scout in the coming Indian campaign. At first he resisted, but six weeks after Kit's death he closed out the run early, telling audiences that he was off to fight real Indians.

As so often before in his life when struck by sorrow or beset with anxieties, Cody turned his face to the West and headed for his beloved plains, where one of the most memorable—and controversial—episodes of his scouting career was about to take place.

Of all the Indian fights Cody engaged in—fourteen altogether after he became chief scout of the Fifth Cavalry in 1868—none carries with it more controversy than the famous fight with Yellow Hand. It has been called by various writers, who apparently did not check the official records, "The Duel on the War Bonnet," "The Death of Yellow Hand," and "The First Scalp for Custer." It has also been argued that Cody did not kill Yellow Hand. Contemporary records, however, prove otherwise.

To start with, it was not a duel. It did not take place on the War Bonnet; and the Indian's name was Yellow *Hair*, not Yellow Hand. The fight in which Cody killed him took place on Hat Creek, near today's Montrose, Nebraska. Yellow Hair, whose Indian name was Hay-o-wei, was a subchief, a son of Cut Nose, a Cheyenne chief. Contemporary accounts gave Cody credit for killing Yellow Hair, and he described the fight in both autobiographies, though with added embellishments.

When Cody told his audience in Wilmington, Delaware, that he was off to fight Indians, he was on his way to join the command of Major General George Crook, one of the officers assigned to deal with the hostile Sioux. Historians of the Sioux campaign of 1876 have concentrated almost entirely on Custer's Last Stand, but it is important to put Custer's defeat into perspective, along with the other engagements that were fought, especially the one in which Buffalo Bill took part. The Sioux war of 1876 grew out of Custer's 1874 expedition, which discovered gold in the Black Hills. The Sioux considered the land sacred—though it had been sacred only for a decade or two, ever since they had chased the Kiowa out of the Black Hills.

In his annual report for the year 1875, the commissioner of Indian affairs stated: "It is not probable that as many as 500 Indian warriors will ever again be mustered at one point for a fight; and with the conflicting interests of the different tribes, and the occupation of the intervening country by advancing settlements, such an event as a general Indian war can never occur in the United States."

How wrong the commissioner was would become apparent when Custer reached the Little Big Horn. "Yet up until this moment," said General of the Army Sherman, referring to Custer's last stand, "there was nothing official or private to justify an officer to expect that any detachment could encounter more than 500, or at the maximum, 800, hostile warriors." In November of 1875 there were some 30 or 40 lodges under Sitting Bull, and 120 lodges under the Oglala Sioux Crazy Horse; other lodges, instead of returning to the reservations where they had been ordered, were on the way to join them. The tribes that were gathering for war were by now a long way from the Black Hills, and more than a thousand in number.

On arriving in Chicago, Cody learned that the Fifth Cavalry was in the field and that General Carr had written Sheridan inquiring about Cody's whereabouts. He changed his plans accordingly. Crook was already on the march, so Will decided to rejoin the Fifth. He determined that the best way to reach the regiment was by taking a train to Cheyenne, Wyoming. There he was met by Lieutenant Charles King, who took him to camp. A press report of the day stated:

> At noon on the 9th [of June] W.F. Cody (Buffalo Bill) joined the command as scout and guide. There is very little change in his appearance

. . . except that he looks a little worn, probably caused by his vocation in the East not agreeing with him. All the old boys in the regiment upon seeing General Carr and Cody together, exchanged confidences, and expressed themselves to the effect that with such a leader and scout they could get away with all the Sitting Bulls and Crazy Horses, in the Sioux tribe.

On June 10, 1876, Cody was again on the quartermaster's payroll as a scout. The following day he left Cheyenne for Fort Laramie with General Carr and the battalion. At Laramie, on June 14, they were joined by General Sheridan and other officers. From there, with a company of cavalry as escort, Cody and Sheridan went to the Red Cloud Agency, while the Fifth Cavalry was sent out to scout the country between the Indian agencies and the Black Hills. While Cody and Sheridan were at Red Cloud, Crook fought the Battle of the Rosebud on June 17, and on June 25 Custer and his command were wiped out on the Little Big Horn. The outcome of these engagements was unknown on July 1, when Brevet Major General Wesley Merritt took over command of the Fifth from General Carr. The following day Merritt, with Cody as guide, led the battalion closer to the Indian trail, after which the troops traveled about the country for several days, camping at Sage Creek in Wyoming on July 6. It was Cody who brought the battalion the news of Custer's fate.

In his memoir, Lieutenant King wrote:

A party of junior officers were returning from a refreshing bath in a deep pool in the stream, when Buffalo Bill came hurriedly towards them from the general's tent. His handsome face wore a look of deep trouble, and he brought us to a halt in stunned, awe-struck silence, with the announcement "Custer and five companies of the Seventh wiped out of existence. It's no rumor—General Merritt's got the official dispatch."

It had taken twelve days for the news to reach the Fifth.

On July 11 the Fifth Cavalry was ordered to join Crook's command and set out at once for Fort Laramie. At reveille on July 14 a report came from the commander at Camp Robinson that one thousand Cheyenne were planning to bolt the nearby Red Cloud Agency. Merritt at once turned back toward Rawhide Creek Crossing, on the trail between Camp Robinson and Fort Laramie, hoping to get ahead of the Cheyenne and turn them back. This was on Saturday. By Monday night the troops had reached Hat Creek, after marching eighty-five miles in thirty-one hours to reach their objective. Lieutenant King commanded an outpost toward the southeast, the direction from which the Cheyenne were expected. On a butte not far from King's position was trooper Chris Madsen, ready to send messages with a signal torch or flag to Merritt's headquarters. At first light the following morning, Cody, who had been reconnoitering, joined Madsen and told him to signal the command that the Cheyenne, encamped not far away, were getting ready to move. At the same time, Lieutenant King sent word that the Indians were coming over a ridge from the southeast. By five o'clock Indians were in view across a three-mile front, all unaware of the soldiers.

Meanwhile the troops' wagon train of supplies had been coming up the trail behind the marching cavalry. When the Cheyenne saw the train, they began to race about on various ridges and hilltops, watching its movement. Cody, with scouts Tait and Buffalo Chips White, had ridden up to Merritt's hilltop to watch. Two couriers bearing messages for General Merritt had been sighted some distance away, and a small band of Cheyenne rode after them. Seeing this, Cody suggested riding down to cut the Indians off. Merritt gave the order, and Cody was told to lead the charge. There were approximately eight men with him, two of them his fellow scouts, and the rest troopers. At this point seven Cheyenne dashed away in pursuit of the couriers.

Cody awaited the signal to charge, which was to come from Lieutenant King who, from his hilltop, was watching the approach of the seven Indians through his binoculars. As the Indians dashed by in front of his hill, he shouted to Cody, "Now, lads, in with you." Merritt and the rest of the group were out of sight of the point at which Cody and his men intercepted the Indians, but Madsen, who was still on signal duty, had a clear view of the action. This is what he wrote in a manuscript years later:

> Cody was riding a little in advance of his party and one of the Indians was preceding his group. I was standing on the butte where I had been stationed. It was some little distance from the place where they met but I had an unobstructed view of all that happened. Through the powerful telescope furnished by the Signal Department the men did not appear to be more than 50 feet from me. From the manner in which both parties acted it was certain that both were surprised. Cody and the leading Indian appeared to be the only ones who did not become excited. The instant they were face to face their guns fired. It seemed almost like one shot. There was no conversation, no preliminary agreement, as has been stated erroneously in some novels written by romantic scribes.

"They met by accident and fired the moment they faced each other," Madsen wrote. "Cody's bullet went through the Indian's leg and killed his pinto pony. The Indian's bullet went wild. Cody's horse stepped into a prairie dog hole and stumbled but was up in a moment. Cody jumped clear of his mount. Kneeling, he took deliberate aim and fired the second shot. An instant before Cody fired the second shot, the Indian fired at him but missed. Cody's bullet went through the Indian's head and ended the battle. Cody went over to the fallen Indian and neatly removed his scalp while the other soldiers gave chase to the Indian's companions. There is no doubt about it, Buffalo Bill scalped this Indian, who, it turned out, was a Cheyenne sub-chief called Yellow Hair."

Madsen, who later earned fame with Bill Tilghman and Heck Thomas as the "Three Guardsmen," distinguished peace officers in the Oklahoma Territory, is considered a reliable witness. So is Sergeant John Powers of Company A, Fifth Cavalry, who was riding in a wagon train that morning. What he saw from the other side of the hill, after Cody crossed the ridge, was reported in a dispatch from Fort Laramie, dated July 22 and printed in the Ellis County *Star* on August 3. It might come as a surprise to readers today that the *Star* had more correspondents in the field than the New York *Herald*, the Chicago *Times*, or the San Francisco *Call*. That is because so many of the men in the Fifth hailed from Ellis County, and local readers were interested in what was going on in the field. As a result, regular dispatches were filed by "Powers," "Brown," or "Mac," all from Ellis County.

Powers's account is substantially the same as Trooper Madsen's. Other official reports confirmed the facts related by Madsen and Powers, though without naming either Cody or Yellow Hair. "The Record of Events" of the Fifth Cavalry for June 30–August 31 states: "Early on the morning of July 17th, a party of seven Indians was discovered trying to cut off two couriers, who were on their way to the company with dispatches. A party was at once detached in pursuit, killing one Indian."

Cody himself described the fight in a brief letter written the following day from the Red Cloud Agency to his wife: "We have had a fight. I killed Yellow Hand a Cheyenne Chief in a single-handed fight. You will no doubt hear about it through the papers. I am going as soon as I reach Fort Laramie the place we are heading for now [to] send the war bonnet, shield, bridle, whip, arms and his scalp to Kerngood [a family friend who owned a clothing store in Rochester] to put up in his window. I will write Kerngood to bring it to the house so you can show it to the neighbors. . . . I have only one scalp I can call my own that fellow I fought single handed in sight of our command and the cheers that went up when he fell was deafening."

The New York *Herald* carried the following account of the fight on July 23, a day before the Ellis County *Star*: "Company K was instantly ordered to the front. But before it appeared from behind the bluff, the Indians, emboldened by the rush of their friends to the rescue, turned savagely on Buffalo Bill and the little party at the outpost. The latter sprang from their horses and met the daring charge with a volley. Yellow Hand, a young Cheyenne brave, came foremost, singling Bill as a foeman worthy of his steel. Cody coolly knelt, and, taking deliberate aim, sent his bullet through the chief's leg and into his horse's head. Down went the two, and before his friends could reach him, a second shot from Bill's rifle laid the redskin low."

The final evidence that Cody killed Yellow Hair is contained in the regimental history: "William F. Cody, the favorite scout of the regiment, was conspicuous in the affair of the morning, having killed in hand-to-hand conflict, Yellow Hand, a prominent Cheyenne chief."

It wasn't long before the mythmakers went to work on the story, forever confusing the details. Louisa Cody, for example, tells it this way in her book with Cooper: "For long fearful weeks I knew only that Will was somewhere in the West, and I daily lived in hopes of a letter from him, and in dread of bad news from some other source. And then one day the expressman delivered a small box from Fort McPherson. It was from William F. Cody. I pried open the lid, and a very unpleasant odor caught my nostrils. I reeled slightly, reached for the contents, and then fainted. For I had brought from the box the scalp of an Indian. When Will came home again, he told me the scalp was Yellow Hand's and that he had killed him in a duel."

Cody's sister Helen Cody Wetmore further embroidered the "duel" in her book, written to practically deify her brother, and incidentally to hawk tickets to the Wild West show:

> Here something a little out of the usual occurred—a challenge to a duel. A warrior, whose decorations and war bonnet proclaimed him a chief, rode out in front of his men, and called out in his own tongue, which Will could understand:
>
> "I know you, Pa-has-ka! Come and fight me, if you want to fight!"
>
> Will rode forward fifty yards, and the warrior advanced a like distance. The two rifles spoke, and the Indian's horse fell; but at the same moment Will's horse stumbled into a gopher-hole and threw its rider. Both duelists were instantly on their feet, confronting each other across a space of not more than twenty paces. They fired again simultaneously, and though Will was unhurt, the Indian fell dead.
>
> The duel over, some two hundred warriors dashed up to recover the chieftain's body and to avenge his death.

By 1879, when Cody's first autobiography appeared, the *New York Weekly* had already published "The Crimson Trail; or, Custer's Last Warpath, a Romance Founded Upon the Present Border Warfare, as Witnessed by Hon. W.F. Cody," and Cody himself had appeared on stage in *The Red Right Hand; or, Buffalo Bill's First Scalp for Custer*. In both the *Weekly* story and the play the fight ended with the chief's death in hand-to-hand combat with knife and tomahawk and Cody holding the Indian's scalp and war bonnet aloft and shouting "The first scalp for Custer."

In his 1879 autobiography Cody described a running fight that lasted several minutes, during which three Indians were killed. He then picked up the challenge from "one of the Indians, who was handsomely decorated with all the ornaments usually worn by a war chief when engaged in a fight, sang out to me, in his own tongue: 'I know you, Pa-he-haska; if you want to fight, come ahead and fight me.'"

Cody's version of the fight continued much as the official record has it, but it ended this way: "My usual luck did not desert me on this occasion, for his bullet missed me, while mine struck him in the breast. He reeled and fell, but before he had fairly touched the ground I was upon him, knife in hand, and had driven the keen-edged weapon to its hilt in his heart. Jerking his war-bonnet off, I scientifically scalped him in about five seconds. . . .

"As the soldiers came up, I swung the Indian chieftain's top-knot and bonnet in the air, and shouted:

"'*The first scalp for Custer.*'"

Later in his life, Cody continued to insist that he had stabbed the Indian warrior with his Bowie knife, that in fact he kept the same knife on the mantel at his home in North Platte. However, there is no independent verification of his claim.

In 1928 Richard J. Walsh wrote, in *The Making of Buffalo Bill*: "Over what General Sheridan described as an almost totally unknown region of about ninety thousand square miles, the Sioux and their allies were supreme and aflame with hatred. There were twenty-nine thousand well-armed Indians at large in a country in which they knew every canyon and ford."

Walsh quotes Cody's 1879 autobiography account of the fight, and adds: "It was not strange that the enemy picked on Buffalo Bill. . . . His comrades wore buckskin, corduroy or flannel so indiscriminately that officers and privates could hardly be told apart. Cody went into that fray all dressed up in one of his stage costumes—a handsome Mexican suit of black velvet, slashed with scarlet and trimmed with silver buttons and lace. Why he should be wearing such regalia, far in the hills, at dawn, after an eighty-mile ride, when the regiment was in its working clothes, is impossible to explain, except as studied showmanship."

Don Russell agrees with Walsh that Cody wore the vaquero stage outfit, and reasons that he had donned it very early that morning, knowing there was soon to be an engagement, so that, when wearing it on the stage the following winter, he could tell his audiences he was wearing the proper attire of a scout on the plains. Or, with dramatic flair, he could truthfully announce to his audience that this was the very same outfit he was wearing when he killed Yellow Hand—studied showmanship indeed. As for his transformation of a theatrical version of the famous fight into his own life story, it is perhaps forgivable artistic license. He was, after all, in some measure the creator of his own legend.

Over the years other claimants to the mantle of Yellow Hair's killer emerged. One early candidate was Baptiste Garnier, "Little Bat," a scout with the Fifth Cavalry during the campaign, though there is no mention of him having been with Cody during the fight of July 17. Little Bat did not claim to have killed Yellow Hand, but his son, John Garnier, known as Johnny Bat, is quoted as saying "When Yellow Hand challenged someone to come out and meet him with knives Bill rode out to meet him despite Dad and the rest telling Bill the Indian would cut him to pieces." Then, to save Bill's life, "my Dad just pulled up on his rifle and took a single shot at Yellow Hand and he rolled off his horse."

Sergeant Jacob Blaut, Company I, Fifth Cavalry, is mentioned as having thought that he himself might have killed Yellow Hand: "Bill and I fired at the same time, and I think my bullet killed him." In one of Blaut's many tales of the affair he says definitely that he shot and stripped the Indian, and that he and the other troops also killed eleven other Indians and captured twelve horses and a mule before the fight was finished. Another soldier, Jules Green, says Cody killed the chief but only because he, Green, chased Yellow Hand out of a canyon so Bill could fire the fatal shot into him.

Billy Garnett, sometimes called Billy Hunter, made the Denver *Post* on February 23, 1923, with his version of the duel. Cody and the chief fought with knives, he said, for more than an hour, and within sight of the garrison at Camp Robinson, thirty-five miles from the spot on Hat Creek where the army said Yellow Hair died.

The author Mari Sandoz claimed to have a complete file on the engagement at Hat Creek, gathered from military records, personal contact with Indians who were knowledgeable about the affair, and personal research in various libraries. From all this, her conclusion was that, after an exchange of a dozen or so shots between the soldiers and Indians, both sides ceased firing. "Yellow Hand," Sandoz wrote, "a young warrior who desired to win honors and prove his courage, then rode up and down between the Indians and the cavalrymen, challenging the soldiers to come and fight.

"He continued to call them old squaws and dared them to meet him in combat. At length, one of the troopers, unable to withhold his anger, disobeyed Merritt's order to hold his fire and took a shot at Yellow Hand. The warrior's horse stumbled and fell to its knees. Yellow Hand stuffed his warbonnet under his belt and struck off towards safety. Another well placed shot killed the braggart. The trooper who downed Yellow Hand scalped him. We assume he took the warbonnet also. Cody paid him five dollars for the scalp that night, and it is presumed he came into possession of the warbonnet by similar means."

In her book *The Buffalo Hunters*, Sandoz was highly critical of Cody and failed to treat his claim to have killed Yellow Hair objectively. What is also self-evident is that a medieval tourney-type battle between opposing foes, or any kind of duel, is completely foreign to Indian warfare, as Don Russell carefully points out.

On July 22, 1876, a brief notice in the *Western Nebraskian* said that there were eight hundred Sioux and Cheyenne bolting their reservation and that Buffalo Bill shot one. A week later the paper reported, "The Indian killed by Buffalo Bill was Yellow Hand, a young chief." Still, conflicting stories of the fight continued to appear for years. As late as May 24, 1917, under the headline "Memorable Duel with Gun and Pistol Fought in Early Days A Matter of History of the West," a purported eyewitness account appeared of "the duel with knives between Colonel William F. Cody (Buffalo Bill) and Yellow Hand, chief of the Sioux Indians, which is accurately pictured in Essanay's current feature, *Adventures of Buffalo Bill*." Essanay was the early motion picture studio founded by George Spoor, the "S," and "Broncho Billy" Anderson, the "A," star of the first Western ever filmed, *The Great Train Robbery*, in 1903.

In this "eyewitness" account, the Indian's horse is yellow, and he is a Sioux, not a Cheyenne. The two duelists use up all their ammunition without either scoring a hit. The commanding general is given as Carr, when it was Merritt who led the troops that day.

Don Russell sums up the Yellow Hand controversy this way: "No other of his race ever died so often, in so many different places, by so many different hands."

The following month, in Deadwood, Dakota Territory, Wild Bill Hickok was sitting in a poker game in Carl Mann's saloon, when a young hoodlum named Jack McCall crept up behind him, poked a .45-caliber Colt close to his ear, and fired once. Asked on the witness stand why he didn't go around front and shoot Bill in the face like a man, McCall said, with simple candor, "I didn't want to commit suicide."

When Doc Pierce, the undertaker, came to take charge of Hickok's remains, he found the gunfighter's fingers crooked as though still holding cards. The cards, strewn on the floor, showed aces and eights. "Since that day," said Doc, "aces and eights have been known as the 'dead man's hand' in the western country." The undertaker also said, "I have seen many dead men on the field of battle and in civil life, but Wild Bill was the prettiest corpse I have ever seen. His long mustache was attractive, even in death, and his long tapering fingers looked like marble."

Wild Bill's Sharps rifle was buried in the coffin with him, and on a stump at the head of his grave these words were carved:

A brave man, the victim of an assassin,
J.B. Hickok, (Wild Bill) age 39 years;
murdered by Jack McCall Aug. 2, 1876.

"Thus ended the career of a good friend of mine," Buffalo Bill recalled, "who, in spite of his many faults, was a noble man, ever brave and generous hearted."

Was there any military significance in the fight at Hat Creek? Some, certainly. It was one of the few instances in which a large war party of Indians was successfully ambushed by federal troops. That the trap was sprung too soon, in order to save the lives of two couriers, limited the casualties to one Indian, but it did keep some eight hundred Cheyenne out of Sitting Bull's camp.

The accounts of Buffalo Bill's fight with Yellow Hand inspired much discussion of scalping. Most Americans are horrified by stories of scalping and attribute it to the Indians, but it seems likely that the white man was largely responsible for the brutal practice, beginning with the Spanish. In America, the wolf-tail bounty of colonial times apparently led to a bounty for Indian scalps. In their ancient intertribal disputes, Indians did little scalping. They "counted coup," which simply meant that the first warrior to touch an enemy with a coup stick in battle was honored. The tribes of the northeastern part of North America, particularly the Iroquois, did some scalping along the lower St. Lawrence in precolonial days. The practice spread because early colonial governments offered to pay bounties to friendly Indians for the scalps of enemies, particularly during the French and British wars.

*   *   *

As Company K came up to the ridge shortly after Yellow Hand's death, the Indians fired a scattering volley. The remaining troops advanced cautiously in open order to the ridge, but after it was gained they saw the Cheyenne fleeing in all directions, leaving in their wake a vast array of ammunition, arms, and blankets, which they flung to the ground as impediments in their efforts to outdistance their pursuers—sure evidence of their intention to join Sitting Bull's and Crazy Horse's campaign. The seven troops of the Fifth Cavalry pursued the Indians into Red Cloud Agency, a march of thirty miles or more that took most of the day, but they were unable to kill or capture any of them. At Red Cloud, the eight hundred hostiles, once they had washed off the war paint, were indistinguishable from the peaceful "blanket Indians" at the reservation, so nothing was done to punish the Cheyenne.

After this brief engagement no more southern Cheyenne attempted to reinforce Sitting Bull. According to Lieutenant King, "one and all they [the Indians] wanted to see Buffalo Bill, and wherever he moved they followed him with awestruck eyes." The fact that Bill was still wearing the black velvet vaquero costume slashed with scarlet was undoubtedly responsible for their awe.

On the afternoon of July 18, Merritt's command was on the march to Fort Laramie. On his arrival at the fort, Cody found a wire from James Gordon Bennett asking for a report on the fight. He asked King to write this for him, and King composed what he later referred to as "a brief telegraphic story, say one-eighth of a column." He read it to Cody, who suggested no changes at the time, though King recalled the scout's remarking "It's fine only—" and then saying no more. The *Herald* story, with banner headlines, was nearly a column long. Lieutenant King did not read the *Herald* story until 1929. He then said that the newspaper had made a few alterations in his story. King rose in the army to become a general, and wrote a number of accounts of the Yellow Hand fight. The definitive and most accurate version appeared in his book, *Campaigning with Crook*, which was published in 1890.

Although the men were eager for a rest after their long marches, the Fifth Cavalry did not linger at Laramie. The troopers had arrived at three o'clock on Friday afternoon. Saturday was spent drawing supplies, shoeing horses, and preparing for a long campaign. Soon they were on the march to Fort Fetterman, where they arrived on Tuesday, July 25. The next morning they picked up additional reinforcements and continued the march toward General Crook's forces.

King's account tells us that somewhere between Crazy Woman's Fork and Clear Fork on August 1, "several small herds of buffalo were sighted, and some few officers and men were allowed to go with Cody in chase," surely to get additional rations. Late in the afternoon of August 3 the Fifth reached General Crook's camp on Goose Creek, about where Sheridan, Wyoming, now stands. Crook's own command, supplemented by the Fifth, was designated the Big Horn and Yellowstone Expedition, commonly abbreviated to the "B. H. & Y." William F. Cody was officially designated as "Chief Scout with the Big Horn and Yellowstone Expedition" and was paid $150 a month by Lieutenant W. P. Hall, the quartermaster. Some twenty civilian scouts were employed by various units of the B. H. & Y., but Bill was "primus inter pares," first among equals.

Among the scouts in the B. H. & Y. were two unusual men. One was Frank Grouard, often called Crook's favorite scout, as Cody was Carr's. Grouard had lived among the Hunkpapa Sioux for several years and was on intimate terms with Sitting Bull and Crazy Horse. Half Polynesian, the son of a Mormon missionary and a Polynesian princess, he was often mistaken for an Indian. He left the Sioux in 1875 and was employed at the Red Cloud Agency. Because of his years with the Sioux, he was regarded with suspicion by some officers and scouts, and the Sioux considered him a renegade.

The other scout worth mentioning is Captain Jack Crawford—the "Poet Scout." He was credited with carrying dispatches for four hundred miles through perilous territory to Fort Fetterman, where he had arrived on July 29. When he reached Crook's camp on August 8, he sought out his old friend Bill Cody. "While we were conversing," said Cody, "Jack informed me that he had brought me a present from Colonel Jones of Cheyenne, and that he had it in his saddle-pockets. Asking the nature of the gift, he replied that [it] was only a bottle of good whiskey. . . . Jack is the only man I have ever known that could have brought that bottle of whiskey through without *accident* befalling it, for he is one of the very few teetotal scouts I ever met." Cody shared the bottle with General Carr and Barbour Lathrop, a reporter with the San Francisco *Call.*

Born in Ireland, County Donegal, John Wallace Crawford was brought as a child to Pennsylvania, where he went to work in the coal mines. When his father left for the Civil War, Jack followed him, and managed to enlist in the Union army at the age of fifteen. Badly wounded first at the Battle of Spotsylvania Courthouse and again at Petersburg, he spent some time in a hospital, where he learned to read and write.

Crawford's mother, on her deathbed, had made him promise never to touch liquor; and though he spent most of his life among heavy drinkers, he kept his promise. He was one of the early settlers in the Black Hills, and chief of scouts of the Black Hills Rangers. He was also a correspondent for the Omaha *Bee.*

Pawnee and Sioux chiefs with Buffalo Bill on Staten Island, 1886. The Pawnee, all scouts, are, from left, Brave Chief, Eagle Chief, Knife Chief, and Young Chief, and on the right, the Sioux American Horse, Rocky Bear, Flies Above, and Long Wolf. (Buffalo Bill Historical Center, Cody, Wyoming)

*   *   *

General Crook was described by King as wearing a "worn shooting jacket, slouch felt hat, and soldier's boots, with ragged beard braided and tied with tape, with twinkling eyes and half-shy embarrassed manner." He may not have looked the part of a soldier, but to most of those who served with him, he was considered the greatest Indian fighter of them all, as well as the one who had the best understanding of Indian nature. He was eager for another blow, but he wisely waited until his forces were at full strength.

That came when Crook's command joined the command of Brevet Major General Alfred H. Terry, brigadier general commanding the Department of Dakota, whose troops included Major Reno of the ill-fated Seventh Cavalry. As the senior officer, Terry was technically now in charge of the expedition. According to King, "Terry had with him a complete wagon train, tents and equipage of every description. We had a few days' bacon and hard-tack, coffee and sugar, and a whole arsenal of ammunition on our mules, but not a tent, and only one blanket apiece. He had artillery in the shape of a few light field pieces, and was making slow, cautious advances up the Rosebud [Creek] at the rate of eight or ten miles a day. . . . Even the Seventh Cavalry were housed like Sybarites to our unaccustomed eyes. 'Great guns!' said our new major, almost exploding at a revelation so preposterous. 'Look at Reno's tent—he's got a Brussels carpet!'"

Cody also noted that Terry's camp presented a great contrast to that of General Crook, "who had for his headquarters only one small fly tent; and whose cooking utensils consisted of a quart cup—in which he made his coffee himself—and a stick, upon which he broiled his bacon. . . . I came to the conclusion that General Crook was an Indian fighter; for it was evident that he had learned that, to follow and fight Indians, a body of men must travel lightly and not be detained by a wagon train or heavy luggage of any kind."

In his book *On the Border with Crook*, Captain John G. Bourke described how Generals Crook and Terry sat down on a strip of canvas, drank coffee, and talked about what to do about the Sioux. "Terry was one of the most charming and affable of men," said Bourke. "He won his way to all hearts by unaffectedness and affability." He was a man who looked like a scholar, with kind blue eyes and a gentle face bronzed by sun, wind, and rain to the hue of an old sheepskin Bible. Because of his intellectual achievements, the whole army felt proud of him, said Bourke, but reading between the lines, it is plain that in his judgment General Crook, not Terry, was the significant commander, equaled only by Sheridan and Grant.

Crook and Terry camped at the mouth of the Powder River while supplies were distributed, and there they organized their plan of attack. Terry would pursue some hostiles who had crossed to the north side of the Yellowstone; Crook would follow the broad trail east because this large party of Sioux might be headed for the Black Hills.

Late in August the columns separated. Terry and Brevet Major General John Gibbon headed northeast, accompanied by Buffalo Bill. Custer biographer Evan Connell, not one of Cody's fans, calling him "a curious admixture of thespian and assassin," reports that there were men in the command who were unimpressed by his presence. "When he joined us," one soldier remarked many years later, "he was wearing all the accoutrements befitting a moving-picture scout. He had an entire suit of creamy buckskin, all beaded and fringed. A rich silk scarf encircled his neck and covered his shoulders. His headwear was a fine-quality big white hat having three or four eagle feathers standing up from its band."

Gibbon accepted Buffalo Bill pleasantly and turned him over to Lieutenant James Bradley, who was in charge of the civilian scouts.

"You'd better be careful of your clothing," Bradley said, "or it may get wet and dirty while you are with us."

It is not known how Buffalo Bill answered Lieutenant Bradley.

Cody's first assignment was to board the supply steamer *Far West* with another scout, Louis Richaud, and accompany Lieutenant General Nelson A. Miles down the Yellowstone River as far as Glendive Creek. "We were to ride on the pilot house and keep a sharp lookout on both sides of the river for Indian trails that might have crossed the stream," says Cody. "The idea of scouting on a steamboat was indeed a novel one to me, and I anticipated a pleasant trip." When Cody saw some objects he thought might be Indian ponies, he and Richaud were landed with their horses and two companies of infantry. The objects turned out to be Indian graves.

At the mouth of Glendive Creek, Miles sent Will overland with reports to Terry; Cody says he "rode seventy-five miles that night through the bad lands of the Yellowstone, and reached General Terry's camp next morning, after having nearly broken my neck a dozen times or more."

On August 22 Cody was discharged as chief of scouts of the B. H. & Y., saying "There being but little prospect of any more fighting, I determined to go East as soon as possible to organize a new 'Dramatic Combination,' and have a new drama written for me, based upon the Sioux war. This I knew would be a paying investment, as the Sioux campaign had excited considerable interest." The Chicago *Times* had a report that Cody told off both Crook and Terry, accusing them of not wanting to fight, and demanded his pay vouchers. He might well have done so; it was a characteristic gesture. When interviewed in Chicago, Cody said that he would ask Sheridan for permission to raise a company of one hundred frontiersmen to fight through the winter. Nothing came of this proposal.

Although he was discharged on August 22, Cody's scouting was not quite over. On August 24 he boarded the steamer *Yellowstone*, headed for Fort Buford and civilization. The *Yellowstone* had only gone about twenty miles downstream when it met the *Josephine* coming upstream with reinforcements for Terry under Brevet Brigadier General Joseph Whistler. When the steamers stopped to exchange news, Cody was pleased to find Texas Jack on board the *Josephine*, carrying dispatches for the New York *Herald*. Whistler asked Cody if he would take some dispatches to General Terry, "saying that it would only detain me a few hours longer; as an extra inducement he offered me the use of his own thorough-bred horse, which was on the boat. I finally consented to go. . . . I delivered the dispatches to General Terry that same evening." Cody's delay of a few hours would actually turn into two weeks. Terry asked Cody if he would carry some dispatches back to General Whistler, and Cody replied that he would. "Captain Smith, General Terry's aide-de-camp, offered me his horse for the trip, and it proved an excellent animal; for I rode him that same night forty miles over the bad lands in four hours and reached General Whistler's steamboat at one o'clock.

"During my absence," says Cody, "the Indians had made their appearance on the different hills in the vicinity, and the troops from the boat had several skirmishes with them." He then goes on to quote Whistler as saying "Cody, I want to send information to General Terry concerning the Indians who have been skirmishing around here all day. I have been trying all evening long to induce some one to carry my dispatches to him, but no one seems willing to undertake the trip, and I have got to fall back on you. It is asking a great deal, I know, as you have just ridden eighty miles; but it is a case of necessity, and if you'll go, Cody, I'll see that you are well paid for it."

Cody says he answered, "Never mind about the pay, but get your dispatches ready, and I'll start at once." This was not the first time Cody had gone on a mission no one else wanted to undertake. Cody left Whistler at two o'clock in the morning and reached Terry's camp at eight o'clock, just as he was about to march. He had ridden 120 miles in twenty-two hours.

Terry then asked Cody to accompany his forces on a scout north of the river toward the Big Dry Fork of the Missouri, where it was expected they would find Indians. After marching three days, the troops found fresh signs of Indians, who evidently had been killing buffalo. Cody was asked to carry this news to Glendive Creek. Cody started at 10 P.M. in a drizzling rain through a part of the country with which he was unacquainted. By daylight he had made only thirty-five of the eighty miles. He decided to spend the day in a ravine, for he considered it dangerous to cross the prairies in broad daylight. He went to sleep, and was awakened by the rumble of a herd of buffalo pursued by twenty or thirty Indians. Cody watched the Indians for two hours, while they killed and butchered their game.

At nightfall he resumed his journey, making a wide detour to miss the Indians, and reached the Glendive stockade at daybreak. He was asked to make a return trip to advise Terry of Indian skirmishes. Cody says he overtook Terry at the head of Deer Creek and guided the general's column toward the stockade. On arriving there, Bill found the *Far West* just leaving for Fort Buford, and went aboard headed for Bismarck, where he took a train for Chicago and his home in Rochester.

According to the official records, on September 6, 1876, the acting assistant quartermaster of the Seventh Cavalry paid William F. Cody $200 for services as a scout with General Terry's Expedition in Montana Territory. One hundred dollars a week was the highest pay Cody had ever received as a scout, but it was hard earned, for he was almost constantly riding alone through country infested with hostile Indians. Nor did he mind that "the few hours" and "just one more ride" had stretched into two weeks, for he had no firm plans as yet for his next combination.

Cody and Texas Jack had come to a parting of the ways, and Jack and his wife, Guiseppina Morlacchi, had organized their own combination for that season. Buffalo Bill was now on his own. With some old stage friends, he put together a show based on the so-called battle of the War Bonnet, billed as *The Red Right Hand; or, Buffalo Bill's First Scalp for Custer*.

The new show, as its star admitted, "was a five-act play, without head or tail, and it made no difference at which act we commenced the performance. . . . It afforded us, however, ample opportunity to give a noisy, rattling, gunpowder entertainment, and to present a succession of scenes in the late Indian war, all of which seemed to give general satisfaction."

The dissolution of the partnership with Texas Jack apparently came without any hard feelings on either side. Undoubtedly both felt they could do better financially as singles than in tandem. Texas Jack's combination looked every bit as strong as Buffalo Bill's, if not stronger. He had, of course, his wife, "the peerless Morlacchi," and a cast including "the great chief and scout Donald McKay and his Warm Springs Indians," who had been outstanding in the Modoc War of 1873; he also had Major John M. Burke, advance man and actor. Said the St. Louis *Globe Democrat* in reviewing *Texas Jack in the Black Hills* that winter: "Arizona John, whose other name is Burke, is a member of the Texas Jack Combination. . . . In all of Texas Jack's retinue there is no one who can annihilate whole tribes of Indians with greater facility than 'Arizona John.' Armed with a revolver filled with blank cartridges, he kills six of the 'red demons' at a single fire." In addition to acting, Burke was honing his craft of press-agentry, which would later serve Buffalo Bill so well.

In 1877–1878, Texas Jack was well received in the old war-horse *The Scouts of the Plains*. In 1880 he appeared in Denver in *The Trapper's Daughter*, and a few weeks later Mlle. Morlacchi was billed in Leadville, Colorado, in *The Black Crook*, considered the first true American musical comedy. In Leadville, Jack prospected for silver, and there he died of pneumonia, on June 28, 1880, at the age of thirty-three. After his death, John Burke joined Cody as advance man and press agent. With all the skill of a kingmaker, Burke would fix the heroic, larger-than-life image of Buffalo Bill in the public mind, with a stream of articles, interviews, and reviews.

Cody's 1876 drama opened in the Rochester Opera House. Captain Jack Crawford, the "Poet Scout," he who had ridden "through 300 miles of hostile country" bringing Buffalo Bill a bottle of whiskey, came to

Rochester at Cody's behest and was added to the combination. The troupe then traveled to New York City for an engagement at the Grand Opera House of Poole and Donnelly. Cody's combination then hit all the principal cities in the East and Midwest, and was a success wherever it went. To advertise the show, Bill displayed the scalp and headdress of Yellow Hand in shop windows, until the squeamish clergy and press of New England denounced "the blood-stained trophies of his murderous and cowardly deeds," an unexpected attack on the hero of Hat Creek, Summit Springs, and a dozen other battles. Cody wisely ceased the practice, which merely stimulated public curiosity to see them at the theater, thereby enhancing box office receipts. Then as now, the American appetite for blood and gore, for sensationalism of all kinds, was insatiable.

That season Cody also staged an alternative play from the previous season, *Life on the Border*, described as "depicting true Frontier life," in which Bill took the part of "Buffalo Bill, a Western Judge, Jury, and Executioner." In this sentimental melodrama, Captain Jack played "Capt. Jack, can trail an Indian from the Missouri to the Pacific."

When he went on the stage, Captain Jack also turned to writing poems and succeeded in getting most of them published. He enjoyed reciting them, especially one of his most popular, "Mother's Prayers":

Mother, who in days of childhood
Prayed as only mothers pray;
Keep him in the narrow pathway
Let him not be led astray.
And when danger hovered o'er me
And when life was full of cares,
Then a sweet form passed before me
And I thought of Mother's prayers.

A Chicago journalist who offered Crawford a drink had to submit instead to a recital of "Mother's Prayers." The reporter apparently needed several shots of the hard stuff himself to serve as an antidote to that saccharine dosage, but Wild Bill Hickok was moved by the poem: "You strike a tender spot, old boy, when you talk mother that way," he said. Wild Bill would surely have appreciated the Poet Scout's eulogy for him:

Under the sod in the land of gold
We have laid fearless Bill;
We called him Wild, yet a
    little child
Could bend his iron will.
With generous heart
    he freely gave
To the poorly clad, unshod—

Think of it, pards
    —of his noble traits—
While you cover him
    with the sod.

Later Captain Jack wrote three successful plays and published more than a hundred short stories. As for his poetry, he was one of the first, if not the first, of the cowboy balladeers, whose works are published and recited out West to this day. In January 2000, nearly 8,000 cowboys attended the sixteenth annual Cowboy Poetry Gathering in Elko, Nevada: before submitting their verses, entrants had to prove to a screening committee that they are real cowboys.

In 1877 Cody announced "a farewell tour." An unidentified contemporary newspaper clipping gives the details: "This will be the last season that Buffalo Bill (W.F. Cody) will travel as a theatrical star. The company he now has is engaged for fifteen months, one month of which is to be passed on vacation. The troupe, about the middle of June, will arrive in Omaha, and then they will be transported at the manager's expense to his ranch on the North Platte, where they will be at liberty to do as they please. Toward the end of June they will start for San Francisco and play there for four weeks. Thence through California, Oregon, Nevada, and Utah, back to Omaha, where they will disband, Buffalo Bill going to his ranch, to remain there the rest of his life as a cattle dealer and gentleman farmer. He now has 4,500 head of cattle, and hopes to have 10,000 by the close of next year. He will, therefore, retire from the stage with an ample competence."

This newspaper report turned out to be premature, both as to his retirement and his becoming a gentleman farmer.

"Except that Cody did not stay on his ranch for the rest of his life," writes Don Russell, "this program was generally carried out." Cody now decided to take his new combination to the Pacific Coast, "against the advice of friends who gave it as their opinion that my style of plays would not take very well in California." Cody was the first to discover what all producers of "Westerns" ever since have proved—that the wholly imaginary and fictitious West of stage, book, or screen is most popular in the real West it mistakenly represents. It is a matter of local pride. When Owen Wister's *The Virginian* was criticized for the unrealistic language of its cowboys, one old-timer remarked with candor, "'Well, maybe we didn't talk that way before Mr. Wister wrote his book, but we sure all talked that way after the book was published.'" Similarly, real cowboys took their wardrobes and mannerisms from fictional misrepresentations of what they really wore and how they behaved.

In San Francisco Cody's play opened at the Bush Street Theatre—and he drew a house of $1,400, substantial money when you consider that theatergoers paid one dollar for dress circle and parquette, fifty cents for the second tier, and twenty-five cents for the gallery. Cody had engaged the theater for only two weeks but stayed five. Unlike now, there were no booking agents in those days; the managers of combinations like Buffalo Bill's sent advance men ahead to book the theaters for them. Cody's earnings for the 1876–1877 tour, which ended at Virginia City, Nevada, were reported at $13,000. At its close he met his family in Denver, where his sisters May and Nellie, or Helen, lived. The Buffalo Bill Combination disbanded at Omaha, as scheduled. It was there that the first rift between Will and his wife, Louisa, occurred. Will does not mention it in his autobiographies, but in a divorce suit, filed in 1905, he testified:

> In paying the company, I went to one of the rooms where the four ladies who were the four actresses of the company were waiting to receive their final settlement, which I paid them and got their receipts in full. The ladies were having a glass of beer in this room, and one or two gentlemen, members of the company, were in this room and we all had a glass of beer or two, or a drink of some kind, and we were talking of the past season, and we were a little jolly, laughing and talking. When I went to leave the party the ladies all jumped up and they said, "Papa, we want to kiss you good bye." They called me papa. the ladies did in the company that season. And I kissed them good bye and we were all laughing and joking.

Louisa was not present in the room where Will kissed the girls goodbye, but she heard what was going on from an adjoining room and was incensed. Cody was puzzled by her reaction.

> I do not think that most wives would have felt a little angry to know and hear her husband in an adjoining room on Sunday morning, drinking beer and kissing the theatrical girls of his company. I think they would be rather proud of a husband who had six or seven months work with a party of people who were in his employ, to know and feel they were on a kindly footing with their late manager, that they were sorry they were going to be separated from a good, kind manager who had always paid their salaries himself. Not only one of them got up and kissed papa good bye, but all four of them rushed up and kissed papa, their old manager, good bye and wished him well and much happiness and success. Actresses are not a narrow-minded people. They do not go behind the door or to some dark room if they want to kiss a man. They boldly walk up to him and with their enthusiasm, they are willing to let the world know that they like him and do not hesitate to show it in their voice and by their lips. . . . You ask how old papa was at that time? He wasn't too old to be kissed then, and that was a good many years ago, and he is not too old now. I was just 31 then, just the right age.

Poor "Papa"! He proved in 1905 that if you talk long enough, ramble on long enough, you are bound to make a sorry situation far worse. Cody simply couldn't understand that his wife, raised in the Age of Victoria, might form quite a different view of what to him was just "showfolk" expressing their affection for one another. His farewell to the actresses of his company in 1877 would not be the last time Lulu would have occasion to take her Will to task for his indiscreet behavior.

Cody actually did take up ranching as promised in his swan song. Early in the spring of 1877, he stopped off in Sidney, Nebraska, where he met the North brothers, Frank and Luther, and there, according to Luther, Will and Frank made arrangements to go into the cattle business together. While Cody was in California with his show, the Norths were to locate grazing range for the cattle and build the ranch headquarters. The ranch was established on the South Fork of Dismal River, sixty-five miles north of North Platte. Cody met North at Ogallala, then the end of the trail for Texas cattle drives. There they bought and branded their first herd of 1,500 head, hired a crew, and drove it to their range, an undertaking that took up most of the summer. Two of the crew were Texans, Buck and Baxter Taylor, both well over six feet tall. Buck, nineteen years old that summer and the taller of the two, was later to be famous as the "King of the Cow-Boys" in Cody's Wild West show.

Will's sister Helen, imprecise in details as she so often was, stated that at the close of the season after he killed Yellow Hair, he "bought a large tract of land near North Platte, and started a cattle-ranch," adding that in partnership with Major North he already owned a ranch some distance to the north. There were 7,500 acres in the North Platte ranch, she wrote, with 2,500 acres in alfalfa and the same in corn. The ranch house, when "seen from the foothills, has the appearance of an old castle."

Cooper has Louisa locate the North Platte farm "near the Wyoming line" and wrote that Cody also "bought a tremendous ranch on the Dismal River in partnership with Major North." Another writer claimed that "Cody owned many valuable tracts of land, as well as large herds of cattle. The land was presented to him by the government for his outstanding services as a scout during the many Indian skirmishes."

Nellie Snyder Yost cleared up the matter of Cody's land. Will did not own any land at North Platte until 1878, when he sent some money to banker Charles McDonald to buy land for him. On February 4 the banker bought 160 acres for $750 in Lincoln County. For the next several years Will sent money back to the banker, earmarking it for the purchase of more land, but it was some time before the ranch attained its maximum size of 4,000 acres.

Buffalo Bill Cody's Scout's Rest Ranch, North Platte, Nebraska. (Buffalo Bill Historical Center, Cody, Wyoming)

Also, according to Nellie Yost, not one acre of land was presented to Buffalo Bill by a grateful government for any reason whatsoever, nor did Cody or North buy any land on the Dismal. During the time they operated their ranch there, from 1877 to 1882, all that part of Nebraska was open range, and the first rancher to put cattle on it held it by the simple right of first use.

Leaving the cattle in the charge of Frank North, Cody visited the Red Cloud Agency early in the fall, and there, for the first time, he engaged reservation Sioux Indians for his next show. Although "Real Indians" had been advertised earlier as part of the cast, for the most part the redskins were white supers in war paint. Taking his family and the Indians with him, he went to Rochester. There he left his oldest daughter, Arta, at a young ladies' seminary, while Louisa and Orra Maude traveled with him during the theatrical season. This was by no means a state of affairs that pleased Louisa, who had no taste for life on the road, and after five months she was thoroughly tired of it. It is possible that she stuck it out that long in order to make sure that Will kept his distance from the actresses in his company.

The season of 1877–1878 featured a timely new play based on the Mountain Meadows massacre of 1857, the notorious slaying of emigrant men, women, and children by the Mormons. The massacre was in the news again because John D. Lee, a Mormon leader, had just been convicted of complicity in it and had been executed by a firing squad on March 23, 1877. Since Cody had played a minor part in the Mormon War while working for Russell, Majors and Waddell, he decided to commission a play based on the episode. The play was *May Cody; or, Lost and Won*. May Cody was Will's sister, who made several appearances in dime novels, although the story bore no relation to her or any of her experiences. An actress named Constance Hamblin played the part. The play's author was Major Andrew Sheridan Burt, a captain in the Ninth U.S. Infantry when he became a dramatist; later he became a brigadier general of volunteers in the Spanish-American War.

As for the supporting cast, hiring supers at twenty-five cents a performance was easy but did not suit the expanding vision of Major John Burke, who demanded genuine Indian braves. Gordon W. Lillie, later known as Pawnee Bill, then an interpreter at an Indian reservation in Oklahoma, borrowed a number of Sioux Indians for the show.

Major Burt's drama opened on September 3, 1877, at the Bowery Theatre in New York. Included in the cast, in addition to the six Sioux braves, were some prairie ponies and a Mexican burro. After its run at the Bowery, *May Cody* played at the Eagle Theater in Brooklyn. "It was the best drama I had yet produced," said Cody, "and proved a grand success both financially and artistically." A cash book for a part of this season has been preserved, and it shows that the take, on the whole, was well over double the expenses. There were good days, such as $599 at Springfield— and bad, only $118 at Waterville.

The Cody-Crawford partnership did not last out the season. At Virginia City, Montana, in July of 1877, Crawford "shot himself in the groin, inflicting a serious wound." One unsympathetic editor remarked that the incident was not without its "counterbalancing advantages, for they had to ring down the curtain." Apparently, Major Burt's drama was no artistic advance over Ned Buntline's *The Scouts of the Prairie*.

"In February, 1878," according to Cody, "my wife became tired of traveling and proceeded to North Platte, Nebraska, where, on our farm adjoining the town, she personally superintended the erection of a comfortable family residence, and had it all completed when I reached there, early in May. In this house we are now living (as of 1879) and we hope to make it our home for many years to come." This was wishful thinking on Cody's part, since he wasn't actually there all that often.

Of this first Cody home in North Platte, little is known. Helen calls it by its popular name, "Welcome Wigwam," and says that it "was built according to the wishes and under the supervision of the wife and mother." In *Memories of Buffalo Bill*, Cooper had Louisa saying: "Furnishings came all the way from Chicago and New York. . . . The lumber had been hauled across country, and there, out on the plains, we built a house that was little less than a mansion."

Frances Fulton, who visited Welcome Wigwam in 1883, said of it: "the Cody's [sic] beautiful home is nicely situated one-half mile from the suburbs of North Platte." Years later, long after the house was gone, a North Platte resident who remembered it described Welcome Wigwam as "an ordinary story and a half frame house with a small stable or shed on the back of the lot and a low white wooden fence around the yard." By then, of course, many larger and finer houses had been built in the town, making the Cody house seem plain, even humble, by comparison. A miniature replica of the house can be seen at the Buffalo Bill Historical Center in Cody, Wyoming; it is anything but a "mansion."

Cody spent the summer of 1878 at his ranch, where he found that the cattlemen had organized a regular "round-up." The word was unfamiliar in 1879, and Cody found it necessary to define it. "The word 'round-up,'" he wrote, "is derived from the fact that during the winter months the cattle become scattered over a vast tract of land, and the ranchmen assemble together in the spring to sort out and each secure his own stock. They form a large circle, often of a circumference of two hundred miles, and drive the cattle toward a common centre, where, all the stock being branded, each owner can readily separate his own from the general herd, and then he drives them to his own ranch."

Although the cowhand's life was to become an integral part of Cody's Wild West show, the ranch was more of a diversion for Cody than a serious business, and he was happy to leave its actual running to Frank North. Even at thirty-one he was getting a bit soft and unsuited to the cow-punching life. "As there is nothing but hard work on these round-ups," he remarked, "having to be in the saddle all day, and standing guard over the cattle at night, rain or shine, I could not possibly find out where the fun came in, that North had promised me." Still, he found it an exciting life, and "the days sped rapidly by; in six weeks we found ourselves at our own ranch on Dismal River, the round-up having proved a great success, as we had found all our cattle and driven them home."

One rancher, J. J. Douglas of Custer County, who was with Cody on the roundups, wrote of him, "Buffalo Bill . . . was a liberal fellow, never cared to lay up money, said he always believed in keeping it in circulation, always carried plenty to drink and smoke, and quite frequently set 'em up to the round-up." If it looked as if his original supply of refreshments might run short, he would send a wagon to North Platte to lay in more.

John Bratt, in his book *Trails of Yesterday*, also mentions Cody's hospitality at the ranch. There was always "something doing besides actual round-up work when Buffalo Bill was there," he recalled.

> Some of the cowboys would take advantage of the Colonel's hospitality by going to his wagon and helping themselves to his cigars and sampling his liquors that had been brought along as an antidote against snake bites and other accidents. There would be broncho riding, roping, racing, riding wild steers, swimming contests, and sometimes a friendly poker game to see who could stand on night herd the longest. The cowboys were glad to see the Colonel and the other cattle owners and foremen would vie with each other in showing him a good time, and would prepare special feasts . . . for him when he came to or near their ranches. Nothing was too good for Colonel Cody.

Later in the summer of 1878 Will spent a few weeks with his family at North Platte, where he was visited by his sisters Helen and May, both now married. He also traveled to Kansas to see his sister Julia, now Mrs. J. A. Goodman, and his fourth sister, Eliza, now Mrs. George Meyers.

When it came time to organize his new Dramatic Combination, he went to Indian Territory and hired a band of Pawnee, with C. A. Burgess as interpreter and Edward A. Burgess as "Boy Chief of the Pawnees." His season opened in Baltimore at the opera house managed by John T. Ford, whose Washington, D.C., theater was the scene of President Lincoln's assassination.

When Cody's troupe reached the capital, he learned that the Indian Bureau was unhappy that he was employing Indians. He went to see Carl Schurz, secretary of the interior, and was told that the commissioner of Indian affairs, E. A. Hayt, claimed that the Pawnee were wards of the government, now absent without leave. Cody says he told the commissioner that the Indians were frequently off their reservations out west, as he had a distinct remembrance of meeting them on several occasions "on the warpath," and that, further, he thought that he was benefiting the Indians as well as the government by taking them all over the country, and "giving them a correct idea of the customs, life, etc. of the pale faces, so that when they returned to their people they could make known all they had seen."

Schurz had to agree with Cody, and the commissioner told him he could keep his Indians provided he was appointed a special Indian agent, putting him under bond to return his actors to their reservation at the end of their contract. The combination then proceeded to Richmond, Virginia, and to Savannah, Georgia, where an epidemic of yellow fever caused Cody to head for Philadelphia instead, and then to the Northeast.

At the same time, he arranged to have "the well-known author and dramatist, Colonel Prentiss Ingraham, to write a play for me." This was *The Knight of the Plains; or, Buffalo Bill's Best Trail*, which had its premiere in New Haven and was so successful that Bill took it on a six-weeks tour of the Pacific Coast and the Far West early in 1879. In San Francisco, Cody and Captain Jack had a violent argument, provoked when Captain Jack was given a fund-raiser that he felt was inadequate. Seeking to persuade him to come back, Cody wrote, "I have just finished a big engagement at the California Theatre. My share was nearly $6,000 . . . I think you had better stayed with me when I offered you $200 a month." Captain Jack, however, did not return to the company.

Cody often found that his amateur actors could be difficult. To Buckskin Sam Hall, who had been a Texas Ranger during the settling of the West, he wrote on July 5, 1879: "In regard to you going on the boards again. I must think of it. I have no part in either my dramas that would be suitable for you to play as I did say that I would never have another Scout or western man with me. That is one whom I would work up. For just as soon as they see their names in print a few times they git the big head and want to start a company of their own. I will name a few. Wild Bill Texas Jack John Nelson Oregon Bill Kit Carson and Capt. Jack all busted flat before they were out a month and wanted to come back. Because I would not take them then they talked about me."

The Kit Carson whom Cody mentioned was not the famous scout but a Kit Carson Jr. who may not even have been related to Kit. Cody was also concerned about Sam Hall's drinking. "Sam," he wrote in September 1879, "realy [*sic*] I don't think we could agree. I am all business and I would expect a man to be prompt and reliable agreeable and quick to understand. . . . But old fellow I fear the Texas Boys would keep you *full* all the time and that would hurt my business. . . . I see you are like most of the prairie boys. Tangle foot gets away with you. And I will have no one with me thats [*sic*] liable to let whisky get away with him in this business a man *must* be perfectly reliable and *sober*."

Cody concluded his letters to Hall at this time by insisting that when he could afford it, he would help the old Ranger financially. He also urged Hall to write rather than attempt to act. Several years later he wrote Hall: "Yours recd. I met Ingraham yesterday. Do you know I begin to beleive like your self that he is a bad egg or that he is a forked tongue. He told me or at least wrote me he had placed your mss. [manuscripts] in B & A

[Beadle and Adams's] hands. Yesterday he says B & A dont want them. But that he has them ready Whether he has or not I cant say. I have so much to do I cant take time to see B & A for a few days. But when I do I will ask them."

Cody readily admitted that he drank heavily at times, and his various partners all complained about the difficulty of keeping him sober, so it is hard to know what to make of his lecture to Sam Hall. Do as I say, not as I do, perhaps?

When the *Knights* played in Central City, Colorado, the *Daily Register Call* on July 31, 1879, found the enterprise wanting. "As might be expected," ran the notice, "the opera house was filled to overflowing last night to see the great scout of the plains, his wild Indians, black bears, buffaloes and jack rabbits, all of which the flaming posters on the dead walls announced would be present. But the small boy and the lover of western romance were disappointed. There were no buffalo, no black bears, no wild Indians; but instead a third-rate dramatic company, playing at some sort of sickly play without point or pith. There was not a passable artist in the crowd, and if there had been there was nothing in the play to bring him or her out. Bill himself did remarkably fine in a character he has created and which he has played thousands of times. The support was simply vile, and unworthy the Alhambra Varieties in its palmy days. But yet the house was crowded." Even though this critic disliked the play and the cast, he still praised Cody.

Prentiss Ingraham, like Ned Buntline, was a colorful character in his own right. Like Buntline, Prentiss was the son of a writer, the Reverend J. H. Ingraham, author of *The Prince of the House of David* and other books, which his son rather irreverently called "dime novels about the Bible." Again like Buntline, Prentiss preferred to write about pirates. He was a genuine warrior. His adventures included fighting with the Confederates during the Civil War and with Juarez in Mexico. A colonel of Cuban rebels, he was condemned to death by the Spanish but made a daring escape. By 1872 he averaged two dime novels a month. He was later to write dozens of Buffalo Bill dime novels, beginning in 1879. He was still churning them out at the time of his death in 1904. He also wrote dime novels signed by Texas Jack and Dr. Frank Powell—and some of those signed by Buffalo Bill. It is through the work of Prentiss Ingraham that the fame of Buffalo Bill would spread throughout the world.

"MORE LIKE FICTION
THAN REALITY"

The town of North Platte, Nebraska, in which the Codys would live for the next thirty-five years, was still a frontier village in 1878. According to Nellie Snyder Yost, it was "a village of modest homes and dirt streets, with a few planks thrown across the muddiest intersections along Front Street in the spring." There were no trees anywhere in the town, no lawns or flowers in the summer. A few homes, one of them the Codys', were somewhat more pretentious, with picket fences to keep out wandering livestock. There was a two-story courthouse, topped by a tall, many-windowed cupola; and a two-story schoolhouse, where Arta Cody and her younger sister Orra went to school for a few years.

As for the streets themselves, they were quite dreadful: ankle-deep in dry, choking dust in summer, with hub-deep mud in the season of melting snows and spring rains. They were so muddy in the spring that four-horse teams could scarcely pull empty wagons, while ducks and mud hens swam in the sloughs spread throughout the town. The alleys were even worse, and the town's three newspapers frequently called attention to their filthy condition, especially during the first warm days of spring. The *Enterprise* bluntly requested that "the gentleman who owned the dog that died near this office to be kind enough to remove same," and the *Republican* noted that "the hog in the alley back of this office has been dead for several months," and "the foulness of the air caused by dead animals in and around the town [makes it] smell like an 'offal' place." The *Republican* went on to say that "Old hoop skirts, wornout corsets, shoes, dirty socks, old hats and underwear, tons of tin cans and old whiskey bottles, a half ton of gunny sacks, 17 dead dogs, 1 horse, 3 cows and a bull, 7 hogs and

11 pigs . . . compose a tithe of the nastiness, rubbish and filth found in the alley in the rear of Front Street."

Like all frontier towns, North Platte had its saloons, barbershops, blacksmith shops, and livery stables. A dozen doctors and lawyers practiced their trades. The barbershops, or "tonsorial parlors" as the gentlefolk called them, were numerous and sometimes elegant. Each shop featured a public bathtub; one North Platte shop had five tubs—a public necessity, since few houses had indoor plumbing. "Bath water," writes Nellie Yost, "was heated on a coal oil stove in the 'bathroom,' and the used water ran through a drain pipe into the alley behind the shop. Freighters and men off the long cow trails, after many days on the road, made the barbershop-bath house their first stop in town. Often the man—bathed, barbered, and shaved—who sauntered out the door was scarcely recognizable as the one who had gone in, hidden beneath long hair, long whiskers, and many layers of dust and sweat."

Buffalo Bill, the townspeople knew, was quite particular about his long hair. Years later Ed Weeks, a classmate of Cody's youngest daughter, Irma, said: "It was a treat to see Buffalo Bill come into a chair with his hair folded up under his big hat, the way he usually wore it. It was sure interesting to see those barbers take the pins out of his hair. He wore more pins than any three women. His hair was very dark but was streaked with grey, and he was very proud of it."

Again like all frontier towns, North Platte boasted more saloons than any other kind of business. There were at least seven on the three main streets of the town, and the general stores also sold liquor and wine. "If half the stories told of Buffalo Bill and his drinking are true," says Yost, "he must have patronized all of them."

On the outskirts of town, there were brothels, unlicensed saloons, and gambling dens that were wide open every day of the week and all hours of the night. Archibald R. Adamson, in his book *North Platte and Its Associations,* writes: "Cowboys would ride long distances to have a 'good time' at North Platte. They were a frolicsome lot . . . and it was not uncommon for one or more to ride into a saloon, order drinks and in wild glee shoot out the lights; or ride at a furious pace through the town, whooping and yelling and shooting. Then, many a man died with his boots on, and it was a question whether the law abiding feared white men or Indians the most." Allowing for some hyperbole, life in early North Platte was certainly no less lively than it was in Dodge City or Tombstone.

One of the first businesses to be established in any new frontier town was a newspaper; North Platte in the early years had three, all publishing at the same time and the editor of each disagreeing violently with the others. Freedom of the press was never in danger in the West, although more than one editor was attacked on occasion, even horse-whipped, for exercising that right. It is because there were so many newspapers publishing then that we have such an abundant and valuable written record of frontier life.

On August 24, 1878, one of these newspapers, the *Western Nebraskian*, reported that Cody had done some very fancy and difficult shooting at his place. There followed the first mention of Cody's shooting at glass balls. The newspaper then went on to say that after running out of glass balls "he shot most of the potatoes from his garden on the fly. He intends to shoot glass balls on the stage when he starts his new season, and after more practice hopes to shoot against Dr. Carver." In the spring, Dr. W. F. Carver, "the greatest of all living riflemen," who would play a considerable role in Cody's career as a showman, had given a very fancy shooting exhibition in Omaha.

The *Nebraskian* also mentioned that Mr. Cody owned a stallion, Silver Clay, which had taken two premiums at a fair in Jefferson County, Kansas, and that the stallion was to be brought to North Platte the next year. Buffalo Bill was clearly planning the showplace he meant to develop at North Platte, a ranch with the loveliest house, the biggest barns, and the finest blooded livestock in the country.

He called it Scout's Rest Ranch.

The year 1879 marked the official debut of Buffalo Bill, Author. At the close of his prosperous western tour in the spring, the *Nebraskian* observed on May 10: "The Honorable W.F. Cody returned from California last Tuesday and was gladly greeted by his many friends." Three weeks later the North Platte *Republican* noted that Cody had ridden about town disguised in one of his stage costumes. After this diversion, Bill joined the spring cattle roundup, then in progress, returning to North Platte about the middle of June. On June 28, according to the *Republican*, *The Life of Hon. William F. Cody, Known as Buffalo Bill, the Famous Hunter, Scout and Guide: An Autobiography* was just off the press, and the newspaper's editor, James M. Ray, promised he would review it for his readers himself, just as soon as he had time to read it.

The autobiography was not the first literary production attributed to Buffalo Bill. Don Russell identifies that as "The Haunted Valley; or, A Leaf from a Hunter's Life," in *Vickery's Fireside Visitor* for April 1875. This was the first of twenty-five dime novels signed "by Buffalo Bill," published from 1875 through 1903, issued by such publishers as Street & Smith's

New York Weekly, The Saturday Evening Post, Saturday Journal, Beadle's Half-Dime Library, and *Pocket Library.*

But how many of these stories were actually written by Buffalo Bill? And did he write his own autobiographies? In *The Lives and Legends of Buffalo Bill,* Don Russell analyzes at length the books, stories, and articles written *by* Cody and those written *about* him. It is Russell's conclusion that at least four "Buffalo Bill" dime novels published in 1875 were actually written by Cody. Albert Johannsen, the foremost authority on dime novels, has assembled evidence to indicate that this is the case, and maintains that "early productions signed by Buffalo Bill are not of such literary excellence as to be beyond Cody's capacity."

It is probably "The Haunted Valley" that Helen Cody Wetmore referred to when she said "Our author would never consent to write anything except actual scenes from border life. As a sop to the Cerberus of sensationalism, he did occasionally condescend to heighten his effects by exaggeration. In sending one story to the publisher he wrote 'I am sorry to have to lie so outrageously in this yarn. My hero has killed more Indians on one war-trail than I have killed in all my life. But I understand this is what is expected in border tales. If you think the revolver and bowie-knife are used too freely, you may cut out a fatal shot or stab wherever you deem it wise.' Even this story, which one accustomed to border life confessed to be exaggerated, fell far short of the sensational and blood-curdling tales usually written, and was published exactly as the author wrote it."

Helen added: "The first sketch Will wrote for publication was destitute of punctuation and short of capitals in many places." Said Cody, "Life is too short to make big letters when small ones will do; and as for punctuation, if my readers don't know enough to take their breath without those little marks, they'll have to lose it, that's all."

Helen continued: "Will now had leisure for study and he used it to such good advantage that he was soon able to send to the publishers a clean manuscript, grammatical, and well-spelled and punctuated." This agrees with the fact that he spent the summer of 1875 at his home in Rochester, and the stories and dime novels began to appear in August of that year.

R. Farrington Elwell, a noted western artist who served his apprenticeship painting subjects for Buffalo Bill's Wild West lithographs, has said, "As to the Colonel's literary work, yes, he did write some of his very earlier work himself; I really should say that quite a number of novels were written entirely by him and used just as written."

We shall never know for sure which of the dime novels signed by Cody he actually wrote, but, according to Don Russell, "It seems doubtful that he ever read a Buffalo Bill dime novel, or anything else printed about himself, including books signed with his name." In fact, it is unlikely he read much of anything. He said he read the Bible and "a few other books" when he was marooned with a broken leg as a boy, during his trapping expedition with Dave Harrington. An English reporter, visiting Cody's tent at the Wild West in 1887, saw a library of three books—*Life of General Custer, U.S. Infantry Tactics*, and a book of newspaper clippings.

Leaving aside the question of whether Burke or Prentiss Ingraham or somebody else actually wrote the novels signed by Cody, it is possible to cherish the diction of this bit of dialogue from *Death Trailers:* "He hissed forth gloatingly: 'I've got yer ag'in, my beauty. Now I'll see that yer don't git away.'"

As for his 1879 autobiography, it was published by Francis Edgar Bliss of the American Publishing Company of Hartford, Connecticut. It has been widely assumed that Cody must have had a ghostwriter for the book, and there are several candidates. The first is Ned Buntline, but Will's association with Buntline had ended years before the publication of the autobiography. Another possibility is Major John Burke, the Wild West general manager, but his style is florid, and the book, for the most part, is simply told, and contains revelations that a general manager would have suppressed, such as Cody's enlistment in the Union Army while drunk. Even Frank E. Bliss has been mentioned as a possible ghostwriter, because the book was copyrighted in his name. But it was the custom at that time for the publisher to hold the copyright, not the author. Russell's emphatic conclusion is that Cody himself wrote the book, though he probably incorporated some of his theatrical material in a few episodes as an *aide-memoire*, or to save time and energy.

Francis Edgar Bliss was born September 23, 1843, the son of Elisha Bliss Jr., head of the American Publishing Company, publisher of works by Mark Twain, Bret Harte, and Twain's good friend Charles Dudley Warner. Frank joined the firm in 1866 and is said to have been the first publisher to sell books by subscription agents, a popular book marketing operation of the late nineteenth century. The agents, who would be called "commission reps" today, were then called "drummers." They traveled from door to door and farmhouse to farmhouse with prospectuses announcing a work to be published, took advance orders, and then delivered the finished products. A surviving prospectus for Cody's autobiography records a long list of subscribers living in Hartford.

Subscription selling was hardly a new phenomenon, having been around for some five hundred years. Napoléon Bonaparte was once a book agent; so were Bismarck, George Washington, Jay Gould, Mark Twain,

Henry Wadsworth Longfellow, Daniel Webster, and Rutherford B. Hayes. And while selling door to door may be much less common today, what are mail-order books but a form of subscription selling?

The Life of Buffalo Bill—Illustrated, as the title is printed on the spine, sold for $2.00 bound in cloth and $2.50 bound in leather. A door-to-door book agent would keep half the purchase price and could make a decent living at a time when Cody was paying his actors $18.00 a week. Mark Twain, several of whose books were sold by subscription agents, once said: "When a subscription book of mine sells 60,000 copies I always think I know whither 50,000 of them went. They went to people who don't visit bookstores . . . the factory hands and farmers," readers who had to be hunted down by the publisher's agents.

At first, Frank Bliss proposed to start his own house, secretly, by raiding his father's firm for authors, one of them being Mark Twain, who was disaffected from the elder Bliss. That effort failed, but when Elisha died in 1880, Frank succeeded him as head of the American Publishing Company.

Helen Cody Wetmore, as usual, got her facts wrong when she said, "During the summer of 1877 I paid a visit to our relatives in Westchester, Pennsylvania. My husband had lost all his wealth before his death, and I was forced to rely upon my brother for support. To meet a widespread demand, Will this summer wrote his autobiography. . . . I, anxious to do something for myself, took the general agency of the book for the state of Ohio, spending a part of the summer there in pushing its sale. But I soon tired of a business life, and turning the agency over to other hands, went from Cleveland to visit Will at his new home in North Platte." The husband Helen mentions was her first, Alexander C. Jester. The publication of her brother's autobiography took place not in 1877 but two years later.

True to his promise, editor James Ray of the *Republican* published a long and highly favorable review in which he wrote, in part, that Cody's "exploits as mule driver, Pony Express rider, hunter, trapper, soldier, scout, legislator and actor read more like fiction than reality, so many are the incidents and so rapidly do they crowd one upon another. . . . Buffalo Bill's life has been varied, exciting, fascinating and successful; his book . . . is just like him." The editor added: "Miss Arta Cody is canvassing the city to sell the book, a work which will meet with a ready sale wherever offered." Arta was thirteen years old at the time but reputed to be both beautiful and mature for her age.

Buffalo Bill did not stay long in town to enjoy his book's success, if he was there at all, for, less than two weeks later, he was in Denver with his combination, playing to capacity houses, according to the *Republican* for July 26, which reported: "Buffalo Bill's show in Denver is a great success. Every inch of space was sold out and the aisles packed in spite of the heat."

From Denver he went on to Cheyenne, where he made his debut on August 2 with Major Burt's *May Cody; or, Lost and Won*, and on August 3 offered Prentiss Ingraham's *Knights of the Plains; or, Buffalo Bill's Best Trail*.

At the conclusion of his 1879 autobiography, Cody told of plans to take *Knights of the Plains* to London for the following season. That trip overseas would have to wait until the Wild West show had been born. Meanwhile, Ingraham wrote a new play for the 1879–1880 seasons, *Buffalo Bill at Bay; or, The Pearl of the Prairies*; it was in four acts and employed sixteen actors.

In his book *Famous Gunfighters of the Western Frontier*, W. B. (Bat) Masterson, a famous gunfighter and frontier lawman himself, recorded an incident in 1880 in which Cody figured prominently. Masterson asserted at the start that Cody was not the original Buffalo Bill; that title belonged to William Mathewson. Masterson described Cody in his prime as "the finest specimen of young manhood in the West. Standing full six feet, as straight as an arrow, strong as a lion and as quick and nimble as a cat." Masterson described how Cody killed buffalo, riding his horse "full tilt into a herd . . . and with a pistol in each hand, the bridle reins between his teeth, was almost sure to bring down the day's supply of meat in the first run. . . .

"Although the country fairly swarmed with desperate men during those years when Buffalo Bill was making history in the West," continued Masterson, "it is not on record that he ever engaged in a deadly duel with a white man. This was perhaps due to the fact that he had never been called upon for such a purpose. That he would fight if his hand was forced was no secret among those who knew him best. He had been known on more than one occasion to take a swaggering bully by the neck and after relieving him of his lethal decorations soundly shake him until he promised to behave himself."

The incident in which Bat Masterson called on Buffalo Bill for help took place in the summer of 1880. Masterson, who was then sheriff of Dodge City, traveled on the Union Pacific Railroad to Ogallala, Nebraska, about sixty miles west of North Platte, to straighten out a serious difficulty in which a friend of his, Billy Thompson, a brother of the famous gunfighter Ben Thompson of Texas, had become involved. To spirit Billy Thompson out of the law's clutches, Masterson enlisted the aid of a bartender he knew in the town. The barman prepared a Mickey Finn to put Billy Thompson's guard out of commission. Then, while the sheriff, who was also the town fiddler, was at a nearby dance hall, Masterson carried Thompson, who was badly injured, out of the hotel room in which he was imprisoned and got him on a train headed for North Platte before anyone knew he was missing.

Masterson picked up the story from there: "We arrived about two o'clock in the morning. When the train pulled up at the station, I again put Thompson on my back and carried him out on the platform. After being informed by one of the station hands which direction to go, in order to reach Dave Perry's saloon, I again picked up my burden and lit out along the dark street and was soon inside the saloon, where I found Buffalo Bill and a dozen others all having a good time. As a matter of course, we were given a royal welcome and were immediately taken in charge by Colonel Cody, who found a safe place for us to remain until he could outfit us for the trip across the country to Dodge City, which was about two hundred and fifty miles south from there.

"'The Ogallala authorities will take you from here,' said Cody to us that night, and we slept quite comfortably. The next day I went up to Colonel Cody's home, a beautiful place in the suburbs of North Platte, and found him busily engaged in raising a flag pole in honor of General Hancock, who had just been nominated by the Democratic party for President of the United States. I may here state that Buffalo Bill is a Democrat, but that should not be held against him, for he is a splendid fellow, and perhaps regrets it as much as any genuine American could. The next day Cody gave us a fine big Texas horse, and his wife's phaeton to carry us across the country, home."

Cody, Masterson, and Thompson then joined a hunting party of "distinguished foreigners" sent to Nebraska by General Sheridan, who asked Cody to take charge of the party. "There were fully twenty persons in the party," said Masterson, "and as everybody was feeling good, when we left North Platte the trip . . . was a right royal one, you may be sure. I was driving a double team hitched to Cody's specially made mess wagon, which was loaded down with everything imaginable. . . . The caravan would stop every little while and liquor up, and then go on until the next liquoring-up point was reached, when the caravan would again come to a halt.

"What a time those foreign gentlemen were given that night after the supper table had been cleared away. Buffalo Bill was then in his prime, and the stunts he did with pistol and rifle and in horse-back riding, were nothing short of wonderful. When Cody got back home to North Platte, his wife asked him what had become of her fine phaeton and harness. I don't know exactly what he told her or how he accounted for their disappearance, but he afterwards told me that a much more expensive outfit soon replaced the one he had given us."

This was not the first time that both Bat Masterson and Will Cody acted outside the law, nor would it be the last time that Will ran afoul of his Lulu and had to make up for it with an expensive gift.

Also in 1880, Cody wrote the following letter to General Nelson A. Miles, who had been Cody's commander when he served as Chief of Scouts for the Big Horn and Yellowstone Expedition:

North Platte, Neb.
June 15th, 80

My Dear General:

I have long had a desire to visit England but might have been deterred from doing so by the thought that I might be classed among the many impostors who have gone before me claiming to be Scouts and Frontiersmen. I wish to be treated like a gentleman by those I may meet over there and as it is possible that I may make the trip in the near future I would like to add your testimony to the credentials I am securing from other distinguished officials that I am the veritable W.F. Cody known as Buffalo Bill and have acted as Scout and Guide for you. If you will please answer this. I am yours to command personaly [sic] or in the service of the Government at any moment.

Very sincerely yours,
W.F. Cody

While the proposed trip to England did not take place during 1880, the letter must be similar to the ones Cody or his staff wrote soliciting testimonials to be used in the Wild West program and for the various tours of Europe that Cody eventually took with the show. Ten years later General Miles was to call on Cody for one more important mission in the West.

That same year, 1880, Cody and J. V. Arlington, a former character actor in the combination, and Colonel Prentiss Ingraham joined forces to produce plays and skits. Cody also considered taking his combination to England but then abandoned the idea. For two more seasons Buffalo Bill's combination toured the East, with considerable financial success. In the fall of 1881, a "thoroughly successful drama," *The Prairie Waif* by John A. Stevens, opened at Sprague's Olympic Theatre in Chicago for one week only, beginning September 5. It got this notice in the *Tribune*: "A crowd that filled every seat, sweltered in the aisles, and filled the lobbies was present at the Olympic Theatre last evening to welcome back Buffalo Bill and his Indian warriors in their soul-stirring, blood-curdling drama of *The Prairie Waif*. The audience appeared to thoroughly enjoy the entertainment offered for their amusement." The troupe of twenty-four included four Winnebago chiefs, a Pawnee chief, and an Indian maiden.

It was clear that Buffalo Bill was still a strong box office attraction. In addition to the colorful Indians in his cast, he included some spectacular shooting exhibitions onstage. Occasionally there were also shooting exhibitions by Dr. Frank Powell, known as White Beaver, a contract surgeon at Fort McPherson while Cody was there as chief of scouts. There is a report that they were together in at least one Indian fight—it took place in the green room of the Olympic on Friday night of the week's engagement when the Winnebago took on too much firewater.

In the season of 1880–1881, Cody is said to have netted $48,000, and the two following seasons were also successful. It apparently didn't matter whether he chose to stage *From Noose to Neck* or *Vera Vance; or, Saved from the Sioux*; audiences flocked to the theaters. In his final season before founding the Wild West show, 1882–1883, when he played *Twenty Days; or, Buffalo Bill's Pledge*, Cody said, "I found myself richer by several thousand dollars than I had ever been before, having done a splendid business at every place where my performance was given that year."

At the close of his highly successful season of 1881–1882, Buffalo Bill returned to North Platte in early June. Once again there was trouble at the Welcome Wigwam.

On March 9, 1882, Will wrote his sister Julia from Albany; he stated indignantly that he was "in a peck of trouble" because Lulu had gotten most of the North Platte property put into her own name. In his letter to Julia Cody he wrote: "I have been sending money to her [Louisa] for the last five years to buy property, not dreaming but what she was buying it in my name. . . . I don't care a snap for the money, but the way she has treated me. My beautiful house. I have none to go to. Al [Al Goodman, Julia's husband] and I will have to build another. I can't write more—to day."

Since his initial investment in Lincoln County real estate in 1878, Cody had been putting the profits from his show business and cattle ranch into more and more land. William McDonald, a family friend, claims that Buffalo Bill sent his father, banker Charles McDonald, money for the purchase of land to build up the ranch. Louisa Cody asserted in her *Memories*: "I added to his ranch, and attended to the thousand and one details of farming life that must be looked after, while he was away on the stage."

According to Nellie Yost, "That Louisa was a shrewd businesswoman has been well proven, and not the least of her acumen is the fact that she did put the property she bought in her own name." By this time she was well aware of her husband's impulsive generosity as well as his speculative ventures. Accordingly, with Will's money, Louisa bought various tracts of land in and around the town. The North Platte *Telegraph* for April 14, 1881, reported that "Mrs. Cody is planning to erect several buildings soon." Louisa, however, could not act completely independently in her financial dealings. While a married woman in the Nebraska of the 1870s and 1880s could buy property, it automatically belonged to her husband as well, and neither could dispose of it without the other's consent.

In the ten years he had been before the footlights, William F. Cody had become a moderately wealthy man. There was another reason why Louisa had been careful to put the property in her own name: Will was planning to get involved in a lawsuit over $15 million worth of property in the heart of Cleveland, Ohio. The suit was best described in an Omaha newspaper, probably the *Herald*, on May 13, 1882. A reporter interviewed Cody as he was passing through on his way to North Platte:

> Bill has recently struck a bonanza for himself and the Cody family gen-
> erally, and he has assurances of able lawyers that his claim to valuable
> real estate in Cleveland is well worth fighting for, and if he wins the suit
> he will realize an immense fortune. He began an active investigation
> into the claims of the Cody family . . . some months ago, and it has
> resulted in his bringing a suit . . . for its recovery.

This was the basis for the suit: In 1832 Philip Cody Sr. moved from Canada to Cleveland and purchased land in Cleveland proper and adjoining the city. He was regarded as quite a well-to-do man for the time. He had seven children, of whom four were sons: Elijah, Isaac (the father of Buffalo Bill), Philip Jr., and Joseph. What happened afterward was a tangle of family intrigue, in which one son, Joseph, persuaded his father, then suffering from dementia, to sell the family homestead; he possibly forged the documents of sale. On his deathbed in 1880, Joseph made a statement to the effect that there was property coming to the heirs of Elijah and Isaac Cody.

The Omaha newspaper article continued:

> The lands to which the Cody heirs lay claim comprise fifty-five acres of
> Euclid Avenue, one of the principal thoroughfares of Cleveland. Their
> claims seem to be so strong that the property owners cannot sell with
> any safety or make any improvements. Two parties, who are in posses
> sion of a large part of the dispute property, offered Buffalo Bill while he
> was in Cleveland, the sum of $300,000 to settle the suit so far as they
> were concerned, but he refused to do so. The suit proper is against 113
> different parties who now occupy the land, and was begun on the 10th
> of this month.

Louisa's concern arose because, alone among his relatives, her Will was the only one with money to pursue the suit. Cody ought to have taken the $300,000, but blinded by the vision of a vast fortune, he chose litigation, thus illustrating Ambrose Bierce's definition of a lawsuit: "A machine which one enters as a pig and emerges as a sausage."

In an article published in the New York *Daily Graphic* of August 10, 1886, it was reported that the case was now in United States Court, and that the value of the property was estimated at $15 million. "During tedious negotiations Buffalo Bill succeeded in buying off one by one the other heirs, so that now he is the sole claimant. This morning he received a letter from his chief counsel, who informs him that a number of the defendants have offered to compromise but that he and his associates are certain of winning the cause, and he, therefore, refused to entertain any propositions. Mr. Cody is highly jubilant."

His jubilation was premature; his unquestioning faith in his attorneys was misplaced, as is so often the case; and Louisa, who refused to sign a paper in connection with the suit or let Will use any of the property she had bought to raise funds for the legal processes, was right to distrust his business sense. The case dragged on for years and in the end came to nothing.

At the time Cody wrote his angry letter of protest to his sister, Julia and her husband, Al Goodman, were living in Kansas, but all that winter Cody had been urging them to move to North Platte and take over the management of his ranch. On April 29, the last day of his theatrical season, Cody wrote to Julia, who was still in Kansas, telling her that he would be home about May 12, after a trip to Cleveland to look into the progress of the lawsuit. He was still angry about Louisa, for he said: "I hear from Al [in North Platte] regular. He does all the writeing [sic] now Lulu has quit writing to me altogether."

Was there an estrangement from his wife at that time? It seems unlikely, for it was not in Cody's nature to hold a grudge or hard feelings for long, and in spite of his statement that he had no home to go to, he must have gone to Welcome Wigwam that summer, for his youngest daughter, Irma, was born the following February, and he stayed at home with Lulu the next spring before taking his Wild West show on the road.

In the summer of 1882, Cody and Frank North sold the Dismal River ranch to John Bratt for $75,000. It was a good time to sell, for the days of the open range were about over. Since there was no land involved—only cattle, horses, some log buildings, wagons, and harness—the price was a good one and showed a handsome profit for the few years spent in the business. It is also quite likely that Cody's exposure to rounding up herds and observing the life of the cowboys was instrumental in forming some of the material he was to put into his Wild West within a relatively short time.

Buffalo Bill's Wild West was undoubtedly years in germinating. For several years before the show was created, Cody had become dissatisfied with the limitations of the stage. The entertainment he envisioned demanded an outdoor setting. Ned Buntline had considered mounting his stars on horseback and staging *Scouts of the Prairie* outdoors, and when Texas Jack and Buffalo Bill broke with him, Buntline tried the idea out with Arizona Frank and Dashing Charlie—unsuccessfully.

There were other precursors as well. The first was undoubtedly the artist George Catlin, whose travels in the West had begun in 1830 and culminated in what was called "Catlin's *Gallery Unique.*" Catlin's exhibition featured a large assemblage of Indian artifacts: a Crow tepee, Comanche lances, shields, headdresses, painted robes, along with the artist's portraits and scenes of Indian life. Catlin described the Crow tepee as a "very splendid thing, brought from the foot of the Rocky Mountains, twenty-five feet in height, made of Buffalo Skins, garnished and painted."

In 1837 the artist opened Catlin's Indian Gallery at Clinton Hall in New York City. The New York *Morning Herald* on October 3 observed that "Mr. Catlin dressed himself in the attire of a Crow Indian. There is no modern civilized raiment that we have ever seen that can compare with it for beauty." One biographer of Catlin called his exhibition "the first Wild West show. It was a rip-roaring success." At first that was true, but when the artist expanded his show with *tableaux vivants*—live reenactments of Indian scenes, first with actors and then with real Indians—his troubles began. The hopeful showman took his enterprise first to England, where he entertained the young Queen Victoria, and then to Paris in 1845; there, his Indian warriors began to die of illness or walked out on him, homesick for the real West. Chastened, Catlin returned to his true forte, painting the West.

Another forerunner was P. T. Barnum. In 1843 the great showman bought fifteen starved and weary calf buffalo, all about a year old, from C. D. French, an expert rider and lasso artist, for $700. Barnum's purchase included French's services to tend and help exhibit the animals. Barnum first exhibited them in a tent at the Bunker Hill Monument celebration when Daniel Webster dedicated the monument. He then took his buffalo to Hoboken, New Jersey, where he advertised a "Grand Buffalo Hunt— Free of Charge." His profit came from renting all the ferries for the day and collecting the fares. Barnum's show included Indian dancers and attracted twenty-four thousand people. The buffalo calves, however, spooked by the crowd's shouts, stampeded, crashed through a fence, and wound up in a swamp. It was reported that the crowd panicked, and at least one man was killed and another injured. With all his genius, Barnum was unable to master the subtle elements of western lore. Thereafter, he confined himself to wild animals, acrobats, and freaks. In 1860 he contracted with Grizzly Adams of California for another menagerie. The animals had been trapped by Adams, who then trained them. Wrote Barnum in his *Struggles and Triumphs*:

> A band of music preceded a procession of animal cages down Broadway and up the Bowery, old Adams dressed in his hunting costume, heading the line with a platform wagon on which were placed three immense grizzly bears, two of which he held by chains, while he was mounted on the back of the largest grizzly, which stood in the centre and was not secured in any manner whatever. This was the bear known as "General Fremont," and so docile had he become that Adams said he had used him as a pack-bear to carry his cooking and hunter apparatus through the mountains for six months, and had ridden him hundreds of miles.

That such a display, with its potential for danger, given the grizzly's unpredictability, could be mounted in the heart of Manhattan is a commentary on nineteenth-century New York's lack of either liability insurance or a live-entertainment license.

Another stab at outdoor western entertainment was Tyler's Indian Exhibition in 1855, which featured simulated buffalo hunting. The familiar tale of Captain John Smith and Pocahontas, Indian dances, and a corn festival were also part of the attraction. The Tyler show traveled first with Van Amburgh's menagerie and Don Stone's circus, then with the Mable Brothers menagerie and Don Stone. These were basically circuses, with western overtones.

Wild Bill had also attempted an outdoor show in 1871, but without adequate preparation; he had met disaster when his buffalo ran away in the streets of Niagara Falls. In 1868 Joseph G. McCoy, in an effort to attract Texas cattlemen and to promote a recently established rail link between Chicago and Abilene, Kansas, loaded wild horses, three buffalo, and two elk onto a railroad car. Accompanied by two Mexicans from California, a Kansan named Thompson, and several assistants, he visited a number of cities en route to Chicago. This Wild West type of exhibit proved very successful, and McCoy followed it up by organizing a "Grand Excursion to the Far West! A Wild and Exciting Chase after the Buffalo, on his Native Plain." Aimed primarily at men in the cattle business, it attracted a large number of sportsmen. McCoy supplied horses and camp equipment, but people were asked to "bring their own firearms." Spectacular though such an isolated event might have been, it was never intended to sustain itself.

Other acts that were precursors of the Wild West were a July 4 commemoration in Deer Trail, Colorado, in which one Emil Gardenshire was crowned "Champion Bronco Buster of the Plains," and another Fourth of July celebration in Cheyenne, Wyoming, in 1872, featuring the riding of an unruly steer. And certainly Cody's buffalo hunt with Grand Duke Alexis was a harbinger of things to come, as were his hunting trips with General Sheridan, James Gordon Bennett and their friends, as well as the Earl of Dunraven. All that was needed, then, was to put the right elements together.

Cody realized that he needed to earn a lot of money to launch a big show, and he was too proud to ask his wealthy friends for funds. Then, in the spring of 1882, he met Nate Salsbury, when they both were playing in New York. Salsbury, who later became Cody's partner, claimed to have thought of the idea of the Wild West when returning from a tour of Australia with the Salsbury Troubadours in 1876. On the boat he had discussed the merits of Australian jockeys in comparison with American cowboys and Mexican vaqueros with J. B. Gaylord, an agent for the Cooper and Bailey Circus.

As a result, said Salsbury, "I began to construct a show in my mind that would embody the whole subject of horsemanship and before I went to sleep I had mapped out a show that would be constituted of elements that had never before been employed in concerted effort in the history of the show business." In the end, of course, Buffalo Bill's Wild West went well beyond horsemanship to embody features of the West that had not been part of Salsbury's plan. Several years later Salsbury "decided that such an entertainment must have a well known figure head to attract attention and thus help to quickly solve the problem of advertising a new idea. After careful consideration of the plan and scope of the show I resolved to get W.F. Cody as my central figure."

When the two men finally met, Salsbury recalled, "As he was about at the end of his profit string on the theatrical stage I dare say he was pleased at the chance to try something else, for he grew very enthusiastic over the plan as I unfolded it to him and was sure that the thing would be a great success. It was arranged at the lunch that I would go to Europe the following summer and look the ground over with a view to taking the show to a country where all its elements would be absolutely novel. I was quite well aware that the Dime Novel had found its way to England especially and wherever the Dime Novel had gone Cody had gone along. . . .

"I went to Europe the following summer," continued Salsbury, "and looked the ground over. I came to the conclusion that it would take a lot of money to do the thing right and told Cody that we must be well provided with money when we made the plunge and that as far as I was concerned I did not feel rich enough to undertake my share of the expense and that I would have to wait another year before I could go into the scheme in proper shape. To this Cody did not demur but said that he was in about the same fix as myself. So far we had arrived at a perfect understanding that we were to share and share alike in the venture. . . .

"But Cody must have agreed to drop the matter for another year with a strong mental reservation for I was astonished in the Spring of 1883 to get a telegram (which I now have in my possession) asking me if I wanted to go into the show for this country if *Dr. Carver did not object.* Of course I was dumfounded and replied that I did not want to have anything to do with Doctor Carver who was a fakir [*sic*] in the show business and as Cody once expressed it 'Went West on a piano stool.' Events proved that Cody did not wait for our plan to go to Europe to ripen but no sooner had my ideas than he began to negotiate with Carver who had a reputation as a marksman to go in with him and was kind enough, when they had laid all their plans, to let me in as a partner. Of course I turned them down and they went on the road and made a ghastly failure."

Back in North Platte that June, however, an event took place that would shape Cody's future and crystallize into what became the Wild West. It was called the "Old Glory Blowout" and took place on July 4, 1882.

At that time in American history, the birthday of our republic was one of the most celebrated days of the year. Plans for its observance usually were made well in advance, and communities vied with each other to see who could stage the most spectacular celebration—and every community hoped to outdo its celebration of the year before.

There are varying stories concerning the celebration in North Platte in the summer of 1882. According to Nellie Snyder Yost, "Some say the town hadn't gotten around to making any definite plans for the Fourth before the Honorable W. F. Cody came home for the summer. Others say plans were already under way to do something big for the occasion but that the planners were waiting until Cody arrived to help them decide just what to do."

William McDonald, just turned twenty-one in 1882, remembered the circumstances sixty years later. He recalled that the town had been planning to celebrate the occasion with some horse races, but "that wasn't big enough to suit Cody," who wanted to put on "something big," or try to. "They had sixteen buffalo down on the 'points' between the rivers," McDonald said, "and Cody rounded them up and put on an exhibition of riding them. And that was the beginning of his Wild West show."

Twelve years later, when he was past ninety, McDonald recalled things differently. He said that upon Cody's return to North Platte after the close of his stage season, Cody joined a group of men in the store owned by Charles J. Foley, when Charles F. Ormsby, a former mayor, and other prominent citizens were there. Cody asked what kind of celebration was shaping up for the Fourth. When told what little had been planned, "Cody mumbled something to the effect that he was surprised that nothing had been planned for the Fourth of July," said McDonald, "then went up the street to the saloon, but he hardly stayed long enough to get a drink. He wasn't one to take a drink just to get his mouth wet. He came back, protesting that it was not patriotic not to have a Fourth of July celebration. Ormsby and Foley said, 'O.K. Bill, you are chairman to get up a celebration.' Cody promptly replied, 'I'll take it.'"

McDonald remembered Cody's taking him aside and saying "I want to show folks how we rope and run and tend cattle. Then I'll stage an imitation buffalo hunt and show them how I used to hunt and shoot buffalo. If it's a success I'm going to call it Buffalo Bill's Wild West Show and Congress of Rough Riders." McDonald's memory was faulty in at least one respect: The Rough Riders were not added to the title until a decade later. And it was McDonald himself who recalled that M. C. Keefe had a small herd of buffalo and suggested that perhaps they should be used.

In the West of 1882, roping, racing, and bucking contests were regular Sunday affairs, where "the cow-boys" gathered at one ranch or another to try their skills "just for the fun of it"; to see who could rope, throw, and tie a steer the quickest, or who could ride the toughest bucking broncs. Similarly, cowboy sports sometimes were presented before gathered crowds, usually as part of Fourth of July celebrations. One was held in Deer Trail, Colorado, in 1869. The riding of a wild steer was featured at an Independence Day celebration in Cheyenne in 1872. Other early contests took place in Pecos, Texas, and Prescott, Arizona. The exhibition that Buffalo Bill mounted in North Platte that summer, though, is considered the beginning not only of the Wild West show but also of the rodeo, although that word was not applied to the contests until 1911.

The most complete version of what happened in North Platte that day is to be found in Nellie Snyder Yost's biography of Buffalo Bill. Not only were there buffalo available—anywhere from five to sixteen—but a private racetrack owned by Isaac Dillon, nephew of Sidney Dillon, president of the Union Pacific, lay a short way north of the depot. His track was a good one, half a mile long and fenced all around with a solid six-foot board fence, and Dillon put it at Cody's disposal for the day. As for cowboys, the big western Nebraska roundup would be winding up, and at the end of June, within three miles of town, there would be some twenty wagons, two hundred cowboys, and two thousand head of horses.

To be sure that everyone within a hundred miles knew about the big celebration, Cody, who was well aware of the power of advertising, ran the following notice in the *Telegraph* on June 15, 1882:

4TH OF JULY CELEBRATION
ATTENTION ALL

All parties interested in a general celebration of the 4th of July in this city are requested to attend a meeting at the courthouse on the 17th at 8 P.M., for the purpose of arranging a program. By the request of I. Dillon, W.F. Cody, Anth. Ries, L. Eels, M.C. Keith, A.J. Miller, C.F. Groner, Chas. McDonald and others.

Following this meeting, five thousand handbills were printed and distributed, advertising the big free celebration. Cody had persuaded the town fathers to offer prizes for shooting, riding, and bronco busting— something new in such events. He had estimated that he might get one hundred cowboy entrants; actually, he got a thousand, "an amazing figure," according to *American Rodeo* by Kristine Fredriksson, "considering that the richest rodeo in the United States, the Cheyenne Frontier Days, in 1982 attracted more than eleven hundred contestants."

The Omaha *Bee* carried this rousing account of the day:

NORTH PLATTE
THE NATION'S HOLIDAY CELEBRATED
AT A LIVE AND ENERGETIC TOWN

A special reporter of the *Bee* left Omaha on the 3rd of July for North Platte, one of the most live and energetic towns on the U.P. [Union Pacific], arriving there on the morning of the Fourth.

The place was found alive to the importance of the occasion, and in full trim to celebrate the nation's anniversary.

At 10:30 there was a regular street parade, the programme having been duly arranged beforehand. The procession was a fine one, including the band, the G.A.R., a number of Sunday-school children, and a long line of citizens and visitors in carriages. Hon. W.F. Cody acted as marshal of the day, ably assisted by Mr. Con Groner, the well-known sheriff of this county. Mr. Cody was resplendent in a suit of white corduroy pants, black velvet coat of military cut, etc., and was strikingly handsome.

The procession was marched to the race track . . . and a regular programme of speaking and singing was gone through with. Following this came a most interesting feature of the day. Hon. M.C. Keith had four or five buffalo, one with a calf, which he turned loose and one of the boys lassoed and rode an animal for which he received $25. After this a Texas steer was turned loose, which was also lassoed and ridden to its great disgust.

In the afternoon there were trotting and running races. . . . There were also running races of one hundred, three hundred and six hundred yards and a half mile race. At night there was a fine display of fireworks and the G.A.R. ball, both of which were largely attended. Notwithstanding the immense crowd, the utmost order and quiet prevailed, and not a single occurrence to mar the pleasure of the occasion was noted.

Charles McDonald also recalled that Cody had told him he was going to have some Indians in the celebration, since "I can get them and no one else can." Sell and Weybright, in their *Buffalo Bill and the Wild West,* also mention Indians as well as a stagecoach holdup in the 1882 show, and say that Cody bought the coach especially for the North Platte blowout. No one else mentions either Indians or the coach, so it is highly unlikely that either of them came on the scene until the following year. Strangely, Cody says nothing about the Fourth of July celebration in his *Life Story.*

In a burst of typical rhetoric, John M. Burke said of the show, "Cody not only scored a howling success, if possible adding to his popularity, but the casualties were few and the result a revelation, even to those familiar with the possibilities of excitement, reckless daring, skill, and devil-may-care fun, represented in a program where all were untrammeled and unconventional stars."

It was Cody's idea to launch his Wild West in 1883, a time when the outdoor show was just entering its period of greatest prosperity. In 1885 more than fifty circuses were on the road, the most ever to tour the United States. The circus lives on today, of course, but in a greatly diminished fashion. Gone are the tents—the big tops—and most of the hoopla that formerly attended "the Greatest Show on Earth."

So the time was ripe for Cody's plan, and he set right to work after the Old Glory Blowout to implement it, signing up talent and seeking properties, despite continuing his theatrical season of 1882–1883 as usual. "Will never enjoyed this part of his career," wrote his sister Helen, "he endured it simply because it was the means to an end. He had not forgotten his boyish dream—his resolve that he would one day present to the world an exhibition that would give a realistic picture of life in the Far West, depicting its dangers and privations, as well as its picturesque phases. His first theatrical season had shown him how favorably such an exhibition would be received, and his long cherished ambition began to take shape. He knew that an enormous amount of money would be needed, and to acquire such a sum he lived for many years behind the footlights."

Helen seems unmindful of Cody's extravagances and his generosities to his family, which also prolonged his theatrical career. She tells of having attended one of his last performances in a Leavenworth theater—in which he played the part of "a loving swain." When the curtain fell on the last act, Helen went behind the scenes and congratulated her brother on "his excellent acting."

"Oh, Nellie," he groaned, she said, "don't say anything about it. If heaven will forgive me this foolishness, I promise to quit it forever when this season is over."

In his *Story of the Wild West*, Cody writes, a bit pompously:

When the season of 1881–83 closed I found myself richer by several thousand dollars than I had ever been before, having done a splendid business at every place where my performance was given in that year. Immense success and comparative wealth, attained in the profession of showman, stimulated me to greater exertion and largely increased my ambition for public favor. Accordingly, I conceived the idea of organizing a large company of Indians, cow-boys, Mexican vaqueros, famous riders and expert lasso throwers, with accessories of stage coach, emigrant wagons, bucking horses and a herd of buffaloes, with which to give a realistic entertainment of wild life on the plains. To accomplish this purpose, which in many respects was a really herculean undertaking, I sent agents to various points in the far West to engage Indians from several different tribes, and then set about the more difficult task of capturing a herd of buffaloes.

Cody went on to say that after he had secured his cowboys, vaqueros, riders, and livestock, he found that all the difficulties had not been overcome, because an exhibition such as he planned had to be staged in an open-air enclosure, and these spaces were not always to be rented, or were inaccessible by street cars. "The expenses of such a show as I had determined to give were so great that a very large crowd must be drawn to every exhibition or a financial failure would be certain."

Because Cody's *Life Story* was published after his death, we will never know how many hands, or whose, were at work on it, but the diction of the above passage does suggest some generous editing of Cody's rough-and-ready prose. Also, the preparations for the show, which probably took about ten months, have been compressed into a shorter time frame.

William H. McDonald, a North Platte native who knew Buffalo Bill well, says that immediately after the Fourth, Cody told his brother-in-law, Al Goodman, to start buying wild horses for his show. By this time Julia had joined her husband in North Platte, but Will was unable to persuade them to stay and manage his ranch. Instead, they returned to Kansas, and would not take up residence at the North Platte ranch until two years later. It is possible, however, that Al bought some horses for the show before he left for Kansas.

Cody's last stage show was *Twenty Days; or, Buffalo Bill's Pledge*. On February 3, 1883, he wrote Julia on a discouraging note: "Dear Sister, your letter rec'd. found me still playing in poor luck. Money is awful scarce." Still, by the end of the season, the show had cleared around $50,000.

Was Cody in North Platte on February 9, 1883, when his fourth child and third daughter, Irma, was born? Nellie Snyder Yost thinks so. Cody doted on all children, especially his own, and would surely have wanted to see the baby, yet his rather poor record of attendance at home argues otherwise. By mid-May, in any case, he was back on the road.

It was during that 1882–1883 season, his last with a combination, that Cody met Nate Salsbury and found him unable to back the venture with cash. He may have thought that Salsbury had cooled on the idea. On this same tour, Will met Dr. W. F. Carver, the self-billed "Champion All Round Shot of the World," in New Haven and discussed a partnership. As Carver once told it, "Cody came to my home in New Haven, Conn., down and out. I told him I was getting ready to bring out the Wild West Show, and he gave me his promise not to drink another drop if I would take him outdoors with me, and I agreed to do so. The result was that I invested $27,000 in the enterprise and signed a note with the First National Bank of Omaha for $2,000, all of which I had to pay. In addition to this, he failed to live up to his promise and was dead drunk all summer. So we separated."

That is how Carver's boastful and defamatory account ran. To begin with, Cody was not "down and out," certainly not at this time, or even at the sad end of his life, when he still spoke of coming back, "bigger and stronger than ever." Carver liked to boast that the Wild West was his idea, yet one of his disputes with Cody was over that title; Carver preferred "Golden West." In addition, according to Charles McDonald, whose family's bank in North Platte backed Cody's show, Carver put up no money at all for the Wild West. Cody's drinking that summer may well have contributed to the show's problems, but observers reported that Carver hit the bottle quite as often as Cody.

Carver's claim to have originated the Wild West has little to back it up. For one thing, he was in Europe on an exhibition-shooting tour while Cody was planning the Old Glory Blowout and was too busy with his own shooting exhibitions to take any part in the show on the Fourth, according to his own accounts.

Who *was* Doc Carver? His name is inextricably linked with Cody's, and in the western collection of the Denver Public Library, he occupies a substantial amount of microfilm space. During his early years in Nebraska, Carver moved about a great deal, from one town to another, practicing as a dentist. After he became a crack shot, Carver spent more time arranging rifle matches than caring for teeth. He began to advertise himself as the "Champion Buffalo Hunter of the Plains," a title he said he won in 1873, when he killed "in the neighborhood of 30,000 buffaloes"—which was possible (unlikely, but possible) if he killed them over two years, 1872 and 1873, at the rate of 1,250 a month, or more than 41 every day of both years.

How about his marksmanship? He was a good shot, there is no doubt about that, but his title "world's champion marksman" was self-conferred, and though he did set several records shooting glass balls and wooden blocks, the records did not stand long. As for his assertions that he was a veteran plainsman, in 1888 a biographical sketch in a program for the Adam Forepaugh Jr. circus, combined with Carver's Wild West, claimed that he played an important part in the Sioux war in Minnesota in 1862, in these words: "Dr. Carver's acquaintance with the country, his familiarity with the savages' methods of fighting, together with his magnetic influence over the band of scouts—of which he was the chief—united in crowning his labors with brilliant success, and the defeat, capture and subsequent hanging of 'Little Crow' was due largely to his courage, strategy, and sleepless zeal." Yet it is said that Carver was hundreds of miles away at the time of the Sioux war in Minnesota and did not even know about it until it was over.

Born to William and Deborah Carver in Winslow, Illinois, on May 7, 1840, William Frank Carver was called "Little Doc" by his father, because the boy cared for wounded and maimed animals and wildfowl. He claimed later that his father so abused him that he ran away as a child and headed West, where he lived some time with the Santee Sioux. His extraordinary marksmanship was credited by the Indians to his Spirit Gun. When he shot a white buffalo and an elusive old gray or "silver" elk, the Indians concluded that only an Evil Spirit could have accomplished such a feat, and Carver proclaimed himself the "Evil Spirit of the Plains."

According to Joseph G. Rosa, the facts were much less dramatic. William Frank Carver was trained by his father as a dentist. By the time he headed West, however, he was already a marksman of note. In the summer of 1872, he reached Fort McPherson, where he became acquainted with a number of well-known frontier personalities, including Wild Bill Hickok,

Texas Jack, and Cody, whom he met in the summer of 1874, when the dentist accompanied the Thomas P. Medley hunting party, of which Cody was guide, for a few days. "He also shot against the frontier's foremost woman 'shootist,' Ena Raymond," writes Rosa. "She taught him nothing about shooting, but he taught her the rudiments of dentistry, which she apparently practiced upon her friends. On one occasion, she recalled, a tooth that she had 'hammered' for Texas Jack gave him some trouble." Painless dentistry was obviously not one of Carver's skills, but then, the care of the teeth in the frontier West was usually a crude affair at best.

Moving to Oakland, California, in 1875, Carver set his sights on becoming the champion rifle shot of the world. He attained one major step toward his goal on February 22, 1878; with a rifle, he broke 885 aerial glass balls out of 1,000. Carver then left on a cross-country tour that drew national recognition. In matches in more than thirty cities between San Francisco and the East Coast (including New York City and Boston), he took on all comers. His skill was such that the press lauded him as "the California Deadshot," "the Rifle King," and "the Magical Marksman." Touring the Continent, Carver claimed to have shot before the crowned heads of Belgium, Saxony, Dresden, and Vienna, besides a command performance at Sandringham before the Prince of Wales. After his European tour, he returned to America in 1882. From his performing and match-shooting exhibitions, he reportedly had cleared $80,000, an enormous sum in those days.

Though Carver's marksmanship was well documented, his alleged western adventures are not. Some time before his death, says Rosa, he produced a manuscript in which he claimed to have been involved in adventures with Wild Bill Hickok and other frontier personalities. He fooled one well-known writer, Raymond W. Thorp, into believing his stories and publishing a fictionalized biography of Carver that is still controversial. At the time he joined forces with Buffalo Bill, the handsome and flamboyant ex-dentist was already teamed up with Captain Adam Bogardus, an excellent exhibition shooter, who also agreed to appear in the proposed Cody-Carver venture.

Others in the cast of the first Wild West show included Major Frank North, Buck Taylor, John Y. Nelson, Con Groner, and Johnny Baker.

William Levi (Buck) Taylor, the cowboy who had come to Ogallala from Texas with the first of Cody and Major North's longhorn herd in 1877, had wound up working at Cody's Scout's Rest Ranch and was on hand for the Old Glory Blowout. The six-foot-five Texan was billed as being able to throw a steer by the horns or the tail and tie it single-handed, pick up a handkerchief from the ground while riding a horse full speed, as well as ride the worst bucking broncs.

Because he had married an Indian woman, John Y. Nelson was known as a squaw man; Cody had first met him at Fort McPherson. He had guided Brigham Young's Mormon migrants to Utah in 1847 and had been a scout at the fort on the Platte when Will was there. Nelson had accompanied Cody on some of his tours with the combinations, and in the new Wild West show he would double as a stage driver and rider of wild horses. Another of his duties was to throw glass balls for his employer to shoot. John Nelson had a full flowing beard, a Sioux wife, and five children. He and his Indian family were frequently front and center when photographers took pictures of the cast of the Wild West.

Con Groner, a formidable physical specimen, was billed as the "Cow-Boy Sheriff of the Platte." The sheriff of Lincoln County since the early 1870s, he had been involved in the preparations for Cody's Fourth of July celebration.

Last, there was Johnny Baker. Johnny's real first name was Lewis, like his father. He was thirteen when Buffalo Bill organized the Wild West show. Johnny, limping because of a railroad accident in 1879, when part of his heel was cut off, worshiped Buffalo Bill and dogged his footsteps all that spring, begging to be taken along with the show. Cody felt a deep affection for the boy, who was the age his own son, Kit, would have been had he lived. Still, when Johnny begged to be in the show, Will laughed, according to Courtney Ryley Cooper and Louisa Cody, and said: "What would you do in a Wild West show, Johnny?" "Well, I could black your boots—and—make myself awful handy," replied the boy. "Will," to quote Louisa, "had taught him to shoot in the days in which he played around our house—in fact, there never was a time when guns were not booming around there and Will was not shooting coins out of his children's fingers, while I stood on the veranda and gasped a remonstrance that the first thing he knew, he would have a fingerless family!" Cody was unable to adopt Johnny because of the Baker family's objections but made him his foster son and took him along with the show, a relationship that was to last till the end of his life.

The preparations and planning in order to get the show ready to leave in May—assembling scouts, cowboys, Mexican vaqueros, Indians, buffalo, elk, mountain sheep, bucking horses, stagecoach and emigrant wagons— must have been a logistical nightmare, but finally what was now known as The Wild West, Hon. W. F. Cody and Dr. W. F. Carver's Rocky Mountain and Prairie Exhibition was ready for a dress rehearsal, which took place in Colville (later Columbus), Nebraska, Major North's hometown. It was a near disaster, an unhappy omen of the season ahead.

As Don Russell tells the story, "The stagecoach was hitched to a team of almost unbroken mules, with a veteran driver, Fred Mathews, at the reins. Mayor 'Pap' Clothier and members of the town council were passengers and honored guests. Frank North headed the Pawnees who were to make the attack. When the Pawnees shrieked their war whoop and charged, firing blank cartridges, the mules bolted. The Indians took up the chase with noise and vigor. Buffalo Bill's rescuers tried to head off the stampede, but were swept along with it. Around the track went the entire company until the mules tired and could be halted."

Mayor Clothier leapt out of the coach and made for Buffalo Bill, eager for a fight. At that point, a young lawyer, Frank Evors, climbed to the top of the coach and addressed the spectators: "Fellow citizens, it fills my breast with pride and swells my heart with joy to point to your view our noble mayor and city council. Look at them, gentlemen. They risked their lives . . . for your entertainment." The mayor turned his attention from Buffalo Bill to Evors, who was well advised to make a quick getaway.

At this point Major North, his Indian war party now under control, galloped up to Cody and remarked, "Bill, if you want to make this d——— show go, you do not need me or my Indians. . . . You want about twenty old bucks. Fix them up with all the paint and feathers on the market. Use some old hack horse and a hack driver. To make it go you want a show of illusion not realism."

To his credit, Cody began with the determination to make his show as realistic as was physically possible. To that end he insisted on authenticity wherever possible. For example, the stagecoach, always billed as the old Deadwood stagecoach, was genuine. Will had wired Luke Voorhees, manager of the Cheyenne and Black Hills Stage line, for a coach. Voorhees sent him one that had originally cost $1,800. Cody himself had ridden it in 1876. At one time it had been abandoned for three months after having been attacked by Indians near Indian Creek, and it survived the sinking of the show on a Mississippi River steamboat the following year. Reportedly it is still in existence in the museum of the United States Post Office Department in Washington, D.C. A handsome surviving stagecoach of the period, similar in all respects to the Deadwood stage, can be seen in the Buffalo Bill Historical Center in Cody, Wyoming.

From Colville, the show traveled eighty-five miles to Omaha, considered "The Gateway to the West," for its scheduled opening on May 17. Cody's arrival on May 12, 1883, along with Major North and thirty-six Pawnee Indians—including squaws and children—caused a flurry of excitement in the crowd gathered at the depot. Cody was introduced to the Indians. There was a vigorous "How! How!" from the braves, and they gathered around to shake hands with Buffalo Bill, who then produced a large box of cigars, which were promptly passed around.

Cody informed the press that ten Sioux Indians were also expected to arrive, making the Indian contingent about sixty. The Indians would carry their own tepees and implements, and there would be little change in their way of life. "Good medicine" also arrived in the form of a buffalo calf, "Western Lillie," that had been born in the encampment.

Buffalo Bill also remarked that "forty odd thousand dollars" had already been spent on putting the entertainment together and the figure would soon reach fifty thousand, not including transportation, printing costs, salaries, or daily provisions. All the same, he and Carver had high hopes of success. Major John Burke prepared the billboards and the program. His posters declaimed "The Green Sward Our Carpet, Azure Canopy Our Canvas, No Tinsel, No Gilding, No Humbug! No Side Shows or Freaks!"

Major Burke also provided what he called a "Salutatory" at the beginning of the program; this feature was to be part of every Wild West program from that time on. Burke described the stars as "a part of the development of the great West." These men were "keen of eye, sturdy in build, inured to hardship, experienced in the knowledge of Indian habits and language, familiar with the hunt, and trustworthy in the hour of extremest danger, they belong to a class that is rapidly disappearing from our country."

Because of rain, the opening was put off until May 19. Of the opening, Cody writes only "In the spring of 1883 I opened the Wild West Show . . . in Omaha, and played to very large crowds, the weather fortunately proving propitious. We played our next engagement at Springfield, Ill., and thence in all the large cities, to the seaboard. The enterprise was not a complete financial success during the first season, though everywhere our performances were attended by immense audiences."

On May 20, 1883, an Omaha newspaper published an enthusiastic account of the show. CODY'S CYCLONE, ran the headline. "The 'Wild West' Sweeps All Victorious Before It. Eight Thousand People Attend the Initial Performances, And Go Wild With Enthusiasm—The Races, Fights And Feats Of The Big Amusement Hit." The newspaper article went on to say that "fully 8,000 people of all classes from frontiersmen to bankers were on hand at 2 o'clock yesterday afternoon at the driving park and after the first three or four acts the show was stamped with popular approval and it was evident that it was a 'go.' . . . There was no mistaking the fact that the show was a success. The swiftest and most daring Indians, the most expert lassoers and riders among the cowboys, and above all Cody, Carver and Bogardus, and the best talent in every line to be had, deserved and won the favor of the people."

A twenty-piece band led the opening parade and was followed by Little Standing Bull in his traditional headdress and war paint, riding a pony.

Behind him rode three Pawnee. Then came three grown buffalo and the newborn calf, "a frisky young thing." More mounted Indians followed, and then came Buffalo Bill and Carver accompanied by cowboys, other animals, the Deadwood stage, drawn by six fine mules, and, bringing up the end of the parade, a second band. "Pop" Whitaker, a noted caller at athletic games as far off as New York, introduced all the acts, which included the Pony Express ride, the attack on the Deadwood stagecoach (saved in the nick of time by Cody and Carver and a contingent of scouts), an exhibition shooting match, and the final act, a "buffalo chase." At the end Cody made a speech, which was greeted with tremendous applause, particularly when he announced that the enterprise was "a thoroughbred Nebraska show," in which, evoking Shakespeare, "they should hold the mirror up to nature."

On May 19 Doc Carver had an off day with his shooting, perhaps because of too much celebration of the opening—a celebration that lasted five weeks, according to some accounts. When the crowd yelled for Buffalo Bill, Cody tried his hand at the glass balls with a borrowed gun. Despite the opening day celebrations, Cody shot so well that his act became a permanent part of the show.

Another feature of the 1883 Cody and Carver Rocky Mountain and Prairie Exhibition, which went along with the Wild West show throughout its long life, was a statement in the program about the role of the rifle in the conquering of the West. The essay, entitled "The Rifle as an Aid to Civilization," was taken from Buel's *Heroes of the Plains*. It began:

> There is a trite saying that "the pen is mightier than the sword." It is an equally true one that the bullet is the pioneer of civilization, for it has gone hand in hand with the axe that cleared the forest, and with the family bible and school book. Deadly as has been its mission in one sense, it has been merciful in another; for without the rifle ball we of America would not be to-day in the possession of a free and united country, and mighty in our strength.

In Omaha, Captain A. H. Bogardus, billed on the program as the Champion Pigeon Shot of America, joined the show. Adam Bogardus was born in Albany County, New York, on September 17, 1833. He moved to Illinois in 1856, where he became a market hunter, a marksman who hunts game for profit, in the town of Elkhart, Logan County. He defeated the Illinois champion wingshot, Abe Kleinman, then challenged Ira Paine, champion wingshot of America. After a series of matches, Paine conceded the title to Bogardus in 1871. On August 6, 1878, Bogardus defeated English champion Aubrey Coventry at Brighton, England, seventy-nine to seventy-eight, in a hundred-bird match. His four sons, Eugene, Peter,

Edward, and Adam Jr., all expert shots, appeared with Bogardus in the Wild West show.

On the show's program, Bogardus was credited with an exhibition "using the Ligowsky clay pigeon." Prior to that time, pigeon shooting meant using live passenger pigeons, which were lured to the marksman's trap by a captive pigeon with its leg tied to a stool, a "stool pigeon," thereby adding a colorful expression to the language. The practice was extremely hard on the pigeon population. Bogardus first invented a trap for launching glass balls and thus was responsible for creating the sport of trapshooting. The new glass-ball targets and the trap for launching them devolved into yet another innovation: clay pigeons, the origin of the target for today's skeet and trapshooting competitions.

The program for the 1884 Wild West show stated: "In deference to the humanitarian sentiment, [our exhibition] matches are all shot at Ligowsky 'clay pigeons,' an ingenious mechanical contrivance that furnishes an exact imitation of the bird's flight. . . . Ladies and children can, therefore, witness and enjoy this unique exhibition with no violence to the feelings, while the expert and experienced sportsman can still appreciate the excellence of the shooting, the clay pigeons heightening rather than diminishing the sport." The pigeons were made of red clay in the shape of a saucer. They measured four inches in diameter, were slightly over an inch in thickness, and were quite light.

The use of artificial targets did reduce the pressure on live pigeons. Unfortunately, passenger pigeon populations had already been widely decimated by market hunters. Between 1878 and 1882 the heavy demand for squabs as a delicacy resulted in the killing of millions of the birds. The last passenger pigeon in America died in the Cincinnati zoo in 1914.

The addition of Bogardus gave the show three of the nation's finest marksmen and ensured that the shooting events would be popular. Besides featuring Bogardus, the show gave top billing to Major Frank North. North brought along as an interpreter for the Pawnee twenty-three-year-old Gordon William Lillie, who had been a secretary to the agent at the Pawnee agency, Indian Territory, and a teacher at the reservation's industrial school. Lillie later became known as "Pawnee Bill" and "the White Chief of the Pawnees." He was born in Bloomington, Illinois, on February 14, 1860. As a trapper, ranch hand, and agency employee, he spent some seven years on the frontier. He joined the Wild West at its second stand, not Springfield, as Cody said, but Council Bluffs.

According to Richard Walsh, Lillie was shocked by his first meeting with Buffalo Bill. The young interpreter explained that his mental picture of Cody had long been one of "a fine looking man, well groomed, with a beautiful buffalo robe coat." Instead, the great man had been sleeping in some hay, his hair was matted, and he was drunk. "Cody was drunk every day for our first five weeks out," added Lillie.

Carver also claimed that his partner was "dead drunk all summer." During their association in show business, Cody had trouble with both Lillie and Carver, but never wrote disparagingly of either of them, though they both recited exaggerated tales of his drunkenness.

After Omaha and Council Bluffs the exhibition headed to Springfield and then eastward, reaching Boston's Beacon Park on July 2. In Boston Cody astonished the sedate citizens by the skill with which he drove his strange cavalcade of wagons, buffalo, elk, steers, mules, ponies, and Indians through the narrow curves of Washington Street. Because fairgrounds were not adequately lighted, the exhibition was limited to afternoon crowds only—but wherever the Wild West went, it played to capacity crowds. At the Aquidnuck Fair Grounds in Newport, Rhode Island, in mid-July, Lord Mandeville rode in the Deadwood stage in the Indian ambush and cowboy rescue segment, the first of many noble and royal passengers to occupy the venerable coach in the coming years. Mandeville swooned dramatically as if wounded. "Half a dozen cowboys sprang to the coach door and tenderly brought the Duke of Manchester's son and heir out and conveyed him carefully to the judge's stand, where he was tended by loving hands, beneath the influence of which he speedily recovered."

The show's program contained many of the features that were to make Buffalo Bill's Wild West a continuing success. The Pony Express and "The Startling and Soul-Stirring Attack Upon the Deadwood Mail Coach" were permanent fixtures, as was "Cow-Boys' Fun!" introducing kicking and bucking ponies. Roping, tying, and riding wild Texas steers was another event that would continue past the Wild West into rodeo, which did not exist in an organized fashion at the time of Cody's show. There were various races: a hundred-yard race between a mounted Indian and an Indian on foot, turning a stake at fifty yards; a bareback pony race of Indians; and a charge of mounted cowboys. The closing spectacle was "A Grand Hunt on the Plains," deriving from the Old Glory Blowout. It introduced buffalo, deer, elk, cattle, and wild horses.

One outstanding event, however, was seen only that first season. It was billed as "Lassoing and Riding the Wild Bison of the Plains." According to Pawnee Bill, the top riders in the show had succeeded in riding every buffalo but one, a big bull called Monarch. Everyone was afraid of him, and they deliberately avoided roping him. At Indianapolis, Cody insisted that Monarch finally be ridden. Buck Taylor and Jim Lawson threw the bull, but Jim Bullock, the top steer rider, refused to attempt the ride. Cody himself then mounted the buffalo. Monarch ran a short distance, then bucked and threw Cody high in the air. He was carried to a hospital and remained there for two weeks. Pawnee Bill says that the first time he had seen Cody free of alcohol that summer was when Will rejoined the show in Chicago. The following season a simulated "Buffalo Chase, by Buffalo Bill and Pawnee Indians" was substituted for roping and riding the wild buffalo of the plains.

In her *Memories*, Louisa Cody, through her mouthpiece Cooper, suggests that she accompanied the show through the entire season and returned with her husband to North Platte in the fall "to plan and scheme again, and to dream of greater things for the coming season." Mrs. Cody and her daughters were quite probably at the Omaha opening, but they would not have traveled any farther with the show. Daughter Orra was in frail health, and the baby was barely past three months old. The rigors of traveling with the show would have taxed grown men, still less a mother and her three young children.

From Youngstown, Ohio, Will wrote on September 24 to his sister Julia, who was still in Kansas, that he had at last filed a petition for divorce against "that woman," and repeated his declaration that "she has tried to ruin me financially this summer. . . . I could tell you lots of funny things how she has tried to bust up the horse ranch and buy more property [and] get the deeds in her name."

All the performances that season were given in fairgrounds with the exception of Coney Island, in Brooklyn, New York, where a temporary stand was erected, and the company remained there for five weeks. On August 16 Cody wrote Julia again from Coney Island:

> Darling Sister, I am now located at this place, have went to a big expense fixing up a place here—and as the watering season is about over it wont be worth much this year, but will be good for next. I am not much ahead on the summer in cash but I have my show all clear, and a fine place built here. I have over a hundred head of stock . . . ten head of fine race horses, the finest six mule coach train in the world and seventy head of good saddle horses—and the foundation laid for a fortune before long. The papers say I am the coming Barnum. . . . I am improving wonderfully in shooting, don't take a back seat from Carver or Roger. Tell Al I broke 87 glass balls out of one hundred thrown from a trap 21 yards rise with a shotgun riding a horse at full speed. I have broken 76 out of a hundred with a rifle horse running full speed. Our Cleveland suit didn't come off yet but it will. . . . Write me Hotel Brighton, Coney Island, N.Y. Love to all, Brother Will.

The 1883 season was a stressful one both for Cody on the road and Louisa at home, lonely for her seldom-seen husband and constantly worrying about Orra's health. Her doubts about the success of the Cleveland lawsuit, compounded by the uncertainty of the Wild West's future, despite the assurances she gave to Cooper in her *Memories*, were probably behind her desire to accumulate more property before Will could turn the land into ready cash. In her book Louisa makes no mention of marital difficulties with her husband at any time in their long marriage; for that matter, the tone of the book throughout is relentlessly rose-colored.

As for Buffalo Bill, not only did the Cleveland suit bedevil him, the problems of building up the big show that first crucial season were a heavy burden. Because of the less-than-efficient business management of the two partners, the show was costing a good deal more than was necessary and, in spite of record attendance figures, was barely making money. There is good reason to believe that Cody was drinking too much that summer, thanks to the constant presence of his friends and hangers-on who wanted to bend an elbow with the famous showman. Then there were the ever-increasing difficulties with Dr. Carver, difficulties that would end in a rupture of the partnership. Neither Cody nor Carver had had any experience in handling such a variegated troupe; even Cody's combinations had not been so logistically complex. Many of the cowboys spent most of their time in saloons and could not be found when called upon to perform their riding and roping stunts.

In the sixteen-car train, one whole car was devoted to a supply of liquor. For the first few weeks, according to Courtney Ryley Cooper, "it was an eternal gamble as to whether the show would exist from one day to the next, not because of a lack of money, but simply through an absence of human endurance necessary to stay awake twenty hours out of twenty-four, that the birth of a new amusement enterprise might properly be celebrated. When the show got into town and the biggest saloon announced an open house for the company, it was quite all right with Bill Cody. In fact, striving always to be the good fellow, he would be in the thickest of the celebration, whooping it up as long as anyone else—and sometimes a bit longer. Then, at the last possible moment, there would be a rush to the show lot, and as much attention paid to business as possible under the conditions."

The whole outfit lacked discipline, and Buffalo Bill had not yet acquired the easy ability to assert his authority—that would come later. Often Cody made the mistake of being "one of the boys."

Although complaining about Cody's drinking, his partner, the "Evil Spirit of the Plains," was also drinking heavily. Jealous and hot-tempered, Dr. Carver was constantly irritated by the fact that the lion's share of the adulation went to Buffalo Bill and not to him. Cody's reference to himself as the "coming Barnum" came from such reviews as the one in the Hartford *Courant* calling it "the best open-air show ever seen. . . . Thunder of hoofs, clank of spurs, rattle of pistols, glint of shattered glass balls, odor of gunpowder and cattle made it authentic. . . . Cowboys rode bucking broncos, roped and tied Texas steers, lassoed and rode wild bison. . . . The real sight of the whole thing is, after all, Buffalo Bill, a perfect model of manly beauty. Mounted on his blooded horse, he rode around the grounds, the observed of all observers. Cody was an extraordinary figure, and sits on a horse as if he were born in the saddle. His feats of shooting are perfectly wonderful. . . . He has, in this exhibition, out-Barnumed Barnum."

Carver, who considered himself a handsome man and a better shot than Cody, was surely incensed by such reviews, and the two men quarreled frequently. Yet Carver simply did not have the personality to put himself over. In addition, he had a vile temper. When he missed his shot one day at Coney Island, he smashed his rifle over his horse's ears and punched his helper. It did not help matters that Cody was regularly outshooting Carver, whose aim, perhaps, suffered from his consumption of alcohol. In any case, he was no one to point an accusing finger at his partner.

In July they appeared at the Prospect Park Fair Grounds in Brooklyn and in August at Brighton Beach, where they found a spot between the Iron Pier and the Brighton Hotel. The place was brilliantly lighted, so they put on their first night performances. P. T. Barnum, who may have felt the least bit jealous, commented, "The virtue of the show is that it did not need spangles, being of itself all life and movement, the effect of which was easily grasped by everybody."

When the show stopped at Chicago's Driving Park for a four-day stand on October 17 to 20, Bill found Nate Salsbury playing in a Chicago theater and went to see him. According to Salsbury, Cody said he was through with Carver and would not go through another summer with him, not even for $100,000. Salsbury had seen Cody's show in New York and found it lacking in merit because "they had not developed my ideas in putting it together at all." Nate, with perhaps a touch of sour grapes, declared the season "a ghastly failure," which, though financially disappointing, it certainly was not. The most important development of that first season was that Cody's show had proven itself as a sure-fire crowd-pleaser. Apparently Salsbury and Cody arrived at some kind of agreement; as soon as Cody had shaken himself loose from the erstwhile dentist, they would join forces. Meanwhile, Salsbury's Troubadours were fully booked a year ahead.

The Wild West was supposed to travel on to Omaha and break up there a short time later, but before it left Chicago Cody was called home to North Platte by the death of little Orra. Louisa wrote a sorrowing note to her friend Frances Sims: "Orra, my precious darling, that promised so fair, was called from us the 24th of October . . . and we carried her remains to Rochester . . . and laid them by the side of her little brother, in a grave lined with evergreens and flowers. When we visited the sacred spot last summer, she said: 'Mamma, won't you lay me by my brother's side when I die?' Oh, how soon we have had to grant her request! If it was not for the hope of heaven and again meeting there, my affliction would be more than I could bear." Her grief, though couched in conventionally sentimental terms, was surely profound—as was Cody's. Once again he had to suffer the loss of a beloved child. Now there were only two left— Arta and little Irma.

Apparently Orra's death put Cody's plans for a divorce on the back burner, and the breach between him and Lulu was healed. After the funeral, Cody returned to the show, and it quickly closed for the season in Omaha. Carver wanted to continue the show into a winter season, but Cody flatly refused, so the two partners divided their assets equally. Richard Walsh writes that they "flipped a silver dollar and chose in turn horse and horse, steer and steer, wagon and wagon." In one of the tosses, it was Cody's good fortune to win the Deadwood coach.

It was time to move on, to firm up plans for the new Wild West. The attorney John P. Altgeld, later governor of Illinois, drew up the contract of partnership among W. F. Cody, Nate Salsbury, and A. H. Bogardus, the third partner in the show they now called Buffalo Bill's Wild West— America's National Entertainment. In Omaha Dr. Carver teamed up with Captain Jack Crawford, the Poet Scout, and took his share of the Wild West on a winter tour. Their show played Nashville, Atlanta, Augusta, Charleston, Columbus, Montgomery, Mobile, and New Orleans. In 1884 Carver took his show to Canada and in 1885 to New England, where he ran afoul of Buffalo Bill's Wild West. A series of court actions ensued. Carver's version is that he won his case but lost his show. In 1886 Carver's Wild West was combined with W. W. Cole's New Colossal Show, and for the two following seasons he joined the circus of Adam Forepaugh Jr.

A revived Carver's Wild West toured Europe in 1889 and Australia in 1890 and 1891. Despite his dogged persistence, Dr. Carver's Wild West always lingered in the shadow of Buffalo Bill's much more successful show; it is not surprising that a bitter Carver was intensely jealous of his more popular rival, and in 1890 their rivalry would nearly escalate into violence.

Nate Salsbury, a consummate showman, was a far cry from the Evil Spirit of the Plains. Born two days after Cody—on February 28, 1846, in Freeport, Illinois—Nate ran away from home at fifteen and enlisted in the Union army during the Civil War as a drummer boy. He was discharged from the army because of his age. Later he reenlisted and served with

General Sherman in the Georgia campaign, where he was celebrated for his singing of "Oh, Susanna." Nate was captured and imprisoned at the Confederacy's notorious Andersonville prison. He is said to have ended the war rich because of his prowess at poker. After the war, Salsbury began the study of law, but was attracted by amateur theatricals and served an apprenticeship in stock companies at Grand Rapids, Baltimore, and Detroit. He then organized his own comedy troupe, The Troubadours, with which he toured quite successfully for twelve years, including the trip to Australia, which he claimed led to his conception of the Wild West show. By the 1890s he was living in high style on Ninety-third Street near Central Park.

Although he remained as manager of the Wild West as long as his health permitted, Salsbury nursed a series of grievances against Cody and the show from the onset. To begin with, he probably resented playing second fiddle to the more popular Buffalo Bill. Even though his photograph frequently appeared on the show's programs, he never appeared in the arena and audiences were unaware of his part in the production. His original concept called for Cody to be no more than a figurehead; Will had other ideas—he also wanted to be part of management, especially when it came to selecting cast members. Finally, Nate felt that Cody and his entourage—especially Major John Burke—obscured his importance in the scheme of things. That he was important is beyond question; his was the steady hand on the rudder of Buffalo Bill's sometimes wayward craft.

He revealed the depth of his dissatisfaction in an article later published in *Colorado Magazine*, "The Origin of the Wild West Show." Among other aspersions, he dismissed Major Burke in these terms: "I should never have put this relation of the origin of the Wild West Show on paper if there had not been in all the years that have passed a most determined effort on the part of John Burke and other hero-worshippers who have hung on to Cody's coat tails for their sustenance to make Cody the originator of the show for in so doing they edge in their own feeble claims to being an integral part of the success of the show. The men I speak of were all participants in the failure that followed the first venture by Cody and were retained in the management of the show by me at the request of Cody, who lives in the worship of those who bleed him."

And then, in a strange combination of tribute and condemnation: "In his peculiar position of almoner general [almsgiver] to the newspaper men of the world Burke has more personal friends than any man I ever knew. I do not believe there is another man in the world who could have covered as much space in the newspapers of the day as John Burke has done and I do not believe there is another man in the world in his position who would have had the gall to exploit himself at the expense of the show as much as John Burke!

"Burke and Keen and the rest of the Codyites who have followed the show from the day I took hold of it have never forgiven me for taking the reins of management out of their hands where they had been placed by Cody and Carver. . . . Mr. Keen is honest and able in his department but that lets him out."

Jule Keen, a friend of Cody's, who had acted in and stage-managed the theatrical combinations, was treasurer of the Wild West for many years.

Salsbury's opinion of Burke was not shared by Major Gordon Lillie, Pawnee Bill, a later partner in the show. Burke, he said, "was the highest salaried press agent in the country. He knew more managing editors and owners of big publications, and called them by their first names, than any man who ever lived. . . . I never in my life saw such liberal treatment of any show, any place, as was accorded us by the press of New York City."

In late November of 1883, Will wrote to Al and Julia Goodman, saying that he still had hopes of winning his lawsuit, but added that it was costing him heavily, although even if he lost he would have the consolation of knowing he had done what he promised his mother—namely, all in his power to take care of his sisters.

During the winter, Cody was occupied with preparations for the Wild West's next season. In a letter to Salsbury, from North Platte on April 12, 1884, he wrote:

> My dear Nate,
>
> Here I am foot loose and ready for work. But no money neither do I know what I am going to do about giving bonds for Indians. . . . I can get Pawnees without any permission but as Burke has agitated the question it is best now to give the bonds but I know nothing what he agreed to do—so I am up a stump until I get money and hear about how to give bonds for Indians. I have bought twelve head of horses and paid for them, including five buckers. Nate what can or had we better do about gambling privileges. I can get the best man in the world to run them and do it in a nice quiet way if you say so. What do you think about it? Write me and tell me what to do—and if we don't get that *money* what in K Christ are we to do?
>
> Write soon,
> CODY

Gambling on the lot was taboo as far as Salsbury was concerned. He did, however, supply money and also arranged for the Indians' bonds.

Con Groner, Buck Taylor, and Captain Bogardus, who had taken part in the blowout, continued with the show. Frank North, though, had missed the first season. His wife was ill—she died later in 1883—and he was also due to serve in the state legislature, so he returned home after the Omaha opening but was back for the second season. Seth Hathaway was the Pony Express rider, and a group of top cowboys known from Texas to Montana were hired to ride the bucking horses and to head the other cowboy acts. A new spectacle was the "Attack on a Settler's Cabin by Indians and Rescue by Buffalo Bill with his Scouts, Cowboys and Mexicans." Like the attack on the Deadwood stage, which it joined, this act became one of the most popular continuing features of the show.

It remained to fill out the cast with Indians. Probably Cody selected the Indians for the show himself. The Indians under consideration, five or six hundred of them, would come to Rushville, a Nebraska town near the South Dakota border, where the selections were made. They came in their finest buckskins, feathers, and beads. Only a small number could be chosen, which meant that most were bound to be disappointed. The government required that the Indians be well fed while away and that they be returned to the reservation in good health and with a new suit of clothes.

C. D. O'Kieffe, who lived in the area in the 1880s, recalled, "I'll never forget seeing Buffalo Bill coming each spring to get his braves. They left in paint and feathers and returned, after a year, in Prince Albert coats, Stetsons, patent leather shoes and long, well-groomed glossy hair."

Of his work that winter, and the resulting new show, Cody wrote: "Immediately upon forming a partnership with Salsbury we set about increasing the company and preparing to greatly enlarge the exhibition. Nearly one hundred Indians, from several tribes, were engaged. . . . We also captured a herd of elk, a dozen buffaloes and some bears with which to illustrate the chase."

Although Cody does not mention him, another guest star was Dr. Frank Powell, White Beaver. Powell was now practicing medicine in La Crosse, Wisconsin, when he wasn't active in show business as an exhibition marksman.

The Wild West show, in all its extravagant glory, was about to be seen by millions both here and abroad.

"THE VASTLY ENLARGED AND
REORGANIZED WILD WEST"

When Nate Salsbury visited the show, ready to open the season at St. Louis in the spring of 1884, he found his partner "boiling drunk . . . surrounded by a lot of harpies called old timers who were getting as drunk as he at his expense. . . . He had taken a plug hat from someone in the crowd, and jammed it on his head, and as his hair was long and thick in those days, a more ridiculous figure could not be imagined than he cut with his arm around White Beaver while they rehearsed the exploits of the frontier to the gaping gang of bloodsuckers that surrounded them."

This scene prompted Salsbury to write a letter to Cody, which he hoped Bill would read in a sober moment. Cody replied: "Your very sensible and truly rightful letter has just been read and it has been the means of showing me just where I stand. And I solemnly promise to you that after this you will never see me under the influence of liquor. I may have to take two or three drinks today to brace up on; that will be all as long as we are partners. I appreciate all you have done. Your judgment and business is good and from this day on I will do my work to the letter. The drinking surely ends today and your pard will be himself, and on deck all the time."

From this incident grew a legend that, as such tales do, grew larger in the retelling. The first version of the story was that Nate Salsbury limited Cody to one drink a day, whereupon Bill poured his drink into a schooner with the capacity to last him all day. In his book *Timberline*, Gene Fowler made it twelve drinks a day poured in twelve large tumblers. Fowler also went on to say that Nate sued Bill under their contract, but that the judge who heard the case held that the contract specified glasses of whiskey without any limitation on their size. This is pure nonsense, since Salsbury and Cody never had such a contract, nor did Nate ever sue Bill.

A performance of the Wild West show in the arena. Cast members watching the show. (Gift of Jess Frost. Buffalo Bill Historical Center, Cody, Wyoming)

Whatever Cody's capacity for drink might have been, and it was probably considerable, there is no evidence that alcohol ever impaired his performances with the Wild West; on the contrary. He may have fallen off the wagon at work occasionally, but there is every reason to believe that Cody stuck pretty well to his bargain to quit drinking on the job. How much whiskey he put away when the season was over is another matter, of course. He had never claimed, to Salsbury or anyone else, that he intended to give up drinking altogether.

Cody once wrote to Captain Jack Crawford, "I would have answered at once from Frisco, but I was on a hell of a toot and I seldom attend to anything but hoof her up when I am that way." His alcoholic excesses were always planned to take place when the show's season closed and he returned to North Platte. Dexter Fellows, who traveled with the show as press agent, recorded an occasion when the show closed at North Platte, and the entire company, with the exception of Johnny Baker and Annie Oakley, the reigning female star of the show, went on a memorable binge. Fellows also observed, however, "No doubt during the winters there were big doings at his camp, but while he was with the show, except for that visit to his home State, I never saw him under the influence of liquor. . . . Because of the need to entertain, Cody kept a stock of liquor in his private car, but I never saw any in his tent on the show grounds. In fact, when General Fitzhugh Lee visited him in Richmond, Cody had to send a messenger to the car to provide the nephew of General Robert E. Lee with the drink of his choice." Lee had heard that Cody made "the best old-fashioned cocktail ever put together. . . . When the messenger brought back the makings, Cody mixed the drink, pouring only a small one for himself."

William McDonald, Cody's business representative in North Platte, states emphatically that Cody quit drinking altogether, under his doctor's orders, during the last nine years of his life. Certainly Cody had the reputation of never missing a performance because of drinking, for all his years in show business.

The 1884 show had an exceptionally strong cast. Two of its proprietors—Buffalo Bill and Captain Bogardus—were there while the third, Nate Salsbury, continued to tour with his Troubadours. All the billing featured Major Frank North, the Pilot of the Prairie, and Buck Taylor, King of the Cow-Boys. William Levi "Buck" Taylor was the first and original King of the Cow-Boys. Though undeservedly forgotten today, he was America's first cowboy hero, in fact as well as in fiction.

Before Buffalo Bill's Wild West, the word "cowboy" had a negative connotation, dating back to the mid-eighteenth century, when New York Colony's landowners so described their rebellious tenants. In the American Revolution, cowboys were Loyalist guerrillas who stole Patriot cows, and when the word headed west it remained uncomplimentary. President Chester Arthur asserted in his annual message to Congress in 1881, "A band of armed desperadoes known as 'Cowboys' were menaces to the peace of Arizona Territory." In 1882 the Cheyenne *Daily Leader* reprinted the following article from an eastern publication:

> As you mingle with the boys, you find them a strange mixture of good nature and recklessness. You are as safe with them on the plains as with any class of men, so long as you do not impose upon them. . . . Morally, as a class, they are foulmouthed, blasphemous, drunken, lecherous, utterly corrupt. Usually harmless on the plains when sober, they are dreaded in towns, for then liquor has the ascendancy over them. They are also improvident as the veriest "Jack" of the seas. Employed as cow-boys only six months in the year—from May till November— their earnings are soon squandered in dissoluteness, and then they hunt to get odd jobs to support themselves until another cattle season begins.

The *Annals of Kansas* noted: "When he feels well (and he always does when full of what he calls 'Kansas sheep-dip') the average cowboy is a bad man to handle. Armed to the teeth, well mounted, and full of their favorite beverage, the cowboys will dash through the principal streets of town yelling like Comanches. They call this 'cleaning out a town.'"

Memories of the Civil War played a part in the animosity between cowboys and townspeople. The drovers were primarily Texans; more than a few were Confederate veterans, bitter about the outcome of the war, and they did not relish being locked up by marshals they considered "abolitionists" because their loyalties had been to the Army of the Potomac. As a consequence, some of these drovers provoked quarrels and, on occasion, got themselves killed.

The annual descent of the cowboys into western towns after the end of the cattle drive, eager to spend their pay, ready to shoot up the town like the feared "Bad Man of Bodie," has become a cliché of the movie or television western. Still, it is well grounded in reality. To put a more compassionate face on what the townspeople considered an outrage—having to submit to an invasion of armed and dissolute cowhands—think of the cowboys' circumstances: half the year working under the most grueling conditions, far away from women or any other civilizing influences. Is it any wonder they ran wild as soon as they reached an oasis, however primitive? They were starved for pleasure, for feminine companionship, for fun, crude as it might have been. By welcoming cowboys into his show and giving them heroic parts to play, Buffalo Bill transformed the image of the cowboy from hellion or desperado to a mythic figure on horseback, a sort of centaur—and Buck Taylor was the avatar of this new breed.

Buck Taylor, who stood six foot five inches tall in his socks (he liked to say he was five feet seventeen inches tall), was matinee-idol handsome. He weighed over three hundred pounds. Eventually he became so heavy that he allegedly had to resign from the show because it was hard to find mustangs big enough to carry his increasing bulk. Patrons of the Wild West were assured that this "critter" was as "amiable as a child." Like Cody, Buck also starred in dime novels, the first of which was *Buck Taylor, King of the Cowboys*, by Prentiss Ingraham, published in Beadle's Half-Dime Library in 1887. Other dime novels, all completely fanciful, followed. As a hero, he was a natural.

Born in Fredericksburg, Texas, in November 1857, Taylor lost his father, a Confederate cavalryman, in the Civil War; his mother died when he was six. He once said, "I was dependent on myself at an age when ordinary children are still in the nursery. . . . There was only one thing to do; which was to be a cowpuncher. . . . By the time I was 14 I was able to ride and rope with some of the best of them and was known around our section as the best cowpuncher of my age that had ever been seen." At the age of seventeen Taylor first rode on a cattle drive from his home state to Wyoming. After returning to Texas, he repeated the feat, this time with his brother, Baxter. Together they took up a homestead on Long Creek, some sixty miles from Lander, Wyoming. Drifting, he wound up on Buffalo Bill's ranch, where, as one of Cody's youthful protégés, he learned to read and write. On hand when the Wild West was organized, he epitomized the "new cowboy": respectable, honest, good-hearted, and neither reckless nor dissolute—a forerunner of Gene Autry and Roy Rogers, though it is unlikely that Buck ever sang or played the guitar. Buck Taylor was the first genuine cowboy hero. In 1894, he tried his own show, known as "Buck Taylor's Wild West"—thereby earning Cody's disfavor.

Presiding over the "genuine blanket Indians"—that is, peaceful or reservation Indians—was John Nelson, the squaw man, also known as Cha-sha-sha-o-po-ge-o, meaning "Red Willow Fill the Pipe." He was featured in the program as one who "by general honesty of character and energy has gained fame and respect among whites and Indians." It was Nelson who was to sit atop the Deadwood stage for many years, his full beard floating in the breeze. At the ribbons of the coach was Fred Matthews, also well bearded. Law and order was represented by Con Groner, "the cow-boy sheriff of the Platte" and the "Nemesis of the Lawless." Audiences read in the program that "Over fifty murderers, more than that number of horse-thieves, cattle-cutters, burglars and outlaws have been caught and convicted through his efforts, notably the Doc Middleton and his allied gangs, and when Doc in conjunction with Jesse James's party surrounded North Platte in their contemplated attack on the Union Pacific train at Garnett Station, six miles east, Groner's strategy frustrated their plans, captured six, scattered the rest, and saved the train. He has followed horse-thieves 1,900 miles through Nebraska, Idaho and Montana, through sand hills, deep canyons, strange valleys, up mountain peaks, in forest fastnesses, facing the fierce blizzards, sleeping out at night with his saddle blanket for a bed, his saddle for a pillow, his horse and rifle for companions, and hardly ever failed to bag his game." This red-blooded prose was Colonel Prentiss Ingraham at his finest, assisting John Burke in spinning a web of rugged romance around the show that clung for thirty years.

It was announced that at some of the large cities the show would include shooting by White Beaver, or Dr. W. F. Powell, "chief medicine man of the Winnebago Sioux—a reckless adventurer on the boundless prairies, and yet in elegant society as amiable as a school-girl in the ballroom; evincing the polish of the aristocrat and a cultured mind that shines with vigorous lustre where learning displays itself."

The press agents may have hyped the show relentlessly, but the show itself was honest, true to its period, and free from all faking. Nate Salsbury's advertising proclaimed: "The Only Real Novelty of the Century. The Amusement Triumph of the Age. The Romantic West Brought East in Reality. Everything Genuine. Each Scene Instructive. Civilizations' Reception to its Pioneers. Amusement, Instruction and Education to All. Air, Light, Life and Health to the Auditor. A Year's Visit in Three Hours. Actual Scenes in the Nation's Progress Delight, Please, Gratify, Chain and Interest the Visitor." Cody signed a "card to the public" that read: "A true prescript of life on the frontier as I knew it to be, and which no fictitious pen can describe."

The "vastly enlarged and reorganized Wild West," in Cody's words, opened in St. Louis, and two weeks later turned out a crowd of 41,448 people for a single show at the Driving Park in Chicago. As advance man, Colonel Ingraham beat the drums for the show's New York opening on June 16, 1884, at the Polo Grounds. The critics commented favorably on the riding and roping acts that had been added to the show. The first year's show had been heavy with shooting acts, but, in fact, despite Nate Salsbury's criticisms of the Cody-Carver ensemble, the program wasn't much changed. The buffalo chase had replaced the unfortunate attempt to ride buffalo.

The reviewer for the *Spirit of the Times* wrote: "The only artistic interest in the show is that it seems to us to contain the germ of the circus of the future. Even the smallest boys of the present generation must be weary of seeing bespangled persons riding around a small ring upon the broad, padded backs of horses trained to gallop as gently as rocking chairs. The circus is behind the times. For years it has introduced no novelties. . . . Why should not Buffalo Bill engage some Comanche braves and show us the real feats? His cowboys, Mexicans and Indians may not be as wild as the playbills assert, but they know how to ride. . . . Let him take this hint for next season and he will make Barnum and Forepaugh shake in their shoes, despite their white elephants, gilded chariots, Roman races and triple rings. He has hit upon one good idea already, and has only to enlarge and perfect it in order to eclipse all rivalry. As for money, when he is tired of touring this country, there is an immense fortune awaiting him in England. . . . "

When the tour reached Hartford, a tragic accident took place. Frank North was thrown from his horse when his saddle girth broke; he fell beneath the hooves of the other charging horses. All but one of the skillful riders managed to pull his pony aside, but that one ran full over him. North's ribs were crushed and his spine injured. He remained in a hospital for several months with little Johnny Baker to keep him company, while the tour continued. North later rejoined the show briefly but left it again in New Orleans early in 1885. He died of his injuries in Columbus, Nebraska, on March 14 of that year.

Because the show was now making one-night stands, which proved expensive, by fall, despite the excellent crowds, the Wild West had not made much money. Hoping to improve their prospects, the partners decided to go south, where they could give outdoor performances all winter. The World's Industrial and Cotton Exposition was scheduled to open in New Orleans for a winter's run, and so it was decided that Salsbury would take the Troubadours on the road again to make money, while Cody would open the Wild West in New Orleans.

At this point Pony Bob Haslam, Cody's old friend and one of the most famous Pony Express riders of a quarter century before, turned up, in need of a job. With his typical generosity, Cody hired him as advance man for the southern tour. His job was to take the boat down the Mississippi, booking the show and renting show grounds along the way. The idea was to earn money on the trip south, arriving in New Orleans in time to open just before Christmas and play through the spring. Haslam, though he was eager to please, had neither the experience nor the capacity for such a job. The boat and navigator he hired in Cincinnati proved to be one of his biggest mistakes, and his other blunders—primarily in choosing sites for the Wild West to play—began to show up in greatly diminished receipts. Losses mounted as the decrepit old tub chugged south.

By the time they neared New Orleans, Cody decided that he'd better go on ahead and look into Pony Bob's arrangements himself. At the site of the exposition, he hired a hack and headed through a pouring rain for the show grounds. The first man he saw there was traveling across the arena in a rowboat. Fortunately, Cody was able to rent the Metarie Race Track, which, while muddy, was usable.

Then disaster struck. Near Rodney Landing, Mississippi, the showboat collided with another river steamer and sank within an hour. "In this accident," Cody wrote, "we lost all our personal effects, including wagons, camp equipage, arms, ammunition, donkeys, buffaloes, and one elk. We managed, however, to save our horses, the Deadwood coach, band wagon and—ourselves. The loss thus entailed was about $20,000." Captain Bogardus also lost all his exhibition equipment.

Cody sent a priceless telegram to Salsbury, who was appearing with the Troubadours in Denver: OUTFIT AT BOTTOM OF RIVER, WHAT DO YOU ADVISE? Nate wired back: GO TO NEW ORLEANS, REORGANIZE, AND OPEN ON YOUR DATE. HAVE WIRED YOU FUNDS. Those who rate Cody as having little talent for management must give him full credit for his resourcefulness here. He sprang immediately into action. "In eight days I had added to the nucleus that had been saved a herd of buffalo and elk, and all the necessary wagons and other properties, completing the equipment so thoroughly that the show in many respects was better prepared than at the time of the accident—and we opened on our date."

Back in North Platte, the new Lincoln County *Weekly Tribune* on January 24, 1885, informed the townspeople that the big show was exhibiting at the New Orleans World's Exposition and "is reported to be drawing crowds in its usual mustard plaster style, while Johnny Baker, the Cowboy Kid, is now one of the leading characters and has seemingly taken the laurels from Con Groner, the Cowboy Sheriff, as Con is no longer starred."

The New Orleans engagement, which had begun with a shipwreck, ended with a deluge. It rained for forty-four days, exceeding the biblical downpour by four, and always at showtime. On one day the ticket seller told Cody that only nine people had shown up, and he had better cancel the show. Cody, proving himself the true professional, replied: "If nine people came out here in all this rain to see us, we'll show."

On February 14 Cody wrote his partner from New Orleans:

My dear Pard,

The camels back is broken. This day I looked forward to as one to help us out, worked every possible means to make it a success, but God, Christ, and the devil is against me. the morning opened bright I started with a full parade, thousands of people in the damned City. And we would surely have played to $2000 had it not been so ordained that we should not. At 10:30 it clouded up all of a sudden and poured rain until 4 P M then it cleared up again Just as pleasant as before. its plain to me now. I can read it clearly. *fate* if there is such a thing is against me. there is not one bit of use trying more the longer we stick at this the worse off we are—the sooner we give this outfit away the better— I am thoroughly discouraged. I am a damned condemned Joner and the sooner you get clear of me the better for you. . . .

I am an *Ingersol* man from this out. [Cody meant he was now an atheist.] And a damed Joner disgusted with myself and the world— there is no *heaven*—if so it can stay there and be damed—

Your pard and take my advice and quit him

CODY

In March the Lincoln County *Weekly Tribune*, revising its earlier bullish report, dolefully declared that "the Wild West didn't do as well as expected in New Orleans because of excessive wet weather, causing the show grounds, fitted up at a cost of several thousand dollars, to become a perfect mudhole, which had to be abandoned."

At the end of the winter of 1884, the show was about $60,000 in the red. In a letter to Salsbury in early March 1885, Cody listed his assets: "About the same number of horses we had last summer . . . about twenty-five Indians in the saddle, 7 Mexicans and 8 cowboys." But some of the Indians would be returning to the reservation, as ordered by the government, to put in their spring crops. Cody sent Frank North back to Nebraska to get more Indians, offering him $5,000 if he could do so. It was on this ill-fated trip that Frank died from the injuries in his fall. In the same letter Will promised Nate: "As I told you that I am to do my best for another season yet next winter when the show is laid up for winter I am going to get on a drunk that is a drunk. Just to change my luck I will paint a few towns red hot—but till then I am staunch and true—With my shoulder to the wheel." In a postscript to the letter, Cody added, "Johnnie Baker is shooting to beat L. breaks balls in the air like an old timer. I want to star him this summer."

It was in this season that the Wild West took its final shape. There would be changes over the years, but the show remained virtually the same until the end. After the disastrous weather in New Orleans, the show moved to St. Louis, where it scored a much-needed triumph in a weeklong engagement. Said the *Globe-Democrat:* "The most remarkable fact is that among so many thousands there were heard no grumbling nor expressions of dissatisfaction, and those who were present will have nothing but agreeable recollections of the Buffalo Bill Wild West."

The next stop was in Chicago's Driving Park, where the show played for two weeks. The opening performance attracted more than twenty thousand spectators, which the Chicago *Tribune* estimated "was more than a twentieth of the population, a fraction greater than all the local preachers had attracted that Sunday morning." General Sherman praised the shows as "wonderfully realistic and historically reminiscent."

Reviews and the show's own publicity always stressed its "realism." There is no doubt it was more realistic, visually and in essence, than any of the competing Wild Wests. There were four other Wild West shows that year: Adam Forepaugh had one, Dr. A. W. Carver another; there was a third called Fargo's Wild West and one known as Hennessey's Wild West. Cody criticized all their claims and their use of the words "Wild West." He had copyrighted the term according to an act of Congress on December 22, 1883, and registered a typescript at the Library of Congress on June 1, 1885. The copyright title read: *The Wild West or Life among the Red Man and the Road Agents of the Plains and Prairies—An Equine Dramatic*

Exposition on Grass or Under Canvas, of the Adventures of Frontiersmen and Cowboys.

Additional copy was headed

BUFFALO BILL'S "WILD WEST"
PRAIRIE EXHIBITION
AND ROCKY MOUNTAIN SHOW,
A DRAMATIC-EQUESTRIAN
EXPOSITION
OF
LIFE ON THE PLAINS,
WITH ACCOMPANYING MONOLOGUE
AND
INCIDENTAL MUSIC
THE WHOLE INVENTED AND
ARRANGED BY
W.F. CODY
W.F. CODY AND N. SALSBURY,
PROPRIETORS AND MANAGERS
WHO HEREBY CLAIM AS THEIR
SPECIAL
PROPERTY THE VARIOUS EF-
FECTS INTRODUCED IN
THE PUBLIC PER-
FORMANCES
OF
BUFFALO BILL'S "WILD WEST"

Although the show's first year under enlarged and reorganized management had not been a financial success, at least one good thing had come from it. Also showing in New Orleans that winter had been the Sells Brothers Circus. One of its performers who had wandered over to visit the Wild West lot was Annie Oakley.

The story of Annie Oakley's life was so much in the American grain that it might have come from the pen of Horatio Alger Jr., the minister turned best-selling author, who chronicled the fictional lives of poor boys who made good. *Ragged Dick: or, Street Life in New York, Ragged Tom,* and *Luck*

MISS ANNIE OAKLEY,
(LITTLE SURE SHOT.)
BUFFALO BILL'S WILD WEST.

Miss Annie Oakley. (Courtesy The Annie Oakley Foundation, Greenville, Ohio)

and Pluck were typical titles. But Annie's success story was so much more remarkable than any of Alger's tales, for she was born in truly daunting circumstances, into a world where women were not even allowed to vote and were not expected to have careers. They were homemakers or, if they worked at all, teachers or nurses. The only avenues to prosperity open to a woman in the latter part of the nineteenth century were show business and prostitution—and in some minds, they were the same.

Oakley was born Phoebe Ann Moses on August 13, 1860, to Jacob and Susan Moses, Quakers who moved from Blair County, Pennsylvania, to Darke County, Ohio, in 1855. Together they had seven children; one, a daughter, died in infancy. Jacob died of pneumonia, after exposure in a blizzard, on February 11, 1866. Susan did her best to raise her family as a practical nurse, but jobs were scarce and she was paid little. The widow

Moses then married Dan Brumbaugh, who died in an accident shortly afterward, leaving another daughter.

When she was seven, Annie frequently fed the family with quail she had caught in homemade traps, much as young Will Cody had trapped small game. In an interview she once said: "I was eight years old when I made my first shot, and I still consider it one of the best shots I ever made. I saw a squirrel run down over the grass in front of the house, through the orchard and stop on the fence to get a hickory nut. I decided to shoot it and ran into the house to get a gun which was hanging on the wall and which I knew to be loaded. I was so little I had to jump up on a chair and slide it down to the mantel and then to the ground. I laid the gun on the railing of the porch, and then recalled that I had heard my brother say about shooting: 'It is a disgrace to shoot a squirrel anywhere but in the head because it spoils the meat to hit him elsewhere.' I took the remark literally and decided, in a flash, that I must hit the squirrel in the head, or be disgraced. It was a wonderful shot, going right through the head from side to side. My mother was so frightened when she learned that I had taken down the loaded gun and shot it that I was forbidden to touch it again for eight months."

Mrs. Crawford Edington, the matron at the Darke County Infirmary, offered to take Annie in and train her in exchange for help with the children. The infirmary was in fact a poorhouse, apparently a dumping ground for the elderly, the orphaned, and the insane. Mrs. Edington taught Annie sewing, a skill that came in handy later when she made her own costumes. Annie was then offered the opportunity to work as a mother's helper on a farm, taking care of a baby for pay and schooling, but she was beaten, half starved, and kept in virtual slavery for two years—until she ran away in search of her mother, with whom she had lost touch. She discovered that in her absence she had acquired a new stepfather, Joseph Shaw, a Civil War veteran with a pension, who had built a cabin for his new wife and her children. The cabin was modest but had an orchard, a garden, and a cellar. It would be Annie's home for a few years, and she returned there in later life between show tours.

For a pioneer family like the Moseses, a large family was a necessity, and every child was expected to do farm chores before being allowed to play. The three eldest daughters had married and left home, so Annie, now the eldest, had many household duties. When she picked up the gun again, it was to shoot game to help support her family. In an interview in 1914 Annie said: "When I first commenced shooting in the fields of Ohio, my gun was a single-barrel muzzle loader and, as well as I can remember, was 16-bore. I used black powder, cut my own wads out of cardboard boxes, and thought I had the best gun on earth. Anyway, I managed to kill a great many ruffled grouse, quail and rabbits, all of which were quite plentiful in those days."

Annie's stepfather was a mail carrier who made two trips a week to Greenville, the county seat. There he exchanged the game at Charles Ketzenberger's general store for ammunition, groceries, and necessities. Ketzenberger in turn sold some of the game to hotels in Dayton and Lebanon, and to Jack Frost, a Cincinnati hotelkeeper, whose customers appreciated finding that there was no shot in the game they ate. Annie had shot every one of the animals straight through the head. Legend has it that she was able to pay off the mortgage on the family farm with the game she sold.

The performer Fred Stone, Annie's friend in later years, said she once told him, "From the time I was nine, I never had a nickel I did not earn myself."

Because she didn't care much for the family name, which was the subject of jokes like "Moses Poses," at the age of ten Annie changed it to "Mozee," a name she had carved on the family tombstones. It was her stage name that was to endure, however.

When she was fifteen, Annie visited her older sister, Lyda, Mrs. Joseph Stein, in Cincinnati. When Jack Frost, the local innkeeper who had bought Annie's game, learned Annie herself was in town, he was curious about the girl who shot squirrels in the eye and decided to match the young sharpshooter with a professional marksman. Frost put up $50 for a Thanksgiving Day match with his guest Frank Butler, who, with his partner Billy Graham, did exhibition shooting between acts of a stock company show. Butler agreed to the contest but thought a joke was being played upon him when he found his opponent to be a little country girl in a pink gingham dress and sunbonnet, dragging an ancient rifle taller than she was. Although she had never shot trap-released pigeons before, Annie wound up winning the match by one bird. As far as can be determined, the contest was held in 1875, northeast of Cincinnati near the route of the Cincinnati Northern Railroad, in a district called Oakley. The acquaintance with Frank Butler ripened into a romance, and the couple were married a year later, although Frank may not have seemed the ideal husband— he was divorced and in debt.

Frank Butler had run away from his home in Ireland and emigrated to the United States when still a boy. Unskilled but hardworking, he managed to go from street Arab—that is, ragamuffin—to show business performer, with a variety of jobs. First he delivered milk, then worked as a stable boy, a fisherman, and after taking care of a group of trained dogs, finally developed a shooting act. In 1877 Frank became an American citizen. He later teamed up with a performer named Baughman, and in the

Sells Brothers Circus they were billed in 1881 as "The Creedmoor Champion Sharpshooters and Most Illustrious Rifle Dead-Shots."

In his 1948 musical comedy *Annie Get Your Gun*, Irving Berlin was apparently unwilling to let the course of true love run smooth, for he took considerable dramatic license, putting obstacles in the way of Frank and Annie's love story and ignoring the fact that they were already married when they joined the Wild West. Probably because Annie could outshoot him, Frank shelved his masculine pride, gave up his own shooting, and devoted himself to managing Annie's far more successful career. Their partnership and their marriage both lasted half a century, ending only with their deaths in 1926, twenty days apart, and they are buried side by side.

On May 1, 1882, the act of Graham and Butler was booked into Crystal Hall, Springfield, Ohio. Billy Graham was ill one night, and Annie took his place in the act. Even though she was unaccustomed to appearing before an audience and to shooting by artificial light, she was determined to do her best. Courtney Ryley Cooper, in *Annie Oakley, Woman at Arms*, described the occasion:

> That was an attribute of Annie Oakley that she took nothing into consideration save her determination to do the thing upon which she had set her mind. A strange combination of human nature, this little woman of Darke County beginnings. As mild as an April shower, apparently as unsophisticated as though she had come but yesterday from the backwoods. . . . her nature contained also a quality that savored of the strength of steel. Perhaps it came from the exigencies of her youth, the trials, the sufferings; perhaps it was ingrained from a mother who had been forced to smile in the face of misfortune for the greater part of her life, but it was there, a sublime form of self-confidence, wholly without ego, which caused Annie Oakley, once she had considered a feat or a task, to believe wholly and utterly that she could perform it—and then go ahead and do that which she believed! It was with this attitude that she looked upon a future career as a stage shot, and she went to her first performance with the assurance of one who had been doing it always.

After that night Billy Graham disappeared from the act, which became Butler and Oakley—a stage name that Annie took from the shooting grounds in Ohio where she and Frank had first met.

On May 9, 1881, Frank sent the following poem to his wife:

> There's a charming little girl,
> She's many miles from here.
> She's a loving little fairy
> You'd fall in love to see her.
> Her presence would remind you
> Of an angel in the skies,

And you bet I love this little girl
With the raindrops in her eyes.

In addition to giving herself a new surname, Annie decided she needed a costume appropriate for the theater. She designed and sewed her own costumes: practical short skirts and leggings, done with such flair that they were often copied by couturiers during her European tours. She avoided leather because it was too hard to keep clean, but used other durable materials.

For the first few years Butler and Oakley played in stock companies, skating rinks, and variety theaters, often appearing as a "specialty" with their acting dogs, Jack and George. As part of their act, George, a standard-bred poodle, sat on a pedestal with an apple on his head, which he allowed Frank to shatter with a rifle shot. "At the end of the performance," writes Isabelle S. Sayers in *Annie Oakley and Buffalo Bill's Wild West*, "he too would bow." An elderly George accompanied the Butlers during their first season with Buffalo Bill's Wild West in 1885. When the dog died in Cleveland, Ohio, his casket was fashioned by one of the Wild West carpenters, and he was wrapped in the elaborate pedestal cover that had been part of his act.

During those early years the couple traveled on a budget and lived in moderately priced hotels. "I owe whatever I have to [my husband's] careful management. Of course, we were poor when we started, and I remember him saying to me, 'Well, Annie, we have enough this week to buy you a pretty hat.'"

In 1883 the Butlers joined the Sells Brothers Circus, an Ohio company organized in 1871 with one tent and a few sideshow features, by Lewis, Ephraim, Allen, and Peter Sells of Dublin, Ohio. By 1878 they had added additional performers and tents and were traveling by railroad. In the early 1880s the circus was enjoying excellent business wherever it went.

Now that the Butlers were a team, Annie naturally wanted to travel with her husband. The first season she did not perform as a sharpshooter but as an equestrienne. She was not altogether happy with the Sells Brothers management, protesting on one occasion that her saddle was unsafe; told the saddle was fine, she jerked the rotted girth and the saddle fell to the ground. On another occasion she complained about the poor living quarters provided them by the owners of the circus.

In the fall and winter of 1883–1884, the Butlers toured with a three-act play, *Slocum's Oath*. The publicity described the drama as a "poetical sensation replete with thrilling situations and wonderful mechanical effects."

While appearing in St. Paul, Minnesota, Annie and Frank had a famous backstage visitor—Sitting Bull. Although still a political prisoner, Sitting Bull was permitted to leave the Standing Rock Agency at Fort

Yates, Dakota Territory, on several occasions, after permission was given by James McLaughlin, Indian agent at the fort. One of Sitting Bull's trips was to the St. Paul gala that marked the completion of the Northern Pacific Railway in 1883, and it was during this trip that the famous Sioux medicine man met Annie Oakley. So impressed was he by her marksmanship that he thought she was certainly possessed of the Good Spirit—that no one could ever hurt her, that only one who was supernaturally blessed could be such a dead shot. When he was introduced to her, they exchanged photographs and he adopted her into his Hunkpapa Sioux tribe, giving her the name "Watanya cicilia," which means "Little Sure Shot." At the time, Annie was only twenty-four years old.

The year 1884 was the first time Annie Oakley was billed by the Sells Brothers as a marksman in an outdoor show. Oakley and Butler appeared as "The Great Far West Rifle Shots." For seven months that year the circus traveled through the Midwest, hitting Texas in October. By December 1 they reached New Orleans, there to entertain crowds expected at the Cotton Centenary fair, marking the hundredth anniversary of cotton export. Unfortunately, the circus ran into the same rainy weather that had buffaloed Buffalo Bill, and the company left earlier than planned for its winter quarters at "Sellsville" outside Columbus, Ohio. During the season they had traveled eleven thousand miles.

It was while they were in New Orleans that Annie and Frank visited the grounds of Buffalo Bill's Wild West. The Butlers were impressed by the care given the Indian ponies, steers, and buffalo. While they were there, Annie and Frank opened negotiations to join the show, offering to try out their act. Cody and Salsbury at first were reluctant; they felt they already had enough shooting acts; moreover, they were short of money to hire any new routines. However, A. H. Bogardus withdrew from the partnership, discouraged by the bad winter in New Orleans, and when Butler proposed that they put their act on trial for a few days, they were invited to join the show in Louisville.

"America's Greatest Entertainment" was encamped at Louisville's baseball park in late April, where the Butlers found the corral, the wigwams, and the mess tent. They got out their guns and Annie practiced while waiting to see Buffalo Bill. She sighted with a hand mirror and shot backward as Frank threw glass balls in the air. She hit them all. Just at that moment a tall bearded man in a bowler hat approached them and introduced himself as Nate Salsbury. "Major Burke told me all about you," he said. Salsbury took the Butlers to the mess tent, where Buffalo Bill joined them, dressed in his best buckskin jacket, the silk handkerchief around his neck held by the diamond pin that Grand Duke Alexis had presented to him. He swept his sombrero off his flowing locks with a courtly flourish. "They told me about you, Missy. We're glad to have you."

Annie later recalled, "I went right in and did my best before 17,000 people and was engaged in fifteen minutes." Cody introduced her to his company with irresistible gallantry: "This little missie here is Miss Annie Oakley. She's to be the only white woman with our show. And I want you boys to welcome her and protect her."

Annie herself described her introduction to the troupe this way: "The cowboys, Mexicans and Indians . . . were all lined up on one side, Mr. Cody and Mr. Salsbury were on the other side, and my husband and I were called upon to pass down the line, meeting all of them. There I was facing the real Wild West, the first white woman to travel with what society might have considered an impossible outfit."

Of Cody, Annie said, "He was the kindest, simplest, most loyal man I ever knew. He was the staunchest friend. He was in fact the personification of those sturdy and lovable qualities that really made the West, and they were the final criterion of all men, East and West. Like all really great and gentle men he was not even a fighter by preference. His relations with everyone he came in contact with were the most cordial and trusting of any man I ever knew.

"I traveled with him for seventeen years—there were thousands of men in the outfit during that time, Comanches, cowboys, Cossacks, Arabs, and every kind of person. And the whole time we were one great family loyal to a man. His words were more than most contracts. Personally I never had a contract with the show after I started. It would have been superfluous. . . . " Annie's tribute to Buffalo Bill was published in the Cody *Enterprise* not long after his death. During one stay in Europe, Cody wrote in Annie's autograph book: "To the loveliest and truest little woman, both in heart and aim, in all the world—W.F. 'Buffalo Bill' Cody."

All through their years together, Bill called her Little Missie, and there is no doubt she was the single greatest asset the Wild West ever had, as well as its highest-paid performer, second only to Cody himself. Though the show's advertising rarely listed performers, after Nate Salsbury saw her at rehearsal, he ordered $7,000 worth of printing featuring Annie, who was billed as "The Peerless Wing and Rifle Shot."

Annie started in the show the same afternoon she met Buffalo Bill— the first act on the program after the grand entry. Major Burke explained to newspapermen once why afterward she always started the show:

> It was our first thought, when we planned the show, that so much shooting would cause difficulty, that horses would be frightened and women and children terrified. It was when Annie Oakley joined us that Colonel Cody devised the idea of graduating the excitement. Miss

Oakley comes on early in the performance. She starts very gently, shooting with a pistol. Women and children see a harmless woman out there and do not get worried. Gradually, she increases the charge in her rifles until at last she shoots with a full charge. Thus, by the time the attack on the stagecoach comes, the audience is accustomed to the sound of shooting. In all our history of Wild West there has never been a horse frightened sufficiently to run away at any of our outdoor performances.

Most accounts of the Wild West give pride of place to Annie Oakley's performance as the opening act of the show, immediately following the Grand Entry. In fact, according to Sarah J. Blackstone in *Buckskins, Bullets, and Business*, the most comprehensive study of Buffalo Bill's Wild West available, Annie "only performed in this position for eight seasons of the seventeen she was with the show. Until 1893 she was usually preceded by Johnny Baker, a race, and 'The Pony Express.'"

Annie Oakley's fame has endured from that day to this, not only in books but in films as well. Barbara Stanwyck played the title role in the movie *Annie Oakley*, with Moroni Olsen as Buffalo Bill; Betty Hutton was Annie in the movie version of Berlin's musical *Annie Get Your Gun* (a role Judy Garland was originally slated to play). The musical itself was revived on Broadway in 1999—its book altered to be politically correct— with Bernadette Peters as Annie. It won Tony awards for both the play and its star.

Even Annie's name achieved a certain amount of fame: It was often attached to complimentary tickets in show business. The comps were called "Annie Oakleys," a singular honor, because often they were punched in the middle to help in counting the show's gate. They resembled the cards that Annie used to perforate with unerring accuracy. One card target was about five by two inches with a small picture of Annie at one end and a one-inch heart-shaped bull's-eye at the other. Such cards, after being hit, were thrown into the audience as souvenirs.

Because her act was made up of masterful shooting skills, combined with humor, drama, pantomime, and even pouting, Oakley's show enchanted audiences wherever she went, and left them—after only ten minutes—always wanting more. The New York *Sun* reported that "when she doesn't hit a ball she pouts. . . . She evidently thinks a good deal of her pout, because she turns to the audience to show it off." Columnist and friend Amy Leslie said that Oakley was "an actress of no mean pretensions, in which comedy was 'half the performance.'"

Dexter Fellows, a press agent for the show, remembered her as "a consummate actress, with a personality that made itself felt as soon as she entered the arena. Even before her name was on the lips of every man, woman and child in America, the sight of this frail girl among the rough plainsmen seldom failed to inspire enthusiastic plaudits. Her entrance was always a very pretty one. She never walked. She tripped in, bowing, waving, and wafting kisses. Her first few shots brought forth a few screams of fright from the women, but they were soon lost in round after round of applause. It was she who set the audience at ease and prepared it for the continuous crack of firearms which followed." According to Fellows, she was considered a tightwad, rarely joining the other troupers on a holiday on the town. Every day she filled a small pitcher with lemonade from a big one provided for Cody. She drank no liquor but occasionally took a glass of beer—when someone else was treating.

How good a shot was she? In April 1884, at Tiffin, Ohio, in an attempt to beat the world record held by Dr. (John) Ruth, she broke 943 out of 1,000 glass balls thrown in the air, using a Stevens .22-caliber rifle. Also at Tiffin, she shot a ten-cent piece held between the thumb and forefinger of an attendant, at thirty feet. At Cincinnati, in February 1885, she broke 4,772 out of 5,000 glass balls at fifteen yards' rise with shotguns in nine hours, loading her own guns. At Gloucester, New Jersey, in 1888, a bet was made that she could not kill 40 out of 50 pigeons, thirty yards' rise. She killed 49. Even in her last years, she never lost her skill; at Pinehurst, North Carolina, in April 1922, she broke 100 targets straight at sixteen yards. Although she met all comers in America or overseas, she was never advertised in the show programs as the woman champion, only as the "Celebrated Shot, who will illustrate her dexterity in the use of Fire-arms."

In 1885, in addition to Annie Oakley, Cody, as he had promised Nate Salsbury, featured Johnny Baker as "The Cowboy Kid." Con Groner and Buck Taylor were top stars, along with Antonio Esquivel, champion vaquero, for years one of the show's outstanding horsemen.

In May the show played Chicago, where crowds packed the West Side Driving Park. Forty thousand people tried to get in on the first Sunday; they kept coming from noon to four o'clock. The Chicago *Tribune* reported on May 28, 1885, that "Buffalo Bill was the object of admiration, especially among the youthful romancers who saw in him the incarnation of their young ideals." On the next Sunday twenty thousand people packed the park. The *Tribune* remarked that "Many of them were the kid type who hope someday to rival the famous scout."

Salsbury and Cody treated the Chicago newsmen to a roast-beef barbecue dinner, which was served without forks, Indian style. As a special attraction, Broncho Bill Irving rode a steer brought from the Chicago stockyards. On that stop Buffalo Bill was the lion of Chicago society. General Phil Sheridan took him to Hooley's Theater, where they sat in a box; the audience recognized them and applauded. The Chicago Reform Alliance protested against the Sunday performances, asking Mayor Carter Harrison to prevent what they called the desecration of the Sabbath. The mayor told the group that he could not refuse the Wild West a license, for if he did, he would have to stop all theater performances on Sunday.

And in June 1885 another luminary joined the troupe—none other than the bane of Custer's Seventh Cavalry, the legendary Sioux chief Sitting Bull.

"PURELY AND DISTINCTIVELY AMERICAN"

When Sitting Bull joined the Wild West in 1885, he was fifty-four years old. Born in 1831 on the Grand River in present-day South Dakota, at a place the Lakota called Many Caches, for the number of food storage pits they had dug there, he was the son of a Hunkpapa Sioux named Returns-Again. The year of his birth, Andrew Jackson was serving his first term as president—though his election would certainly not have concerned the Hunkpapa. The Hunkpapa—the name means "Those Who Camp by the Entrance"—roamed the territory of what is now North Dakota and eastern Wyoming and Montana, nomads and warriors, living off the land, unreconciled to white rule or life on the reservation as blanket Indians.

"Of all the Indians I encountered in my years on the Plains," wrote Buffalo Bill in his *Life Story*, "the most resourceful and intelligent, as well as the most dangerous, were the Sioux. They had the courage of daredevils combined with real strategy. They mastered the white man's tactics as soon as they had an opportunity to observe them. Incidentally they supplied all thinking and observing white commanders with a great deal that was worth learning in the art of warfare. The Sioux fought to win, and in a desperate encounter were absolutely reckless of life. But they also fought wisely, and up to the minute of closing in they conserved their own lives with a vast amount of cleverness. . . .

"They were a strong race of men, the braves tall, with finely shaped heads and handsome features. They had poise and dignity and a great deal of pride, and they seldom forgot either a friend or an enemy.

"The greatest of all the Sioux in my time, or any time for that matter, was that wonderful old fighting man, Sitting Bull. . . ."

*   *   *

Sitting Bull's father, Returns-Again, was a great warrior—his name meant that he always returned to fight again—but when Sitting Bull was a child, Returns-Again saw nothing remarkable in the son who would become one of the greatest of the Sioux warriors. Therefore, his family gave the boy the name of "Slow"—until he could earn a better one for himself. Slow's childhood, like that of other Sioux boys, was a happy one, because no restrictions were placed on his conduct.

As a youth, he had to decide whether he would become a warrior or a *wintke*. *Wintkes* were men, found in many camps, who adopted the ways of women. They dressed as women and performed women's work. They were regarded with scorn, except that they were reputed to have magical powers and often were consulted on matters of grave importance. But Slow had no desire to be a *wintke*. He wanted to be a mighty warrior like his father. As a consequence, the games he favored drew on the art of warfare: shooting rapidly with his bow, sending several arrows in the air at once, and riding a horse swiftly and Indian-style, keeping the body of the horse as a shield between him and his enemies.

At fourteen, about the age of young Will Cody when he rode the Pony Express, Slow was allowed to go on a raid against the Crow. He had no weapons, carrying only a coup stick, which his father had given him. A coup stick was especially decorated, and when a Sioux brave struck the first blow with it against the body of an enemy, he was said to have "counted coup," which the Sioux considered more important than actually killing the foe. On his first hunt, riding ahead of the other warriors, Slow struck an enemy warrior on the arm with his coup stick. Returns-Again was jubilant, for his son's feat would reflect honor on him and his family; now he surely deserved a better name. After careful thinking, he was given the name Sitting Bull, "Tatanka Yotanka," one of four names that Returns-Again had heard a buffalo bull speak in a vision. He himself then became Jumping Bull.

Sitting Bull's name was meant to picture a strong buffalo bull, sitting on its haunches, resolute in the face of danger; he more than lived up to it. In time, Sitting Bull led the Strong Heart warrior society, whose members attributed their triumphs in battle to the extraordinary visions of their leader—and later he was a distinguished member of the Silent Eaters, a group concerned with tribal welfare. His courage was legendary. Once, in the middle of a fight with soldiers guarding a railroad crew near Yellowstone, he strolled out with two of his warriors in front of the troops and sat down. Bullets buzzing all around him, he calmly lit his pipe and smoked it, passing it back and forth to his companions until it was empty; then he carefully reamed it out and walked away from the fighting.

He adamantly refused to accommodate to the white man. "Look at me!" he once shouted to a group of Assiniboin Indians who had made peace with the whites. "See if I am poor, or my people, either. The whites may get me at last, as you say, but I will have good times until then. You are fools to make yourselves slave to a piece of fat bacon, some hard-tack, and a little sugar and coffee."

He also said, "I will remain where I am until I die, a hunter, and when there are no more buffalo or other game I will send my children to hunt and live on prairie mice, for where an Indian is shut up in one place his body becomes weak."

After the defeat of Custer, Sitting Bull and his people migrated to Canada, where he was safe from pursuit. Five years later, after most of his followers had deserted him and gone home, he too returned to the United States and surrendered. After two years in custody at Fort Randall, South Dakota, as a prisoner of war, he was sent to Standing Rock Reservation, which occupied a plateau on the west bank of the Missouri near the present North Dakota line.

At the Standing Rock Agency, Sitting Bull was unable to reclaim his former glory; many of his one-time followers were fed up with his stubborn resistance to the whites, which caused them so much suffering. Oddly enough, the whites, who had been his enemy, were the first to embrace him; visitors to the reservation almost always asked to see the great chief.

For years promoters had attempted to sign the Sioux chief to a personal appearance contract, but Indian agent Major James McLaughlin, who had jurisdiction over Sitting Bull at Standing Rock, refused. The agent felt that Sitting Bull was already hard to handle, that he might misinterpret what he saw in the eastern cities and return to the reservation more intractable than ever. Sitting Bull himself was willing to visit the cities of the East—as long as he had an acceptable deal.

Finally, in the hope of impressing on Sitting Bull and his people the importance of farming and education, McLaughlin agreed to let the chief see the outside world. In March 1884 he took Sitting Bull on a ten-day trip to St. Paul. It was there he met and was enchanted by Annie Oakley. The chief also visited schools, stores, churches, and banks. He was visibly impressed, and McLaughlin felt the trip had shown Sitting Bull some of the grandeur and power of the white nation.

A month after the St. Paul trip, Will Cody made his first attempt to sign up Sitting Bull and a number of other Sioux for a tour with the fledgling Wild West. McLaughlin expressed his feeling to Cody that "he could not accept any such proposition at the present time when the late hostiles are so well disposed and are just beginning to take hold of an agricultural life." This was far from true in Sitting Bull's case; his hand was accustomed to holding a lance or a rifle, not a hoe or a spade. "However," the agent allowed, "if permission was granted, he would prefer to have them in your troupe to any other now organized that I have knowledge of."

The secretary of the interior, Henry M. Teller, was brought into the discussions. He gave approval—provided Sitting Bull was in agreement—and McLaughlin then sought to implement a tour. It was too late to join the Wild West season, so arrangements were made for an eastern trip, under the auspices of Colonel Alvaren Allen of St. Paul. The troupe, known as the Sitting Bull Combination, was composed of eight Indians and two interpreters. Sitting Bull was advertised as "the slayer of General Custer." The tour began on September 2, 1884, and ended on October 25. Twenty-five cities were visited, from Minneapolis to New York. Sitting Bull was promised a meeting with the president, which never took place. Allen's tour proved unprofitable, but McLaughlin believed that Buffalo Bill's Wild West would have shown the chief to greater advantage.

Cody made another attempt on April 29 the following year, with this wire to the secretary of the interior: "Sitting Bull has expressed a desire to travel with me and requests your permission for himself and seven of his tribe. I will treat him well and pay him a good salary." Through the commissioner of Indian affairs, Secretary Teller refused Cody's request. Undeterred, Cody then asked General William Tecumseh Sherman and Colonel Eugene A. Carr to send letters of support. This time the secretary agreed to allow Sitting Bull and some of his tribe to join the Wild West.

Within two weeks Major John Burke was at Fort Yates, organizing the company and signing up new performers—one of whom was Sitting Bull. The chief, unhappy with the treatment he had received on the Allen tour, was at first reluctant. When Burke saw the photograph of Annie Oakley in Sitting Bull's tepee, he promised the chief that if he joined the Wild West he would be able to see "Little Sure Shot" every day. Sitting Bull was persuaded. He signed a contract on June 6, 1885, agreeing to appear with the show for four months at $50 a week. He got a $125 bonus for signing and the sole right to sell his autographs and photographs. Five Sioux warriors went with him for $25 a month each, three women for $15 each, and William Halsey, interpreter, for $60 a month. Burke also agreed to pay the reservation contingent's expenses to join the show—appropriately—in Buffalo, New York, and the return trip to Standing Rock when the season was over.

Sitting Bull's name was featured in the Wild West advertising almost as prominently as Buffalo Bill's. In the United States, Sitting Bull played the villain's role—he was frequently hissed by audiences more sympathetic to Custer than to the Sioux. When greeted by derision, his response was a look of disdain and contempt. While appearing in Pittsburgh, the chief was attacked by the brother of a trooper killed at Little Big Horn. In self-defense, the chief smashed his assailant in the face with a sledgehammer, knocking out several teeth. In Boston an elaborate ceremony was held in which Nate Salsbury became a member of the Hunkpapa tribe, an event well attended by the press. A barbecue was held in connection with the festivities. Salsbury's Indian name was Little White Chief.

In Boston the *Transcript* reporter, on July 31, 1885, after noting that the attendance at the show was "immense, numbering more than six thousand," commented on a resemblance between Sitting Bull and Daniel Webster. The advertisement in the Boston *Post* called Sitting Bull "the Renowned Sioux Chief." The *Globe* ran an interview with Sitting Bull, in which an interpreter asked the chief how he liked the East "and the people of this section." Sitting Bull replied that the more he saw of the white men the more he liked them. "They treat me very kindly," he continued, "and when I return to my people I shall tell them all about our friends among the white men, and what I have seen."

The show played Montreal in August, where the reviews were raves, both in English and in French, especially for "le fameux chef indien."

On October 5 the St. Louis *Republican* reported that "Buffalo Bill's Wild West attracted an immense crowd to Sportsman's Park yesterday afternoon. About 9,000 people were in attendance. On the road leading to the park, the streets were black with people. The performance was an excellent one in every respect."

The *Republican* correspondent interviewed Sitting Bull and his "right hand man," Crow Eagle. "Sitting Bull and Crow Eagle expressed themselves as highly pleased with the show busines [*sic*]," ran the concluding paragraph of the interview, "they enjoyed the traveling and seeing so many different cities and so many people, but they were beginning to get a little tired of so much noise and bustle and found themselves longing for the fresh air of the prairie; the grand romantic scenery of the mountains and the quiet . . . of their native wigwams."

On this tour, Sitting Bull finally got to meet the Great White Chief. As the show neared Washington, D.C., arrangements were made for him to be presented to President Grover Cleveland, to whom he told his troubles. On the stationery of "Buffalo Bill's Wild West, America's National Entertainment," a two-page letter written by a cast member, signed by Sitting Bull, addressed "To My Great Father" and dated Washington, June 23, 1885, is now in the National Archives.

In Canada, where the Wild West played Montreal, Ottawa, Kingston, Toronto, and Hamilton, it was quite a different story. Although Sitting Bull and his followers had been asked to leave Canada four years earlier and had been escorted to the U.S. border by mounties, there was considerable sympathy for the chief. He was honored by mayors and members of Parliament as a virtual monarch, and stole the show. His stock of souvenir cabinet cards sold so well that they had to be replenished. In Montreal a famous photograph of Sitting Bull with Cody was taken and captioned: "Foes in '76—Friends in '85."

Opinions varied on whether Sitting Bull enjoyed his one season with the show. Apparently the chief relished the limelight and seemed unhappy when he was not the center of attention. With a natural flair for self-promotion, he did well selling photographs of himself—as well as autographs, once he had learned to trace his name crudely. He also picked up the trick of selling more than one of such personal possessions as his tobacco pouch, of which he maintained a reserve stock. Both Johnny Baker and Annie Oakley asserted that whatever money Sitting Bull did not send home to his family, he spent on newsboys, bootblacks, and other urchins who hung around his tent. Like Buffalo Bill, he was an easy touch for a hard-luck story. He simply could not understand how there could be so much obvious poverty in the midst of the white man's great wealth. On the tour he also met General Carr and other old opponents, from whom he learned much. In his words: "The white people are so many that if every Indian in the West killed one every step they took, the dead would not be missed among you. I go back and tell my people what I have seen. They will never go on the warpath again."

Sitting Bull was gravely concerned about living conditions on the Standing Rock Reservation. Nate Salsbury wrote on his behalf to the commissioner of Indian affairs. Among his complaints: the trespassing of army personnel and cattlemen on reservation lands, the possible loss of timber, the presence of only one agent, and that one McLaughlin, on a large reservation, and the inability of teachers sent to train the Indians as farmers to speak the Sioux language. Salsbury's letter was meant to inform the commissioner "what [Sitting Bull] considers will be for the benefit of his people, leaving it entirely to your sense of justice to give him a hearing."

The 1885 program set the format of the Wild West, which, despite later additions, remained virtually the same until the end. The cowboy band, its members suitably dressed in western gear with white hats, entertained the crowd while Frank Richmond, the show's announcer, introduced the proceedings with his splendid voice. The "exhibition," he claimed, was not the result of "what is technically called 'rehearsals.'" Anyone could see that "men and animals alike are the creatures of circumstances, depending for their success upon their own skill, daring and sagacity." Then came the Grand Processional Review and the Entree,

Sitting Bull and Buffalo Bill Cody. Sitting Bull made only
one tour with William F. Cody's Wild West show—this
photograph was taken during that tour, in Montreal, 1885.
"Foes in '76—Friends in '85." (Photograph by David Notman)

when celebrities and groups were introduced. In 1885 the Pawnee Indians
came first, followed by White Eagle, their chief. Then came the Mexican
vaqueros, followed by the Wichita. After them the cowboys rode in, followed by Buck Taylor and Con Groner. It was then the turn of the Sioux
warriors, led by Sitting Bull—and finally the "star of stars," hailed by
Richmond as "chief of scouts of the United States Army under ten generals, the Honorable William F. Cody, 'Buffalo Bill.'" A bugle sounded, and
Cody entered on his horse "Charlie." Richmond then turned to the
assembled company and called out: "Wild West, are you ready? Go!"

First on the program was Annie Oakley, "Celebrated Shot, who will
illustrate her dexterity in the use of Fire-arms," followed by a race among

a cowboy, a Mexican, and an Indian, riding ponies. Then came the Pony Express, ridden by Billy Johnson, which accurately depicted the switch of the rider and his *mochilla*—the mail pouch—from one horse to another. Buffalo Bill's famous duel with Yellow Hand followed, winding up with a fight on foot, spear against knife, and the scalping of Yellow Hand; after that came a feature called "The Cow-Boy's Fun," throwing the lariat, riding bucking ponies and mules, by Buck Taylor, Tony Esquivel, and the other cowboys. Buck was the last to perform, picking up both his hat and his handkerchief from the ground at full gallop. Again Buffalo Bill rode into the arena, hailed by Frank Richmond as the Champion All-Around Shot of the World. Cody shot both clay pigeons—twenty of them within a minute and thirty seconds—and composition balls, including hitting a ball thrown in the air while he rode by it at full gallop. After he had dazzled the crowd with his prowess with a Winchester, he finished by shooting the balls with his Colt army revolver.

The ever-popular attack on the Deadwood stage was followed by other races, and phases of Indian life, including the attack of a hostile tribe—and scalp, war, and other dances—which were colorful but rather meaningless to most spectators. Mustang Jack came next, a rider who thrilled the crowd by jumping over horses and burros. After an exhibition of riding and roping of wild Texas steers by cowboys and Mexicans, there was a buffalo hunt, with Buffalo Bill leading a band of Sioux, Pawnee, Wichita, and Comanche Indians. Last act of all was the "Attack on a Settler's Cabin." John Nelson played the settler whose cabin is surrounded by Indians. In came the cowboys on a gallop, led by Buffalo Bill, and a running fight on horseback ensues, "with enough firing of pistols in it to make the small boy howl with delight, men shot from their saddles and riderless steeds dashing around, the cowboys won their victory and the cabin was saved."

In what the program called a "Salute," Cody gathered the entire cast in front of the grandstand, bade the audience farewell, and dismissed his cast. Frank Richmond then invited all the spectators to visit the Wild West camp before they went home. By all reports, this was a superb piece of public relations, which delighted audiences and was repeated wherever the show performed.

In late September Cody entertained the staff of Fort Hays, his old post, including the commander, Colonel Offley, at the performance at the Columbus, Ohio, fairgrounds. The 1885 Wild West tour ended in St. Louis on October 11. Following the last performance, in an interview with the press, Sitting Bull remarked that "the wigwam is a better place for the red man. He is sick of the houses and the noises and the multitude of men." Cody sent him home as agreed, giving him as a farewell present a gray trick horse to which he had become attached and a white sombrero, size eight. Later, when one of his relatives wore the hat, angering the chief, he said, "My friend Long Hair gave me this hat. I value it very highly, for the hand that placed it upon my head had a friendly feeling for me."

The only negative note in the relationship of Cody and Sitting Bull was sounded in W. Fletcher Johnson's *The Life of Sitting Bull and the Indian War,* in which Cody was quoted as follows:

> I do not know for certain whether I met Sitting Bull or not during the campaign of '76. He was not at that time a chief of any note; in fact, he was not much of a chief but more of a medicine man. It was General Sheridan who really made him a "big Indian." They had to have some name for that war, and I was on the mission at Red Cloud Agency when they were talking about what name to give it. They spoke of Chief Gall, Crazy Horse, and others, all bigger men than Sitting Bull, but finally decided to call it Sitting Bull's war, and that made him seem to be a great man, and his name became known all over the country.
>
> The first time I ever saw him to know him was when he joined my show at Buffalo, coming with eight or nine of his chosen people from Grand River. He appeared there before 10,000 people, and was hissed, so it was some time before I could talk to the crowd and secure their patience. The same thing occurred at almost every place. He never did more than appear on horseback at any performance, and always refused to talk English, even if he could.
>
> At Philadelphia, a man asked him if he had no regret at killing Custer and so many whites. He replied, "I have answered to my people for the Indians slain in that fight. The chief that sent Custer must answer to his people." That is the only smart thing I ever heard him say. He was a peevish Indian, always saying something bad in council. He was an inveterate beggar. He sold autographs at a dollar apiece and during the four months he was with the show picked up a good deal of money.

Cody is correct in saying that Sitting Bull was not as important a figure in Custer's defeat as many Americans thought—and still think—he actually was, for he did not lead the combined Indian forces into the fateful battle; that mantle rested on Crazy Horse. Sitting Bull was, however, a revered elder whose vision of soldiers falling from the sky inspired Crazy Horse and his warriors to attack Custer's forces. However, it ill behooved Cody to criticize the old chief for selling autographs, when the permission to do so was part of his contract.

When Sitting Bull got back to Standing Rock, Agent McLaughlin, as he had feared, found the chief's attitude and outlook had taken a turn for the worse. Said McLaughlin:

> He is inflated with the public attention he received and has not profited by what he has seen, but tells the most astounding falsehoods to the Indians. He tells every person who he sees that the "Great Father" in his interview with him told him that he was the only great Indian living, that he made him head chief of all the Sioux, that all Indians must do his bidding, that he was above his agent and could remove the agent or any employee whom he chose and that any Indian who disobeyed him or questioned his authority must be severely punished. Also that all Indian dances and customs that have been discontinued should be revived, "sun dance" included, and rations be issued in bulk.

Whether it was due to Annie Oakley or Sitting Bull, the 1885 tour of Buffalo Bill's Wild West had been a huge success, playing to more than a million people in some forty cities for a profit of $100,000. All the same, Cody did not feel he could safely follow Mark Twain's advice to "put all your eggs in one basket, and then watch that basket." He returned to the legitimate stage for the last time that winter, playing *The Prairie Waif* with Buck Taylor in a tour that included Topeka and Kansas City in February 1886. From that time on, both Cody and Salsbury would devote their full time to the Wild West.

Mark Twain saw the Wild West on that tour. The celebrated author, whose book *Roughing It* told the story of Twain's own adventures as a young man in the early West, sent an enthusiastic endorsement from Elmira, New York, dated July 14, 1885:

> I have now seen your Wild West show two days in succession, enjoyed it thoroughly. It brought back to me the breezy, wild life of the Rocky mountains, and stirred me like a war song. The show is genuine, cowboys, vaqueros, Indians, stage-coach, costumes, the same as I saw on the frontier years ago.
>
> Your pony expressman was as interesting as he was twenty-three years ago, when he used to come whizzing by from over the desert with his war news. Your bucking horses were even painfully real to me, as I rode one of those outrages once for nearly a quarter of a minute. On the other side of the water it is said that none of the exhibitions which we send to England are purely and distinctively American. If you will take the Wild West show over there you can remove that reproach.

When Cody requested Sitting Bull for the coming season, McLaughlin responded by saying that the chief wanted to go but that it was unlikely the request would be approved by the Department of the Interior. Cody kept trying, but in April McLaughlin wrote a letter calling Sitting Bull a "consummate liar" who was "too vain and obstinate to be benefitted by what he sees, and makes no good use of the money he thus earns." The agent added that Sitting Bull "spent money extravagantly among the Indians in trying to perpetuate baneful influences which the ignorant and non-progressive element are too ready to listen to and follow. Of the money and property that he brought home last fall, he did not have a dollar, or anything else (except for the gray circus-trained horse) left, after being three weeks at home & it was all used in feasting the Indians and trying to impress upon the Indians his own great importance, and I had a great deal of trouble with him and through him with other Indians caused by his own bad behavior and arrogance. I, however, have him under control again and would dislike to run similar risks."

There would be no more public appearances by Sitting Bull. Annie Oakley, however, except for an occasional lapse, would remain with the show for the next sixteen years.

At about the time John Burke was signing up Sitting Bull for the Wild West, Cody had written to his brother-in-law Al Goodman in Kansas, urging him once again to come to North Platte to take charge of his ranch. It "is one of the finest in America today," he said. "And with you at its head to *Stay* we could make it the best by long odds of any ranch in America. . . . if you come . . . I want you to come for life—no more hoffing [hoofing] around the country." Once again he asserted his belief that he would win the Cleveland lawsuit, and added that his daughter Arta was coming to see him in St. Louis. He would be returning to North Platte by November 1 and hoped to see the Goodmans installed at the ranch by then. Three weeks later the North Platte *Telegraph* reported the homecoming of the town's most famous citizen:

> The Honorable W.F. Cody, North Platte's Buffalo Bill, arrived in the city last Saturday and the flag which denotes his presence was raised at the ranches on his lands west of town. He was not seen by many as business occupied much of his time. He left Monday evening for Omaha to meet a party of Englishmen whom he will pilot on a hunt of six weeks to two months in the vicinity of Rawline [Wyoming].

The Lincoln County *Tribune* also hailed "the far-famed scout and plainsman whose name has become household words in nearly every home in the U.S. by reasons of his daring deeds."

While awaiting the arrival of Julia and Al Goodman and their five sons and two daughters, Cody had hired a Mr. C. A. Dillon as ranch foreman. In June Dillon was busy making improvements at the ranch "calculated to make it more comfortable as a home and popular as a summer resort." A straight road leading from the south gate to the corral was nearly finished, "giving an opportunity to let the fast steppers spin if desired." Visitors could also try out the "half-mile speed ring, constructed on scientific principles, than which there will be none better on these fertile plains." A fish pond was also under construction, and would be stocked with fish when finished. At Lincoln County's first fair, held September 30 through October 2, Dillon had exhibited both horses and cattle from Cody's well-bred herds, and the ranch had garnered several blue ribbons.

It is interesting to see that Cody was still guiding hunting parties. No information is available about this particular party, except that it was composed of "distinguished English gentlemen," according to the local press. Undoubtedly Cody was extremely well paid for his services; it is difficult to see how he would have taken on the assignment otherwise—although there was always the chronic need for large infusions of money to support his role as North Platte's squire, the gentleman rancher.

About a month after the fair closed, having been considered a great success, the Omaha *Herald* sent a writer to North Platte to report on the town's progress. Several pages of the newspaper were devoted to descriptions of North Platte homes and businesses, and its prominent citizens, especially the Honorable W. F. Cody; a review of Buffalo Bill's life up until that time was included. The same issue also carried a rhapsodic one-and-a-half-column portrait of Cody's ranch, called "one of the finest on the continent." Among the tributes paid the ranch: "The waters of the great Platte flow through no prettier or more natural stock ranch. Nature in all her bounteous gifts or freaks never designed a place more fitting. . . . He [Cody] has a tract of nearly four thousand acres here, the eastern portion adjoining the city's limits, which the rapid growth of North Platte is making very valuable."

At this time, Cody had a herd of 125 of the best blooded cattle, including Herefords, Shorthorns, and Polled Angus. His imported Hereford bull, Earl Horace, was pedigreed. He also had a herd of 181 horses, most of them Thoroughbred, and described by the *Herald* reporter as "some of the best ever brought out west."

Given the obvious success of C. A. Dillon in managing Cody's ranch, why then was he discharged? The most likely explanation is Cody's desire to have his sister Julia and her husband well situated, where he could take care of them and their family. He would also be able to rest easier once his relatives were in charge of his beloved ranch. Lulu, who is seldom mentioned in this period, was comfortably installed in the Welcome Wigwam in town; he could depend on Julia and Al to look after his interests on the ranch.

While Cody enjoyed all the fame and adulation that accompanied him as the star of the Wild West, according to Nellie Snyder Yost, he also regretted missing out on the North Platte fair. He promised that next year he would be sure to attend and bring along some of the Roman racing chariots used in his show, and put on a truly spectacular exhibition at the new fairgrounds. Meanwhile, there was his last combination, or "house show," to stage. It was called "Buffalo Bill's Dutchman and the Prairie Waif Combination." John Burke had completed the arrangements for a Chicago opening on November 2; however, it wasn't until toward the end of November that Cody returned from his Wyoming hunting trip with the visiting Englishmen, so an actor named Matt Snyder, Cody's understudy, had to open the play in the Windy City.

At the time, Cody proposed to bring his stage show, *The Prairie Waif*, to North Platte, for the opening of the new Lloyd's Opera House. Unfortunately, he would not be able to bring the show to his hometown until the middle of February, after the opera house had already opened. As an alternate attraction, he set about helping the opera house's management secure "the celebrated Milan Opera Company of Milan, Italy" with which to open the new theater.

Cody's combination finally arrived in North Platte on Saturday, February 20, 1886, and by February 17 every chair in the opera house had been sold, and additional seats were put in. The week after the show, Ira Bare, the young editor of the *Tribune*, reported: "The Hon. W.F. Cody (Buffalo Bill) was greeted at Lloyd's Opera House last Saturday evening by the largest audience that has gathered in that building this season. The company is a strong combination of excellent actors and presents *The Prairie Waif* with happy effect. Jule Keen, the Dutch comedian, bringing in enough fun to keep the audience in a roar of good humor. Mr. Cody [is now] on his way to California and is meeting with grand ovations at every stopping point. He expects to return to 'the states' by the first of May."

Cody would retain a fond attachment to Lloyd's Opera House, which in the following years showcased a number of traveling productions. When he was in town, and there was an outstanding show at Lloyd's, small boys would seek him out in whatever barroom he could be found and tell him they wanted to see the show. He would always arrange with the box office that the boys be admitted, and he would "pay the count." According to one of the boys, who spoke fifty years later: "No one was ever turned away, and I'm afraid to tell you how many there would be of us. You wouldn't believe me if I told you."

After staging *The Prairie Waif*, Cody again got down to the business of the Wild West. He and Nate Salsbury decided to try an experiment in 1886: Instead of traveling around in one-night stands, they would open the show for a lengthy stay in one location. They chose a summer resort on Staten Island called Erastina, owned by a man named Erastus Wiman, where twenty thousand people could watch the two daily performances, at 12:30 and 8:00 P.M., according to an advertisement in the New York *Times* on June 26, 1886. Admission was fifty cents; children, twenty-five cents. "A fleet of steamers" was chartered to take patrons to Erastina Woods, Mariner's Harbor, on Staten Island. The evening performance was given under artificial light, still something of a novelty.

Buffalo Bill's Wild West showed at Erastina for six months. Spectators from Manhattan were happy to take the ferry from the Battery to Staten Island—a five-cent trip. General William Tecumseh Sherman attended the opening performance; Mark Twain came to see the show twice. Old P. T. Barnum, suffering from the gout and hobbling on crutches, came all the way from Bridgeport, Connecticut, to see it, though in forty years he had seldom if ever attended any show not his own. Nate Salsbury introduced him as "a man of world-wide celebrity, whose name is known from the freezing zones of Greenland to the torrid regions of upper South America, the greatest showman of the world, Mr. Phineas T. Barnum."

"It is the coming show," said Barnum. "Will I gobble it up? Oh no. Mr. Salsbury is going to take it to Europe. We have had a long talk over it."

The New York *Times*'s review of June 26, 1886, predicted that "if every day's performance of the season brings him in as many shekels as did yesterday's he will be able to buy himself a ranch as large as Rhode Island and spend the remainder of his days in luxurious idleness. The show was a decided success."

The New York *World* reporter declared that Buffalo Bill "could ride with a cup of water on his head and not spill a drop." This same feature writer, who signed his stories "Nym Crinkle," spent the night at Erastina and wrote of his bivouac "within half an hour of City Hall." He especially praised Buck Taylor, "who can stand in the path of any Mexican steer and turn it over by the horns." He also admired Con Groner, "the Sheriff of North Platte, who took Jesse James and his gang off a train"; Broncho Bill, "full of bullets . . . You can't help fancying that the toot of the absurd Staten Island railroad is the yelping of the coyotes."

Burke put on special western demonstrations for the press and informed the newspapermen that Cody and Salsbury had spent $8,000 on four miles of railroad track to serve their show-ground encampment. Even though there were no shows on Sunday, the crowds still came to see the Indians, and old soldiers came to visit Sergeant Bates and hear him re-create the battles of the Civil War, which he did at great length. Bates was a war veteran who had traveled around the country giving patriotic lectures.

George Armstrong Custer's widow, Libbie, called the Wild West "that most realistic and faithful representation of a western life that has ceased to be, with advancing civilization."

Prior to opening at Erastina, a shakedown tour had hit St. Louis in May and then showed in Indiana, Ohio, West Virginia, and Maryland before a week's run in Washington, D.C., ending on Memorial Day. By then the company had been joined by two cowgirls who rode in a horse race: Georgia Duffy of Wyoming and Della Farrel of Colorado.

At Erastina, another rifle-shot, fifteen-year-old Lillian Frances Smith, the "California Girl," joined Annie Oakley in trick shooting. Lillian was born in Coleville, Mono County, California. She started riding as soon as she could sit a saddle and began shooting at the age of seven. She claimed forty mallard and redhead ducks in a single day. At her first attempt at glass balls she made 323 consecutive shots without a miss and broke 495 out of 500, using a Ballard .22. In her act with the Wild West, she was able to hit a plate thirty times in fifteen seconds, break ten balls hung from strings and swinging around a pole, and fire four times after a glass ball had been thrown into the air, breaking it with the last shot.

Cody had added Lillian Smith to his troupe while he was in California, touring with the Waif Combination, and he billed her as "the Champion Rifle Shot of the World." When the show broke up in Denver, he retained her for the Wild West and brought her on to North Platte, where she was advertised to give an exhibition of shooting with rifle, shotgun, and revolver at the opera house on the evening of April 20.

In the next issue of the *Tribune*, editor Bare referred to Lillian Smith as "the best shot in the world." Her performance, he wrote, "borders on the marvelous, breaking twenty glass balls in twenty-four seconds with a Winchester rifle, and twenty balls with a single loading rifle in fifty-four seconds. That is shooting as fast as an ordinary gunman can shoot his piece, to say nothing of taking an aim at a fast-moving target. A beautiful feat was breaking two balls with one shot as the balls swung past each other in the air." Despite her exceptional skills, Lillian Smith never caught the public's fancy as Annie Oakley did, while arousing Annie's jealousy of the younger woman. As a result, Annie took six years off her age.

On February 14, 1886, Cody wrote to his sister Julia from Staten Island: "I think our poor days are over for I really believe the public now looks on me as the one man in my business. And if they will only think so for a year or two I will make money enough for us all for our life time."

Johnny Baker, under Annie's coaching, was slowly becoming a worthy rival of the popular star. That rivalry developed into one of the show's main features; many spectators hoped to be present when Johnny outshot Annie. That never happened. When asked in later years whether their contests had been rigged in Annie's favor, Johnny denied the charge, admitting frankly that he could never quite beat Little Sure Shot.

Buffalo Bill's own shooting continued as another headlined feature of the show. The program described Buffalo Bill not as a "fancy shot" but rather "a practical all-around shot. . . . That is, a man of deadly aim, in any emergency, with any weapon." The show program also stated that "Mr. Cody will give an exhibition of his ability by shooting objects thrown in the air while galloping at full speed, executing difficulties that would receive commendation if accomplished on foot, and which can only be fully appreciated by those who have attempted the feat while experiencing a rapid pace while occupying 'a seat in the saddle.'" In the 1902 show program, an advertisement cites Cody as saying: "As you know, I always use Winchester rifles and Winchester ammunition. I have used both exclusively for over twenty years for hunting and in my entertainments."

"It is a well-known fact," announced master of ceremonies Frank Richmond, "that Mr. Cody performs his feats of marksmanship under the most difficult circumstances, riding at break-neck speed, and with flying objects. And I can positively assert that the feats are accomplished with a 50-caliber Winchester rifle, shooting 50-caliber solid head cartridge, containing no shot, and furnished by the Union Metallic Cartridge Company."

Richmond's zeal in promoting his boss was slightly misplaced. Cody did not use solid head cartridges. From Dr. Carver on, Cody's detractors have accused him of "trickery," using small shot fired from a rifle instead of rifle bullets. The actual truth is that Cody broke his glass balls not with rifle bullets but with what are called "shotted shells," shells of .44 caliber loaded with about 20 grains of black powder and 7 1/8 ounces of chilled shot. The pellets made a pattern of about the same size as the glass ball at the usual range of twenty yards. According to Johnny Baker, it was just as hard to hit an object at twenty yards with the shot as it would have been with a rifle ball. Moreover, how many skeet or trap shooters could expect perfect scores while firing their shotguns from horseback?

Baker stated that at the first performance of the Wild West both Cody and Carver actually did use rifle bullets—and got a bill for broken glass from a greenhouse eight blocks away for their pains. Cody and Carver then decided that, for safety's sake, they had better use shot, which would drop harmlessly inside the grounds. There is no doubt about Cody's marksmanship when he was in his prime. Johnny Baker himself had seen him split the edge of a playing card with a rifle bullet. At North Platte in March 1892, he found swans swimming in a lake north of the ranch buildings. "If I can get them lined up right I won't need but one bullet," Cody said, according to A. B. (Pinnacle Jake) Snyder, who was breaking horses on the ranch at the time. "Sure enough," said Jake years later, "when the swans were swimming with their heads in line, Cody drew a bead and got 'em both with one shot, and that a long one and a sixty-mile wind blowing to boot." Added Jake: "Cody's reputation as a dead shot with almost any kind of gun was well known at that time but there are some in these times who'd like to make folks believe that his marksmanship was exaggerated and that he actually wasn't such a good shot at all. Well, the best they've told about old Bill's shooting was no exaggeration."

One of the stories about Cody's shooting that he especially enjoyed telling concerned his efforts to kill a prairie chicken with a revolver. He fired once and missed, fired again and missed, and kept firing—and missing—until all the barrels were emptied, while the chicken flapped about unharmed. Angered, Cody hurled the empty revolver at the bird, hitting it on the head and killing it instantly.

The 1886 Wild West program provided

A FEW REASONS WHY YOU SHOULD VISIT "BUFFALO BILL'S WILD WEST"

You will see the GREATEST MARKSMEN in America. . . . You will see BUFFALO BILL (Hon. W.F. Cody) . . . and You will see an Exhibition that has been witnessed and endorsed by—

PRESIDENT ARTHUR AND CABINET

GEN. SHERIDAN AND STAFF;

GENERALS SHERMAN, CROOK, MILES, &C.;

RISTORI, PATTI, NEVADA, BOOTH, IRVING, BARRETT;

BENNETT, WATTERSON, CHILDS, VANDERBILT,

BELMONT, DREXEL,

and tens of thousands of well-informed people in

EVERY WALK OF LIFE.

While marksmanship may have been a prime attraction of the show, the Wild West was not all shooting. Doc Middleton, the Nebraska bandit whom Sheriff Con Groner had pursued so relentlessly, was there, along with his pursuer. An English spectator described the riding of a black mare called Dynamite by Jim Mitchell: "It was necessary for four men to hold her and she had to be blindfolded before he could get on her, and then letting out a scream like a woman in pain, she made a headlong dash and plunged with all her force into a fence, turning completely overhead head first and apparently falling upon the rider. . . . Poor Jim was dragged out, bleeding and maimed, and led away. What was the astonishment of the multitude, when the other refractory animals had had their sport, to see Dynamite again led out, and the cowboy, limping and pale, come forward to make another attempt to ride her. . . . For fifteen minutes the fight went on between man and beast. . . . The cowboy got upon her back by some superhuman skill, and then he was master."

Thomas A. Edison was a visitor to the Erastina grounds. Although the great inventor had created the first practical incandescent lamp in 1879 and had overseen, in 1882, the construction of the Pearl Street plant in New York City, the first central electric-light power plant in the world, his inventive genius was not behind another Wild West innovation—the first night performances of the show. The advertising touted "Night made day by 100 electric lights." Lamps, gas flares, and the use of considerable red fire for the Indian dances and the attack on the stagecoach were all the special lighting effects that could be mustered by the show's staff. The shooting acts suffered, and Cody demanded that something be done. A back-lot handyman soaked wads of cotton in alcohol and glued them to the clay pigeons, lighting the flares just before the trap was sprung. Don Russell describes what happened: "Often the pigeon went one way and its light another. Then came a night when this was corrected. The clay targets were all well lighted—but Annie Oakley chalked up ten straight misses, and Will followed with the same zero score. The inventor had fastened his lights to the pigeons with masses of court plaster—the predecessor of adhesive tape—and the shot went through without breaking them!"

The 1886 Erastina engagement was a triumph. Twice a day all summer, except Sunday, the Wild West performed to capacity crowds of twenty thousand. Every weekday seventeen steamboats brought full loads of passengers to the island. In July Buffalo Bill announced in the New York newspapers that he would give free tickets to all newsboys and bootblacks riding to the island on the first boat on a certain day. Fifteen hundred boys showed up and were given tickets as well as sack lunches, distributed by Ed Goodman, Cody's nephew, and Johnny Baker. Cody addressed the boys, urging them to go to school and Sunday school and to do their best to be good citizens. From that day on, newsboys and boot-blacks dogged his footsteps everywhere he went in New York, urging free papers and shoeshines on the showman.

In a letter from Erastina, Ed Goodman expressed his concern about Johnny Baker. "Johnie runs out very near every night with some of the boys and does not come in until 2 or 3 oclock in the morning and then half the time he is *drunk* but gets sobered up by morning and Uncle Will does not know anything about it. . . . Johnie & I make it all right [but] he is as big a gambler as there is in camp and there is a good deal of it going on. . . . Uncle Will never touches a drop I don't think I ever hear of him doing so." Apparently Cody was living up to his promise to Nate Salsbury.

During the 1886 season, Al and Julia Goodman were managing Scout's Rest Ranch, and Cody frequently wrote them about specifications he wanted in the new home that was being built there. First, he insisted on a three-room suite for himself—parlor, bedroom, and bath. Next, he suggested ten-foot porches. The contractor had agreed to build a two-story, nine-room house, with numerous closets and pantries, for $3,500, which covered all materials, plastering, and painting. Cody asked only that it be finished by October 15 at the latest. In one letter quoted in Stella Foote's book *Letters from Buffalo Bill*, he made this specific request on September 16:

> I want a side board in the house someplace, probably just as well in my bedroom upstairs, with some nice decanters and glasses. I don't propose to make a barroom out of your home, but must have a side board. All we big dogs have a side board so put it up in my bedroom—then if anyone gets full I can put them to bed.

Could he have been thinking primarily of himself getting "full"—after a night of partying with his friends or the members of his cast?

From Erastina the show moved on to Philadelphia, where the *Evening Bulletin* observed that "a recent addition to the show, and one who has attracted great attention, is Gabriel Dumont, the famous fighting man and trusted lieutenant of Louis Riel, the Canadian insurrectionist, during his fated although enthusiastic stroke for liberty a short time since." The reviewer also remarked that "No better opportunity was ever offered the people of the East to witness the various features of wild Western life and to study the habits and customs of the Aborigines than is now afforded by the exhibition at the Gentleman's Driving Park."

Cody must have been pleased by this last sentence in the review; he insisted on always calling the Wild West an "exhibition" and an "educational experience," never a "show," which of course it was.

Toward the close of the 1886 season, a newspaper story reported that Buffalo Bill had presented a gold watch to Johnny Baker inscribed:

> Presented to Master Johnny Baker
> Champion Boy Shot of the World
> by his guardian
> William F. Cody
> Erastina, Aug. 18, 1886

The summer run proved so successful—attendance one week in July totaled 193,960—that Cody and Salsbury leased Madison Square Garden from Adam Forepaugh for a winter exhibition, at a rent of $18,000 a month.

First, though, the show took a two-month rest; during that break Cody returned to North Platte to check on the progress being made at his ranch. He was given the royal treatment. "Let everybody pull together," urged the Lincoln County *Tribune,* "and give Buffalo Bill the handsomest reception ever known in this city. North Platte has reason to feel proud of the world-wide reputation her honored citizen has received and should show her appreciation of him."

The Omaha *Republican* as well reported that the "Hon. W.F. Cody will soon be roaming over the boundless plains of Nebraska which he loves so well, and inhaling huge draughts of life-giving ozone that exhilarates but does not intoxicate."

The new house on Scout's Rest was finished just in time to welcome its owner home, and when his sister Julia showed him through its rooms, he assured her that he was well satisfied.

The old Madison Square Garden, demolished after the Democratic National Convention of 1924, occupied a full block between Madison and Fourth avenues, from Twenty-sixth to Twenty-seventh Street. Designed by Stanford White, who was later shot by Harry Thaw in its Roof Garden, it was a huge brown structure of marble, masonry, and brick, with colonnades covering the sidewalks. It housed circuses, horse shows, and band concerts. At the Garden, Cody's director was Louis E. Cooke, whose visions of the show were grand indeed; he called it "a gigantic new era and departure in colossally realistic scenic production," a phrase even John Burke or Prentiss Ingraham might have envied. The impresario Steele Mac-Kaye wrote a scenario to match the scenery, called *The Drama of Civilization.* Matt Morgan created the historical panoramas that served as heroic backgrounds for the show, and Nelse Waldron, inventor of the first double or moving stage, was responsible for the mechanical effects. Their plans were so ambitious that the roof of the Garden literally had to be raised twenty-five feet to accommodate all the marvels down below.

One of the wonders was a scene in which a mining camp, Deadwood City in the Black Hills, was re-created—tavern, post office, stage station, and all—and then destroyed in a cyclone. But where was the cyclone to come from? Stage manager Lew Parker came up with the answer: ventilators. One of these machines, placed in a wall, blew fresh air into the building; another machine on the opposite side of the building, revolving the same way, blew out foul air, keeping a current of fresh air circulating at all times. Although this sounds rather like an electric fan, it was actually driven by steam. Parker ordered three of the fans, each five feet in diameter. The Stevenson Car Company, across Twenty-seventh Street from the Garden, allowed Parker to run a pipe under the street and use steam from the factory at night. Not troubling to get a permit to take up the paving, Parker had a trench dug across the street, the pipe laid, and the street completely repaved, between midnight and three-thirty one morning.

To add a note of realism, one hundred bags of dried leaves were opened in front of the fans; the leaves blew wildly over the vast stage. The cyclone was a smashing success, blowing not only the leaves but also toppling mining shacks and hurling passengers from the Deadwood coach. A prairie fire also thrilled the spectators.

Johnny Baker, who was now a crack shot, had an act all his own. Finally the audience saw the Battle of the Little Big Horn with Buck Taylor as General Custer. When Custer and his men were slaughtered, Buffalo Bill rode in, a majestic figure in the spotlight. As he viewed the carnage, head bowed, the words "Too late!" appeared on a giant screen.

The show opened the night of November 24, 1886, with General William Tecumseh Sherman in one box, Henry Ward Beecher in another. The next day was Thanksgiving, and the newspaper advertisement on the front page of the *Herald* the next day announced:

The Greatest Triumph Ever Known
in the History of the City

———

Thousands Turned Away

———

Grand Thanksgiving Matinee Today, Tonight
and Every Night with regular matinees Thurs-
days and Saturdays, Buffalo Bill Has Grand
Army of Scouts, Cowboys, Indians, United States

Troops, Mexican Vaqueros and Women and
Children in a mighty Drama of Civilization.
The Grandest Stage Pictures, the Most Thrill-
ing Tableaus, the Most Amazing Episodes. An
Aggregation of Marvelous and Entrancing
Scenes and Occurrences. Never before placed
before any public. Admission 50c, Children 25c
Reserved Seats 75c, $1, $1.50. Boxes $8, $10,
$15. Doors open at 1 and 7 P.M.

Not everyone was pleased with the *Drama of Civilization*. One reviewer
felt that it was no longer quite the old Wild West: "Steele Mackaye has
tamed it and transformed it into a circus of living pictures. He has not
changed it into a drama, because there is no actor in the company, except
Buffalo Bill, who says nothing, shoots badly and is kept pretty much in the
background. . . . This new scheme to combine the show and the theatre
and give the Wild West on a tanbark stage and the border drama without
actors is not a success. . . . Adam Forepaugh, who has invested a great deal
of money in the enterprise, advertises it like a circus. It used to be better
than a circus, because the horses were supposed to run wild and the riders
had to risk their limbs in mounting them; but now the animals are cribbed,
confined and have to be whipped into a display of a little animation. . . .
We hope that Buffalo Bill, the Indians, the cowboys and the bisons will be
let loose in the open again and that, when they go to Europe, all of Matt
Morgan's scenery will be carefully left behind."

At first the Garden was filled, even the $15 boxes, and people were
being turned away, but by the middle of December Ed Goodman wrote his
mother, Julia: "The show is not paying too well but do not know what it
will do as the show business is all a lottery anyway." Ed added that because
the buffalo had all been stabled underground at the Garden, they had
developed "Neumonia," and sixteen of them died.

Still, a million people saw the show in New York that season. The
engagement at Madison Square Garden was profitable—and even greater
triumphs for the Wild West lay just ahead. Queen Victoria's Golden
Jubilee—celebrating the fiftieth year of her reign—was scheduled for 1887,
and a group of American promoters, encouraged by an enterprising Yorkshire businessman named John Robinson Whitley, organized "An Exhibition of the Arts, Industries, Manufactures, Products and Resources of the
United States." The promoters offered their facilities and a percentage of
the gate receipts to Cody and Salsbury if Buffalo Bill's Wild West could be

a part of their exhibition for six months. The partners accepted. Next stop: Blighty.

The preparations for the Wild West's trip to England in 1887—it could as well be called an *invasion*—was, like the Madison Square Garden epic, carried out on a grand scale, though without the wind machines. A wind machine of another sort was provided by Major John Burke, tireless in his efforts to collect endorsements from leading army officers to certify that Buffalo Bill Cody was indeed what he was heralded to be: a genuine frontiersman and scout. For it was Cody who would be the centerpiece of the show in England, its reigning star and the symbol to the Brits of what the American West had been—a romantic and adventurous chapter of our history. In the process he would become a figure of worldwide stature.

The letters of introduction and endorsement of Cody came in a series of brief notes dated from December 25, 1886, to February 14, 1887, and they could not have been more gratifying to both Burke and Cody.

Sherman, then the only living four-star general, recalled that Cody had guided him in 1866 "up the Republican, then occupied by the Cheyennes and Arapahoes as their ancestral hunting grounds." Lieutenant General Sheridan, then commanding general of the army, commended Cody as a scout who "served in my command on the western frontier for many years. He was always ready for duty, and was a cool, brave man, with unimpeachable character." Said General Miles, "Your services on the frontier were exceedingly valuable," and "your Exhibition is not only very interesting but practically instructive." General H. C. Bankhead, who had once arrested Cody in a dispute over a government mule, chimed in: "I fully and with pleasure indorse you as the veritable 'Buffalo Bill,' U.S. scout, serving with troops operating against hostile Indians in 1868 on the plains. I speak from personal knowledge, and from reports of officers and others, with whom you secured renown by your services as scout and successful hunter."

Similar kudos came in from Generals Crook, Merritt, King, and Emory; from Colonels W. B. Royall, N. A. M. Dudley, and James W. Forsyth. These testimonials from the highest-ranking army officers of the period, all of whom had personal knowledge of Cody's career as a scout, were indeed impressive, although there may have been the slightest hint of a desire on their part to be reflected somehow in Cody's glory—for his fame now was as great as or greater than any of theirs.

There was only one snag in all this. The letters referred to him as "Mr. Cody," for he had never been other than a civilian scout; his only army rank was private. He was accustomed in the United States to preface his name with the title "Honorable," given him when he was elected to the Nebraska legislature. This honorific, however, would never do overseas. He needed something grander and more impressive.

By this time the State of Nebraska was immensely proud of its most distinguished citizen. Some hoped that he would be to Nebraska what Barnum had been to Connecticut. One last endorsement sought by John Burke came from John M. Thayer, the governor of Nebraska, who obliged his fellow Nebraskan by giving him a commission dated March 8, 1887: "reposing special trust and confidence in the integrity, patriotism and abil-ity of the Hon. William F. Cody, on behalf and in the name of the State, do hereby appoint and commission him as Aide-de-Camp on my staff, with the rank of Colonel." Now he finally had the coveted title he would bear for the rest of his life. To the world at large he would be "Colonel Cody," although to the real colonels in the real army he would surely always remain "Mr. Cody," or just "Buffalo Bill." His colonelcy, of course, was quite ordinary, of little worth in the United States but, borne by a governor's aide, commissioned in the National Guard, it would sound impressive enough abroad.

The Omaha *World* carried a dismissive report of Colonel Cody's new commission. The Lincoln County *Tribune* countered the criticism this way:

> The *World* utters a deep groan because Gov. Thayer has seen fit to appoint W.F. Cody as a representative at the coming World's Fair to be held at London. Having been a resident of Nebraska since a boy, Mr. Cody has had an opportunity to witness its wonderful development and is thoroughly conversant with the needs of this great common-wealth. It is just recognition of the services Buffalo Bill gave the state while she was clothed in infantile garments and we are glad to know that the Governor appreciates the men who helped by deeds of valor to make Nebraska what she is. But then, the *World* wouldn't be happy if it didn't have something to kick about.

Army officers presented the newly minted colonel with a jeweled sword to wear, while Major Burke devised a new designation for publicity purposes: "Col. W.F. Cody, Chief of Scouts, U.S. Army." Burke and Cody both must surely have known that the U.S. Army had no chief of scouts with the rank of colonel. Still, no one was about to challenge Burke's harmless piece of puffery.

The endorsements from the army officers, glowing as they were, were in any case superfluous. Thanks to advance publicity for the Wild West and its hero, and to Cody's fame as a guide for so many British noblemen on big-game hunts on the plains, he was already well known in England—and highly esteemed.

"Brick" Pomeroy, an American who knew Buffalo Bill and was in England before the show arrived, wrote a letter to the Lincoln County *Tribune* describing the preparations for the show's arrival in England. Both Pomeroy and Major Burke, who was also there, readying a seven-acre tract near the American Exposition for the Wild West, were besieged by British citizens who wanted to know all about Buffalo Bill, his size and habits, how he came to have such a singular name, where and how he lived. Burke also had to field questions about Buck Taylor and Con Groner, Jule Keen and old John Nelson, the white Ingomar of the Sioux, and little Johnny Baker.

Hundreds of teams were at work in London, smoothing and grading the show's grounds. "The grand stand," wrote Pomeroy, "will be covered and will easily accommodate 25,000. The private boxes for the royal family and the crowned heads and courts of Europe are to be modern. . . . Besides the tent headquarters and fittings for Buffalo Bill, there will be tents and offices for all the lieutenants and chief assistants. Also adobe houses for the Mexican cowboys, tents for the Texas cowboys, tepees, tents and lodges for the different bands of Indians . . . buildings for refreshments, water tanks, telegraph and telephone offices and accommodations for reporters, artists and newsgatherers."

Meanwhile, in Madison Square Garden, Will treated his Indians to a Christmas feast of stewed dog and entertained ten thousand schoolchildren at his show. Louisa, with Arta and baby Irma in tow, visited Cody in New York City. What happened between them is not a matter of record, but a letter written by Ed Goodman to his father on March 17 suggests that there was trouble. One young woman named Miss DeValasco, who lived at the Hoffman House, where Cody also boarded, was mentioned by Louisa. It is likely that she and Will quarreled again.

Louisa and her daughters returned to North Platte on February 27. Buffalo Bill closed his winter engagement on the twenty-second. On February 26, 1887, his forty-first birthday, he and Salsbury incorporated the Wild West by issuing one hundred shares of stock, of which each partner held thirty-five. Three of their close friends divided the remaining thirty shares. The corporation held its first official meeting two days later on Salsbury's forty-first birthday.

The following week Cody was busy lining up Indians, horses, and riders for the trip abroad. A few days before his March 17 departure for New York, Cody sent an agent to the Pine Ridge Reservation to recruit the Sioux Indians he would take with him to England. Before they left the reservation, the Indians he chose bade a sad farewell to other members of the tribe. The Sioux believed that if any of their people attempted to cross "the Big Water," they would sicken, waste away, and die. One Indian, Chief Broken Horn, complained: "You know, you get in that big canoe and pretty soon it goes up and down. You, also, go up and down. You throw up so much that you die. Then the white man throws you into the Big Water. How do you find the trail to the Great Mystery when you are at the bottom of the Big Water?" Many a transatlantic traveler before and since might heartily agree with the chief's sentiments.

The Sioux also dreaded taking the big canoe out so far onto the water "that when you look back, there is no land and when you look ahead, there is no land." Still, Cody was able to gather 97 Indians for the trip, along with 18 buffalo, 10 mules, 10 elk, 5 wild Texas steers, 4 donkeys, 2 deer, 180 horses, tents, wagons, the Deadwood stagecoach, band instruments, arms, ammunition, as well as brand-new costumes for the invasion of England. Also on board the State Line ship *State of Nebraska*, which Cody chartered for the voyage, were 83 salon passengers and 38 steerage passengers, including cowboys, Indians, Mexican vaqueros, and Annie Oakley. A great deal was at stake in this trip; by the time the show opened in London, expenses would mount to $165,000, an exceptionally large sum for the period.

CROSSING THE "BIG WATER"

On Thursday, March 31, the ship weighed anchor from New York harbor, while Bill Sweeney's thirty-six-member cowboy band, wearing uniforms of gray shirts, slouch hats, and moccasins, played "The Girl I Left Behind Me."

The New York *Times* said "Good-Bye to Buffalo Bill" in an editorial on March 31: "Buffalo Bill tears himself away from his native land this morning . . . to show the effete Europeans just what real life in America is like. . . . Mr. Cody expects to make the trip to London in 12 days. The demonstration he expects to make when he lands on the other side will give the stolid Britishers new ideas of the magnificence of this Western Hemisphere. A good many friends will be down at the dock this morning to say good-bye to the Wild West heroes."

Once out on the high seas, almost all the passengers were seasick at one time or another. The Indians kept pinching themselves to see if they were wasting away; and now and then, the Sioux death song was heard. Buffalo Bill, "sick as a cow with hollow-horn" himself, did his best to keep his passengers calm. Annie Oakley, who did not suffer from seasickness, said that the worst came as the ship rolled in a stormy sea for forty-eight hours until a damaged rudder could be repaired. After the third day out, there was smoother sailing, all recovered, and the rest of the voyage was fairly pleasant. Various entertainments were devised: Cody and Red Shirt, a Sioux chief, addressed a Sunday prayer meeting, and Salsbury revived some acts from his Troubadors. During the transatlantic crossing, only one horse was lost—a remarkable accomplishment, considering the weather—and not a single Indian wasted away.

On April 3, 1887, even as the *State of Nebraska* was on the open Atlantic, a controversy erupted. An American who signed himself "INQUIRER" wrote a letter to the New York *Times* in which he attacked that "curious

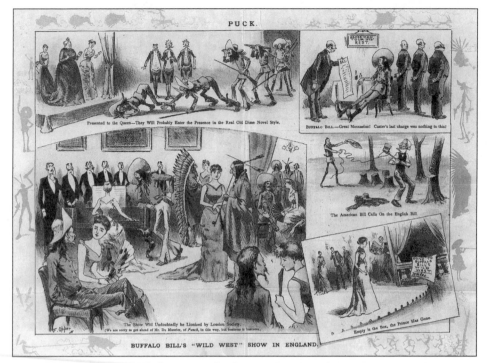

Buffalo Bill's "Wild West" show in England, 1887. (Western History Department, Denver Public Library)

hybrid," the "American Exhibition and the 'Wild West' Show . . . The Wild West Show which the Hon. W.F. Cody, better known as 'Buffalo Bill' is to open in London on May 2, promises to be, what it deserves to be, a great success. In connection with this show there will be another, known as the American Exhibition, to be run by a Yorkshire man named Whitley, who has propped himself in his venture by tacking his show on to the deservedly popular one of Buffalo Bill. The name of the American Exhibition can only be claimed for the show because of Buffalo Bill's connection with it."

Apparently both Cody and Salsbury had been deceived by Whitley's claims to have the backing of the Prince of Wales for his exhibition, by means of which he secured the endorsement of President Cleveland. When Cleveland learned through the American Legation in London that the prince had nothing to do with this enterprise, the president ordered that his name be removed from the letterheads. By April 3 the "American Exhibition" was in trouble. Its buildings had not been completed, it was short of money, and it was unlikely to be open on May 2. INQUIRER urged American manufacturers "to consider the management and the financial status of this exhibition before shipping their goods for display therein." Whitley did recover and managed to open the exhibition, but INQUIRER's points were well taken. No display of American manufactured products could compete with the glamorous hero of the plains.

The colorful invaders, with the Indians out on the deck in full ceremonial regalia, sailed into the Thames Estuary on April 14 and cast anchor at Gravesend, England, two days later. The first sight to meet the passengers of the *State of Nebraska* at Gravesend was a tug flying the Stars and Stripes. Three cheers went up, and a band on the tug responded with "The Star-Spangled Banner." The cowboy band on board, not to be outdone, struck up "Yankee Doodle." The tug had been chartered by a committee headed by Lord Ronald Gower, official director of the exhibition, to welcome the Wild West to Britain; his lordship was accompanied by Major Burke and a group of reporters.

Gazing at the approach to the world's busiest port, Cody's thoughts turned to the reality of "all of us combined in an expedition to prove to the center of old world civilization that the vast region of the United States was finally and effectively settled by the English-speaking race." In his Anglo-Saxon fervor, Cody neglected to consider the many other races and nationalities that had played their parts in the settlement of the West, from the black descendants of African slaves to the Chinese immigrants who had helped build the transcontinental railroads and had remained to put down roots in a strange land. Going ashore, Cody was given a warm welcome in the town where the Indian princess Pocahontas lies buried. The Indian princess, daughter of the great Chief Powhatan, had traveled to England in 1616 with her husband, the Virginia planter John Rolfe. She was presented at court and lionized by English society. Pocahontas died of smallpox in Gravesend, just as she was about to embark for America.

From the moment of its arrival at Gravesend, Cody and his show were given every consideration. British officials at the port waived their usual regulations in honor of the American Exhibition. Despite recent outbreaks of rinderpest and foot-and-mouth disease, the buffalo and cattle were released after only a brief quarantine. The company was not allowed to bring in ammunition, so the Woolwich Arsenal supplied specially loaded blanks for arena use, and the supply of underloaded ammunition used by Cody and other sharpshooters was turned over to the arsenal, which issued it to the show as needed. Three trains transported the show from the port of London to the Midland station, close by the exhibition grounds, where the show people set up camp the same day, for a May 9 opening. The speed with which this was done attracted wide attention among the English.

Ed Goodman said of their hosts: "The working class of people are the slowest people I *ever* saw . . . one good American man can do as much work as 4 English men." At the close of the day, the United States flag was raised while the cowboy band played "our national air [to] a storm of shouts and cheers . . . from the thousands that lined the walls, streets and housetops of the surrounding neighborhoods. So gratifying was this that the Colonel had his band play 'God Save the Queen.'"

The arrival of Buffalo Bill's Wild West in England in 1887 was especially timely. To begin with, the people of Great Britain were understandably pleased with themselves; their empire stretched across the globe, and they were the most powerful and prosperous nation on that globe. For another, sixty-eight-year-old Queen Victoria was just coming out of her retirement after the death of Albert, the Prince Regent, in 1861. Moreover, twenty-two years had passed since the end of the Civil War, in which most of the British aristocracy supported the Confederacy, while the working classes were staunch Unionists. In the years following the war, relations between the two countries steadily improved, resulting in a growth of "Anglo-Saxonism" on both sides of the water. As Henry James wrote his brother William, "I can't look at the English-speaking world . . . save as a big Anglo-Saxon total."

In addition, Buffalo Bill Cody seemed to the British to represent the ideal of Anglo-Saxon manhood—and he was an authentic hero as well.

The ingenuity of the show people in setting up shop was not the only thing that attracted attention. American publicity methods also sparked comment. One newspaper denounced the show's posters as "mural enormities . . . colossal daubs, splashes of red and yellow." The *Globe* commentator set his remarks to verse:

> I may walk it, or 'bus it, or hansom it; still
> I am faced by the features of Buffalo Bill.
> Every hoarding is plastered, from East-end to West,
> With his hat, coat, and countenance, lovelocks and vest.

The show's promotion may have been garish to British tastes, but it paid off handsomely. All the major English newspapers carried vivid and lengthy accounts of Buffalo Bill, the Indians, especially the Sioux Ogila-Sa (Red Shirt), the animals, and the huge camp. It was not long before distinguished visitors came to the camp: Lady Randolph Churchill, Grand

Duke Michael of Russia, and scores of other titled people. People of the theater also flocked to the grounds. Henry Irving, soon to be knighted, was one of the first. He was then starring in *Much Ado About Nothing* with Ellen Terry. Irving had written an article in the *Era*, a theatrical paper, warmly praising the Wild West, which he had seen at Erastina. "It is an entertainment," he wrote, "in which the whole of the most interesting episodes of life on the extreme frontier of civilization in America are represented with most graphic vividness and scrupulous detail. You have real cowboys with bucking horses, real buffaloes, and great hordes of steers, which are lassoed and stampeded in the most realistic fashion imaginable. Then there are real Indians who execute attacks upon coaches driven at full speed. No one can exaggerate the extreme excitement and 'go' of the whole performance. It is simply immense, and I venture to predict that when it comes to London it will take the town by storm."

Irving's costar, the great actress Ellen Terry, also came; as did Mary Anderson, an actress who had visited North Platte and had briefly considered buying a ranch there; and Justin McCarthy, a member of Parliament and author of the melodrama *If I Were King,* long a popular vehicle for E. H. Sothern and later made into the musical *The Vagabond King.*

On April 12 the *Morning Post* announced: "The famous huntsman, Buffalo Bill, the idol of the *petit peuple* of America, arrives next week and ere long the Aborigines of the Great Republic will be as familiar in London streets as need be."

On April 16 the London *Daily News* reported: "One could not help recalling the delightful sensations of youth, the first acquaintance with the Last of the Mohicans, the Great Spirit, Laughing Water, and the dark Huron warrior." This newspaper story and others started a boom in the bookstores for the works of James Fenimore Cooper. Prentiss Ingraham's *Border Romances of Buffalo Bill* also had a tremendous vogue, selling edition after edition at the bookstalls. It seemed that the entire British population could think or talk about nothing except the American West.

Getting the show ready for performances in London was no easy matter; the Wild West had come from the indoor confines of Madison Square Garden to an arena bounded by a track one-third of a mile in circumference, and the weather stubbornly refused to cooperate. Rainy England that April was no place to be. When William Ewart Gladstone, former prime minister, showed up with a party on April 25, two weeks before the formal opening, the cowboy band welcomed the visitors, and Cody gave an abbreviated show for them, in spite of the muddy arena and uncompleted track. After the exhibition, Cody hosted a luncheon for Gladstone's party, where he sat beside Mrs. Gladstone. In the *Pall Mall Gazette* on April 28, it was reported that "the manly frankness of the American

Backwoodsman highly interested Mr. Gladstone, and he remained in conversation with him [Cody] for some time." The Colonel, who by now cut an extremely distinguished figure, could hardly object to being called a "backwoodsman" if it would bring in paying customers.

On May 5 Cody invited Albert Edward, Prince of Wales—later King Edward VII—to attend a special performance, four days before the grand opening. In the party were the Princess of Wales, Alexandra; their three daughters, Princesses Victoria Louise, Maud, and Louise; Princess Alexandra's brother, Crown Prince Frederick of Denmark; the Comtesse de Paris; the Marquis de Lorne; and "other highly placed attendants on the assembled royalties." The show was underrehearsed, and the grounds were still in "unspeakably bad condition," according to Cody, but the royal box was "handsomely rigged out with American and English flags," and the event served as a dress rehearsal for Buffalo Bill's show.

Cody need not have worried about the outcome of this preview. The prince and princess were both unassuming and friendly, and when the Indians, "yelling like fiends, galloped out from their ambuscade and swept around the enclosure like a whirlwind, the effect was instantaneous and electric," said Cody, with pardonable pride. "The Prince rose from his seat and leaned eagerly over the front of the box and the whole party seemed thrilled by the spectacle. 'Cody,' I said to myself, 'you have fetched 'em.' From that moment we were right—right from the word 'Go.' Everybody was in capital form—myself included—and the whole thing went off grandly." "Fetched 'em" he surely had.

The royal party then visited the whole camp. In Cody's tent, the prince was much impressed with the gold-mounted sword given him by his army friends. Albert also insisted on tramping through the mud to inspect the stables where two hundred horses were kept, in what Cody proudly considered "apple-pie" order. The prince endeared himself to his host by praising Old Charlie, the famous twenty-one-year-old horse that had long been Cody's favorite mount. Cody told the prince the story of how Old Charlie had won a $500 bet for him by riding over the prairie a hundred miles in ten hours. Actually, Charlie made it in nine hours and forty-five minutes. Despite his advanced age, the horse usually stole the show.

"The Royal party cottoned greatly to John Nelson's half-breed papoose," said Cody. Then Salsbury, Burke, the announcer Frank Richmond, Lillian Smith, and Annie Oakley were introduced.

Annie recalled: "I had heard a great deal about how women tried to flirt with the Prince while the gentle Princess held her peace and now it all ran before me. An English-born lady would not have dared to have done as I did—they must speak to royalty according to the station of the Royal personages. The Prince's hand came over the low front of the box as they all rose to their feet. I ignored it and quickly proffered my hand to his Princess. She did not offer the tips of her fingers, expecting me to kneel down and kiss them, but took my hand gently in her own, saying: 'What a wonderful little girl.' Nor was His Highness displeased at what I had dared to do, for he, too, shook my hand warmly when I turned from the Princess to him, and after I had bowed far enough to turn my back, he made this remark, loud enough for the whole assembly to hear: 'What a pity there are not more women in the world like that little one!'"

Cody deemed Annie's decidedly unroyal behavior "a small solecism," but it obviously went over well with the royals themselves.

On May 9, the day of the opening, the weather fortuitously shifted, and there were sunny skies and gentle spring breezes to greet the twenty thousand or so people who poured onto the grounds. The admission price, according to Ed Goodman, "was $5 or 1 pound," for that performance only. Inflation makes it hard to calculate the actual value of a pound sterling at that time, but some idea of its worth may be obtained by recalling that a British working man with a small family could live in a city on just over one pound a week. For regular performances, tickets ranged from one to four shillings.

According to Cody, the daily expenses of the show were $2,500, and it cost him a great deal more to feed his company in England than it did in the United States. An "English laborer thinks he is lucky if he gets meat to eat once a week, while the American must have it two or three times a day. Fresh beef costs a shilling a pound over there, and when it comes to feeding such a large number of hungry Indians, whose principal article of food is meat, the expense is enormous."

The London press raved about the show. *Sporting Life* concluded its review by observing that such a "vast concourse of the cream— . . . the *creme de la creme*—of society is seldom seen at any performance. The number of chariots waiting at the gates outnumbered those of Pharaoh, and the phalanx of footmen constituted quite a small army."

Another London paper described the show in detail, praising the shooting of Annie Oakley and Buffalo Bill, marveling at the Pony Express and the Deadwood stage, and at the amazing acrobatic feat of Mustang Jack, who covered thirteen feet with a standing jump and then leapt over a horse that stood sixteen hands high. To the Londoners, however, the most unusual part of the entertainment was the bucking horses. "No cruelty is used to make these animals buck," the reporter assured his readers. "It is simply a way they've got."

All the crowd-pleasers in the show were pulled out for the London performances: the attack on the settlers' cabin, an attack on an emigrant train with teams of oxen and mules, a buffalo hunt, and, a great novelty to the British, bucking broncos.

Said the *London Review*: "Buffalo Bill's specialty is shooting while riding at full gallop, and he does this to wonderful perfection. Lillian Smith smashed a glass ball revolving horizontally at high speed, and struck eggs in rapid and slow motion." In addition to their marksmanship, Lillian and Annie Oakley competed in a horse race.

After the report of her son Albert Edward, Queen Victoria sent a "command" that it be shown to her. When it was explained to her majesty that the Wild West could not be brought in its entirety to Windsor Castle, she agreed to go to the Earl's Court arena to see the show. It was a precedent-setting appearance of sorts on the queen's part; in the more than a quarter of a century since the death of her husband, she had not attended any kind of public entertainments, though she had on rare occasions commanded some companies to give private performances of plays at the castle—and she also had attended concerts, laid foundation stones, and opened exhibitions.

She arrived at five in the afternoon on May 12, in a carriage-and-four, with the princes and princesses, a military escort in brilliant uniforms, and a bevy of ladies-in-waiting who, as Major Burke described them, formed "a veritable pottiere of living flowers about the temporary throne." Before the show, a large American flag was borne around the arena by Buffalo Bill, while Frank Richmond intoned that it was "an emblem of peace and friendship to all the world." The queen rose and bowed. The rest of the party stood, the ladies bowing, the noblemen raising their hats, the military men saluting. The Americans looked on, and as Cody described it later, "there arose such a genuine heart-stirring American yell from our company as seemed to shake the sky." It was a thrilling moment. "For the first time in history since the Declaration of Independence," exclaimed John Burke, "a sovereign of Great Britain saluted the Star Spangled Banner—and that banner was carried by Buffalo Bill." Cody himself recalled that "all present were constrained to feel that here was an outward and visible sign of the extinction of that mutual prejudice, amounting sometimes almost to race hatred, that had severed two nations from the times of Washington and George the Third to the present day. We felt that the hatchet was buried at last and the Wild West had been at the funeral."

The queen had stipulated that she would remain at Earl's Court for just one hour. However, she was so fascinated by this unusual entertainment that she stayed till the end of the program—and fifteen minutes overtime—and then commanded that Buffalo Bill and the other leading members of the company be personally presented to her. These included Nate Salsbury, Annie Oakley, Lillian Smith, two Indian women with their babies, and Ogila-Sa, Red Shirt, whose regal bearing she had admired. When Buffalo Bill presented Annie Oakley, the queen said, "You are a very, very clever little girl." When Red Shirt was presented, through an interpreter he said, "It gladdens my heart to hear words of welcome."

When Buffalo Bill wrote his book *Story of the Wild West and Camp-Fire Chats*, he mentioned Lillian Smith but not Annie Oakley. Of Queen Victoria Cody said, "A kindly little lady, not five feet in height, but every inch a gracious queen. I had the pleasure of presenting Miss Lillian Smith, the mechanism of whose Winchester repeater was explained to her Majesty, who takes a remarkable interest in firearms. Young California spoke up gracefully and like a little woman."

The omission of Annie's name is perhaps explained by her having left the show after the last London performance in the fall of 1887, while the balance of the company went to Manchester. There may have been a rift between Cody and Annie; we cannot be sure. It is also possible that Buffalo Bill was a bit jealous of Annie's celebrity in England, which rivaled his own, although that would not have been characteristic of Cody, who was always willing to share the limelight and who knew the value of having a strong cast to back him up.

When she returned to Windsor Castle, the queen sat down and described what she had seen that day in her personal journal:

> . . . to Earl's Court, where we saw a very extraordinary and interesting sight, a performance of "Buffalo Bill's Wild West." We sat in a box in a large semi circle. It is an amphitheatre with a large open space, all the seats being under cover. All the different people, wild, painted Red Indians from America, on their wild bare backed horses, of different tribes,— cow boys, Mexicans, &c., all came tearing around at full speed, shrieking and screaming, which had the weirdest effect. An attack on a coach & on a ranch, with an immense deal of firing, was most exciting, so was the buffalo hunt, & the bucking ponies, that were almost impossible to sit. . . .
>
> Col: Cody "Buffalo Bill" as he is called, from having killed 3000 buffaloes, with his own hand, is a splendid man, handsome, & gentleman-like in manner. He has had many encounters and hand to hand fights with the Red Indians. Their War Dance, to a wild drum & pipe, was quite fearful, with all their contorsions [sic] & shrieks, & they came so close. "Red Shirt" the Chief of the Sioux tribe, was presented to me & so were the squaws, with their papooses (children) who shook hands with me. . . . The performance ended, we drove straight to Paddington Station & returned to Windsor, getting there by 1/2 p[ast] 7.

The first visit of Queen Victoria resulted in another command performance on June 20, given for her royal jubilee guests. This time the audience included the King of Denmark, the King of Greece, the King of the Belgians, the King of Saxony, the Crown Prince and Princess of Germany (he was soon to become Kaiser Wilhelm II), and Crown Prince Rudolph of Austria who, two years later, would commit suicide in the tragedy at Mayerling. It was Rudolph's fate to fall in love with a commoner. Sadly, the customs of his country would not permit a morganatic marriage, so the pair killed themselves rather than separate. The story was turned into a highly romantic French film in 1936, starring Charles Boyer and Danielle Darrieux. More than a dozen other princes and princesses completed the royal contingent.

It was at Windsor Castle that the Deadwood coach carried the kings of Denmark, Greece, Saxony, and Belgium, along with the Prince of Wales, and Buffalo Bill as driver, during the Indian attack. This led to a much-repeated anecdote. In 1871 President Grant had appointed General Robert Cumming Schenck as ambassador to the Court of St. James. Schenck proceeded to introduce the game of poker to British society. The Prince of Wales must have studied with Schenck, for he said to Cody after the ride: "Colonel, you never held four kings like this before."

"I've held four kings," said Cody, "but four kings and the Prince of Wales makes a royal flush, such as no man ever held before." The prince roared with laughter, and was then faced with the unenviable task of explaining the joke to the four monarchs, not all of them familiar with English. A later version of the story, probably told by Cody, has him saying "four kings and the Royal Joker," a nice improvement on the original story. Did it actually happen that way? It certainly could have, since all the kings and the Prince of Wales were there that day.

Back in North Platte, the newspapers kept readers informed of the triumphs of "Bison William." One article in the Omaha *Bee*, taken from a British newspaper, told of a visit to the Drury Lane Theatre by Buffalo Bill and some of his Indians and cowboys. "They occupied half a dozen boxes and the Indians, being in their paint and feathers, created a great sensation. Some of the Indians had never been in a theatre before and none had ever seen anything like the performance, in which there is much brilliant spectacle and many ballet girls." At one point, Buffalo Bill signaled his Indians, who then joined in the applause with a loud war whoop that stunned the other spectators.

Red Shirt and his fellow Indians, along with some cowboys, also attended a performance of Goethe's *Faust* at the Lyceum Theatre. The reviewer for the *Times* noted that the redskins had been "greatly scared at its horror" as they watched the show unfold from their boxes. Henry

Irving played Mephistopheles, and his version of the play was a great success, both in London and in New York the following year. Asked what he thought of the performance, Red Shirt summed it up as "a big dream."

In mid-May twenty-year-old Arta Cody left North Platte for New York City, on her way to join her father in England. Although an earlier news item had stated that Louisa Cody would spend the summer in Europe with her daughters, she did not make the trip. In *Memories*, she— or Cooper—says "I was to stay at home and look after the business of the ranch, while Will was away [and] it was through [his] letters that I followed him on that trip." We know that Lulu remained in North Platte with four-year-old Irma that summer, though it is unlikely she had much to do with the management of the ranch; the Goodmans were looking after Will's interests at Scout's Rest. Nor is there a record of any letters from Cody to his wife during this period, except for passages quoted by Cooper, as usual the least reliable of sources.

Once again, the Omaha *Herald* was taking its share of potshots at Cody and his family. "Some of the New York newspapers had gone fairly frantic over the beauty of miss Arta" is the way the article began. "A prophet has little honor in his own country and it is possible we have had a gem of purest ray dwelling among us and did not know it. . . . Miss Arta Cody, daughter of Buffalo Bill, is not the remarkably handsome person she has been represented to be by the New York papers. In place of being petite and slender she is quite stout and, though bright and intelligent, she has never been considered beautiful. There are many hundreds of Nebraska girls handsomer than she, but still it is pleasant to observe that the effete East is startled by her beauty."

Many Britishers felt differently about Arta. The Lincoln County *Tribune* reprinted one article from a British publication that described Arta as "a young lady who inherits her father's handsome features and graceful bearing, and whose well-bred manners compare to her credit . . . a singular contrast to the blatant loudness of the American women who come here in search of notoriety, a goal which they attain, if ever, by the aid of stuffed corsets, pearl powder and bad language."

Apparently some Omaha residents were peevish because Cody, with scant formal education and only his service as a plainsman and scout to recommend him, had been appointed by Governor Thayer to serve as Nebraska's ambassador to the Queen's Jubilee and World's Fair in London. It may also have been a source of some envy that his Wild West so far outshone the rest of the American Exhibition, which consisted of a rather dull display of "coffee-mills, stoves, Gatling guns, [and] liquid fish-glue."

In June Buck Taylor was seriously injured. During the performance of a quadrille on horseback, Taylor's horse, a new and relatively untried steed, became unmanageable, throwing his rider against the cantle of the saddle of the horse next to him. Taylor fell to the ground and sustained a compound fracture of his thigh bone. The King of the Cowboys was taken to London's St. George's Hospital. As soon as Buck was released from the hospital, Cody gave him a gambling concession until he was able to ride again. (Apparently Nate Salsbury had reconsidered his original disapproval of gambling on the show's grounds.)

Buffalo Bill became "the hero of the London season," said the London *Times*. "Notwithstanding his daily engagements and his punctual fulfillment of them, he found time to go everywhere, to see everything, and to be seen by all the world. All London contributed to his triumph." It was the "first year of the American invasion," and the handsomest American of them all made the most of it.

Soon after his arrival, Buffalo Bill was made an honorary member of a number of the most prominent London clubs. At the Reform Club he was formally presented to the Prince of Wales and the Duke of Cambridge. At the Savage Club he met Wilson Barrett, the actor, and Henry Irving again. He was entertained at the United Arts and dined at Lord and Lady Randolph Churchill's, where he met their son Winston Spencer Churchill, then thirteen years old. The future prime minister of England attended the Wild West and was thrilled by the spectacle. Lord Charles Beresford took him frequently to the Coaching Club. He was also honored by a lunch given for him by the Lord Mayor and Lady Mayoress of the City of London.

Many Americans in London also called on Cody, and he and Salsbury decided to throw a rib roast breakfast. The meal was cooked by the Indians, all of whom ate with the visitors; Red Shirt was one of the speakers. Invitations for the afternoon's performance were offered to all the guests.

Back in North Platte, editor Bare of the *Tribune* marveled: "A few years ago W.F. Cody was shooting buffalo and dodging Indians and playing 7-up and drinking bad whiskey in western Kansas. Then everybody called him Buffalo Bill. Now he is the social lion in London and Lords and Ladies are running over each other to get an introduction to him and they call him 'Colonel, the Hon. William F. Cody.' There is nothing wilder than this in any romance."

Despite all his social engagements, Buffalo Bill was appearing twice a day in his show, playing to audiences of twenty to forty thousand people daily. There were detractors, of course. "The Buffalo Bill furore is becoming ridiculous," said one London newspaper, criticizing Lord Beresford for inviting Cody, "chiefly famed as an adroit scalper of Indians," to the hallowed Coaching Club meet. James Russell Lowell, former U.S. Minister to the Court of St. James, wrote: "I think the true key to this eagerness for lions—even of the poodle sort—is the dullness of the average English mind." One critic saw the Wild West as an "overgrown circus . . . neither more nor less than a hippodrome on an enormous scale. All the best of it we have seen before, either at Covent Garden or Olympia."

A quite contradictory opinion came from Marshall P. Wilder, comedian, entertainer, and author, then enjoying a successful tour in Europe. Wilder was moved to say: "I must express my pride and delight, as an American, at the figure Bill cuts in society. He fills a dress suit as gracefully as he does the hunter's buckskins, carries himself as elegantly as any English gentleman . . . uses good grammar, speaks with a drawing-room tone of voice, and moves as though he had nothing to do all his life but exist beautifully. He tells a good joke, but knows when not to carry the fun too far. Every friend he has made over there I am sure he has kept. I ought to know, for [the English] have told me so themselves."

Some of Cody's detractors spread rumors that he went about in an alcoholic haze among his aristocratic friends, or engaged in amorous dalliances with this lady or that. Actually, Cody spent most of his weekends at the Oatlands Park Hotel at Weybridge, Surrey, a place that had a history dating back to Henry VIII. Cody was not above criticism on occasion, though those who have labeled him a "bum" or a "drunken bum" would find no agreement among the Britons who met him in the summer of 1887.

Altogether, two and a half million people came to see the Wild West. Business was so good that in July Buffalo Bill wrote Al Goodman: "If you see a good place where I can invest some money, I can send it for we have a few scads now—and am liable to have more."

Buffalo Bill was not the only one lionized that summer. All during the London engagement, Annie Oakley's tent was filled with flowers and gifts sent by her many admirers. She even received love letters, because few people realized that she was already married, and Frank Butler stayed in the background. One badly smitten young man was so crushed when he learned she was married that he migrated to Africa. Years later he turned up in America, bringing with him, as trophies, horns from game he had killed in Africa; he presented these to a bemused Annie and Frank.

Both Wimbledon and the London Gun Club invited Little Sure Shot to give them exhibitions of her shooting skills. "A fee was never mentioned," writes Isabelle Sayers, "but the day after an exhibition a purse of around $200 was brought to her. This, in addition to her Wild West salary, enabled her to indulge in some luxuries, such as having some really elegant gowns made for her many social engagements. The London designers copied *her* ideas for riding habits and brought the Western theme into their collections . . . a real honor for the Ohioan who had learned to sew at the Darke County poor farm."

At the written request of the Prince of Wales, Cody arranged for a match with Annie and Grand Duke Michael of Russia. Out of fifty pigeons shot as targets, she won, forty-seven to thirty-six. Following their departure from the Wild West, Annie and Frank accepted an invitation from the kaiser to come to Germany, where she performed for the Union-Club Berlin, at the Charlottenburg Race Course on November 13, 1887.

It was a chilly afternoon when Annie performed for a fur-coated crowd at the race course. As usual, during the course of her performance, Annie offered to shoot the ashes from the cigar of some gentleman in the audience. It was always Frank Butler, however, who volunteered to be her target. This time, to Annie's shock and horror, Prince Wilhelm himself leapt out of the royal box and strode into the arena. German policemen standing by attempted to stop the stunt, but Wilhelm waved them off. Annie could not retract her challenge without losing face, so she paced off as usual, turned, raised her Colt, took aim, and fired, blowing away the prince's ashes.

Years later, after World War I began, Annie had second thoughts and wrote Wilhelm, now the kaiser, offering to repeat the stunt for him. He never responded.

Toward the end of October, as the London season drew to a close, Cody remarked, "from the day of opening our show in London until the close of our engagement . . . I had not missed a single one of the three hundred performances given." Along with his social engagements, he had been, he said, "occupied nearly eighteen hours out of every twenty-four."

During his six months at Earl's Court, his headquarters tent had been visited by thousands of guests. The tent consisted of two large rooms; a first-class hotel could not have been more elegant. The first room was his parlor, its floor covered with robes and fine skins, and its supporting posts hung with animal horns and heads. The adjoining bedroom was furnished with a lace-covered bed and other pieces of fine furniture. Hot and cold water added to its comfort. His dressing table was covered all season long with scented invitations, some "stamped with armorial bearings," requesting Buffalo Bill's appearance at dinners, balls, receptions, and various other affairs. On the mantelpiece were portraits of the Prince and Princess of Wales, Henry Irving, and other noted figures of the period, all of whom had visited the Colonel in his baronial tent, some more than once.

Among the invitations he received was this one, dated May, 1887, 19th Week:

16 TITE STREET,
CHELSEA, S.W.

Dear Colonel Cody,

We hope so much that you will be able to come and have tea with us on Wednesday, as we would be much disappointed not to see you.

Yours sincerely,
/s/ Constance Wilde

It is tempting to speculate how the famous writer and wit Oscar Wilde and Buffalo Bill would have gotten along together. Cody undoubtedly accepted Mrs. Wilde's invitation; he seems to have accepted every invitation he received in London, for he was constantly on the go. In 1882 Wilde had traveled to the United States on an extended lecture tour, and in the spring of that year he made stops at Leadville and Denver, Colorado, Leavenworth, Kansas, and a number of other cities in California, Nebraska, Kansas, and Missouri. He would have his own memories of the West to share with the famous scout—and if anyone in London cultivated celebrities energetically, it was Oscar Wilde.

It was reported that Wilde showed some jealousy of the attentions lavished on Buffalo Bill. However, Oscar did attend the opening, and *Vanity Fair*, the society gossip magazine, reported tongue-in-cheek that during the attack on the Deadwood coach, Mr. Wilde "was greatly alarmed for the safety of his scalp."

A telegram addressed to The Hon. Colonel Cody, American Exhibition, read:

I have only invited gentlemen to meet you on Sunday otherwise would have been delighted to have the honour of receiving your Daughter.

Randolph Churchill

And there was this invitation:

Mr. Henry Irving
requests the pleasure of
The Hon. Col. W.F. Cody's
Company at Dinner
at The Lyceum Theatre
on Sunday the 26 June
at 7:30 o'clock

Despite his busy schedule, Cody did not neglect affairs at home. With his ranch manager Al Goodman, he had made plans for a barn at Scout's Rest, a huge structure that would be 148 feet long, 70 feet wide, and 40 feet high. The foundation was laid early in October; seven carloads of lumber were used in its construction, and its hundreds of rafters were sawed in the shape of gunstocks. At its peak, the barn stabled eighty horses, while the ranch employed thirty men, the number rising to fifty or sixty at certain seasons. The barn, along with the ranch house and the original outbuildings, has been preserved by the Nebraska Game and Parks Commission as a state historical park.

On October 7 Cody wrote his sister Julia that he believed that the English climate did not agree with him. "If I don't get my health back soon," he said, "I will be tempted to leave it and come back to my own good country. . . . Oh how I would love to spend a month with you at the Ranch." Clearly the frantic pace of the past few months was beginning to tell on him. However, in three more weeks he would have fulfilled his Earl's Court contract; that realization probably kept him going.

Buffalo Bill's Wild West remained in London through October. Although it was always a part of Mr. Whitley's so-called American Exhibition, it was without any doubt the centerpiece of the whole affair. As for the rest of the exhibition, British newspapermen found little to write about except Frederic Auguste Bartholdi's diorama of New York harbor, including his Statue of Liberty, dedicated less than seven months before the exhibition opened. One reporter declared that we "did not come to the exhibit to see the false teeth and the Christmas cards."

Cody appeared in top form at the closing performance of the Wild West's London engagement on the evening of October 31. A London theatrical journal reported that he was called upon for a speech and, prancing upon his old war-horse Charlie, who seemed to fully appreciate the importance of the occasion, said, among other remarks: "The stay of the Wild West in London had been attended by such genuine hospitality as to mark it a red letter epoch in the history of the world's amusements. The fast disappearing page of Western American pioneer history that we have the honor to portray consists simply of scenes in which we have all more or less participated. . . . Personally, I dare not express myself fully for fear, in my exuberance, I might be misunderstood, but I have been overwhelmed with kindness, friendship and hospitality on every hand. Ladies and gentlemen of England, I owe you more than my most grateful remembrance can ever repay. But while my life shall last, the memory of this parting will live in my heart, and in conclusion I have but one sentiment to express—long life and general prosperity to you of Old England. Good bye and God bless you." It was a well-turned farewell speech by any standards.

At the close of the American Exhibition, its sponsors called a meeting to propose a court of arbitration to settle any differences that arose between the United States and the British Empire. The *Times* of London credited the goodwill built up by Buffalo Bill and his Wild West to the approval with which the proposal was received. "It is no paradox," concluded the *Times*, "to say that Colonel Cody has done his part in bringing America and England nearer together. . . . Colonel Cody can achieve no greater triumph, even if he some day realizes the design attributed to him of running the Wild West Show within the classic precincts of the Colosseum at Rome. *Civilization itself consents to march onward in the train of Buffalo Bill.*"

Thus, there were other important results of the Earl's Court engagement beyond simply entertaining the English. Cody and his troupe were superb emissaries for their own country. On one occasion Cody, Major Burke, and Broncho Bill, the interpreter, took Red Shirt, Flys Above, and some other chiefs to the Savage Club at the Savoy Hotel. Buffalo Bill and Red Shirt made speeches, and Red Shirt promised to send a peace pipe from his home for the London Savages to hang on their dining-room wall. Red Shirt was also the first American Indian to venture inside the halls of Parliament, introduced in the House of Commons by Mr. Justin H. Mc-Carthy. The chief, who wore war paint for the occasion, was a big hit among the M.P.'s.

From London the show moved on to Birmingham on November 5 for the beginning of a six-month tour; other English cities were also eager to see the wonders of the Wild West. Annie Oakley and her husband, however, remained behind, preparing for a trip to Germany, though they would be back with the Wild West again during the 1889 season.

In Birmingham, said Cody, "we met with a prodigious welcome from the screwmakers, the teapot turners and the manufacturers of artificial jewelry and 'Brummagem goods' in general." It was getting rather late in the year for an open-air show, but fortunately the autumn weather was not too severe. Tickets at the Aston Lower grounds went for one shilling; reserved seats were one to three shillings extra.

The Birmingham *Gazette* was less than rapturous in its response to the Wild West. "In spite of London's lavish praise," said the *Gazette*, "Birmingham's thousands insisted on their right to criticize. . . . There was nothing remarkable about the 'genuine buffalo hunt.' Of course the buffaloes were genuine. There was nothing very remarkable about the roping and riding of 'wild' Texas steers by cowboys and Mexicans. . . . The Indian war cry is a decided failure. It is apparently a shrill and feeble screech, and not at all the blood-curdling yell that Fenimore Cooper and other writers have led us to believe. . . . I fear, too, that the 'war dance' as performed at Aston has not made a great impression on the popular mind. It is a tame—one might say almost a childish—jig, without rhythm or measure, and thus another hallucination of our boyhood is disposed of."

Turning things around with a somewhat left-handed compliment, the *Gazette* concluded: "The show is worth seeing—if it is worth anybody's while to put himself to some trouble to go and see it. Nothing like it has ever been shown in Birmingham before. A better idea of the dangers pioneers confront, of the resource and skill that difficulties bring out, of the way in which the Wild West has been 'settled' and civilized, can be obtained from one visit to this exhibition than by reading a score of histories and a cartload of exhibitions."

In any event, the Brummagem folk, or "Brummies," gave the show a hearty welcome. By November 14 the entire electrical installation from the American Exhibition in London was installed at Aston: ten carbon arc lights with a total of 150,000 candlepower.

Not all of the Wild West company appeared in Birmingham. In addition to Annie Oakley, Broncho Charley Miller and Marve Beardsley—a former Pony Express rider—remained in London at Agricultural Hall, Islington, taking part in a six-day race on their horses against two English cyclists riding penny-farthings, the popular cycles of the day with a large front wheel and a small rear wheel. The racers competed for eight hours each day, and the cowboys used thirty horses, which were changed every hour. There was a prize of £300, a handsome sum in 1887, and the cowboys won by two miles and two laps, at an average pace of twenty miles an hour. The race was a huge success with the public, and not incidentally a source of some extra publicity for Cody's Wild West.

Manchester, a city of 6 million, was the last stop of the season, and while preparations were made to set up the show there, Cody and Arta made a hurried two-week trip to Italy. Cody and Salsbury had thought they might be able to give a Wild West exhibition in the Colosseum at Rome, but after looking at the ruins, the idea was abandoned.

At a racetrack, across the river from Manchester in Salford, Cody and Salsbury had "the largest theater ever seen in the world" built for their show. Next to the theater, a building was erected large enough to contain the tents and tepees of the entire troupe. All the structures were heated by steam, for it was already winter, and lit by electricity. The animals were housed in the barns and stables already on the track. The previous year's indoor exhibition at Madison Square Garden was used as a model for the winter engagement that opened on December 17. At a cost of $40,000, Matt Morgan painted elaborate western scenery for a "Depiction of American Pioneer History." There were seven panoramas, each two hundred feet long, operated on drums thirty feet high.

The Manchester Sunday *Chronicle* applauded the installation: "The theater, brilliantly lighted and warmed throughout, is like nothing else ever constructed in this country. . . . The illusion, indeed, is so well managed and complete, the boundless plains and swelling prairies are so vividly counterfeited, that it is difficult to resist the belief that we are really gazing over an immense expanse of country from some hillside in the far West. The pictures . . . are singularly beautiful in themselves. . . . Buffalo Bill has come, we have seen, and he has conquered."

In Manchester Cody received a number of requests from schools and charitable institutions for seating space for their "waifs." His reply was always the same: "Let me know your numbers and come on Wednesday afternoon . . . and we will fix you up for nothing at all, if we have to turn money away for you."

Ed Goodman wrote his mother in January that "The winters in this country are the worst kind . . . Slopy [*sic*], wet, nasty, damp and many fogs." At the end of his letter, he asked Julia if she had ever heard from Miss DeValesco, and if she might be coming back to North Platte in the spring.

A month later Cody was ill with bronchitis and "terribly homesick besides," wrote Ed. On March 4 Ed reported that although his Uncle Will complained that the climate did not agree with him, he had gained eighteen pounds since arriving in Manchester, "and now ways [*sic*] 218 pounds in his light clothes. I believe it is only *home-sickness* that is the matter with him." The bad news was that the terrible weather had probably accounted for the poor business the shows had done during the past month.

Back in North Platte, the *Tribune* informed its readers that "it is reported that Buffalo Bill is pining for his ranch in Nebraska and expresses himself this way: 'I want to come home. We are doing an immense business here, but the country cramps me and the climate chokes me. There is not air enough. If I start out to take a ride on my horse, just as soon as I get warm in my saddle I've come to the end of the island. If I get comfortably fixed in their damn railway coaches the guard announces that we've arrived. There isn't territory enough for the people. They tread on each other and their biggest country needs ventilation. You forget how to breathe here in six months. You're afraid of robbing someone else of atmosphere.'"

At first the Wild West repeated its London triumph in Manchester. Dignitaries flocked to the show grounds. The local Freemasons greeted Cody as one of their own—and one evening the Colonel was presented with "a magnificent rifle, decked in flowers and gaily adorned with ribbons," the gift of "the artistic, dramatic, and literary gentlemen of Manchester." To present the rifle, a delegation of London's *elite* of the metropolitan *literati*, one hundred strong, came up to Manchester to take part in the ceremony. Afterward, Bill entertained all the celebrities at a camp dinner of fried oysters, Boston pork and beans, Maryland fried chicken, and a real "Indian rib-roast," eaten with the fingers, aboriginal style.

By February business had fallen off. There was some thought of returning to London, but what if they returned and failed to repeat their first triumphant success on the return stand? The company's reputation would suffer badly. So they chose to remain in Manchester and take their losses. At one time Cody and Salsbury had considered staying in Europe for two years, but when it appeared in January 1888 that the British had had enough of the Wild West for now, on the tenth of the month Nate Salsbury returned to the United States to arrange for a summer tour back home.

A few days before the troupe was to leave Manchester, his worship the Mayor of Salford proclaimed three new streets in his town to be Buffalo Street, Bill Street, and Cody Street. On April 30, when the Wild West gave its final Manchester performance, Cody was cheered to the rafters and covered with flowers by enthusiastic spectators; it was five minutes before the cheering subsided enough for the show to begin.

A "Farewell Day" was announced for May 1, when Cody was given a benefit by the race course owners; it was held outdoors on the Salford arena, and nearly fifty thousand people paid admission. It was, in effect, a rodeo, and the main event was a ten-mile relay race between English Thoroughbreds and American broncos, for a £500 purse. Antonio Esquivel rode thirteen broncs for America. Each rider changed mounts every half-mile, without assistance. Because of his experience in the Pony Express act, where the rider leapt from one mount to another while both were in motion, Esquivel was adept at changing horses, while the English rider dismounted and mounted motionless horses. Accordingly, Esquivel won by some three hundred yards, completing the race in twenty-one minutes. Twenty thousand spectators enthusiastically applauded both riders.

Again attended by cheering crowds of well-wishers, the Wild West pulled out of Windsor Bridge Station on the morning of May 4, headed for the port of Hull, where they would take ship for America. All along the way, crowds gathered to cheer and wave to them. Then, on May 5, the final English performance was given at the Hull Football Field. The Hull *News* reported: "Numerous excursion trains were run to Hull not only from the immediate neighborhood, but from the West Riding and the Midland districts, and large numbers of persons were brought to the town. The Holderness road during the latter part of the morning and the afternoon presented a lively scene, for as early as eleven o'clock the spectators began to enter the ground, and the trams and waggonettes plying in that direction were heavily laden, the traffic being for a time congested, and was only carried on with difficulty, so great was the crowd of vehicles. Early in the afternoon very many thousands had gathered on the field and the grand stand, for entrance to which a charge of 5s each was made, was quite filled." Temporary stands had been erected to seat the overflow crowd.

At the very end, England seemed unwilling to let the Wild West depart. By nine o'clock on the evening of May 5, the entire troupe, along with all their possessions, including the guns, jewelry, and other gifts lavished on Buffalo Bill, were on board the *Persian Monarch*. Between then and three o'clock in the morning, when the ship hoisted anchor, faithful admirers lined Hull's Alexandra dock, singing, cheering, and waving. Homesick or not, the Americans could only marvel at such devotion. They would hear cheering again, but perhaps never with such unbridled frenzy.

The trip home saw none of the apprehensions of the outward voyage. Everyone on board was glad to be homeward bound. The Indians by now had realized that they would not "waste away" on the high seas and that, in fact, travel *was* broadening; a few of them had elected to remain in England.

There was one sad note on the return trip: Old Charlie, Buffalo Bill's best-loved horse, his companion of the past fifteen years, sickened and died. On the morning of May 14, 1888, Cody went down into the hold to see Charlie and gave him some sugar. Less than an hour later his groom told the Colonel the horse was sick. At two o'clock on the morning of May 17, Charlie died. Mourned almost as if he were human, he was buried at sea on the eighteenth. During the day he lay in state on the deck, wrapped in a canvas shroud and covered with the Stars and Stripes. According to the Aurora, Nebraska, *Register,* "at the appointed hour the entire ship's company assembled. The band played 'Auld Lang Syne,' lights were burned and as the faithful creature glided gently into the water, the ship's cannon boomed a last farewell." Say what they would about Cody, he was a grand master of entrances and exits—nor is there any question that his grief at Old Charlie's death was genuine. "We could almost understand each other," he said, "and I felt very deeply."

Early on the morning of May 20, the *Persian Monarch* steamed into New York harbor to a tumultuous welcome. The New York *World* captured the moment unforgettably:

The harbor probably has never witnessed a more picturesque scene. . . . Buffalo Bill stood on the captain's bridge, his tall and striking figure clearly outlined, and his long hair waving in the wind; the gayly painted and blanketed Indians leaned over the ship's rail; the flags of all nations fluttered from the masts and connecting cables. The cowboy band played "Yankee Doodle" with vim and enthusiasm which faintly indicated the joy felt by everybody connected with the "Wild West" over the sight of home.

Cody's words on the occasion were "I cannot describe my joy upon stepping again on the shore of beloved America. . . . 'There is no place like home,' nor is there a flag like the old flag." "The Hero of Two Continents," as the New York *Evening Telegram* put it, "had come home."

While Buffalo Bill, his daughter Arta, and Major Burke, along with several reporters, were debarking in New York City, Nate Salsbury was getting the rest of the show settled in Erastina, to open another engagement there.

On December 15, 1887, Charles Dana Gibson drew a two-page cartoon entitled "The Triumph of the West" in the American humor magazine *Life* (which bore no relationship to the weekly or monthly *Life* of later years). The central figure in the cartoon was Buffalo Bill, rifle in hand, receiving the homage of Queen Victoria and her court and preceded by three peers in their robes. The British lion, garbed as an Indian with a tomahawk in its belt, marched alongside.

While *Life*'s objective was probably to make England's enthusiasm for this unlikely American ambassador look faintly ridiculous, there was no doubt, as Don Russell put it, "that in 1887, the man of the year was William F. Cody."

Shortly after returning to the United States from England, Cody received a gratifying letter from William Tecumseh Sherman, written at the Fifth Avenue Hotel in New York, and addressed to Colonel Wm. F. Cody:

> *Dear Sir*—In common with all your countrymen, I want to let you know that I am not only gratified but proud of your management and success. So far as I can make out, you have been modest, graceful, and dignified in all you have done to illustrate the history of civilization on this continent during the past century. . . .
>
> As nearly as I can estimate, there were in 1865 about nine and one-half million of buffaloes on the Plains between the Missouri River and the Rocky Mountains; all are now gone, killed for their meat, their skins, and their bones. This seems like desecration, cruelty, and murder, yet they have been replaced by twice as many cattle. At that date there were about 165,000 Pawnees, Sioux, Cheyennes, and Arapahoes, who depended upon these buffaloes for their yearly food. They, too, have

gone, but they have been replaced by twice as many white men and women, who have made the earth to blossom as the rose, and who can be counted, taxed, and governed by the laws of Nature and civilization. This change has been salutary, and will go on to the end. You have caught one epoch of this country's history, and have illustrated in the very heart of the modern world—London—and I want you to feel that on this side of the water we appreciate it.

This drama must end; days, years, and centuries follow fast; even the drama of civilization must have an end. All I aim to accomplish on this sheet of paper is to assure you that I fully recognize your work. The presence of the Queen, the beautiful Princess of Wales, the Prince, and the British public are marks of favor which reflect back on America sparks of light which illuminate many a house and cabin in the land where once you guided me honestly and faithfully, in 1865–66, from Fort Riley to Kearney, in Kansas and Nebraska.

Sincerely your friend,
W.T. SHERMAN

It was, of course, the policies of Sherman, and his commander in chief, President Ulysses S. Grant, that led to the extermination of the buffalo and the near extermination of the Indians. Were these policies genocidal? Most certainly—and most deliberately. Can they be defended? Yes, if you believe, as Grant and Sherman, and much of the white population of America wholeheartedly believed, in the policy of manifest destiny, or what Kipling called "the White Man's burden." There were always voices strongly raised in support of the Indian's rights, in criticism of the official government policy; and they were not voices in the wilderness, they were voices in the civilized cities of the East—but they were seldom heeded.

In 1888 the Wild West made only a brief tour, opening at the old site at Erastina on Memorial Day, a "coincidence" probably arranged by Major Burke, since it allowed Cody, Salsbury, and two hundred of their cowboys and Indians to ride in the hugely popular Decoration Day parade in New York City. As the New York *Tribune* reported: "Buffalo Bill, dressed as a scout and mounted on a powerful young horse, rode with the staff of the Grand Marshal. He was received with shouts of applause."

Not long afterward, the New York *World* described Cody as "probably the best known man in New York city. Wherever he goes he is recognized and pointed out by the crowds." Children followed him in the streets, and workmen paused to see him go by. "Colonel Cody bore it all," continued the *World*, "with that quiet, gentle modesty which is so becoming to him. What a candidate for Vice President he would make to help out a chilly ticket." The election that year pitted the incumbent Democrat Grover Cleveland against Republican Benjamin Harrison; Harrison was victorious.

The Erastina booking was only for the month of June, but the opening-day crowd of twenty thousand on May 31, with another ten thousand people waiting at the gates unable to get in, encouraged the showmen to remain there until mid-August. During the Erastina run Buffalo Bill lived at the Waldorf-Astoria Hotel in New York, holding open house in his suite every night for the city's most fashionable socialites. The transformation of rough plainsman into the *beau-cavalier* was now complete; only in the arena was there any vestige left of Buffalo Bill the plainsman. When Cody patronized the fashionable bars of New York, he was frequently approached by well-wishers who would offer to buy him a drink. His response to the offer was always: "Sir, you speak the language of my tribe."

Near the end of July, Cody wrote his sister Julia:

> I am feeling some better. . . . But I am tired out. . . . Two weeks from tomorrow we close here then go to Philadelphia and I am only going to give one show a day there, so I can rest of evenings. . . . I will be with you in October and take a whole month's rest, then I am going into a new scheme—start a new show for the winter and one that nobody can get up immitations on. . . . I ain't even going to tell you & Al what it is till I spring it on the public in December.

After playing Erastina and the New York area, the show made stops in Philadelphia, Baltimore, and Washington, closing the season late in October at the Richmond, Virginia, Exposition and then going into winter quarters and disbanding, for the first time in the two years and seven months since they had opened in St. Louis.

Before heading for North Platte, Cody took some seventy-five of his Indians to Washington, D.C., where they visited the White House and saw the U.S. Senate and House of Representatives in action. The Indians smoked a peace pipe at the Bureau of Indian Affairs and called on the Great Father himself; Grover Cleveland received the Indians in the East Room and was impressed with their majestic bearing as they filed by.

From Washington the Indians returned to their reservation, and Cody finally went home to Nebraska. The *Tribune* recorded his arrival in North Platte on November 6, election day. He received a warm welcome from his friends and for the first time in several years was able to cast his ballot at the polls.

Cody was pleased with his splendid new barn, which, as editor Bare described it, "looms up against the skyline like a mountain." Across its southern roof slope, SCOUT'S REST RANCH had been painted in letters four feet tall, readable from the trains passing on the tracks one and a half miles to the south; the letters are still there today.

While Cody was gone, a "brick block," the town's first, had been built; a waterworks plant had been completed, making it possible for residents to have running water in their homes. A new drink, called the "milk shake," had been introduced, and a group of townsmen had set up a rifle range on the fairgrounds and organized the W. F. Cody Rifle Club. A Mr. Horton S. Boal, who would figure prominently in the life of the Cody family, had opened a real estate, loan, and insurance agency. "Mr. Boal, a Chicagoan," wrote the local *Journal,* "comes to this city full of vim and enterprise, characteristic of the people of Chicago," and editor Bare predicted that his business would do well.

A reception in Will's honor was arranged by the Cody Grand Army of the Republic (GAR) Post of Wallace, Nebraska, an association of Union veterans that had been organized in Cody's absence. The veterans had named the post for their Man of the Year, W. F. Cody, a signal honor, since it was customary to name GAR posts only for men who had died in some heroic action. The rest of the Codys' winter season in North Platte, according to Nellie Snyder Yost, was filled with parties, banquets, plays, symphonies, and operas. In a more serious vein, the Buffalo Bill Hook and Ladder Company was organized, officers were elected, and uniforms ordered; this company was to be "the pink of the North Platte fire department."

"It must have been during this extended visit home," wrote Nellie Snyder Yost, "that Cody's tallyho arrived in North Platte; he had, no doubt, purchased the vehicle while in England and had it shipped home. . . . Actually, it was not a tallyho, which is an open rig used on English fox-hunts, but a British four-in-hand, a fourteen-passenger covered carriage with seats on top as well as inside. In North Platte, however, it was always called 'the tallyho.'"

The carriage caused quite a sensation among the locals and was used on special occasions when the Colonel was in town; he drove its four or six horses himself, and used it to transport his guests to and from the ranch or the Welcome Wigwam, or for his hunting parties.

While Cody rested with his family—dividing his time between his wife and daughters at the Welcome Wigwam house and his beloved Scout's Rest Ranch—Nate Salsbury made the final arrangements for the next tour: this time an invasion of the European continent. Salsbury followed an already-proven formula in his plans: Go where the crowds were already gathering. This meant being in Paris during the Exposition of 1889, marking the one-hundredth anniversary of the Fall of the Bastille on July 14, 1789, where great numbers of people would gather with money in their pockets and a thirst for novelty. Also, many of the visitors that summer would be Britons, already enchanted with Buffalo Bill. The well-known travel agent Thomas Cook arranged it so that his tourists could take in Buffalo Bill's Wild West on their excursions—or, for those with more macabre tastes, the occasional public execution by guillotine. One of the other features of the *Paris Exposition Universelle* was the recently completed Eiffel Tower.

There would be no American tour in 1889 before the Wild West's engagement in Paris, so Cody was able to relax—so much so that, after celebrating while seeing in the new year 1889, he was fined one dollar for being drunk and incapacitated.

Annie Oakley and Frank Butler had left the show at the end of the first London engagement, accepting an invitation from Crown Prince Wilhelm of Germany, later Kaiser Wilhelm. In Germany, Oakley performed one of her most astonishing feats of marksmanship: tossing six balls into the air herself and bursting each one of them faster than the shots could be counted. For this stunt she used the new pump-action Spencer rifle.

While the Wild West was on tour in 1888, Annie and Frank, after returning from Europe in the spring, signed up with a rival show, probably one organized by Charles M. Southwell of Philadelphia. Accustomed to Buffalo Bill's beautifully trained and groomed horses, they were appalled at the condition of the animals they saw. Moreover, Southwell's cowboys could not ride, and his cast, with the exception of a few wretched Indians, had all been recruited no farther west than Philadelphia.

At the same time, Pawnee Bill Lillie, who had been an interpreter for the Indians of Buffalo Bill's Wild West in the early years, had organized a huge show that he planned to take to Belgium for a six-month stand at the Grand Exposition in Brussels. When Emperor Wilhelm of Germany suddenly died, the contract was canceled, and Lillie had to find bookings in the United States. His show was a large one: 165 horses and mules; 85 Indians; 50 riders; and 30 trappers, hunters, and scouts. By the time Lillie reached Pittsburgh, he was having box office troubles. Learning of Pawnee Bill's problems, the Butlers decided to arrange a merger.

The reorganized Pawnee Bill Frontier Exhibition opened July 2, 1888, at Gloucester Beach, New Jersey, with two performances daily. Featured were Annie Oakley, Pawnee Bill—showcased as "White Chief of the Pawnees—young daredevil who performs miracles with a rope and six-shooter and rides like a fiend on a big black stallion"—and his wife, May

Lillie, "World's Champion Woman Rifle Shot." The show drew big crowds at Gloucester Beach, but when it started south in the fall, playing fairs, unfavorable contracts and bad weather combined to devastate Pawnee Bill's finances. In Euston, Maryland, the show was attached by the sheriff. Lillie could not pay his hotel bill, and his trunks were seized.

Annie and Frank were once more at liberty, though not for long. Annie appeared in a variety bill at the opening of Tony Pastor's Opera House in New York City, took part in a few shooting matches, and appeared in a new melodrama, *Deadwood Dick, or The Sunbeam of the Sierras*. Annie was the "Sunbeam" of the title. The play was not a hit and closed at the end of January 1889.

Whatever differences Annie may have had with Salsbury and Cody during the tour of England were now resolved, and the two partners asked Annie to come back and star in their show during their forthcoming European tour. Lillian Smith had now left the Wild West; her departure may have been a condition for Annie's return. Cody planned to take 250 people with him to Europe—cowboys, Indians, and other performers, along with three hundred head of stock, including fifty-seven buffalo from his North Platte ranch. The Indians were Sioux, Cheyenne, and Arapaho, because he believed they were "more hardy than the others."

Once again the *Persian Monarch* was engaged, its destination Le Havre. The Wild West opened at the *Exposition Universelle* in Paris on May 19, 1889, and immense crowds thronged to see the show. The opening performance was attended by the French president, Sadi Carnot, several members of his cabinet, and American ministers Whitelaw Reid and Louis MacLean. Fewer crowned heads attended the show in Paris than at Victoria's Jubilee, but Shah Naz-er-el-den of Persia attended and former Queen Isabella II of Spain rode in the Deadwood coach.

In the beginning of the engagement, the Paris crowds did not understand the Wild West show. As Annie Oakley put it: "[The French audience] sat like icebergs at first. . . . There was no friendly welcome, just a 'you must show me' air. . . . I wanted honest applause or none at all." Fortunately, her performances were so dazzling that, according to Nate Salsbury, she saved the show and became the darling of Paris, as she had been the toast of London.

The artist Rosa Bonheur, the most famous animal painter of the day, was then nearing seventy. After Cody met her in her chateau outside Paris, he gave her the freedom of the show, and she spent many hours in the back lot of the Wild West's "Buffalodrum" during its seven-month run at the Paris Exposition; at least seventeen paintings of Cody, his Indians, horses, and buffalo, were the result. The most famous of these paintings was one of Buffalo Bill on his white horse, which was copied on posters, programs, and postcards and in many books. The original was shipped home to North Platte, where Louisa hung it on her parlor wall and invited all of North Platte to come and admire it. Cody was apparently dissatisfied with Bonheur's depiction of him and later had the face repainted by the artist Robert Lindneux.

Cody wrote Julia from Paris on July 5: "Yesterday was a busy day for me, first I went with the American Minister to the tomb of General LaFayette then to the unveialing [sic] of Barthold's Statue, then to a reception & dinner we gave in camp—then the afternoon performance—then to the Legation reception—back for the evening show—then into my evening dress and to Minister Reids reception, turned in at daylight—and today I am off my feed.

"I can't stand as much as I used to," Will continued, "and I am not all well this summer. Now we are getting old we must not kick at our breaking down, it can't be helped, but I don't want to break down until I get out of debt and ahead of the hounds for enough to take it easy."

Cody was only forty-six when he wrote that letter, but the way he drove himself was beginning to tell—that and his worries about debt and "taking it easy," concerns that would dog him for the rest of his life.

Not all his news was depressing. He cabled Louisa that same month that he had been decorated with "the badge of the Legion of Honor," a distinction, remarked the editor of the North Platte *Telegraph*, that he believed was enjoyed by no other Nebraskan.

While the Wild West was in Paris, Black Elk, one of six Indians who had inadvertently missed the boat in Hull two years before, suddenly reappeared. He had made his way to London and from there to France, as a member of Mexican Joe's traveling show. When Joe learned of Cody's presence in Paris, he brought Black Elk to him. Cody asked the Indian whether he would rather join the show or go back home. Said Black Elk: "He [Cody] was glad to see me. He had all his people give me three cheers. Then he asked me if I wanted to be in the show or if I wanted to go home. I told him I was sick to go home. So he said he would fix that. He gave me a ticket and ninety dollars. Then he gave me a big dinner. Pahuska had a strong heart."

Thirty-two million people altogether attended the Paris Exposition of 1889, and it is a safe bet that a good many of them wound up at the Wild West. Among the visitors was forty-one-year-old artist Paul Gauguin. Cody reported that "everything American became the fad during our stay. Fashionable young men bought American and Mexican saddles for their rides in the Bois. Cowboy hats appeared everywhere on the street. There was a great cry for stories of the Plains and all the books that could be found that dealt with the West were translated into the French language.

Relics from the plains and mountains, bows, moccasins, and Indian baskets, sold like hot cakes in the souvenir stores." Popcorn was first introduced to the French at the show, and was avidly consumed.

Buffalo Bill's Indians were allowed to move freely around the city; some wandered off, and a few found their way back to America. One of these was White Horse, who told a reporter from the New York *Herald* that there was cruelty and starvation in the Wild West camp. The rumor spread and reached scandalous proportions. When the story reached the Wild West in Berlin, Major Burke, the original spin-doctor, immediately went to work to refute the allegations. He invited the consul general and the secretary of the legation there, as well as the consul in Hamburg, to inspect the Indians. All three agreed that "they are certainly the best looking, and apparently the best fed Indians we have ever seen." A refutation of the original story was then published in the European edition of the New York *Herald*. Cody, however, felt that it would be best to take the matter up directly with the commissioner of Indian affairs, so he decided that instead of planning a winter tour in 1890–1891, he would take the Indians home that fall and straighten the matter out personally.

After the Paris Exposition the Wild West toured southern France, including Lyon and Marseilles. At Lyon a can of French gunpowder almost resulted in disaster for Annie Oakley. Using a wet-weather load on a hot day caused the smokeless gunpowder to burst the gun barrel. Fortunately, Annie was not hurt.

The next stop was Spain. There a band of Cody's American Indians landed at Barcelona—398 years after Columbus returned to that port after discovering America. Major Burke had the Indians photographed in front of a statue of Columbus, which led one of the braves to remark, "It was a damned bad day for us when he discovered America." No newspaper published the picture, and despite his best efforts, Burke was unable to generate much enthusiasm for the show among the Spanish, probably because it did not feature any bullfights.

At Barcelona the Wild West suffered one of the worst months in its history. The city was in partial quarantine for Spanish influenza and typhoid fever as well as being economically depressed. Frank Richmond, the show's dynamic announcer, died suddenly of influenza, as did four Indians who all lacked immunity to the white man's diseases. Seven ailing Indians were sent home. Annie Oakley, too, was taken seriously ill. As soon as the quarantine was lifted, Salsbury booked passage for Naples, where they opened on January 26, 1890. Understandably depressed, the show people were happy to leave Spain alive.

The Wild West tour through Italy was much more encouraging. It was spring in Italy and the crowds were huge. In Naples, instead of a painted backdrop depicting the Wyoming mountains, Vesuvius supplied the background. An imaginative Neapolitan had counterfeited two thousand or more reserved-seat tickets, which led to unimaginable confusion on opening day. The company made stops in Rome, Florence, Bologna, Turin, Verona, Padua, and Venice. In Rome mounted Indians were photographed in front of St. Peter's, and on February 20, 1890, Pope Leo XIII received a Wild West delegation at an audience; the occasion was the anniversary of his coronation. Major Burke instructed the Indians ahead of time how to behave in the pontiff's presence. While the pope was carried out in his *sedia gestatoria,* wearing the tiara, or triple crown, the solemn and silent Indians lined the corridor to watch the spectacle. One of the Indian squaws fainted, and another died that night at camp, which greatly upset the superstitious Indians.

The show also put up a temporary camp in the Colosseum, the closest Buffalo Bill came to fulfilling an old dream of his—putting on a show in that ancient arena, but it was too cluttered with rubble and stonework for showing horses or driving the Deadwood coach. However, the whole company was photographed there.

The high point of the Roman engagement—perhaps of the entire tour—was provided by Don Onorio Herzog of Sermonetta, Prince of Teano. The prince challenged Cody's cowboys to ride his untamed Cajetan stallions, a wild and unmanageable breed of horseflesh. It was rumored that the beasts were so fierce they ate people. Don Onorio claimed that no cowboy in the world could conquer his stallions. On March 4 Cody accepted the challenge. Special barricades were set up in Rome for fear of what would happen to the crowd if the horses should get loose. Two of the prince's horses were released inside the improvised corral, and Buffalo Bill announced that they would be tamed in full view of the audience.

"The brutes made springs into the air, darted hither and thither in all directions, and bent themselves into all sorts of shapes, but all in vain," wrote the Rome correspondent of the New York *Herald.* "In five minutes the cow-boys had caught the wild horses with the lasso, saddled, subdued, and bestrode them." There were twenty thousand spectators at this event, most of them betting that these beasts would defeat the Americans, and some hoping for mortal injuries. When it was over so quickly, Italian pride was hurt, and some in the crowd booed the cowboys; others applauded wildly. Cody's recollection was that "The audience, always strong for the winners, forgot their disappointment in the absence of fatalities, and howled with delight."

Buffalo Bill then challenged the Italians who had come from the south of Italy with their wild horses to break the American broncos. Every

The Wild West show cast in the arena at Mt. Vesuvius in Italy, c. 1889. (Buffalo Bill Historical Center, Cody, Wyoming)

Italian rider was tossed and on the ground in less than a minute. Cody then allowed the Italians to try their own methods of breaking horses, which employed chains and irons. After half an hour the Colonel called the affair off, because the Italian methods were too cruel to the horses.

In Florence there was a bothersome delay when the customs officials insisted on charging entrance duties for the horses in accordance with their weight. At Verona Buffalo Bill finally got to exhibit his show in an ancient Roman amphitheater, that of Diocletian, built in A.D. 260 and restored by Emperor Napoleon. It was estimated that forty-five thousand people saw the show that day. When the company reached Venice, some of the Indians were pictured in a gondola on April 16 and were described in the press as "the first American Indians that have visited the Adriatic."

In the industrial city of Milan, one spectator was the composer Giacomo Puccini, not yet famous, who loved the show, and who shared his enthusiasm with his brother in a letter written on April 24. David Belasco's *The Girl of the Golden West* was the source of Puccini's opera

La Fanciulla del West, but Buffalo Bill's Wild West may also have turned the composer's thoughts toward the American frontier.

From Italy the Wild West moved to Innsbruck and the Tyrol, and then on to Munich. While in Munich at the end of April, Joseph William Louis Luitpold, the Prince Regent of Bavaria, visited the show with his daughters. So impressed was the prince with Annie Oakley's shooting prowess that he sent her the following message: "If convenient, His Majesty requests the honor of an audience with Fraulein Oakley at 10:30 this morning." As was her custom, Annie granted the request. After inspecting the guns in her tent, the prince also asked if she would toss coins for him. While they were in the arena, the prince was threatened by a fractious horse, Dynamite. Annie, casting protocol aside, tackled the nobleman to knock him out of the horse's path. As a token of his gratitude for saving his life, the prince sent her a handsome gold bracelet bearing the crown and monogram of his family, with a diamond solitaire.

The Wild West spent most of the 1890–1891 season in Germany, where enthusiasm for the show seems to have been greater than anywhere else in Europe. One German was so moved by the performance that it set him off on a career that, according to the *Enyclopaedia Britannica*, made him "one of the world's all-time fiction best sellers." The man was Karl Friedrich May. Born in 1842, the son of a weaver, May became a schoolmaster, was imprisoned for theft, and then embarked on a criminal career that had him in and out of prisons for thirteen years. Released from prison one last time, he decided to become a writer. Drawing on atlases and encyclopedias, he wrote travel and adventure stories for young people, many dealing with American Indians in the Wild West. The stories were remarkable for the realistic detail that the author was able to achieve, despite having never set foot in the country he wrote about. Some of May's stories were inspired by Buffalo Bill Cody, though his most famous character was called Old Shatterhand. When his criminal career became common knowledge, his reputation suffered; still, by the time he died in 1912 he was idolized by generations of Germans. Among his passionate readers were Albert Einstein, Albert Schweitzer, and Alois Schickelgruber, who changed his name to Adolf Hitler.

Though virtually unknown in the United States, May is still widely read in Europe, and there is a museum in Munich dedicated to his work. One of the museum's treasures is a painting titled *Custer's Last Stand* by Elk Eber, who got his information from an eyewitness of the fight, a Sioux woman who left Buffalo Bill's Wild West to marry a German.

Buffalo Bill Cody with five Indian chiefs from the Wild West show, in Italy, c. 1890. (Buffalo Bill Historical Center, Cody, Wyoming)

It is interesting to note that the American film director Billy Wilder, born in 1906 in what is now a part of Poland, worked as a young man in the German film industry, doing silent film treatments. While in Germany, Wilder learned to speak English from Karl May. Wilder's first name was actually Samuel, but his mother renamed him Willie because she had been so impressed by Buffalo Bill's Wild West.

Back home in North Platte, the social event of the season was the marriage of Arta Cody to Horton Boal. Since his arrival in North Platte, the young Chicagoan had supplanted Arta's other suitors in her affections. Boal's cause may have been helped along when his horse threw him in the vicinity of Welcome Wigwam; he was carried with a broken leg into the Cody house, where a doctor was called to treat him. It is not known whether this accident preceded or followed Arta's interest in Boal, but by Thanksgiving they were married.

Helen Cody Wetmore wrote: "It was impossible for the father to be present, but by cablegram he sent his congratulations and check." The Grand Island (Nebraska) newspaper reported: "H.S. Boal and Arta Cody were married at the Cody residence. The young people left after the ceremony for Denver and points west. Among the presents was a draft from the bride's father, Col. W.F. Cody, for $5,000 and a deed to a cottage in which Mr. and Mrs. Boal will take up their residence after their return."

As if Buffalo Bill didn't have enough to worry him with his European tour and the false charges that he had abused and starved his Indians, there was a storm gathering on the home front as well. Like many naturalized Englishmen before him, Horton Boal hankered to run his own western ranch. Both Arta and her mother, Louisa, thought he ought to be put in charge of Scout's Rest and were doing their best to displace Al and Julia Goodman as Cody's managers. This maneuver probably grew out of the jealousy that had long existed between Will's wife and his favorite sister. Having an unseasoned son-in-law run his beloved ranch was the last thing Cody wanted to happen. He had every good reason to put his show in winter quarters and return to the United States.

Moreover, another matter of some urgency would occupy his attention when he returned home: His old friend and onetime adversary Sitting Bull was in trouble—and needed his help.

THE LAST OF THE INDIAN WARS

Though the Indian campaigns of 1872 to 1877 were sometimes called Sitting Bull's War, Sitting Bull was not necessarily the most militant of the Sioux leaders, or the most intractable. His followers considered him a beloved elder statesman, a tribal Benjamin Franklin whose advice was sought after and trusted, an orator, a philosopher, a propagandist, a healer of the sick, a psychiatrist, and a political leader. The Sioux also believed that he had mystical powers, which made him a spiritual leader as well. Historian Stephen Ambrose said of him: "Sitting Bull was an extraordinary man for any race at any time, and such a man is of necessity complex."

"Sitting Bull had great power over the Sioux," said Lewis Dewitt, a white scout. "He was a good medicine man. He made good medicine. . . . He told the Sioux many times he was not made to be a reservation Indian. The Great Spirit made him a free Indian to go where he wanted to go, to hunt buffalo and to be a big leader in his tribe."

After surrendering to General Miles in the summer of 1881, Sitting Bull and his 158 ragged followers had had no choice but to give up their nomadic, hunter-warrior existence and adapt as best they could to reservation life at Standing Rock. Unfortunately, if the Sioux thought by accepting a sedentary existence they would put an end to white pressure for lands assigned to them by treaty, they were horribly, tragically wrong.

By 1881 almost all the Indian peoples within the United States had been forced to sign treaties that confined them to reservations and made them dependents of the federal government. That year Helen Hunt Jackson, a New England–born writer, wrote A Century of Dishonor, detailing the many broken promises that the government had made to Indian tribes. She also described the corrupt practices by which white settlers, with government connivance, were continuing to encroach on the remaining tribal lands and to violate the Indians' rights. Jackson thought of the plight of the Indians much as the abolitionists had felt about slavery.

In 1881 western tribes still held title to almost a quarter million square miles of reservation tracts. However, both ranchers and sodbusters were constantly putting pressure on Congress to pass laws that would open Indian-occupied territory for new white settlement. In this they were abetted by do-gooders, particularly evangelical reformers, who hoped to help the Indians by weaning them from their "savage" customs and turning them into God-fearing family farmers. In 1886, in answer to these pressures, Senator Henry Dawes of Massachusetts put forth a proposal that would effectively strip the Indians of much of their birthright. Dawes devoutly believed that the best way to civilize the Indian families was to give each one 160 acres of land for farming—plus a share in the profits gained from the sale to whites of the rest of their land. No matter that 160 acres in arid parts of the plains was not enough arable land to give an Indian family a living. The Dawes act was in truth intended as a "mighty pulverizing engine," which would break up the "tribal mass."

The Dawes Severalty Act passed Congress easily in 1887, and at once the uncomprehending Indians were persuaded to sign away huge chunks of land for as little as fifty cents an acre—an outrageous piece of chicanery. By 1889 the Dawes act had cost western tribes about 61,000 square miles of reservation land—16,000 acres cut out of the ancestral hunting grounds of the Sioux alone. Indian landholdings fell from about 138 million acres in 1887 to 48 million by 1934. One old Sioux remarked to a minister that the white men "had made us many promises but only kept one; they promised to take our land and they took it."

As Bernard Weisberger wrote in American Heritage magazine, "the break-up of the reservations drive radiated the spirit of the 1890s. It was an age that launched 'Americanization' programs to bring the 'new' immigrants into line in the public schools, that celebrated the farm family on its homestead as the backbone of the nation (when in fact the nation was rapidly urbanizing) and that imbibed a social Darwinism holding that all must yield to the inevitable march of progress."

Sitting Bull, though, was not as complacent as his fellow chiefs when it came to negotiating the sale of tribal lands. In 1887 Buffalo Bill invited him to travel to London with the Wild West show and attend Queen Victoria's Golden Jubilee. Even the chance to meet the Great Mother was not enough to tempt the old chief, now nearing his sixtieth birthday. "It is bad for our cause for me to parade around," he said. "I am needed here. There is more talk of taking our lands." He was right. The government wanted to sweep away another 10 million acres of the great Sioux preserve in western Dakota, offering fifty cents an acre—even for those times a pitiful price.

Sitting Bull, using his formidable powers of persuasion, was able to convince his fellow Sioux leaders to stand fast. When the U.S. Government commissioners arrived at the Standing Rock Agency in July 1888, there was no contest. The tribal leaders were asked to sign one of two papers, indicating either acceptance or refusal of the government's offer. Most of them refused to sign either one and simply walked away.

In October of that year, Sitting Bull traveled to Washington with a delegation of sixty Sioux leaders. Keeping them in closed ranks, he argued with Secretary of the Interior William Vilas that the offer was too low. Vilas countered with $1.00 an acre. The Indians rejected this, too, as inadequate, knowing that the government was planning to sell the land to white settlers for $1.25 an acre. In 1889 Congress stepped in and increased the offer to $1.25 an acre, promising at the same time to give the head of each Indian family 320 acres of land, with the title to be held in trust by the government for twenty-five years so speculators could not swindle the Indians out of it. Sitting Bull was determined to refuse this offer as well—but this time, unfortunately, he could not hold his other chiefs in line. There were now enough signatures on the agreement for it to carry. Sitting Bull had lost the battle. It is quite possible that the old chief would have turned down every offer the government made, no matter how generous. When asked later what he thought the Indians' sentiments were about the deal, he snorted: "Indians! There are no Indians left but me!"

From that point on, the Sioux's fortunes declined rapidly. Now that they were no longer regarded as a dangerous enemy, only a people on welfare, an economy-minded Congress ordered the tribe's beef ration cut in half. In 1889 and 1890 epidemics of measles, influenza, and whooping cough killed many undernourished Indian children. Adding to their woes, the Sioux suffered crop failures, which had been predicted by Sitting Bull. Tatanka Yotanka still received messages from the birds in the air, but where once an eagle had told him he would lead his people in battle, a meadowlark now informed him that "The Sioux will kill you." Sitting Bull resigned himself to the inevitable. His visions had never proved themselves wrong.

In the tragedy of the Sioux Nation, the stage was now set for a bloody climax.

In 1889 rumors of a miraculous Indian revelation came from farther west. In Nevada, during a solar eclipse on January 1, 1889, which the Indians called "the day the sun died," a young Paiute mystic named Wovoka had fallen into a trance. When he awoke, he told others that he had been taken up into the spirit world—what today would be considered an alien abduction. While in his trance, Wovoka had had a revelation that called for great things to come—as far as he could determine, in the spring of 1891. At that time the dead would rise from their graves. Indians already alive would live forever. The buffalo would return in their old herds of millions. The white man would disappear, buried under the earth. Wovoka told the Indians if they would follow God's commandment and perform "ghost dances," their old days of prosperity and happiness would return.

As with any other religion, there were commandments—no-nos, mostly. Wovoka's strictures called for purity of heart and immaculate behavior: no fighting, no war, nothing that savored of aggression, no lying, no stealing, no cruelty. It was a better religion than they had ever had before, one white man commented. Because it called for the appearance on earth of a Messiah, it was, in fact, Christianity in a new dress—the Gospel in buckskin and beads.

In January 1889 on the Walker Lake Reservation, the first Ghost Dance was performed on a dancing ground chosen by Wovoka. In the dance, the Paiute formed a large circle, dancing and chanting as they narrowed the circle; the circle then widened and narrowed again. The dancing continued for a day and a night. Wovoka sat in the center of the circle before a large fire, head bowed. At the end of the second day, he stopped the dancing to describe the visions that God had sent him. Then the dancing resumed for another three days.

The new religion spread quickly, to tribes eager for hope, for good news of any kind. First, several Ute visited the ceremony out of curiosity and told their neighboring Bannock about it. Before long the Shoshone sent a delegation to Nevada to learn the new religion from Wovoka himself. The Cheyenne and the Sioux, too, felt the need for a Messiah who might lead them back to their days of glory. In the autumn of 1889 Porcupine, a Cheyenne, made the trip to Nevada by train, traveling free of charge—a perk available to Indians—and not long afterward Short Bull, Kicking Bear, and other Sioux leaders traveled all the way from Dakota to see Wovoka.

The Sioux took zealously to the Ghost Dance religion and its Messiah. In the spring of 1890 they began dancing the Ghost Dance at Pine Ridge Reservation, adding new elements to Wovoka's original ceremony. They danced until they fell in an exhausted frenzy or went into trances, muttering messages from their ancestors. They took to wearing ghost shirts made of cotton cloth, painted blue around the necks, with designs of great originality: stars shaped like peyote birds; stars in the shape of Maltese crosses; bright-colored thunderbirds; bows and arrows and suns and moons. And to accompany the dance they wrote ghost songs:

The whole world is coming,
A nation is coming, a nation is coming,
The Eagle has brought the message to the tribe.
The father says so, the father says so.
Over the whole earth they are coming,
The buffalo are coming, the buffalo are coming.

It was the ghost shirts that caused alarm in governmental and army circles. They were said to be bulletproof, that a brave wearing one could not be killed. This seemed to prove to the whites, ever suspicious of their Native American neighbors, that the Indians were planning an armed uprising—why else would they need such protection?

"Mainly because they misunderstood the meaning of the Ghost Dance religion," wrote Dee Brown, "the Government's policy makers who ran the reservations from Washington decided to stamp it out. If they had taken the trouble to examine its basic tenets, they would have found that in its original form the religion was opposed to all forms of violence, self-mutilation, theft and falsehood."

The movement probably would have withered away under official disapproval had not Sitting Bull seen in Wovoka and his Ghost Dance yet one more opportunity to torment the white man. It is doubtful he believed in such superstition himself, not with his knowledge of the white man and his deadly weapons, but he knew how to use the incredulous to play upon the minds of the gullible and excite their emotions. When Kicking Bear, one of the early emissaries to Wovoka, visited Sitting Bull in late 1890 to teach him the Ghost Dance, Indian agent James McLaughlin ordered him escorted off the reservation. Kicking Bear was hardly off the camp on the Grand River before Sitting Bull set up a dance camp and started instructing his followers in the new religion. The peaceful ghost songs soon became warlike chants. By November 1889 the movement had taken on the alarming proportions of an uprising, though still a peaceful one, serious enough, however, for President Benjamin Harrison to order the War Department to take whatever steps were necessary to quell it. General Nelson A. Miles was ordered to move a large number of troops into the area.

Miles, who commanded the Division of the Missouri with headquarters in Chicago, and who was a veteran Indian fighter, believed that "It was a threatened uprising of colossal proportions, extending over a far greater territory than did the confederation inaugurated by the Prophet and led by Tecumseh, or the conspiracy of Pontiac, and only the prompt action of the military prevented its execution."

Agent James McLaughlin was convinced "that the new religion was managed from the beginning, as far as the Standing Rock Sioux were concerned, by Sitting Bull, who . . . having lost his former influence over the Sioux, planned to import and use it to re-establish himself in the leadership of the people, whom he might then lead in safety in any desperate enterprise which he might direct."

McLaughlin was considered the ablest Indian agent of his time. His wife was a Sioux, and he did sympathize with the Indians—he just didn't understand them. McLaughlin represented the prevailing Indian Bureau policy. He banned the notorious Sun Dance and discouraged Indian customs and habits. It was his conviction that the Indians had no real history or traditions. He did everything in his power to discredit Sitting Bull among his followers and destroy the chief's influence. He believed that if the older chiefs were rendered powerless, the younger Indians would be more tractable, more willing to adopt white ways. In this he was completely wrong; it was the younger braves who embraced the Ghost Dance most avidly, while the older chiefs, like Red Cloud, counseled prudence.

McLaughlin went out of his way to defame Sitting Bull. "Crafty, avaricious, mendacious, and ambitious" is how the agent described the chief. He "possessed all the faults of an Indian and none of the nobler attributes which have gone far to redeem some of his people from their deeds of guilt. . . . Even his people knew him as a physical coward, but the fact did not handicap the man in dealing with his following." In his attempts to discredit Sitting Bull, McLaughlin also spread the false report that, at the Battle of the Little Big Horn, Sitting Bull "took to the hills, there to make medicine, while the fight was in progress."

After Kicking Bear had been evicted from Sitting Bull's camp by Lieutenant Chatka of McLaughlin's Indian police, Sitting Bull broke his peace pipe, which he had kept sacred since his surrender at Fort Buford in 1881. McLaughlin recommended the arrest of Sitting Bull; his request was turned down by the Indian Bureau, which left the matter in the hands of the army. Disappointed, McLaughlin went to Sitting Bull's camp, accompanied only by an interpreter, an act that took considerable courage, what with several thousand fanatical Sioux about. He found Sitting Bull leading a Ghost Dance. When McLaughlin scolded him, accusing him of leading his people astray, Sitting Bull challenged McLaughlin to go with him to "seek the men who saw the Messiah, and when we find them, I will demand that they show him to us, and if they cannot do so I will return and tell my people it is a lie." McLaughlin, who apparently did not believe that Wovoka existed, said "such an attempt would be like catching up with the wind that blew last year" and ordered Sitting Bull back to the agency. Sitting Bull refused.

It is with the situation at an impasse that General Miles decided to call on Buffalo Bill. When the showman arrived in New York, he planned to accompany Major Burke and his Indians to Washington to resolve once and for all the charges of mistreatment, which still hung over the Wild West. Instead, when he stepped off the ship, he was handed a telegram from General Miles asking him to come to Chicago at once. Leaving Major Burke to deal with the Indian problem, he immediately boarded a train to Chicago and met with the general. Miles, believing that he was faced with a full-scale Indian war, wanted information about the Badlands from Cody, who was familiar with the country. Miles also suspected that Sitting Bull was behind the Indians' unrest. It is probable that out of their conversations Miles conceived the idea that Cody, as the chief's trusted friend, might be a useful intermediary in any negotiations with the Indians.

Said Cody: "Miles said that Sitting Bull had his camp somewhere within forty or fifty miles of the Standing Rock Agency, and was haranguing the Indians thereabout, spreading the Messiah talk and getting them to join him. He asked me if I could go immediately to Standing Rock and Fort Yates, and then to Sitting Bull's camp. He knew I was an old friend of the chief and he believed that if anyone could induce the old fox to abandon his plans for a general war I could. . . . I was sure that if I could reach Sitting Bull he would at least listen to me." The plan was for Cody to persuade the chief to come into the Standing Rock Agency and there await a meeting with General Miles. "Sitting Bull might listen to you," Miles told Cody, "when under the same conditions he'd take a shot at one of my soldiers."

It seems clear in hindsight that Sitting Bull had no intention whatever of starting a full-scale war; he just enjoyed twitting Agent McLaughlin. To give Cody the authority he would need on his mission, Miles drafted the following order:

Confidential

Headquarters, Division of the Missouri
Chicago, Ill., Nov. 24, 1890

Col. Cody,

You are hereby authorized to secure the person of Sitting Bull and and [sic] deliver him to the nearest comd'g officer of U.S. Troops, taking a receipt and reporting your action.

NELSON A. MILES
Major General
Comd. Division

On the back of a visiting card Miles wrote in pencil:

Comd'g officers will please give Col. Cody transportation for himself and party and any protection he may need for a small party.

NELSON A. MILES

Richard Walsh, in his biography of Cody, claims that when he met with General Miles in Chicago, Buffalo Bill advised him to arrest Sitting Bull, saying that "of all the bad Indians, Sitting Bull is the worst." There is no evidence to support this, however, and it is inconsistent with Cody's other statements about the old chief, nor does it make any sense in the light of the two men's friendship. Be that as it may, two days later Cody got off the train at Bismarck. It was his first appearance in Indian country since 1876.

When McLaughlin learned of Cody's mission, he was horrified. Both he and Lieutenant Colonel William Drum, the military commander, believed that Cody's actions might precipitate a general outbreak throughout the area. McLaughlin planned to have Sitting Bull arrested by Indian police during the winter, on ration day, an alternate Saturday, when all the Indians except Sitting Bull came into the agency. "I knew that any attempt by outside parties to arrest Sitting Bull would undoubtedly result in loss of life, as the temper of the ghost-dancers was not to be doubted," McLaughlin wrote later. The agent's thinking makes little sense, however. Although Cody's order implied that he was empowered to arrest Sitting Bull, he surely had no such intention. He wanted only to persuade the chief to come into the agency to meet with General Miles, and he would undoubtedly have succeeded.

When Buffalo Bill turned up at Standing Rock, Major McLaughlin tried to frighten him off. But Buffalo Bill was certainly not afraid of Sitting Bull; he knew the old man too well. So confident was he that he asked for no military escort at all; instead, he filled a wagon with presents, chiefly candy and pastries. As Johnny Baker later put it, "If they had left Cody alone, he'd have captured Sitting Bull with an all-day sucker."

McLaughlin telegraphed the commissioner of Indian affairs in Washington: "William F. Cody (Buffalo Bill) has arrived here with commission from Gen. Miles to arrest Sitting Bull. Such a step at present is unnecessary and unwise, as it will precipitate a fight which cannot be averted. A few Indians still dancing, but it does not mean mischief at present. I have matters well in hand, and when proper time arrives can arrest Sitting Bull without bloodshed. I ask attention to my letter of November 19. Request Gen. Miles order to Cody be rescinded and request immediate answer."

The officers at nearby Fort Yates, serving in the Eighth Cavalry and Twelfth Infantry, also resented Cody's interference. They considered Buffalo Bill only a civilian scout, "just a beef contractor" with a rank given him by the governor of Nebraska. Moreover, they thought, he was just a showman and a dime novel hero, more famous than his deeds warranted.

Together with McLaughlin, the officers conspired to keep Cody from his mission, until the agent's wire had been answered. The plan was to get Cody over to the Officer's Club and, working in relays, drink him under the table. Obviously, they did not know their man. As Assistant Surgeon Alonzo R. Chapin, apparently the only survivor, tells the story: "Colonel Cody's capacity was such that it took practically all the officers in details of two or three at a time to keep him interested and busy through the day."

Cody enjoyed the hospitality of the officers, but outlasted them all and kept his head. He slept late but was on his way by eleven o'clock in the morning in a spring-wagon drawn by a span of mules and loaded with presents for Sitting Bull and his two squaws. With him were his two old comrades Pony Bob Haslam and White Beaver Powell, who had known Sitting Bull in the Wild West show. Cody took his time, stopping for a visit with an old soldier, William Presley Zahn, married to a Sioux woman and living on the reservation. Zahn says that Cody was confident of success, and said, "Why, I've got a hundred dollars' worth of stuff in that wagon for every pound old Bull weighs." What Cody did not know is that McLaughlin had no intention that he should meet with Sitting Bull; he sent Indian horsemen to meet and mislead Cody, delaying him until he could hear from Washington.

Was there ever any danger to Cody? It is highly doubtful, even though he and his party were armed with nothing more deadly than lead pencils. On the same day that Cody arrived at Standing Rock, Sam Clover, a Chicago newspaperman, went with Jack Carignan, the agency teacher, to see the Ghost Dance—and Clover photographed it from the seat of a wagon; no one threatened him. The only danger was manufactured by McLaughlin, who wanted no interference with his authority. Already the newspapers in the East were calling him incompetent, and the Indian commissioner was known to dislike him because he was a Roman Catholic and a friend to the military.

McLaughlin got his answer before Cody was able to reach Sitting Bull's camp on Grand River. His plea had been bucked up through channels to President Harrison, who ordered Cody recalled, and he was headed off. When Sitting Bull asked Jack Carignan about his visitors, he was told that Cody was at the agency and wanted to see him. Sitting Bull, of course, refused to go to the agency, thereby ensuring his own destruction. He made one last vain effort to avert a conflict; in a letter to the agency, he wrote: "I wish no one to come to me in my prayers with gun or knife."

Agent McLaughlin was then ordered by the commissioner "to cooperate with and obey the orders of the military officers commanding." On December 12, when the War Department ordered Colonel Drum to arrest

Sitting Bull. (Photograph by David F. Barry, c. 1884)

Sitting Bull, McLaughlin protested that "a military demonstration would precipitate a collision and bloodshed," and again urged that "if I could make provision to make the arrest by Indian police, at an opportune time and in my own way, there would be no necessity for shedding blood."

McLaughlin's decision was precipitated by a request for a pass from Sitting Bull. Early in December Short Bull, the leader of the Ghost Dancers in the Pine Ridge Agency, had a revelation that the Messiah was to hasten his coming, because of white interference in the dance. Now that the time was at hand, Short Bull felt that Sitting Bull ought to be present to greet the Indian Christ. Sitting Bull consulted his people, who voted that he ought to go by all means. McLaughlin viewed Sitting Bull's request for a pass as a defiance of his orders, despite the fact that at the time many Indians went off the reservation without one; Short Bull and

Kicking Bear, for example, went all the way to western Nevada and were gone six months without a pass.

McLaughlin mobilized forty-three Indian police under Lieutenant Henry Bull Head. This was his most serious mistake, if he hoped to avoid bloodshed. According to Don Russell, "The Indian police, authorized in 1878, were an Indian Bureau device for civilizing the Indian by depriving him of tribal government, thus putting an end to the power and influence of chiefs. The fact that Indian police were answerable only to the agent was in direct conflict with Indian ideas of democracy, and sending Indian police to arrest a leader of the stature of Sitting Bull was a direct challenge."

Also, there was bad blood between Lieutenant Bull Head and Catch-the-Bear, the head of Sitting Bull's personal following. Just a few months before, Bull Head had seized a bag containing Catch-the-Bear's rations, dumped the contents on the ground, and used the bag for his own rations. Catch-the-Bear warned Bull Head: "Look out in the future. I am going to get you."

On a bitterly cold and starless winter night, a party of some forty Sioux police—called Metal Breasts by other tribesmen because of their badges—converged on Sitting Bull's Grand River camp. At dawn they surrounded the chief's cabin. Bull Head burst through the door and dragged Sitting Bull from his bed. A kerosene lamp was lighted. Bull Head told Sitting Bull he was under arrest. Shave Head, a sergeant, said, "If you fight, you will be killed here."

At first Sitting Bull put up no resistance, saying "All right. Let me put on my clothes and I will go with you." Then, as the police started to manhandle him, attempting to hold him and dress him at the same time, he began to protest. One of his wives cried out, "What are all you jealous people doing here?" By now a curious crowd had gathered outside the cabin.

Tightly gripped by the Metal Breasts, Sitting Bull was dragged out into the cold. He had had enough. "I'm not going!" he shouted. When his followers heard him cry out, one of them, Catch-the-Bear, suddenly threw off his blanket and fired a rifle point-blank at Bull Head. As the police chief fell, mortally wounded, he managed to put a bullet in Sitting Bull's body. Sergeant Red Tomahawk, who had been pushing the chief, fired a shot into the old man's brain. Either shot would have been fatal. Now there was gunfire from both sides, rapid and devastating. When it was over a half hour later, fourteen people were dead: six policemen and eight of Sitting Bull's followers. Four Indian police were killed outright, besieged in the cabin, and both Lieutenant Bull Head and his second-in-command, Sergeant Shave Head, were fatally wounded.

Two messengers got through to two troops of the Eighth Cavalry under Major E. G. Fechet, camped within two miles of the proposed arrest. Fechet's men galloped up to the rescue, backed by a Gatling rapid-fire gun and a breech-loading steel Hotchkiss gun. Major Fechet reported that "The Indians fell back from every point upon the approach of the troops, not showing any desire to engage in hostile action against the soldiers." One can hardly blame them for falling back, given Fechet's armament, and in any event, the Sioux hostility was directed only against the hated Indian police.

And so it unfolded almost as if Sitting Bull had planned it that way. Perhaps he had tired of the battle. Perhaps he knew he could not defy the prophecy of the meadowlark, that he was bound to die at the hands of his own people, and was resigned to his destiny.

By a strange twist of fate, when the shooting started, Sitting Bull's horse thought it was the cue for his Wild West act and began going through his routine. With bullets flying all around, he sat down in the middle of the battleground and raised one hoof in the air. The Indian police were terrified, supposing that Sitting Bull's spirit had possessed the horse. Onlookers thought he might be performing the Ghost Dance—the dance to raise the dead—but soon he stopped and walked away from the scene of the tragedy. Unhurt, the horse was ridden to Fort Yates with the news of Sitting Bull's death. There Cody recovered him, and he was ridden by the cavalry standard-bearer in the Wild West at the Columbian Exposition of 1893 in Chicago.

Cody always regretted what he considered Sitting Bull's tragic and unnecessary death. "If I could've talked to him," he said later, "it never would have happened."

In an interview with a reporter from the New York Times on March 7, 1891, Cody said that he had seen "a sister of the old chief, who was injured at the battle of Wounded Knee Creek, and is now in the hospital at Pine Ridge Agency. She says that her brother was anxious to see Cody at the time he [Cody] started to capture him, and had expressed a wish to have the long-haired paleface come for a friendly pow-wow with him. Had the Government at Washington allowed Cody to go on when he started out to take him, Sitting Bull would doubtless have come into camp without trouble."

All this is speculation, of course. Of Agent McLaughlin's role in this sorry business, the best that might be offered in his defense is that he meant well; he genuinely believed that the situation was too tense to be handled in any way other than by the Indian police. What is unfortunately true is that he did not understand the fervor of Sitting Bull's followers, or their resentment of his use of force in a situation that called for tact and diplomacy—the kind of intervention Miles asked Cody to undertake. Despite his claims, McLaughlin did not "have the situation well in hand," not at all.

On January 19, 1891, James McLaughlin prepared "An Account of Sitting Bull's Death" for the Office of Indian Rights Association in Philadelphia. Herbert Welsh, corresponding secretary of the association, paid special tribute to McLaughlin, calling him "a good example of what an Indian Agent should be—experienced, faithful and courageous."

In his report, McLaughlin branded the newspaper reports of the great chief's death "ridiculously absurd." His own account was painstakingly detailed, laying the blame for the unrest among the Indians on Sitting Bull's "baneful influence" on his followers. Similarly, McLaughlin exonerated the Indian police from any responsibility in their badly mismanaged treatment of Sitting Bull. "I desired to have the police make the arrest, fully believing that they could do so without bloodshed, while, in the crazed condition of the Ghost Dancers, the military could not."

McLaughlin ended his report with a list of all the dead and wounded, and concluded: "This conflict . . . is much to be regretted, yet the good resulting therefrom can scarcely be overestimated, as it has effectually eradicated all seeds of disaffection won by the Messiah Craze among the Indians of this Agency, and has also demonstrated to the people of the country the fidelity and loyalty of the Indian police in maintaining law and order on the reservation."

In his book, *My Friend, the Indian,* McLaughlin again defended his own actions and deplored those of Buffalo Bill. Some critics suggested that Cody's intervention was nothing but a publicity stunt for his show—but there were no reporters with him when he set out to meet with Sitting Bull; in fact, this episode was one of the most poorly reported in Buffalo Bill's career.

McLaughlin spoke of the "ridiculously absurd" press reports of Sitting Bull's death. The New York *Herald,* in a dispatch from the Standing Rock Agency on December 16, 1890, implied that "there was . . . cruel as it may seem, a complete understanding from the Commanding Officer to the Indian Police that the slightest attempt to rescue the old medicine man should be a signal to send Sitting Bull to the Happy Hunting Ground." If there was such an understanding, and it is highly doubtful, it was badly botched.

Even after his death, Sitting Bull was not allowed to rest in peace. Loved and hated in equal measure, his body was not buried with the dead of the Indian police. It was deemed wise not to give the old chief a public funeral. Instead, his body was buried just as it came in to the Fort Yates carpenter shop, wrapped in a blanket frozen stiff with blood. According to J. F. Waggoner, the soldier detailed to make Sitting Bull's coffin, "He was not scalped. He had seven bullet wounds in his body, and his jaw was around under his left ear. He was a big man; he filled that box chock-a-block. They had to sit on the lid to close it. The lid was not nailed down."

Waggoner and another man held up the coffin lid while "five gallons of chloride of lime were poured into the box, and on top of that a suitable amount of muriatic acid." Then the lid was nailed down and the box lowered into a grave at a corner of the Post Cemetery. In this manner, like a felon, the great chief Sitting Bull was buried—among his enemies, not his friends.

For some time there was only a wooden marker at his grave, with the simple inscription:

Sitting Bull
Died Dec. 15, 1890

The wooden marker was ultimately replaced by an iron railing, a cement slab, and a modest marble tombstone with the words:

SITTING BULL
Died
Dec. 15, 1890
Chief of the
Hunkpapa
Sioux

In 1953, according to Don Russell, relatives kidnaped his remains and reburied them at Mobridge, South Dakota, on the Standing Rock Reservation—ironically, quite near the town of McLaughlin.

Sitting Bull's death may have been the climax of the Sioux wars, but it was not the denouement. That came before the new year was rung in—at a place known as Wounded Knee Creek.

McLaughlin was wrong in claiming that all the seeds of Indian dissatisfaction had been eradicated with the death of Sitting Bull—that was far from accurate. In fact, the killing of Sitting Bull very nearly provoked the general Indian war it was designed to prevent. News of Sitting Bull's death sent shock waves across the reservations. Some of the chief's followers were frightened and headed for the Standing Rock Agency to surrender. Others fled to the Badlands, where other frightened and rebellious Indians were already hiding out.

About a hundred of the fugitive Sioux headed for the camp of an aging Minneconjou chief named Big Foot, an ardent Ghost Dance believer. For some time Big Foot had been gathering followers at a small village near the mouth of Deep Creek on the Cheyenne River. Big Foot's band had grown in size as the Ghost Dance craze had spread, and the army had taken notice. His camp was kept under close watch by a small party of cavalrymen under Lieutenant Colonel Edwin V. Sumner Jr. On December 17 the War Department issued an order for Big Foot's arrest, as one of the "fomenters of disturbances."

When the news of Sitting Bull's death reached Big Foot, he prepared to break camp, telling Colonel Sumner that the Indians were preparing to proceed eastward to the Cheyenne River Agency, where they would spend the winter. Big Foot told Sumner that his intentions were entirely peaceful, that he had welcomed the Sioux fugitives into his ranks only in order to lead them back to the reservation. Sumner, believing that the chief was sincere, allowed the band to keep their weapons—in retrospect, a costly mistake.

On his way toward the Pine Ridge, South Dakota, agency, Big Foot came down with pneumonia and began to hemorrhage. He was placed in a wagon, wrapped in blankets. On December 28 the Indians sighted four troops of cavalry approaching. At once, Big Foot ordered a white flag run up over his wagon. The troops were from Custer's old regiment, the Seventh, led by Major Samuel Whitside. Whitside told Big Foot that his orders were to take him to a cavalry camp on Wounded Knee Creek. Whitside then intended to seize the Indians' weapons, but was dissuaded by his half-breed scout, John Shangreau, who argued that disarming them might precipitate a fight. It was finally decided that Big Foot and his band would be taken to Wounded Knee and there disarmed.

Once bivouacked at Wounded Knee, the Indians were issued rations and provided with shelter. Whitside stationed two troops of cavalry to guard the Sioux tepees and placed two Hotchkiss guns on top of a rise overlooking the camp. The barrels of these guns, which could hurl explosive charges for more than two miles, were positioned to rake the full length of the Indian tepees. During the night Whitside was relieved by Colonel James W. Forsyth, who now commanded the Seventh Cavalry. Along with the balance of his troops, Forsyth set up another two Hotchkiss guns. Then he and his officers settled down with a keg of whiskey to celebrate the capture of the notorious Big Foot. Meanwhile, the chief lay in his tepee, too ill to sleep, while his people worried that the palefaces meant to take revenge for the Little Big Horn.

"The following morning there was a bugle call," said Wasumaza, one of Big Foot's warriors. "Then I saw the soldiers mounting their horses and surrounding us. It was announced that all men should come to the center for a talk and that after the talk they were to move on to the Pine Ridge

Agency. Big Foot was brought out of his tepee and sat in front of his tent and the older men were gathered around him and sitting right near him in the center."

After issuing hardtack for breakfast, Colonel Forsyth told the Indians that they were now to be disarmed. "They called for guns and arms," White Lance said, "so all of us gave the guns and they were stacked up in the center." Apparently the troopers were not satisfied with the number of guns surrendered, so they began to search the tepees, bringing out axes, knives, and tent stakes. Still not satisfied, the soldiers ordered the Indians to remove their blankets and be searched for weapons. The Indians were angry about this invasion of their privacy, but only one, the medicine man Yellow Bird, protested. He danced a few Ghost Dance steps and chanted in Sioux: "The bullets will not go toward you. The prairie is large and the bullets will not go toward you."

According to Captain Edward Godfrey, who recorded what happened, "The medicine man was exhorting the warriors that the ghost shirt would protect them from the bullets of the soldiers. Major Forsyth forbid him from exhorting, and the medicine man threw a handful of dust into the air."

Accounts of what happened next vary; there is general agreement that an Indian fired, though not necessarily with intent to kill or wound anyone. One deaf Indian, Black Coyote, apparently meant to put his gun down but was manhandled by a trooper; right after he was spun around, there was a shot. At least one Indian, Turning Hawk, accused Black Coyote of firing the shot, and said that he was "a crazy man, a young man of very bad influence and in fact a nobody."

In any event, wild and indiscriminate firing broke out. The Hotchkiss guns opened up, firing point-blank into the tepees, raking the Indian camp with shrapnel and killing men, women, and children alike. In the first few seconds the volleys of carbine fire were deafening, and the air was filled with powder smoke. Big Foot was one of the first to fall; soon dozens lay dead or dying on the frozen ground. The carnage was devastating. When it was over, according to historian Dee Brown, "153 were known dead, but many of the wounded crawled away to die afterward. One estimate placed the dead at very nearly three hundred of the original 350 men, women, and children in the camp. The soldiers lost twenty-five dead and thirty-nine wounded." Since the Indians had few weapons, the military dead were probably killed by their own bullets or shrapnel—what has become known as "friendly fire."

Because a blizzard was heading toward Wounded Creek, the dead were left where they had fallen. When they were found by burial parties after the storm had abated, their bodies were frozen into grotesque, twisted shapes. The Indians who were still alive were gathered up, loaded into wagons, and carried into Pine Ridge, where they were left lying in the open wagons in the bitter cold while a hapless army officer looked for shelter.

The army sought ways to turn this disgraceful episode into a heroic feat of arms, calling the massacre a "battle," as was the custom during the Indian Wars. Few were deceived. Hastening to the scene from Chicago, General Miles declared the incident "a most abominable, criminal military blunder and a horrible massacre of women and children."

One survivor, Black Elk, recalled: "I did not know how much was ended. When I look back from the high hill of my old age, I can still see the butchered women and children lying heaped and scattered all along the crooked gulch as plain as when I saw them with eyes still young. And I can see that something else died there in the bloody mud, and was buried in the blizzard. A people's dream died there. It was a beautiful dream. . . ."

Buffalo Bill was not present at the Wounded Knee massacre, although he later reenacted it for the Wild West and in a motion picture. A voucher dated February 28, 1891, shows that he was paid $505.60 as "reimbursement of expenses in complying with order by Gen. Miles." After Miles's order had been rescinded by President Harrison, Cody had returned to his home in North Platte. He had been commissioned a brigadier general as aide-de-camp on the staff of Governor John M. Thayer of Nebraska on November 23, 1889, and on January 6, 1891, Thayer issued an order to Cody. He was to proceed to the scene of the Indian troubles and communicate with General Miles. He was also to call on Brigadier General L. W. Colby, the commanding general of the Nebraska National Guard, and inquire about the probability of the Indians "breaking through the cordon of regular troops. Your superior knowledge of Indian character and mode of warfare, may enable you to make suggestions of importance. All officers of the State Troops, and all others, will please extend to you every courtesy."

As Don Russell interpreted Cody's "special service," it was to act as a liaison between the National Guard and Miles's troops, to prevent any irresponsible action on the part of some local officer that might set off the general war Miles was trying to avoid.

Cody found all quiet along the Nebraska front and traveled on to the Pine Ridge Agency, where he joined Major Burke and the Wild West show Indians. The Indians had all been questioned about the pay, clothing, food, and general warfare while they had been abroad, and all spoke highly of Cody; not one made a complaint. Said the Lincoln (Nebraska)

Journal: "This is a pretty effectual denial of the various charges lodged against Buffalo Bill and his managers."

On January 11, only a few days after General Cody received his orders from Governor Thayer, General Miles announced the end of the campaign, with a commendation addressed to Brigadier General W. F. Cody: "I am glad to inform you that the entire body of Indians are now camped here (within a mile and a half). They show every disposition to comply with the orders of the authorities. Nothing but an accident can prevent peace from being re-established, and it will be our ambition to make it of a permanent character. I feel that the State troops can now be withdrawn with safety, and desire through you to express to them my thanks for the confidence they have given your people in their isolated homes."

The Indians formally surrendered on January 16, 1891, giving up nineteen leaders as hostages. On that day General Miles reviewed his troops, the largest army assembly since the Civil War, in company with Buffalo Bill. More than twenty years had passed since Cody had scouted out of Fort McPherson; it was quite fitting that he should be there at the finale. It was his last service for the government, though with his Wild West he would continue to be an unofficial American ambassador of goodwill for many years.

Now he was "General" Cody. Shortly after he was commissioned, one of his show Indians called to pay his respects and asked: "You big general now, Bill?"

"Yes, I'm a general now," Cody replied.

"Big general same as Crook, Terry?"

"No, my commission is in the Nebraska National Guard."

"M'lish!" exclaimed the Indian. "Oh, hell!"

Whether that Indian's scorn of the National Guard had anything to do with Cody's reluctance to wear his general's star, he did not take much advantage of his higher rank; perhaps he felt uncomfortable with it and was accustomed only to being addressed as "Colonel." On March 30, 1895, Nebraska governor Silas A. Holcomb issued a new commission to Cody as aide-de-camp on the staff of the commander in chief of the Nebraska forces, this time with the rank of colonel. The demotion may have been at Cody's request; at any rate, he reverted to the title of "Colonel" from that point on.

Back in North Platte, he arranged a truce of sorts at the ranch, and Al and Julia Goodman remained in charge—for now at least. Cody, at Scout's Rest, had signed on most of his riders for the show when Major Burke's telegram arrived, telling him of the successful hiring of the Indians. Shortly afterward, the major himself arrived, and the following day the *Telegraph* announced that "a display of horsemanship will be tendered

Buffalo Bill Cody, c. 1890. (Buffalo Bill Historical Center, Cody, Wyoming)

by the boys before they leave for Europe that is seldom equalled and never surpassed in any country." The riders "already here are famous in their respective districts and those who are to come are equally good."

Under Al Goodman's management the ranch had become so well known for its good horses that buyers came from all over the country to bid for them.

Early in 1891, Cody wrote the Butlers two letters, which are now preserved at the Garst Museum in Greenville, Ohio. In a letter of January 19, addressed to Annie, he spoke of his activities in the Sitting Bull affair. He also mentioned an erroneous report of Annie's death in Buenos Aires, first published in French newspapers. The last line of the letter was cryptic: "I hear V.C. is in N.Y." This was probably a reference to Cody's former friend and protégée Viola Katherine Clemons, whom he had met in 1887 when the Wild West first played London and with whom he was rumored to have had an affair.

In his second letter, dated January 27, from Cody to Frank Butler, he acknowledged receipt of a registered packet containing letters from "V.C." and asked the Butlers "if you have any more send them along. . . . She is to[o] swift & dishonest for me—Those were all lies about her getting letters & cables from me. Would like to know what she done in London & . . . who was the favorite she smiled upon there."

When Cody first met Viola Clemons (her last name is sometimes spelled "Clemmons"), he called her "the finest looking woman in the world." Confusing her appearance with acting ability, Cody financed a tour of England for the young woman, in the play *Theodore*. He then brought Viola Clemons to the United States and backed the play *A Lady of Venice* for her. The vehicle was a flop, costing him $50,000. Viola complained because Will went bear hunting instead of spending time with her. Cody was quoted as saying "I would rather manage a million Indians than one soubrette."

One Washington, D.C., news release had reported a fight over the lovely Viola between Cody and one Fred May in Chamberlin's restaurant. Cody, who decked May, was quoted as saying that it was "just a difference of opinion between gentlemen."

In 1898 Viola Katherine Clemons married Howard Gould, whose family name was well known on Wall Street. Later, when he attempted to get a divorce, Gould accused Cody of "criminal and meretricious" behavior with Viola before their marriage. Cody threatened to sue Gould to reclaim the money he had lost on Viola's ill-fated theatrical career. At one point, Gould's attorneys came to Cody at a time when his finances were at their lowest point, offering him $50,000 if he would testify against Viola; Cody told them to get the hell out of his tent.

Whether Cody was unfaithful to his wife, Louisa, cannot be said for certain. Unlettered Buffalo Bill may have been, but he was a gentleman in every sense of the word, and in an age of chivalry, a gentleman never kissed and told, so we have only supposition to go on when it comes to his marital fidelity. He was an uncommonly attractive man, often away from home for long periods of time—the births of his children could almost be plotted by his infrequent visits home, so there can be no question of his virility. Before his marriage, and even afterward, he lived on the frontier, where the only women were usually schoolteachers, housewives, or prostitutes. As a showman, he was constantly in the company of actresses and female admirers, always exposed to temptation. It would have been highly surprising, not to say incredible, if he had *not* been unfaithful, especially given that he and Louisa were so plainly incompatible. It might be said of him what was said of Alexander Hamilton: "His right eye was a good right eye, but his left eye loved to roam."

That Louisa was aware of his wanderlust was evident in their divorce trial of 1905. She accused Cody of intimacies with a number of different women, not only with an "Olive Clemons," who resided with him in Chicago during the 1893 World's Fair, but also with Queen Victoria, the most unlikely liaison imaginable. Another possible paramour was Bessie Isbell, a press agent for the Wild West after 1900. It is known that Cody invited her to his Wyoming ranch, but the nature of their relationship is a matter of conjecture.

Annie Oakley occasionally stayed at the Cody ranch about this time, and often she would throw the glass balls that Cody shot. He had a racetrack at the ranch where the two of them practiced, getting ready for the show. Whenever Cody was at home and had time for it, there were shooting matches, either at the ranch or on the firing range at the fairgrounds. When Cody shot, it was always while riding at full gallop around the ranch racetrack; it was said that he never missed. At this time Cody made the famous shot in which he killed, with a single bullet, two swans that were lined up on the lake.

In the aftermath of the Sitting Bull episode, the nineteen prisoners of war of the Ghost Dance outbreak were sent to Fort Sheridan, Illinois. Their "punishment," according to one historian, was to be sent to Europe with Buffalo Bill's Wild West show. Although Cody had been cleared of any charges of abusing his Indians, a major roadblock had to be overcome before any Indian could travel to Europe: Indian Commissioner Morgan. As the New York *Times* reported on March 7, 1891, "when the Colonel got ready to take his Indians back to Europe, Commissioner Morgan flatly refused to permit a single red man to leave the reservation. He had been told that the Indians did not have proper surroundings abroad, and he considered it much better that they should remain on the reservation than be demoralized by foreign travel."

General Miles and Colonel Forsyth both recommended that Cody be allowed to take one hundred Indians out of the country, as the best way to prevent renewal of any troubles, but the commissioner was adamant. The matter was finally laid before Interior Secretary Noble, who overruled the commissioner, issuing an order that Cody be allowed to take as many of the Sioux Indians to Europe as he wished.

As the *Times* summarized the affair, "A fortnight hence 100 of the redskins will sail with Buffalo Bill and Commissioner Morgan, who boasted that he never attended a theatre or a circus in his life, will have to give them up to the demoralizing and degrading influences of foreign travel and contact with the civilization of the white man."

The Indians left from Philadelphia on the Red Star steamer *Switzerland* and landed at Antwerp, joining the show at Strasbourg. Among the prisoners allowed to take part in the show were Kicking Bear, Short Bull, Lone Bull, Scatter, and Revenge as well as Long Wolf, No Neck, Yankton Charley, and Black Heart—these last four peacemakers. They had all been hired not to give up their ancient ways but to put those ways, including the Ghost Dance, on public display for the entertainment of the multitudes.

"A CONGRESS OF ROUGH RIDERS"

There were major changes in store for the Wild West during the 1891 season. Nate Salsbury, who had kept the show in winter quarters in Europe while Cody was back in America dealing with Indians both warlike and pacific, had not been idle. Needing a new attraction, and fearing that they might not be able to get any Indians for the show, the general manager had returned to his original concept for the Wild West—a show that "would embody the whole subject of horsemanship." Salsbury set about signing up horsemen of as many nationalities as he could find. The idea was so popular that by 1893 the show's name had been changed to "Buffalo Bill's Wild West and Congress of Rough Riders of the World." It is not clear where the name "rough riders" came from, but Cody's use of it preceded Theodore Roosevelt's by five years. Don Russell believes it might refer to a bronco-busting term; the cowboy who had the hardest broncos to bust was called "riding the rough string." There was also an Illinois Cavalry regiment during the Civil War with that name. At any rate, the picturesque name stuck.

The full complement of Cody's show, as organized in 1891, had 640 "eating members." There were 20 German soldiers, 20 English soldiers, 20 soldiers from the United States, 12 Russian Cossacks, 6 Argentine gauchos, along with the familiar cast of characters: 20 Mexican vaqueros, 25 cowboys, 6 cowgirls, the 100 Sioux Indians, and the Cowboy Band of 37 mounted musicians. Altogether, it was a spectacular ensemble, an exhibition of horsemanship that for speed, style, and color would soon be the talk of Europe.

The 1891 tour picked up the swing through Europe that had been interrupted by Cody's trip home. Stops in Germany included Karlsruhe, Mannheim, Maxinz, Wiesbaden, Cologne, Dortmund, Duisburg, Krefeld, and Aachen. Kaiser Wilhelm II was a frequent patron of the show.

Another military offshoot of the show was the lesson in logistics it gave the German army. Buffalo Bill's Wild West had fine-tuned the organization of the show to a point where it was a model of its kind. Both overseas and in the States, it had a special railway train, making it possible to travel long distances between shows. Its payroll, maintenance, and other costs were extremely high, while the season was short. Ideally, each stop on the tour would begin with a parade and be followed by two shows—a matinee and an evening performance—sometimes three shows. Then it was on to the next stop. This required split-second timing in packing, moving, and setting up at the next stop. German officers watched these procedures with interest. "American shows," wrote Don Russell, "originated the method of unloading a train of flatcars in continuous procession by linking the cars with runways and using a single ramp at the end for bringing all vehicles to the ground in order—virtually ready for the parade. This method was applicable to the unloading of artillery and other heavy military equipment." Also, the Wild West served three meals a day to all employees, and from this practice the Germans developed their rolling kitchens.

There is no doubt that the Germans profited from the Wild West's example. Wrote Annie Oakley: "We never moved without at least forty officers of the Prussian Guard standing all about with notebooks, taking down every detail of the performance. They made minute notes on how we pitched camp—the exact number of men needed, each man's position, how long it took, how we boarded the trains and packed the horses and broke camp; every rope and bundle and kit was inspected and mapped." Given Europe's subsequent history, there is something chilling about this—American know-how applied to imperial aggression. However, there was no way of knowing how the Germans would apply this knowledge—even improve on it, with typical Teutonic efficiency.

The German army was not alone in its interest in Buffalo Bill's show; the general public, too, loved it. Translations of Buffalo Bill dime novels were published in Germany long after they were out of print in the United States, and there is considerable interest in the American West in Germany to this day. "In Germany each year," according to an article in Time magazine for June 18, 1979, "there is a three-day camp out, where Germans relive the American frontier days in full dress with almost complete historical veracity."

Queen Wilhelmina attended the show in Holland, recalling how much she had enjoyed it at Victoria's Jubilee. From Brussels, Belgium, where the company raised the American flag on the battlefield of Waterloo, the Wild West embarked at Antwerp to cross the North Sea to Grimsby. There a tour of provincial England began.

The Liverpool *Mercury* on July 7 greeted the performance as "a piece of the Wild West bodily transported to our midst. . . . It is not a show in the ordinary acceptance of the term, because the actors are each and all real characters—men who have figured not on the stage, but in real life. . . . The exhibition, moreover, is not merely entertaining, but most instructive." John Y. Nelson, Annie Oakley, Johnny Baker, and Antonio Esquivel were singled out for praise.

A special performance was staged in Manchester to benefit the survivors of the immortal Charge of the Light Brigade, the "brave six hundred" who had ridden into the Russian guns at Balaclava on October 25, 1854, during the Crimean War. Nineteen veterans of the charge, some of whom had fallen on hard times, were present, and it was a highly emotional occasion, for the Yanks as well as the British. At Cardiff, Wales, a six-day stand, September 21 to 27, brought in £10,000, nearly $50,000 in those days. Successful engagements in Bristol, Brighton, and Portsmouth followed. In Glasgow, another highlight occurred when six thousand orphans in the stands, at the sight of the Stars and Stripes, sang "Yankee Doodle."

In August a company was organized to play in theaters during the winter. The Wild West went to Glasgow, where Steele MacKaye's indoor pageant—which had been such a hit in Madison Square Garden—was revived in the East End Exhibition Building. Cody now planned a trip back home; with the show losing its stellar attraction, new acts were sorely needed. Lew Parker went to Boulogne, France, where he hired a troupe of performing elephants. When he learned that Henry Morton Stanley—of "Dr. Livingstone, I presume" fame—had arrived in Hamburg with a group of Zulus, Parker signed up thirty men and thirty women of the tribe. When they arrived in Glasgow, they were lined up opposite Cody's Indians for a photo opportunity. Broncho Bill called on the Sioux Rocky Bear to try the sign language of the plains. To everyone's astonishment, the Zulu chief not only understood but responded in a similar sign language.

Buffalo Bill had several reasons for wanting to return home just now. He complained of "feeling poorly" and of nervous strain, even though at the same time he was "shooting better than I ever did in my life." Homesick, he asked for the North Platte papers. He was angry because the newspapers in America were still attacking him for his treatment of the Indians, despite all he had done to allay criticism. Al wrote him the bad news that two of his best bulls, for which he had paid $500 apiece, had been killed by lightning.

He was concerned about the ranch itself too. In August he had written Al: "Boal is no man to run it. When you get to[o] old to work you can ride around in a buggy & look after it." He had instructed Al Goodman to build a big barn with "shelter enough to keep all our stock at home this winter." He wanted it painted white. "Then in the spring we could put a fresh coat of red paint on the Big Barn, and paint the House blue with green borders. . . . Red White & blue." He also told Al to see that "if Mrs. Cody has any grain or grass on her place to be cut, I wish you would have it done for her—if she ain't there just go over and do it for her. I often feel sorry for her," he wrote. "She is a strange woman but don't mind her—remember she is my wife—and let it go at that. If she gets cranky, just laugh at it, she can't help it." At the time, Louisa Cody lived on the 160-acre farm she had occupied since 1878.

The new barn—"the big T barn," as it was called—was built that fall. Al was also buying bulls from the best bloodlines; Cody wanted to know if he needed more money.

In November 1891 Louisa's house burned down. In *Last of the Great Scouts*, Helen Cody Wetmore wrote that in November 1890, "while Will was away at the seat of war," on his mission for General Miles, Welcome Wigwam burned down. "The little city is not equipped with much of a fire department," said Wetmore, "but a volunteer brigade held the flames in check long enough to save almost the entire contents of the house, among which were many valuable and costly souvenirs that could never be replaced. Will received a telegram announcing that his house was ablaze. . . . [His] reply was characteristic: 'Save Rosa Bonheur's picture, and the house may go to blazes.'"

The *Tribune* gives the year of the fire as 1891, which is undoubtedly correct. It was clear when the volunteers arrived that the house itself could not be saved, so people turned to and helped carry out the contents, including the piano, a heavy sideboard, and, of course, the Rosa Bonheur painting. The loss on the house was estimated at $5,000; insurance covered only $3,000 of this sum. Mrs. Cody moved into one of her other houses, and early in 1892, the Colonel returned home. In December he had written that he had "hay fever or Grippe or something." He wanted to come home soon, he said, to get to a country where he could see and feel the sun again.

As soon as Cody reached North Platte, Horton and Arta Cody Boal prevailed in their determination to manage his ranch. Al and Julia Goodman resigned and returned to Kansas. It was not likely to be a restful visit home, although at least Cody was out of public view for a while; also, there was work to be done. He needed to restock his show with more horses and replacements for the cowboy, Indian, and rough-riding acts.

While Cody was in the United States attending to his ranch and his preparations for the next season, his company remained abroad. Frank Butler spoke later of the many men in Europe who attempted to ride the bucking broncos of the Wild West, without success. A prize of $100 was offered to anyone who could stay on one of the broncs. After depositing their eyeglasses and hats, the aspirants mounted their horses—and, shortly afterward, were back on the ground again.

"We had a surprise in London, though," Butler said. "A young fellow, wearing a monocle, derby, stiff collar and carrying the indispensable cane, dropped in to ride. We trotted forth the wildest bronco we had. Our hearts went out to this young man and we had a mental picture of his immaculate appearance all deranged. He rode the animal hands down. He turned out to be a wealthy Australian ranch owner. He sent the $100 prize to a charity organization. Incidentally, he was the husband of Madame Melba, the opera singer."

Actually, Charles F. Armstrong, Nellie Melba's husband, was not Australian but British, the youngest son of Sir Andrew Armstrong of Ireland.

American newspaper reporters in Europe enjoyed describing for their readers the swift taming of the wildest horses of the Continent by Cody's rugged western cowboys. Theodore Roosevelt also rang in on the subject in his book *The Wilderness Hunter*, about his hunting exploits in the early 1880s.

"When Buffalo Bill took his cowboys to Europe," wrote Roosevelt, "they made a practice in England, France, Germany, and Italy of offering to break and ride, in their own fashion, any horse given them. They were frequently given spoiled horses from the cavalry services in the different countries through which they passed, animals with which the trained horse-breakers of the European armies could do nothing; and yet in almost all cases the cow-punchers and broncobusters with Buffalo Bill mastered these beasts as readily as they did their own western horses. At their own work of mastering and riding rough horses they could not be matched by their more civilized rivals."

Roosevelt went on to suggest that if the cowboys had tried riding to the hounds, or steeple-chasing, kinds of horsemanship alien to the West, it would have been a different story.

On May 7, 1892, with Cody on hand, feeling much rested and in greatly improved health after his sojourn at home, the Wild West opened at Earl's Court, London, the scene of its first European triumph in 1887. The artist Frederic Remington, who, along with Cody, virtually invented the Wild West with his immensely popular paintings and drawings, was in London at the time. In the September 3 issue of *Harper's Weekly*, Remington wrote, among other things: "The Tower, the Parliament, and Westminster are older institutions than Buffalo Bill's show, but when the

The Wild West show in Europe, c. 1891. (Buffalo Bill Historical Center, Cody, Wyoming)

New Zealander sits on the London Bridge and looks over his ancient manuscripts of Murray's Guide-book he is going to turn first to the Wild West. At present everyone knows where it is, from the gentleman on Piccadilly to the dirtiest coster in the remotest slum of Whitechapel. The Cabman may have to scratch his head to recall places where the traveler desires to go, but when the Wild West is asked for he gathers his reins and uncoils his whip without ceremony.

"The Wild West is a great educator," continued Remington, "and with its aggregate of wonders from the out-of-the-way places, it will represent a poetical and harmless protest against the Derby hat and the starched linen—those horrible badges of the slavery of our modern social system. . . . "

Queen Victoria was particularly eager to see the Cossacks, led by Prince Ivan Rostomov Macherdaze. Nate Salsbury, in his article "Origin of the Wild West Show," described this second "command" performance at length. The queen had indicated that she would be "highly honored" if the Wild West management would allow the Cossack riders to perform at Windsor. Since that portion of the program lasted only about twelve minutes, it did not seem worthwhile to Salsbury to go to the trouble of getting just the Cossacks there, so he decided to "do something worthy of the occasion. To this end," wrote Salsbury, "I engaged a train of cars and loaded enough of our outfit to give a representative performance, leaving enough members of the company in London to satisfy the public."

During the performance at Windsor, Salsbury remained at the queen's side, acting as "Scout, Guide and Interpreter," to explain anything she did not understand about the proceedings. When the queen asked Nate what weapon the Colonel was using, he said that it was "'the Winchester rifle, Madame, an American firearm.' 'Ah!' exclaimed the Queen, 'a very effective weapon and in very effective hands.'

"When the show was over," Salsbury continued, "the Queen requested that Cody be presented to her. . . . I sent for Cody, who came in his buckskins, and he was presented to the Queen, just before she started on her afternoon drive around the grounds of the castle. Her Majesty was very gracious to Cody, complimented him highly for the delightful afternoon she had enjoyed, and wished him good luck for the future, while presenting him with a magnificent signet ring." Salsbury was given a scarf pin set in diamonds.

Cody and Salsbury were both invited to stay for lunch, where "we compromised by another act of self-sacrifice on my part, for as Cody did not drink anything that summer, I did duty for both of us in a glass of wine." When this incident was publicized, it brought great joy to the leaders of the Salvation Army, who spread the word about Cody's abstinence.

In her journal, Victoria confided her pleasure in the show, which lasted an hour, and added: "At the conclusion of the performance, all advanced in line at a gallop and stopped suddenly. Col. Cody was brought up for me to speak to him. He is still a very handsome man, but has now got a grey beard."

The London season ended on October 12, 1892—bringing to a close a European tour that had spanned three years and four months. This tour may not have matched the 1887 season, but it was still a resounding success. After the show closed on October 12, the troupe boarded the ship *Mohawk* and arrived back in New York on October 26.

Between the rigors of mounting the show and his troubles at home, it is no wonder Buffalo Bill's beard had turned gray. Then, too, he was now in his late forties—middle age in a time when men aged faster and died earlier. However, there was no letup in his performances or his social life. In fact, the Wild West was now on the threshold of its greatest single season—the Columbian Exposition of 1893 in Chicago.

On his arrival back in America, Buffalo Bill went straight to his home in North Platte; the animals, rolling stock, and equipment for the show were sent to winter quarters in Bridgeport, Connecticut. The winter of 1892–1893 was spent getting the show ready to open at the World's Columbian Exposition the following spring. Celebrating the four-hundredth anniversary of Columbus—although a year late—it would be one of the most memorable world's fairs ever mounted. Between May 1 and October 30, 1893, more than 21 million people visited the fairgrounds. There they could admire the monumental classical architecture of the fair's "White City," laid out by Frederick Law Olmsted, the codesigner with Calvert Vaux, of New York City's Central Park. One beautiful architectural work still survives from the fabled White City, left behind after the crowds had departed as a gift to the people of the city; it is now the Chicago Museum of Science and Industry.

Fairgoers undoubtedly also dropped in at the many attractions along the Midway Plaisance, including the exotic dancer Little Egypt. On Chicago Day, October 9, 716,881 people paid admission to the fair. It is likely, Don Russell believes, that this stands as a record for ticket sales to a single place of entertainment.

Nate Salsbury had gone ahead to arrange with the exposition officials Wild West accommodations on the fairgrounds; he was denied space in the park, probably because Buffalo Bill's show did not fit in the midway, nor was it in harmony with the classical motif of the pavilions. Salsbury then leased a fifteen-acre tract between Sixty-second and Sixty-third streets, directly opposite the entrance to the fairgrounds, and hired workers to grade and landscape the area. A grandstand large enough to seat eighteen thousand people was then built on the site. Over the Wild West gateway was a pictorial banner showing Columbus on his quarterdeck emblazoned "Pilot of the Ocean, the First Pioneer," facing Buffalo Bill on horseback, "Pilot of the Prairie, the Last Pioneer." The same design appeared on the 1893 Wild West letterhead.

Buffalo Bill's Wild West and Congress of Rough Riders of the World opened on April 3, 1893, a month ahead of the exposition itself, and attracted a large crowd, despite a heavy spring downpour. It is said that there were those who thought the entrance to Buffalo Bill's Wild West was the entrance to the Columbian Exposition proper and, after seeing the show, went away satisfied. Don Russell quotes a Chicago city editor who considered the 1893 Wild West to be the greatest show he had ever seen in his life.

On opening day 130,000 people attended the fair; crowds were turned away from the Wild West. Adam Forepaugh's circus attempted to compete with Cody's show but failed to make a perceptible dent in its business.

The Wild West had played to American audiences only once since its first invasion of the Old World—in 1888—so anticipation to see the show was high. Moreover, the dispute over the mistreatment of the Indians in Cody's show—in which Cody was soundly vindicated—had turned public opinion in his favor. He was also widely acclaimed for his role in the last of the Indian Wars—by those who exaggerated the importance of that role. Americans were more than ready to applaud their great western star.

Like the crowds in Europe, the Chicago audiences enjoyed wandering around Cody's camp, which was more exotic than ever, with its Indians, cowboys, Russians, Mexicans, Arabs, French, German, English, and American soldiers to attract attention. Always open for inspection, it was, wrote one Chicago reporter, the "cleanest, coolest and most comfortable resort, as well as one of the most attractive spots in or about Chicago, and visitors would do well to get to the grounds in ample time to spend an hour strolling about and studying the life and customs of these people."

On payday the Indians, in their turn, enjoyed the attractions of the midway. Chief Standing Bear, wearing his headdress of two hundred eagle feathers, rode the giant Ferris wheel. Sioux and Cheyenne braves ate Crackerjack and drank colored soda water. At the merry-go-round, they mounted the painted horses; the engineer speeded up the turntable, and, while the steam organ played "Maggie Murphy's Home," the Indians whooped with delight.

The Chicago papers devoted many columns to describing and praising the show. Additional transportation facilities were necessary to carry "the fantastic numbers of people clamoring to get to the show." The Illinois Central, which served the South Side of Chicago, had to extend the run of its special World's Fair train, while the Chicago Elevated had to establish a station only a few feet from the entrance to the Wild West. The *Globe* summed it up with a big headline: ALL ROADS NOW SEEM TO LEAD TO BUFFALO BILL'S BIG SHOW.

Indeed, twenty-five thousand people a day found their way to the Wild West, many coming so often that the ticket sellers and takers became familiar with their faces. When the Nebraska building opened on the fairgrounds, Governor Lorenzo Crounse arrived in Chicago to ride in the parade, and Buffalo Bill rode with him. A reporter described Cody as "crusted with gold lace and, with the genius he usually displays in such matters, usurped a large share of the governor's glory and accepted the plaudits of the crowd with engaging candor."

Amy Leslie of the Chicago *Daily News* spent hours in Cody's tent, visiting the Colonel, his daughters Irma and Arta, and various members of the company.

"No such an engaging story-teller as Buffalo Bill figures in history or romance," Leslie wrote. "He is quiet, rich in humor and mellow in his style as a bottle of old port . . . and not a dozen men I know have his splendid magnetism, keen appreciation and happy originality. He sticks to truth mainly and is more intensely beguiling than the veriest maker of fiction."

How far the Colonel may have wandered from the truth in this interview can only be surmised—particularly when the subject was horse-racing. At forty-seven, Cody was still vigorous, his voice as powerful as ever, and his shooting as accurate, even though his hair was thinning now and quite gray.

"No other exhibition," declared the *News* on June 17, "has received the plaudits of the people as has Buffalo Bill's Wild West." And on June 18 the Chicago *Post* said that "No other entertainment in the city can or does accommodate the half that daily visit the Wild West." The *Dispatch* observed that "those portions of the program most familiar to the public, . . . the attack on the Deadwood stage, the Pony Express, the Indian encampment, meet with the heartiest approbation and applause. The new troop of Arab horsemen, the Cossacks and cavalry of the four great armies of the world, in a grand international musical drill, were magnificent." Added the *Tribune*: "The dash and vim of Buffalo Bill's horsemen at the Wild West exhibition keep that place of amusement easily in the fore-front of the World's Fair attractions. Up to date the attendance has increased steadily and there seems to be no reason why Colonel Cody should not duplicate his London success." Back in North Platte, the papers reported that "our people are glad to learn that Buffalo Bill is draw-ing immense crowds."

Not one performance was canceled during the 186-day season. At first, the show was dark on Sunday, but because of public demand, the Wild West finally ran a schedule of two performances a day, seven days a week. To appreciate the scope of the spectacle offered by Cody and Sals-bury, it helps to look at the "Programme" prepared for distribution at the 1893 Exposition (see page 371).

The 1893 "Historical Sketches, & Programme" was actually a book of some sixty-five pages, "COPYRIGHTED BY CODY AND SALSBURY, CHICAGO, ILL., 1893" and selling for a dime. Beginning with a "SALU-TATORY" by Major Burke ("the performance, while in no wise partaking of the nature of a 'circus,' will be at once new, startling, and instructive"), the book included biographies of the major performers; tributes from army officers; episodes from Cody's career on the frontier; descriptions of the Wild West's adventures in Europe; tributes to the Indians; and informa-tion about the Cossacks and the gauchos. The text was illustrated with photographs, drawings, and paintings, and was bound in a full-color cover. There was nothing in the least halfhearted about the Wild West's con-summate mastery of public relations. Programs of this nature and length became staples of the show in its subsequent tours.

Of the show Indians who performed at the Wild West that season, the most famous was Rain-in-the-Face. After Sitting Bull's death, Rain had become the most celebrated survivor of the Little Bighorn; it was he who tomahawked George Custer's brother Tom. Another unique attraction was

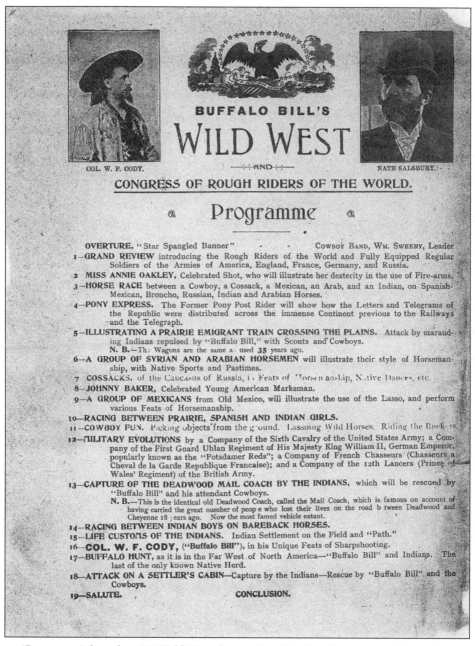

BUFFALO BILL'S

WILD WEST

COL. W. F. CODY. —∵ AND ∵— NATE SALSBURY.

CONGRESS OF ROUGH RIDERS OF THE WORLD.

❦ Programme ❦

OVERTURE, "Star Spangled Banner" - - COWBOY BAND, WM. SWEENY, Leader

1—**GRAND REVIEW** introducing the Rough Riders of the World and Fully Equipped Regular Soldiers of the Armies of America, England, France, Germany, and Russia.

2 MISS ANNIE OAKLEY, Celebrated Shot, who will illustrate her dexterity in the use of Fire-arms.

3—**HORSE RACE** between a Cowboy, a Cossack, a Mexican, an Arab, and an Indian, on Spanish-Mexican, Broncho, Russian, Indian and Arabian Horses.

4—**PONY EXPRESS.** The Former Pony Post Rider will show how the Letters and Telegrams of the Republic were distributed across the immense Continent previous to the Railways and the Telegraph.

5—**ILLUSTRATING A PRAIRIE EMIGRANT TRAIN CROSSING THE PLAINS.** Attack by marauding Indians repulsed by "Buffalo Bill," with Scouts and Cowboys.
   N. B.—The Wagons are the same as used **35** years ago.

6—**A GROUP OF SYRIAN AND ARABIAN HORSEMEN** will illustrate their style of Horsemanship, with Native Sports and Pastimes.

7 COSSACKS, of the Caucasus of Russia, in Feats of Horsemanship, Native Dances, etc.

8—**JOHNNY BAKER**, Celebrated Young American Marksman.

9—**A GROUP OF MEXICANS** from Old Mexico, will illustrate the use of the Lasso, and perform various Feats of Horsemanship.

10—**RACING BETWEEN PRAIRIE, SPANISH AND INDIAN GIRLS.**

11—COWBOY FUN. Picking objects from the ground. Lassoing Wild Horses. Riding the Buckers

12—**MILITARY EVOLUTIONS** by a Company of the Sixth Cavalry of the United States Army; a Company of the First Guard Uhlan Regiment of His Majesty King William II, German Emperor, popularly known as the "Potsdamer Reds"; a Company of French Chasseurs (Chasseurs a Cheval de la Garde Republique Francaise); and a Company of the 12th Lancers (Prince of Wales' Regiment) of the British Army.

13—**CAPTURE OF THE DEADWOOD MAIL COACH BY THE INDIANS**, which will be rescued by "Buffalo Bill" and his attendant Cowboys.
   N. B.—This is the identical old Deadwood Coach, called the Mail Coach, which is famous on account of having carried the great number of people who lost their lives on the road between Deadwood and Cheyenne 18 years ago. Now the most famed vehicle extant.

14—**RACING BETWEEN INDIAN BOYS ON BAREBACK HORSES.**

15—**LIFE CUSTOMS OF THE INDIANS.** Indian Settlement on the Field and "Path."

16—**COL. W. F. CODY**, ("Buffalo Bill"), in his Unique Feats of Sharpshooting.

17—**BUFFALO HUNT**, as it is in the Far West of North America—"Buffalo Bill" and Indians. The last of the only known Native Herd.

18—**ATTACK ON A SETTLER'S CABIN**—Capture by the Indians—Rescue by "Buffalo Bill" and the Cowboys.

19—**SALUTE.**   **CONCLUSION.**

"Programme" from the 1893 Wild West show at the Columbia Exposition in Chicago. (Library of Virginia, Richmond, Virginia)

Sitting Bull's cabin—which had been dismantled, shipped from Fort Yates to Chicago, and reassembled. Customers of the Wild West could see where the old medicine man had lived out his last days and examine the logs pocked with bullet holes.

Annie Oakley, who was always the first performer to appear, after the Grand Review, designed thirty-five different costumes for the long Chicago summer, according to Isabelle Sayers. "She enjoyed being on location for the season, which made it much easier to care for guns and wardrobe. Her brightly carpeted tent was a rendezvous for the children of the company and headquarters for visiting friends. No queen received more admirers in court that summer than did little 'Missie.'" A bed of flowers bordered her tent, primroses and geraniums flanked by tall-blooming hollyhocks. Inside the tent were her books and pictures, her couch and rocking chairs, her guns and her banjo, her embroidery stand and dressing table. Wherever Annie traveled, she took her creature comforts with her and set up a cozy home on the road.

"She welcomes us royally," wrote Amy Leslie in the *Daily News*. "Her tent is a bower of comfort and taste. A bright Axminster carpet, cougar skins and buckskin trappings all about in artistic confusion. She has a glass of wine awaiting and a word of welcome." Apparently Annie had loosened up a bit from the days when she only drank Buffalo Bill's lemonade and beer if someone else was picking up the tab.

At the end of July, Carter Harrison, Chicago's mayor, proclaimed a day's outing for the poor children of the city and asked fair officials to admit the kids free. The officials denied the request. Major Burke was quick to seize on the opportunity. The Wild West offered every child in Chicago who could not otherwise afford it a free ride on the Illinois Central to Sixty-third Street, a free pass to the Wild West grounds, a free seat in the arena, and free candy and ice cream. It was called "Waif's Day," and fifteen thousand children showed up to marvel at the Wild West and cheer it wildly.

The outstanding event of the 1893 season was the Thousand-Mile Cowboy Race, a publicity bonanza for the Wild West. The previous winter, in the western cowtown of Chadron, Nebraska, a group of stockmen got together and talked about organizing a thousand-mile horse race. The intention was to break a French endurance record of fifty miles a day on horseback for twenty days—and, incidentally, to prove that the speed and stamina of the western horse was the greatest in the world. Someone realized that the distance from Chadron to Chicago was almost exactly a thousand miles; why not run the race so that it finishes in Chicago at the site of the Columbian Exposition? Enthusiasm for the idea was immediate and widespread. Chadron put up a purse of $1,000 for the winner of the race; Colonel Cody, recognizing a surefire publicity angle, added another $500 and a fine saddle—provided that the finish be at the Wild West arena.

The cowboy race was to be run in thirteen days, with an average distance covered each day of seventy-seven miles. Every rider was allowed two horses, which he could ride alternately, leading the other. The riders were to register themselves and their horses at stated checkpoints along the road in Nebraska, Iowa, and Illinois—and each rider was to come into Chicago riding one of the horses he started with.

To ride seventy-seven miles a day is nothing extraordinary—in his Pony Express days and as a scout, Cody himself surpassed that more than once. However, to do it for thirteen days straight would tax both horses and riders to the extreme. Humane societies protested the race, as cruelty to the animals; Governor Altgeld of Illinois issued a proclamation against it. All objections were overcome when the humane societies were asked to supervise the race.

Several men, among them John Berry, a Chicago & North Western Railway civil engineer, were delegated to lay out the route and set up the checkpoints. On a sunny June day in 1893, the racers lined up in front of the Baline Hotel in Chadron, and the starting gun was fired. According to Don Russell, there were ten entrants, of whom five finished. Richard Walsh's account lists eight men in the race; others say nine. One of the riders was Doc Middleton, Nebraska's most famous bandit, who had formerly been in the Wild West. Middleton rode for the honor of Chadron but gave up at Dixon, Illinois, when one of his horses was injured. It is generally agreed that John Berry finished first, riding up to Buffalo Bill's show entrance at 9:30 on the morning of June 27, after thirteen days and sixteen hours on the road. Joe Gillespie, a Chadron stock farmer, was second. Berry's eligibility to compete in the race had been contested because he was one of the men who drew up the route, but he rode anyway. Although he had come in ahead of the pack, one source reported that Berry, after the starting gun was fired, had gone to the Chadron depot, sent his horses ahead by express, and rode the train for the first hundred miles. As a result of this violation of the rules, he was given only the saddle.

The $1,500 purse was divided among the four others who finished the race, with George "Stub" Jones awarded the largest share for being the fastest. It's not really important who won the race, however; as the first horse race of its kind ever staged in the United States, it established the superiority of the tough western horse over the European breed once and for all.

And it brought additional customers to the Wild West—not that Cody needed the flamboyant publicity. Buffalo Bill's show was all action from the moment when he swept off his sombrero and announced, in his booming voice, "Ladies and Gentlemen, permit me to introduce to you a Congress of Rough Riders of the World." The run of the Deadwood coach was guaranteed to thrill audiences. The Pony Express ride in Cody's show was far more successful—more profitable at any rate—than the original had been. In the numbers called "Cowboy Fun" and "A group of Mexicans from Old Mexico, will illustrate the use of the lasso," the origins of rodeo were established.

One unfortunate episode during that season further widened the rift between Cody and his wife, Louisa. Mrs. Cody came to Chicago to pay her husband a surprise visit and, as is frequently the case in matters of that kind, was herself surprised. She went to his hotel and inquired for Mr. Cody and was told that she would be shown to "Mr. and Mrs. Cody's suite." Russell wrote that "Lulu, having heard rumors of her husband's association with one 'Olive Clemons,'" and, though she found no Olive Clemons "at the house where he lived during the show season . . . wrecked the place on general principles."

To make amends, after Cody put the show up for the winter in November and went home to North Platte, he presented his wife with a deed to the finest residence in town—the McKay mansion. Nothing apparently mollified Lulu more when she was upset than another piece of real estate.

The house, originally owned by the North Platte silk merchant and dry goods store owner George McKay, Nellie Snyder Yost tells us, "was an ornate three-storied affair with inlaid parquet floors and a fine, open stairway ascending from the front parlor to a wide landing with a window above it, then on up to the spacious, many-bedroomed second floor." This house became the new Welcome Wigwam, and Louisa lived there for the next sixteen years.

While Buffalo Bill's Wild West was turning away thousands of World's Fair visitors for lack of space, another important event in the history of the real West was taking place in Chicago. In the second week of July 1893, the American Historical Association met with the World's Historical Congress in morning and evening sessions at the Chicago Art Institute. On Tuesday evening, July 11, thirty-two-year-old Professor Frederick J. Turner of the University of Wisconsin read a paper entitled "The Significance of the Frontier in American History."

"Up to our own day," said Turner, "American history has been in large degree the history of the colonization of the Great West. . . . In this advance, the frontier is the outer edge of the wave—the meeting point between savagery and civilization." The whisper of traffic along Michigan Avenue provided an undertone to Turner's words.

Professor Turner continued: "Since the days when the fleet of Columbus sailed into the waters of the New World, America has been another name for opportunity, and the people of the United States have taken their tone from the incessant expansion which has not only been open but has even been forced upon them. . . . And now four centuries from the discovery of America, at the end of a hundred years of life under the Constitution, the frontier has gone, and with its going has closed the first period of American history."

It is a virtual certainty that Buffalo Bill was unaware of Frederick Turner's paper; nor was Turner one of the crowds thronging daily to see the Wild West, though he and the other historians were invited. But there was a link between them nonetheless, a link more profound than their presence at the same time in the city of Chicago.

In his essay "Frederick Jackson Turner and Buffalo Bill," Richard White writes: "The two master narrators of American westering had come together at the greatest of American celebrations with compelling stories to tell. . . . Turner and Buffalo Bill told separate stories; indeed, each contradicted the other in significant ways. Turner's history was one of free land, the essentially peaceful occupation of a largely empty continent, and the creation of a unique American identity. Cody's Wild West told of violent conquest, of wresting the continent from the American Indian peoples who occupied the land. Although fictional, Buffalo Bill's story claimed to represent a history, for like Turner, Buffalo Bill worked with real historical events and real historical figures.

"These stories," White continues, "demanded different lead characters; the true pioneer for Turner was the farmer; for Buffalo Bill, the scout. . . . As different as the two narratives were, they led to remarkably similar conclusions. Both declared the frontier over."

In the opening paragraph of the Wild West's 1893 program, there is this line: "*This last* [the existence of a wild, "rapidly expanding frontier"] *while perfectly true when written (1883), is at present inapplicable, so fast does law and order progress and pervade the Grand West.*"

It is interesting that in later years, Cody would state that he sometimes felt he had stood alone "between savagery and civilization," a patent but perhaps forgivable exaggeration of his actual contribution to the settlement of the West.

Turner's Chicago paper, which employed arresting literary imagery in combination with incisive reasoning, led to what came to be known as the "frontier school" of historiography. Turner held that the American character was decisively shaped by conditions on the frontier, which evoked such qualities as "coarseness and strength . . . acuteness and inquisitiveness, that practical, inventive turn of mind . . . restless, nervous energy . . . that buoyancy and exuberance which comes with freedom."

Buffalo Bill's Wild West program, on the other hand, celebrated the rifle and the bullet—the bullet as "the pioneer of civilization."

By the end of September, with autumn in the air, the Columbian Exposition was preparing to shut down, having played host to 21 million visitors. From across America came reports of unrest, labor strife, lockouts, economic disruption. A severe financial crisis in England and the United States in 1890 led to a stock market panic in 1893, followed by widespread bank failures and a severe depression. Thousands of firms were suddenly bankrupt; one out of every four American railroads passed into the hands of receivers. On one September day in Chicago, twenty-two thousand people showed up at the Kopperl relief agency. Even as far west as Denver there was poverty and homelessness. It was a crisis that would not be equaled in severity until the Great Depression, almost exactly forty years later.

In Massillon, Ohio, Jacob Coxey, a self-made businessman, proposed that the federal government launch a $500 million relief program; the following year he would lead a march of unemployed people—never more than five hundred—to the national capital. This was Coxey's Army, so-called, sometimes referred to as the Commonweal of Christ. This "petition in boots" ended ignominiously when Coxey and a number of his followers were arrested for trespassing on public property.

In Chicago's Jackson Park at the end of October, the sunset gun boomed its last salute and all the exposition flags came down. (They came down half-staff because Mayor Carter Harrison had been shot three days earlier by an angry citizen.) "Within a few months," wrote author Walter Havighurst in *Annie Oakley of the Wild West*, "Chicago would be paralyzed by the great railway strike. Governor John Peter Altgeld, who as a young Chicago lawyer had drawn up the partnership of Cody and Salsbury in 1883, would refuse to muster Illinois troops to protect trains from strikers' violence. Then President Cleveland would order two thousand federal troops to Chicago. So in 1894 the Seventh Cavalry, Custer's regiment, would ride through the streets of Chicago, throwing a guard around the railroad shops and terminals. General Miles at the head of his men might recall his meeting with Sitting Bull on the plains of the Yellowstone and his pursuit of Geronimo through the harsh valleys of Arizona. Hearing the troops sing 'Garry Owen' while protecting the property of the Pullman Company and the New York Central, he would have his own thoughts about the passing of the frontier."

It had been a fabulous season for Cody and company. The Wild West partners were able to clear nearly $1 million profit from the 1893 exhibition in Chicago, a record box office take for the show. When Cody returned to North Platte, the local band and practically everyone in town was waiting for him at the train station. He complimented the band on its playing but suggested that they might sound better if they had new uniforms. "I want each man measured for a new outfit, the best possible, and send the bill to Buffalo Bill." He also paid off the mortgages of five North Platte churches. As always, Cody was prodigal with his money; one resident recalled that Cody came home with "barrels of money, and it was good for a five for a kid just to open the door to Guy Laing's saloon for him."

Nellie Snyder Yost said that one old-timer claimed Bill also bought bloomer outfits for the North Platte girls' drill team and presented every saloonkeeper in the city with a fine gold watch and chain. Before the year was out, he would also invest many thousands of dollars in a Duluth printing plant, a cereal company, and a Wyoming reclamation project.

In July, while the Wild West was in Chicago, his sister Helen, whom he called Nellie, married Hugh Wetmore, editor of the Duluth *Press*. At Helen's request, Cody bought the paper for the newlyweds and put up a fine new brick building to house it.

Earlier that year Cody had discovered Alexander Majors, the old employer of his youthful teamster and Pony Express days, now impoverished and living in Denver. The old man was attempting to write his memoirs. Cody took the manuscript to Prentiss Ingraham, dime novel biographer, and paid Ingraham to edit the book. He also paid $750 to have the book printed. As *Seventy Years on the Frontier*, the book was published in Chicago that summer, and sold at the show grounds. The profits all went to Majors.

As for the cereal company, Cody and Dr. Frank Powell had been associated in a number of business enterprises, most of them having to do with patent medicines. Powell had also appeared in the Wild West as a marksman and had accompanied his friend on Cody's abortive trip to "arrest" Sitting Bull. Now the two men went into the manufacture of a roasted bran coffee substitute in La Crosse, Wisconsin, where Dr. Powell occasionally resided, and where Cody sometimes visited and also bought property. At one time the Colonel owned part of Barrons Island in La Crosse. An early incarnation of Postum or Sanka, the brew was called "Panamilt." The partners hoped to sell huge quantities of it to the Mormons, who did not drink coffee. In August Will wrote to Julia, then living in Denver, and urged her to try his new "coffee" and let him know what she thought of it. "Its creating a great excitement already we are getting orders faster than we can make it," he wrote. "And we are going to start a big factory or Mill where we can turn out thousands of pounds daily.

I own one half interest in it. I am ashamed to tell you how cheap we can make it."

Cody and Powell were also involved in the distribution of a nostrum known as White Beaver's Cough Cream, the Great Lung Healer, selling for fifty cents a bottle. Its advertising claimed that it was made from ancient Indian herb preparations and would cure almost any respiratory ailment. Powell always insisted that he was a member of the Beaver clan of the Seneca through his mother, who was of Iroquois ancestry, and had been given the name White Beaver by the Sioux. Be that as it may, neither the coffee substitute nor the lung healer, while they may have prospered for a brief while, brought Cody the riches he hoped for. In fact, at the end of 1893, thanks to his extravagances, he was already cash-poor—and Panamilt had proved a costly failure.

In 1893, two years after applying for a patent on his Kinetograph, a primitive movie camera, Thomas Edison built the first movie studio. It was a black tar-paper building mounted on a swiveling mechanism, which made it possible to turn the entire structure to catch the strongest rays of sunlight while filming. On May 8, 1894, Buffalo Bill and some of the Sioux braves from the Wild West were filmed before the Kinetograph—as was Annie Oakley, who performed some of the shooting feats that had made her famous.

The films were viewed in a Kinetoscope. Each one ran only eighty seconds and cost a nickel to see, whence came the term "Nickelodeon." A store might have rows of Kinetoscopes, each with a different offering; the public flocked to see these crude motion pictures.

Under Al Goodman's management, the North Platte ranch had been at least self-supporting if not profitable most of the time, but, under Horton Boal's aegis, Scout's Rest suffered, as Cody had feared. Nor could Boal get along with his neighbors as Al and Julia Goodman had done. Although Scout's Rest was the place where Cody went to recharge his batteries, so to speak, to rest from his strenuous show seasons and let down his hair, his thoughts had begun to turn even farther west—to Wyoming.

Cody's work as a scout and leader of hunting parties had taken him often into the gloriously scenic Bighorn country of Wyoming, which he believed was ripe for development. The 1890s were a time of increasing travel by Americans in search of new experiences and entertainments; Cody, looking to the future, saw great possibilities for anyone who could provide reliable transportation and lodging for the many tourists who found the Rocky Mountains an attractive place to visit.

The Colonel was able to convince officials of the Burlington & Missouri River railroad and the Sheridan Land Company to build a large hotel in the thriving town of Sheridan, once a railroad had been completed to that Wyoming city in 1892. Although Cody did not own any part of the hotel, he did buy the furnishings for the luxurious establishment, which boasted both steam heat and running water. Cody also had two stagecoaches shipped from Deadwood to Sheridan by train. One was a six-horse coach, the other a four-horse outfit. For years afterward the Colonel was often the host to large parties at the Sheridan Inn, and transportation was always by coach, with Cody himself handling the reins many times. Moreover, when he entered a saloon in Sheridan he often treated everybody in the house, paying with twenty-dollar bills.

At the same time, the Colonel wanted his beloved Scout's Rest Ranch to thrive. Irrigation, he felt, was the way to make the land fertile. To achieve this, in January 1894, in partnership with Isaac Dillon, an old friend and fellow rancher, he purchased two hundred acres of land west of his ranch, thereby gaining access all the way to the North Platte River for an irrigation canal, which he planned to dig through his valley holdings.

As originally planned, the ditch was to be twelve miles long, and 600,000 cubic feet of water was to be taken from the river per second to irrigate some twelve thousand acres. The ditch, completed that year, cost Cody and Dillon $10,000, and in the end irrigated only about four thousand acres. With this land now ready for development, Cody planned to divide his acreage into small holdings of forty to eighty acres each, and invite a Quaker family to occupy each holding. This colony of Friends never materialized, nor did the Colonel become a Quaker himself, though there were rumors to that effect.

The 1894 season could hardly help but be a disappointment after the Columbian Exposition. A successful formula for the show had been found, and there were few changes for the rest of the decade. "The main elements of the Wild West were horses, guns, heroes, and villains," according to Sarah J. Blackstone. "Each act made use of at least one of these elements and the most complex of them used all four." In 1894 there was added the "Hurdle Race between Primitive Riders mounted on Western Broncho Ponies that never jumped a hurdle until three days before the opening of the present exhibition."

The 1894 season was played in Brooklyn, New York. A covered grand-stand seating twenty thousand spectators was built at Ambrose Park, South Brooklyn, adjoining the Thirty-ninth Street ferry. The Wild West played two performances a day, rain or shine, general admission fifty cents.

Cody's sister Julia was now in Kansas, while her husband, Al, was back at the ranch; Horton and Arta Boal had given up ranching, presumably because it involved more work and headaches than the young couple had bargained for.

In a letter to Julia, urging her to join Al at the ranch, Cody wrote: "I am too worried now to think of anything—This is the worst deal I ever had in my life—for my expenses are $4000 aday, And I cant reduce them, without closeing entirely. You can't possibly appreciate my situation—this is the tightest squeeze of my life. Don't mention it to anyone, but it's close papers this time." Cody was expecting several big excursion parties, but they did not come because of the railroad strike. Moreover, he had to close his coffee factory down. "I am getting it on all sides" is how he ended this letter—a far cry from his euphoria the year before. From being a near millionaire in 1893, he had now come close to bankruptcy. The entire country was suffering from a money shortage as well as a drought, and none of Will's investments had paid off.

Attendance at the 1894 engagement in Brooklyn was simply not large enough now to support its overhead. Although the Wild West had made a record profit in 1893 despite the panic, by 1894 people were cutting back on their expenses, particularly for entertainment. The show's final performance was on October 6; this was the last time the show ever remained in one place for an entire season.

Worse was to come; at the end of 1894, Nate Salsbury took sick and was never again able to manage the show. In January 1895 Cody asked Salsbury to cosign his note for $5,000. A deal was closed with James A. Bailey to provide transportation for the Wild West and local expenses, for a share in the profits. Bailey, though less famous than his senior partner, Phineas T. Barnum, was, in Don Russell's opinion, "the greater circus name of the two." Bailey had run away with a circus as a boy, and circuses were his entire life. By the time he was thirty, he was half owner of the Cooper and Bailey Circus. When an elephant was born on the circus lot, Barnum offered $100,000 for it. By advertising Barnum's offer, Bailey was able to outshine the older man's circus. Barnum, recognizing the inevitable, joined forces with Bailey. The newly constituted Barnum and Bailey then acquired the Forepaugh and Sells Brothers Circus in 1890, when Adam Forepaugh died. The next year Barnum died, leaving Bailey in charge of the two largest circuses in the country. By adding Buffalo Bill's Wild West to his empire, Bailey could mount a serious challenge to the ascendant Ringling Brothers, his principal competition. It might seem hard to believe today that circuses were so deeply ingrained a part of American life—particularly rural American life—that no summer in the late nineteenth and early twentieth centuries would have been complete without the big top on tour of the hinterlands.

For the past twelve years the Wild West had generally played in large cities or at expositions for long runs, but the poor box office receipts in New York in 1894 suggested it was time to try something different. In 1895 Bailey provided railway cars and equipment to send the show to 131 stands in 190 days, over a 9,000-mile route. This required fifty-two railway cars, ten more than the Barnum and Bailey circus used, and fourteen more than the Ringling Brothers required.

Sleeping on trains, rolling out at dawn, rain or shine, unloading at the lot in a jumble of animals, canvas, wagons, equipment, and weary men, parading through unfamiliar streets, giving two performances, and striking the show in the dark, dead tired, moving on to play another stand the next day—this was circus business, grueling, unlike anything Cody and his people had ever seen before.

Weeks before the show came to town, advance men—up to three railway cars full for Buffalo Bill—would blanket the area with posters ranging from small handbills to enormous, multisheet emblazonments that could cover the side of a barn or up to 140 feet of running fence. Cody's success inspired more than a hundred imitators, from shoestring operations to huge shows with their own trains. These companies studiously copied Cody's buckskin-clad scouts, sharpshooting cowboys, and war-bonneted Indians and promoted performances with the flashiest posters they could afford.

In March of 1894 the Kearny (Nebraska) *Hub* interviewed Cody and spoke of the Wild West as "the largest show that has ever been put on wheels. There will be six hundred people in his company and six hundred animals. His portable grandstand will be the largest ever built and will seat 18,000 people. . . . Few people supposed that his Wild West venture would ever pan out as an average success, much less the great proportions it has attained, and at the same time makes originators both rich and famous.

"Not content, however, with his laurels, won with his great exhibition and delineation of the old frontier life, Mr. Cody has planned another great original enterprise of as great, if not greater, magnitude than the first. The new enterprise will be . . . a grand exposition of the history of American slavery."

This grandiose scheme, which Cody envisioned as employing a thousand of the most talented Negroes in the country, was carried out in 1895

Buffalo Bill Cody on horseback, c. 1895. (Buffalo Bill Historical Center, Cody, Wyoming)

by the ailing Nate Salsbury, along with the versatile Lew Parker, a veteran of minstrel shows. The show was called "Black America," and employed three hundred Negroes, transported in fifteen railway cars. Within three weeks Salsbury predicted failure and was ready to drop the show; Cody insisted that it be given a further trial. However, the show did not catch on with the audiences of the day and died a slow death by autumn.

Buffalo Bill's Wild West, on the other hand, was as successful as ever. In 1895 the company consisted of seven hundred people: performers, blacksmiths, canvasmen, electricians, musicians, cooks, sailmakers, watchmen, porters, and candy butchers, or vendors. The barnstorming tours in 1896 took the show ten thousand miles in 132 stops. Cody was hardly happy with the one-night stands, however, which took their toll on his health. He was growing older and was increasingly burdened by management duties, now that Salsbury was no longer at his side. In addition to the work on the irrigation canal on his Nebraska ranch, he now owned acreage in the Big Horn Basin of Wyoming, where he built a new ranch, the TE. He was negotiating with the State of Wyoming to build a huge irrigation canal from both the North and South Forks of the Shoshone River out across his ranch. The project would cost approximately $2 million, but the company Cody organized hoped to make back its initial investment and show a profit by selling the irrigated lands to interested settlers. Expenses and equipment for the Shoshone Land and Irrigation Company would be a huge drain on his income for the next several years.

In 1895–1896 Lincoln County staged an Irrigation Fair in North Platte, with Cody's enthusiastic support and leadership. "I will do my part," he wrote to the chairman of the North Platte committee. "You may advertise the Wild West for October 12. Although it is a big run for my two trains from Omaha to North Platte, when I could play a much larger town directly on the route, and will cost me $5,000, I will do it." Although the population of the town was only four thousand souls, Cody instructed the head canvasman to "stretch the full canvas."

The fair officials ordered a life-size marble statue of Buffalo Bill in his scout's costume, to be set up at the entrance to the fairgrounds in time for the grand opening. By noon on October 11, 1896, the streets of North Platte were jammed with buggies, carriages, and wagons; by sundown it was estimated that some four thousand wagons were parked among the tents, the largest camp in Nebraska's history.

On the following day, a big parade took place, in October's bright blue weather. The Colonel headed the march, driving a spirited gray Arabian team on a high-seated carriage, with a footman on a stool at the rear. Mrs. Cody and Nebraska governor Silas Holcomb followed in the Deadwood stagecoach. Both thirteen-year-old Irma and her older sister Arta were also there.

The North Platte Wild West show took in some $20,000 at admission prices of fifty cents for adults and twenty-five cents for children under nine; some eighteen thousand people attended the two performances, according to one newspaper account. Cody, Annie Oakley, and Johnny Baker, the hometown boy who had achieved stardom in his own right, were the center of attention, although one local matron was shocked at Annie's "mannish attire." After the end of the evening performance, Cody visited the headquarters tent of the Grand Army of the Republic at the campground, where he mingled with the other veterans, walking among the campfires, greeting old comrades and making new friends.

From North Platte the Wild West backtracked to Hastings, Nebraska, on to Lincoln, and from there to St. Joseph, Missouri, where Buffalo Bill was arrested and charged with putting on a show without a license. The Wild West Company had a license for a sideshow, for which it had paid $20. A license for a circus would have cost $250, but Cody insisted, as always, that his show was not a circus. The case was given a continuance to allow the Colonel time to engage counsel; meanwhile, he stated publicly that he would take the case to the highest court in the land before he would buy a license to put on a "circus exhibition." The case never came to trial, and a short time later the Colonel put the show in winter quarters.

During the year 1897, Buffalo Bill's Wild West traveled 6,108 miles and appeared in 104 cities in the United States and Canada. It was billed in jaw-breaking terms as an "Ethnological, Anthropological and Etymological Congress—Greatest Since Adam."

With George T. Beck, a Wyoming rancher and Cody's partner in his irrigation project, the Colonel laid out the town that was to be known as Cody early in 1897. By August they had established the Cody post office and appointed Cody's nephew Ed Goodman as its postmaster. A hotel had been opened, and several saloons and a store were thriving. A new little newspaper, the *Shoshone Valley News*, started up, and in February the paper wrote an effusive article of welcome to "the charming wife and lovely daughter of the renowned Colonel W.F. Cody."

As for the Cody Canal, it was moving about as fast as the Colonel could pour money into it. (Unfortunately, the project was never completed. Buffalo Bill gave up his rights to the land in 1904 but continued to lobby his friend President Theodore Roosevelt for support of his cherished project. Later that year the U.S. Department of the Interior was given the funds to begin the Shoshone Reclamation Project—largely because of Cody's continued insistence. By 1910 two dams, the Buffalo Bill and the Corbett, were in place and more than 16,000 acres were being irrigated.)

By now the Codys were grandparents. Arta Clara, a daughter, had been born to Horton and Arta Boal on November 7, 1890, in North Platte, and a son, William Cody Boal, in March 1896, in Wyoming. "That the Codys were proud and loving grandparents," wrote Nellie Snyder Yost, "is evident from the many visits exchanged between the two families during those years. In fact, the whole family seems to have been very close during this period. . . . and both girls usually came home to North Platte whenever their father was there."

On April 20, 1898, Cody's voice was recorded by the Berliner Gramophone Company. After opening his talk with a statement in support of Cuba in its quest for independence from Spain—a guerrilla insurrection that would lead to war only days later—Cody suddenly switched to his opening statement from his Wild West show. "Ladies and Gentlemen, permit me to introduce to you a Congress of the Rough Riders of the

World." These are the words he uttered more than any others in his life-time, and if he resorted to them then because only a few seconds of time remained on the recording machine, it is nevertheless wonderful to have his voice come down to us through the years.

The summer of 1898 was to see another long, triumphal tour for the Wild West. The show opened in New York in April, outshining even its previous successes there, according to the press reports. The New York *Telegram* summed them all up by saying "All over the world there are circuses and museums and sideshows and red lemonade, but there is only one Buffalo Bill."

Tim McCoy, a Wyoming cowboy from 1909 until he became a famous Hollywood cowboy of the 1920s and 1930s, had his "initial exposure to the West" during Buffalo Bill's tour of the Midwest that summer of 1898. McCoy remembered the day, July 16, when Cody's Wild West came to Saginaw, Michigan. Young Tim was thrilled with the show—"a fantastic spectacle"—but doubly thrilled when he actually got to meet his hero in person. Tim's father, Saginaw's chief of police, took him to Buffalo Bill's tent after the show. Years later McCoy recalled that Cody "sat in his tent holding court in a dark cutaway coat. . . . Around his neck was a four-hand tie, half a size larger than is fashionable now, and in that tie was a stickpin with the three feathers of the Prince of Wales, given to him as a token by the Prince when he was touring England. . . . Cody was the most impressive man I had ever seen, unmatched either before or since. As someone once said, he was the 'greatest one-man tableau that ever lived.'"

The summer of 1898 was the period of the short-lived Spanish-American War, and Buffalo Bill's Wild West featured a "Color Guard of Cuban Veterans, on leave to give their various wounds time to heal." Another innovation in 1898 was "A Bevy of Beautiful Rancheras, genuine and famous frontier girls in feats of daring equestrianism." The coinage "rancheras" never caught on, but the cowgirls were a popular addition to the Congress of Rough Riders of the World.

After the American battleship *Maine* was destroyed in Havana harbor on February 15, 1898, President McKinley requested, and Congress voted, a declaration of war against Spain on April 25. Cody had expected and hoped to take part in it, though he was fifty-two years old and responsible for an enterprise employing 467 people. On April 18 he proposed to raise a company of cavalry scouts, offering his services to General Miles. He also offered 400 horses, of the 453 the show carried that year. Cody's services were promptly accepted by the commanding general of the army,

Bill's old friend and comrade the former Indian fighter Nelson A. Miles, with an appointment to his staff. Cody sent two horses, Knickerbocker and Lancer, to Washington to be sent with headquarters property whenever such a move might be made.

After the declaration of war, while the Wild West was still playing in Greater New York, it was announced that Colonel Cody would stay with the show until his services were needed. On April 29 Cody wrote a friend: "I will have a hard time to get away from the show—but if I don't go—I will be forever damned by all—I must go—or lose my reputation. And General Miles offers me the position I want. . . . America is in for it, and although my heart is not in this war—I must stand by America." This at a time when Buffalo Bill's adventures as a dime novel hero were at their peak, and his biographer Prentiss Ingraham was suggesting that Cody was seeking ever new and more perilous adventures. How could he disappoint his vast public—which included so many children? Nevertheless, he did not make it to Cuba.

Nor did General Miles, for that matter, at first. When the Wild West moved on to Washington, after a stop in Philadelphia, General Miles was still there. On July 1 Theodore Roosevelt, who had formed the First Regiment of United States Volunteers, universally known as the Rough Riders, led his regiment up San Juan Hill—on foot; their horses had been left behind in Florida. On July 3 Admiral William T. Sampson's fleet destroyed the Spanish fleet off Santiago. On the seventh of July Miles finally left Washington to accompany reinforcements to Cuba; he arrived to find surrender negotiations in progress. He stayed until the formal surrender took place on July 17.

Four days later General Miles sailed for Puerto Rico with 3,300 troops—and this time he did send for Cody. Miles fought six small and forgotten battles in Puerto Rico, but it was obvious by this time that the war was winding down. When Cody advised Miles that it would cost $100,000 to shut his show down, the general told him to stay at home. All hostilities ceased on August 13, 1898. General Miles rode Buffalo Bill's horses in Puerto Rico and then brought them back to Washington.

It would have made no sense for Cody to have fought in the Spanish-American War, his press agents' talk of heroic adventures notwithstanding. The heroic thing was to stay with the show and protect those whose livelihoods depended on it. It is unlikely, at his age, that he would have gotten anywhere near the fighting in any case. Meanwhile, his show caught the martial fever and added "two great guns, each drawn by six powerful horses, thundering across the arena at full gallop with their drivers and cannoneers hanging on like monkeys."

The year 1898 was also the time of Omaha's great Trans-Mississippi Exposition, where the Colonel enjoyed what Dexter Fellows called "the happiest day in his life during the years I was with him." On August 31 Nebraska honored its favorite native son with "Cody Day"—and Buffalo Bill had arranged to bring his Wild West to Omaha, to play on the same spot where it had held its first performance fifteen years earlier.

Nellie Snyder Yost described the occasion: "Twenty-four thousand people came to pay their respects that day, thirteen thousand of them in the evening. When Buffalo Bill rode into the arena at the head of his brilliant cavalcade, the crowd surged to its feet as one and gave voice to wave after wave of cheers. Dismounting at the grandstand, the handsome old scout took his place among the dignitaries and his old friends of the frontier days in the box seats."

After the obligatory remarks and fulsome tributes paid by half a dozen politicians, an old man stepped forward. It was Alexander Majors, one of the owners of the famous Pony Express. Of Buffalo Bill Majors said: "He stands not at the head of the showmen of the United States of America, but of the world." He made a moving speech, recalling the days when he had first employed Cody, "giving him a man's pay because he could ride a pony as well as a man can." Majors spoke of how Billy had been paid $25 in half-dollars for his first month's work and had taken his pay home to his mother and spread it out over the table.

"I have been spreading it ever since," Cody put in. Many Nebraskans knew how true this was, but few knew that Majors himself, old and impoverished by then, now lived on an allowance paid him regularly by Buffalo Bill.

"Bless your precious heart, Colonel Cody," Majors said, and sat down. Cody himself then concluded the program with an appropriate speech of his own, in which he reminisced: "How little I dreamed in the long ago that the lonely paths of the scout and the pony-express rider would lead me to the place you have assigned me today. . . . we who are called old-timers cannot forget the trials and tribulations which we had to encounter while paving the path for civilization." This was followed by more cheering and the National Anthem played by the assembled bands.

John Burke later wrote of this day, in his typically high-flown prose: "Yet to him 'Cody Day' was infinitely and inexpressibly the most gloriously gratifying triumph of his memorable life, involving the highest compliment ever paid by any sovereign state, community or association to a private citizen."

From Omaha Cody brought his show back to North Platte for a single afternoon performance on Saturday, September 3. Again, thousands from all over western Nebraska turned out for the show. "Colonel Cody is very dear to the hearts of the people of North Platte and adjacent territory," said the *Telegraph*, which then provided these statistics, which give a good idea of the magnitude of the Wild West at its peak. "The mammoth tent covers eleven acres of ground, the grandstand four-and-one-half acres. The working arena is 70,000 square feet in area. The tent-wall canvas stretches for 22,750 yards; 1,104 stakes and twenty miles of rope hold the massive tents together. The show's electric plant is valued at $15,000. Sixty men are employed in the cook tent alone."

The organization of the Wild West had grown apace. The staff now included a crew of ticket sellers; a blacksmith and repair department; a publicity department of ten, led by Major Burke; and an enthusiastic band of billposters, who sometimes plastered over the advertisements of competing shows with "Wait for Buffalo Bill Next Week."

A month after Cody Day in Omaha, according to Richard Walsh, Buffalo Bill fainted three times during a performance. Numerous explanations for his uncharacteristic weakness could have been the cause: He suffered from a cold or typhoid fever or perhaps a nervous breakdown; he was broken-hearted because his protégée Katherine Clemons was in love with Howard Gould; or, "most unkindest cut of all," he was too drunk to stay on his horse.

In 1899 the show's Rough Riders of the World included sixteen of Roosevelt's Rough Riders. The spectacle they reenacted was the Battle of San Juan Hill with the war-horses Knickerbocker and Lancer, which Cody had lent to General Miles, featured. Adding to the Spanish-American War atmosphere were eight Cubans, three Filipinos, and seven Hawaiians. The Wild West was already beginning to lose some of its western flavor.

Another innovation during the 1899 season was the appearance of typical circus sideshows on the Wild West lot, in which the fine hand of James A. Bailey may be detected. Spectators had to pay an additional charge over the price of admission to the main show to see midgets, a snake enchantress, a Japanese magician, a boy giant, a sword swallower, a king of cards, some Venetian glass blowers, and a group of South African Bantus.

The 200-day season ended at Urbana, Ohio, with the 341st performance on October 14, 1899. In that last season of the nineteenth century the show had traveled 11,110 miles.

In the 1899 program Cody went out on a limb and endorsed the concept of votes for women, twenty years before the Nineteenth Amendment to the Constitution was passed. People in the West were in general more favorably disposed to women's suffrage, because western women had to be more self-reliant than their sisters in the East; Utah was the first state to grant them the vote, in 1870. Cody's support for women's independence went beyond the right to vote.

"Do you believe that women should have the same liberty and privileges that men have?" was the leading question put to the Colonel by a prominent feminist. "Most assuredly I do," Cody replied. "I've already said that they should be allowed to vote. Why, of course, if a woman is out earning her living she keeps up with what is going on in the world, and she knows the best man to vote for. . . . What we want to do is give our women even more liberty than they have. Let them do any kind of work that they see fit, and if they do it as well as men give them the same pay. Grant them the same privileges in their home life and club life that men have and we will see them grow and expand into far more beautiful and womanly creatures than they are already."

Cody was not only ahead of his own time but slightly ahead of ours as well. When it comes to earning power, women still have not achieved parity with men.

That year, 1899, and for the rest of his life, one of Colonel Cody's primary interests would be the fledgling town of Cody, Wyoming. In 1896 he had started its first newspaper, which was aimed not so much at keeping the locals informed—there were so few of them that they knew each other's business anyway, and there was not much space for reprinting outside news—as at promoting the town of Cody to the outside world and assisting local advertising and commerce.

In 1899 Cody persuaded Colonel J. H. Peake, one-time editor of the North Platte *Enterprise*, to come to Wyoming as editor. In hiring Peake, he was telling the world that his namesake community had come of age. Cody bought a steam-driven Babcock printing press originally purchased for the Duluth (Minnesota) *Press*, which had been run by his sister Helen and her husband Hugh Wetmore. Peake brought out the first issue of the Cody *Enterprise* on August 31, 1899, boosting the new town as enthusiastically as he had boosted North Platte back in 1874. Now the *Enterprise* had the look and feel of a big-city newspaper—and the town of Cody, established on a dry, treeless plain downwind from the sulfur springs on the aptly named Stinking Water River, would flourish. That, at least, was Buffalo Bill's dream.

"ON THE THRESHOLD OF 1900"

On December 31, 1899, the New York *Times* ran an editorial reviewing the past century and looking forward to the next. "We step on the threshold of 1900 . . . facing a still brighter dawn for human civilization," the editors declared. Everywhere the prospects were encouraging. Factories were busy manufacturing products; incomes were steadily rising. Incredible new inventions—the telephone, automobile, and light bulb, to name only three—were transforming daily life. "Laws are becoming more just, rulers humane," said a Brooklyn pastor, "music is becoming sweeter and books wiser."

Already the United States was the world's largest industrial power. After a severe economic slump in the early 1890s, our annual output of goods and services was nearly $19 billion. In just thirty years the number of Americans had doubled and now stood at 76 million. Three new states had been added in the past decade, for a total of forty-five. The entire nation, it seemed, was getting bigger, stronger, more prosperous.

Massive changes were under way, however. The great American frontier—that vast expanse of unsettled land beyond the Mississippi—had largely disappeared. Thanks to the efforts of pioneers like Isaac Cody and his son William, the plains had been tamed. The last Indian outbreak—the massacre at Wounded Knee, South Dakota—was a decade past; the former Indian territory of Oklahoma now teemed with thousands of new settlers.

Buffalo Bill Cody, though a child of the nineteenth century, was quick to sense the prevailing winds and take advantage of them. Despite his celebration of the past in the Wild West show, he was a visionary who had always looked to the future and who was perfectly positioned to thrive in the new century.

In February 1900, after visiting with friends and family in North Platte, Cody headed for Wyoming to look after his business interests there. He had turned down a $400,000 offer from the Mormons for all his Big Horn Basin holdings. Shortly thereafter traces of copper and gold had been found on his lands, and he was busy organizing a million-dollar mining company. He was also working on a petition to be sent to Congress, urging the construction of a road from Cody to Yellowstone, a much shorter route into the park than any then in existence. He conceived the idea of establishing a military school for boys near the town, the Cody Military College International Academy of Rough Riders, and tried to persuade the Elks to locate their retirement home in Cody. And, as always, he was actively involved in his wildly expensive irrigation project, described by the New York *Times* as "the most extensive irrigation scheme ever attempted in the world." Cody, Nate Salsbury, and their partners had secured a concession of 300,000 acres of arid land from the government, on the condition that they would irrigate it within five years. The plan of Cody's company was to induce emigrants to settle upon the land and then sell it to them at a nominal price. The first two thousand acres had been ready for cultivation in 1896, and the town of Cody was laid out in the center of that reserve.

At about that time, February 1900, Cody estimated that in addition to the people in his show, he was employing more than four thousand men. He wanted, he said, "to be known as a pioneer and developer of civilization," rather than only as a scout and showman. He also told reporters that he was "connected with eleven different enterprises and president of five companies. I have lost several fortunes in outside ventures." And he was about to lose several more.

As became a man of far-flung affairs, he switched his political stance from his Democratic beginnings to a more conservative point of view. "I was a Democrat until I found out my mistake," he said. "There is nothing to the Democrats. The Republicans have all the wealth. The Democrats have nothing." He now supported protective tariffs and the gold standard—and voted for McKinley in both 1896 and 1900. In the latter year he was mentioned as a possible vice-presidential candidate—a trial balloon that never took flight.

In March 1900 Cody traveled east again to put his show on the road. One of his first acquisitions was a new private railroad coach, the very one in which the Spanish diva Adelina Patti, one of the great coloratura sopranos of the nineteenth century, had made her last tour of the American continent. Cody's first private coach, originally owned by P. T. Barnum until his death in 1891, had burned in New Haven winter quarters in February. It was in this magnificent new coach that his daughter Irma traveled with Cody later in the season. The 1900 season itself was largely the same as 1899. The Wild West's American seasons were now committed to long tours with many one-night stands.

The year 1901 was different for the Wild West. At fifty-five, Cody was growing old; his voice had lost its booming resonance and his thin hair and goatee were nearly white. In place of the great chiefs of previous seasons, the Indian camp was headed by stone-faced Has No Horses, dour Iron Tail, boyish Sammy Lone Bear, and shrunken old Flat Iron. Johnny Baker was now a widower, a thickset man in a derby hat with a cigar clamped in his mouth.

Nineteen hundred one—and the world was changing. It was a time of billion-dollar trusts, spectacular crimes, ever new, titillating sensations. The liner *Celtic* with nine decks above the water had docked in New York harbor. The New York Central was tunneling under Park Avenue, and New York's first skyscraper, the Flatiron Building, was rising twenty stories on lower Fifth Avenue. The first automobile show had opened in Madison Square Garden, and horses took fright from auto wagons in the streets. Marconi sent the letter "S" across the Atlantic by "Hertzian waves," and the Wright brothers were preparing the first winged flight on the sands of Kitty Hawk, North Carolina.

In the spring of 1901 Nate Salsbury was on hand for rehearsals at Bridgeport. Though thin and worn from his illnesses, he was in better health than he had been in recent years. Ever abreast of the times when it came to acts for the Wild West, Cody had added a spectacle drawn from the previous year's Boxer Rebellion in China: "The Allied Powers at the Battle of Tien-Tsin and the Capture of Pekin." In that battle, an international force had rescued diplomats besieged by the Boxer rebels. Uniforms of the Ninth Regiment of U.S. Infantry, U.S. Marines, British Marines, Welsh Fusiliers, East Indian Sikhs, and German, Russian, French, and Japanese forces were represented in the pageant.

A Gatling gun, which had earned considerable acclaim at Santiago, was another new feature. It was a light machine gun of several barrels fired in succession, mounted on a light artillery carriage. The gun fired blanks with rapidity and exciting noise—though, once again, it had little to do with the Wild West.

As the show left Charlotte, North Carolina, on October 28, 1901, for its last engagement of the season at Danville, Virginia, its second section had a head-on collision with a freight train at 3:20 A.M. One hundred ten horses were killed outright or had to be shot, including Cody's mount, Old Pap; only two survived. Cody was devastated. No one was killed, but Annie Oakley suffered serious internal injuries. Little Sure Shot was never again to appear in the Wild West arena. She told friends that her hair had turned white within seventeen hours after the accident. However, the true cause of the end of Annie's career was revealed by Amy Leslie in the Chicago *Daily News*: She was left in a fierce, hot bath in a health resort for forty minutes instead of the usual sixty seconds. "When released, Annie's bonny, imperishable brown hair had turned white clear to her crown, her face and hands were speckled with dark brown patches and one side of her back was blistered. She was in a dead faint and restoration was a question for an hour or so." She was white-haired and forty-two when she retired. In August 1903 William Randolph Hearst's Chicago *Examiner* and *American* published articles claiming Annie was a cocaine addict, destitute, and serving a jail term for theft. She sued and won libel suits against fifty-four of the fifty-five newspapers she targeted.

In the fall Annie began rehearsals for a play, *The Western Girl*, written especially for her by Langdon McCormick and including a cast of sixteen. The play opened in Paterson, New Jersey, on November 6, 1902, and closed in April 1903. For the next nine years Annie and Frank traveled in the East, visiting friends and family. Annie still shot, but not professionally. In 1906 she became friends with the actor Fred Stone, star of *The Wizard of Oz* and *The Red Mill*. She taught him to shoot at his Amityville, Long Island, farm. Annie toured again in 1912 with the Young Buffalo Wild West and Col. Cummins Far East Combined show. After 1915 Annie's only stage appearances were in theatricals at the Carolina Hotel in Pinehurst, New Jersey, though she never lost her skill at marksmanship. Her last public appearance was at the Grand American Trapshoot at Vandalia, Ohio, in 1925; both she and Frank Butler died the following year, and are buried side by side in a Darke County, Ohio, cemetery. They had been married fifty years.

The year 1901 brought other tragedies and anxieties into Cody's life. His "Brother Al," who suffered from a kidney ailment, became too ill in January to oversee the ranch, even from a buggy. Julia moved into North Platte to give him proper care. In March the Colonel wrote his brother-in-law from New York, urging both Al and Julia to be ready to move to Wyoming as soon as the railroad into Cody was completed, to take advantage of DeMaris Springs, a place of "God healing waters" near the town. He would arrange for transportation and lodging, and they must plan to stay at least three months.

Al was never to bathe in the "healing waters." He died in October, before the railroad reached Cody. Will's grief was compounded when he was unable to attend the funeral services because of the demands of his show. It was not the first nor the last event in his life he must have longed to attend but could not because of his show business career. He was at a point where, as Don Russell put it, "he was not making enough to quit, while at the same time he was making too much to quit." He needed huge sums of money to fund his ambitious plans in Wyoming; at the same time, he realized that to keep the show going, he had to make his daily appearances in the arena. If the famous Buffalo Bill did not ride out at every performance, smiling and bowing, the audience would feel cheated. So he soldiered on, despite the many onerous burdens he had saddled himself with.

Nate Salsbury, seriously ill and unable to travel with the show, worried about Cody's spending. The irrigation project in Wyoming, he insisted, was being handled in a way that made him sick to his stomach, and too many people were cheating the Colonel in too many ways. The mining company in Wyoming had come to nothing, for there was not enough gold or copper to pay to mine it.

Now that Al Goodman was dead, Cody's sister Julia became another of those burdens; he assured her that she would never want for anything as long as he was able to look after her. To Julia he wrote many long letters, telling his "sister mother" of all his troubles—financial, domestic, complaints about his health—everything, probably to arouse her motherly sympathy. Even while showing a smiling face to his public and claiming that he felt fine, he would write Julia that he was suffering from overwork, sleeplessness, hay fever, grippe, chills, nerves, and whatever ailment suggested itself.

In October, in an attempt to cheer Cody up, the ailing Nate Salsbury wrote:

> My dear Cody:
>
> . . . We cannot regulate the universe and we must get along
> with as little friction and worry as possible if we care to stay on earth
> much longer. You complain of the worry and work in the Wild West.
> I understand it perfectly, for I carried the load for ten years without an
> hour's vacation from the job, and I know what it means, but I could
> not help myself and tried to take it as philosophically as possible, and
> succeeded pretty well if I do say so. . . .
>
> Yours,
> NATE SALSBURY.

According to Richard Walsh, this was the last recorded letter to Cody from his partner.

Although he was traveling again with the show, most of Cody's attention was centered on the town of Cody and his Big Horn holdings. He visualized Cody as the jumping-off place for Yellowstone Park, which to a large degree, it has become. He now opened the Buffalo Bill Barn, with coaches and rigs for hire. The federal government was building "Cody Road," at a cost of $50,000, from the town of Cody to the east entrance of the park, where a hunting lodge named Pahaska Tepee was rapidly being built. Halfway between Pahaska and Cody, he was building another hostelry, Wapiti Inn, and at Cody itself, another beautiful hotel was taking shape. Meanwhile, to put his namesake town on the map, the canvas coverings on the Wild West wagon train carried the phrase "Take the Burlington-Northern to the Big Horn Basin."

After a long coast-to-coast tour in 1902, with more stops than the show had ever made before, the Colonel returned to Cody, Wyoming, in November for the grand opening of the Irma Hotel, named after his daughter. The hotel was built of native wood and sandstone, at a cost of $80,000. It was soon embellished with a $100,000 cherrywood bar, made in France and shipped first to the East Coast, then carried by rail to Red Lodge, Montana, and finally by wagon to Cody. The bar is still in the Irma, in what was the original lobby, but is now the Buffalo Bill Bar and Silver Saddle Lounge. The Colonel also bought a farm ten miles from Cody and hired the farmer and his wife to raise chickens, make butter, and grow vegetables for the hotel. Even before the building was finished, he had bought more than two hundred "etchings from the paintings of artists like Fred Remington" and the very best of furniture. There would be a piano for the parlor and another for the dining room. "I tell you . . . I will make it [the hotel] the talk of the West," he boasted. For himself, as on his ranch, he reserved a private parlor and two bedrooms, with bath and closet.

When his sister Julia wrote to ask him his advice about mortgaging her house in North Platte, he urged her to sell instead and move to Cody. She was just the person to "mother" his new hotel. He was furnishing the hotel in a "fine and costly manner"; he had sent a man from the Hoffman House to be the head cook and line up a staff of uniformed waiters. Julia could oversee everything, supervise the chambermaids, do all the buying, and, in general, run the hotel. In return, the Irma would be a home for Julia, her schoolteacher daughter Josephine—called Josie—and Julia's son Walter. Josephine then lived in North Platte with her mother and little brother and taught in the city schools.

But even before the gala opening of the Irma Hotel, tragedy struck. In Sheridan, Wyoming, in late October, Horton Boal killed himself. As is so often the case with suicide, mystery clouds his death. The son of the first manager of the Sheridan Inn, Sherman Canfield, wrote that Horton used to stay at the inn for several days at a time and did not care to have himself introduced as Buffalo Bill's son-in-law. According to Canfield, on the night of his death, Boal stayed late in the bar and then took a bottle

The Irma, Cody, Wyoming, 1907—Buffalo Bill's hotel in the Rockies. (Courtesy Park County Archives)

of brandy to his room, saying that he had letters to write. About three the next afternoon he was missed, and someone went to his room and knocked on the door. Smelling chloroform, they forced his door open and found him lying dead on his bed with his face in his shoe, in which he had placed the chloroform. By his bed was a gun and a note, in which he said he had used the chloroform instead of shooting himself because the gun belonged to Arta. He asked in his note that his saddle horse follow the hearse to the cemetery and be shot over his grave.

Another Wyoming historian claims that the suicide did not take place in the inn—that Horton took his chloroform, wad of cotton, and rubber shoe to a big cottonwood tree beside the railroad tracks several blocks from the inn, and there asphyxiated himself.

As for Horton's reasons for killing himself, money is ruled out; he stood to inherit a small fortune from his mother. It is probable that a rift had developed between him and Arta, for an article in the North Platte *Telegraph* in September 1902 informed its readers that "Mrs. H.S. Boal will go to Kansas City Thursday, where she will make her future home."

At the funeral, Horton's horse did indeed follow the hearse, with his boots reversed in the stirrups, but the local authorities, showing both good sense and good taste, would not allow the horse to be shot, despite Arta's request that her husband's last wishes be carried out.

Two weeks after Horton's funeral, Colonel Cody, Arta, and her two children went up to Cody for the opening of the Irma. Irma Cody was already there, helping her aunt Julia and cousin Josie put the finishing touches on the hotel, a handsome two-story building with sixteen-foot-wide porches. A thousand engraved invitation cards, ornamented with a gold buffalo, had been sent out for the party—though at the time there were only six hundred residents in Cody. The town put on its Sunday best for the occasion, flags flying, bunting and portraits of Buffalo Bill decorating the local businesses.

That same evening, in the dining room of the Irma, where a dancing party was in progress, Cody announced the engagement of his daughter Irma to Lieutenant Clarence Armstrong Stott, stationed at Fort Mackenzie, Sheridan, Wyoming.

Conspicuous by her absence from the festivities was Louisa Cody, who remained at her home in North Platte. One can only wonder why—though it would not be long before Cody's barely suppressed disaffection from his wife would come to the surface.

Cody was now fifty-six years old and had just finished his longest and most tiring season. His show had toured coast to coast, making more stops than ever before. His sick partner, Nate Salsbury, was failing fast, and he must have felt shaken by the suicide of his son-in-law. He had time for a big-game hunting party on the TE with his friends, Dr. Frank Powell and other "old scouts," the only "rest" he got that year, and then he was on the move again. On December 6 the hunting party returned; on the fifteenth the Colonel sailed for England with his show. Bailey sent the show to Europe that winter, for a tour of more than four years. In London Cody and Bailey were notified by cable that Nate Salsbury had died on Christmas Eve, 1902. The show opened on schedule the day after Christmas, with all flags at half-staff and the banner carried by the cavalry draped in crepe. It was the end of an era for Buffalo Bill's Wild West—and Nate Salsbury would be sorely missed. Although it was Cody's fame and glamour that attracted the huge crowds to the show, it was Salsbury's showmanship, his formidable energy, and his managerial skills that had propelled Buffalo Bill to stardom. Without his guidance, the show would and did suffer—and Buffalo Bill Cody began his long and sad decline.

On Tuesday, February 24, 1903, Cody's youngest daughter, Irma, was married to Lieutenant Stott, now with the Twelfth U.S. Cavalry. The newlyweds left for Fort Clark Texas, where the Twelfth was to be stationed before leaving for a two-year tour of duty in the Philippines.

* * *

Irma Cody (left) and her husband, Lt. Clarence A. Stott, c. 1900. (Buffalo Bill Historical Center, Cody, Wyoming)

The Wild West's tour of Europe was planned by James A. Bailey, who, like Salsbury, would also die before the show returned to America. There is speculation that Bailey sent the Wild West to Europe so that it would not compete with his show in America, but that seems unlikely, since he stood to profit handsomely from a successful tour of Buffalo Bill's show, and may well have decided that the Wild West would do better in Europe at the time than in the States.

Between the years 1897 and 1902, Bailey had made a successful European tour with the Barnum & Bailey circus. If he sent the Wild West to Europe, he could effect an exchange of transport and other equipment between the two shows, thereby saving a considerable amount of money. The European tour of the Wild West was a continuation of the tours Bailey had directed in the States, where he routed the show to every city large enough to support a one-night stand.

After the opening at Earl's Court, early public enthusiasm for the show started to wane, and business fell off until the visit on March 14, 1903, of King Edward VII, who had done so much to arouse interest in the show in 1887 as the Prince of Wales. The king brought his wife, Queen Alexandra, the duke of Connaught, the duke of York, Princess Mary, and both Prince Edward, who became Edward VIII until his abdication, then duke of Windsor, and Prince Albert, "Bertie," later to be crowned George VI. Both princes, according to the *Daily Telegraph*, were "evidently keenly interested in the prospect of seeing Buffalo Bill." Thus did a succession of monarchs and future monarchs become patrons of Buffalo Bill's Wild West.

The young princes were especially charmed by the Indian village, complete with tepees. Remarked Cody: "I have never seen children more delighted than the little princes were. It was a joy to see and hear them."

Sir Robert Baden-Powell, hero of the siege of Mafeking during the Boer War and the founder of the Boy Scouts, was a great admirer of Buffalo Bill and a frequent visitor to the show grounds. Cody returned the admiration, and it was Cody's interest that contributed to the formation of a similar scouting organization in America.

When the tour began, Cody hoped for a big summer, "then quit the show business for ever," but it was not to be. Bad weather and bad luck would see to that.

From London, the show moved to Manchester, opening on April 13, where the first misfortune occurred. As the Colonel was leaving the arena, his horse shied at some shifting scenery and fell back; Cody could not clear himself in time, and one of his legs was injured. At the evening performance, and for the next two weeks, he rode around the arena in an open carriage. Both the Battle of San Juan Hill and the Indians—Arapaho, Brulé Sioux, and Cheyenne—were great crowd-pleasers on the tour. As one Manchester paper noted, "considering the arctic weather the attendances have been surprisingly good," and the show "as a thrilling and realistic exhibition has never been surpassed."

After Manchester, the Wild West staged mainly one-night stands except in major cities such as Liverpool, Cardiff, and Leeds. The 1903 season included 333 performances, with one canceled, and seven street parades. The show closed down on October 23 at Burton-on-Trent after weather that appalled Cody—fifty hours of steady rain "and the worst wind storms I ever experienced in all my life. We stood it off for 43 hours But had to give up. And to night have lost our first show this season. We commenced pulling at 8 15. At 8 37 a house adjoining our big top was blown down and fell on our seats. had we had an audience in there it would have been many killed so we were lucky to not attempt a show."

The 1903 and 1904 seasons, according to Joseph Rosa and Robin May, "were highly successful financially. Winter quarters were at Stoke-on-Trent each year. The last English town to see Buffalo Bill was the

neighboring one of Hanley, on October 10, 1904. The company was better off than its chief, for . . . early in 1905 he was in the midst of his
divorce hearing."

By 1905 it was no secret from anyone who knew Will Cody that he was
profoundly unhappy in his marriage and wanted a divorce. On March 21,
1902, he wrote his sister Julia:

> I have tried & tried to think that it was right for me to go on through
> all my life, living a false lie—Just because I was too much of a Morral
> coward to do otherwise, But I have decided that if the Law of man can
> legally join together the same law can legally unjoin. And that it's more
> honorable to be honest than to live a life of deceipt. There is no use of
> my telling you of my Married life—more than that it grows more un-
> bearable each year—Divorces are not looked down upon now as they
> used to be—people are getting more enlightened. Some of the very best
> people in the world are getting divorced every day. They say it's better
> than going on living a life of misery for both. God did not intend joining
> two persons together for both to go through life miserable. . . . As it is I
> have no future to look forward to—no happiness or even contentment.
> Lulu will be better contented. She will be her absolute master—I will
> give her every bit of the North Platte property. And an annual income.
> If she will give me a quiet legal separation—if she won't do this then it's
> war and publicity. I hope for all concerned it may be done quietly.

He wrote Julia from Manchester, England, on April 12, 1903: "I think
when Lou and Arta sees I am determined—they will agree to a mutual
separation. Lou likes to be boss. She loves to be the whole thing—And if
I give her all the North Platte property, and money besides, she will take
it. She will be a rich woman. And her own boss." Cody apparently did
sign over the North Platte property to his wife, expecting that she would
agree to a divorce, but she did not.

When word of the Cody divorce proceedings got out, the citizens of
North Platte were sharply divided. Some took the Colonel's side, others
Louisa's. According to Nellie Snyder Yost, the affair "became personal,"
dividing friends and even families. Louisa Cody had many friends in town,
while Buffalo Bill's visits had been infrequent. In his favor was his largesse
whenever he did come back home.

All that spring Cody bombarded his sister with letters, advising her what
to do and telling her what his plans were. For some reason letters from
home were not reaching him, and he was frantic for news. He com-

plained: "no one tells me—who we owe or how much. I have sent $6000 & I know I did not owe that much."

Already the Colonel wanted to build an addition onto the Irma, although Julia told him there was not enough business to justify it. He insisted there would be soon and meant to go ahead with the addition anyway. He also warned her against allowing any gambling in the hotel.

Prior to leaving for Europe, Cody had bought a large mining estate in Arizona, the Oracle, and he had high hopes for great riches from that source. He was so confident of this that he began to call himself a "millionaire" and was already spending the fortune he anticipated. After Liverpool, Birmingham, Bristol, and Leicester, Cody complained of nervous strain and told Julia, "I do not go to hotels any more for I haven't the strength to be even talked to." In September he was less optimistic about the Arizona mines, though he wrote: "I will make more money after this with the show for I will be sole owner. I am buying the Salsbury interests." He did not succeed in this, however.

Still, he was promising Julia a new house of her own, telling her to get it started right away, "on 90 days time," and he would send her the money soon. He told her to buy additional Cody town lots, also on time, and he would pay for them with profits from the mine—profits delayed now because of the necessity of building a mill to process the ore. If she could just "run that dear old face" for a little while longer, she would be rich and could "sit around and give orders, & look nice" and have her own carriage with a driver.

On the upside, Will's daughter Arta had pitched in to help Julia manage the Irma Hotel. Near the end of March Arta cabled her father that the books, statements, hotel, ranches, and everything else in Wyoming were fine.

On the downside, there was trouble with Nellie (his sister Helen). Helen and her newspaperman husband Hugh Wetmore had built a mansion called Cody View in Duluth after the Colonel bought the local newspaper, the *Enterprise*, for them; Helen had badly mismanaged the paper. When the bills for the construction of the house came due and the contractors threatened to sue for their labor and materials, Brother Will, as usual came through and paid the bills. He took the precaution, however, of deeding Cody View to Louisa, with Helen and her husband to have lifetime occupancy. When Hugh Wetmore died in 1901, Helen wanted to sell the house, but Louisa refused to sign the note deeding the house to her sister-in-law. Helen then quarreled with Will, who told Julia to keep Helen out of Cody when he returned.

Louisa apparently had also attempted to drive Julia out of the Irma, for Cody wrote Julia in June 1901: "My Dear Poor Tired Sister, don't you think for a moment you are going to be turned out of my house. I gave every thing at North Platte up to Lulu, now she want to run me out of Cody its all Lulu work . . . and I won't stand for it. I have just cabled Ridgely you remain. . . . No one shall put you out of my house. God bless you, Brother."

H. S. Ridgely was a former North Platte attorney who had stayed on in Cody after its opening to look after the Colonel's many interests there and to advise Julia in her management of the hotel. He was also called upon to serve divorce papers on Louisa.

Cody returned home on November 3, 1904, bringing friends from England for a big hunt in Wyoming. Also on the hunt were Dr. Frank Powell, Lieutenant General Nelson Miles, Major Burke, and Iron Tail. The Colonel's Arizona mine was still devouring cash greedily; the Irma's ledgers were written in red ink; and there was as yet little income from his irrigation canals in the Big Horn Basin. In addition, Helen quarreled with Judge Peake, the editor of the Cody *Enterprise*, and went back to Duluth in a huff. To placate his sister, Cody gave her his interest in the Wyoming newspaper.

On New Year's Day, 1904, Arta was married again, to Dr. Charles W. Thorp. After the wedding, the couple traveled to Spokane, Washington, where Dr. Thorp had been appointed chief surgeon for the Northern Pacific railroad. Just before the end of January, Louisa Cody received a letter from her daughter, telling her that an operation for "organic trouble" was necessary, that it was of a critical nature, and that she, Arta, had grave doubts as to her survival. On January 30 Mrs. Cody had packed a bag and, accompanied by little Cody Boal, had gone to the depot to take a train to Washington. While waiting at the station, she was handed a telegram informing her of Arta's death. When he received the news, Cody telegraphed his wife urging that they overlook all their past differences. Lulu rebuffed his overtures, claiming that he had broken Arta's heart and caused her death. Louisa and Will took Arta's remains on a train to Rochester, where she was buried beside her little sister Orra and brother Kit. During the train ride, Lulu refused to speak to him and threatened to air her grievances with him at Arta's grave. Of the Codys' four children only one, Irma, was now still alive.

Before the end of March, Cody filed suit for divorce and gave his deposition. The trial was set for April in Cody, but before that time, the Colonel was sailing for Europe. In April 1904 the Denver *Post* ran an article stating that W. F. Cody had charged his wife with "nagging." His testimony proceeded along the lines of incompatibility rather than cruel and inhuman treatment. One of the grounds for divorce in Wyoming was that one of the partners in a union made the marriage "intolerable."

According to the *Post*:

Buffalo Bill claims that Mrs. Cody began making things intolerable for
him even in the early days of their wedded life and has kept it up. . . .
Aside from the charge that his wife had tried to poison him when he was
ill three years ago, Colonel Cody's testimony was not severe against his
wife. He told of many petty quarrels and related many instances of her
alleged ill temper. "It has been nag, nag, nag," he said, "it has worn me
out and I want to get away from it."

That same month a group of witnesses from North Platte traveled to
Cody to give testimony, but because of the Colonel's absence, the trial
was postponed to June. Postponement followed postponement until
November 1904, when Cody, back in the States once again, filed an
amended divorce petition against his wife in Sheridan. The charges were
much the same as before: intolerable indignities; a regular and systematic
course of ill treatment of himself from 1878 to the present. He repeated
the charge that Lulu had attempted to poison him, adding that his wife
had accused him of causing his daughter Arta's death and had threatened
his life, declaring that she would "fix" him.

Louisa Cody's attorney went up to Cheyenne in January 1905 to file
her answer to the Colonel's charges. Mrs. Cody's statements, as reported
in the North Platte *Telegraph*, were not sensational, merely detailing the
life of the couple during "their married state." A later article in the *Telegraph*
was headlined WE'RE LIABLE TO HEAR NAUGHTY THINGS and noted
that Mrs. Cody had denied attempting to poison the Colonel or submitting
him to indignities, but made "a countercharge of his infidelity."

H. S. Ridgely, Cody's attorney, spent several days in North Platte,
taking depositions, while Cody went to Omaha, where his deposition of
rebuttal to Mrs. Cody's answer was taken. The deposition was taken at the
Merchants Hotel, where Cody had the bar opened and treated everyone
in the house to a popular new drink called the "Horse's Neck," a mixture
of whiskey and lemon.

The celebrated divorce case of *Cody v. Cody* came up for trial on February
16, 1905, in a packed Cheyenne district courtroom, before Judge
R. H. Scott. Press interest was also intense, although a number of newspapers
regarded the trial as more of a circus than a serious legal action. One
of the many journalists who covered the trial was Arthur Sears Henning
of the Chicago *Tribune*. His first dispatch was headed "BUFFALO BILL"AT
LAST STAND:

Intrenched [sic] in a legal fastness and surrounded by a band of brave
attorneys, who know every bypath of the Wyoming divorce laws, the
hero of the thrillers of two generations started today to fight his way to

marital freedom. . . . The colonel declares he is seeking to escape the indignities and insults from which he has suffered for thirty years, and that he feels free to attempt it now that his children are married.

Mrs. Cody . . . surrounded by another brave band of attorneys, is determined to fight to the last ditch, for she asserts the colonel wants the divorce only in order to marry another woman.

The complete transcript of the testimony is available at the Mc-Cracken Research Library of the Buffalo Bill Historical Center and makes quite entertaining reading. To the Codys, however, it was all deadly serious.

Mrs. Cody's defense laid particular stress on Will's heavy drinking, but testimony was offered that she too drank on occasion, and that when she did, she became quarrelsome and abusive; that she sometimes refused to feed her husband's guests and otherwise insulted them.

The Colonel's charge that his wife had attempted to poison him was based on an incident that took place the day after Christmas in 1900. Mrs. John Boyer, wife of the superintendent at Scout's Rest Ranch, testified: "She gave him Dragon's Blood. It was a drug she had. She gave it to him in his coffee." After Cody drank it, he collapsed and found himself unable to speak. It turned out that Dragon's Blood was a love potion that Lulu had obtained from a gypsy; it was intended to revive the Colonel's moribund affection for her and perhaps to cure his drinking habit. However, Mrs. Boyer said that she believed that Mrs. Cody "never tried to poison the Colonel, but only gave him the powders to try to get sway over him." Mrs. Boyer also reported that Mrs. Cody had told her that her husband was immoral "with any woman he met, it didn't make any difference who she was."

Mrs. Boyer also testified that Mrs. Cody was often rude to guests and had once had one of her children drop the piano lid on a lady guest's hand. She had driven her husband's guests out of the house by discharging the servants, appearing in old, dirty wearing apparel, and telling the guests they had made her a lot of trouble and she hoped they would never come to her house again, all the while using forceful and unbecoming language.

Another witness, Mrs. H. S. Parker, testified that Mrs. Cody was jealous of the attentions paid to her husband by Queen Victoria and Queen Alexandra. Judge Scott immediately struck from the record any mention of the two queens as "manifestly unjust, preposterous, false, and brutal." That the charge was preposterous there is no doubt, though in the course of the trial it appeared that both plaintiff and defendant were doing their best to outdo each other in absurdities.

Louisa's jealous suspicions of Will went all the way back to 1877, when he kissed the girls of his company good-bye—his defense in the divorce trial of his actions back then was both muddled and insensitive to his wife's point of view. Here, in Don Russell's apt phrase, was "the hero less heroic."

Testifying in the box on March 6, which happened to be his thirty-ninth wedding anniversary, Cody proved to be a poor witness. He described what he called his youthful gullibility, saying that he had agreed to his engagement to Louisa as a joke and had not realized that she had taken him seriously. Her letters reminding him of his promise prompted him into "keeping his word," and agreeing to the marriage.

The most damning—and the most titillating—testimony against Cody was offered by John W. Claire of Brooklyn, New York, and reported in the Denver *Post* on March 2, 1905. Although Cody's petition had recited sensational things in a general way, and Mrs. Cody's answer was a general denial, Claire's deposition was quite specific. Filed on March 1, and the last one entered by the defense, it cited many occasions on which Cody was "intimate with one Bessie Isbell, the comely Iowa girl who, the deponent alleges, followed the Wild West show for several years."

Claire was Buffalo Bill's valet, and obviously no great fan of his master, while Bessie Isbell was one of the Wild West's press agents. The *Post*'s story ran like this:

> Statements made in the Claire deposition would indicate that Col. Cody and his pretty press agent . . . were quite fond of each other and spent much of their time together while Buffalo's Wild West show was on the road, as well as during the time it was not. Col. Cody has always claimed his feeling for Miss Isbell was purely of a platonic character, and that his frequent visits to her apartments was for the purpose of transacting business connected with the show. In order to have his press agent near him, Buffalo Bill has repeatedly stated he usually arranged that they were assigned to adjoining rooms at hotels and other places where they stopped. Callers upon Cody frequently found him in Miss Isbell's and quite as frequently found Miss Isbell in the Colonel's apartment. At times she was dressed in street clothes, while frequently she had on gowns used only for indoor purposes, such as kimonas [sic] and loose fitting wrappers.

Here at last was the stuff that supermarket tabloids thrive on. At the time of the trial the Denver *Post*, under Fred Bonfils and Harry Tammen, was not the sedately respectable journal it would later become—nor was it a fan of Buffalo Bill.

Claire testified that he first met Cody in 1887 and was employed as a booking agent for the show in 1890. Later he became Cody's messenger and valet, and in this capacity he dressed the Colonel for his performances, cared for his clothing, and was close to Cody at all times. Among the other questionable occasions he cited, Claire stated that one morning "he saw Miss Isbell in her room. She was clothed in a loose-fitting wrapper, or kimona, and the colonel was asleep in her bed. There was but one bed in Miss Isbell's room."

Bessie Isbell began to travel with Buffalo Bill's Wild West in 1900 as a press agent—and a good one, according to Cody. He gave her a silver-mounted saddle but denied that it was a token of his affection. On one visit to the Big Horn country she was "sick all over the ranch," according to testimony, which mentioned that Bill had kissed her good-bye (that habit of Cody's cropping up again), but the Colonel said he could not remember the kiss. Judge Scott asked Mrs. Cody's attorneys to strike out all charges relating to Bessie Isbell.

Katherine Clemons, the young British actress Cody had befriended and sponsored, was mentioned in the trial, but only in passing. In 1898 Lulu, then staying at the Astoria in New York, again sought Will out, this time in the Hoffman House, his favorite home away from home in Gotham. Her phone call was answered by a voice she claimed was that of "Bessie Bell." This time Lulu wrecked her own room, breaking mirrors and vases—the damage all charged to Will Cody, who paid up this time, dutifully but no doubt begrudgingly.

Letters and a photograph in the Cody file of the Denver Public Library's Western History Department reveal the existence of another possible rival of Lulu's for the Colonel's affections: a strikingly handsome woman named Nadeau Piatt. The letters begin with the salutation "B.B.," for "Beautiful Baby," and are signed "B.B.," for Buffalo Bill, of course. The letters, disappointingly enough for anyone in search of scandal or even a hint of passion, relate mostly to the activities of Cody's various relatives. According to Don Russell, it appears that the Piatt family had some connection with the Colonel's Arizona mining ventures. In 1902 Cody had joined Colonel D. B. Dyer, a former Indian agent, to form the Cody-Dyer Mining and Milling Company. The mine presumably contained tungsten, gold, and lead. In March 1903 Cody wrote his sister Julia that a long-sought vein of ore had been struck after seven months of drilling night and day; he predicted that the mine would begin to pay off within four months. Although Cody never lost faith in Dyer, his mining venture, wrote Russell, "cost him more money than all the women in his life, possibly even including Lulu." Dyer apparently fleeced Cody of $500,000 by padding payrolls and falsifying bills while sending him glowing reports of bonanzas soon to come.

After asking the attorneys for Mrs. Cody to strike out all charges naming other women, Cody's conduct in Chicago, and other early excesses at Fort McPherson, Judge Scott handed down the decision that "all the allegations in the amended answers of the said defendant, Louisa Cody, are true, and that the allegations in the plaintiff's petition and amended petition and supplemental petition are hereby disproved." Thus, Cody lost his suit and was ordered to pay Mrs. Cody's court costs, which came to $318. The case was dismissed on March 23, 1905.

When it came to his divorce, Cody did not fare well in the columns of the North Platte *Tribune;* Editor Ira Bare ended his report of the affair with the words "Shame on you, Mr. Cody."

Colonel Cody at once announced his intention to appeal Judge Scott's decision. His attorneys argued the case before a Cheyenne judge in May, claiming they had new evidence. When his right to a new trial was denied, he stated that he would take the case all the way to the Supreme Court. Immediately after this announcement, Cody departed for Europe to rejoin his show.

It seems clear from both the trial testimony and accounts of friends and North Platte townspeople that Louisa Cody genuinely loved her husband, even though she was unable to make him happy. Perhaps no one woman could; this was a man who flourished best in the adulation of crowds. Also, her insistence on putting his property in her name rather than his was undoubtedly an effort to ensure that he would have something to fall back on in his old age; she knew all too well how extravagant, even improvident, he could be. Although there was a serious rift between Lulu and Will's sisters, they, too, wished only the best for him— with the possible exception of Helen (Nellie), whose approval of her brother waxed and waned according to his generosity to her. Of all the Cody family, she comes off as the least admirable. Cody's devotion to his sisters, his efforts throughout his life to carry out his mother's dying wishes that he take care of them, is surely one of the most admirable of his many qualities. In that determination, if he sometimes quailed at the sheer magnitude of the task, he never wavered.

On July 11, 1905, the New York *Times* reported that "Col. W.F. Cody (Buffalo Bill) to-day cabled to Dr. D. Frank Powell, his business manager . . . to withdraw the appeal in his suit for divorce."

The *Times* squib continued:

> "Col. Cody will withdraw the appeal," said Dr. Powell, "in compliance with the earnest request of his only living child, Irma, the wife of Lieut. Stott of the regular army. She has long been seeking to effect a reconciliation between her parents."

That reconciliation would have to wait another five years, until 1910, when the pair finally repaired the breach between them.

In the aftermath of his divorce suit, Cody faced another serious legal problem: His Masonic lodge planned to hold a trial for the purpose of ejecting Buffalo Bill from their fellowship, because of the publicity of his divorce case. Cody was horrified at this prospect. He had been a charter member of the Fort McPherson lodge in 1869 and had risen through the ranks to reach the thirty-third degree, "the Order of the Mystic Shrine," the Masons' highest. In Manchester, England, in 1888, the Prince of Wales, Grand Master of the Free Masons, had presented him with a gold watch of that order. Cody was in France and unable to defend himself in person, but both Julia and her daughter, Josie, wrote letters on his behalf, and their intercession was successful; his lodge brothers at home dropped their plans for a trial.

Thus ended one of Cody's worst years—though worse was still to come.

THE OLD SCOUT ON
"HIS NATIVE HEATH"

While the good Colonel was pursuing his hapless divorce litigation, in its fecklessness so reminiscent of his Cleveland real estate suit so many years earlier, his show had moved from England to France. Huge crowds turned up in Paris. Absent Annie Oakley, Johnny Baker was now the undisputed star marksman of the show; he was also its equestrian director, and he was almost as popular in France as Cody. So well known and loved was the Colonel, however, that posters heralding his show needed only to display his picture with the words *"Je viens"*—I am coming—to bring in eager audiences. The Paris engagement from April 2 to June 4 has been called the most prosperous in tent history. An elaborate program was published for the show, with eighty pages devoted to *Le Dernier des Grand Eclaireurs*, a literal translation of the title of Helen Cody Wetmore's book. Featured acts were *"Le Dernier Combat du General Custer"* and *"Attaque du Dead Wood Mail Coach."* One-day stands followed the Paris engagement: Chartres, Alencon, Fleury, St. Lo, and Cherbourg. The first four days of July were spent at Lille, where James Bailey paid his last visit to the show.

There was competition for the Wild West in France—principally from J. T. McCaddon's International Shows, which included a Wild West. Cody was so successful in outdrawing his rival that McCaddon was forced to flee across the English Channel to escape his creditors. A more serious setback to the show's prosperity came when there was an outbreak of glanders, a highly contagious disease that can be controlled only by slaughtering the infected animals. Cody had to destroy two hundred out of his three hundred horses. This blow, which put the show deeply in debt, was followed close on by the sudden death of James Bailey early in 1906. A note with Cody's signature on it for $12,000 was discovered, and Bailey's estate wanted it paid. Cody insisted that he had already paid it, and Don Russell

Buffalo Bill Cody outside his tent at the Wild West show, c. 1907. (Buffalo Bill Historical Center, Cody, Wyoming)

firmly believes that if Cody said he had paid it, then he had, and Bailey had just neglected to release it.

The Bailey heirs not only demanded payment of the $12,000 but took over the mortgaged Salsbury share as well, leaving Cody with only a one-third interest in the show, and that third mortgaged. Moreover, Bailey's widow and the other heirs to his estate wanted nothing to do with show business—which meant that Cody, who still spoke longingly of "retirement"—simply could not afford to leave the show. With all his other debts, his financial burden was crushing—and he would never manage to unload it.

After successful stops in France and Italy, the company visited Austria, Germany, Hungary, Luxembourg, and Belgium in 1906. Business was especially strong in Germany. There was also a brief but unsuccessful stop in Russia, where the Cossacks in his Rough Riders company surely would have felt at home. While the show was in Italy, Vesuvius erupted, and Buffalo Bill, feeling prosperous, promptly sent $5,000 to the "sufferers" in the stricken villages. He also sent $1,000 to San Francisco to aid the victims of the earthquake. The 1906 season ended in Van Gogh country, Arles, France, on October 30. During the European tours, the Wild West used fifty railroad cars, each fifty-four feet long and eight feet wide, moved in three sections. There were twenty-two flats, eighteen orange stock cars, nine red sleepers, including one box sleeper, and an advance car. Cody himself boasted that his company was the best behaved he had ever had— "No swearing or drinking in my Company since I got good"—which meant he had stopped drinking.

The Wild West returned to America for the 1907 season, just months after the sudden death of James Bailey. On April 23, 1907, Cody made the following public announcement: "After nearly five years absence in foreign lands my foot is on my native heath again and I desire to let my friends and patrons know that the Old Scout is still alive and active, and with the same fidelity and sense of duty to the public will be found in the saddle twice daily, rain or shine, at the head of the ORIGINAL and the ONLY morally and RIGHTFULLY entitled 'Wild West and Congress of Rough Riders of the World.'"

From New York, Cody wrote Julia from his office in the Bailey Building: "I am very busy as I have no partner I must put the show together alone. So I will be here some time. I am at My desk every morning at 8 30 and work all day. And office work is not my fort."

For the next two seasons, Cody managed the show by himself, though not without considerable nervous strain. The Bailey estate, through its representative Joseph T. McCaddon, was in charge of the purse strings. On May 25, 1907, Cody wrote McCaddon that "it's got down to one show a day. And our great success will end if we cant get men to put and take down the show. Would like to hear from you. I am personally wore out trying to keep things going. . . . We must have men or its all off." It was not until the end of July that Cody had worked out his problems with the Bailey interests.

After its long absence, the show was as popular as ever. Once again the Wild West played Madison Square Garden. There were two new western acts in the show. One was a staging of the controversial 1869 Battle of Summit Springs, in which Cody killed Tall Bull (or did not kill him, according to his detractors); to re-create the battle, Cody asked General Carr for his recollections, to supplement his own. The second new addition was "The Great Train Holdup and Bandit Hunters of the U.P." This act was patterned after the numerous train holdups that had plagued the Union Pacific since 1877. A realistic steam locomotive pulled a string of cars into the arena, where it was held up by the bandits, who broke into the express car and blew up the safe. Then they lined up the passengers and relieved them of their cash and jewelry. Just in time, the U.P. Bandit Hunters galloped in and shot or captured the robbers. The steam locomotive was actually a motor car that had been outfitted with larger driving wheels; its mechanical effects included a puffing engine, black smoke, and an electric headlight—a quite effective illusion.

While he was running the 1907 show, Buffalo Bill was working on articles and writing the book that became *True Tales of the Plains.* "I work every day in my tent," said Cody, "and two hours before I leave my private car I spend with my secretary, dictating. That's the way I write stories. Sit down and talk them off." Both Richard Walsh and Don Russell believe that John Burke's fine hand can be detected in Cody's articles and also in his book.

That same year the Katherine Clemons scandal popped up again, when Howard Gould sued the actress for divorce. Gould's lawyers offered Will $50,000 if he would testify against Katherine in the trial—a sum Cody could have used to pay off some of his pressing obligations. He told the attorneys to "get the hell out" of his tent. Gould was unable to prove that Cody had behaved improperly with his wife—and lost his divorce suit in the bargain.

On April 25, 1907, Cody wrote that "the show has started great The biggest send off I have ever had Press & Public unanimous in praise. Have showed to four big rousing cheering audiences. If it continues this way all summer I will be glad I came home back to Wyoming country."

One of the Wild West's triumphs during the 1907 season was its financial victory over the Barnum and Bailey circus. Box office receipts showed Cody's show to be the most popular, and he couldn't resist crowing about it in a letter to R. Farrington Elwell, a young Western artist who had become a good friend.

Well the Wild West have beaten the Greatest Show on Earth. The *Barnum Circus* in receipts in newspaper notices and applause of the public. Its been just a few years a go that the Proprietors of the Barnum Circus

Chief Iron Tail, c. 1907. (Buffalo Bill Historical Center, Cody, Wyoming)

told their agents to pay no attention to me. That I didnt amount of much . . . Not to recognize me at all & c.

Beating the Barnum Circus may not have been quite the triumph Cody painted it. The Barnum and Bailey show at that time was sadly run down; in 1907 it was bought by the Ringling Brothers and merged with their much more successful show.

By the end of the 1907 season, Cody was obviously exhausted and badly in need of a long rest. On October 12 he wrote Elwell from Jacksonville, Florida, that he was "quite ill and these terrible long runs and hard work has put me about all in. We had 134 miles run to get here now a 172 mile run out of here. . . . I expect to be at T.E. [his TE ranch in Wyoming] by the 28th."

At this time, Cody was staying away from North Platte, possibly because he did not feel comfortable in his hometown after the unpleasant publicity fallout from his divorce trial; then, too, he had not yet reconciled with Louisa.

On December 16, 1907, Irma's husband, Lieutenant Stott, died of pneumonia in White Horse, South Dakota. On March 18, 1908, she married Frederick Harrison Garlow, the son of a prominent Omaha family. After the wedding, the couple moved into Scout's Rest Ranch, where Garlow became the manager, much to Cody's satisfaction. Garlow proved a good ranch manager. Though he was a hard taskmaster with those who worked for him, he was also a gentleman. Like the Colonel himself, he did not care much for the actual hard work of running a ranch. Unlike Al Goodman, he did not pitch in with the physical labor himself, but delegated it to others.

During the winter of 1908–1909, Cody decided to merge his show with that of Major Gordon "Pawnee Bill" Lillie. Lillie's admiration for Cody began when he was a nine-year-old boy and saw Buffalo Bill, Wild Bill Hickok, and Texas Jack Omohundro in Bloomington, Illinois, where they were playing in *The Scouts of the Prairie*. That admiration lasted throughout Lillie's life. Lillie had replaced Major Frank North as interpreter for the Wild West in 1883 and at the time had been harshly critical of Cody's drinking. After two seasons with Buffalo Bill, he put together several shows of his own—none, however, as successful as Cody's. In 1904 he enlarged his show, calling it Pawnee Bill's Historic Far West and Great Far East Show, and toured with it until 1908. His show featured camels, elephants, Arabs, and other so-called Far East performers. When the two shows teamed up, the hybrid became "Buffalo Bill's Wild West and Pawnee Bill's Far East." It was popularly known as the Two Bills show.

The union was providential for Buffalo Bill. Pawnee Bill paid off his debts with the Bailey estate and put up the cash needed to keep the Wild West in winter quarters and open it again the following spring. Cody was relieved of many of his managerial burdens. Lillie also made Cody an equal partner in the new show—the cost of Cody's share to be paid off out of the show's earnings, after which he would receive his half of the profits in cash. As for Pawnee Bill, while his own show had paid expenses and made a modest profit, it had never been the windfall he expected. He badly needed a headliner like Buffalo Bill. Despite the merger, ostensibly of equals, the new enterprise was much more "Wild West" than "Far East."

One new act was added after the merger: football on horseback. As one North Platter who saw the show in 1911 described the game, it was played with a ball about four feet in diameter. The horses would rear up and strike the ball with their hooves, attempting to put it across a goal line before the defenders could boot it back. After the first game, the riders dismounted and the horses played a game by themselves, in which Colonel Cody's snow-white horse always put the ball over the goal line first—to win the game. Harry Webb, a cowboy with the Wild West, said: "Football on horseback between cowboys and Indians [was] little less than murder." Audiences loved the excitement of the game.

The Cody-Lillie partnership lasted until 1913. During the show seasons, the two men lived together, traveling in the same private railroad car, touring the United States and Canada. Perhaps the greatest favor Lillie paid Cody was to redeem his notes from the Bailey heirs. Almost from the beginning, there was interference from the heirs' agents. First, they were unhappy with the expense of subway advertising, which had proved successful for other shows. At one point, they demanded that Lillie fire Major John Burke, widely considered the best press agent in the business, and also Louis E. Cooke, the show's veteran general agent, who had been with James Bailey before joining the Wild West. Like Burke, Cooke was considered without a peer in his profession. Burke, Cooke, and Johnny Baker were the only three men Cody insisted should remain with the show as long as they filled their positions properly. Lillie quite rightly refused to fire Burke and Cooke, precipitating a showdown with the Bailey interests. In due course, Lillie paid off the Baileys and became the sole owner of the Two Bills show—though he later deeded one-half of his equity in the shows to Buffalo Bill.

Cody's partnership with Major Lillie was, on balance, a success. Lillie well understood the Colonel's temperament. When badgered by a creditor, Cody might take to his bed and threaten not to appear in the arena—or even burst into tears. Will's constant advances against his earnings at times jeopardized the show's financial health. However, Lillie also recognized, as the Bailey heirs did not, that Cody was the show's greatest asset; without him, there would be no headliner. Gordon Lillie was a shrewd manager and businessman, but Pawnee Bill was not a star of the first magnitude, like Buffalo Bill.

Moreover, the Great Far East was merely the seventh episode out of eighteen. It was a show within a show, "a dream of the Orient," with camel caravan, Rossi's Musical Elephants, acrobatics by Bedouin Arabs and Imperial Japanese, Australian boomerang throwers, a Hindu fakir who "caused a beautiful young lady of the Orient to gracefully float in the air without any visible means of support," and Whirling Dervishes, South Sea natives, Moors, Persians, Musselmen, and Syrians, making up "An Ethnological Congress of Strange Tribes, Clans, Races, and Nations of Peculiar People." The bulk of the Two Bills show was still the Wild West.

At the close of the 1910 season, Cody saw the Cody-Dyer mine in Arizona for the first time. He visited it with Johnny Baker and his wife. The Campo mine, which Cody and Dyer had leased, was located about seven miles northeast of the town of Oracle in Pima County, in the Catalina Mountains. The two partners hired L. W. Getchell and his son Noble to manage the property, and they began to pour money into it, hoping always to find gold.

Cody did not remain at the mine for long, but went to North Platte for Christmas, then for a brief stay in Wyoming. Before he could return to Arizona, he was called to Pasadena, where his sister Helen was critically ill. Helen died there on February 8, 1911.

His North Platte stop coincided with a reconciliation with his wife, Louisa, which took place on July 28, 1910. Cody had first returned to North Platte in the spring of that year. The North Platte *Telegraph* announced on March 24 that Lincoln County's cowboy band would "meet the train and greet him with joyous music." The band did meet the train, along with several hundred townspeople, who struck up a cheer that lasted until their hero appeared on the platform of the rear coach. In Nellie Snyder Yost's words: "Standing there, the Old Scout swept his big hat from his snow-white head and bowed his thanks to his old friends."

On Sunday afternoon Fred and Irma Garlow hosted a huge barbecue at the ranch in the Colonel's honor. More than a hundred of his old friends, some of them men who had been on his hunting and scouting expeditions forty years ago, attended the reception. During the height of the party, he was handed a telegram from the New York *World:* "Your friends read with interest today of your welcome home. What were the sensations of home-coming after ten years' absence? A sentiment from you would be appreciated by thousands of newspaper readers who have followed your career as a national figure in American life. Please answer at our expense."

Cody's reply expressed his great pleasure at being with upward of 150 of his good friends.

Louisa had said many times to friends in North Platte that she longed to have her husband come home, and knew that he would be there "if it weren't for wild women and whiskey." Even during the divorce proceedings, when she denounced him, she stated that "Will is one of the kindest and most generous of men." On this visit, however, she refused to see him. While he was there, she had her meals sent up to her room, and when Cody came and knocked on her locked door and pleaded with her to let him in, she wouldn't open the door. So it was not until the July 28 visit that the couple reconciled. On that occasion the Wild West was touring Nebraska, and Cody's grandson, William Cody Boal, urged Will to come to North Platte. While he was there, the family conspired to leave Will and Louisa alone in a room together. When they came out, all was apparently forgiven—or at least they had decided to preserve their stormy union as best they could.

Back in 1905, Cody had written his sister Julia from France that he planned to retire in 1910, when he would be sixty-four, "the age all my old Army friends retire." In May 1910, attempting to keep to this resolve, he made a farewell speech in Madison Square Garden.

"Col. William F. Cody, 'Buffalo Bill,' gave his final salute in the saddle last night," wrote the New York *Times* reporter on May 15, 1910, "to an enthusiastic audience that packed Madison Square Garden to its capacity. When he rode into the arena with the rough riders from all corners of the earth the applause from 7,000 admiring New York men, women, and children rang through the huge hall. . . .

"In his brief farewell speech to the people he thanked them for the kind manner in which they had received him for so many years in New York, and felt sorry that the time had come when he had to say good-bye.

"'I have always looked forward to coming to New York every year,' said Buffalo Bill, 'and seeing the smiling faces of the women and children welcoming me. It has been a great gratification to me to see how the show has been appreciated in the East by the rising generations and the interest that has been taken by you all in the buffaloes and the Indians which have now disappeared from the plains to make way for the homesteads of the thousands who have gone West. Once more I thank you all for your kindness and say good-bye.'"

With these words and a final wave of his sombrero, bowing to the right and left of the Garden, Cody backed slowly away on his white horse toward the exit, while the audience rose to its feet and cheered.

It was Cody's original plan, which he worked out with Pawnee Bill, to do two years of farewell tours, stopping at every city he had ever played—but only once. He was confident that the two partners would clear a million dollars, half a million each, because the people who had seen him before would surely wish to see him again one last time. "The biggest and best gold mine you or I will ever have," is how Lillie put it to Cody.

He refined the farewell speech as the tours unfolded, until it sounded like this: "I am about to go home for a well-earned rest. Out in the West I have my horses, my buffaloes, my sturdy, staunch old Indian friends—my home and my green fields, but I never see them green. When my season is over the hillsides and the meadows have been blighted by a wintry frost and the sere and yellow leaves cover the ground. I want to see nature in its prime, to enjoy a rest from active life. My message to you tonight is one of farewell. Thirty years ago you gave me my first welcome here. I am grateful for your continued loyal devotion to me. During that time many of my friends among you and many of those with me have been long since gathered to the great unknown arena of another life—there are only a few of us left. When I went away from here each year before I merely said good night—this time it will mean good-bye. To my little friends in the gallery and the grown-ups who used to sit there, I thank you once again. God bless you all—good-bye."

In his book *Thrilling Lives of Buffalo Bill and Pawnee Bill*, the Wild West press agent Frank Winch wrote, "There was not a dry eye in the Garden." Actually, Cody would make more than one farewell appearance in the Garden. His "farewell exhibitions" were extended through 1912, though clearly he meant what he said in 1910—that he did plan to retire. Unfortunately, he couldn't afford to—and so, like many an opera diva or concert soloist before or since, he continued his farewell tours until he could no longer justify them, until his audiences and the press could no longer take them seriously. His refrain of "just one more big season and then I'll quit" dates all the way back to his combinations in the 1870s.

The show's take in 1910 was $1 million, of which $400,000 was profit. A portion of Lillie's share went to buy the show's winter quarters and equipment from the Ringling Brothers, to whom they had been paying rent. Lillie had invested his fortune in his Buffalo Ranch in Pawnee, Oklahoma, and in a $75,000 "Bungalow." (The word was capitalized because the concept of the house was so new at the time.) The value of the furnishings in Lillie's Bungalow, according to publicity agents Burke, Cooke, and Winch, was estimated at between $100,000 and $200,000, including specially commissioned paintings by several leading western artists, among them Charles Schreyvogel and H. H. Cross, both good friends of Buffalo Bill. Cody's share of the profits, on the other hand, were sunk in the Oracle mine.

An article in the New York *Times* for December 15, 1910, from Pawnee, Oklahoma, is headlined BUFFALO BILL'S LAST BULL. The report goes on to say that while visiting with Major Gordon W. Lillie on the latter's buffalo ranch, Cody shot and killed his last buffalo during an early morning hunt. Lillie's ranch contained 500 acres and was home to 150 buffalo, making Pawnee Bill one of the early conservators of an almost extinct species; Buffalo Bill was another.

"For some time," the story continued, "an unruly old buffalo bull has been attacking the other animals, and Major Lillie determined to kill him for a barbecue feast in honor of Col. Cody and a party of friends from the East. Buffalo Bill had the distinction of shooting the bull. He was accompanied by all members of the party, with numerous Pawnee and Osage Indians, and executed the death sentence with one shot."

On March 13, 1911, a special bulletin to the New York *Times* from Tucson, Arizona, noted that "Col. William F. Cody ('Buffalo Bill') plans to round out his career as one of the great pathfinders of the West by becoming the first United States Senator from Arizona."

On his way through Omaha Cody was interviewed about this possibility. He stated that he would do so if statehood were granted Arizona that year. The story broke in newspapers across the country. "Senator Buffalo Bill" in Philadelphia; "Buffalo Bill for the Senate" in Arizona; "Buffalo Bill Belongs in Senate" in Washington, D.C.; and "Cody Not Shying at Senatorship Job" in New York *Times*. "With a senator on the floor able to snuff out a candle at forty paces," quipped the Washington *Post* in March of 1911, "decorum could be preserved . . . without the services of a presiding officer."

Cody reveled in the attention this coverage brought him. He told the New York *Journal* that he absolutely favored women's suffrage. "I'd like to know of any boy t'other side of an idiot who didn't go to his mother with all his troubles and who didn't take her way as settling the matter."

"Arizona doesn't care how I stand on public questions as long as I can shoot straight," he declared. On the subject of conservation, Cody cracked, "Here, just a second, I'll show you." He produced a whiskey bottle. "Here's something I've been conserving for years. What'll you have?"

The New York *Times*'s editorial on the subject, however, took a different tack, suggesting politely that "war and the camp are no longer considered—even in Arizona—training schools for statesmen. . . . Offices are awarded more for merit and skill in the application of governmental principles. They go to eminent lawyers like ex-Gov. Hughes, or to professors of history and political economy like Woodrow Wilson. . . . [Colonel Cody] knows nothing of the problems of ballot reform, control of public utilities, conservation of natural resources—indeed, a chief part of his life was given up to destroying our resources—and the reform of the great municipalities which, linked together by railroads, have sprung up in the places of the rude camps of shacks, tents, and prairie wagons along the Western trails."

The *Times* also published a satiric political cartoon in a section called "The Passing Show." The cartoon pictures "U.S. Senator Buffalo Bill" sitting at a senatorial desk, a six-shooter in each hand, booted and spurred, with a rifle leaning against his desk and a lariat dangling from it.

The Cody for Senate boomlet—for such it was—petered out in due course. Arizona was admitted to the Union the following year, but without Senator Cody. It is perhaps a good thing that he did not actually run for the Senate and win. His experience as a no-show in the Nebraska legislature when he was elected to that body—or thought he was elected to it—does not inspire confidence in his dedication to statecraft.

Still, it is possible to question the *Times*'s disparagement of his qualifications. In our time, we have seen at least two military heroes elected to the Senate with little or no prior experience in government—John Glenn and John McCain. In an age when we send a professional wrestler to a governor's mansion, putting a showman in the nation's capital doesn't seem at all far-fetched.

During the years 1910 through 1912, Cody bombarded the manager of his Campo Bonito mine, L. W. Getchell, with letters begging for information, many of them sounding a note of desperation. On August 25, 1910, he wrote to "Dear Pard L.W., Today I am going to have Major Burke to come and spend a day with you before I get there and I am going to arrange to be with you two full days at Campo Bonito, and won't we enjoy it. The mill is getting good values but there will be two sorry old chums if things are going badly. . . . If there are no values in our ores we will eat snowballs, and they are scarce in Arizona. So get there, old pard, God bless you and yours, and may we be two happy old chaps this winter. I'll stick right to my work rustling up money to keep things going while you are at work at that end."

By November of that year Cody was writing to "Dear Getchell: I wish you would take two or three good men and put them to work in the Gideon Silver Mine. Show them where you thought the old workers lost the vein and let them start in and see if they can strike that silver vein. If we could strike it, up would go our stock—that vein is sure there someplace. . . . "

On May 24, 1911, a rail wreck near Lowell, Massachusetts, spread the Wild West and Great Far East all over the landscape. Elephants and buffalo stampeded; burros ran wild; Indians, Cossacks, and Arabs huddled in nearby fields while the cowboys rounded up the livestock. Some of the animals and their keepers were imprisoned in the wrecked railway cars, many with severe injuries. Cody's private car was part of the wrecked second section, but, with Johnny Baker's help, he managed to restore order.

Buffalo Bill Cody on horseback, 1911. (Buffalo Bill Historical Center, Cody, Wyoming)

After tending to the injured, Cody led the company by "foot parade" into the town of Lowell, where they set up tents without missing a performance. Business was poor in the New England mill towns, which were suffering from a recession. In September and October, when the show swung into the South, it ran into bad weather and heavy losses. Cody was sick with *la grippe* and feeling miserable. The tone of his letters to Getchell soon turned desperate.

On June 1, 1911, he wrote, "I am yet hit hard down east since leaving Boston. The railroad wreck will cost about $10,000 damage. And we are loosing money in every town. And I had several big notes due in June. So its going to make me sweat to meet June 15th pay day. . . . You see you are working over 40 men instead of 30 which we calculated. No telegram yet saying vein in drift struck. If nothing struck things at Bonito will look bad."

And on June 12: "I have gone on nearly bankrupting my self. Beleiveing on what you have told me, written me, and telegraphed me. And I still believe in you. At least I hope you are right. . . . Your expenses this spring have been much heavyer than I told you to spend or I could raise. I can get no satifactory answer to any of my questions Telegraph me whether I shall go ahead or quite. My old friend I am nearly crazy."

As early as 1910 Cody had attempted to sell his interest in the mine. He had also done his best to interest Major Lillie in putting up money for it. Lillie, who apparently had confidence in Getchell, did visit Campo Bonito, but wisely decided not to invest in it.

During the 1911 season, the Two Bills show faced serious competition from the Miller Brothers 101 Ranch Wild West show—the only Wild West that competed with Cody after 1910. At the beginning of the season, the 101 did its best to put Buffalo Bill out of business by playing cities on Cody's scheduled route before Cody arrived. This attempt at sabotage was thwarted when Cody's show arrived in Philadelphia first and did close to $70,000 worth of business. "Guess 101 Ranch wish they had never got ahead of us," said Cody.

Philadelphia was an exception, though, and by the end of the season, profits were low, and Cody offered to sell Scout's Rest Ranch to Lillie for $100,000. Of this, $80,000 went to Louisa Cody and $20,000 toward Cody's debt of $30,000 to Lillie. The balance was covered by a $10,000 mortgage on the Irma Hotel, which Cody transferred to Lillie. Through this deal Cody became half owner of the show at the end of 1911. Meanwhile, the Arizona mine was producing scheelite, a form of tungsten ore that had proven useful in manufacturing electric light bulbs. It seemed possible that at last the mine would cease to hemorrhage Cody's money and begin to pay for itself. It never did, not in Cody's lifetime, and must be counted as his greatest folly. And yet other contemporaries of Cody— George Hearst and Meyer Guggenheim in particular—made vast fortunes in mining.

Were Colonel Getchell and his son Noble systematically robbing Cody of his money? Certainly Nate Salsbury thought so, and Gordon Lillie became convinced over time that the money his partner spent on the mines in Arizona was largely wasted. E. J. Ewing, a mine expert, was asked by Colonel Dyer in 1912 to examine Campo Bonito and offer his opinion. Ewing later concluded that the Getchells conspired to separate as much money from Cody and Dyer as they possibly could. Informed by Ewing of certain kickbacks received by the Getchells, Cody threatened them with arrest and prosecution, forcing them to give up their stock in the mine and return some of the Colonel's money to Cody, who decided not to prosecute, because he did not want the notoriety. Richard Walsh also writes that the mines, like the Wyoming irrigation project, were not properly managed. Johnny Baker, after a visit to one of them, reported he had found only four men working, although there were thirty-six names on the payroll. On the advice of his "experts," Cody had spent somewhere between $300,000 to $500,000 on the Oracle. However much it was, it was enough to ruin him financially.

* * *

As the Wild West continued across the country on its "farewell" tours, Buffalo Bill was shooting better than ever. At an afternoon performance in Washington, D.C., on April 17, 1911, fifty balls were thrown into the air as he galloped around the arena, "and not one was missed by old scout as the applause from thousands of hands and throats followed him," reported the Washington *Star* on April 18.

An advertisement in *The Show World*, typical of the promotion, read: "Positively Last Personal Appearance in Chicago . . . July 15–23." The magazine also reminded its readers of "the announced farewell appearance of Col. William F. Cody (Buffalo Bill) in the saddle."

Many of the cities the Wild West visited commemorated the occasion by presenting Buffalo Bill with elaborate loving cups, so many that he complained he was being crowded out of his private coach. In all these appearances he stressed that Major Lillie—Pawnee Bill—would be taking his place in the arena in years to come.

When it was announced in May that the Colonel would pay a farewell visit "in the saddle" to North Platte on August 19, the excitement in town was unbridled. The local newspapers outdid themselves in accounts of Cody's exploits; reminded readers that their hometown had been the place where the old idea of the Wild West was put together, "where the baby of his brain was born," as one scribe put it. In expectation of thousands of visitors from around Nebraska, residents were urged to clean up all ashes, garbage, and manure from their property.

Nor did North Platte want to skip the obligatory loving cup. One was ordered early and put on display in a local store. Posters and lithographs were plastered all over town a month in advance of the show's arrival. On the morning of August 18, two forty-seven-car show trains pulled into the North Platte depot. Hundreds of people were on hand. Hundreds more arrived from every town for miles around.

When the hometown loving cup was presented to Cody at the end of the afternoon performance of the Wild West, the old showman accepted the cup and thanked North Platte for its testimonial, which, he said, "I prize more than gold or silver. It will ever remind me of the deep debt of gratitude I owe to you, dear friends, and when the time comes that I retire I shall again make my home among the old friends and neighbors I have known so long and love so well." At that point, the mayor of North Platte filled the cup—with water—and Cody drank deeply of it.

It was on this tour that Cody had his confrontation with "Buffalo Bill" Matthewson. There are conflicting versions of this episode. One, which Don Russell endorses, was given by Frank Winch, the Wild West's press agent. In this version, Matthewson was found virtually destitute, and Cody secretly subsidized the old man as well as recognizing him as the "original" Buffalo Bill. Another contemporary version had Colonel Matthewson—yet another "colonel"; was there no end to them in the old West?—financially well off. A Wichita newsman interviewed Matthewson before Cody arrived in town; he portrayed a healthy, generous, eighty-one-year-old man who did "not and never did worry about the matter in the least, even though he feels that he has been very much imposed on." Matthewson insisted that "the name of Buffalo Bill was tacked onto me before Bill Cody knew the difference between a buffalo and a jack rabbit. . . . I don't care what Cody has said or done, for my friends know where and how the name of 'Buffalo Bill' was given to me and if he has been successful in commercializing my reputation, I can only say, 'He is welcome.'" As for being hard up, the newspaperman claimed that Matthewson "can now write a check for close onto a hundred thousand."

It became clear to Buffalo Bill that if he was to continue feeding his insatiable Arizona mine, he needed to liquidate some of his other holdings. A natural choice was his Big Horn Valley property, most specifically the three hotels he owned there: the Irma, the Pahaska Tepee, and the Wapiti Inn. In 1912 these hotels were worth much more than he had put into them, and selling them would save him the trouble of attempting to run them while he was on the road with the show. He made an effort to sell them to the Busch family of Anheuser-Busch Beer, which he felt could use them to advertise their beer, but the deal was never consummated.

As early as 1898, Buffalo Bill had been put on film by Thomas Edison, at the same time as Edison shot footage of Annie Oakley at his West Orange, New Jersey, studio. Cody was filmed firing his Model 1873 Winchester—his favorite rifle. None of this film has survived. In 1902 Biograph made films of the Wild West, including shots of Cody hunting buffalo on horseback, firing blanks—and firing at glass balls, still on horseback. An Indian throws up the targets as the two ride around the show ring. There is also footage of the old Deadwood stagecoach and of cowboys and Indians shooting at each other.

In 1912 the Two Bills formed the Pawnee Bill and Buffalo Bill Film Company, which produced *The Life of Buffalo Bill (Col. Cody)*, starring, of course, the old scout himself. In three reels, the movie does have a story line, and features the First Scalp for Custer as well as an encounter with Cheyenne Indians. The plot, such as it is, unfolds as a dream sequence, "A Dream of the Days of His Youth."

It is interesting to see that Cody recognized the potential of motion pictures early and hoped to capitalize on his personal fame and the reputation of the Wild West. *The Life of Buffalo Bill* can certainly be considered one of the first movie westerns, though not the first; that title belongs to *The Great Train Robbery*, filmed in 1903 by Gilbert A. Anderson. Then in his sixties, Cody was obviously too old to become a matinee idol, but he did not relinquish his hopes of re-creating the exploits of his frontier days on film.

Cody had publicly denied that 1911 was positively his last season. "I will remain in the saddle and at the head of the organization until November, 1912. Then my partner, Major Lillie, and John Baker, both men who started with the Wild West in 1883 and are now with it, will continue the exhibition."

And in fact, Cody did retire in 1912. But not for long. That year the show's profits came to only $125,000—not enough to cover the Colonel's debts and investments. His partner Pawnee Bill had been absorbing the $40,000 cost of keeping the show in winter quarters, recovering Cody's share from the show's earnings. That winter he asked Cody to do his best to raise $20,000 somehow. In the fall the Colonel put 116 acres of the first land he had ever owned at North Platte—the site of the first Welcome Wigwam—up for sale as town lots and acre tracts. The streets in his new development were named after the army officers he had once served under: Sherman, Sheridan, Miles, Carr, Custer, and Mills. Sixty-seven lots were sold on opening day, but at $75 to $150 a lot, with terms of $10 down and $5 a month, or a 10 percent discount for cash in full, the lots wouldn't have brought enough to ease the Colonel's financial pressures.

Then, while visiting his sister May Decker in Denver, the Colonel ran into Harry H. Tammen, the publisher, with Frederick G. Bonfils, of the Denver *Post*. It was an encounter he would come to regret.

"THE MAN WHO BROKE
MY HEART"

Bonfils and Tammen, in Don Russell's opinion, were "probably the most amoral and unscrupulous partners ever to publish a newspaper." Tammen, a native of Baltimore, went to work as a porter's helper in a beer garden at the age of seven and at twenty-one was the bartender at Chicago's famous Palmer House. He later tended bar at the Windsor in Denver, where Cody probably met him. The Windsor was built in 1880. There were two bars on the first floor—one off the lobby, and a back bar off the billiard room. There were usually six bartenders on duty. If a celebrity such as General Grant, Buffalo Bill, or the heavyweight champion John L. Sullivan visited Denver, the bar staff was doubled. A Chinese boy in full costume kept the floor clear of cigar butts and tobacco juice.

Bonfils had made a small fortune running a lottery in Chicago. Tammen met him there, and in his account of the meeting, "walked smack in on him. . . . He eyed me up and down, and said: 'Who are you? And what do you want?' 'Kid,' I said, 'I hear you've got a million dollars in safety-deposit boxes, and I'm going to shake you down for half of it.'

"This sort of floored him," continued Tammen. "He said: 'Sit down, and we'll talk it over.' Then he imitated me. 'Kid,' he said, 'if you get a nickel out of me, you'll be doing more than anyone else ever did, or ever will do.'"

The proposition Tammen made to Bonfils was that they buy "a piddling little paper" in Denver called the *Evening Post*. Bonfils put up the money—$12,500—and Tammen supplied the brains. They also bought the equipment of the defunct Denver *Democrat* and rechristened their new acquisition the Denver *Post*. They then proceeded to turn it into the most successful paper in Denver—building circulation in William Randolph Hearst fashion—by making the *Post* loud, vulgar, and sensational.

426

No cheap trick was beneath their brand of blatant journalism. At the same time, they were perceived as populists, for their ardent support of the working man. They were indeed an odd couple, faithfully portrayed by Gene Fowler, who once worked for them, in his book *Timber Line*.

"Tammen was a dreamer," Fowler wrote, "Bonfils was haughty, dynamic, publicly taciturn (except when his Peer Gynt temper broke through and words or fists commenced to fly).

"Tammen was forever on the lookout for new and tinkling toys. A boys' band, a coal company, Geronimo's authenticated scalps . . . all these were excellent treasures, but Tammen sought a more glamorous field."

The glamorous field he sought was the sawdust. In short, he wanted to acquire a circus. Bonfils didn't object to his partner's indulgence, as long as it made money "from the grass up." They started on a small scale with a dog and pony show. Because Tammen wanted an impressive name, he called it the Floto Dog and Pony Show, after his sports editor, Otto C. Floto, who owned no part of the show. Then, in order to attach a well-known circus name to their show, they hired a relative of the Sells Brothers, of Sells-Forepaugh fame, gave him a few shares of stock, and advertised their enterprise as the Sells-Floto Circus. Their posters showed pictures of Otto Floto and all four Sells Brothers. The Brothers Ringling were furious at this invasion of their turf; they had bought Sells-Forepaugh, along with Barnum and Bailey, in order to eliminate competition; now this upstart outfit was following their routes and plastering over their bills. (Of course, the Ringlings did the same thing to their rivals, including the Wild West and Great Far East.) In the pages of the *Post*, the Greatest Show on Earth was labeled the "Circus Trust," casting Sells-Floto as a beleaguered underdog, fighting a giant monopoly.

The dispute ended up in court, and ended with an order that Tammen and Bonfils must cease picturing the Sells Brothers in their promotion but could continue using the name—which did, after all, belong to a genuine Sells—William.

There was one other "toy" that Harry Tammen wanted to acquire: Buffalo Bill. Cody unwittingly put himself in Tammen's clutches in that 1911 meeting. Tammen learned that Cody was looking for a loan and was quick to offer one—$20,000 for six months, at 6 percent. That $20,000, while a godsend at the time, would become the most costly note Cody ever signed.

Once he had the money in hand, Cody left for New York, where he chatted with a reporter for the New York *Clipper*. "I will not be in the saddle," he said cheerfully, "but I will be with the show and appear at every performance. It will be my pleasure to meet my friends and introduce Major Gordon Lillie as my successor." Once more, he said, there would be street parades—a practice that had been discontinued some time earlier. He would no longer make his entrance to the arena on horseback, but would be driven in behind a pair of spanking bays in a fancy phaeton with driver and footman in full livery.

Back home in North Platte, Cody was still hopeful that his mines would be "heavy producers." He now made an effort to sell stock in Oracle. To his cousin J. Frank Cody, he sent a night letter in October 1912: "Wait till I come, wonderful report from mines. Mill running on forty dollar ore. Tucson Bank buying our consentrates as come from mill, get busy. Waldorf Hotel first November, telegraph there. High Jinks [a new tunnel in the mine] will be a winner too." In February 1913 he sent another night letter to Cousin Frank, "Have just heard from Mines Have made a rich strike on Southern Bell claim The ore simpliy carries gold all through it I will send you a sample Have you received stock books."

In February 1913 Cody left for Canada in a vain attempt to sell mining stock to some of his relatives there. The relatives seemed to be interested, and in June he reported to Julia that they had organized a syndicate and sent an engineer to Arizona to evaluate the mines. The engineer's report had been "excellent," he wrote, "[a]nd the Canadians will finance and take over the properties if we can come to terms. I'll sure come to terms." Nothing more is heard of financial assistance from his relatives. As in the unhappy Cleveland lawsuit, they either did not have the money to invest or were too wary to buy Cody's mining stock.

On his return from Canada, the Colonel discovered that he was about to become part of the Sells-Floto Circus. An announcement in the Denver *Post* on February 5, 1913, stated: "Colonel W.F. Cody (Buffalo Bill) put his name to a contract with the proprietors of the Sells-Floto Circus, the gist of which is that the two big shows consolidate for the season of 1914 and thereafter. The Pawnee Bill interests now associated with Colonel Cody's Wild West Show are not included in this agreement—the idea being that the Sells-Floto Circus shall continue in its entirety and the 'Buffalo Bill Exposition of Frontier Days and the Passing of the West' with the historic incidents associated with them, shall also be preserved, added to, and given with the circus performance."

Whatever the wording of the agreement he had signed when he borrowed the $20,000 from Tammen, it is unlikely that he realized he was selling the publisher his services—most important, his name—by accepting the loan. There is, however, a "Memoranda of Agreement, Made and Entered into this twenty-eighth day of January, A.D. 1913, by and between the SELLS-FLOTO SHOWS COMPANY, a corporation, organized and existing under the laws of the state of Colorado, party of the first part, and

WILLIAM F. CODY, (generally known as 'Buffalo Bill') of North Platte, Nebraska, party of the second part."

This agreement called for Cody to travel with Sells-Floto in a private car, manage a "Wild West" feature, appear in parades as well as in and about the tents where performances were given, in order to please the public. He was not, however, required to appear in the saddle, or give any other performance, except of his own volition. This agreement was to begin with the season of 1914. Tammen was hardly generous in his terms; he, "party of the first part," was to keep strict account of all receipts, pay himself $3,000 a day for each circus day, with the excess of the receipts to be divided sixty percent for Tammen and forty percent for Cody. The Memoranda of Agreement was duly signed and sealed by Tammen and Cody. Did the old scout know what he was signing? It's hard to believe that he could have been completely taken in. At this point in his life he was, though, a desperate man.

When Lillie asked what was going on, Cody telegraphed, "Pay no attention to press reports; I have done nothing that will interfere with our show."

Cody must actually have believed this, in which case, his general faith in the good nature of everyone he associated with would have led him both to misjudge and to underestimate Tammen; in any case, his was a sad case of naïveté. Despite Cody's reassurances, Lillie believed that he had been double-crossed by Cody. He did not worry about the fate of the show, because it had been incorporated and could not be held liable for the Colonel's personal obligations. At the same time, Lillie no longer felt any need to be further concerned about Cody's debts.

At the opening performance of the 1913 show in Philadelphia's Constitution Hall, Cody made his arena entrance seated in a trap behind a team of spanking horses. It was the first time in thirty years that he had not appeared before his audiences in buckskins, mounted on his favorite horse. He told his audience, "I feel bad about this, but I decided to dismount before Father Time bucked me out of the saddle."

A new addition to the show that year was Goldie Griffith, leader of the cowgirl contingent. Years later an old-timer said of her, "She was a heller in skirts, half man, but all woman, and pretty, and she could ride better than half the men in Nebraska." In New York City a parade had been planned, but the city fathers declined to issue a permit, because of the many automobiles now clogging Fifth Avenue. The Wild West paraded anyway, for there was no law against sightseeing—even on horseback.

Goldie Griffith rode her horse up the steps of Grant's Tomb, to wild applause.

All of the show people liked Colonel Cody, said Goldie, especially the Indians, for he "never bawled anybody out," nor would he allow anyone else to do so. When the weather was cold and wet he had his striker, an Indian named Carlos Miles, mix hot toddies in the big silver punch bowl Queen Victoria had given him. All who came to his tent on such days were given a cupful to keep them warm. The toddies were very good, Goldie remembered, and she and some of her friends used to wish it would rain more often.

They got their wish when the show headed south. The year 1913 was a flood year, and the show's routing was ill-conceived. In early spring they were hit by cold and freezing rains. At the same time, the South was reeling from a fall in cotton prices. Canvas was twice blown down by high winds. The crowds were so sparse that for the first half of the season the show showed only red ink in its account books. From Jackson, Tennessee, Cody wrote Julia: "I am much better. One week ago to day I was very ill in Knoxville. I am not at all strong. I have had lots of trouble for years financially. And no vacation work and worry has broken my once iron constitution. . . . This is a killing life."

This was also the third year of Buffalo Bill's "farewell" tours. It was one good-bye season too many for the show, because there was no city where they had not previously said farewell. Sarah Bernhardt may have made year after year of farewell tours, but Colonel Cody was no Bernhardt.

For one hundred successive days the show lost money—one matinee in good weather netted only $7.15. Rations were cut in the dining tent and many Indians, discouraged by the prospect of going hungry, deserted. Replacements had to be found at the Pine Ridge Agency in midseason.

By July 1913 the show was in Chicago, where it was threatened with foreclosure by the United States Printing and Lithograph Company, whose home office was in that city. The company held a $16,000 note against Cody and Lillie for advertising and posters printed in 1912. Out of a high regard for Cody, the lithograph company had agreed to print $50,000 worth of material for the 1913 show. The company was now prepared to attach the show for some $40,000 worth of advertising, in addition to the $16,000 note. Lillie agreed to send $10,000 on account if they would let the show run for two more weeks. "We felt friendly to Colonel Cody," said a company spokesman, "and didn't want to embarrass him."

The show continued on its way, passing through North Platte on July 19, heading toward Denver. There a disastrous season was about to end in a blow from which the Wild West could not possibly recover.

Pawnee Bill Lillie was warned ahead of time, by a representative of the United States Printing and Lithograph Company, not to go to Denver, that if he did take the show there, he would never take it out of the city—Tammen would see to that. Cody's note with Tammen was about to fall due, putting Tammen in a strong position to foreclose on the show. Lillie apparently did not believe that Tammen actually would wreck the show; in any event, it couldn't be attached for a debt of Cody's—or so he thought.

At the close of the evening performance, according to Richard Walsh, Cody saw the sheriff and his men come on the lot and, fearing the worst, sent one of his men hurrying to the treasury wagon to save the day's receipts. Unfortunately, the sheriff got there first and seized the money. This meant that Cody could not pay his performers, or even feed them. On the following day, the trunks of his company were also attached, leaving them only the clothes they were wearing.

Lillie could have saved the situation by paying the $60,000 note for posters, programs, and other show advertising, which Tammen now controlled, out of his own funds, or by signing over Cody's mortgaged property to the lithography company. He did not, knowing that Cody was going to join Sells-Floto next year anyway. Instead, Lillie fled to New Jersey to file a petition in bankruptcy, but was thwarted by Denver attorneys who had earlier filed a petition in involuntary bankruptcy on behalf of two of the show's creditors. Tammen persuaded Cody to sue Lillie for an accounting of the $30,000 the show had taken in since Chicago, none of which Lillie used to reduce the show's indebtedness, and to dissolve their partnership; Tammen then attached the show for the $20,000 note and got what he had wanted all along—Buffalo Bill. Lillie, however, whose machinations had been blocked by Tammen at every turn, kept his personal fortune but was through in show business.

Cody's primary concern was the well-being of his people, who had been left penniless by Tammen's actions, and the show's animals, now without shelter. Any cash the Colonel could scrape up—and it wasn't much—he used to help the members of his company. When a sympathetic friend sent him $500, he divided that among them too. A place was found in a stable in Overland Park for the horses; the show people soon moved in with them, slept in the hay, and washed out their clothes at night, to wear them the next day. Cast members took jobs wherever they could find them. Goldie Griffith, for one, took part in a wrestling match at the Denver Auditorium. Whatever money the performers had, they shared with each other. The Indians, it was said, had to sell their costumes to get back to their reservations, although Adolph Marks, general counsel for the lithography firm, claimed that he had arranged to send them home. The rest of the company went home however they could. Some Boy Scouts who had traveled with the show since it left Chicago were particularly unfortunate; broke, they headed home on foot, giving exhibition drills along the way and passing the hat to buy food. During the third week in August they stayed in North Platte, put on their drill, then headed for Omaha. The following week the Omaha *Bee* reported a letter from Boy Scout national headquarters advising the public that the Buffalo Bill show refugees walking to Chicago were not Boy Scouts at all. "What of it?" challenged the *Bee*. "What is the difference between a Boy Scout and a scouting boy when it comes to such straits?"

Through all this turmoil Louisa Cody, who had remained in Denver, stood by her bewildered husband. Adolph Marks was highly critical of Lillie's behavior and assigned no blame whatever to Cody, who could not bear to watch on September 15 as his beloved show went under the auctioneer's hammer. Even Cody's favorite horse Isham was sold. Fortunately, two of Cody's friends bid against each other for it, each determined to give Isham back to the Colonel. The horse was knocked down for $150, and the buyer, Colonel C. J. Bills of Lincoln, Nebraska, sent it to Cody's TE Ranch. Tammen bought only a pair of black mules.

Cody later spoke of Tammen as "the man who had my show sold at a sheriff sale, which broke my heart." The Colonel was old, ill, tired—only a few years from death; anyone would have assumed he was finished, washed up. His show was gone, along with Scout's Rest Ranch and the Irma Hotel. Nevertheless, he was already making plans to start over. In a letter to an old friend, Tom Foley, he wrote: "I am not down and out . . . although I regret the scandal and publicity. . . . I will soon be on the road with a new and better show, under new management with unlimited capital."

Once he was back on the TE ranch, offers from vaudeville managers came pouring in. One offer from a London agent was for $2,500 a week; Cody replied that his price was $5,000; this demand was rejected. Tammen, still going through the motions of friendship, made him an offer of a part in a motion picture. Cody refused but proposed a plan of his own—a series of grand historical films depicting events in his life and the Old West, where possible with the original participants. He would re-create the Battle of Summit Springs, the fight with Yellow Hand, even Wounded Knee. Tammen and Bonfils, eager to cash in on their "investment," agreed. The secretary of war was visiting Denver, and he approved the use of army troops for the project. The secretary of the interior agreed to the use of Pine Ridge Reservation as well as agency Indians. Cody's old friend General Miles, now retired, was also willing to take part. And so "The Col. W.F. Cody (Buffalo Bill) Historical Pictures Company" was organized by the Essanay Film Company of Chicago. At Essanay the "S" was George K. Spoor, who started making movies in 1895, when they were first projected on a screen; "A" was Gilbert M. "Broncho Billy" Anderson, who first appeared in *The Great Train Robbery* in 1903, which he also directed. Since then he had made some six hundred Broncho Billy features and had become the first true western star.

By early fall of 1913 they were ready to make pictures at Pine Ridge. The Twelfth Cavalry, six hundred troopers strong, was there, along with General Miles and other Indian Wars veterans. The Indians included Short Bull, No Neck, Woman's Dress, Flat Iron, and others who had been in Buffalo Bill's Wild West. The project was touted by the newspapers as "the greatest film ever made, a lasting pictorial history of these early campaigns to hand down to posterity." This claim is especially ironic, since none of the films Cody made have survived; the only record we have is in still photographs.

When the time came to shoot the Yellow Hand episode, Lieutenant King—now a general—once again gave Cody the signal for his famous dash to glory. Johnny Baker, a tower of strength to the old scout, was the director. The Battle of Wounded Knee was staged in Rushville, Nebraska. In this episode, General Miles demanded authenticity—he wanted the six hundred cavalrymen to march past the camera until all eleven thousand of his 1891 command had been filmed. What the general did not know was that for most of the march the cameramen, to save film, had surreptitiously closed their lenses.

Since the Indian tepees were set up precisely where they had been when their ancestors were slaughtered almost twenty-five years earlier, some of the young Indians thought of using live ammunition instead of blanks in the battle scene, thus avenging the massacre of their grandparents. The older warriors, who knew better, prevailed, and only blanks were fired that day. Still, the Hotchkiss gun that was set up, again as in 1891, did cause some stirrings of alarm among the Indians, who wondered if the whites planned to mow them down a second time. During filming, Indian extras "died" convincingly enough, but then kept lifting their heads to look at the continuing action.

Eight one-reel subjects were filmed by the company. They were sometimes shown on eight successive afternoons. The "Historical Pictures," despite their advance billing, created no great excitement, but perhaps it was too soon for the Nickelodeons to move on to more sophisticated fare. Meanwhile, the Colonel sent his son-in-law Fred Garlow to Omaha to handle the promotion of the films. Cody himself traveled to Washington, where he premiered *The Indian Wars* for members of President Wilson's cabinet and Congress at the New Home Club on February 27, 1914. Cody then made a brief tour with his pictures, showing them and lecturing at the same time, in Chicago, in the American Theater in Omaha, and finally in Denver.

In April Cody went out to California for the 1914 season with Sells-Floto Circus and Buffalo Bill's Wild West—Two Big Institutions Joined Together at One Price of Admission—twenty-five cents. The Colonel was to receive $100 a day plus 40 percent of the receipts over $3,000. Although he led the parades in his buggy, he was required to introduce the show from the saddle, tired as he was. He was not obligated to do any shooting or other acts. Most of his work was to promote the show by chatting with reporters and meeting local dignitaries. The show toured up the coast to Canada, and on May 13 and 14, Fred Garlow was running the eight reels of Indian war pictures in North Platte. Johnny Baker, meanwhile, was in London to shoot in the Anglo-American Exhibition and while there sought to raise British capital for the Oracle mine and to get bookings for Historical Pictures.

The circus closed in Texas in mid-October, and Cody went directly to Denver, where he stayed with his sister May Decker and her husband, Lew. He had been sick through the last week of the season, mainly because of his anxiety over his debts. A few days of rest restored his energy, and he traveled to his TE ranch, where he killed a deer by moonlight. He spent the winter devising new ways to pay his debts. One scheme was to start a dude ranch at DeMaris Springs in Wyoming.

While the Colonel was sick in Denver, Tammen paid him a call and persuaded him to sign a new contract. Cody had been unhappy with his share of the 1914 profits—so much smaller than Tammen's—but he failed to notice that this time his 40 percent was for receipts above $3,100 instead of $3,000. Tammen had bilked him again.

Cody had two staunch admirers on the Sells-Floto lot. One was Karl L. King, then bandmaster with the show. "The Colonel," King said, "had a certain amount of dignity about him. . . . Was a handsome man for his age and still looked wonderful on a horse. He made a definite impression on me, and it is one of my favorite memories of my years in show business. In other words I liked the old boy." King composed an intermezzo dedicated to Cody called "Passing of the Red Man," which Cody liked to have played for him.

The other admirer was Courtney Ryley Cooper, then acting as the Sells-Floto press agent. This is how Gene Fowler, who knew Cooper well, described him: "Cooper was a sprightly, colorful chap, skinny and balding in his late twenties, a dancer of surpassing grace, and full of wit and the

Buffalo Bill Cody with cast members, c. 1915, the last year he toured with his own show. (Buffalo Bill Historical Center, Cody, Wyoming)

juice of living." According to Fowler, Cooper idolized Buffalo Bill, and his newspaper articles helped sustain the ego of Pahaska, the long-haired one.

On his sixty-ninth birthday, February 26, 1915, the Colonel was entertained by the Cody Club of Cody, Wyoming. Sixty-nine guests were invited to a party given for him at the Irma Hotel. He seemed fit and rested when the nightmare season of 1915 opened on April 13. By the end of May, they had enjoyed only four days of sunshine, which meant no profits for Cody—still, he was getting his $100 a day, he was rested and fairly fit, and his wife, Louisa, was with him. He had a private car with a porter, a cook, and a carriage driver. The admission price was to be raised to fifty cents, which gave him hope that his 40 percent override would begin to kick in. To his dismay, however, he learned that the advertising still listed the show's ticket price as a quarter. Cody considered this outright robbery, and demanded that his name and photograph be removed from any misleading advertising.

At Fort Madison, Iowa, the show tent was pitched near a swamp, and when a sudden cloudburst flooded the lot, a thousand spectators were in danger. Cody and five of his men stayed to carry out the children and

Buffalo Bill Cody with his wife, Louisa, in front of his private railroad car, c. 1915.
(Buffalo Bill Historical Center, Cody, Wyoming)

help the women escape, while the rest of the four hundred circus men panicked and fled. In addition to his complaint about the admission price to the show, Cody was upset about the condition of the tent, which was old, with rotting ropes. He threatened to leave the show unless the tent was repaired, fearing he would be blamed if there was an accident. Tammen struck back.

In Cody's words: "After everything was sold . . . at the sheriff's sale in Denver I asked him if he was satisfied. He said yes and that I should be satisfied as my debts were paid. I said are you paid in full he said yes. Now as I am going to leave him, I get a letter from him yesterday August 21 saying that Lawyers and thieves had gotten away with all the money and I still owed him $20,000. Of course I have got to see Tammen and I have got evidence enough to land him in the Penitentiary. I may not stay with the show two weeks probly not a day. I am going to Denver to see Tammen." What Tammen proposed to do was to withhold $50 of wages every day until the $20,000 loan was satisfied. To say that Tammen was unscrupulous would be putting it too mildly.

To Julia Will wrote despairingly in August: "Everything I attempt to do goes wrong. . . . I have two buyers [for my mine] and Tungstun is five times higher than it ever was but I am so unlucky nothing comes my way. . . . I expect to pull off a big hunt this fall but I am in such bad luck that might fall—down—

"I am very tired and nervous and discoraged. . . . Such things won't let me get well."

Cody wrote old friends seeking help against Tammen. Pawnee Bill offered assistance, even though Cody's suit against Lillie was still in the courts. Tammen finally went to Lawrence, Kansas, to see Cody, who had written to one friend, "There must be a law to protect me from him robbing me. Ask some good lawyer to stop this. I have stood between savagery and civilization most all my early days. Won't someone who knows the law come to my rescue. God bless you. I am old and tired."

He added a scribbled postscript: "This man is driving me crazy. I can easily kill him but as I avoided killing in the bad days I don't want to kill him. But if there is no justice left I will."

Cody meant what he said; he was angry enough now to kill Tammen on sight, and Tammen knew it. Instead of summoning Cody to Denver, he did meet with the old showman in Cody's tent, but only after being assured by Cody that he would be safe. Tammen got Cody to agree that he would stay with the show till the end of the season, in return for which he dropped his attempt to dock the Colonel's daily fee—though he did not waive the $20,000 obligation. He also told Cody he would sue him for $100,000 if he broke his contract.

Buffalo Bill Cody and "the man who broke my heart," Harry Tammen, 1916. (Courtesy Park County Archives)

After 366 performances over 183 days, the show closed in Texas. It had traveled over a route of 16,878 miles. "And with Gods help," said Buffalo Bill, "I haven't missed a performance." Although business had been good for the show's last four weeks and Cody figured that Tammen owed him some $18,000, he didn't expect to collect it, and probably felt only relief to have Tammen off his back—or so he thought.

Cody went on a lecture tour with his western films in the spring of 1916, but despite considerable publicity, the films failed to make the profits that he had anticipated. The theme of his lectures was "preparedness," for war was raging in Europe, and it was thought that America would soon be drawn into the conflict.

Tammen, meanwhile, was not quite through with Cody. In addition to claiming a share in any profit from the motion pictures—Spoor talked him out of that—Tammen demanded $5,000 for the use of the name "Buffalo Bill" in any future show. Cody, who indeed planned to start another show, paid Tammen off and was finally rid of his nemesis for good.

In the winter of 1915–1916, Cody still had hopes for the Oracle, though they were fading fast. In order to raise money, he leased 1,400 acres of oil land in Wyoming and organized the Buffalo Bill Oil and Gas Co. There was talk of selling prints of the Rosa Bonheur painting. Cody also began writing a series of autobiographical articles for *Hearst's International* magazine, entitled "The Great West That Was: Buffalo Bill's Life Story." These articles were published from August 1916 to July 1917. In 1920 they were brought out in book form as Cody's last and least reliable autobiography, and a few years later Universal Pictures Studio drew on the material for a series of western serials.

In 1916 "preparedness" was in the air, because of America's position regarding the Great War in Europe. President Wilson had been elected to a second term because "he kept us out of war." Officially we were neutral, but with the sinking of the *Lusitania* in 1915 with the loss of American lives, and Germany's threats to wage all-out submarine warfare against neutral as well as enemy shipping, it was becoming increasingly difficult to maintain neutrality. Preparedness, however, had a solid ring to it; "be prepared" was the Boy Scout motto, after all; and it was always considered wise to be ready for any threat to our security.

Buffalo Bill conceived an idea for "A Pageant of Preparedness," which could also be combined with a Wild West show. He proposed the idea to Major General Hugh L. Scott, the chief of staff of the U.S. Army, and got swift approval. He would be able to draw on soldiers on reserve furlough as well as obtaining artillery pieces.

Still, he needed a venue for his pageant. He chose the Miller Brothers and Arlington 101 Ranch Wild West. Founded after the Civil War, the 101 Ranch took up the better part of 110,000 acres in northeastern Oklahoma for several decades. The ranch became virtually self-sufficient, spreading over four counties, producing its own corn, wheat, oil, and fruit, with its own telephone system, schools, churches, and roads. Its rodeos blossomed into a touring show, which competed at first with Buffalo Bill's Wild West, although, according to Don Russell, it "had a good reputation but never seemed quite sure of itself financially."

Buffalo Bill first sought backing to buy into the Millers' show. Unsuccessful in this, he became a 101 employee. He made a deal by which he was paid $100 a day and one-third of all profits over $2,750 daily. In one week he made $4,161.35. The show was billed as "Miller & Arlington Wild West Show Co., present The Military Pageant Preparedness, 'Buffalo Bill' (himself) Combined with the 101 Ranch Shows." Clearly, Cody's name had not lost its magic.

The Pageant of Preparedness featured charging cavalry and batteries of field guns. As the program promised, "the frontier features always naturally associated with the name of Buffalo Bill, have not been neglected, and scores of Indians, cowboys, cowgirls and other characteristic people of the ranch and prairie present a vivid picture of life on the border." The Pony Express was a part of the new show, as was marksmanship, although Cody was not called upon to shoot—only to lead the parades and perform his now-classic introduction, sometimes riding around the arena in a carriage or an automobile, sometimes on horseback. Other events included bucking-horse riding, trick and fancy roping, wild-horse racing, and roping steers.

One amusing sidelight to the 1916 tour took place in Chicago, whose mayor, "Big Bill" Thompson, proudly boasted that his city was "the sixth German city in the world," and he wanted no part of "preparedness." Consequently, the show was renamed "the Chicago Shan-Kive and Roundup." It was explained that "Shan-Kive" meant "a good time" and "roundup" attracted Big Bill, who fancied himself a cowboy and wore a ten-gallon hat, even on his campaign buttons.

Cody liked the Miller Brothers show and found it a happy place. He wrote W. H. Curtis from Baltimore on May 31: "Say Billy its different with this show—no friction. Johny [sic] Baker has full charge of the rear and . . . I have full access all over. Parades out on time baring late arrieving, which no one can help. Our business fine. We had a capacity matinee and turned them away tonight."

Johnny Baker was serving as arenic director, and Major Burke was the show's press agent. Cody's share of the money was paid promptly, and he traveled in a private railroad car with a valet. He was still plagued with debts, however, and frequently had to draw his salary in advance to satisfy his creditors. Also, ill advisedly, he was suing both Major Lillie and Sells-Floto. As the season wore on, the show's profits dropped. To make matters worse, cold, rainy weather set in, followed by hot, sticky days and an epidemic among children that brought business almost to a standstill. About this time, Cody learned that holders of the Medal of Honor were eligible for pay, and in June he wrote to the adjutant general of the army applying for it, saying "I need that ten dollars in my business as it rains all the time." He signed the letter "William F. Cody," but also added a line in the corner of the show stationery: "Bill Cody of the Old Army." He had been misinformed. There was no provision for payment to Medal of Honor holders; in fact, *Army Regulations, 1913* called for the medal to be awarded only to "an officer, noncommissioned officer, or private in the Army of the United States." Because Cody had been a civilian employee when he received his award, his name was now stricken from the list of Medal of Honor holders by a board of review. Only much later was his name reinstated on the list.

In July Cody wrote Julia that he had not missed a parade or a performance all summer. Occasionally he shot glass balls from the saddle. He reported that his stories in the Hearst magazine had created more demand than the publisher could fill. Hearst, he said, now wanted him to write a book about his life as a showman, including his tours of Europe and the royalty he had met. He still talked grandly of new moneymaking schemes—"I am climbing toward another fortune"—but there was no question that the old scout was nearing the end of his long and epic journey. At the age of seventy, his once-magnificent body was exhausted; uremic poisoning provoked a deterioration of his kidneys and heart, and he could not sit on a horse without agony from his ailing prostate. A photograph taken at about that time shows him gaunt and pale, his cheeks shrunken, an overcoat hanging loosely about his lanky frame. His hair, once his crowning glory, had gone completely white, and was so thin on top that he wore a toupee when performing. Once, as he swept off his hat in his trademark salute to his audience, the toupee came off as well. He swore he would never wear it again, but he did.

Toward the end of the 1916 tour, Johnny Baker had to hoist the Colonel up on his horse at showtime. There he sat slumped on his saddle, eyes closed, awaiting his cue. When the curtains opened, he straightened up and spurred his horse into the lights and the applause. He kept his chin up and his hat, as always, held up in the air until his horse brought him back into the shadows. Somehow he hung on. It is probable that he was never more of a hero than at those moments when, suffering extreme pain, he rode out to take his bows. Toward the end of the season, it became evident that he could not mount a horse at all, and he was brought into the arena in an open carriage. Cody was afraid of "dying before all these people in the arena," according to Johnny Baker.

Apparently he did not realize himself how ill he was, or did not wish to admit it, for on October 26 Cody wrote his sister from North Carolina, telling her that he was feeling fine, investigating two or three deals for a show next season. "Now that my health is good, I must get to makeing big money." The show would close in a few days, he told Julia, and then he would be seeing her "about Nov. 21st."

When the show closed in Portsmouth, Virginia, on November 11, Cody traveled to Denver for a four-day visit with his sister May, Mrs. L. E. Decker. From there he went to his beloved TE Ranch in Wyoming for a few weeks' rest, returning to Denver in early December, where he planned to write a series of autobiographical articles for William Randolph Hearst. While at May's, he caught a cold. His physician, Dr. James H. East, told reporters that "a complication of ailments has developed, including an affection of the heart and stomach trouble," complications that alarmed East enough so that Cody's wife, Louisa, and daughter, Irma Cody Garlow, were summoned. By the time they arrived he had rallied and was out of bed, though Dr. East insisted that he give up smoking, to ease the burden on his heart. His wife and daughter, meanwhile, returned to Cody, Wyoming.

On January 3 he traveled to Glenwood Springs, Colorado, where Dr. East hoped the mineral waters would restore Cody's health. His body, however, once so powerful, had been too weakened by years of alcohol abuse, and his heart could no longer sustain him.

On January 5 Cody suffered what was described by the Denver *Post* as "a grave nervous breakdown." Accompanied by the sanitarium physician, Dr. W. W. Crook, he started for Denver that Saturday afternoon.

"If able to travel after reaching Denver," the *Post* reported, "Colonel Cody will be taken by his family to his old home in Wyoming."

Before leaving Glenwood Springs with Cody, Dr. Crook gave out this statement:

> Colonel Cody is slowly but surely nearing the end. There is no hope whatever for him. He suffered a nervous collapse yesterday and his mental faculties are seriously threatened. In fact, his memory is virtually gone. The colonel shows flashes of his old-time fire, telling his friends he soon will go on the road with a new show, bigger and better than ever.

But it is evident his mind is wandering. He cannot recall the events even of yesterday.

It is very doubtful whether he can live through the trip. If he does, it is certain the end will come soon.

Cody was not quite ready to go, however. He lingered on for a few days more in the home of his sister May. There Louisa, Irma, his sister Julia, and son-in-law Fred Garlow joined him. Dr. East returned to his bedside and, in an interview with newspapermen, suggested that his patient's condition was being worsened by "an eclipse of the moon," a curious diagnosis, to say the least.

During the next two days, almost hourly bulletins on the old Colonel's condition went out from the Decker home. Boy Scouts, eager to be of service, kept vigil on the porch. Telegrams, letters, and phone calls poured in from all over.

In North Platte, Nebraska, where the Codys had lived for many years, the *Telegraph,* under a big headline COLONEL CODY IS DYING IN DENVER, reported:

> A hush hung over the city this morning, such a hush as is known only in a city where some great disaster is pending. Sad faced men and women gathered in little groups and talked in subdued tones, now and then seeming to stop and listen as though waiting for the end of something unknown. It was as if they listened, yet feared to hear, the galloping of the pale horse that would bear the grim reaper on his final journey. For North Platte's most famous and most beloved citizen is dying in Denver. . . . Colonel W.F. Cody, the greatest plainsman the world ever knew, is calmly awaiting the end, watching the sands of life's hourglass run out.

Cody asked the doctor what his chances were. "There is a time," said East, "when the physician must commend his patient to a higher power."

"How long?" asked Cody.

"The sand is slipping slowly . . . " East told him, but Cody interrupted: "How *long,* Doctor?"

"About thirty-six hours, sir."

"All right," said Buffalo Bill, and called in his brother-in-law, Lew Decker. "The doc says I've got thirty-six hours. Let's forget about it and play some cards."

William Cody Boal, his grandson, wrote: "We played a game of high five and I remember when I played as his partner, his opponents sluffed a trick to him, and even in his weakened condition he called them on it. He was always a square shooter and demanded fair play."

To those who dropped in to pay their respects to the old man, he seemed unconcerned. "It was the last handshake," said Chauncey Thomas, an old friend. "I knew it; he knew it, but on the surface not a sign."

Cody's main concern, however, was that Johnny Baker should get there on time. "I wish Johnny would come," he kept saying, and Johnny, broken-hearted, was on the way, traveling by night train from New York, although he did not arrive in time to join the family at the old showman's bedside.

Challenging the contention that his mental faculties were impaired, the Colonel began to make arrangements for his own funeral. On January 9 he expressed a desire to join the Catholic church, although Louisa was an Episcopalian, and he had previously told his sister Julia, a Presbyterian, that "your church suits me." Be that as it may, he was promptly baptized by Father Christopher V. Walsh, assistant at Denver's Cathedral of the Immaculate Conception, and one of Buffalo Bill's greatest admirers. As a boy in Ireland in 1887, when Cody was exhibiting his Wild West show in Europe, Father Walsh saw the famous frontiersman and resolved that when he grew old he would follow the example of Cody, permit his hair to grow long and, in other ways, pattern himself after Buffalo Bill.

On the same day the New York *Times* reported that the vitality shown by Cody "was a source of amazement to his medical attendant and members of the family at the bedside . . . the noted scout gained strength during the day, although the heart action was very weak. He was breathing spasmodically, Dr. East said, which was considered a grave symptom. At intervals during the day, when the patient rallied from the effects of medicines, the physician said, he was irrational."

According to Nellie Snyder Yost, various sources related that the dying Cody, when told he had only thirty-six hours to live, calmly told his family to let the Elks and Masons take charge of his funeral.

"During his last illness," Cody Boal wrote, "the house was full of reporters from all the news syndicates, asking numerous questions pertaining to his life, experiences and personal affairs, and elaborating on any scrap of news available." Telegrams, letters and phone calls came from all over the country.

Shortly after breakfast the following day, Cody called out that he was going to die. An hour later he was unable to speak, and resorted to the sign language he had learned among the Indians.

The end came at 12:05 in the afternoon on January 10. The word went out to an expectant nation. Buffalo Bill Cody, the idol of millions, was dead.

EPILOGUE

THE LEGACY

When the legend becomes fact, print the legend.

—*The Man Who Shot Liberty Valance*

At first his death was mourned worldwide, and the accolades poured in—yet William F. Cody had no sooner been laid to rest in his solid granite grave on Lookout Mountain than detractors stepped forward to attack his character and reputation. In their efforts to belittle or deny his achievements—efforts that continue to this day—some undoubtedly acted out of jealousy, others out of envy. When we look at his legacy, however, we will understand that Cody was indeed the real thing, and not a papier-mâché hero manufactured by the hype of press agents like Major Burke and Frank Winch.

After his death a cowboy named Teddy Blue Abbott remembered working briefly for Cody as a cowboy. "Buffalo Bill was a good fellow," Abbott said, "and while he was no great shakes as a scout as he made the eastern people believe, still we all liked him and we had to hand it to him because he was the only one that had brains enough to make that Wild West stuff pay money."

"*No great shakes as a scout?*" Ridiculous! Cody's scouting record speaks for itself. His service with the U.S. Army during the Indian Wars is unequaled.

Abbott also remembered that on one occasion when Buffalo Bill entered a North Platte saloon, he took off his hat and his long hair fell to his shoulders. He rolled it up again under his hat, as the bartender said,

"Say, Bill, why the hell don't you cut the damn stuff off?" Cody replied wryly: "If I did, I'd starve to death." Cody always wore his fame, and his image, lightly.

More recently, in an essay in a 1981 exhibition catalog, Leslie Fiedler, the Samuel Clemens Professor of English at State University of New York, Buffalo, remarked that Cody's sentiments that "the West could only be redeemed from 'savagery' by 'the march of the Anglo-Saxon race,' reminds us uncomfortably of the sheeted riders of the Ku Klux Klan."

The Native American scholar and author of *Custer Died for Your Sins*, Vine Deloria Jr., strongly disagrees with this contemporary assessment of Cody's character. Says Deloria: "When judged according to the prevailing standards of the times, Buffalo Bill's relationship with the Indians, absent the aura of show business, seems above average in the positive human qualities of justice and fair play. . . . No strain of racial antagonism seems to have motivated Cody; his ethics and personal integrity appear solid and admirable."

As for the Indians' view of Cody's character, Sitting Bull not only toured with the showman for a season but also declared, when a relative was rash enough to touch the white Stetson Buffalo Bill had given him: "My friend Longhair gave me this hat. I value it very highly for the hand that placed it on my head had friendly feeling for me." Nor ought we to forget that when Sitting Bull felt beleaguered by the army and Indian Agent McLaughlin, it was Buffalo Bill he wanted to see. Other Indian chiefs who knew him also respected him.

Another bizarre viewpoint was that of Evan Connell. In *Son of the Morning Star*, his biography of Custer, he said of Cody: "Like Wild Bill Hickok, Buckskin Frank Leslie, Rowdy Joe Lowe and other borderline personalities, Cody seems to have been a curious admixture of thespian and assassin." Cody would have been the first to admit that if he was an actor, he was a poor one. As for assassin, the *American Heritage Dictionary of the English Language* defines the word as "A murderer, especially one who carries out a plot to kill a public official or other prominent person."

To repeat what Annie Oakley, who knew him well, wrote about the Colonel: "I traveled with him for seventeen years. . . . And the whole time we were one great family loyal to a man. . . . His words were more than most contracts."

Cody hardly fared well in Arthur Kopit's 1969 play, *Indians*. Here the Indians were given center stage and the more sympathetic roles. The play features Buffalo Bill (played by Stacey Keach), Wild Bill Hickok, Sitting Bull, other Indians, and a committee of mulish congressmen, to whom Bill attempts to explain the Indian point of view.

During the play, Buffalo Bill is unable to persuade the congressmen of the justice of the Indians' cause, or the Indians of the right of the white men to take their land. The Indians, in turn, shame the old scout.

At the end of the play, Cody sits trembling while the stage goes completely black. Then, suddenly, all the lights blaze up, there is rodeo music, the Rough Riders of the World enter, followed by Buffalo Bill on his white stallion. "*He tours the ring, a glassy smile on his face. He waves his big Stetson to the unseen crowd.*" The Indians approach—and the lights fade to black once more.

Fiedler believes that "there is a kind of vestigial, qualified sympathy for Cody" in Kopit's play, "a sense that to be trapped as he was in an outlived myth, even of his own making, was at least pitiful, if not downright tragic."

Unfortunately, when Robert Altman made his 1976 film, *Buffalo Bill and the Indians or Sitting Bull's History Lesson*, "suggested" by Kopit's drama and starring Paul Newman as Cody, the script by Altman and his screenwriter Alan Rudolph turns Buffalo Bill into a flamboyant fake, a hopeless drunk, and an aging ladies' man slouching into impotence.

A more amusing caricature of Cody appears in Elmore Leonard's western novel, *Gunsights*. The book's two heroes are standing off a hundred angry "hard-eyed cutthroats"—hired by the villain of the story to kill them—when a man "in a white Stetson and fringed buckskin" appears and introduces himself as "Colonel Billy Washington, here to extend a personal invitation to both of you to join the world-famous Billy Washington All-American Wild West Show as star attractions and performers." The Colonel is described as having "gleaming store teeth and waxed guardsman mustache twirled to dagger points." There's no mistaking the provenance of the good Colonel Billy Washington.

Going to the record, to the scorecard, so to speak, Cody's treatment of the Indians in his Wild West show was exemplary. Though accused of abusing them and feeding them poorly, he was cleared of all these charges and commended for the way he dealt with them. The Indians themselves, certainly, were quite willing to join his company; in fact, some vied with each other to be chosen—and this, strange as it may seem, was for the chance to portray themselves as savages.

It must be added that Cody was always even-handed in treating *all* his show people. On one occasion, when the Indians in the company were fed leftover pancakes for breakfast, Cody dressed down the manager of the restaurant and demanded that they get the same food as everyone else.

On still another occasion, when he saw during one matinee performance that the cowboys in his troupe were giving the Indians the most intractable horses to ride, he quietly saw to it that the cowboys rode the more vicious mounts that evening.

In summing up the legendary figure of Buffalo Bill, as complicated a man as he was as colorful a personality, we might best approach him by following Deloria's caveat and judge him "by the prevailing standards of the times." Cody cannot be fairly judged by contemporary standards, such as those applied by Evan Connell and Leslie Fiedler. Nor can he be held accountable as a spokesman or representative of opinions or positions he would have forsworn, had he known what posterity might make of his acts and public statements.

Like most of the leading figures of his time—Grant, Sherman, Sheridan, and Theodore Roosevelt—Cody believed that the white or Anglo-Saxon race was inherently superior to the other races, which does not mean he approved of the brutality with which the other races were so often treated. In a Toronto newspaper he was quoted as saying "In nine cases out of ten when there is trouble between white men and Indians, it will be found that the white man is responsible. Indians expect a man to keep his word. They can't understand how a man can lie. Most of them would as soon cut off a leg as tell a lie."

On another occasion Cody said: "The defeat of Custer was not a massacre. The Indians were being pursued by skilled fighters with orders to kill. For centuries they had been hounded from the Atlantic to the Pacific and back again. They had their wives and little ones to protect and they were fighting for their existence."

Deloria also notes that Buffalo Bill wisely kept his distance from any treaty negotiations, nor did he ever attempt to persuade an Indian chief to sign a treaty, though plenty of traders and Christian missionaries did so. Cody understood full well that any treaty's provisions would be violated by his countrymen at the first opportunity.

It is hard for us today to come to a balanced opinion of the struggle between the whites and the Indians for the American land. The Indians were by no means always "noble," nor were the whites justified in their policies of extermination and in seizing land the Indians had occupied for centuries. It is a pity that some way could not have been found for the two races to live peaceably alongside each other. I believe that Buffalo Bill would have been the first to argue that such a rapprochement of the two peoples was both desirable and possible.

As it is, the Indians' travails continue unabated in our own time. Since the 1880s, the Bureau of Indian Affairs (BIA), under the tragically misguided Dawes Severalty Act of 1887, has acted as a trustee for the Indians, leasing their lands to farmers, loggers, and oil companies; these accounts generated $400 million in 1998. However, the BIA has no nationwide accounting system for the trusts, and in 1996, five plaintiffs sued the government on behalf of 500,000 Indian beneficiaries to repay the estimated $10 billion—that's 10 *billion*—lost over the last century in undervalued lease payments and unsent checks, money owed in many cases to unemployed and impoverished tribespeople. The government repeatedly failed to comply with court-ordered requests for documentary evidence, and so, on February 22, 1999, U.S. District Court Judge Royce C. Lamberth declared Secretary of the Interior Bruce Babbitt and Secretary of the Treasury Robert Rubin in contempt. "I have never seen more egregious misconduct by the federal government," wrote Lamberth in his ruling. The suit has not yet come to trial as of this writing. Apparently many of the subpoenaed records were either lost or stored in facilities contaminated by vermin.

In this unending conflict between the palefaces and the redskins, the only redskin victory is apparently the spread of Indian gambling casinos, which have succeeded in separating thousands of *wasicus* from their money.

In considering Buffalo Bill's career, there remains the question of whether he was a true hero. "Show me a hero," wrote F. Scott Fitzgerald, "and I'll write you a tragedy." There are elements of tragedy in Cody's long life— the loss of a beloved son and two of his three daughters; a dysfunctional marriage; his attempts to prolong his youthful persona, the dashing cavalier of the plains; and perhaps saddest of all, his persistent conviction that his fortune lay always elsewhere and just around the corner: in his mining investments, his town-building enterprises, his irrigation plans, his hotels, rather than in his Wild West, where his true fortune lay, if only he could have held on to it.

Yet Cody's investments were not complete failures—merely ahead of their time. His fondest dream was to see his beloved Big Horn country grow, and it has, mightily. As Cody became a small city of 7,000 residents—more than a million tourists a year visit the town—the Irma Hotel prospered with it. Today oil wells around Cody are pumping black gold, and the Buffalo Bill Reservoir provides precious irrigation for ranches in the area. Even the Campo Bonito mines in Arizona were operated profitably from 1918 to 1943 after wolframite was found—too late to help Cody, but in time to pay off the indebtedness of the Cody-Dyer Company. In 1927 Johnny Baker and others completed construction of a ranch at the Campo Bonito site, called the High Jinks. The ranch housed many artifacts from Cody's life, including his Medal of Honor, until 1945, when the last of the mementos were taken to the Cody Museum in Golden, Colorado. The High Jinks ranch house has been beautifully restored and its cattle spread is still thriving; both were added to the National Register of Historic Places in 1996.

As for his heroism, he was in fact what he later claimed to have been: a freighter, a Pony Express rider, a buffalo hunter, a scout, and an Indian fighter. All these exploits were attested to by the unimpeachable testimony of leading army officers and civilian leaders of the time—most of whom were proud to call him a friend. True, many other men performed in these capacities, too, but few as well as Cody—and only Cody won the Medal of Honor for his scouting—or remained on the army payroll, as he did, continuously from 1868 to 1876. He can hardly be blamed for capitalizing on that authentic career as a frontiersman in show business; it was his stock-in-trade, his "shtick," if you will. He would have been a fool not to seize on the opportunities that were thrust at him—for it was he who was sought after, cultivated, and, yes, exploited. His marksmanship has been well documented; how about his horsemanship? Wrote Nebraska Ned in his book *Buffalo Bill and His Daring Adventures in the Romantic Wild West*: "He is the complete restoration of the Centaur. No one that I ever saw so adequately fulfills to the eye all the conditions of picturesque beauty, absolute grace, and perfect identity with his animal."

The three men who figure most prominently in the history of the Old West are Wild Bill Hickok, George Armstrong Custer, and Buffalo Bill Cody. Cody has been frequently associated in historical memory with Custer—in large part perhaps because of his re-creation of "Custer's Last Stand" in his show. In that episode he comes riding up on his white horse after the carnage is over, and the legend TOO LATE is lit up on a screen. (Cody, of course, was nowhere near the Little Big Horn during that epic battle.)

Consider the similarities, first. Both men were superb horsemen and crack shots. Both were flamboyant and articulate—which made them attractive subjects for newspaper reporters. Both were called "Long Hair" or "Pahaska" by the Indians. Leslie Fiedler implies that Buffalo Bill deliberately modeled his persona on Custer's—though it is far more likely that the young Cody borrowed his long locks and facial hair from his longtime friend Wild Bill Hickok.

Cody admired Custer greatly, though I think it unlikely, from his record as a scout, that Cody would have led the Seventh Cavalry into that fateful ambush if he had been in Custer's place; he would have been far more prudent, much less eager to play the hero's role. In fact, there is little in the record to show that Cody sought out glory for its own sake. The killing of Tall Bull came about because he coveted the chief's horse; only the so-called duel with Yellow Hand (or Yellow Hair) seems to be an exception. He wanted that "first scalp for Custer," and he got it. As far as his show was concerned, Custer's widow, Libbie, saw it in New York more than once and thought it was wonderful in its fidelity to the history of the West.

Cody's biographer Don Russell puts it this way: "In an age that is skeptical of heroism, anyone who does bother to find out what William F. Cody really amounted to may turn up a record that is impressive in its universal acclaim from a wide variety of sources as well as in its lack of any hint that he ever faltered or blundered. What more could possibly be asked of a hero? If he was not one, who was?"

It is when we turn to William F. Cody the man as distinguished from Buffalo Bill the public figure that we come to his contradictions. On the plus side, first: He made friends easily and apparently kept them for years; it seems that virtually everyone he ever encountered liked him, unlikely as this seems. A skeptic might suspect that some of those friends were drawn to him by his generosity, which was legendary; he spread money around lavishly wherever he went. Many of those friends, however, dated back to his days as a young scout, far from wealthy, and they remained loyal to him even when he suffered financial reverses.

He was dedicated to his family and came to the aid of his sisters whenever they needed his help. He loved children, who must have sensed that quality in him, for they loved him in return and were his most devoted fans. When a cousin wrote to ask him if she might bring some of her students to his show, he told her to "bring them all. I love children." When he was at Campo Bonito at Christmastime, he played Santa Claus to the children of the miners, dressed as Saint Nick and riding in an open touring car with a bag full of gifts.

He was a good manager, if a poor businessman. Gordon Lillie, "Pawnee Bill," who knew him well over a number of years, at one point called him "an irresponsible boy," but at the end, even after their break, Lillie said that the Colonel "still lives in my memory as the ideal of my boyhood days . . . one of the biggest and best men I ever knew."

On the minus side: He probably drank far too much, though there is no reason to believe that alcohol ever kept him from performing. Most of his binges took place after the end of his show's season. Heavy drinking, after all, was commonplace on the frontier at the time. He had an unusually strong constitution; even so, his drinking did contribute to his final illness, although there is testimony that he did not drink during the last nine years of his life—abstinence that apparently came too late.

No one would claim that he was a model husband. He was probably unfaithful from time to time, but he provided well for his wife, Louisa, and undoubtedly meant what he said in seeking a divorce, that she would be better off alone, to "run things her way." Certainly she didn't rely on him to keep the home fires burning. He was a devoted and generous father to his daughters, who usually made an effort to be back in North Platte whenever he returned home.

We come next to his supposed braggadocio. Even here, there is credible evidence that Cody was essentially a modest man, who did not boast privately of his exploits but was more inclined to make good-natured fun of them, or to pass them off as inflated. Much of the nonsense that clung to his public persona was generated by press agents to enhance the box office receipts for the Wild West. Is it any wonder that on occasion he may have "borrowed" one of the questionable feats attributed to him and included it in one of his numerous autobiographies? Many if not most of the books bearing his name were the handiwork of other writers; only his first 1879 autobiography can be relied upon. He was in no way, shape, or form a practiced liar, though like all the westerners of his day, he was fond of tall tales, which nobody was expected to take seriously.

As a showman, he was second to none. "The next Barnum," as some thought of him, performed before an audience estimated to be in excess of 50 million spectators around the world over thirty years and became, in museum director David H. Katzive's words, "America's first media hero." As he toured abroad, he served as the most popular and effective ambassador ex officio of his time. For much of the world, he *was* the Wild West; for thousands of American schoolchildren, he was the hero they dreamed of becoming. Cody thought of "Buffalo Bill's Wild West and Rough Riders of the World" as an educational exhibition more than a "show," and would have been horrified to have it considered a circus. According to Helen Cody Wetmore, as a boy he always wanted to be a showman. He told his sisters in intervals between "playing Indians" that "I believe I'll run a show when I get to be a man." When they objected that he was instead destined—as a fortune teller had once told their mother—to be President of the United States, he replied, "I don't propose to be President, but I do mean to have a show."

Here's an interesting what-if? scenario. What if Cody had been nominated as the vice-presidential candidate with McKinley in 1900? He was mentioned as a possible nominee. If so, when McKinley was assassinated by Leon Czolgosz in Buffalo, New York, Cody would have become president. What kind of president might he have made? One rather like Reagan, perhaps, a "great communicator," or, like his friend Teddy Roosevelt—"that damned cowboy," as Mark Hanna called him—a strong advocate of American expansion and the conservation of natural resources.

One other element of his legacy is the contemporary rodeo, which grew out of the "cowboy fun" that Cody incorporated in his Wild West. Kristine Fredriksson, in her book *American Rodeo: From Buffalo Bill to Big Business,* said of Cody's 1882 Independence Day celebration in North Platte, Nebraska, the appropriately termed "Old Glory Blowout," that "The North Platte celebration . . . is considered the beginning both of the wild-west show and of rodeo."

William F. Cody's own view of himself was that he was not merely a showman but a developer, a man who looked not to the past but always to the future. In this respect he was far ahead of his time as a supporter of women's rights, as a defender of the Indian, as a conservationist, a preservationist. He would have been pleased to see the recent efforts to turn at least a portion of the prairie back into the ecosystem it was in his day, a "sea of grass," as one writer put it.

Like Teddy Roosevelt and Pawnee Bill Lillie, he did what he could to help save the few remaining buffalo herds, that once again they might prosper. It would pain him for anyone to think of him as a "butcher." The four thousand or so bison he is reported to have killed were the tiniest fraction of those slaughtered by professional hide-hunters, Indians, and gun-happy tourists. And the buffalo he shot were killed for food.

Readers may make their own judgments of Cody's character from this story of his life. As for me, I have no hesitation in calling him a hero, his flaws as a man notwithstanding—and even those flaws serve in my eyes only to humanize what I consider a fine human being. Toss the legend aside and you still have the man: brave, strong, humane, appealing—and fun to be with. "There was always something doing when the Colonel was around," one of his friends said.

Buffalo Bill's legacy is also to be found in his contributions to art and entertainment. As a patron of the arts, Cody commissioned work from Frederic Remington for one and the western painter Charles Schreyvogel for another. Schreyvogel, according to Peter H. Hassrick, former director of the Buffalo Bill Historical Center, was paid in mining stock and one painted Sioux tepee. The stock, as we know, was never redeemed, but the tepee remained in the artist's studio as a prop. When the Wild West was in Paris, the French artist Rosa Bonheur painted Buffalo Bill's entourage as well as Cody himself. "Charles Russell," writes Hassrick, "N.C. Wyeth and many other turn-of-the-century artists also portrayed elements of Cody's adventurous life." One of these was the Detroit painter Irving R. Bacon, who did numerous commissioned works for Cody. One 1908 allegorical Bacon work was called *Conquest of the Prairie*; it evoked the passing of the frontier, with buffalo, Indians, a wagon train, and the lone figure of Buffalo Bill on horseback. "Cody functioned as both patron and inspiration for a world of artists," said Hassrick.

Turning to the entertainment field, it is safe to say that the western movie would not have been the same without Buffalo Bill. Thanks to his Wild West re-creations of authentic life on the plains, movie Indians ride their ponies instead of stalking their game or ambushing their foe on foot, as they did in the eastern wilderness of James Fenimore Cooper—and they wear Sioux headdresses in their charges, as they did in Cody's scouting days. Cody rode a white horse and wore a white hat, as did many heroes in early westerns. The cavalry rescues he took part in and restaged in his show have been reprised in many a Hollywood horse opera and serial.

As early as 1898, Cody's *Parade of Buffalo Bill's Wild West Show* was filmed by Thomas Edison, who only a few years before had invented the first motion-picture camera, the Kinetescope. The only major film project Buffalo Bill was involved in was the Essanay production *The Indian Wars*, in which Cody served as a consultant and portrayed himself, though not, judging by the stills from the film, all that convincingly. The poses he struck remind us of nothing so much as the artificiality of nineteenth-century melodrama.

When it came to re-creating the Battle of Wounded Knee in *The Indian Wars*, Cody allegedly attempted to film the massacre on the very site where it occurred, a decision that, according to Vine Deloria Jr., "destroyed much of the good will that Cody had painstakingly earned over the decades. But the film was made in Cody's later years when his fortunes were declining precipitously, and can probably be attributed to his urgent desire to recapture his youth and popularity at a time when the public wanted to forget Cody, Indians and West, and enjoy the luxuries of modern life." It is unfortunate that the Indian Wars film has not survived. The government never permitted the film to be released for general distribution, and the prints allegedly decomposed at the Bureau of Indian Affairs during the 1920s.

Film historian William Judson has identified some twenty-seven movies, both silent and sound, in which Buffalo Bill plays a major or minor role, beginning with the Universal Pictures serial *In the Days of Buffalo Bill* in 1923 and John Ford's *The Iron Horse* the following year. These films include the musical comedy *Annie Get Your Gun*, in which

Bill was played by Louis Calhern; *Annie Oakley*, with Moroni Olsen as the great showman; and one French production, *Touche pas la femme blanche* (*Don't Touch the White Woman*), with an actor named Michel Piccoli as Cody. The roster of actors who played the part of Buffalo Bill includes Tim McCoy, Douglas Dumbrille, Roy Rogers, Joel McCrea, Richard Arlen, Charlton Heston, and Paul Newman.

When it comes to the on-screen portrayals, however, filmmakers have fallen far short of doing justice to his life. Perhaps the worst incarnation of Buffalo Bill was in the movie *Pony Express*, starring Charlton Heston as Bill. Heston was much too long in the tooth to play the fourteen-year-old Pony Express rider that Cody actually was, but that might be forgiven if there had been any attempt on the screenwriter's part to deal with historic facts. Cody, with his sidekick Wild Bill Hickok standing by, is credited with carrying out the entire Pony Express operation single-handedly. Moreover, he is portrayed as an overbearing braggart, which he could have been but certainly wasn't, and a gunslinger, which he never was and never could have been. Bat Masterson, who was a gunfighter and knew Cody, vouched for that. Cody packed a gun only when he needed to—as a Pony Express rider, a hunter, and a scout. An interesting historical footnote is provided in the last scene of *Pony Express*, in which the Pony Express statue has this quote from Abraham Lincoln superimposed on it: "A grateful people acknowledge with pride its debt to the riders of the Pony Express. Their unfailing courage, their matchless stamina knitted together the ragged edges of a rising nation. Their achievement can only be equaled—never excelled."

Among the other films in which Cody was portrayed in a leading (and misleading) role are Cecil B. DeMille's *The Plainsman*, with Gary Cooper as Wild Bill Hickok and James Ellison as a rather dour Buffalo Bill; and William Wellman's eponymous *Buffalo Bill*, which made some attempt to follow the course of his career, though it gave Bill a mustache and goatee much earlier in his life than he really sported them, and shows him, at one point in his later life, broke and down on his luck, riding a wooden horse and shooting glass balls in a sideshow—pure invention. In that same film, there is a delicious farewell scene with Joel McCrea, in white buckskins and a white hat, riding a white horse into the arena. (Physically, McCrea made a quite impressive Cody.) Addressing the hushed crowd, he says, "Now the time has come to say . . . goodbye. Hand in hand, my wife and I are returning to our home in the West . . . to the sunset. . . . And so my little comrades up in the gallery and you grownups who used to sit there . . . good bye. God bless you." Then from far up in the peanut gallery a child pipes up: "And God bless you too, Buffalo Bill." There must have been at least a lump in the throat of everyone in 1944 who saw that movie.

Buffalo Bill frequently turns up in print these days but has not been much in evidence on television, although his life and legend certainly would lend themselves well to that medium. He did have at least one exposure on the tube, however: a segment of an A&E series called *The Real West*, with Kenny Rogers as host. This biopic, aired in 1992, includes film footage of the Wild West show as well as vintage still photographs of the great scout in his prime, and is quite faithful to the historical record.

If Buffalo Bill has suffered neglect these days, you'd never know it in Cody, Wyoming, where the locals manage to mount a celebration at the drop of a ten-gallon hat. Nor in Golden, Colorado, where a caretaker once found a container of someone's ashes on Buffalo Bill's Lookout Mountain grave and where, in the summer of 1999, a "grand jury" was formed to decide if Buffalo Bill really wanted to be buried there at all, and if not, where he did wish to be interred. A debate was held between Paul Fees, of Wyoming's Buffalo Bill Historical Center, and Steve Friesen, of Colorado's Buffalo Bill Memorial Museum, to decide the issue. Paul Fees, asked who won, said that he "threw a monkey wrench into the proceedings" by claiming that Cody was really buried in Rochester, New York, along with his children.

Nor is the Colonel neglected in North Platte, Nebraska, where Scout's Rest Ranch welcomes visitors to Cody's hideaway, where he entertained his friends and kept his distance from his wife. Today a movie theater in the barn shows films of the Wild West and Rough Riders of the World. Cody artifacts and Cody memorabilia have turned up in a wide variety of places, from LeClaire, Iowa, Cody's birthplace, where there is a Buffalo Bill Museum, to London, England, where the Royal Armauries mounted a "Buffalo Bill in England" exhibition in 1999; the show also traveled to the Tennessee State Museum in Knoxville and to the Cowboy Hall of Fame in Oklahoma. In Paris, a modern version of Buffalo Bill's Wild West is now staged at EuroDisney. Opened in 1992, it is the most popular live entertainment at the world-famous theme park, playing to sell-out audiences. By 1997, it had reportedly attracted more than three million spectators in almost 4,000 performances, 1,058 for each show. A cast of over thirty and a backstage crew of twenty-five bring the Colonel's celebrated extravaganza to life.

"When the legend becomes fact, print the legend." Poor advice for a biographer, but in Cody's life story, legend and fact are closely intertwined, almost if not quite inseparable, so that no biography can do justice to his life without recognizing that there is indeed a mythic quality to the story of the "Last of the Great Scouts"—a myth that will not die out any time soon, if ever.

SOURCE NOTES

Portions of the information used in this biography come from Don Russell's book *The Lives and Legends of Buffalo Bill* and Nellie Snyder Yost's *Buffalo Bill: His Family, Friends, Fame, Failures, and Fortunes*. Entries from these volumes will be designated "Russell" or "Yost." Other sources include *The Life of the Hon. William F. Cody, Known as Buffalo Bill*, his first autobiography, designated *Life*, and *Buffalo Bill's Life Story*, designated *Life Story*. Additional sources are Richard Walsh's *The Making of Buffalo Bill*, "Walsh," and Sell and Weybright's *Buffalo Bill and the Wild West*, "Sell"; Helen Cody Wetmore's *Buffalo Bill, Last of the Great Scouts*, "Wetmore"; Joseph G. Rosa and Robin May's *Buffalo Bill and His Wild West*, "Rosa and May"; R. L. Wilson with Greg Martin's *Buffalo Bill's Wild West: An American Legend*, "Wilson with Martin"; and *Memories of Buffalo Bill* by Louisa Cody with Courtney Ryley Cooper, *Memories*. For other works, the author and title will be listed for the first use; subsequent citations are listed only by author. Cody's letters, unless otherwise indicated, come from Stella Adelyne Foote's *Letters from "Buffalo Bill,"* "Foote," or Sarah J. Blackstone's *The Business of Being Buffalo Bill*, "Blackstone." Buffalo Bill's distinctive spelling and grammar have not been "improved" in any way—except where absolutely necessary for clarity.

Other citations are specifically identified and dated, unless clearly indicated in the text.

1: *a man of unusual appearance* . . .   Yost, p. 401.

1: *Colonel Cody was a high-minded gentleman* . . .   Russell, p. 469.

2: *an American of Americans* . . .   Russell, p. 469.

2: *He delighted millions* . . .   New York *Times*, January 11, 1917.

3: *I have got a mountain* . . .   Yost, p. 401.

3: *It is my wish and I hereby direct* . . .   Sell, p. 255.

3: *Denver's mayor Robert W. Speer* . . .   *Time*, March 4, 1946.

3: "When the Kids Next Door Called You Buffalo Bill" appeared in the Denver *Post* on January 15, 1917.

4: *indiscreet, prodigal, temperamental* . . .   Gene Fowler, *Timberline: A Story of Bonfils and Tammen*, p. 372.

4: Judge Walls's report on Cody's estate appeared in the Denver *Post* on January 16, 1917.

4: *where the last rays of the sun* . . .   *Memories*, p. 324.

4–6: The descriptions of Cody's funeral were taken largely from reports in the Denver *Post* from January 10 to January 15, 1917.

6: Springer's eulogy of Buffalo Bill was printed by the Denver Lodge #17, Benevolent and Protective Order of Elks, and delivered on Sunday, January 14, 1917.

8: *It was a remarkable funeral* . . . Fowler, *Timber Line*, p. 43.

8: Nellie Snyder Yost's interview with Johnny Baker Jr. appeared in the North Platte *Telegraph* on September 17, 1973.

CHAPTER 1

11: *a lineal descendant of Milesius* . . . Wetmore, p. xiii.

12–13: The family background of Isaac and Mary Ann Cody comes from Russell, pp. 4–5.

14: *a large and powerful animal* . . . Wetmore, p. 7.

16: *dark-skinned and rather fantastically-dressed* . . . *Life*, p. 28.

18: *If I had my way, I'd hang* . . . Alice Nichols, *Bleeding Kansas*, p. 9.

18: *Govern Kansas?* . . . Ibid., p. 139.

18–19: The Salt Creek Valley Resolutions are from Russell, p. 13.

19: *as nearly as I can recollect* . . . *Life*, pp. 40–41.

19: *As father fell* . . . Wetmore, p. 18.

20: *I saw the gleam of a knife* . . . *Life Story*, p. 7.

CHAPTER 2

24: *I worked at this* . . . *Life*, 49.

25: *While I am in the employ of A. Majors* . . . Mary Lund Settle and Raymond W. Settle, *Saddles and Spurs*, p. 8.

26: Cody's "first love affair," *Life*, pp. 53–57.

26: *Dear Old Friend* . . . Russell, p. 30.

27: *About five hundred of them* . . . Ibid.

27: *I have since often met Stephen Gobel* . . . *Life*, p. 57.

29: *The orders were to decoy the emigrants* . . . Geoffrey Ward, *The West: An Illustrated History*, p. 178.

31: *Presently the moon arose* . . . *Life Story*, p. 32.

31: *Bill's story is not so remarkable* . . . Russell, p. 38.

CHAPTER 3

34: The account of the Fort Laramie Treaty is taken from Geoffrey Ward's *The West*, pp. 154–55.

35: *in abject want of food* . . . Evan Jones and the Editors of Time-Life Books, *The Plains States*, p. 39.

36: *The wagons used in those days* . . . *Life*, pp. 66–67.

37: *He was a plainsman* . . . Ibid., pp. 70–72.

38: *The wagon was loaded to full capacity* . . . *Life Story*, p. 14.

38: *made a very hot, fierce fire* . . . *Life*, p. 77.

40: *Surrounding the adobe walls* . . . Sell, p. 23.

40: *Laramie had become the most famous meeting-place* . . . *Life Story*, p. 17.

41: *There was little time to act* . . . *Life Story*, p. 18.

42: *Ain't it splendid, Mother* . . . Sell, p. 26.

42: *We pushed on to the gold streams* . . . *Life*, p. 90.

43: *On the twelfth day* . . . *Life*, pp. 97–101.

ℂHAPTER 4

45–46: *In a little while* . . . Mark Twain, *Roughing It*, pp. 63–64.

47–48: *He [Majors] became intimately acquainted* . . . Settle, p. 3.

48: *that the firm should engage* . . . Ibid., p. 13.

49: *On the night of September 17, 1848* . . . *American Heritage*, September 1998, p. 108.

50: *WANTED—young, skinny, wiry fellows* . . . Jerry Ellis, *Bareback*, p. 12.

52: *the great pony express* . . . *Life*, pp. 91–99.

53: *Among the most noted* . . . Russell, p. 47.

53: *the most bloody* . . . Twain, *Roughing It*, p. 70.

54: *so friendly and so gentle* . . . Ibid., p. 75.

54: *Slade, though rough at times* . . . *Life*, p. 105.

55: *About six or seven years ago* . . . Russell, p. 48.

55: *The Indians came on* . . . *Life*, p. 105.

56: *Twenty miles out from Sweetwater* . . . Ibid., p. 107.

57: *The significant part of this story* . . . Russell, p. 52.

59: *That the business men and citizens* . . . Settle, pp. 5–6.

61: *After a year's absence* . . . *Life Story*, p. 35.

ℂHAPTER 5

62: *A strong Union woman* . . . *Life*, p. 125.

63: *A man by the name of Chandler* . . . *Life*, pp. 125–27.

64: *His instructions were carried out* . . . Ibid.

65: *On our return to Rolla* . . . Ibid., pp. 131–32.

65: *This expedition* . . . Ibid., p. 134.

66: *The Red-Legged Scouts* . . . *Life Story*, p. 36.

67: *more purely an indiscriminate thief* . . . Russell, p. 59.

67: *Thus passed away* . . . *Life*, p. 135.

67: *in a rough lumber wagon* . . . Wetmore, p. 100.

67–68: *My dear sisters* . . . Ibid., p. 106.

68: *entered upon a dissolute* . . . *Life*, p. 135.

68: *I met quite a number* . . . Ibid.

69: *More than any other state* . . . James M. McPherson, *The Atlas of the Civil War*, p. 22.

70: *On several occasions* . . . Russell, p. 64.

70: *General A.J. Smith re-organized* . . . *Life*, p. 136.

70–71: *Busy day here . . .* Russell, p. 65.

71: *skirmishing around the country . . .* Life, p. 136.

72: *As the Indian was pushed west . . .* Sell, p. 49.

72: *We commenced shooting . . .* Ibid.

73: *About 100 yards from the ranch . . .* Ward, *The West*, p. 201.

74: *What shall I do with the Third Colorado . . .* Ibid.

74–75: Details of the Battle of Sand Creek are taken from ibid., pp. 203–6.

76: *Since this . . . horrible murder . . .* Ibid., p. 206.

76: *Although wrongs have been done me . . .* Ibid.

76: *was put in charge . . .* Life Story, p. 45.

77: *You little rascal . . .* Life, p. 136.

77–78: *From this time on . . .* Ibid., p. 140.

78: *One of the members of Company H . . .* Russell, p. 72.

ℂHAPTER 6

79: Louisa's version of her meeting with Bill Cody is related in her book *Memories*, pp. 3–6.

79: *her bridle-rein broke one morning . . .* Wetmore, pp. 122–23.

80: *having made up my mind . . .* Life, p. 141.

80: *Boylike . . . I thought it would be very smart . . .* Russell, pp. 73–74.

80: *While driving stage . . .* Colonel Henry Inman and Colonel William F. Cody, *The Great Salt Lake Trail*, p. 220.

81: *At Leavenworth . . . I took leave . . .* Life, p. 52.

82: *The poor old woman . . .* Russell, p. 77.

83: *Will radiated hospitality . . .* Wetmore, p. 146.

83: *People generally said I was . . .* Life, p. 145.

83: *started alone for Salina, Kansas . . .* Ibid.

84: *Custer had covered nearly one thousand miles . . .* Stephen E. Ambrose, *Crazy Horse and Custer: The Parallel Lives of Two American Warriors*, p. 266.

85: *As a scout, Cody had his share . . .* Russell, p. 81.

85: *the dashing and gallant Custer . . .* Life, pp. 145–46.

86: *In his new apparel . . .* Frederick Whittaker, *Complete Life of Gen. George A. Custer*, p. 169.

86–87: *A few days after my return to Fort Hays . . .* Life, pp. 147–48.

88–89: The Fetterman Massacre is described in Ward's *The West*, pp. 232–33.

90–91: The story of Rome, Kansas, is told in *Life*, pp. 149–52.

91: *a perfect gentleman, a whole-souled, genial-hearted fellow . . .* Ibid., pp. 152–53.

92: *There were eleven buffaloes in the herd . . .* Ibid., pp. 155–56.

94: *During my engagement as hunter . . .* Ibid., p. 162.

95: The chase by Indians is described by Cody in ibid., pp. 162–64.

96: *It was not long before I acquired . . .* Life Story, p. 68.

97: *Buffalo Bill, Buffalo Bill . . .* Russell, p. 90.

97: *All from the area were grateful . . .* Wilson with Martin, pp. 25–26.

98: *You have no right* . . . Ibid., p. 26.

98: *I never laid eyes on him* . . . Walsh, p. 112.

99: *Considering that in the 'sixties* . . . Ibid., p. 113.

100: *Comstock and I dashed into a herd* . . . Life, pp. 172–73.

102: *The white chief seems not to be able* . . . Sell, pp. 64–65.

103: *Many sportsmen traveled to Kansas* . . . The Buffalo Book, pp. 78–79.

106: *The post at that time* . . . Life Story, p. 73.

CHAPTER 7

107: *failed to pay attention* . . . Rosa and May, p. 21.

107: *Bill Cody (Buffalo Bill)* . . . Russell, p. 101.

107: *fifty first-class hardy frontiersmen* . . . Ibid.

109: *After the General had gone* . . . Life, p. 179.

110: *This intelligence required* . . . Russell, p. 103.

111: *a brown, chunky little chap* . . . Roy Morris Jr., *Sheridan: The Life and Wars of General Phil Sheridan*, p. 1.

111: *the only good Indian is a dead Indian* . . . Ibid., p. 328.

112: *I was very favorably struck* . . . Life, p. 207.

112: *All right, Colonel* . . . Ibid.

113: *directing the deployment of his command* . . . Russell, p. 107.

114: *While I was unloading my horses* . . . Rosa and May, p. 27.

114: *a Frenchman by birth* . . . Life, p. 212.

115: *General, I think the scouts are mistaken* . . . Ibid., p. 215.

115: *When we were approaching the stream* . . . Ibid., pp. 215–16.

115–16: *were 'jumped' by about fifty Indians* . . . Ibid., pp. 216–17.

116: *Go ahead in your own way* . . . Morris Jr., *Sheridan*, p. 308.

116: *I rely in everything upon you* . . . Ward, p. 250.

117: *All I'm afraid of is that we won't find* . . . Ibid., p. 251.

117: *The Indians left on the ground* . . . Ibid., p. 252.

118: *If we can get in one or two more [such] blows* . . . Ward, p. 252.

119: *Telling Wilson, the chief wagon-master* . . . Life, pp. 222–23.

120: *It was sold to our boys* . . . Ibid., p. 226.

121: *Among the scouts of Penrose's command* . . . Ibid., p. 227.

122: *General Carr, at my request* . . . Ibid., p. 229.

122: *I could only stare at him* . . . Memories, pp. 155–56.

122: *even with the stories of his prowess* . . . Walsh, p. 137.

CHAPTER 8

123: *I immediately went over* . . . Life, p. 229.

124: *I know that, Bill* . . . Ibid., p. 231.

125: *the most remarkable feat* . . . Ibid., p. 238.

126: *Unfortunately we were in too jolly* . . . Ibid., pp. 244–45.

126: *They all, to this day* . . . Russell, p. 122.

127: *Cody decided it would be best* . . . Ibid., pp. 122–23.

127: *Our scout William Cody* . . . Ibid., p. 123.

127: *I have the honor* . . . Ibid., p. 123. (Carr's report is taken from the Records of the Adjutant General, National Archives.)

128: The description of Fort McPherson is from Yost, pp. 4–6.

129: *It was a somewhat demoralized army* . . . Russell, p. 119.

130: *I be made chief of scouts* . . . *Life*, p. 249.

130: *who shall receive the pay* . . . Russell, p. 125.

130: *had made quite a reputation* . . . *Life*, p. 249.

130: *always been opposed to* . . . Rosa and May, p. 31.

131: *One of the herders* . . . Ibid., p. 251.

132: *Wherever they had encamped* . . . Ibid., p. 255.

133: *Cody's idea was to get around* . . . Russell, p. 134.

133: *By this maneuver* . . . *Life*, p. 256.

133: *. . . the arrival of the guide* . . . Russell, pp. 134–35.

134: *I was in the skirmish line* . . . *Life*, p. 260.

135: *I jumped on his back* . . . Ibid., p. 261.

136: *four years afterward* . . . Ibid., pp. 260–61.

136: *I had a few words* . . . Russell, p. 130.

136: *in a court of law* . . . Ibid., p. 142.

137: *Never before this year* . . . Ibid., p. 148.

137: *I know it was generally understood* . . . Ibid.

137: *a pony which I called 'Powder Face'* . . . *Life*, p. 262.

137: *From there . . . the particulars* . . . Ibid.

138: *on my way voluntarily* . . . Judson's military records are on file at the National Archives. Other details of his life come from Jay Monaghan's *The Great Rascal: The Life and Adventures of Ned Buntline.*

139: Details of the Astor Place Riot will be found in *Encyclopaedia Britannica.*

139: *I take a bound book* . . . Wilson with Martin, p. 13, from *Life and Adventures of Ned Buntline*, Cadmus Book Shop, 1919, p. 6.

140: The history of dime novels will be found in Daryl Jones's *The Dime Novel Western.*

141: *Just then I noticed a gentleman* . . . *Life*, p. 263.

141: *During this short scout* . . . Ibid., p. 264.

141: *one of the swiftest ponies* . . . Ibid., p. 266.

142: *Together . . . we would do our sewing* . . . Yost, p. 26.

143: *Lord and Lady Dunraven* . . . Ibid.

143: *at great expense* . . . Ibid.

143: *When the scouting ended* . . . Walsh, p. 157.

143: *found Fort McPherson* . . . *Life*, p. 268.

143: *Mr. Flynn, and George Boyd Houghton* . . . Ibid.

144: *I rode the horse bareback* . . . *Life*, p. 269.

144: *a good fellow though as a liar* . . . Ibid., p. 272.

144: *a jolly, blustering old fellow* . . . Ibid., p. 271.

145: *Suddenly I heard three or four shots* . . . Ibid., p. 274.

145: *Today we marched 24 miles* . . . Russell, p. 158; Major Frank North, *The 1869 Diary of Frank North*, ed. Donald F. Danker, p. 158.

145: *a traditional plains signal* . . . *Life*, p. 274.

145: *It was afterwards learned* . . . Russell, p. 158; George F. Price, comp., *Across the Continent with the Fifth Cavalry*, pp. 141–42.

146: *I am now able to report* . . . Walsh, p. 154.

🅒HAPTER 9

147: *The wildest and truest story* . . . Russell, p. 159. A copy of *Buffalo Bill, the King of Border Men* is available in the Western History Collection of the Denver Public Library.

149: *I might have paved for myself* . . . Wilson with Martin, p. 20, Pond, op. cit.

150: *When the alarm was given* . . . *Life Story*, p. 115.

151: *The Indians were encamped on a little knoll* . . . Ibid.

151: *The whole Command rushed across* . . . Russell, p. 163.

151: *I knew a shorter route* . . . *Life Story*, p. 118.

151: *The major was hotter* . . . Ibid., p. 119.

152: *This being the first fight* . . . Russell, p. 164.

152: *Lieutenant Thomas especially commends* . . . Ibid.

153: *requesting him to give me* . . . Ibid., p. 165, from the Earl of Dunraven, *Canadian Nights*, New York, 1914, pp. 51–55.

153: *Bill was dressed in a pair* . . . Ibid.

154: *Jack, tall and lithe* . . . Ibid.

154: *Six or seven of us would start* . . . Ibid., p. 166, from Cody, "Hunting Parties," p. 136.

154: *We stood the Indians off* . . . *Life*, pp. 279–80.

155: *He gave me a geological history* . . . Ibid., p. 280.

155: *A gay party it was* . . . Wetmore, pp. 174–79.

155: *I woke up one morning* . . . *Life*, p. 275.

156: *conspicuous and gallant conduct* . . . Russell, p. 169.

156–57: *General Sheridan and party arrived* . . . New York *Herald*, September 23, 1871.

157: *at five o'clock next morning* . . . *Life*, p. 288.

157: *At the camp we were introduced* . . . Russell, p. 171. The pamphlet mentioned is "Ten Days on the Plains," by H. E. Davies, pp. 25, 26, 29.

158: *for years afterward* . . . Cody, "Hunting Parties," pp. 137–40.

158: *a good deal of time and some trouble* . . . Russell, p. 172.

159: *a dismal-looking, dun-colored brute* . . . Ibid.

159: *after our guide* . . . Ibid., p. 173.

159: *Enough game will be left* . . . Salt Lake *Tribune*, October 2, 1871.

160: *Two companies of cavalry were sent* . . . *Life*, p. 292.

160: *During the next few weeks* . . . Ibid.

162: *in ten sleeps* . . . Ibid., p. 297.

163: *Your highness, this is Mr. Cody . . .* Unidentified newspaper clipping dated January 13, North Platte, Nebraska.

163: *a large, fine-looking young man . . . Life,* p. 299.

163: *Buffalo Bill is a famous Western scout . . .* Russell, p. 176.

163: *Buffalo Bill as Guide, Tutor . . .* New York *Herald,* January 16, 1872.

164: *his well-known frontier buckskin . . .* Ambrose, *Crazy Horse and Custer,* p. 316.

164: *he fired six shots . . . Life,* p. 301.

164: *while in some . . . it was stated . . .* Ibid., p. 302.

164: *The hunt was continued for some two hours . . .* Lincoln *State Journal,* North Platte, Nebraska, January 15, 1872.

164: *It was either an extraordinarily . . . Life,* p. 302.

165: *Spotted Tail and his chosen Sioux, . . .* Ambrose, p. 317.

165: *singling out a gigantic bison . . .* W. F. Cody, "Famous Hunting Parties of the Plains," *Cosmopolitan,* vol. 17, No. 2 (June 1894), p. 141.

165: *a heavy, double-seated open carriage . . .* Russell, p. 179.

165: *General Sheridan sang out to me . . . Life,* p. 274.

166: *On arriving at the railroad . . .* Ibid., p. 305.

166: *the Grand Duke invited me into his car . . . Life Story,* p. 136.

167: *AT IT . . .* Kansas City *Times,* January 14, 1872; Russell, p. 180.

167: *Every week, some new thrilling story . . . Memories,* p. 215.

168: *The Admiral [Custer] is all sunshine . . .* Elizabeth B. Custer, *"Boots and Saddles," or, Life in Dakota with General Custer.*

168: *All I looked forward to . . . Life Story,* p. 137.

ℂHAPTER 10

169: *a beautiful little reason . . . Memories,* p. 219.

170: *exhibited some of my backwoods steps . . . Life,* p. 310.

171: *I finally consented . . .* Ibid., p. 311.

171: *I had struck the best camp . . .* Russell, p. 182.

172: *Cody . . . is spare and wiry in figure . . .* Webb, *Buffalo Land,* pp. 149, 161, 194–95.

172: *I was familiar neither with the horse . . . Life Story,* p. 142.

173: *Shortly after my return . . . Life,* p. 313.

173: Captain Meinhold's report is from Russell, p. 187.

174: *While this was going on . . .* Ibid.

174: *I made several other scouts . . . Life,* p. 315.

174: *At one of these lonely little stations . . .* Earl of Dunraven, *Canadian Nights,* pp. 53–54.

175: *Milligan, here's what you've been waiting for . . .* Ibid., p. 317.

175: *I lariated, or roped . . .* Ibid., p. 318.

175: *he didn't know any more about law . . .* Wetmore, p. 180.

176: *There's money in it . . . Life,* p. 320.

176: *I don't know just how bad I'd be . . . Memories,* p. 232.

177–78: *Buntline, who was taking the part . . . Life,* pp. 326–27.

178: *when the scene ended . . .* Ibid., p. 327.

179: *Act I. On the Plains* . . .   Russell, p. 194.

179: *the papers gave us a better send-off* . . .   *Life*, p. 327.

180: *Buntline delivered some opinions* . . .   Russell, p. 196.

180: *On the whole it is not probable* . . .   Ibid.

180: *Buffalo Bill won no laurels* . . .   Ibid., p. 197.

182: *With Arta on my lap* . . .   *Memories*, pp. 248–50.

185: *We closed our tour on the 16th* . . .   *Life*, p. 329.

185: *Unheard extravagance became ours* . . .   *Memories*, pp. 251–52.

186: *Texas Jack and myself longed* . . .   *Life*, p. 328.

186: *We have played New York until we forced* . . .   Rosa and May, p. 49.

189: *Ned Buntline has been trying to murder me* . . .   Ibid., p. 51.

190: *told us from the start* . . .   *Life*, p. 329.

190: *with his weak eyes blinded* . . .   Russell, p. 207.

191: *In New York, where I was raised* . . .   Yost, p. 74.

191: *He will first proceed to New York* . . .   Russell, p. 207.

192: *Deadwood was then hog-wild* . . .   Walsh, p. 194.

192: *I have a hunch* . . .   Ibid.

192: *an English gentleman, Thomas P. Medley* . . .   *Life*, p. 337.

ⓒHAPTER 11

193: *citizens: Two guides* . . .   Russell, p. 209, from Anson Mills, *Big Horn Expedition.*

193: *For years he had been Cody's faithful* . . .   Russell, pp. 209–10, from King's *Campaigning with Crook*, pp. 113–14.

194: *It was worth the money* . . .   *Life*, pp. 338–39.

195: *Mr. Cody (Buffalo Bill) sustained* . . .   Russell, p. 212, from Mills, *Big Horn Expedition.*

195: *At ten o'clock the next morning* . . .   *Life*, p. 339.

196: *was too good for this world* . . .   Yost, p. 83.

197: *It is not probable that* . . .   Russell, pp. 215–16.

197: *Yet up until this moment* . . .   Russell, p. 216.

197–98: *At noon on the 9th [of June]* . . .   *Ellis County Star*, Hays City, Kansas, June 29, 1876, p. 4., as cited by Russell, p. 220.

198: *A party of junior officers* . . .   Russell, pp. 221–22.

199: *Cody was riding a little in advance* . . .   Russell, p. 226, from Chris Madsen's "Comments on King's Campaigning with Crook," MS, 1937.

200: *Early on the morning of July 17th* . . .   Russell, p. 229.

200: *We have had a fight* . . .   Baltimore *Sun*, December 21, 1936.

201: *William F. Cody, the favorite scout* . . .   Russell, p. 235, from Price, *With the Fifth Cavalry.*

201: *For long fearful weeks I knew only* . . .   *Memories*, pp. 267–70.

201: *Here something a little out* . . .   Wetmore, p. 217.

202: *one of the Indians, who was handsomely* . . .   *Life*, p. 343.

202: *Over what General Sheridan* . . .   Walsh, pp. 190–91.

203: *When Yellow Hand challenged someone* . . .   Russell, p. 232.

204: "*Yellow Hand, . . . a young warrior*" . . . Yost, p. 92.

204: *No other of his race ever died so often* . . . Russell, p. 235.

205: *Since that day* . . . Walsh, p. 194.

205: *I have seen many dead men* . . . Ibid.

205: *who, in spite of his many faults* . . . Life, p. 336.

206: *one and all, they [the Indians]* . . . Russell, p. 236.

206: *several small herds of buffalo* . . . Ibid., p. 238.

207: *While we were conversing* . . . Life, p. 349.

208: *worn shooting jacket, slouch felt hat* . . . Russell, p. 238.

208–9: *Terry had with him* . . . Captain Charles King, *Campaigning with Crook: The Fifth Cavalry in the Sioux War of 1876*, pp. 79, 82.

209: *who had for his headquarters* . . . Life, p. 351.

209: *a curious admixture* . . . Evan S. Connell, *Son of the Morning Star: Custer and the Little Bighorn*, p. 335.

210: *We were to ride on the pilot house* . . . Life, p. 353.

210: *rode seventy-five miles that night* . . . Ibid., p. 355.

210: *There being but little prospect* . . . Ibid., pp. 355–56.

210: *saying that it would only detain me* . . . Ibid., pp. 356–57.

212: *was a five-act play* . . . Ibid., p. 360.

212: *Arizona John, whose other name is Burke* . . . Russell, p. 253.

213: *Mother, who in days of childhood* . . . Sell, p. 128.

214: *This will be the last season* . . . Russell, pp. 255–56.

214: *Except that Cody did not stay* . . . Ibid., p. 256.

215: *In paying the company* . . . Ibid., pp. 257–58, from *The Westerners Brand Book*, Chicago, Vol. II (1945–46), pp. 27–31.

216: *bought a large tract of land* . . . Wetmore, p. 135.

216: *near the Wyoming line* . . . Memories, p. 278.

216: *Cody owned many valuable tracts* . . . Yost, p. 98.

218: *It was the best drama I had yet produced* . . . Life, p. 361.

218: *In February, 1878* . . . Ibid.

219: *was built according to the wishes* . . . Wetmore, p. 221.

219: *Furnishings came all the way* . . . Memories, pp. 278–79.

219: *the Cody's [sic] beautiful home* . . . Yost, p. 100.

219: *The word 'round-up'* . . . Life, p. 362.

219: *As there is nothing but hard work* . . . Ibid., p. 363.

219–20: *Buffalo Bill . . . was a liberal fellow* . . . Yost, p. 101.

220: *Some of the cowboys would take advantage* . . . John Bratt, *Trails of Yesterday*, pp. 278–79.

220: *giving them a correct idea* . . . Russell, p. 262.

221: *I have just finished a big engagement* . . . Cody to Crawford, April 22, 1879, Western History Department, Denver Public Library.

221: *Sam . . . realy [sic] I don't think we could agree* . . . Cody to Hall, September 2, 1879.

221–23: *Yours rec'd. I met Ingraham* . . . Cody to Hall, August 17, 188– (before 1883).

CHAPTER 12

223: *a village of modest homes* . . .   Yost, p. 105.

223: *the gentleman who owned the dog* . . .   Ibid., p. 110.

224: *Bath water . . . was heated* . . .   Ibid., p. 108.

224: *It was a treat to see Buffalo Bill* . . .   Ibid.

224: *If half the stories told of Buffalo Bill* . . .   Ibid., p. 109.

224: *Cowboys would ride long distances* . . .   Archibald R. Adamson, *North Platte and Its Associations*, pp. 42–43.

226: *early productions signed by Buffalo Bill* . . .   Albert Johannsen, *The House of Beadle and Adams*, Vol. II, 59–61.

226: *Our author would never consent* . . .   Wetmore, pp. 222–23.

226: *As to the Colonel's literary work* . . .   Russell, p. 267.

226–27: *It seems doubtful that he ever read* . . .   Ibid., p. 283. A comprehensive study of the books by and about Cody can be found in Chapter 20 of Russell's book.

228: *During the summer of 1877* . . .   Wetmore, p. 223.

228: *exploits as a mule driver,* . . .   Yost, p. 113.

229: *the finest specimen of young manhood* . . .   W. B. (Bat) Masterson, *Famous Gunfighters of the Western Frontier*, p. 70.

229: *full tilt into a herd* . . .   Ibid.

230: *We arrived about two o'clock* . . .   Ibid., p. 74.

230: *There were fully twenty persons* . . .   Ibid., p. 75.

231: *A crowd that filled every seat* . . .   Chicago *Tribune*, August 8, 1880.

232: *I found myself richer* . . .   Walsh, pp. 214–15.

232: *I have been sending money* . . .   Foote, p. 27.

232: *That Louisa was a shrewd businesswoman* . . .   Yost, p. 115.

234: *I hear from Al* . . .   Foote, p. 19.

236: The material on Joseph G. McCoy is from Rosa and May, p. 66.

237: *I began to construct a show* . . .   Nate Salsbury, "The Origin of the Wild West Show," *The Colorado Magazine*, July 1955.

238: *Some say the town* . . .   Yost, p. 116.

238: *that wasn't big enough to suit Cody* . . .   Ibid.

239: *Cody mumbled something to the effect* . . .   Ibid., pp. 116–17.

240: *an amazing figure* . . .   Kristine Fredriksson, *American Rodeo: From Buffalo Bill to Big Business*, p. 140.

241: *Cody not only scored* . . .   Sell, pp. 133–34.

241: *Will never enjoyed this part* . . .   Wetmore, p. 231.

242: *When the season of 1881–83 closed* . . .   W. F. Cody, *Story of the Wild West and Camp-Fire Chats*, pp. 693–94.

243: *Cody came to my home* . . .   Russell, pp. 292–93.

244: *Dr. Carver's acquaintance* . . .   Ibid., p. 294.

245: *He also shot against the frontier's* . . .   Rosa and May, p. 68.

245: Discussion of Carver's manuscript, ibid.

246: *What would you do in a Wild West show* . . .   *Memories*, pp. 285–86.

247: *Fellow citizens, it fills my breast . . .* Yost, p. 133.

247: *Bill, if you want to make this d—— show go . . .* L. O. Leonard, "Buffalo Bill's First Wild West Rehearsal," *The Union Pacific Magazine,* August 1922, pp. 26–27.

248: *The Green Sward Our Carpet . . .* Sell, p. 135.

248: *a part of the development of the great West . . .* John Burke's "Salutatory," from the Wild West Programme, 1893.

249: *There is a trite saying . . .* Ibid.

250: *a fine looking man, well groomed . . .* Walsh, p. 229.

252: *to plan and scheme again . . .* Memories, p. 295.

252: *that woman . . .* Foote, p. 33.

252: *Darling Sister . . .* Ibid., p. 31.

253: *it was an eternal gamble . . .* Cooper, as quoted by Walsh, p. 229.

254: *The virtue of the show . . .* Sell, p. 136.

254: *they had not developed my ideas . . .* Salsbury, "The Origin of the Wild West Show," p. 207.

255: *Orra, my precious darling . . .* Yost, p. 142.

255: *flipped a silver dollar . . .* Walsh, p. 231.

256: *I should never have put this relation . . .* Salsbury, "Origin," pp. 207–8.

257: *was the highest salaried press agent . . .* Glenn Shirley, *Pawnee Bill: A Biography of Major Gordon W. Lillie,* pp. 186–87.

257: *My dear Nate . . .* Walsh, p. 232.

258: *I'll never forget seeing Buffalo Bill . . .* Yost, p. 143.

258: *Immediately upon forming a partnership . . .* Ibid., p. 144.

ℂHAPTER 13

259: *boiling drunk . . . surrounded by a lot . . .* Walsh, p. 233.

259: *Your very sensible and truly rightful . . .* Ibid.

260: *I would have answered at once . . .* Russell, p. 303.

260–61: *No doubt during the winters . . .* Dexter W. Fellows and Andrew A. Freeman, *This Way to the Big Show,* 1936, pp. 90–92.

261: *A band of armed desperadoes . . .* Russell, p. 305.

262–63: *I was dependent on myself . . .* Ibid., p. 306.

263: The quotes are from the Wild West programme, 1884.

264: *The Only Real Novelty of the Century . . .* Sell, pp. 137–38.

264: *The only artistic interest in the show . . .* Walsh, pp. 238–39.

265: *In this accident . . .* Yost, p. 146.

266: *In eight days I had added to the nucleus . . .* Ibid.

266: *If nine people came out here . . .* Walsh, p. 242.

266: *My dear Pard . . .* Ibid., pp. 242–43.

266–67: *the Wild West didn't do as well as expected . . .* Lincoln County *Tribune,* March 7, 1885.

267: *About the same number of horses . . .* Walsh, pp. 243–44.

267: *As I told you that I am to do my best . . .* Ibid., p. 244.

270: *I was eight years old* . . . Russell, pp. 311–12.

270: *When I first commenced shooting* . . . Isabelle S. Sayers, *Annie Oakley and Buffalo Bill's Wild West*, p. 4.

271: *From the time I was nine* . . . Ibid., p. 9.

272–73: *There's a charming little girl* . . . Ibid., p. 6.

273: *At the end of the performance* . . . Ibid., p. 11.

273: *I owe whatever I have* . . . Wilson with Martin, p. 123.

273: *poetical sensation replete* . . . Ibid.

274: *Major Burke told me all about you* . . . Sell, p. 141.

275: *They told me about you* . . . Ibid., p. 143.

275: *I went right in and did my best* . . . Russell, p. 313.

275: *This little missie here* . . . Ibid.

275: *He was the kindest, simplest* . . . Sell, p. 240.

275–76: *It was our first thought* . . . Ibid., p. 143.

276: *only performed in this position* . . . Blackstone, *Buckskins, Bullets, and Business*, p. 59.

276: *when she doesn't hit a ball* . . . Wilson with Martin, p. 125.

276: *an actress of no mean pretensions* . . . Ibid.

276: *a consummate actress, with a personality* . . . Sayers, p. 21.

277: *Buffalo Bill was the object of admiration* . . . Sell, p. 144.

277: *Many of them were the kid type* . . . Ibid.

ℂHAPTER 14

279: *Of all the Indians I encountered* . . . *Life Story*, p. 172.

281: *he could not accept any such proposition* . . . Wilson with Martin, p. 59, based on records in the National Archives.

282: *Sitting Bull has expressed a desire* . . . Ibid.

284: *The white people are so many* . . . Rosa and May, p. 91.

284: *exhibition . . . what is technically* . . . Ibid., pp. 85–89, from Deahl, "Buffalo Bill," p. 142, in B. A. Botkin, ed., *A Treasury of American Folklore*, 1944.

285: *Wild West, are you ready?* . . . Ibid.

286: *with enough firing of pistols* . . . Ibid.

287: *My friend Long Hair gave me this hat* . . . Stanley Vestal, *Sitting Bull: Champion of the Sioux*, p. 251.

287: *I do not know for certain* . . . Sayers, p. 22.

288: *He is inflated with the public attention* . . . Wilson with Martin, p. 60.

288: *I have now seen your Wild West show* . . . Letter from Twain to Cody, in Walter Havighurst's *Annie Oakley of the Wild West*, p. 79.

289: *consummate liar . . . too vain and obstinate* . . . Wilson with Martin, p. 61.

289: *is one of the finest in America today* . . . Foote, p. 34. Letter dated September 28, 1885.

289: *The Honorable W.F. Cody* . . . Yost, p. 152, the North Platte *Telegraph*, October 22, 1885.

289: *The far-famed scout* . . . Lincoln County *Tribune*, October 24, 1885.

290: *calculated to make it more comfortable* . . . Yost, p. 153.

290: *The waters of the great Platte* . . . Omaha *Herald*, December 6, 1885.

291: *The Hon. W.F. Cody (Buffalo Bill)* . . . Yost, p. 160.

291–92: *No one was ever turned away* . . . Ibid., p. 161.

292: *a man of world-wide celebrity* . . . Walsh, p. 261.

292: *could ride with a cup of water on his head* . . . Sell, p. 151.

293: *that most realistic and faithful representation* . . . Elizabeth Custer, *Tenting on the Plains*, p. 46.

293: *the best shot in the world* . . . Yost, p. 167.

294: *I think our poor days are over* . . . Foote, p. 36.

294: *It is a well-known fact* . . . Walsh, p. 252.

295: *If I can get them lined up right* . . . Yost, p. 230.

296: *It was necessary for four men to hold her* . . . Russell, pp. 320–21.

296: *Often the pigeon went one way* . . . Ibid., p. 322.

297: *I want a side board in the house* . . . Foote, p. 41.

298: *Presented to Master Johnny Baker* . . . Walsh, p. 253.

298: *Let everybody pull together* . . . Yost, p. 173.

298: *Hon. W.F. Cody will soon* . . . Ibid., p. 174.

300: *Steele Mackaye has tamed it* . . . Walsh, pp. 262–63.

300: *The show is not paying too well* . . . Sayers, p. 25.

302: *reposing special trust and confidence* . . . Ibid., p. 263.

302: *The* World *utters a deep groan* . . . Lincoln County *Tribune*, April 2, 1887. Governor Thayer, as well as commissioning Cody a colonel, had named him Commissioner for the State of Nebraska to the American exhibition to be held in London.

303: *The grand stand . . . will be covered* . . . Yost, p. 181.

304: *You know, you get in that big canoe* . . . Tim McCoy and Ronald McCoy, *Tim McCoy Remembers the West*, pp. 1–2.

ⒸHAPTER 15

305: *sick as a cow with hollow-horn* . . . Yost, p. 186.

307: *all of us combined in an expedition* . . . Rosa and May, p. 102.

308: *The working class of people* . . . Yost, p. 187.

308: The comment by Henry James is taken from Rosa and May, p. 96.

308: *I may walk it, or 'bus it* . . . Russell, p. 328.

309: *It is an entertainment* . . . Sell, p. 162.

310: *yelling like fiends* . . . Rosa and May, p. 111.

310–11: *I had heard a great deal about* . . . C. R. Cooper, *Annie Oakley*, p. 173.

311: *English laborer thinks he is lucky* . . . Leavenworth *Times*, January 29, 1889.

312: *there arose such a genuine heart-stirring* . . . Russell, p. 330.

312: *all present were constrained to feel* . . . William F. Cody, *Story of the Wild West and Camp-Fire Chats*, p. 737.

313: *A kindly little lady* . . . Sayers, pp. 34–35.

313: *. . . to Earl's Court, where we saw . . .* Rosa and May, pp. 118–20. From the Royal Archives, Windsor Castle, Queen Victoria's Journal, by gracious permission of Her Majesty Queen Elizabeth II.

314: *Colonel, you never held four kings . . .* Russell, p. 331.

314: *They occupied half a dozen boxes . . .* Yost, p. 190.

315: *I was to stay at home . . .* Ibid., p. 191.

315: *Some of the New York newspapers . . .* Ibid., p. 196.

315: *a young lady who inherits her father's . . .* Ibid., p. 198.

316: *Notwithstanding his daily engagements . . .* London *Times*, November 1, 1887.

316: *A few years ago W.F. Cody . . .* Yost, p. 199.

316: *chiefly famed as an adroit scalper . . .* Ibid.

317: *neither more nor less than a hippodrome . . .* Russell, p. 334.

317: *I must express my pride and delight . . .* Marshall P. Wilder, *The People I've Smiled With*, pp. 108–21.

317: *A fee was never mentioned . . .* Sayers, pp. 35–36.

318: *from the day of opening our show . . .* Cody, *Story*, p. 749.

320: *If I don't get my health back soon . . .* Foote, p. 33.

320: *The stay of the Wild West in London . . .* Lincoln County *Tribune*, November 26, 1887.

321: *It is no paradox . . .* *Times* (London), November 1, 1887.

321: *we met with a prodigious welcome . . .* Cody, *Story*, p. 748.

321: *In spite of London's lavish praise . . .* Birmingham *Gazette*, November 4–7, 16, 1887.

323: *Let me know your numbers . . .* Cody, *Story*, p. 756.

323: *The winters in this country . . .* Foote, p. 33.

323: *terribly homesick besides . . .* Ibid., p. 34.

323: *it is reported that Buffalo Bill . . .* Lincoln County *Tribune*, February 25, 1888.

324: *a magnificent rifle, decked . . .* Cody, *Story*, p. 757.

324–25: *Numerous excursion trains . . .* Hull *News*, May 5, 7, 12, 1888.

325: *at the appointed hour . . .* Aurora, Nebraska, *Register*, June 14, 1888.

325–26: *The harbor probably has never witnessed . . .* Wetmore, p. 254.

326: *I cannot describe . . .* Cody, *Story*, p. 766.

326–27: General Sherman's letter appears in Wetmore, pp. 254–55.

327: *Buffalo Bill, dressed as a scout . . .* New York *Tribune*, May 28 and 31, 1888.

327: *probably the best known man . . .* Reprinted in the Lincoln County *Tribune*, June 23, 1888.

328: *I am feeling some better . . .* Foote, p. 35.

329: *Mr. Boal, a Chicagoan . . .* Yost, p. 213.

329: *It must have been during this extended visit . . .* Ibid., p. 217.

331: *[The French audience] sat like icebergs . . .* Wilson with Martin, p. 135.

332: *Yesterday was a busy day for me . . .* Foote, pp. 35–36.

332: *He [Cody] was glad to see me . . .* Russell, p. 351.

332: *everything American became the fad . . .* Walsh, p. 276.

334: *The brutes made springs into the air . . .* Russell, p. 352.

338: *It was impossible for the father* . . . Wetmore, p. 262.

338: *H.S. Boal and Arta Cody were married* . . . Grand Island (Nebraska) *Independent*, November 30, 1889.

ⓒHAPTER 16

339: *Sitting Bull was an extraordinary man* . . . Ambrose, *Crazy Horse and Custer*, p. 326.

340: *The break-up of the reservations drive* . . . *American Heritage*, May–June, 1999, p. 16.

340: *It is bad for our cause for me to parade around* . . . Vestal, pp. 251, 255.

341: *Indians! There are no Indians* . . . Dee Brown, *Bury My Heart at Wounded Knee*, p. 431.

343: *The whole world is coming* . . . Dee Brown, *Best of Dee Brown's West: An Anthology*, p. 337.

343: *Mainly because they misunderstood* . . . Ibid.

343: *It was a threatened uprising* . . . Russell, p. 356.

344: *Crafty, avaricious, mendacious* . . . James McLaughlin, *My Friend the Indian*, pp. 25, 180, 182, 192, 263.

344: *seek the men who saw* . . . Russell, p. 358.

345: *Miles said that Sitting Bull had his camp* . . . Cody, *True Tales of the Plains*, pp. 234–35.

345: The original of General Miles's order and visiting card are in the Buffalo Bill Museum, Lookout Mountain, Colorado.

346: *of all the bad Indians* . . . Walsh, p. 284.

346: *If they had left Cody alone* . . . Ibid., p. 286.

346: *William F. Cody (Buffalo Bill) has arrived here* . . . Ibid., p. 286; McLaughlin, pp. 209–10.

347: *Colonel Cody's capacity was such* . . . Vestal, p. 281.

347: *to cooperate with and obey the orders* . . . McLaughlin, pp. 211–12.

349: *The Indian police* . . . Russell, p. 362.

349: *Look out in the future* . . . Vestal, pp. 180–81.

350: *If I could've talked to him* . . . Yost, p. 226.

351: Agent McLaughlin's report is available on the Internet from "Archives of the West: 1887–1914," copyright 1996 THE WEST FILM PROJECT and WETA, Developed by Lifetime Learning Systems.

352: *He was not scalped* . . . Vestal, pp. 309–10.

353: *The following morning there was a bugle call* . . . Dee Brown, *Bury My Heart at Wounded Knee*, p. 442.

354: *They called for guns and arms* . . . Ibid.

354: *The bullets will not go toward you* . . . Ibid.

354: *a crazy man* . . . Ibid., p. 444.

354: *153 were known dead* . . . Ibid.

355: *I did not know how much was ended* . . . Ibid., p. 446.

355: *reimbursement of expenses* . . . The original is in the Buffalo Bill Museum, Lookout Mountain, Colorado.

355: A facsimile of Governor Thayer's order is in the Wild West programme, 1893, p. 52.

356: *This is a pretty effectual denial* . . . Russell, p. 367.

356: *I am glad to inform you* . . . Facsimile in the Wild West programme, 1893, p. 53.

356: *You big general now, Bill?* . . . Walsh, p. 289.

356–57: *a display of horsemanship* . . . Yost, p. 227.

358: *if you have any more send them along* . . . Sayers, p. 49.

358: *I would rather manage a million Indians* . . . Russell, p. 433.

ⒸHAPTER 17

362: *American shows . . . originated the method* . . . Russell, p. 371.

362: *We never moved without at least forty officers* . . . Courtney Ryley Cooper, *Annie Oakley*, p. 236.

363: *Boal is no man to run it* . . . Yost, p. 231.

364: *if Mrs. Cody has any grain or grass* . . . Foote, p. 69.

364: *while Will was away at the seat of war* . . . Wetmore, p. 266.

364: *Save Rosa Bonheur's picture* . . . Ibid.

365: *We had a surprise in London, though* . . . Sayers, p. 52.

365: *When Buffalo Bill took his cowboys* . . . Sell, pp. 183–85.

365: *The Tower, the Parliament, and Westminster* . . . "Buffalo Bill in London," *Harper's Weekly*, September 3, 1892.

366: *do something worthy of the occasion* . . . Nate Salsbury, "The Origin of the Wild West Show."

367: *At the conclusion of the performance* . . . Rosa and May, p. 156. From Queen Victoria's Journal, Windsor Castle, June 26, 1892.

369: *cleanest, coolest and most comfortable* . . . Chicago *Post*, June 18, 1893.

369: *No such an engaging story-teller* . . . Yost, p. 237; Chicago *Daily News*, June 26, 1893.

370: *those portions of the program* . . . Yost, pp. 239–40.

370: *The dash and vim of Buffalo Bill's horsemen* . . . Ibid.

372: *She enjoyed being on location* . . . Sayers, p. 53.

372: *She welcomes us royally* . . . Havighurst, p. 171.

374: *Lulu, having heard rumors* . . . Russell, p. 432.

374: *was an ornate, three-storied affair* . . . Yost, p. 244.

374–75: *Up to our own day . . . Since the days* . . . Turner, "The Significance of the Frontier in American History," *Annual Report of the American Historical Association for the Year 1893* (Washington, D.C.: Government Printing Office, 1894).

375: *The two master narrators of American westering* . . . Richard White, "Frederick Jackson Turner and Buffalo Bill," pp. 7–9.

376: *Within a few months* . . . Havighurst, p. 182.

377: *I want each man measured* . . . Yost, p. 247.

377: *barrels of money* . . . Ibid., p. 250.

377: *Its [sic] creating a great excitement* . . . Foote, p. 75.

379: *The main elements* . . . Blackstone, *Buckskin, Bullets, and Business*, p. 107.

380: *I am too worried now to think* . . . Ibid., p. 76.

380: *the greater circus name of the two* . . . Russell, p. 378.

382: *I will do my part* . . . North Platte *Semi-Weekly Tribune*, May 12, 1896.

384: *That the Codys were proud and loving* . . . Yost, p. 276.

385: *sat in his tent holding court* . . . Yost, p. 278, from Tim McCoy and Ronald McCoy, *Tim McCoy Remembers the West,* p. 17.

385: *I will have a hard time to get away* . . . Russell, p. 417, from Cody to George Everhart, April 29, 1898.

386: *Twenty-four thousand people came* . . . Yost, p. 279.

387: *He stands not at the head* . . . Wetmore, p. 286.

387: *Yet to him 'Cody Day' was infinitely* . . . Havighurst, p. 199.

387: *Colonel Cody is very dear to the hearts* . . . Yost, p. 281.

388: *Do you believe that women should have* . . . Wilson with Martin, p. 169.

CHAPTER 18

391: *to be known as a pioneer and developer* . . . Walsh, p. 327.

391: *connected with eleven different enterprises* . . . Ibid., p. 310.

391: *I was a Democrat until I found out* . . . Ibid., p. 311.

392: *However, the true cause* . . . Wilson with Martin, pp. 142–44.

393: *he was not making enough to quit* . . . Russell, p. 418.

394: *My dear Cody* . . . Walsh, p. 328.

395: *I tell you . . . I will make it* . . . Foote, p. 93.

398: *I have never seen children more delighted* . . . Rosa and May, p. 174.

399: *and the worst wind storms* . . . Russell, p. 441.

399–400: *I have tried & tried* . . . Foote, pp. 89–90.

400: *I think when Lou and Arta sees* . . . Ibid., p. 102.

401: *I do not go to hotels any more* . . . Ibid., p. 106.

401: *I will make more money after this* . . . Ibid., p. 107.

401: *My Dear Poor Tired Sister* . . . Foote, p. 105.

406: *cost him more money than all the women* . . . Russell, p. 434.

CHAPTER 19

411: *No swearing or drinking* . . . Russell, p. 444.

411: *After nearly five years absence* . . . Yost, p. 343, from an unidentified North Platte newspaper.

411: *I am very busy as I have no partner* . . . Foote, p. 129.

411: *it's got down to one show a day* . . . Blackstone, p. 35.

412: *I work every day in my tent* . . . Walsh, p. 334.

412: *the show has started great* . . . Blackstone, pp. 33–34.

412–13: *Well the Wild West have beaten* . . . Ibid., p. 34.

413: *quite ill and these terrible long runs* . . . Ibid., pp. 38–39.

415: *Football on horseback* . . . Yost, p. 349, from Harry E. Webb, "Buffalo Bill: Saint or Devil?" *The Roundup,* p. 5.

415: *caused a beautiful young lady* . . . Russell, p. 449.

416: *Standing there, the Old Scout* . . . Yost, p. 362.

416: *Your friends read with interest today* . . . North Platte *Telegraph*, April 2, 1910.

417: *I am about to go home* . . . Russell, pp. 450–51.

418: *There was not a dry eye* . . . Ibid., p. 451, from Frank Winch, *Thrilling Lives of Buffalo Bill and Pawnee Bill*, pp. 217–24.

419: *I'd like to know of any boy* . . . *Arizona Highways*, March 1999.

419: *Arizona doesn't care how I stand* . . . Ibid.

419: *war and the camp are no longer considered* . . . New York *Times*, March 26, 1911.

420: *Dear Pard L.W., Today* . . . Courtesy of the Western History Department, Denver Public Library.

420: *Dear Getchell: I wish you would take* . . . Ibid.

421: *I am yet hit hard* . . . Ibid.

421: *I have gone on nearly bankrupting my self* . . . Blackstone, p. 51.

423: *Positively Last Personal Appearance* . . . Yost, p. 371; *The Show World*, June 24, 1911.

423: *I prize more than gold or silver* . . . North Platte *Semi-Weekly Tribune*, August 1911.

424: *not and never did worry* . . . Yost, pp. 374–75; Wichita *Eagle*, August 20, 1911.

425: *I will remain in the saddle* . . . Yost, p. 375.

ℂHAPTER 20

426: *probably the most amoral and unscrupulous* . . . Russell, p. 452.

426: *walked smack in on him* . . . Fowler, *Timber Line*, p. 86. (Ed.: I would not vouch for the authenticity of Fowler's recollections, but he always made good reading.)

427: *Tammen was a dreamer* . . . Ibid., p. 87.

427: *Tammen was forever on the lookout* . . . Ibid., p. 207.

427: *I will not be in the saddle* . . . Yost, p. 378; North Platte *Semi-Weekly Tribune*, December 6, 1912, reprinted from New York *Clipper*.

428: *Wait till I come, wonderful report* . . . Blackstone, p. 59.

428: *Have just heard from Mines* . . . Ibid., p. 61.

428: *excellent* . . . [a]*nd the Canadians will finance* . . . Foote, p. 140.

428–29: *Memoranda of Agreement* . . . Blackstone, pp. 195–206.

429: *Pay no attention to press reports* . . . Russell, p. 454.

429: *I feel bad about this* . . . Yost, p. 381; North Platte *Telegraph*, April 19, 1913.

429: *She was a heller in skirts* . . . Yost, p. 381; North Platte *Telegraph*, October 9, 1967.

430: *I am much better* . . . Foote, p. 138.

430: *We felt friendly to Colonel Cody* . . . Yost, p. 383; North Platte *Telegraph*, July 31, 1913.

432: *What of it?* . . . Yost, p. 386.

432: *I am not down and out* . . . Ibid.; North Platte *Telegraph*, July 31, 1913.

434: *The Colonel* . . . *had a certain amount* . . . Russell, p. 459.

434: *Cooper was a sprightly, colorful* . . . Gene Fowler, *A Solo in Tom-Toms*, p. 367.

437: *After everything was sold* . . . Foote, p. 144; Walsh, pp. 361–62.

437: *Everything I attempt to do* . . . Foote, pp. 144–45.

437: *There must be a law* . . . Walsh, p. 352.

437: *This man is driving me crazy* . . . Ibid.

440: *had a good reputation but* . . .   Russell, p. 463.

440: *Say Billy its different* . . .   Ibid., p. 464, Cody to W. H. Curtis, Baltimore, May 31, 1916.

441: *I need that ten dollars in my business* . . .   Walsh, p. 357.

442: *Now that my health is good* . . .   Foote, p. 148.

442: *a complication of ailments* . . .   New York *Times*, December 22, 1916.

442: *Colonel Cody is slowly but surely* . . .   Sell, p. 255.

443: *A hush hung over the city* . . .   Yost, p. 400. From an article in the North Platte *Telegraph*, under the headline COLONEL CODY IS DYING IN DENVER.

443: *There is a time* . . .   Sell, p. 256.

443: *We played a game of high five* . . .   Yost, p. 400.

443: *I wish Johnny would come* . . .   Walsh, p. 359.

444: *During his last illness* . . .   Yost, p. 401.

EPILOGUE

445: *Buffalo Bill was a good fellow* . . .   Ward, p. 375.

446: *Say, Bill, why the hell* . . .   Ibid.

446: *the West could only be redeemed* . . .   Leslie A. Fiedler, "The Legend," exhibition catalog *Buffalo Bill and the Wild West*, pp. 91–92.

446: *When judged according to the prevailing standards* . . .   Vine Deloria Jr., "The Indians," in ibid., pp. 49–50.

447: *He tours the ring, a glassy smile* . . .   Arthur Kopit, *Indians*, p. 94.

447: *in a white Stetson* . . .   Elmore Leonard, *Gunsights*, pp. 493, 497.

448: *The defeat of Custer* . . .   Sell, p. 247.

449: *I have never seen* . . .   "The BIA's Cat-and-Mouse Game," *Harper's Magazine*, May 1999, p. 22.

451: *In an age that is skeptical* . . .   Russell, pp. 479–80.

451: *still lives in my memory* . . .   Wilson with Martin, p. 213.

452: *I believe I'll run a show* . . .   Wetmore, p. 44.

453: *The North Platte celebration* . . .   Fredriksson, p. 140.

453–54: *Charles Russell* . . . *N.C. Wyeth and many other* . . .   Peter H. Hassrick, "The Artists," exhibition catalog *Buffalo Bill and the Wild West*, pp. 25–26.

BIBLIOGRAPHY

BOOKS

Adams, Alexander B. *Sitting Bull: An Epic of the Plains.* New York: G.P. Putnam's Sons, 1973.

Ambrose, Stephen E. *Crazy Horse and Custer: The Parallel Lives of Two American Warriors.* New York: Doubleday and Company, 1975.

American Heritage. *Great Minds of History: Interviews by Roger Mudd.* New York: John Wiley & Sons, 1999.

Arnold, Elliott. *Blood Brother.* New York: Duell Sloan and Pearce, 1947.

Barnum, Phineas T. *Struggles and Triumphs, or, Sixty Years' Recollections of P.T. Barnum, Including His Golden Rules for Money-Making.* Buffalo, NY: The Courier Company, 1889.

Barron, Elwyn A. *Lawrence Barrett, a Professional Sketch.* Chicago: Knight & Leonard Co., 1889.

Blackstone, Sarah J. *The Business of Being Buffalo Bill: Selected Letters of William F. Cody, 1879–1917.* New York: Praeger Publishers, 1988.

———. *Buckskin, Bullets, and Business: A History of Buffalo Bill's Wild West.* Westport, Connecticut: Greenwood Press, 1986.

Bloss, Roy S. *Pony Express: The Great Gamble.* Berkeley, CA: Howell-North Press, 1959.

Botkin, B. A., ed. *A Treasury of American Folklore.* New York: Crown, 1944.

Bradley, Glenn D. *The Story of the Pony Express,* edited by Waddell F. Smith. San Francisco: Hesperian House, 1960.

Bratt, John, *Trails of Yesterday,* introduction by Nellie Snyder Yost. Lincoln: University of Nebraska Press/Bison Books, 1980.

Brown, Dee. *Best of Dee Brown's West: An Anthology,* edited by Stan Banash. Santa Fe, NM: Clear Light Publishers, 1998.

———. *Bury My Heart at Wounded Knee.* New York: Henry Holt and Company, 1970.

Burke, John (Richard O'Connor). *Buffalo Bill, the Noblest Whiteskin.* New York: G.P. Putnam's Sons, 1973.

Burton, Sir Richard Francis. *The City of the Saints.* New York: Harper & Brothers, 1862; repub. Boulder: University Press of Colorado, 1990.

Capps, Benjamin. *The Great Chiefs,* Old West Series. Alexandria, VA: Time-Life Books, 1975.

Chapman, Arthur. *The Pony Express.* New York: A.L. Burt Company, 1932.

Cody, Aldus Morrill. *Phillip and Martha: Their Sons and Daughters . . . The Cody Family in North America.* The International Cody Family Association, 1986.

Cody, Louisa Frederici in collaboration with Courtney Ryley Cooper. *Memories of Buffalo Bill By His Wife.* New York: D. Appleton and Company, 1919.

Cody, William F. *Adventures of Buffalo Bill.* New York: Harper & Brothers, 1904 (Harper's Young People Series).

———. *Buffalo Bill's Life Story: An Autobiography.* New York: Farrar & Rinehart, 1920.

———. *Life of the Hon. William F. Cody, Known as Buffalo Bill, The Famous Hunter, Scout and Guide: An Autobiography,* Hartford, CT: American Publishing Co., 1879.

———. *Story of the Wild West and Camp-Fire Chats.* Philadelphia: Historical Publishing Co., 1888.

Coerr, Eleanor. *Buffalo Bill and the Pony Express.* New York: HarperCollins Publishers, 1995.

Connell, Evan S. *Son of the Morning Star: Custer and the Little Bighorn.* San Francisco: North Point Press, 1984.

Cook, Jeanie, Lynn Johnson Houze, Bob Edgar, and Paul Fees. *Buffalo Bill's Town in the Rockies.* Virginia Beach, VA: The Downing Co., 1996.

Cooper, Courtney Ryley. *Annie Oakley, Woman at Arms.* New York: Duffield and Co., 1927.

Custer, Elizabeth B. *"Boots and Saddles," or, Life in Dakota with General Custer.* Norman: University of Oklahoma Press, 1961.

———. *Tenting on the Plains.* New York: Charles L. Webster & Co., 1893.

Custer, George A. *My Life on the Plains,* edited by Milo Milton Quaife. Lincoln: University of Nebraska Press, 1966.

Dary, David A. *The Buffalo Book: The Full Saga of the American Animal.* Chicago: Swallow, 1974.

d'Aulaire, Ingri, and Edgar Parin d'Aulaire. *Buffalo Bill.* Garden City, NY: Doubleday & Company, 1952.

Deloria, Vine, Jr. *Custer Died for Your Sins: An Indian Manifesto.* New York: Macmillan, 1969.

Ellis, Jerry. *Bareback: One Man's Journey Along the Pony Express Trail.* Thorndyke, ME: Thorndyke Press, 1993.

Foote, Stella Adelyne. *Letters from "Buffalo Bill."* El Segundo, CA: Upton & Sons, 1990.

Forbis, William H. *The Cowboys,* Old West Series. Alexandria, VA: Time-Life Books, 1973.

Fowler, Gene. *A Solo in Tom-Toms.* New York: Viking Press, 1946.

———. *Timber Line: A Story of Bonfils and Tammen.* New York: Blue Ribbon Books, 1933.

Fredriksson, Kristine. *American Rodeo: From Buffalo Bill to Big Business.* College Station: Texas A&M University Press, 1985.

Gilbert, Bill. *The Trailblazers,* Old West Series. Alexandria, VA: Time-Life Books, 1973.

Gilcrease, Thomas, and the Institute of American History and Art. *Treasures of the Old West: Paintings and Sculpture from the Thomas Gilcrease Institute.* New York: Abrams, 1984.

Goetzmann, William H. *Exploration and Empire: The Explorer and Scientist in the Winning of the American West.* New York: Alfred A. Knopf, 1966.

Goodman, Julia Cody, and Elizabeth Jane Leonard. *Buffalo Bill: King of the Old West.* New York: Library Publishers, 1955.

Grossman, James R., ed. *The Frontier in American Culture.* Berkeley: University of California Press, 1994.

Hassrick, Peter H., et al. *American Frontier Life: Early Western Painting and Prints.* New York, Abbeville Press, 1987.

Havighurst, Walter. *Annie Oakley of the Wild West.* New York: Macmillan, 1954.

Henderson, Paul, and Merrill J. Mattes. *The Pony Express, from St. Joseph to Fort Laramie*. St. Louis: The Patrice Press, 1989.

The Henry Art Gallery. *Myth of the West*, essays by Chris Bruce and others. Seattle: Rizzoli International, 1990.

Horn, Huston. *The Pioneers*, Old West Series. Alexandria, VA: Time-Life Books, 1974.

Inman, Col. Henry, and Col. William F. Cody. *The Great Salt Lake Trail*. New York: Macmillan, 1898.

Johannsen, Albert. *The House of Beadle and Adams and Its Dime and Nickel Novels: The Story of a Vanished Literature*. Norman: University of Oklahoma Press, 1950.

Jones, Daryl. *The Dime Novel Western*. Bowling Green, OH: The Popular Press, Bowling Green State University, 1978.

Jones, Evan, and the editors of Time-Life Books. *The Plains States*. New York: Time-Life Books, 1968.

King, Captain Charles. *Campaigning with Crook: The Fifth Cavalry in the Sioux War of 1876*. Milwaukee: NP, 1880.

Kopit, Arthur. *Indians*. New York: Hill & Wang, 1969.

Masterson, W. B. (Bat). *Famous Gunfighters of the Western Frontier*, series of articles in *Human Life* magazine, January 1907 to March 1908, in book form, with line drawings by Frederic Remington and others. Silverthorne, CO: VISTABOOKS, 1996.

Matthews, Anne. *Where the Buffalo Roam*. New York: Grove Weidenfeld, 1992.

McCoy, Tim, and Ronald McCoy. *Tim McCoy Remembers the West: An Autobiography*. Garden City, NY: Doubleday, 1977.

McLaughlin, James. *My Friend the Indian*. Stanford, CA: 1941.

McPherson, James M. *The Atlas of the Civil War*. New York: Macmillan, 1994.

Merington, Marguerite, ed. *The Custer Story: The Life and Intimate Letters of George A. Custer and His Wife Elizabeth*. New York: Devin-Adair, 1950.

Monaghan, Jay. *The Great Rascal: The Life and Adventures of Ned Buntline*. Boston: Little, Brown and Company, 1952.

Morris, Roy, Jr. *Sheridan: The Life and Wars of General Phil Sheridan*. New York: Crown Publishers, 1992.

Moses, L. G. *Wild West Shows and the Images of American Indians: 1883–1933*. Albuquerque: University of New Mexico Press, 1996.

Nathan, Mel C., and W. S. Boggs. *The Pony Express*. New York: The Collectors Club, 1962.

Nevin, David. *The Expressmen*, Old West Series. Alexandria, VA: Time-Life Books, 1974.

————. *The Soldiers*, Old West Series. Alexandria, VA: Time-Life Books, 1973.

O'Neil, Paul. *The End and the Myth*, Old West Series. Alexandria, VA: Time-Life Books, 1979.

————. *The Frontiersmen*, Old West Series. Alexandria, VA: Time-Life Books, 1977.

Price, George F., compiler. *Across the Continent with the Fifth Cavalry*. New York: 1883.

Reader's Encyclopedia of the American West, ed. Howard R. Lamar. New York: Thomas Y. Crowell, 1977.

Reinfeld, Fred. *Pony Express*. Lincoln: University of Nebraska Press, 1973.

Reiter, Joan Swallow. *The Women*, Old West Series. Alexandria, VA: Time-Life Books, 1978.

Root, Frank A., and William E. Connelly. *The Overland Stage to California*. Topeka, KS: 1901; reprinted Columbus, OH: Long's College Book Co., 1950.

Rosa, Joseph G. *They Called Him Wild Bill: The Life and Adventures of James Butler Hickok*. Norman: University of Oklahoma Press, 1964 and 1974.

Rosa, Joseph G., and Robin May. *Buffalo Bill and His Wild West: A Pictorial Biography*. Lawrence: University of Kansas Press, 1996.

Russell, Don. *The Lives and Legends of Buffalo Bill*. Norman: University of Oklahoma Press, 1975.

————. *The Wild West, or A History of the Wild West Shows*. Fort Worth: Amon Carter Museum of Western Art, 1970.

Russell, Don, ed. *Trails of the Iron Horse: An Informal History by the Western Writers of America*. Garden City, NY: Doubleday & Company, 1975.

Sandoz, Mari. *The Buffalo Hunters*. New York: Hastings House, 1954.

Sayers, Isabelle S. *Annie Oakley and Buffalo Bill's Wild West*. New York: Dover Publications, 1981.

Sell, Henry Blackman, and Victor Weybright. *Buffalo Bill and the Wild West*. New York: Oxford University Press, 1955.

Settle, Mary Lund, and Raymond W. Settle. *Saddles and Spurs: The Pony Express Saga*. New York: Bonanza Books, 1955.

Shirley, Glenn. *Pawnee Bill: A Biography of Major Gordon W. Lillie*. Albuquerque: University of New Mexico Press, 1958.

Slotkin, Richard. *Gunfighter Nation: The Myth of the Frontier in Twentieth-Century America*. New York: Atheneum, 1992.

Smith, Henry Nash. *Virgin Land: The American West as Symbol and Myth*. Cambridge, MA: Harvard University Press, 1950.

Stanley, Dorothy, ed. *The Autobiography of Henry Morton Stanley*. Boston: Houghton Mifflin Co., 1909.

Tebbel, John. *The Compact History of the Indian Wars*. New York: Hawthorn Books, 1966.

Time-Life Books, eds. *The Buffalo Hunters*. Alexandria, VA: Time-Life Books, 1993.

————. *The Wild West*, foreword by Dee Brown. New York: Warner Books, 1993.

Trachtman, Paul. *The Gunfighters*, Old West Series. Alexandria, VA: Time-Life Books, 1974.

Turner, Frederick J. "The Significance of the Frontier in American History." *Annual Report of the American Historical Association for the Year 1893*. Washington, D.C.: Government Printing Office, 1894.

Twain, Mark. *Roughing It*, foreword by Leonard Kriegel. New York: New American Library, 1962.

Vestal, Stanley. *Sitting Bull: Champion of the Sioux*. Boston: Houghton Mifflin Company, 1932; Norman: University of Oklahoma Press, 1957.

Wallis, Michael. *The Real Wild West: The 101 Ranch and the Creation of the American West*. New York: St. Martin's Press, 1999.

Walsh, Richard J., with Milton Salsbury. *The Making of Buffalo Bill*. Indianapolis: Bobbs-Merrill, 1928.

Ward, Geoffrey C. *The West: An Illustrated History*. Boston: Little, Brown and Company, 1996.

West, Elliott. *The Saloon on the Rocky Mountain Mining Frontier*. Lincoln: University of Nebraska Press, 1979.

Wetmore, Helen Cody. *Buffalo Bill, Last of the Great Scouts. The Life Story of Colonel William F. Cody*. Lincoln: University of Nebraska Press, 1965.

Wheeler, Keith. *The Chroniclers*, Old West Series. Alexandria, VA: Time-Life Books, 1976.

————. *The Scouts*, Old West Series. Alexandria, VA: Time-Life Books, 1978.

White, Richard. *It's Your Misfortune and None of My Own: A New History of the American West*. Norman: University of Oklahoma Press, 1991.

Whittaker, Frederick. *Complete Life of General George A. Custer*. New York: Sheldon & Co., 1876.

Wilder, Marshall P. *The People I've Smiled With*. Akron, OH: O. M. Dunham, 1899.
Wilson, R. L., with Greg Martin. *Buffalo Bill's Wild West: An American Legend*. New York: Random House, 1998.
Winch, Frank. *Thrilling Lives of Buffalo Bill and Pawnee Bill*. New York: S. L. Parsons & Co., 1911.
Yost, Nellie Snyder. *Buffalo Bill: His Family, Friends, Failures, and Fortunes*. Chicago: The Swallow Press, 1979.

PAMPHLETS, CATALOGS, MAGAZINE ARTICLES

"The Arizona Life and Times of a Darned Good Showman." *Arizona Highways Magazine*. March 1999.
Buffalo Bill and the Wild West: An Exhibition Catalog. Brooklyn Museum, Brooklyn, NY, 1981.
Buffalo Bill Historical Center. Cody, Wyoming, 1977.
Buffalo Bill Museum. Buffalo Bill Historical Center, Peter H. Hassrick, Director, N.D.
"Buffalo Bill's Wild West." *Wyoming Horizons*. August 1983.
Buffalo Bill's Wild West and Congress of the Rough Riders of the World, show programme. Copyrighted by Cody and Salsbury, Chicago, IL, 1893.
Doherty, Jim. "Was He Half Hype or Sheer Hero? Buffalo Bill Takes a New Bow." *Smithsonian Magazine*. May 1981.
Fiedler, Leslie A. "The Legend." *Buffalo Bill and the Wild West: An Exhibition Catalog*. Brooklyn Museum, Brooklyn, NY, 1981.
From Cody to the World: The First Seventy-Five Years of the Buffalo Bill Memorial Association. Cody, Wyoming, 1992.
Hassrick, Peter H. "The Artists." *Buffalo Bill and the Wild West: An Exhibition Catalog*. Brooklyn Museum, Brooklyn, NY, 1981.
Morrison, Tom. "Cody's Home on the Range." *NEBRASKAland Magazine*. July 1986.
———. "The Last of the Great Scouts." *NEBRASKAland Magazine*. May 1996.
Salsbury, Nate. "The Origin of the Wild West Show." *The Colorado Magazine*, 32, no. 3 (July 1955).
Webb, Harry. "Buffalo Bill, Saint or Devil?" *The Roundup*. January 1974.

DOCUMENTS AND NEWSPAPER FILES

Buffalo Bill Ranch State Historical Park, North Platte, Nebraska. Documents, letters.
McCracken Library, Buffalo Bill Historical Center, Cody, Wyoming. Letters, documents.
National Archives, Reference Branch, Textual Reference Division, Washington, D.C. Military Records of E. Z. C. Judson and William F. Cody.
Tuckahoe Branch, Henrico County Library, Richmond, Virginia. New York *Times* articles.
Western History Department, Denver Public Library, Denver, Colorado. Letters, documents, newspaper articles.

INDEX